CONTINUITY AND ANACHRONISM

ARCHIVES INTERNATIONALES D'HISTOIRE DES IDEES

INTERNATIONAL ARCHIVES OF THE HISTORY OF IDEAS

91

P.B.M. BLAAS

CONTINUITY AND ANACHRONISM

Continuity and Anachronism

PARLIAMENTARY
AND CONSTITUTIONAL DEVELOPMENT
IN WHIG HISTORIOGRAPHY
AND IN THE ANTI-WHIG REACTION
BETWEEN 1890 AND 1930

by

P.B.M. BLAAS

1978

MARTINUS NIJHOFF

THE HAGUE / BOSTON / LONDON

*Published with a grant from the Netherlands Organization
for the Advancement of Pure Research (Z.W.O.)*

ISBN 90 247 2063 x

PRINTED IN THE NETHERLANDS

CONTENTS

PREFACE

Several of the themes of this study have been treated in earlier publications, some by means of a general analysis and some through a detailed handling of problems raised by a particular theme or historian. Both the more general theoretical treatment of the theme and the concrete historiographical treatment are, I think, indispensable aids to the proper understanding of the development of historical scholarship in nineteenth- and twentieth-century England.

There are a number of problems in a concrete historiographical approach: there is first the mass of historians to be faced, and then the immense amount of historical themes dealt with in various periods. As a guideline through the tangle of themes we chose the historiography on the development of the English parliament. We can only hope that we have made a responsible choice of the historians concerned. Unfortunately it was not always possible for us to give extensive biographies of some of the more recent historians, as several 'papers' are still firmly in the possession of families, and a number of them must – despite of years – still be labelled 'confidential.'

The Pollard Papers in the London Institute of Historical Research thus remained inaccessible. Fortunately the lack was partly compensated by some important material being found apart from these Papers. Another difficulty was identifying those historians who contributed in those years (1902–1930) to the *Times Literary Supplement*, as there is still a tendency to safeguard their anonymity. The twentieth century sadly needs a 'Houghton' of its own: the reader will soon understand how much we owe to the two volumes of the *Wellesley Index to Victorian Periodicals* of which Houghton was editor-in-chief.

The appropriate function of a preface is to express thanks to all the persons and institutions who assisted during the preparatory stage. What was submitted to the late Professor Presser was a rough draft only; long before our final choice of subject was made, we were lucky enough to have the inspiration of our promotor, Professor Dr. M.C. Brands, an inspiration which persisted throughout the writing of this dissertation. When the work had reached a later stage it was Professor Dr. C. van de Kieft who was willing, as a co-referent, to scrutinize this study with all his scholarly conscientiousness. We quite realize that not all of their objections have been met, although many changes were made.

The Netherlands' Organization for the Advancement of Pure Research (Z.W.O.) made two short trips to England possible. We were thus able to consult the archives for the material needed, as well as posing relevant questions to several people.

For their kind assistance in this respect we owe thanks to Mrs. M. Bindoff, John Brooke, H. Butterfield, V.H. Galbraith, A.T. Milne, Graham Pollard and G. Palgrave Barker. We wish to make grateful mention of the cooperation extended to us by the institutions we visited in England: the Register of National Archives, the British Museum, the University of London Library, the University College of London, the Public Record Office, the Bodleian Library, the Cambridge University Library. The same goes for the University Library of Amsterdam and the Royal Library (Koninklijke Bibliotheek) in The Hague.

The English text corresponds on the whole with the original Dutch text of 1974. However, corrections have been made in every chapter; passages were shortened or left out. Apart from the beginning of the first chapter (translated by Mr. H.S. Lake) the book was translated into English by Tine van Wijk (Bennekom, Gelderland). I am greatly indebted to her for the zeal and capability shown in tackling a difficult job. I am equally indebted to Phyllis Mitzman for her final censorship of the English text. The text was typed out by secretaries of the Historical Seminar of the University of Amsterdam, the brunt of this in many respects very thankless job being borne by Ineke van Dijk: if I name her especially I am equally honouring her colleagues. Although I usually respect her aversion to obligatory public praise, I insist on taking this opportunity of dedicating this work to my wife Tiny in heartfelt gratitude for the indispensable help she gave me during the long preparatory years.

Finally let me say that I am very grateful to the Netherlands' Organization for the Advancement of Pure Research (Z.W.O.) for the aid which rendered both the publication and the translation of this work possible.

INTRODUCTION

The subject of this study is a dual one: Whig historical writing of the nineteenth century and the criticism levelled against it during the first decades of this century. The best-known critics of Whig historiography are L. Namier and H. Butterfield, each of whom, in his own special way, laid bare, during the years before and after 1930, the short-comings of the Whig interpretation of history. Nevertheless, it would be mistaken to see their work as the very first expression of such criticism. If we analyse the development of English historical studies since 1890, it becomes clear that historians, especially medievalists, had been trying laboriously for several decades to free themselves from what Namier and Butterfield imputed to their nineteenth-century predecessors in the field of 18th-century constitutional history. The most serious failing of which earlier historians were repeatedly accused after 1890 was their severely anachronistic manner of interpretation, which represented past reality in far too modern terms. This Whig anachronism was rooted partly in an evolutionism characterized by strong teleological leanings which could scarcely present historical development as anything other than a continuous process moving linearly and purposefully towards the present. The more continuous and linear this development could be considered to be, the more meaningful its interpretation became.

A feature of this pattern of interpretation was the strong tendency to emphasize the similarities rather than the differences in the relation between past and present. The belief in a beneficial and still active continuity in many respects strengthened the anachronistic view of the past, especially that of Parliament and the Constitution.

About 1900, a reaction set in against these more general aspects of Whig history. This reaction took the form of a conscious attempt on the part of many historians to avoid anachronism as far as possible. An attempt was also made to substitute for the linear evolutionary way of thinking an 'accidental view of history,' while a greater appreciation of the 'historical law of unintended consequences' became evident, so that despite historical continuity the reality of change was more than ever emphasized.

The decline of Whig historiography after 1890 was due to a number of causes, principally within the discipline of history itself. The significance of constitutional history, the subject of Whig historical writing *par excellence*, was reduced to its true proportions (at an early stage, by J.R. Seeley) by, among other things, the rise in importance of new fields such as economic and administrative history. Another factor was the increasing professionalization of historical writing, which began with the attention to historical detail of what came to be known as 'record-history.'

These internal changes, however, were only able to make themselves felt at the end of the nineteenth century, when the political climate altered and liberal ideology underwent a change of direction. Certain political concepts which had been so essential to the Whig interpretation of history now became less obvious. For these to be more fully understood, and to test the validity of the anti-Whig reaction which followed, it has been necessary to examine more closely the development of Whig historical writing itself. This we did at some length in the second chapter, re-examining the work of the principal 19th-century Whig historians. We tried to find explanations for the increasing cogency of the Whig view in the 19th century.

Insight into the political constellation of Victorian England made the background and function of several Whig anachronisms understandable. Admittedly the 19th-century Whig historians paid hardly any attention to industrialization and its consequences, yet that does not render their writings 'irrelevant' for that period.[1] The anachronisms can only be understood within the context of their political and social functions, and the same applies to the other – general – characteristics of the Whig view, as, e.g., finalism and continuity. This historical view can only be called 'mythical' with regard to its functioning, for

the mythical account is . . . essentially different from the historical because it uses an exemplary model for action and thought. The myth posits the existence of a continuous meaning which links past and present, giving the im-

---

[1] Cf. G. Kitson Clark in *History and Theory* 13 (1974), p. 155; and Norman Baker in G.G. Iggers, *New Directions in European Historiography*, Middletown, Connecticut, 1975, p. 156.

pression that these belong as it were to the same reality and suggesting a
degree of coherence about the historical process unknown to the historian.[2]

Generally speaking Whig historiography – as did 19th-century continental history – undoubtedly retained some mythical traits in the
above-mentioned meaning. There were however notable exceptions
to this rule; we gave due attention to this fact in the second chapter.
We consider Sir Francis Palgrave to be one of the exceptions.

In the turbulent times before and after 1832, he was by far the most
important historian in the field of early parliamentary history. Significantly, he launched (together with Whig moderates such as J. Allen
and H. Hallam) certain ideas relating to the function and composition
of parliament – ideas which were later, at the end of the century, to be
taken up again by Maitland after they had disappeared or been pushed
into the background in Stubbs's great work. The early Whigs proved
to be more capable of resisting the tendency towards the formation of
historical myths than others like Stubbs. They opposed the myths
relating to early parliamentary history not only on historical grounds
but also by criticizing the advocates of a more radical parliamentary
reform who drew on the history of parliament in justification of their
ideas on annual parliaments and universal suffrage.

When after 1850 this 'radical danger' had disappeared for good, Whig
historians proved more willing to accord early (i.e. Anglo-Saxon) history a more important place within the whole context of constitutional
development. Only with Stubbs do we find a major synthesis of the
medieval constitutional evolution: in an original thesis postulating
continuity since 1066, Stubbs fuses the two political traditions (Anglo-
Saxon and Norman) into a harmonious unity; from this unity developed the English Parliament. Within the framework of Stubbs's synthesis and thesis of parliament there are two main ideas: representation
and (local) self-government. The important part which these concepts
play in Stubbs's work can be explained by a closer examination of certain of the political campaigning points of the second Reform Movement. Neither did Stubbs hesitate occasionally to include in his account of the medieval constitution certain political concepts such as the
idea of party and cabinet government or the principle of ministerial
responsibility – concepts which Stubbs borrowed from historical writing on later periods. The result of this was that during the nineteenth

[2] C.A. Tamse, 'The Political Myth' in *Britain and the Netherlands*, vol. V, Ed. J.S. Bromley
and E.H. Kossmann. The Hague, 1975, p. 7.

century the Whig approach increased, rather than decreased, in its intensity.

It was principally these ideas which formed the background of Macaulay's work on 1688 and of a number of books on the early years of the reign of George III. The gradual emergence of a parliamentary constitutional monarchy in the nineteenth century lent a great topicality to these periods, and whenever these principles were at issue we see the historical debate on them flaring up with renewed vigour. During the second half of the nineteenth century the interest of historians became more and more concentrated on the Civil War and Cromwell. This may have been a consequence of the fact that, under Gladstone, liberalism was increasingly exposed to the influence of nonconformist groups who regarded themselves as being closer to seventeenth-century puritanism than to the Whig tradition of the eighteenth century. Whig historiography, which so strongly emphasized the topicality and usefulness of the constitutional past, was very well in tune with Victorian society, after 1850 so tellingly characterized by Bagehot as a 'deferential society.'

As the end of the century approached, however, this belief in the value of tradition began to wane, and the past came to be thought of as ballast, as something of no use, as an anachronism. A new political slogan, Efficiency (whose precise meaning was not always clear), was used to criticize tradition on a number of counts, and enjoyed a remarkable vogue during a serious crisis which the House of Commons underwent in the years following 1880 as well as during the South African crisis at the turn of the century. The Liberal party itself was beset with troubles. The emergence of modern mass democracy and the growing bureaucracy and centralization within both state and society lessened the power of the old ideas of local self-government and did much to weaken the power of parliament. The more elements of the past came to be seen as anachronistic, the more it seemed possible for historians to put the past in a historical perspective and interpret it less anachronistically.

The importance of this growing tendency for historians to distance themselves from the past and view it more critically may be illustrated by the work of F.W. Maitland. Precisely because for the whole of his life he had been a sharply utilitarian critic of the anachronisms still existing in the English legal system, as a medievalist he was particularly anxious to avoid as far as possible anachronisms in his account of the development of that system during the Middle Ages. Due to his legal training he was acutely conscious, as a historian, of the great and in-surmountable differences between the lawyer's historical interpreta-tion of the law and that of the historian. In his research into the early history of parliament in the Middle Ages, too, he arrived at a less anachronistic view, becoming increasingly aware of the originality, in this respect, of Palgrave's work.

Maitland's study of the parliament of 1305 was an inspiration to many historians, including A.F. Pollard. Pollard, who was in many ways successful in furthering the study of history in London, came to be known after 1900 mainly for his work on the early Tudor period. He is significant for being the first liberal historian to view Henry VIII and Tudor despotism in general as a necessary and indispensable episode in the progression of England's constitutional development. No Whig historian had been capable of this. Unlike J.R. Green, Pollard regarded the period of the New Monarchy in a most positive light, and was clearly influenced by the change which took place in Liberal ideology at the turn of the century. In all his work, particularly his study of the evolution of parliament, Pollard revealed his acute perception of the many unplanned and unforeseen facets which are typical of historical development as such. In this way he expressly distanced himself from the linear historical evolutionism of the Whigs. Rejecting the nine-teenth-century view of history, he repeatedly stressed the enormous differences between present and past and between the Middle Ages and the early modern age – sometimes in so extreme a manner that criticism of his view of parliamentary development from the medie-valists could scarcely have been expected not to be forthcoming.

Modern writing on the history of parliament was given a fresh im-petus by a new discipline within the broad field of history: administra-tive history. This branch of historical scholarship, which was patently a product of contemporary experience of the process of bureaucratiza-tion, attracted the attention of many historians, including Maitland and Pollard. However, the figure (and work) most associated with the field of administrative history is that of T.F. Tout, who had early been impressed by the achievements of French institutional history. In its opposition to the manner of interpretation of constitutional history, which was concerned largely with the history of ideas and was some-times strongly legalistic in its thinking, administrative history dealt with the actual working of the constitution.

Its approach was intentionally de-ideologizing: the 'how' of the or-ganization of government was more important than the 'why,' and the actual working of the constitution was taken to be more relevant than its political content. It was Tout's conviction that it was precisely this branch of historical studies which would lead the historian to a more autonomous (and less anachronistic) interpretation of the past. This view, however, finally proved an illusion. The ever-increasing specialization and splitting up of historical research in 'branches' failed to provide sufficient guarantees against anachronisms. The picture of the past frequently arrived at by a self-enclosed administrative history was, as the critic F.M. Powicke observed, too bureaucratic in the modern sense of the word. The most integrated historical approach possible, consciously supported by thorough historical specialization of time and place, would appear to be a sufficient guarantee against anachronistic elements in the writing of history.

The present study is, for the most part, a historiographic one of the kind which abounds in the history of historical writing. No conclusive studies have yet been published on English and French historiography for the period 1890–1930, and it is this blank which this work – as far as England is concerned – proposes to fill. However, there is more to the study of historiography, in our opinion, than just an examination of political-social and other ideological influence in the work of historians.

Such an approach seems to be too limited, and based on a too easy acceptance of historical relativism. Within those limitations the history of historiography would be merely a history of ideas, almost useless for closer understanding of the way in which historical knowledge is formed.

This book hopes to provide something more than the usual historiographical survey that only places a historical work within the context of its time. Certainly in recent historiography we cannot overlook the outspoken attempts of historians to avoid such contemporary influences. The reaction to Whig historiography was focused on those attempts, and it is for that very reason that the problem of anachronism keeps recurring in the present study.

Amsterdam, November 1976

ABBREVIATIONS

A.H.R.	*American Historical Review*
B.I.H.R.	*Bulletin Institute Historical Research*
B.L.	Bodleian Library
C.U.L.	Cambridge University Library
D.N.B.	*Dictionary of National Biography*
E.B.	*Encyclopaedia Britannica*
E.H.R.	*English Historical Review*
E.R.	*Edinburgh Review*
P.R.O.	Public Record Office
Q.R.	*Quarterly Review*
T.L.S.	*Times Literary Supplement*
T.R.H.S.	*Transactions Royal Historical Society*
U.L.L.	University of London Library

its parliamentary system.[8] In 1930 the American, W.T. Laprade, in a lecture gave an extensive summary of the situation with regard to historical writing about the eighteenth century. The many legendary stories about eighteenth-century England which had been propounded during the nineteenth century received special attention: "Men in the nineteenth century had a distorted view of their predecessors, similar to that which vitiates the judgements pronounced on the age of Victoria by sophisticated youths in the passing generation."[9] As regarded the new 'revisionist' literature on the ruling political élite, Namier's studies were undoubtedly among the best, but, he continued, "a serious weakness in his work, so carefully done in many respects, is his failure to make adequate use of newspapers, periodicals, and pamphlets which the rival politicians and their lieutenants used in their struggles with each other."[10]

From the very beginning it was clear that many of Namier's colleagues shared this ambivalent attitude towards his work: praise for his precision, criticism of his decision to restrict his field of research so narrowly. Later, especially after the Second World War, it was to be reiterated in even stronger terms, principally by Herbert Butterfield.[11]

A year later Namier's second book, *England in the Age of the American Revolution*, again received generally favourable reviews in the specialist journals.[12] Nevertheless, at the beginning of the nineteen-thirties there was no sign at all that there might one day be talk of a 'Namier revolution' or of 'Namierism.' Namier himself was so preoccupied with the political events of the decade that he was never able to devote himself to his favourite century as absolutely as he had wanted, and the historian Plumb rightly observes that the time itself was unfavourable to

---

[8] Cf. e.g. Richard Lodge in *History* 14 (1929–1930), pp. 269–270.
[9] W.T. Laprade, 'The Present State of the History of England in the Eighteenth Century' in *Journal of Modern History* 4 (1932), p. 581.
[10] *Ibid.*, p. 589.
[11] Mainly in H. Butterfield, *George III and The Historians*, London, 1957. His later criticisms were less harsh, cf. his review of the *History of Parliament. The House of Commons, 1754–1790*. (3 vols.) London, 1964 in *E.H.R.* 80 (1965), pp. 801–805. In the preface to this *magnum opus* stated J. Brooke very clearly that it had always been Namier's firm conviction "that the conclusion he had reached about the middle years of the century might not necessarily be true for an earlier or later period" (p. IX). Namier's critics still tend to overlook this, cf., e.g., John Cannon, *The Fox-North Coalition. Crisis of the Constitution, 1782–1784*, Cambridge, 1969, esp. pp. 239–242.
[12] With praise by H.H. Bellot in *E.H.R.* 47 (1932), pp. 677–679, Cf. also Richard Lodge in *History* 16 (1931–1932), pp. 172–176. J.H. Plumb remarked that "the second book had a somewhat poor press," but this does not seem to apply to the professional journals (*New Statesman*, 1-8-1969, p. 141).

CHAPTER I

THE PRESUPPOSITIONS OF WHIG HISTORICAL WRITING

> The decade of the 1890's has a special importance in the history of historical scholarship in Great Britain.
>
> (H. Butterfield)

When in 1903 Bury made his much discussed inaugural speech on the science of history it elicited sharp reaction, particularly from G.M. Trevelyan. Only once, however, did Bury answer his critics, and then only by intimating that the intent of his message had been distorted.[1]

With his pronouncement that 'history is a science, no less and no more,' Bury put into words what many historians of his generation had already felt. In the first place this 'definition' was both a challenge to an existing type of dilettante historiography and a call for professionalization through specialization. It was not a hypothesis founded on scientific theory, nor was it a statement of fact; it was the expression of a fervent desire to break with an older form of historical study and writing, a desire which had grown partly from his reflections on the work of two brilliant Oxford historians, W. Stubbs and E.A. Freeman, which he respected and which, certainly in Freeman's case, had been a considerable source of inspiration to him.[2] What, then, was the difficulty with their work? "It is significant," he said, "that two brilliant historians, to both of whom the study of history in this country is deeply indebted, built perilous superstructures in regard to the English Con-

---

[1] J.B. Bury wrote in the preface of his *Life of St. Patrick* (London, 1905), p. VIII, note 1: "I may be permitted to remark that in vindicating the claims of history to be regarded as a science or *Wissenschaft*, I never meant to suggest a proposition so indefensible as that the presentation of the results of historical research is not an art, requiring the tact and skill in selection and arrangement which belong to the literary faculty." Referring to criticism by John Morley (*Nineteenth Century and After*, October, 1904) and by S.H. Butcher (*Harvard Lectures on Greek Subjects*, 1904) he admitted that his own lack of precision had caused this misunderstanding. For Trevelyan's immediate sharp reaction, see G.M. Trevelyan, 'The Latest View of History' in *The Independent Review* 1 (1903–1904), pp. 395–414. For reactions by other historians, see *E.H.R.* 18 (1903), pp. 605–606; C.H. Firth, *A Plea for the Historical Teaching of History*, Oxford, 1904; G.W. Prothero in *T.R.H.S.*, N.S. 19 (1905), p. 17 ff.; see also A.L. Rowse, *The Use of History*, London, 1946, pp. 86–113.
[2] Freeman's influence on Bury: see esp., N.H. Baynes, *A. Bibliography of the Works of J.B. Bury*. Compiled with a Memoir by N.H. Baynes, Cambridge, 1929, pp. 13, 60, 64–44. Cf. *The Life an Letters of E.A. Freeman*, ed. W.R.W. Stephens, London, 1895, II, p. 453, and J.B. Bury, *History of Greece*, London, 1959, pp. 53 ff., 631, 857, 893.

quest upon speculations which were only superior specimens of the prescientific type."[3] While Trevelyan's reaction could be called contingent and coincidental, Bury's stand in 1903, like the background from which it had emerged, was anything but that.

Putting the study of history on a scientific footing became a demand heard with increasing frequency and formed a regular constituent of the many inaugural speeches made in the years before and after 1900; speakers repeatedly deplored the way in which English historical studies were undeniably lagging behind their German and French counterparts.[4] The pursuit of professionalization was an important element of the desire for a breath of fresh air in English historical studies at the turn of the century. The implications of this will not only be discussed in the first chapter but will also be a recurring theme throughout this dissertation.

Whence came the impulses which gave so much force to this desire? Although the influence of developments within historical scholarship on the continent must not be underestimated, the reformists strengthened their position principally by adopting an oppositional attitude towards the historical writing of an earlier generation. This new view challenged the more traditional one. With some surprise Bury observed in Victorian historiography dangerous superstructures founded on unsound speculation.

Is it possible to come to a more precise definition of this new attitude towards the past and to show why the beginning of this revival should have occurred at the end of the nineteenth century and the beginning of the twentieth? In this introductory chapter I shall confine myself to the first part of this question and propose some theoretical reflections. What aspects of Victorian historical writing were subjected to a particularly severe attack? To say that the attack was directed at the Whig character of nineteenth-century historiography does not explain much unless we first understand clearly what is meant by Whig historiography. It is difficult to work with such vague terms as Whig historical writing or Whig historiography if we do not first agree upon a measure of consensus regarding its characteristics. In my view this is not only possible, but also desirable in order to bring the period 1890–1930 into perspective.

---

[3] *Selected Essays of J.B. Bury*, ed. H.W.V. Temperley, Cambridge, 1930, p. 20.

[4] Cf. C.H. Firth's inauguration speech of 1904 (note 1) and A.F. Pollard, 'The Study of History' 1904 (in A.F. Pollard's *Factors in Modern History*, London, 1948, pp. 234–254). See also F.Y. Powell, 'The Study of History in Universities' in O. Elton, *F.Y. Powell*, Oxford, 1906, II, pp. 80–95.

A. THE 'PRE-NAMIER' PERIOD AND THE GROWING CRITICISM OF THE FEATURES OF WHIG HISTORICAL INTERPRETATION: ANACHRONISM, FINALISM AND HISTORICAL CONTINUITY

In 1929 A.F. Pollard wrote in a review of H. Fisher's lecture Whig Historians that it would be difficult to define precisely of historian. Nevertheless, he hazarded a provisional descript must be a parliamentarian and must write about the eightee tury mainly to justify the English or the American revolutio reform bill of 1832."[5] One of the points to emerge from th ordinary definition is that in his conception Whig historiogra far from limited to the eighteenth century. Elsewhere in review Pollard said of the conservative medievalist Stubbs wrote and thought like a Whig without himself realizing it.

The first major work by L. Namier on the eighteenth cen *Structure of Politics at the Accession of George III*, also appeared i dealt with the British constitution during the eighteenth cer heralded an important reorientation in historical thinking was to become the man who finally eliminated a number myths relating to political corruption and the absolutism of G from the image of the eighteenth century; however in 1929 carried none of its later authority.[6]

Despite this, the real value of Namier's study did not e notice of the reviewers. "No previous writer," wrote D.A. W "has ever made so thorough and gallant an attempt to discove *workings* of the political system of the eighteenth century."[7] take long, however, for praise of this kind to be joined by particularly since the ambitious title of Namier's study did r accord with the content and subject-matter of the eight 'co says' which it comprised. An examination of a nation's entir structure demanded more than simply an analysis of the s

---

[5] *E.H.R.* 44 (1929), p. 690. See H.A.L. Fisher, 'The Whig Historians' in *the British Academy* 14 (1928), pp. 297–339. Reprinted in H.A.L. Fisher, *Page* London, 1939. Cf. also: R.W.K. Hinton, 'History Yesterday: Five Point History' in *History Today* 9 (1959), pp. 720–728.

[6] In Namier's first study few Whig historians were mentioned by name, ti tions being: W. Hunt and W.E.H. Lecky. See *The Structure of Politics at the Ac III*, London, 1961, pp. 121 (note 2), 158 ff., esp. pp. 182–183.

[7] *E.H.R.* 44 (1929), p. 657. Our italics.

Namier. 'The Thirties were riven by ideological strife,'[13] he wrote, and there was scarcely room for a 'structural' method as 'de-ideologizing' as Namier's. Even so, the nineteen-fifties, described by Plumb as 'deeply conservative,' saw a tremendous revival of the Namier method. It became fashionable to refer to 'Namierism' or a 'Namier Revolution'; in short, Namier became 'the creator of a new precision.'[14] These slogans were not only used by his admirers – indeed, they were introduced by his opponents, who in their sometimes sharp criticism strengthened the tendency to ascribe to Namier's influence anything which purported to be original detailed 'biographical' research. Butterfield spoke of a Namier school and called Namier's sympathizers a 'formidable squadron,' by which term differences and nuances were neglected.[15]

The concept of 'disciple' proved to be extremely elastic. Contemporaries such as J.E. Neale, A. Aspinall and the classical historian, H.H. Scullard, who had chosen the path of biographical research at least as early as Namier, subsequently found themselves not infrequently branded as 'Namierites.'[16] A pupil of Pollard's, Neale, took upon himself the task of researching both the composition and the actual functioning of the parliaments of the Elizabethan era, and at about the same time Aspinall started revising the traditional picture of the political structure of the early nineteenth century. Aspinall had been a student of the Manchester History School which had flourished under T.F. Tout, and everyone was aware of the significance of such a qualification. When in 1927 Aspinall's first book was published, on Lord Brougham, H. Temperley wrote: "The author is . . . as might be expected from the Manchester School, very precise and conscientious in his use of material and, in most cases, both moderate and impartial in his statements."[17] This precision led to much reinterpretation: "We shall have to reinterpret the political history of this period from the

[13] J.H. Plumb, 'The Atomic Historian' in *New Statesman* 1-8-1969, p. 142. Cf. also J.M. Price in *Journal of British Studies* 1 (Nov. 1961), p. 76.
[14] David Thomson, *England in the Twentieth Century*, Harmondsworth, 1965, p. 185.
[15] H. Butterfield, *George III and the Historians*, p. 203.
[16] A most informative article is: D.J. Roorda, 'Sir Lewis Namier, een inspirerend en irriterend historicus' in *Tijdschrift voor Geschiedenis* 75 (1962), pp. 325–347, esp. p. 340 ff.; there was initially some scepticism concerning the interpretation of H.H. Scullard in his book *Scipio Africanus in the Second Punic War* (Cambridge, 1930): "The theory that the rivalry between alliances of noble families is the key to Roman politics during the latter part of the third century B.C. is far from winning general acceptance," as Brogan wrote in *History* 18 (1933–1934), p. 357. A Survey of the prosopographic method may be found in L. Stone, 'Prosopography' in *Daedalus* (winter, 1971), pp. 46–79.
[17] *E.H.R.* 44 (1929), p. 313.

new angle of party organisation," wrote Aspinall in 1930 regarding 'his' period, and it was this aspect which became the subject of his first important article.[18]

I do not mean to depreciate Namier's importance: despite his short-comings as a historian there can be no doubt whatever of his significance, nor of his influence in the refinement of historiographical technique and method of research regarding the English parliament of the eighteenth century. The 'Namier method' is neither more nor less than a more efficient research technique, according to John Brooke, a student of his. Whether Namier invented the method himself or whether others may have preceded him 'is not of great consequence.'[19]

This last pronouncement is not wholly convincing. The picture of Namier as the 'inventor' of a new technique of historical research suggests a new beginning, which fails to do justice to the developments that had gradually been taking place in English historical scholarship since the turn of the century. Even if he did come from 'elsewhere,' Lewis Namier was not the *Deus ex machina* which he is sometimes taken for. This representation of him is unfair, because it inevitably leads to underestimation of the previous reforms in English historical circles. It is this Namier legend, and not Namier himself, which threatens to depreciate the importance to English historical studies of the years between 1890 and 1930. At the same time, however, it must again be stressed that depreciating Namier's work on the eighteenth century leads equally to a distorted view of the evolution of English historical studies during the early part of the present century. The most thoroughgoing change effected by Namier's revaluation was in Whig conceptions of the eighteenth century, previously a stronghold of Whig presentism. This was partly because the history of the opposition to George III, as we shall see, directly accorded with liberal ideology in the nineteenth century. Yet what Namier undertook for the eighteenth century was, as it were, a special final offensive by an anti-Whig revisionism which is already discernible among English historians studying other centuries and other eras during the first three decades of the twentieth century.

---

[18] *History* 15 (1930–1931), p. 172, cf. also his reviews on pp. 374–375, and in *History* 16 (1931–1932), p. 364. The title of his first article was: 'English Party Organization in the Early Nineteenth Century' in *E.H.R.* 41 (1926), pp. 389–411. In 1953 N. Gash repeated: "The history of party organization is still to be written even though the outlines of the subject are becoming clearer" (N. Gash, *Politics in the Age of Peel*, London, 1953, p. XVII).

[19] J. Brooke, 'Namier and Namierism' in *Studies in the Philosophy of History*, ed. G.H. Nadel, New York, 1965, p. 101.

THE PRESUPPOSITIONS OF WHIG HISTORICAL WRITING

The decade of the 1890's has a special importance in the history of historical scholarship in Great Britain.

(H. Butterfield)

When in 1903 Bury made his much discussed inaugural speech on the science of history it elicited sharp reaction, particularly from G.M. Trevelyan. Only once, however, did Bury answer his critics, and then only by intimating that the intent of his message had been distorted.[1]

With his pronouncement that 'history is a science, no less and no more,' Bury put into words what many historians of his generation had already felt. In the first place this 'definition' was both a challenge to an existing type of dilettante historiography and a call for professionalization through specialization. It was not a hypothesis founded on scientific theory, nor was it a statement of fact; it was the expression of a fervent desire to break with an older form of historical study and writing, a desire which had grown partly from his reflections on the work of two brilliant Oxford historians, W. Stubbs and E.A. Freeman, which he respected and which, certainly in Freeman's case, had been a considerable source of inspiration to him.[2] What, then, was the difficulty with their work? "It is significant," he said, "that two brilliant historians, to both of whom the study of history in this country is deeply indebted, built perilous superstructures in regard to the English Con-

---

[1] J.B. Bury wrote in the preface of his *Life of St. Patrick* (London, 1905), p. VIII, note 1: "I may be permitted to remark that in vindicating the claims of history to be regarded as a science or *Wissenschaft*, I never meant to suggest a proposition so indefensible as that the presentation of the results of historical research is not an art, requiring the tact and skill in selection and arrangement which belong to the literary faculty." Referring to criticism by John Morley (*Nineteenth Century and After*, October, 1904) and by S.H. Butcher (*Harvard Lectures on Greek Subjects*, 1904) he admitted that his own lack of precision had caused this misunderstanding. For Trevelyan's immediate sharp reaction, see G.M. Trevelyan, 'The Latest View of History' in *The Independent Review* 1 (1903–1904), pp. 395–414. For reactions by other historians, see *E.H.R.* 18 (1903), pp. 605–606; C.II. Firth, *A Plea for the Historical Teaching of History*, Oxford, 1904; G.W. Prothero in *T.R.H.S.*, N.S. 19 (1905), p. 17 ff.; see also A.L. Rowse, *The Use of History*, London, 1946, pp. 86–113.

[2] Freeman's influence on Bury: see esp., N.H. Baynes, *A. Bibliography of the Works of J.B. Bury*. Compiled with a Memoir by N.H. Baynes, Cambridge, 1929, pp. 13, 60, 64–44. Cf. *The Life an Letters of E.A. Freeman*, ed. W.R.W. Stephens, London, 1895, II, p. 453, and J.B. Bury, *History of Greece*, London, 1959, pp. 53 ff., 631, 857, 893.

quest upon speculations which were only superior specimens of the prescientific type."[3] While Trevelyan's reaction could be called contingent and coincidental, Bury's stand in 1903, like the background from which it had emerged, was anything but that.

Putting the study of history on a scientific footing became a demand heard with increasing frequency and formed a regular constituent of the many inaugural speeches made in the years before and after 1900; speakers repeatedly deplored the way in which English historical studies were undeniably lagging behind their German and French counterparts.[4] The pursuit of professionalization was an important element of the desire for a breath of fresh air in English historical studies at the turn of the century. The implications of this will not only be discussed in the first chapter but will also be a recurring theme throughout this dissertation.

Whence came the impulses which gave so much force to this desire? Although the influence of developments within historical scholarship on the continent must not be underestimated, the reformists strengthened their position principally by adopting an oppositional attitude towards the historical writing of an earlier generation. This new view challenged the more traditional one. With some surprise Bury observed in Victorian historiography dangerous superstructures founded on unsound speculation.

Is it possible to come to a more precise definition of this new attitude towards the past and to show why the beginning of this revival should have occurred at the end of the nineteenth century and the beginning of the twentieth? In this introductory chapter I shall confine myself to the first part of this question and propose some theoretical reflections. What aspects of Victorian historical writing were subjected to a particularly severe attack? To say that the attack was directed at the Whig character of nineteenth-century historiography does not explain much unless we first understand clearly what is meant by Whig historiography. It is difficult to work with such vague terms as Whig historical writing or Whig historiography if we do not first agree upon a measure of consensus regarding its characteristics. In my view this is not only possible, but also desirable in order to bring the period 1890–1930 into perspective.

[3] *Selected Essays of J.B. Bury*, ed. H.W.V. Temperley, Cambridge, 1930, p. 20.
[4] Cf. C.H. Firth's inauguration speech of 1904 (note 1) and A.F. Pollard, 'The Study of History' 1904 (in A.F. Pollard's *Factors in Modern History*, London, 1948, pp. 234–254). See also F.Y. Powell, 'The Study of History in Universities' in O. Elton, *F.Y. Powell*, Oxford, 1906, II, pp. 80–95.

A. THE 'PRE-NAMIER' PERIOD AND THE GROWING CRITICISM OF THE FEATURES OF WHIG HISTORICAL INTERPRETATION: ANACHRONISM, FINALISM AND HISTORICAL CONTINUITY

In 1929 A.F. Pollard wrote in a review of H. Fisher's lecture on The Whig Historians that it would be difficult to define precisely this type of historian. Nevertheless, he hazarded a provisional description: "he must be a parliamentarian and must write about the eighteenth century mainly to justify the English or the American revolution or the reform bill of 1832."[5] One of the points to emerge from this extraordinary definition is that in his conception Whig historiography was far from limited to the eighteenth century. Elsewhere in the same review Pollard said of the conservative medievalist Stubbs that he wrote and thought like a Whig without himself realizing it.

The first major work by L. Namier on the eighteenth century, *The Structure of Politics at the Accession of George III*, also appeared in 1929. It dealt with the British constitution during the eighteenth century and heralded an important reorientation in historical thinking. Namier was to become the man who finally eliminated a number of Whig myths relating to political corruption and the absolutism of George III from the image of the eighteenth century; however in 1929 his name carried none of its later authority.[6]

Despite this, the real value of Namier's study did not escape the notice of the reviewers. "No previous writer," wrote D.A. Winstanley, "has ever made so thorough and gallant an attempt to discover *the actual workings* of the political system of the eighteenth century."[7] It did not take long, however, for praise of this kind to be joined by criticism, particularly since the ambitious title of Namier's study did not entirely accord with the content and subject-matter of the eight 'collected essays' which it comprised. An examination of a nation's entire political structure demanded more than simply an analysis of the structure of

---

[5] *E.H.R.* 44 (1929), p. 690. See H.A.L. Fisher, 'The Whig Historians' in *Proceedings of the British Academy* 14 (1928), pp. 297–339. Reprinted in H.A.L. Fisher, *Pages from the Past*, London, 1939. Cf. also: R.W.K. Hinton, 'History Yesterday: Five Points about Whig History' in *History Today* 9 (1959), pp. 720–728.

[6] In Namier's first study few Whig historians were mentioned by name, the only exceptions being: W. Hunt and W.E.H. Lecky. See *The Structure of Politics at the Accession of George III*, London, 1961, pp. 121 (note 2), 158 ff., esp. pp. 182–183.

[7] *E.H.R.* 44 (1929), p. 657. Our italics.

its parliamentary system.[8] In 1930 the American, W.T. Laprade, in a lecture gave an extensive summary of the situation with regard to historical writing about the eighteenth century. The many legendary stories about eighteenth-century England which had been propounded during the nineteenth century received special attention: "Men in the nineteenth century had a distorted view of their predecessors, similar to that which vitiates the judgements pronounced on the age of Victoria by sophisticated youths in the passing generation."[9] As regarded the new 'revisionist' literature on the ruling political élite, Namier's studies were undoubtedly among the best, but, he continued, "a serious weakness in his work, so carefully done in many respects, is his failure to make adequate use of newspapers, periodicals, and pamphlets which the rival politicians and their lieutenants used in their struggles with each other."[10]

From the very beginning it was clear that many of Namier's colleagues shared this ambivalent attitude towards his work: praise for his precision, criticism of his decision to restrict his field of research so narrowly. Later, especially after the Second World War, it was to be reiterated in even stronger terms, principally by Herbert Butterfield.[11]

A year later Namier's second book, *England in the Age of the American Revolution*, again received generally favourable reviews in the specialist journals.[12] Nevertheless, at the beginning of the nineteen-thirties there was no sign at all that there might one day be talk of a 'Namier revolution' or of 'Namierism.' Namier himself was so preoccupied with the political events of the decade that he was never able to devote himself to his favourite century as absolutely as he had wanted, and the historian Plumb rightly observes that the time itself was unfavourable to

---

[8] Cf. e.g. Richard Lodge in *History* 14 (1929–1930), pp. 269–270.

[9] W.T. Laprade, 'The Present State of the History of England in the Eighteenth Century' in *Journal of Modern History* 4 (1932), p. 581.

[10] *Ibid.*, p. 589.

[11] Mainly in H. Butterfield, *George III and The Historians*, London, 1957. His later criticisms were less harsh, cf. his review of the *History of Parliament. The House of Commons, 1754–1790.* (3 vols.) London, 1964 in *E.H.R.* 80 (1965), pp. 801–805. In the preface to this *magnum opus* stated J. Brooke very clearly that it had always been Namier's firm conviction "that the conclusion he had reached about the middle years of the century might not necessarily be true for an earlier or later period" (p. IX). Namier's critics still tend to overlook this, cf., e.g., John Cannon, *The Fox-North Coalition. Crisis of the Constitution, 1782–1784*, Cambridge, 1969, esp. pp. 239–242.

[12] With praise by H.H. Bellot in *E.H.R.* 47 (1932), pp. 677–679, Cf. also Richard Lodge in *History* 16 (1931–1932), pp. 172–176. J.H. Plumb remarked that "the second book had a somewhat poor press," but this does not seem to apply to the professional journals (*New Statesman*, 1-8-1969, p. 141).

But Namier also had his 'predecessors' for the eighteenth century. A quantity of new writing with anti-Whig tendencies had been summarized in 1930 by Laprade, in the lecture previously mentioned. Butterfield, as part of his criticism of Namier, also pointed to forerunners, by which he meant not only continental writers but also English specialists writing on the eighteenth century in the early twentieth century: "Even in English historiography ... the Whig interpretation of the reign of George III was soon to be undermined though in gradual stages."[20] It is the gradualness of this undermining, however, which deserves the most emphasis. The figures named by Butterfield, such as W. Hunt, H. Temperley, W. Anson and finally D.A. Winstanley, unmasked the anachronistic distortions in Whig historiography only with difficulty and often only in minor points of detail. In this context Winstanley's laudatory remarks (quoted above) on Namier's first book are especially relevant: it was Namier who had brought about the breakthrough.[21] Of the four men just mentioned, Hunt and Winstanley were least capable of relinquishing the old Victorian pattern of interpretation. Winstanley's study of the notorious first six years of George III's reign (*Personal and Party Government*, 1910) was described by Hunt as too abstract: too much was seen 'by the light of future events, without making full allowance for the circumstances of their time.'[22] Yet Hunt's own work was anything but free of this kind of anachronistic perspective.[23] Winstanley's second work (*Lord Chatham and the Whig Opposition*, 1912) was in many respects just as traditionally Burkean in its views.[24]

Temperley and Anson were more important 'pre-Namier' pioneers. Temperley sought a 'correct understanding of the machinery of the central executive,' and in order to arrive at a correct interpretation of the operation of political structure in the eighteenth century he concluded in 1912 that it was necessary to shift the first beginnings of the 'modern cabinet system' to the last quarter of the eighteenth century.[25]

[20] H. Butterfield, *George III and the Historians*, p. 182. For more information about these 'precursors' see pp. 169–190.

[21] Cf. note 7.

[22] *E.H.R.* 25 (1910), p. 785.

[23] H. Butterfield on W. Hunt, in *George III and the Historians*, p. 176 ff.

[24] Cf. B. Williams in *E.H.R.* 28 (1913), p. 168: "Like Burke, he (Winstanley) sees in the Rockinghams the great mainstay for enlightened government and like Burke, he tends to see in Chatham the villain of the piece who made united party opposition impossible." See also Butterfield (*Op. cit.*, p. 297). On Winstanley, see G.M. Trevelyan, *An Autobiography and Other Essays*, London, 1949, pp. 235–237.

[25] H.W.V. Temperley, 'Inner and Outer Cabinet and Privy Council, 1689–1783' in *E.H.R.* 27 (1912), pp. 682–699. See, for all the literature on this subject during the thirties,

Two years later Anson produced an excellent piece of work on the same subject, in which it was possible to detect a large dose of revisionism, or for those who preferred the term, 'Namierism.' Anson considered Temperley's account too schematic, and pointed out the meaninglessness and inapplicability of such modern concepts as 'party discipline,' 'party government' and 'ministerial responsibility' when dealing with the eighteenth century. In his criticism he warned against what he called 'a large anticipation of facts': "There is a good deal of unreality about party government in the eighteenth century, and if we allow ourselves to talk of the cabinets of George I and George II as though they correspond to the cabinets of Sir Robert Peel or Mr. Gladstone, we fall into error."[26]

Butterfield is not the only person to have pointed out this first move towards reform in the years before the First World War. In his Ford Lectures Namier himself recognized the importance of this first small step. The Namier legend of the nineteen-fifties tended to underestimate the importance of the 'pre-Namier' period. Namier himself never did so. In 1934 he praised Temperley as a pioneer and appreciated Anson's 'intuitive' understanding of the unique character of the eighteenth century.[27] Furthermore, Namier realized that where the refinement of historical research techniques was concerned, the medievalists had an advantage over the specialists in modern history. For the new era he demanded 'careful and incisive studies comparable with the work on medieval history.'[28] H.W.C. Davis, originally a medievalist, had also rightly held up medieval studies as an example for the study of more recent times: "Is it not legitimate, is it not proper and necessary, that modern history, even the history of the nineteenth century, should be studied as patiently and scientifically as that of the Middle Ages"?[29]

I need not go any further into a question which has already occupied many people: the 'ideological' background to Namier's 'de-ideolo-

---

Trevor Williams's article 'The Cabinet in the Eighteenth Century' (Historical Revision, no. 83) in *History* 22 (1937–1938), pp. 240–252, cf. pp. 332–334. For Temperley, L.M. Penson in *History* 24 (1939–1940), pp. 121–124. His studies on 19th-century dipomacy were also renewing in the 'Namierist' sense, cf. A. Marwick, *The Nature of History*, London, 1970 p. 93: "Both (Webster and Temperley) showed an almost Namierite interest in the mechanics of the Foreign Office."

[26] W.R. Anson, 'The Cabinet in the Seventeenth and Eighteenth Centuries' in *E.H.R.* 29 (1914), p. 65.

[27] L. Namier, *Crossroads of Power*, London, 1962, p. 94.

[28] L. Namier, *Avenues of History*, London, 1952, p. 137.

[29] H.W.C. Davis, *The Study of History*, Oxford, 1925, p. 10. In this connection too F. Powicke considered Aspinall's first study of lord Brougham an important result of Davis' influence in this direction. See F.M. Powicke, *Modern Historians and the Study of History*, London, 1955, p. 124.

gizing' method.[30] I touched on Namier only because any mention of an anti-Whig reaction in English historical scholarship automatically brings his name to mind. My intention has been to show Namier's aspirations and work only as an extension of an evolution. The description and analysis of the developments leading up to 'Namierism' will only be one of the important elements of this work. Let us therefore return to the question posed at the beginning of this chapter regarding the nature of the anti-Whig reaction in English historical circles at the turn of the century and thereafter.

What elements of Whig historical writing came under heaviest attack? In 1931 Butterfield published a short work entitled *The Whig Interpretation of History*. Unlike Namier's book published in the same year, it initially attracted relatively little attention.[31] It was not a full-sized study in depth, but rather a pamphlet in which various thoughts were recorded about the attitude to history taken by the Whigs, scarcely any of whom were ever mentioned by name.[32] It seems to me that the shortness of Butterfield's essay was not the only reason for its inconspi-

[30] More about this in the discussion between H.C. Mansfield and R. Walcott in *Journal of British Studies*, 1962–1964; H.C. Mansfield, 'Sir Lewis Namier Considered' in *Journal of British Studies* 2 (November 1962), pp. 28–55; R. Walcott, '"Sir Lewis Namier Considered" considered' in *Journal of British Studies* 3 (May 1964), pp. 85–108 en H.C. Mansfield, 'Sir Lewis Namier again considered' in *Journal of British Studies* 3 (May 1964), pp. 109–119. Mansfield makes an elaborate attempt to prove the contemporary character of Namier's method and interpretation: "In Namier's practice the destruction of nineteenth-century legends requires the dismissal of eighteenth-century opinions on the basis of twentieth-century and of eighteenth-century opinions which sustain those twentieth-century opinions" (*Journal of British Studies* 3 (May 1964), p. 113.) J. Brooke (cf. note 19) mentions Freud's influence, L.S. Sutherland Pareto's (*Proceedings of the British Academy*, vol. XLVIII, pp. 371–385).

[31] Cf. D.C. Somervell in *History* 17 (1932–1933), p. 86; cf. B.H. Summer in *E.H.R.* 48 (1933), pp. 174–175. There is a more extensive review by C.L. Becker in *Journal of Modern History* 4 (1932), pp. 278–279.

[32] Butterfield's interest in the history of historiography dates from a later period. He regarded his own work of 1931 as the result of a more theoretical view regarding the proper historical method. The matter of the moral judgments in history receives a great deal of attention, especially in his criticism of Acton. There is no denying the moralizing political tone of Victorian Whig historiography, but Acton's fervent plea for the necessity of a moral standard in historiography is not like the usual type of Victorian moralism. It should rather be contrasted to this, as G. Himmelfarb contends (*Victorian Minds*, New York, 1968, p. 177 ff.). Notwithstanding a few typical Whig anachronisms about the 18th-century constitution, Acton is the very opposite of a Whig in his historical ('iconoclastic' says Himmelfarb) stance. See H.G. Wood, *Christianity and the Nature of History*, (Cambridge, 1934, p. 111 ff.) for earlier criticisms of Butterfield's identification of Acton as a Whig. Two chapters of Butterfield's *Whig Interpretation of History* are of interest for our analysis of the general characteristics of Whig historiography. The chapters are 'The Underlying Assumption' (Ch. 2) and 'The Historical Process' (Ch. 3). Cf. H. Butterfield, 'Some Reflections on the Early Years of George III's Reign' in *Journal of British Studies* 4 (May 1965), pp. 78–101, esp. p. 95.

cuous arrival on the scene; his reflections were not so novel as to be assured of a better and more obvious reception. On the contrary, his little work was a summary of a development in English historical studies which had already been existent for several decades rather than a programmed exposé of a new course which one was expected to steer.[33] That Coke was criticized by Butterfield was anything but new; for years, as we shall see, this common lawyer had been a somewhat unpopular figure among historians. In 1931 Butterfield treated the subject in fairly abstract terms, and avoided committing himself on the concrete historical topics of the Whigs: Magna Carta, Lancastrian Constitutionalism, the Civil War, the Glorious Revolution and the opposition to George III, to name but a few. With Butterfield's reflections as our guide, let us now attempt to unravel the more general features of Whig historiography.

No complaint has been so consistently levelled against the Victorian Whigs as their 'present-mindedness': an approach to the past based exclusively on present concepts and directed towards the present, whichever era or course of events in medieval or modern history may be the subject of study. They studied history not 'for its own sake,' for they lacked the requisite historical 'feeling,' the 'past-mindedness' whereby the past could be seen and interpreted within its own context. This was not only Butterfield's main complaint, but also that of many others, including the American R.L. Schuyler in his attack on the presentism of the American 'New History.'[34] The medievalist V.H. Galbraith spoke of 'the pervading anachronism which underlay so much of liberal historical scholarship.'[35] In short, the Whig interpretation is an anachronistic interpretation, and in the words of the French historian Marc Bloch, history as a time-science knows no greater sin that that of anachronism.[36]

The epithet 'anachronistic' brings us to an old and vital problem of the study of history: the possibility of knowledge of the past 'from

---

[33] Cf. e.g. J.H. Plumb: "The fusillade started with the publication by Herbert Butterfield of his *Whig Interpretation of History* in 1931, a most appropriate date, for this year, more than any other, proclaimed the coming dissolution of the British Empire. After that opening shot, bombardment came thick and fast and still continues," in *The Death of the Past*, London, 1969, p. 42, note 1.

[34] H. Butterfield, *George III and the Historians*, pp. 169–171; H. Butterfield, 'Some Trends in Scholarship, 1868–1968, in the field of Modern History' in *T.R.H.S.* 5th. ser. 19 (1969), pp. 169–178. See, among others, articles by R.L. Schuyler. 'Some Historical Idols' in *Political Science Quarterly* 47 (1932), pp. 1–18 and 'The Usefulness of Useless History' in *Political Science Quarterly* 56 (1941), pp. 23–37.

[35] V.H. Galbraith, *Historical Study and the State*, Oxford, 1948, p. 7.

[36] Cf. L. Namier in *Personalities and Powers*, London, 1955, p. 11.

the inside out.' First there are a number of preliminary observations: is it reasonable to apply this term specifically to nineteenth-century Whig historiography? There can be no denying that precisely at the turn of the century outdated 'presentist' conceptions of the past were being unmasked within the English historiographical discipline, and particularly within medievalist circles. More than ever, historians were aware of this evil. Anachronisms in the work of previous historians were removed, the stubbornness of certain all too modern views regarding the past was continually denounced in critical reviews, and pretensions to a better understanding of the past as the past became increasingly common.[37] Thus a sharper eye for anachronisms as such and for the danger to historical studies inherent in them was undoubtedly an important feature of the new movement. We shall come across this repeatedly in the coming chapters.

Neither anachronisms themselves nor the fight against them were in the slightest degree new, so that those who have concerned themselves explicitly with the Whig interpretation of history are right when they state that the Whig approach is far older than the nineteenth century.[38] Anachronistic concepts have been a challenge ever since the beginnings of Western historiography in the sixteenth century. In the abundant literature about Renaissance historical writing no subject is treated more thoroughly or at greater length than that of anachronism – the 'concept of anachronism' by which the new, budding awareness of history may be recognized – to such an extent, indeed, that it is now possible to speak of an anachronistic, i.e. over-modern, use of the term 'anachronistic' itself.[39] It is argued that the modern historical scholarship owes its existence to the victory over the unhistorical, perspectiveless way of thinking of medieval man. But it can be called a Pyrrhic victory when four centuries later eminent historians are still qualifying the fight against anachronisms as an essential, if not *the* essential com-

---

[37] For instance A.L. Smith on H. Hallam: "his habitual vice of reading back into a monarchical age the parliamentary canons of a modern Whig" in *E.H.R.* 14 (1899), p. 749. Cf. J. Tait in *E.H.R.* 17 (1902), pp. 349–350; cf. J.N. Figgis in *E.H.R.* 19 (1904), p. 330 ff. and G.T. Lapsley in *E.H.R.* 24 (1909), p. 339. These examples could be extended with many others.

[38] Cf. F.M. Powicke in *Magna Carta Commemoration Essays*, ed. H.E. Malden, London, 1917, p. 97; V.H. Galbraith, *Roger Wendover and Matthew Paris*, Glasgow, 1970, p. 17 ff.; J.G.A. Pocock presents the best analyis of this medieval 'Whiggism' as it was revived in the 17th century in *The Ancient Constitution and the Feudal Law*, Cambridge, 1957. More about the assumption that Stubbs was re-animating an old view in his *Constitutional History*, see J.E. Neale in *Tudor Studies*, ed. R.W. Seton-Watson, London, 1924, p. 257.

[39] See *History and Theory* 8 (1969), p. 375 ff. for the criticism by F. Smith Fussner of F.J. Levy's *Tudor Historical Thought*.

ponent of the study of history.[40] Are we really sentenced to continue with this Sisyphean labour or should we yield, with Carr or the older 'relativists,' to the inevitability of presentism? The inevitability of anachronism in this broad sense of presentism may be established and demonstrated empirically in the history of historiography. What else does the study of historical writing do, at first sight at least, but detect anachronistic elements? It lives by the grace of this inevitable presentism.

We can even go a step further and attempt to explain this by a theory of interpretation in which this kind of presentism becomes the cornerstone of historical comprehension itself. Presentism then becomes not only inevitable, but also a necessary and positive condition in terms of the totally ineluctable historicity of comprehension itself.[41] The time dimension, the perspective offered by later developments, is then not a disruptive element in interpretation but a *sine qua non* for it. The result of any interpretation of the past which may be described as a 'fusing of horizons' is an inextricable tangle of autonomous and heteronomous elements.[42]

In a number of excellent essays, H.R. Hoetink asserted that anachronism, or what he prefered to describe as anachronistic conceptualization, is indeed unavoidable.[43] He says that although history knows no greater platitude than that the past must be understood from within, few historians have taken the trouble to define more closely the theoretical and practicable degree to which this ideal may be realized. In a very elementary sense the writing of history is ineluctably anachronistic; it is especially so when the historian tries to describe a development or show the future significance of an event. This essential historical

---

[40] Cf. J. Huizinga: "Éviter les anachronismes, c'est la moitié des sciences historiques," as quoted by H.R. Hoetink in *Tijdschrift voor Rechtsgeschiedenis* 23 (1955), p. 2; and C. Vann Woodward: "Anachronisms are pre-eminently the business of historians," in *A.H.R.* 66 (1960), p. 13.

[41] H.G. Gadamer, *Wahrheit und Methode*, Tübingen, 1960, p. 281: "Der Zeitenabstand ist daher nicht etwas, was überwunden werden muss. In Wahrheit kommt es darauf an, den Abstand der Zeit als eine positive und produktive Möglichkeit des Verstehens zu erkennen."

[42] For this characterization see H.G. Gadamer, *op cit.*, pp. 289–290, 359, 375. For a criticism of Gadamer's opinion see E.D. Hirsch, *Validity in Interpretation*, New Haven, 1967 and E. Betti, *Allgemeine Auslegungslehre als Methodik der Geisteswissenschaften*, Tübingen, 1967, pp. 492–493, note 4a. The terms 'autonomous' and 'heteronomous' in this connection are borrowed from N. Elias. See his article 'Problems of Involvement and Detachment' in *British Journal of Sociology* 7 (1956), pp. 226–252.

[43] See H.R. Hoetink, *Historische Rechtsbeschouwing*, Haarlem, 1949; *idem*, 'Les notions anachroniques dans l'historiographie du droit' in *Tijdschrift voor Rechtsgeschiedenis* 23 (1955), pp. 1–20, or its German version 'Über anachronistische Begriffsbildung in der Rechtsgeschichte,' in *Zeitschrift der Savigny-Stiftung für Rechtsgeschichte*, Romanistische Abteilung 72 (1955), pp. 39–53.

activity would be impossible without knowledge of consequent or subsequent events. It is the knowledge of later events that provides the
basis for the particular selection of earlier events in any outline of
developments. The occurrence of a later event is a necessary element
in the meaningful elucidation of an earlier one. Churchill's statement:
'With the fall of Singapore we are beginning to realize the meaning of
Pearl Harbour' is only one of the countless examples of 'retrospective'
historical reconstruction, where the retrospectiveness must be seen as
a highly essential component. The 'after-mindedness' (to use another
expression dear to Whig critics) that was considered so detrimental to
historical thinking would, if eliminated, render any description of a
historical development totally impossible.

Convinced not only of the inevitability but also of the necessity of
retrospective knowledge, must we now praise it as a happy and divine
privilege as F. Lot did when he wrote: "nous qui, au regard de nos
ancêtres, sommes des dieux, puisque nous savons leur avenir"?[44]
Assuredly, there are many more historians who prefer to stress the
diabolical side of the privilege and never cease to demonstrate its
crippling effect upon historical insight. Privilege does have its faults.
McIlwain's lament: 'The changing world always makes earlier times
incomprehensible' has been often voiced in the past as it will be in the
future.[45] Historical research and interpretation ought not to be directed
towards bringing about a fusion of horizons between present and past
perspectives, but rather the opposite: the separation of the two within
the limits of what is possible. Even if we assume the basic impossibility
of a completely autonomous evaluation, there is nevertheless a whole
range of means of eliminating heteronomous elements. That this elimination is an essential part of a historian's work is not even denied by
Hoetink.

Despite this, however, Hoetink states that there are two stages of

[44] Quoted by Ch.E. Perrin, *Un historien Français, Ferdinand Lot, 1866–1952*, Genève, 1968,
p. 73. Cf. also pp. 66–96. Also cf. Th.J.L. Locher's remark: "This final knowledge (awareness
of the ending) also makes a historian of him, gives him an advantage, an extra dimension.
But this wisdom becomes folly, if he does not realise that he is being wise after the event,"
in *Forum der Letteren* 5 (1964), p. 158. For the inevitable anachronistic conceptualization, cf.
Barrington Moore's pronouncement: "In discussing bourgeois revolutions the justification
for the term rests on a series of legal and political consequences." (*Social Origins of Dictatorship
and Democracy*, Boston, 1967, p. 429).

[45] C.H.McIlwain, *Constitutionalism: Ancient and Modern*, New York, 1966, p. 79. McIlwain
quoted here the perspicacious Sir Henry Spelman: "When states are departed from their
original Constitution, and that original by tract of time worn out of Memory; the succeeding
Ages viewing what is past by the present, conceive the former to have been like to that they
live in."

historical research where anachronistic conceptualization must still be considered permissible or even inevitable: at the beginning, when the problem or hypothesis is formulated, and at the end, when the historical events studied are presented in a manner comprehensible to the contemporary reader. But the admissibility of anachronistic thinking is clearly restricted, since at a later stage of the research the problem or hypothesis may be found irrelevant for an earlier period and must therefore be rejected as anachronistic. In the second case the copious use of quotation marks serves as a warning to the reader to be aware of the different use of some terms as compared with his own time, for example, the 'democracy' and 'public opinion' of the Greek *polis*. Especially when the subject is taken from a strange and distant past is it difficult to avoid this kind of presentism if one wishes to remain comprehensible. Even so, such modernization will always have to be no more than a means towards an end; it is never *carte blanche* for one's own creations. "Vergegenwärtigung geschieht," writes J. Vogt in this connection, "indem der Historiker sich in die Vergangenheit versetzt, wie ein Gast in ein fremdes Land, nicht indem er die Vergangenheit hervorbringt und Menschen formt nach seinem Bilde."[46] If such anachronistic terminology becomes an end instead of a means, it does violence to history itself. A similarity must never be allowed to seduce us into seeing or assuming an identity.[47]

Thus we may again wonder whether there is really any point in condemning the nineteenth-century Whigs for something that is intrinsic in historiography – even for the anti-Whig writing in the years following 1900. Indeed, in a number of cases we shall see that the 'presentism' of these revisionists had its uses for the perception of anachronisms in Victorian historical writing. Nevertheless, there are wide differences in the 'presentism' between English historical writing before 1900 and after. It then becomes necessary to define anachronism itself rather more carefully. Before turning to the problem of anachronism itself, however, we must first point out some other elements in the Victorian anachronistic approach to the past that figure prominently in post-1900 criticism. These elements were so essential to Whig anachronism that

---

[46] J. Vogt, 'Geschichte und Gegenwartsverständnis' in *Geschichte und Gegenwartsverständnis. Festschrift für Hans Rothfels*, Göttingen, 1963, pp. 61–62.
[47] Cf. H.G. Gadamer: "Es geht einfach darum, dass unser historisches Bewusstsein, das mit dem Wissen um das Anderssein, die Fremdheit fremder historischer Welten getränkt ist, das seine eigene Begriffe und die Begriffe jener fremden Zeiten und Welten mühsam, nur mit einer ungeheuren Anstrengung des denkenden historischen Erkennens, auseinanderzuhalten strebt, doch am Ende beide Begrifflichkeiten immer miteinander vermittelt" (*Kleine Schriften*, Tübingen, 1967, I, p. 158). The objective at the end of the quotation seems contestable.

Victorian historical writings must indeed be regarded as more anachronistic than those of the post-Victorian period: it is thus with a comparative notion, one of 'more' or 'less' that we are concerned here.

The second characteristic of Whig interpretation is what I shall call 'finalism,' a form of interpretation strongly oriented towards the present, which is complacently regarded as some sort of climax. Here, too, we can postulate that no interpretation is possible whithout finalism.[48] The accusation levelled at the Whigs, however, is that they put too great an emphasis on finalism in the historical process. There was an excess of teleology which resulted in a stress on the linearity of history. The more purpose history was credited with, the more meaningful it became. In a generalizing vein, V.H. Galbraith wrote: "The Victorian view of history depended, as everything Victorian depends, on the assumption of finality, that beyond Victorianism the force of nature could no further go."[49] Another error arising from finalism was underlined by Butterfield: "The Whig historian is apt to imagine the British constitution as coming down to us safely at last, *in spite of* so many vicissitudes; when in reality it is the result of those very vicissitudes of which he seems to complain."[50] The Whig historian lacked, one might say, any feeling for the 'dialectic within history,' for the creation of the present not in spite of but precisely because of so many vicissitudes. In a collection of essays interesting for the light it sheds on the development of English historical thinking, W.H. Woodward wrote in this connection: "The teacher will point out how good men, if weak, may do greater harm than worse men who are strong; how bad motives may somehow end in results which are for the welfare of the many."[51] The obsession with directness within historical thinking heightened the tendency to see the present as already contained within the past, and thus reinforced the habit of 'modernizing' and 'anachronizing' the past. Schuyler referred to 'background history.'[52]

G.M. Trevelyan, considered by many to have been the last Whig

[48] W.H. Walsh, *An Introduction to Philosophy of History*, London, 1951, p. 61 ff.
[49] V.H. Galbraith, 'Historical Research and the Preservation of the Past' in *History* 22 (1937–1938), p. 310.
[50] H. Butterfield, *The Whig Interpretation of History*, London, 1931, p. 41.
[51] *Essays on the Teaching of History*, ed. W.A.J. Archbold, Cambridge, 1901, p. 78.
[52] R.L. Schuyler, 'The Usefulness of Useless History' in *Political Science Quarterly* 56 (1941), p. 24 ff.; the most remarkable characteristic of this 'background' history was the anachronism: "it exaggerates the similarities and obscures the dissimilarities between past and present" (p. 35).

historian, confessed in his autobiography to a predilection for 'those bits of history that have clear-cut happy endings.'[53] In general this predilection is also to be observed in all Victorian Whig historians, with their sharply delineated and 'happy' historical topics. The result of their one-sided finalistic approach to their own glorious past was justifiably described by G. Himmelfarb, referring to the historiography of the second Reform Bill, as 'imposing order upon chaos, necessity upon contingency, principle upon expediency.'[54] The course of history was as it were ironed smooth, the unevennesses removed.

One remarkable phenomenon would seem to be the reaction of 'anti-finalism' after 1900. Ways were (and still are) sought to avoid the excessive finalism and teleology which tended to cripple the science of history.[55] As we have already seen, the reactions to Victorian finalism took various forms. One remedy occasionally recommended in this connection is known as 'possibilistic history' – the study of historical movements which 'had no future.'[56] In a sense there is a certain 'tasting of another medicine' by deliberately avoiding description of a development (as far as that is possible), and preferring to give an analysis of situations rather than of movements or developments.[57] An antidote to an excess of finalistic historical interpretation was seen by some in what is called an 'accidental view of history.'[58]

In his attack on 'accidentalism' Carr said it would be a mistake to attach to it the consequence of a denial of causality in history.[59] However, his accusation of intellectual sloth in those inclined to view history as a 'chapter of accidents' testifies at the very least to a lack of understanding. It seems to me that this accidental view is first and foremost a reaction against Victorian Whig finalism. Bury, with whom this

[53] G.M. Trevelyan, *An Autobiography and Other Essays*, p. 34.

[54] G. Himmelfarb, *Victorian Minds*, p. 335. Cf. about G.M. Trevelyan, pp. 181–182.

[55] See for this paralyzing effect H.R. Hoetink, *Historische Rechtsbeschouwing*, pp. 27–28. We shall return to this point in our chapter on law and history.

[56] Cf. F. Braudel, 'Pour une économie historique,' in *Revue économique* 1 (1950), pp. 37–44, reprinted in F. Braudel, *Écrits sur l'histoire*, Paris, 1969, pp. 123–133. Cf. A.J.P. Taylor, in *The New Statesman and the Nation*, 5-5-1950, p. 518. Cf. J.C. Boogman, *Vaderlandse Geschiedenis in Hedendaags Perspectief*, Groningen, 1959.

[57] R.W. Southern in *History and Theory* 6 (1967), p. 111.

[58] For this characterization by Bernard Berenson, see I. Berlin, *Historical Inevitability*, London, 1954, p. 3.

[59] E.H. Carr, *What is History?*, Harmondsworth, 1964, p. 99. Cf. the following remark of Bury's: "The principle known as the law of causation does not affect the problem. It is probably true that every phenomenon is the consequent of antecedent causes, and that no phenomenon contains any element which is not determined by a sequence of causes and effects. In any case it is a hypothesis which we are obliged to assume if the world is not to become a chaos and science to commit suicide" (*Selected Essays*, p. 60). Bury was trying to attain a 'systematic study of contingencies' (*Ibid.*, p. 67).

chapter began, perhaps best exemplifies this reaction. Though the extremism of his 'accidentalism,' particularly in his last years, may be considered exceptional, his views on this point were certainly not unusual. True, his reaction was aimed not so much at the English Whigs as at the generalizing philosophical and sociological theories of history which sought to exclude all coincidence. From this point of view his 'theory of coincidence' was frequently taken to be synonymous with 'the role of the individual in history.' Although Bury does not himself regard these two matters as totally identical, Collingwood, for whom Bury always remained a 'positivist,' did thus represent Bury's thought.[60]

The finalism often encapsulated in these general theories of history was also one of Bury's targets – possibly even the main one. His intent was not (and here too Collingwood's interpretation was biased) to saturate the past with coincidences and contingent factors so that the historian would be doomed to sink without trace into a morass of impenetrability. He was naturally aware that the assumption of total contingency would mean the death of history as a science, since all scientific research into cause and effect would become impossible.[61] Despite this, his sharp reaction held a more positive message for widening historical understanding by drawing his colleagues' and others' attention to the capriciousness and the unexpected and para-doxical elements in historical development that were neither unimportant nor 'accidental' for an improved understanding of history and hence could not for simplicity's sake be effaced from the historical picture. From his point of view it was this very tendency to ignore factors and phenomena which might be called insignificant when seen in terms of a later result or aim that formed an obstacle to improved understanding of the course of history. His targets were the blind acceptance and love of ease which abounded in an attitude to history permeated by too strong a sense of finality. Although the way in which he formulated his theory was incomplete and not always equally felici-tous, it will be worth considering more closely several of Bury's ideas.

In a lecture given in 1904 Bury attacked a childishly naive nine-

---

[60] See R.G. Collingwood on Bury in *E.H.R.* 46 (1931), pp. 461–465; and Collingwood's *The Idea of History*, Oxford, 1946, pp. 147–151. ("the contingency of history is simply a name for 'the role of the individual' seen through the spectacles of a positivism for which nothing is intelligible except what is general," p. 151).

[61] For R.G. Collingwood's mistaken interpretation, see *The Idea of History*, p. 151 ("Contingency means unintelligibility"). Bury could have agreed with this, cf. his pronouncement quoted in note 59.

teenth-century interpretation of history where one's own time was seen as the final goal. For Bury this vision was a childish delusion, a product of 'the spell of the present' so admirably suited to the nineteenth century, which saw all that had gone before as only the means to, or a feeble foreshadowing of what had then been achieved.[62] This lecture may have been the first step in Bury's study *The Idea of Progress*. We hear more of this in his lecture on 'Darwinism and History' of 1909, an account of the origins of the theory of historical and genetic evolution in which the eighteenth-century idea of progress was seen as a 'forerunner' of Darwinist evolutionism. The emerging prominence of the idea of progress was an important step forwards in the growth of historical consciousness: "it helped effectively to establish the notion of history as a continuous process and to emphasize the significance of time."[63] The idea of progress also enabled one to see more clearly the diversity between the various periods and thus promoted the perception of historical periodization. Nevertheless, such a concept carried with it an unfavourable aspect as well: a teleological hypothesis which equated procession and progression.[64] In 1909 Bury saw the importance of evolutionary ideas as found in the works of Darwin, because of their secularizing and, above all, neutralizing effect. In 1920 he placed evolutionism within the 'third' phase of the 'idea of progress,' where 'progress' is replaced by 'evolution,' 'a neutral, scientific conception, compatible either with optimism or with pessimism.'[65]

In 1909 Bury was one of the few English historians to have any great regard for Lamprecht's *Deutsche Geschichte*: 'the ablest product of the sociological school of historians.'[66] What he did reject in Lamprecht's work, despite this praise, was the idea that the course of history followed a straight line: "Historical development does not proceed in a right line, without the choice of diverging."[67] Lamprecht's thinking on historical development was too direct, too one-sidedly finalistic; Bury sought, as he later wrote in the epilogue to his book, to combat 'the illusion of finality,' and to nullify the optimism in the idea of progress.[68]

However, Bury was not always lucid – sometimes he even contra-

[62] *Selected Essays*, pp. 50, 57.
[63] *Ibid.*, p. 27, cf. p. 24.
[64] *Ibid.*, p. 25.
[65] J.B. Bury, *The Idea of Progress*, Introduction by C.A. Beard, New York, 1955, p. 335; just before that: "Evolution itself ... does not necessarily mean, applied to society, the movement of man to a desirable goal."
[66] *Selected Essays*, p. 41.
[67] *Ibid.*
[68] J.B. Bury, *The Idea of Progress*, p. 351.

dicted himself – about the precise meaning of the concept of progress for the development of historical thinking. In his work of 1920 he devoted an entire chapter to the 'new conceptions of history,' and stated that with the emergence of the concept of progress the study of history was undergoing a revolution.[69] But what constituted this revolution? In 1909 he had clearly stressed the importance of the concept of progress for the evolution of developmental thinking; in 1920 this aspect of the matter received little or no attention – even in his discussion of the *Querelle des Anciens et des Modernes* and its origins in Bodin, LeRoy or Bacon.[70] The historiographical revolution to which he now referred emerged from the eighteenth-century's general perception of progress in the historical process, where this view became the principal component of historical writing. The idea of progress became a dynamic ordering principle for a new conception of history which replaced the Christian view of providence and in which, moreover, there was no place for 'accidentalism.' "If progress was to be more than the sanguine dream of an optimist [i.e. the Abbé de Saint-Pierre] it must be shown that man's career on earth *had not been a chapter of accidents* which might lead anywhere or nowhere, but is subject to discoverable laws which have determined its general route, and will secure his arrival at the desirable place."[71]

This seventh chapter of Bury's *The Idea of Progress* is a curious one. The three thinkers whom he cites (Montesquieu, Voltaire, and Turgot) certainly do not exemplify this revolution. The various stages in the development of human civilization are not emphasized by Montesquieu; he was unclear, and because he lacked the idea of progress there is little periodization in his work. "Whatever may be the value of the idea of progress, we may agree with Comte that if Montesquieu had grasped it, he would have produced a more striking work."[72] A figure such as Voltaire is particularly difficult to reconcile with Bury's 'revolution.' Voltaire succeeded in eliminating optimistic finalism through irony. Unlike Montesquieu, he was perhaps the perfect representative of the 'accidental view of history.'[73] And Turgot laid great emphasis on the twisting, unplanned path of human progress, in Bury's

---

[69] *Ibid.*, p. 144. Cf. also p. 5.
[70] *Ibid.*, chapter 1 and 2.
[71] *Ibid.*, p. 144.
[72] *Ibid.*, p. 148.
[73] *Ibid.*, p. 151: "He eliminated final causes altogether" and p. 152. "Montesquieu sought to show that the vicissitudes of societies were subject to law; Voltaire believed that events were determined by chance where they were not consciously guided by human reason."

words, his motto was: "Man advances by committing errors."[74] Thus he was able to include in the course of history, with a clearly defined place, such seemingly 'unprogressive' periods as the Middle Ages. This his more radical contemporaries, including his own pupil Condorcet, could not do because of their 'resentment against history.'[75]

Bury's analysis of the idea of progress during the first two decades of this century is significant. In the first place it is important as a critical reaction against the oversimplified historical finalism of the nineteenth century. Second, it is an important topic of the twentieth century because it is linked with the 'uncertainty crisis' which let loose an avalanche of literature on the idea of progress.[76] Carr rather hurriedly traced Bury's accidentalism back to this uncertainty, and postulated that Bury's first thoughts on the subject appeared in 1909 'after a long interval.'[77] Certainly it does look at first sight as though nineteenth-century historical writing, particularly Whig writing, showed few signs of any 'accidentalist' tendencies. Both the optimism of the idea of progress and Victorian earnestness, which was in any case hostile towards irony, were to show little or no tolerance of an ironic accidentalism.[78] At a later stage I shall return to the time-bound quality pointed out by Carr; first, however, I shall attempt to summarize what has already been said on the value of the idea of progress for the study of history.

In *The Idea of Progress* Bury was mainly concerned with summarizing the facts; he was less specific in his assessment of the value of the concept for historical thinking. All we read in the epilogue is that the idea of progress ought to have overcome a psychological obstacle 'which may be described as the illusion of finality.'[79] The origins of the idea and its breakthrough after the *Querelle* were, one might say, of no small significance for historical studies, and especially for the idea of evolution. The future was seen as being more open, and even attitudes towards antiquity and the past in general became freer and hence more critical once the 'slavish' ideal of imitation was no longer *en vogue* (in 1920 Bury spoke in somewhat too definite and uncompromising terms

---

[74] *Ibid.*, p. 156.
[75] *Ibid.*, pp. 206–207, Cf. p. 171.
[76] A source of literature, J. Romein, 'Gedachten over de vooruitgang' (Thoughts on Progress), in *Carillon der Tijden*, Amsterdam, 1953, pp. 12–40.
[77] E.P. Carr, *op. cit.*, p. 100.
[78] Cf. W.E. Houghton, *The Victorian Frame of Mind, 1830–1870*, New Haven, 1967, pp. 149, 300, 357.
[79] J.B. Bury, *op. cit.*, p. 351.

of the 'yoke' of the Renaissance).[80] Without this breakthrough, without this criticism of the *reverentia antiquitatis*, without this dethronement of classical Antiquity to a definitely limited historical stage, the concept of actual historical progress and development could hardly have come into being. However, despite the 'historical' merit of the idea of progress, criticism of its usefulness for the science of history at the beginning of the century was widely disseminated among historians – in the Netherlands, I need only mention Huizinga and Romein.

Huizinga's criticism of the idea of progress and his considerable reservations regarding the concept of 'precursor' was, as J. Kamerbeek put it, 'historiographically fruitful.'[81] Romein presented his 'dialectics of progress' as one of the many attacks since 1914 on the genetic-finalistic historical thinking of the nineteenth century, which 'projected the present directly back to the past as far as its supposed origins.'[82] It was indeed the directness in the teleological view of the course of history that was considered a serious shortcoming in earlier historical writing. Despite all progress it suggested a permanent qualitative identity between present and past, and led in effect to an anachronistic view of that past. Moreover, it tended towards an effacement of any 'unevenness' which did not suit a historical outline of development. There were also, within English historical writing, many attacks on what was termed by Vinogradoff and others the 'retrogressive' nationalism and constitutionalism attributed to earlier historical writing.[83]

With his accidentalism Bury, too, attempted above all to combat the 'illusion of finality' which in his view had characterized the second (nineteenth-century) stage of the idea of progress. In his seventh chapter, referred to above, Bury described an eighteenth-century view of history which had undoubtedly grown within the climate of the idea of progress; yet it could not be called finalistic, as was to be the case later in the nineteenth century. In Voltaire, after all, he had found a

[80] *Ibid.*, p. 78. An important correction in H. Baron, 'The *Querelle* of the Ancients and the Moderns as a Problem for Renaissance Scholarship' in *Journal of the History of Ideas* 20 (1959), pp. 3–22; cf. A. Buck, 'Aus der Vorgeschichte der *Querelle des anciens et des modernes* in Mittelalter und Renaissance,' in *Bibliothèque d'Humanisme et Renaissance* 20 (1958), pp. 527–541. See also H.R. Jauss, 'Ursprung und Bedeutung der Forschrittsidee in der *Querelle des anciens et des modernes* in *Die Philosophie und die Frage nach dem Fortschritt*, München, 1964, pp. 51–72.
[81] J. Kamerbeek, 'Huizinga en de Beweging van Tachtig' in *Tijdschrift voor Geschiedenis* 67 (1954), pp. 145–164, esp. pp. 160–161.
[82] J. Romein, 'De dialektiek van de vooruitgang, bijdrage tot het ontwikkelingsbegrip in de geschiedenis' in *Het Onvoltooid Verleden*, Amsterdam, 1937, pp. 9–64, quotation p. 55.
[83] P. Vinogradoff, *English Society in the Eleventh Century*, Oxford, 1908, p. 5. Cf. P. Vinogradoff, *Villainage in England*, Oxford, 1892, p. 38.

form of accidentalism, and Turgot's 'ironic view of history' offered a perfect antidote to direct finalism. This accidental 'view of history' implied a feeling of what Wundt at the end of the nineteenth-century called the *Heterogonie der Zwecke*.[84] This sense of the paradoxical had not been absent in historical writing of the Enlightenment. Turgot was far from being alone: Bury could equally have pointed to Hume, Ferguson or Millar, the Scottish Enlightenment writers, whose significance in this respect was only rediscovered in this century.[85] The idea of progress, in itself, had little or no effect on their thinking regarding the development of history. In their view of the course of history they discounted what Duncan Forbes calls 'the law of the heterogeneity of ends,' the law of unintended or even opposite results.[86] It was this concept that lurked behind Adam Smith's 'invisible hand' theory; it was in this ironic fashion that Millar interpreted that most holy of documents, the Magna Carta, and Ferguson repeatedly stressed the unplanned quality of the change in historical progress. But the high point was reached with David Hume's description of the excellent British constitution as a 'great mixture of accident.'[87]

In English historical writing at the turn of the century this idea returns again and again, precisely where it was thought necessary to resist the old Whig interpretation, precisely where everything was centred on British freedom and the constitution whose origins could be directly traced back only by completely misunderstanding the past. Namier's later paradoxical description of sound historical consciousness as 'an intuitive understanding of how things did not happen' is also clearly embodied in the work of authors of the 'pre-Namier' period. The paradox of the 'unfree' origins of English freedom was to become a favourite topic. The American, Charles Beard, who was trained in

---

[84] W. Wundt, *Ethik, eine Untersuchung der Thatsachen und Gezetze des sittlichen Lebens*, Stuttgart, 1892, pp. 266–267, pp. 446–447, 502. The gradual spread of this conception throughout different branches of science is worth a closer study. Cf. the praise in a review by E. Durkheim, 'La science positive de la morale en Allemagne' in *Revue Philosophique* 24 (1887), pp. 113–142; F. Meinecke, *Die Entstehung des Historismus*, Berlin, 1936, pp. 62, 419 ff.

[85] See W.C. Lehmann, *Adam Ferguson and the Beginnings of Modern Sociology*, New York, 1930; Gladys Bryson, *Man and Society: The Scottish Inquiry of the Eighteenth Century*, Princeton, 1945; W.C. Lehmann, *John Millar of Glasgow*, New York, 1960; D. Kettler, *The Social and Political Thought of Adam Ferguson*, Ohio, 1965; finally, too, the excellent preface by Duncan Forbes in *Adam Ferguson, An Essay on the History of Civil Society, 1767*, Edinburgh, 1966.

[86] Duncan Forbes, 'Scientific Whiggism: Adam Smith and John Millar' in *The Cambridge Journal* 7 (1954), pp. 643–670, esp. pp. 651, 654, 667. Forbes also points out that this very conception was lost in the work of James Mill and other 19th-century heirs of the Scotch Enlightenment (p. 670). See also J. Romein, 'Gedachten over de vooruitgang' in *Carillon der Tijden*, p. 31.

[87] Quotation in S.R. Letwin, *The Pursuit of Certainty*, Cambridge, 1965, p. 98.

the new anti-Stubbsian school of medieval studies, also wrote (in 1899) about the beginning of English freedom: "It began its career as an instrument of power and convenience in the hands of the state, the monarch and those who shared with him efficient sovereignty."[88] The perception that a great historical irony lay at the roots of English freedom became stronger, and it is shortly after 1900 that the most vicious attack on Magna Carta is found. Here I do not refer to the well-known moderate revisionist work of W.S. McKechnie, whose study of the Magna Carta as a feudal document was very significant, but Edward Jenks's article in the *Independent Review* of 1904. Jenks's criticism of the 'reactionary baronial document' was so thorough-going that he threw out the baby with the bathwater.[89] Two years previously Jenks had committed the same sacrilege regarding the Writ of Habeas Corpus, where the original intention had been 'not to get people out of prison, but to put them in it.'[90]

It was not only the increasing social and political uncertainty to which Carr refers that opened people's eyes to the coincidence, irony and heterogeneity within history; contributions were also made by the increase in detail, specialization and refinement of research. A.J.P. Taylor, for instance, whose own work is prone to accidentalism – sometimes to an absurd extent – wrote: "There is much to be said for the accidental view of history. The details usually happen by accident

[88] C.A. Beard, 'The Teutonic Origins of Representative Government' in *American Political Science Review* 26 (1932), p. 44. For the date of this article see p. 31, note 12.

[89] E. Jenks, 'The Myth of Magna Carta', in *The Independent Review*, 4 (1904–1905), pp. 260–273. On Edward Jenks generally, see R.W. Lee, 'Edward Jenks, 1861–1939' in *Proceedings of the British Academy* 26 (1940), pp. 399–423. The historical world rejoiced when the 'troublesome' Jenks left Oxford in 1903. R.L. Poole wrote to J.H. Round on 17-1-1904: "We are looking forward to having Vinogradoff here as professor. It is an admirable appointment and the more so since it has delivered us from Jenks" (L.U.L.I.H.R. MSS, no. 664). See for Barraclough's characterization *The Observer*, 13-6-1965. McKechnie's study caused a shock at the time, for which see H. Butterfield, *Magna Carta in the Historiography of the Sixteenth and Seventeenth Centuries*, Reading, 1969, p. 25. Jenks and McKechnie had a strongly 'feudal' interpretation of the Magna Carta, in which they had been preceded in 1894 by Petit Dutaillis. Their reaction to Stubbs resulted during the twenties in a reaction in favour of Stubbs, as in F.M. Powicke's Ford Lectures. (cf. the interesting review by V.H. Galbraith in *The Scottish Historical Review* 25 (1927–1928), pp. 348–349). Powicke had already proceeded in that direction in 1917, in his contribution to the *Magna Carta Commemoration Essays*. In this he gave a 'disjunctive' interpretation of the notorious *vel* of article 39 ('*nisi per legale judicium parium suorum vel per legem terrae*'). In 1918 Tait wrote about Vinogradoff's 'conjunctive-feudal' interpretation and Powicke's 'disjunctive' one: "Their divergence on the meaning of the little word 'vel' is vital for the question of the aims of the baronage of 1215. It means all the difference between a reactionary attempt to reverse the judicial progress of half a century, and a constitutional effort to secure adequate protection against abuse of prerogative." See *E.H.R.* 33 (1918), p. 263. Cf. J.C. Holt, *Magna Carta*, Cambridge, 1969, p. 227 ff., and pp. 175–177.

[90] E. Jenks, 'The Story of the Habeas Corpus' in *Law Quarterly Review* 18 (1902), pp. 64–77, quotation, p. 65.

and the historian who sticks to detail is inclined to believe that everything happens that way."[91]

Before considering the underlying causes of this sudden switch to an
anti-Whig school of historical thinking, we must first deal with a third
feature of Whig historiography against which similar opposition sprang
up: its exaggerated sense of continuity. We have already discussed the
accusation of extreme anachronism and finalism in connection with
Victorian historical writing. Anachronism and finalism were closely
interrelated: the straight-line thinking of finalism unintentionally
related the past too quickly and too directly to the present, so that an
exaggeratedly modernistic impression of the past became virtually
inevitable. The strong tendency towards a hasty appreciation of continuity was a natural concomitant; the less unbroken the course of
history was taken to be, the more finalistic the picture of historical
development appeared. Breaks and discontinuities would merely
detract from this directness and finalism. There is overmuch finalism in
the disinclination or inability to identify essential hiatuses in history.

The concept of continuity is frequently thought to be one of the most
essential in the science of history. But how is it essential? Alexander
Gerschenkron differentiated between no fewer than five meanings
attached to this concept.[92] There is unlikely to be much discussion
regarding continuity viewed very broadly as 'connectibility' (Gerschenkron's fourth definition). In this formal sense, where the essence
of historical scholarship is described as a search for historical antece-
dents, the concept of continuity may indeed be regarded as specifically
historical.[93] According to this definition, it is also possible to agree with
Hoetink that history stands and falls by the 'construction' of historical
continuity.[94] However, this extremely formal meaning does not yet
embody any pronouncement on the nature of historical change. This
is stressed because I believe that the concept of continuity was of much

[91] A.J.P. Taylor in *The Observer*, 23-7-1967, p. 20. (review of M. Cowling, *1867: Disraeli,
Gladstone and Revolution*, Cambridge, 1967). Taylor, however added to this: "In fact, tendencies cannot be wholly accidental, even though they are composed of accidental details."
More about Taylor's own 'accidentalism' in A. Marwick, *The Nature of History*, London,
1970, pp. 189, 192.
[92] A. Gerschenkron, *Continuity in History and Other Essays*, Cambridge Mass., 1968, pp.
11-39.
[93] *Ibid.*, p. 29: "This connection of historical events is inherent in the very concept of
history." Cf. also p. 44.
[94] H.R. Hoetink, *Historische Rechtsbeschouwing*, p. 19.

greater import in nineteenth-century historical writing. It referred to a constancy of direction within the historical process and was often a synonym for the concept of stability.[95] It did not exclude the possibility of historical change, but nevertheless expressed a view, in principle, of the nature of any such change, which was assumed always to be gradual. "Ce qui fait le fond de la science historique, c'est l'observation de la continuité des choses et de leur lentes modifications," was written at the very end of the nineteenth century by Fustel de Coulanges who had himself written much to eliminate many of the mythical and anachronistic misconceptions about the history of France.[96] In England, as we shall see, Freeman, and in fact the entire 'Oxford School,' strongly supported this idea of continuity. This kind of thinking was undoubtedly able to anchor itself in the historical consciousness of the time because it pointed to a significant anti-revolutionary political ideal when revolution appeared to be a permanent feature of the historical scene. The concept of continuity was an ideological weapon against revolution, for revolution was viewed as a violent break with the past. The growing nationalism of the Romantic period reinforced this tendency and made of the historian a seeker for continuity in this specific sense.

Much has been written describing the influence of the French Revolution on the development of historical thinking in the nineteenth century, which was to push it in a conservative direction, emphasizing continuity rather than revolution.[97] The unique value of the historical-genetic method, as it was developed and refined, consisted in the search for what had 'grown' organically and gradually, which was preferred to what had been constructed suddenly and on an *ad hoc* basis. The search was not only for permanent, interrelated data, but also ap-

---

[95] A. Gerschenkron, *op. cit.*, pp. 12, 21.

[96] *Histoire des institutions politiques de l' ancienne France*, vol. V, Paris, 1890, p. XV. Cf., however, also p. 206. As Fustel de Coulanges was quite aware of the dangers of anachronism, the introduction to his *La Cité Antique* (Paris, 1864) is still worth reading. An English view of the significance of his work and of the part filled by '1870' in his romanist thesis is given by E. Jenks, 'Fustel de Coulanges as a Historian' in *E.H.R.* 12 (1897), pp. 209–224.

[97] See M.C. Brands, *Historisme als Ideologie*, Assen, 1965, pp. 53–76; F. Gilbert in J. Higham, L. Krieger, F. Gilbert, *History*, Englewood Cliffs, 1965, p. 320 ff.; Hedva Ben-Israel, 'The French Revolution and the Romantic Movement in Historiography, in *English Historians on the French Revolution*, Cambridge, 1968, pp. 110–126. Acton never lost his conviction that the French Revolution had been a decisive influence, as witness his remark in *E.H.R.* 1 (1886), p. 8; his article on Doellinger, in *E.H.R.* 5 (1890), pp. 700–744 ("revolution, as the break of continuity, as the renunciation of history, was odious to him . . ." p. 719), and his remark about Savigny: "His theory of continuity has this significance in political science, that it supplied a basis for conservatism apart from absolutism compatible with freedom" (*E.H.R.* 10 (1895), p. 112).

proached the past in its entirety from the viewpoint of continuity. Continuity, in the specific sense to which I referred above, became a classical historical mode of thought, an attitude of mind. Even the French Revolution, seen at first as a major hiatus, was eventually examined by Tocqueville from this angle, and for many the insight which resulted from this approach came as something of a liberation.[98]

This approach was subjected to an excellent analysis by the American economic historian, V.G. Simkhovitch, who published a series of articles around 1930 sharply attacking the over-teleological idea of continuity prevalent in the nineteenth century.[99] He too sought a more realistic, perhaps more dialectical concept of development. Simkhovitch underlined the limitations of continuity as such for the understanding of the past. We are forced, he wrote, to understand the historical facts "in terms of continuity and to do so we are very apt to emphasize the shell of continuity and overlook its kernel, whose very meaning and very essence is the break."[100] To declare continuity in this sense to be the essence of history is only the result of a deceptive perspective.

If one approaches things in terms of continuity it is only the continuity that one sees, even where the continuity is irrelevant. It cannot be otherwise, for our approach means that we are thinking in terms of continuity, hence it is continuity we are looking for and our mental processes will inevitably produce continuity.[101]

The reality of historical change is not completely denied, but 'the historic-genetic attitude ... gives to that element also a quality of continuity ...'[102] Within the description and analysis of the process of change the prevailing emphasis is on what Simkhovitch called 'a straight-line continuation' over that of the 'departures.'[103]

One feature of this continuity approach is a lack of 'feeling' for what is really new or revolutionary in a period of change, or for the conflicts and tensions which frequently accompany a change.[104] Whereas ear-

---

[98] As a liberation especially of the liberals who were disappointed in the Revolution, see R. Herr, *Tocqueville and the Old Regime*, Princeton, 1962, p. 107, ff.

[99] V.G. Simkhovitch, 'Approaches to History,' in *Political Science Quarterly* 44 (1929), pp. 481–497; 45 (1930), pp. 481–526; 47 (1932), pp. 410–439; 48 (1933), pp. 23–61. See also, on the development idea in general, H. Rickert, *Die Grenzen der naturwissenschaftlichen Begriffsbildung*, Tübingen, 1913, esp. pp. 422–423.

[100] V.G. Simkhovitch in *Political Science Quarterly* 44 (1929), p. 490.

[101] *Ibid.*, p. 491.

[102] V.G. Simkhovitch in *Political Science Quarterly* 48 (1933), p. 24.

[103] *Ibid.*, p. 52

[104] *Ibid.*, p. 53: "... We emphasize continuity but overlook the psychology of struggle that these departures present."

lier, in connection with finalism, I referred to an effacement of the 'unexpected' and of historical vicissitudes, here we are concerned with a tendency towards an effacement of antagonisms and conflicts which threaten to be damaging to the continuity. Since 1900 there is an important reaction in historical scholarship against this obsession with continuity, which disguised the reality of historical change. Such a notion of continuity leads not only to a contradiction of the so-called uniqueness of history, but also directly to a denial of historical reality as historical reality, of the past as the past: or, as F.G. Maier put it: "Sie ist der geschichtlichen Realität überhaupt nicht mehr angemessen."[105]

English historical scholarship, in its reaction against Whig historiography, was also sensitive to this kind of criticism. Hearnshaw's declaration that 'continuity is by no means the most conspicuous feature of history' was a remarkable statement in view of the English historiographical tradition, although certainly not the only one of its kind.[106] Even so, criticism of the idea of continuity was often cast in a somewhat different mould, for, once under the spell of continuity, the historian is eminently predisposed to belittle the differences between past and present and to lay the main stress on their similarities. Thus, in comparing past and present one tends to find the 'similar' predominating over the 'dissimilar'; it was against the 'similar,' which had so set the tone of Whig historical writing, that English historical scholarship began to revolt at the turn of the century.

This was the background against which Butterfield in 1931 summed up the main task of historical work with the following sentence: "The chief aim of the historian is the elucidation of the unlikenesses between past and present . . ."[107] Even in 1901 J.R. Tanner elucidated a similar view when he wrote of the absolute necessity of accentuating the fundamental differences between modern and medieval thinking 'even

---

[105] *Geschichte*, Fischer Lexikon, Hrsg. W. Besson, Frankfurt a. Main, 1961, p. 246, cf. also p. 86. See also H. Rickert, who used the term 'heterogeneous' continuity, *op. cit.*, p. 36; Hedva Ben-Israel, *op. cit.*, p. 123; C.E. Perrin, *op. cit.*, p. 70 ff.

[106] Quoted in G. Barraclough, *History in a Changing World*, Oxford, 1957, p. 4. Cf. what Acton – who did a remarkable job of putting a relative value on the continuity approach – said in his inaugural speech: "The modern age did not proceed from mediaeval by normal succession, with outward tokens of legitimate descent. Unheralded, it founded a new order of things, under a law of innovation, sapping the ancient reign of continuity" (*Essays on Freedom and Power*, sel. by G. Himmelfarb, New York, 1955, p. 27). Cf., however, A.F. Pollard's remark in *Factors in Modern History*, p. 37. About the reaction to the gradualistic thinking of the 19th century, see also E.L. Eisenstein, 'Clio and Chronos,' in *History and the Concept of Time*, 1967 (Beiheft 6 of *History and Theory*) p. 36 ff.

[107] H. Butterfield, *The Whig Interpretation of History*, p. 10.

to exaggeration.'[108] This last point was made particularly to break away from the countless presentist ideas of the nineteenth century. Being fascinated by that strange other world of the past was increasingly seen as an essential quality of a new and correct conception of history. "Our curiosity about the past," wrote V.H. Galbraith, "arises from the contrast it seems to present to the present."[109] Contrast, difference and discrepancy between present and past are all frequently recurring concepts which, after 1900, thoroughly undermined the continuity and sameness of the 'Whiggish' view of English history. This reaction not only became apparent from a new description of the origins of historical consciousness, but was also manifest in a reorientation towards the special function of historical studies.

The direct usefulness and pedagogical value of history perceived by the Whigs because of its supposed 'sameness' was not only called into question but also directly attacked. A dual danger in this 'historic' approach was noticed: an anachronistic distortion of the past when seen in too modernist a way, and of a present which was too exclusively seen as *sub specie praeteritorum*. The function now attributed to history was less direct, yet no less fundamental. It consisted in a liberation of the present from the burden and pressure of the past. That Acton's and Maitland's work was based upon this ethos will be discussed later.[110] The demonstration of 'the death of the past' was seen as a positive function of historical studies, and at first sight it would be impossible to conceive a more radical contrast between Victorian and post-Victorian historical scholarship. But we are also confronted here with an important political factor in the decline of Whig historiography. For it becomes clear that history's direct political devaluation greatly benefited the development of history as a science. This loss of function was one of the causes of a breakdown of Victorian presentism and was in a certain sense a condition for the recognition of the 'pastness' of the past.

[108] *Essays on the Teaching of History*, p. 57: "The natural tendency to become enthusiastic over liberal and modern movements in medieval history is so strong that the teacher will do wisely to lay stress even to exaggeration, upon the fundamental differences."

[109] V.H. Galbraith in *Why We Study History*, Historical Association Pamphlet, no. 131 (1944), p. 6.

[110] Cf. Acton in his inaugural speech: "If the Past has been an obstacle and a burden, knowledge of the past is the safest and the surest emancipation" (*Essays on Freedom and Power*, p. 28). For the applicability of this generalization, valid outside the strict confines of the historians' world, see also H.V. White, 'The Burden of History' in *History and Theory* 5 (1966), pp. 111–134. Cf. also L. Febvre's famous dictum: "L'histoire, qui est un moyen d'organiser le passé pour l'empêcher de trop peser sur les épaules des hommes," in *Combats pour l'histoire*, Paris, 1953, p. 437.

We have now returned, via a detour, to the most basic characteristic of Whig historical writing: the anachronism against which the reaction was primarily directed. Have we come any further? I mentioned already the growing recognition of the danger inherent in anachronistic thinking for both present and past; L.P. Smith, in his well-known short study of the English language, observed: "If we examine our historical vocabulary, the words and phrases by which we express *our sense that the past was not the same, but something different from the present*, we shall find that they are all of them modern, and most of them, indeed of very recent introduction."[111] The late development of this historical vocabulary, which testifies to an understanding of the 'unlikeness' of the past, is a phenomenon which in the present connection deserves close attention. There is perhaps no clearer indication that 'the struggle against anachronism' in historical writing was accomplished only slowly and with difficulty. In this respect the development of the concept of anachronism itself is significant. Not until recently did it assume its secondary meaning: 'something has become an anachronism,' in the sense of being inapplicable to the present. The primary definition of the concept, first used in the seventeenth century as an important result of the Renaissance historical consciousness is given as follows in the *Oxford Dictionary*: "an error in computing time, or fixing dates; the erroneous reference of an event, circumstance, or custom to a wrong date."[112] This relates exclusively to the dangers of anachronistic distortion for the past. This Renaissance 'concept of anachronism' did indeed show the past more clearly in perspective, in its chronological development. The usefulness of the past was still accepted as self-evident; history remained a 'mirror' and a 'theatre' for the present, and the theory of 'similitudo temporum' reflected the search for the most useful periods in the past with which to compare the present.[113]

The second, more practical sense of the concept of anachronism – that something has become 'an anachronism,' 'unusable,' 'out of date,' or has 'outlived its time' – did not develop until the nineteenth century.[114] It was only then that a view of the present could be described as anachronistic. Past and present were now equally susceptible of

---

[111] L.P. Smith, *The English Language*, Oxford, 1952, p. 149.

[112] *Oxford Dictionary*, Oxford 1888, vol. I, p. 300.

[113] See Else-Lilly Etter, *Tacitus in der Geistesgeschichte des 16. und 17. Jahrhunderts*, Basel-Stuttgart, 1966, pp. 16, 51, 109, 123, 171.

[114] *Oxford Dictionary*, vol. I, p. 300: "Anything done or existing out of date; hence, anything which was proper to a former age, but is, or, if it existed, would be, out of harmony with the present: also called a practical anachronism." See also L.P. Smith, *op. cit.*, p. 150.

anachronistic approaches. At the same time, a recognition of the detrimental nature of such an attitude for the present constituted an important step forward in a clearer, less anachronistic, understanding of the past. The way of thinking behind this second meaning is, as L.P. Smith says, of very recent origin. In relation to historical consciousness it implies a budding scepticism towards the value and immediate usefulness of the past as such. The main problem here is the danger of an anachronistic view of the present because the past is seen as an anachronism. The fundamental changes brought about by the French Revolution and the Industrial Revolution provided the basis for this newer meaning of anachronism, which so clearly reveals the greater gap between past and present. It was these changes which generated such a recognition of discontinuity – necessary for the creation of any historical consciousness – that historical insight could grow in the fundamental differences between past and present – a recognition which also gave substance to the conviction that the past was indeed past and that it should thus also be understood as the past.

Despite all this, I have intentionally referred to an unfolding scepticism regarding the 'sameness' and usefulness of the past; I must also add that this scepticism was only a first move towards the conception or experience of the past 'as an anachronism.' Coleridge may have been the first to use the term in its modern sense, but his historical consciousness was not influenced by it, unlike Maitland's at the end of the nineteenth century. Although – or perhaps because of – the past could be called an anachronism compared to the modern age, it became for Coleridge (a romantic) a welcome and useful means of escape from the industrial society which was then emerging. Within the romantic school, which undoubtedly had a sharp awareness of the uniqueness and different character of the past,[115] escapism remained a considerable handicap to the dawning of a non- or at least less anachronistic conception of the past. Because there was a desire to save as much as possible of what was about to be, or had already been lost through the industrial and political revolutions, among romantic historians there emerged a strong body of opinion supporting and furthering the idea

---

[115] Suffice it to remember the origin and development of the idea of *couleur locale*. More about this in J. Kamerbeek, *Tenants et Aboutissements de la notion 'couleur locale,'* Utrecht, 1962. Yet within that very romantic historiography which had allotted so great part to this conception, many unhistorical and even anachronistic elements were discovered at the end of the 19th century, Cf. Ch.V. Langlois, 'L'histoire aux XIX siècle,' in *Questions d'histoire et d'enseignement*, Paris, 1902, pp. 209–241, and esp. p. 232. "On a appris à se méfier de la 'couleur locale,' si souvent artificielle."

of continuity discussed earlier. It was not until late – very late, in England – that it became possible to leave the past alone. In a later chapter I shall return to the persistence of certain presentist Whig myths, which so surprised and irritated historians after 1900.[116] This deserves more detailed elucidation and further differentiation.

We should now sum up this preliminary overview. The presuppositions of Whig historical writing, which I have examined in the light of the triple problem of anachronism, finalism and the concept of continuity, have a bearing on the essentials of any form of historical scholarship: when stripped of their concrete English manifestations and applications they concern all historical writing. From an epistemological point of view it is true that without the three aforementioned characteristics, historical writing would be quite impossible. The perception of historical knowledge occurs essentially after the event: the historian looks ahead in retrospect,[117] and is thus the discoverer of and seeker after a continuity as 'connectibility' in order to make sense of – that is, render comprehensible – the course of historical events. Equally, the same epistemological logic justifies the demand for a certain identity within the historical process, and for this reason it cannot be absent from any theoretical discussion. German and French writing in what was called the idea of congeniality laid especial stress on this aspect during the nineteenth century.[118]

"C'est le postulat nécessaire de toutes les sciences documentaires: si les faits rapportés dans les documents n'avaient pas été analogues à ceux que nous observons, nous n'y pourrions rien comprendre."[119] Anything completely different could never appeal to us, and we should never be able to let it do so. According to the *Introduction* by Langlois and Seignobos of 1898, which was so influential even in England: "Si l'humanité de jadis n'était pas semblable à l'humanité actuelle, on ne comprendrait rien aux documents."[120] In this sense all historical work

---

116 Cf. Namier's lack of understanding of 19th-century political thinking in this respect, in *Avenues of History*, p. 138.
117 H.R. Hoetink, *Historische Rechtsbeschouwing*, p. 24.
118 Compare H. Mommsen's article on the historical method in *Geschichte*, Fischer Lexikon, pp. 78–91, and especially his criticism on p. 86.
119 Ch. Seignobos, *La méthode historique appliquée aux sciences sociales*, Paris, 1909, p. 120.
120 Ch.V. Langlois and Ch. Seignobos, *Introduction aux études historiques*, Paris, 1898, p. 189. Cf. the review by S.R. Gardiner in *E.H.R.* 13 (1898), pp. 327–329. In 1898 an English translation was published with a preface by F.Y. Powell. See O. Elton, *F.Y. Powell*, vol. I. p. 252.

may be called essentially and necessarily comparative, even though it is precisely here – so the two authors continue – that the most important source is hidden from all false interpretation.[121]

From a somewhat more concrete historiographical viewpoint, however, we see the other side. What can and must be postulated epistemologically still only supplies half the truth of the origins of modern historical consciousness. Epistemological reflection is primarily concerned with the conditions, the premises without which no historical perception or the construction of a development would be possible. These premises do not as such offer any explanation for the beginning and growth of historical thought. For a living traditionalism that regards the past as useful and recognizes authority, finalism and continuity may, in the veiled form which I have described, be considered characteristic or even essential.[122] *Historical consciousness* is different; it develops by means of greater separation and does not supplement a *traditionalist consciousness*. It rather breaks it down and corrects it: it is often a criticism of tradition, consisting of critical reflection and the analysis of a traditionalist consciousness.

Thus at the roots of historical consciousness there lies an awareness of the discontinuity between present and past: "There mere affirmation of continuity can produce only traditionalism; historical explanation can arise only where there is some awareness of discontinuity," as J.G.A. Pocock has written.[123] In this connection Marxist writers have

---

[121] Ch. V. Langlois and Ch. Seignobos, *op. cit.*, p. 189: "Ce travail, qui se fait inconsciemment, est en histoire une des principales occasions d'erreur."

[122] We shall discuss this difference again in the chapter on law and history. Here it will suffice to draw attention to the discussion in the German-speaking area between H.G. Gadamer and J. Habermas, and especially to the latter's criticism of Gadamer's *Wahrheit und Methode* in his *Zur Logik der Sozialwissenschaften*, Tübingen, 1967 (Beiheft 5, *Philosophische Rundschau*), p. 174 ff., also to Gadamer's reply in his *Kleine Schriften*, I, (Tübingen, 1967), pp. 113–130. There is little or no place for the historian as 'the critic of the tradition' in the whole of Gadamer's theory, cf. the passages on Droysen, *op. cit.*, I, p. 121. While he acknowledges and portrays the 'discontinuity experience' ('Epochenerfahrungen') as important, he does not view it as functional in the origin and the growth of critical historical scholarship as such. The task of such scholarship seems to be simply to go on building where tradition has already laid the groundwork (cf. also Gadamer's article 'Die Kontinuität der Geschichte und der Augenblick der Existenz,' in *op. cit.*, I, pp. 149–160). Regarding these problems cf. also the pronouncement of J.M. Headley: "Tradition as authority denies any critical review, private investigation, or rational verification, consequently it is opposed to the historical consciousness" (J.M. Headly, *Luther's View of Church History*, New Haven, 1963, p. 57).

[123] J.G.A. Pocock, 'The Origins of the Study of the Past; a comparative approach' in *Comparative Studies in Society and History* 4 (1961–1962), p. 237. See, too, his article 'Time, Institutions and Action: an essay on traditions and their understanding' in *Politics and Experience*, ed. P. King, B.C. Parekh, Cambridge, 1968, esp. p. 223. Pocock points out that the right conditions for the growth of critical historical scholarship are dependent on the rise of alternative versions of the past. In England the rival Whig and Tory versions had long existed side by side, although in the second half of the 19th century the Whig interpretation

expressed the opinion – which it is possible to endorse without being a Marxist – that the problem becomes the more un-historical the more one adopts a traditionalist standpoint.[124] The French sociologist M. Halbwachs even spoke of an 'opposition finale entre la mémoire collective et l'histoire.' Historical consciousness can only grow when tradition, or particular traditions, fall into discredit. "C'est qu'en général l'histoire ne commence qu'au point où finit la tradition, moment où s'éteint ou se décompose la mémoire sociale."[125] In this connection Halbwachs rightly describes the 'mémoire collective' as a 'tableau des ressemblances' and history – emphasizing the *differences* between past and present – as a 'tableau des changements.'[126]

Both Pocock's and Halbwachs's analyses of the origins of historical consciousness are important because I hope later to demonstrate that the reaction against Whig historical writing after 1890 was founded on the abandonment of a social and above all political tradition. Posed in terms of the problem of anachronism, a clear experience of discontinuity, i.e., the experience of the past as an anachronism, was a decisive step forward in a less anachronistic understanding of that past. Maitland's approach to history is particularly illustrative of this development. The discrediting of certain political traditions was an important breeding-ground both for criticism of the presuppositions of Victorian historical writing and for the reorientation in attitudes towards its own past gradually apparent in English historical scholarship. The discussion of this external ideological factor in the breakthrough will be taken up in Chapter III; the rest of this first chapter will be devoted to a number of figures from the transitional period where we may detect the beginnings of a reorientation. We will also discuss a number of

had been dominant. Stubbs, Tory though he was, wrote and thought like a Whig, and the conservative Alison around 1860 abandoned all further historical work in despair because of the omnipresence of the liberal Whig version of the past. (See the summarizing article of G.R. Crosby, 'George III; Historians and a Royal Reputation,' in *Essays in Modern English History, in honour of W.C. Abbott*, Cambridge Mass., 1941, p. 303).

[124] G. Lukacs, *Die Zerstörung der Vernunft*, Berlin, 1954, p. 472: "desto energischer die Wendung zur Vergangenheit, desto unhistorischer, antihistorischer ... die Fragestellung." The Victorian respect for the past and tradition was attended by a great amount of un-historical thinking, and thereby slowed down the development of critical historical scholarschip. Cf. Butterfield's saying: "Yet this respect for the past has been combined with (perhaps even it has been dependent on) what one might call a sublime and purposeful un-historicity." (*The Englishman and His History*, London, 1944, p. 6). The same idea can be found in his article 'Delays and Paradoxes in the Development of Historiography' in *Studies in International History*, ed. K. Bourne and D.C. Watt, London, 1967, pp. 1–15.

[125] M. Halbwachs, *La mémoire collective*, Paris, 1950, p. 68.

[126] *Ibid.*, pp. 75–78. Cf. also p. 73: "En réalité dans le développement continu de la mémoire collective il n'y a pas de lignes de séparation nettement tracées, comme dans l'histoire, mais seulement des limites irrégulières et incertaines."

internal factors which began to undermine the Whig interpretation of history from within historical scholarship itself.

B. THE RELATIVIZATION OF CONSTITUTIONAL HISTORY

The Whig interpretation had left its mark most plainly on the field of constitutional history. That is where the historiographers of the late Victorian and post-Victorian eras continually came up against the evils of anachronism, finalism and continuity. The reaction was not simply an attack on the presentist and finalist way the Victorians chose to view the constitutional development: the very hypostatization of the British constitution also came under attack. The Whig myth concerning the constitution was so irresistible, that the constitution had come to be regarded as the sole explanation for the development of English history as such. It became the ideal angle from which to illustrate the growth of the British nation, and its development was the axis of the history of England, *tout court*, the factor explaining especially the uniqueness of British political development. It came to be almost regarded as an autonomous historical force: the object to be interpreted had developed into a means for interpretation. The saturation point in this constitutional history was reached around 1900. As early as 1901 T.F. Tout wrote to Sydney Lee about new professorships for the London University as follows: "Personally I would lay not great stress on constitutional history. It is much overdone at Oxford and it would be a pity to follow Oxford in its weak points."[127]

Tout voiced the general opinion, his reaction (as well as that of most of his professional colleagues) being rather moderate at first, especially when compared with E.H. Dance's in his pro-Strachey -, anti -Victorian book *The Victorian Illusion*.[128] Dance's book – which reads like a pamphlet – lacks any feeling for nuances, for in this book he accused the most varied historians (the new school included) of the same obsession with constitutional matters.[129] Nevertheless, it is an extremely clear illustration of the discomfort experienced by the post-Victorian generation. Dance saw the Victorians as the creators of 'the tradition of the Constitution,' a tradition accorded inviolability by means of a

---

[127] Letter of 8-2-1901, B.L. Oxford, Sidney Lee Correspondence, MS misc.d. 181. Cf. J.R. Tanner's pronouncement in *Essays on the Teaching of History*, p. 54.
[128] E.H. Dance, *The Victorian Illusion*, London, 1928.
[129] *Ibid.*, p. 321.

mythical, ancient past: "they invented for it a specious antiquity which they valued none the less because it was false."[130] "In this tradition of English Constitutionalism," he continued, "there was no room for an active monarchy, and the Victorians therefore persuaded themselves, with an ease born of the practice in self-deception, that the English monarchy was nothing but what the people made it."[131] Of course the author also stressed both the presentism and the finalism of Victorian historians, "who are often more faithful mirrors of their own times than of the times they set out to paint."[132]

Granted that this book is a simple piece of 'debunking,' granted also that the way in which Dance reduced all the Victorian certainties, traditions, dogma's and ideals to illusions was rather crude – 'it was the age of the parliamentary illusion,' and all this was 'self-deception' and 'a hot-pot of opportunism'[133] – still there is an element of truth in the underlying tone of his charge. The aim of his realistic approach was to unmask the hollow political phrases of the preceding generation, especially the unctuous uncritical verbiage about the Constitution, dismissed by the author as 'hypocritical cant born of the fulsome self-satisfaction of that very complacent people.'[134]

Actually the Whigs did lack realism to a very great extent in their historical writing. We already mentioned the constitution as the key to the interpretation of the English history as a whole. This characteristic description of Victorian constitutionalism might also be paraphrased so that 'constitutional history' does not mean 'history of the constitution' but also 'constitutional interpretation of history.' This constitutional approach to the past and this way of interpreting the past lie at the very root of English Whig historical writing. After 1900 the non-historical elements of this 'legal interpretation of history' began to be more sharply perceived. They concerned mainly the disregarding and abstracting of the historical context, as well as the related tendency to miminalize or eliminate both the elements of chance and conflict. The three characteristics of Whig historical writing that we mentioned before were greatly strengthened by this legalism. The anti-Whig reaction endeavoured to push this 'legal mind' into the background. In the chapter on Maitland we intend to discuss further this internal factor in the breakthrough away from the old pattern of interpretation.

---

[130] *Ibid.*, p. 225.
[131] *Ibid.*, pp. 225–226.
[132] *Ibid.*, p. 321.
[133] *Ibid.*, p. 7. Cf. also pp. 4, 10, 11.
[134] *Ibid.*, p. 17.

Generally a more realistic and functional approach to the constitution came into being as a reaction to the earlier constitutionalism. The administrative history can be seen as a more specific exponent of the new approach. Historians never stopped being attracted by the study of constitutional history, but when the actual working of the constitution became the focal point of interest instead of its imagined permanent content or essence, there was a profound change both in approach and in interpretation. A concrete explanation of this will be given in the chapters dealing with Maitland, Pollard and Tout. First, however, we intend to devote our attention to some early attempts, made in the late 19th century, to break away from the traditional Whig historiography.

1. An attempted breakthrough: Seeley's approach and Gardiner's method

The reaction against the Victorian manner of writing history began with the criticism of constitutional history as the only possible history. The historian J.R. Tanner in 1901 had harsh words in the book mentioned above; in some respects, surprisingly harsh for a historian who would become significant in this area. His restriction concerning the 18th and 19th century was very blunt indeed: "The vital matters do not fall within the province of the historian of the constitution."[135] This strongly relativist approach towards historical problems concerning the constitution in modern times came from his teacher, J.R. Seeley. This Cambridge historian may have been a true 'Victorian' and very old-fashioned in his rejection of original research, but there is no doubt about his merits in displacing the narrowly constitutionalist approach.

Tanner echoed the message of *The Expansion of England* regarding the necessary revision of constitutional history. Because the turn of the century was the heyday of imperialism Seeley's book, written in 1883, was dubbed an example of 'imperalist' historiography. It was regarded solely as a manifesto of 'New Imperialism,' with the consequence that the author's historiographic revisionism was not accorded nearly as much attention as it deserved. However, the work strongly advocated a revision of the Whig historical view, especially concerning the 18th century. A narrow constitutionalism had overlooked the essence of the

---

[135] *Essays on the Teaching of History*, p. 64. He stated clearly that since the 18th century "the striking facts of English history are not longer constitutional facts." See J.R. Tanner on J.R. Seeley in *E.H.R.* 10 (1895), pp. 507–514.

century: the rise of the Empire. "It is a misrepresentation to describe England in George III's reign as mainly occupied in resisting the encroachments of a somewhat narrow-minded king. We exaggerate the importance of these petty struggles."[136] Seeley opposed first what he called a childish mode of arranging history and secondly the identification of history with parliamentary history. "History, I say, is not constitutional law, nor parliamentary tongue-fence, nor biography of great men, nor even moral philosophy. It deals with states ..."[137]

Regarding the first point it should be remarked that Seeley did not seek new facts, but a re-arrangement of the known facts within a new framework, well-constructed because well-selected, and based on 'a new standard of importance for events and a new principle of grouping.'[138] Results determined the importance of a historical event: 'the greatness of the consequences' was Seeley's criterion.[139] Historical writing should not be based on a reconstruction of a contemporary's judgment or point of view, for this vision in itself was insufficient and usually wrong since they had no way of knowing the consequences.[140] Seeley's criticism of the current constitutional history also implied an attack on the romantic literary school of 're-living' history. He believed that this system omitted a consciousness of the problematical in history, and robbed it of its 'futurist' value.[141] He denounced romantic historiography: "History is commonly regarded as a sort of ocean, an immense magazine of miscellaneous facts which no memory can retain, a labyrinth in which the mind loses itself."[142] This was what he had in mind when he spoke of a 'perversion' of the too literary writing of history; for him Carlyle and Macaulay were charlatans, which extreme assertions caused George Macaulay Trevelyan to re-value history as litera-

---

[136] J.R. Seeley, *The Expansion of England*, London, 1925, p. 139; cf. p. 141: "We shall avoid the error commonly committed in these later periods of confounding the history of England with the history of Parliament," and also the daring statement on p. 30: "It is only our own blindness and perversity which leads us to overlook the grandeur of that phase in our history, while we fix our eyes upon petty domestic occurrences, parliamentary quarrels, party intrigue, and court-gossip." In the same place he also objects to the fact that 1760 is represented as a break in English history. See also his criticism on the English insular approach to the American Revolution (p. 169).

[137] J.R. Seeley, *op. cit.*, pp. 175–176. Cf. also G. Hollenberg, *Englisches Interesse am Kaiserreich*, Wiesbaden, 1974, pp. 216–217.

[138] J.R. Seeley, *op. cit.*, pp. 121, 141, 164–165.

[139] *Ibid.*, p. 167.

[140] *Ibid.*, p. 165: "It is in fact one of the chief functions of the historian to correct this contemporary judgment."

[141] *Ibid.*, pp. 166, 193, 202.

[142] J.R. Seeley, *Introduction to Political Science*, London, 1923, p. 380.

ture years before Bury's inaugural speech again attacked the literary approach to history.[143]

Seeley objected to Macaulay, however, on more than only literary grounds. His criticism was mainly concerned with the framework of Macaulay's work dealing with 1688: Macaulay's overestimate of the Glorious Revolution and consequent underestimate of the importance of the Restoration period. He already made mention of this in his *Expansion*[144], but it did not become a recurrent theme until later, when he tried to develop the revisionist programme of *The Expansion* in several aspects. Both Hallam and Macaulay were attacked in his well-known series of lectures of 1885–1886. These contain a number of excellent topical essays on the function of parliament over the centuries. Taking up the cudgels against Macaulay's anachronistic interpretation of 1688, he pointed out the immense importance of the 'Long Parliament of the Restoration'; this was the starting-point for the development of his theory about the 'Second English Revolution' in the 17th century – which unlike the Civil War was hardly an insular affair.[145] In our chapter on the new historiography dealing with Parliament we shall refer to a further development of Seeley's theory by his pupil, Tanner.

When Seeley criticized the old constitutional history he included also the insular approach and insular interpretation. It is this insularism which historians of the following decades repeatedly refer to as a great deficiency of Victorian historiography. The old school, as Seeley remarks, never once inquired about the background of England's emergence as a great power.[146] This question was the main theme of his last book, *The Growth of British Policy*, published posthumously. He saw the study of 'international history,' as the ideal means of breaking through the pattern of constitutional history: international history was the history of British policy as 'the policy of the modern Great Power,' whose foundations went back to the times of Elizabeth, Cromwell and William III. If there is any continuous theme in all Seeley's historical and political work, it is that of the emergence and development of the

---

[143] G.M. Trevelyan, *An Autobiography and Other Essays*, p. 17.

[144] Cf. J.R. Seeley, *The Expansion of England*, p. 142: "The Revolution was not nearly so revolutionary, nor the Restoration so reactionary, as is commonly supposed."

[145] See J.R. Seeley, *The Growth of British Policy. An Historical Essay*, Cambridge, 1895, II, pp. 171–172, 276. Cf. J.R. Seeley, *Introduction to Political Science*, pp. 235, 253, 258 and 261: "It was at the Restoration ... that Parliament began to be a permanent, fixed organ of the English State."

[146] See Seeley's article, 'Our Insular Ignorance' in *Nineteenth Century* 18 (1885), pp. 861–872. Seeley mounted an attack on a wide front (politics, history, education and so on) against English insular complacency. Cf. J.R. Seeley, *The Growth of British Policy*, I, pp. 1–2.

State, as well in his great Stein-biography dating from 1878 as in his last work on the growth of England to a great power. History "deals with states, it investigates their rise and development and mutual influence, the causes which promote their prosperity or bring about their decay."[147] This kind of historical interest was somewhat unusual for an English Liberal, which is exactly what the Regius Professor was in matters of national policy. The basis for his views can be found not only in a strong German influence, but was also inspired by the religious-political ideas of the Broad Church Tradition, ideas to which his earlier works especially bear testimony.[148]

Apart from this exclusive interest in the development of the State, Seeley introduced still another non-Whig element into English liberal historiography. By putting the idea of power at the centre he dealt a heavy blow to the old constitutionalism with its legalistic interpretation of the past. His realistic ideas about power naturally proved unacceptable for many Liberals; Freeman's sharp reaction in his inaugural speech was only one protest.[149] However, the slowly growing consciousness of the reality of power in the Liberal circle was an important factor in undermining the Whig historiography.[150] Seeley was not alone in this respect; the same factor subsequently proved valuable for Pollard's revaluation of Tudor despotism.

On the one hand, therefore, Seeley brought a sense of relativity to the constitutional history after 1700, "George III and all that." On the other hand, he modified the current views about 1688. The Glorious Revolution was unimportant in itself; it was not imbued with the spirit of modern parliamentary democracy. The Restoration period evidenced the most significant break in constitutional history; only

---

[147] J.R. Seeley, *The Expansion of England*, p. 176.

[148] About the glorification of the christian-national State: read the excellent essay by R.T. Shannon, 'John Robert Seeley and the Idea of a National Church' in *Ideas and Institutions of Victorian Britain*, ed. R. Robson, London, 1967, pp. 236–267.

[149] E.A. Freeman, *The Methods of Historical Study*, London, 1886, p. 9. Cf., too, Motley about Seeley in *Macmillan's Magazine*, 99 (1883–1884), pp. 241–258. Cf. further, J.R. Green's unfavourable view of Seeley when the latter was made a professor in Cambridge in 1869, *Letters of J.R. Green*, ed. L. Stephen, London, 1902, p. 248.

[150] R.T. Shannon, *op. cit.*, p. 262: "In thus introducing, more distinctly and effectively than any other publicist, the power factor into the intellectual debate on the politics of the later nineteenth-century England, Seeley performed a much-needed function of revision and realignment." Cf., too, his conclusion on p. 266: "But in any case Seeley had done the important thing. By insisting on the necessity of reinterpreting both English history and English politics in terms of the State and its power relationships, Seeley provided the basis necessary for a revised agenda of national debate." See about Seeley's contribution to a more realistic political science also: F. Nuscheler, *Walter Bagehot und die englische Verfassungstheorie*, Meisenheim am Glan, 1969, pp. 99–103.

then can parliament be said to have become a permanent instrument of the British constitution.

Seeley did not attempt a revaluation of the other great Whig theme of the 17th century: the Civil War. How difficult and slow the breakthrough on this theme was, is seen in *The History of England*, a work of Seeley's contemporary S.R. Gardiner. Gardiner tried to cut loose from the old conceptions, but his methods were different from Seeley's, even diametrically opposed. No rearrangement of known facts for him; he accumulated interminable quantities of new details, stringing them together until they formed one endless chronological story which at long last filled eighteen tomes: a labyrinth laden with anomalies that must have made Seeley shudder.

Gardiner attempted a 'new method': original research. He began his work in the sixties of the last century, just when the Whig conception of the Civil War was predominant. This, and the dryness of his method and presentation, kept the sale figures of his first studies lamentably low.[151] Only after more than a decade did the prominent journals accord him any notice. In 1875 an Oxford historian, Robert Laing, published an extensive article in the *Quarterly Review*. The title was: "The first Stewart in England."[152] As had other reviewers, he too praised Gardiner's research activities as a unique achievement: "He is complete master of the facts; we are indebted in chief to him for our knowledge of them."[153] From this viewpoint it is indeed possible, even now, to concur with Ch. Hill: "We have to start with Gardiner."[154] Despite this praise contemporary criticism was no less apparent. For there was something curious in Gardiner's research, namely his inability to incorporate the evidence resulting from his new facts into his views as a whole: "surely his facts themselves make as evidence against the conclusions which he ultimately inclines to draw from them."[155] A remarkable discrepancy and a short circuiting effect be-

---

[151] Cf. A.F. Pollard, *Factors in Modern History*, p. 251; C.H. Firth, 'S.R. Gardiner' in *D.N.B.*, Suppl. II, London, 1902, pp. 75–78. See further, E.M. Hunt, 'S.R. Gardiner,' in *Some Modern Historians of Britain*, ed. H. Ausubel, New York, 1951,

[152] *Q.R.* 139, (1875), pp. 1–40. Ranke, Pattison and Spedding were also mentioned here. Cf., too, the reviews by A.W. Ward in the *Saturday Review*, included in the latter's *Collected Papers*, Cambridge, 1921, I, pp. 224–265.

[153] *Q.R.* 139 (1875), p. 29.

[154] C. Hill, *Puritanism and Revolution*, London 1958, p. 4. Cf. C. Hill, *God's Englishman. Oliver Cromwell and the English Revolution*. London, 1970, p. 268.

[155] *Q.R.* 139 (1875), p. 29.

tween research procedure and interpretation were noticed. In the last resort his conclusions and his views did not differ from those of the old Whig writers, and it was not just his conclusions but his presuppositions as well that had a similar quality.

More than ten years after Gardiner died, the historian R.G. Usher clearly and succinctly explained this. It was perhaps a hypercritical study, with which Gardiner's successor, C.H. Firth, found it difficult to agree.[156] Usher stated that Gardiner retained the typically vague Whig terminology concerning the old parliamentary constitution like conceptions as nation, people and liberty. He also firmly believed in the existence of a more or less clearly defined 'Elizabethan constitution,' and overestimated the unity of opposition in speaking of a truly national resistance movement. Although he did question certain points and had some doubts, his tale was certainly still anachronistic in this respect; Usher thus considers the differences between Gardiner and his Whig predecessors minimal.[157]

Had he then not made any real progress? A critical observer, Reginald Palgrave, in the *Quarterly Review* of 1882, had the courage to call his work a revolution, a revolution which was the more remarkable because of the author's Liberal origins.[158] With a slightly Crokerian conservatism he praised Gardiner's "annals", stating they formed the ideal approach for understanding the character and the direction of a revolution.[159] He especially remarked on the openness and the great understanding that the liberal Gardiner had for the 17th-century

[156] R.G. Usher, *A Critical Study of the Historical Method of Samuel Rawson Gardiner*, Washington University Studies, vol. III, part II, no. I, St Louis, 1915. Partly because of the First World War, it took four years for the book to come to the attention of English historians. It occasioned a debate in the *T.L.S.* which lasted for months, after an anonymous historian had drawn the readers' attention to it on the 25th of September, 1919 (*T.L.S.* 25-9-1919, p. 515). The historian made no bones about agreeing wholeheartedly with Usher's criticism, and his letter to the editor contained a devastating judgment of S.R. Gardiner's historical method. In fact he went farther than Usher had done: "Critics have been so thoroughly deceived by Gardiner's Berean attitude that they have failed to perceive that he was a subtle and dangerous partisan." "The truth is that nothing that he (Gardiner) says can be trusted. Every reference note should be checked." This letter unleashed a number of highly indignant reactions by A.P. Newton, A.F. Pollard, C.H. Firth, and Gardiner's wife Bertha Gardiner. See *T.L.S.*, 9-10, 16-10, 13-11, 27-11, 4-12, 18-12, 1919. Firth's criticism of Usher mainly in *T.L.S.*, 6-11-1919. Cf. also D.M. Fahey, 'Gardiner and Usher in Perspective' in *Journal of Historical Studies* 1 (1968), pp. 137-150.

[157] R.G. Usher, *op. cit.*, pp. 86 ff., 130, 142. Cf., too, H.E. van Gelder in *Tijdschrift voor Geschiedenis* 76 (1963), p. 300: "de Whig interpretatie had haar afsluitend handboek gekregen." (The Whig interpretation had acquired its manual).

[158] *Q.R.* 154 (1882), p. 2: "This historical revolution is the more remarkable because Mr. Gardiner's bias- and who is not in some way biased? – is towards the Puritan aspect of life and so-called liberalism in politics."

[159] *Ibid.*, p. 4: "The character and tendency of a revolution turns on its daily development."

monarchs. It was this impartiality in Gardiner that the *Edinburgh Review* found difficult to accept: according to them, Gardiner went too far in his revaluation of James I and of Laud's policies.[160]

Gardiner's method expressly aimed at breaking up the Tory-Whig differences in their views of the Civil War: "I am not so vain as to suppose that I have always succeeded in doing justice to both parties, but I have, at least, done my best not to misrepresent either."[161] Connected with this is the recurrent 'thesis' to the effect that England early in the 17th century was facing a choice between either the ideas of Bacon or Coke's, and that the Civil War might have been avoided if Bacon had been followed.[162] However, even Gardiner finally decided in favour of Coke and the Commons, for their views, and for their early Whig interpretation of England's past. One of the ways in which he tried to do justice to both parties was by banning all reference to later happenings, reporting rather the opinions of contemporaries from year to year and from month to month, and as far as possible avoiding a clear summing-up in order to postpone a final interpretation until the very end. In the end this method failed because it was based on an internal impossibility.[163] The mass of new facts weakening the Whig standpoint, or putting it in a different light, was not sufficient to convince Gardiner to abandon the Whig view. G. Lapsley once said of Stubbs that "zwei Seelen wohnten in seiner Brust": (two souls dwelt in his breast), the one belonged to a cautious methodical student, and the other to an interpretator imprisoned by an idealistic Whig view. The same applies to Gardiner. Despite the amount and importance of the newly available published sources during the second half of the 19th century, it was not yet possible to gain the needed distance from the Whig example. Moreover Gardiner's method had robbed his work of the necessary coherence and consistency. Usher cites many examples of this inconsistency.[164]

---

[160] *E.R.* 143 (1876), p. 123 and *E.R.* 148 (1878), p. 387.

[161] S.R. Gardiner, *England under the Duke of Buckingham and Charles I*, London, 1863, p. VI.

[162] Cf. Brian Manning in *Crisis in Europe, 1560–1660*. ed. Trevor Aston, New York, 1967, p. 27, note 23. See also Gardiner's article on Bacon in the *D.N.B.* and H.R. Trevor-Roper in *Crisis in Europe*, p. 98, note 28. The significance of Harrington for Tawney's 'Rise of the Gentry' is similar to Bacon's significance for Trevor-Roper's theory of a 'General Crisis.' See H.R. Trevor-Roper, *Religion, the Reformation and Social Change*, London, 1967, p. 245: "We can easily agree with the greatest of English seventeenth-century historians, S.R. Gardiner, that if only Bacon's programme had been carried out, England might have escaped the Great Rebellion."

[163] R.G. Usher, *op. cit.*, pp. 20–24. "Is it possible for any one to forget what he knows and place himself where a contemporary stood?'" (p. 24). Cf. also the question on page 144.

[164] *Ibid.*, esp. ch. 3 and 4.

Gardiner's fantastic accumulation of detail resulted after all only in a juxtaposition of Tory and Whig thinking; he could never obtain a truly original view nor a real integration of the two viewpoints, because his approach and way of regarding problems was essentially the old one. To him the struggle still was mainly one between different religious-constitutional ideas. He was not sufficiently interested in the actual functioning of the constitution and the actual political relationships; here his analysis was found wanting.[165] Only with the rise to prominence of economic history did really important innovations occur in this field.

2. The Rise of Economic History: W. Cunningham and G. Unwin

We saw that Seeley attempted a breakthrough on the field of 17th- and 18th-century history through a wider (i.e. non-insular) approach and a different focus. Constitutional history, whose importance he had questioned, was partly replaced by what he called 'international history.' In Gardiner's case we find a similarly broadened approach, though to a lesser extent; but in his case the international aspect is not lacking either. In this respect Seeley even cited Gardiner as an example.[166] Gardiner was also more interested in the military aspects of the Civil War, although the real pioneer in this field was his friend, C.H. Firth. For Firth, the Civil War was no longer the idealistic battle in defence of the Constitution which the 19th century and Gardiner had perceived: "a civil war is not only the conflict of opposing principles, but the shock of material forces."[167]

[165] Cf. C.H. George, 'Puritanism as History and Historiography' in *Past and Present*, no. 41 (1968), pp. 77–104, esp. p. 96: "His (Gardiner's) idealism was as naive as it was unobtrusive in the monumental narrative of seventeenth-century England which he created. Gardiner's puritanism is, in fact, not really an analytical concept." Yet there are some bright flashes of analysis in his work, e.g., about the social function of Scottish Presbyterianism (cf. C. Hill, *Puritanism and Revolution*, p. 5, note 1). Apart from this, his work also possesses a greater realism than was found in the work of his Whig predecessors. This was pointed out by Esmé Wingfield-Stratford and others. Stratford's characterization and his 'thesis' regarding Gardiner's work exaggerate in our opinion, esp. when suggesting that Carlyle's hero worship had a strong influence. "Gardiner was the very man to effect the marriage of the old Parliamentary Liberalism and the new Carlylese Satanism overlaid with godliness," and: "Gardiner tried to bring the Civil War melodrama up to date by adding such frank supermen as Strafford and Cromwell to the alleged champions of constitutional liberty in his category of heroes," (Esmé Wingfield-Stratford, *Truth in Masquerade*, London, 1951, resp. pp. 137, 173). Cf. also P. Zagorin, *The Court and the Country*, London, 1969, p. 266; and Duncan Forbes' Introduction in David Hume, *The History of Great Britain*, Harmondsworth, 1970, pp. 19, 48–49.
[166] J.R. Seeley, *The Growth of British Policy*, I, p. 2.
[167] C.H. Firth, *Cromwell's Army*, London, 1902, Univ. Paperback, London, 1962 (Introd. by P.H. Hardacre), p. XIII. Significant is the opening sentence by C.H. Firth: "The His-

There is no doubt, however, that the greatest breakthrough in Civil War historiography, one that freed this area from a pure constitutionalism, was made by economic history.[168] The rise of this new branch in the study of history occurred simultaneously with the decline of Whig historiography. Not only did a new subject area join the existing field of science, a new approach was implied as well, and in that sense an 'economic interpretation' (not used in any monocausal sense) came to replace the old 'legal interpretation.' Replace is perhaps putting it rather strongly, but we certainly may call it an important correction. No longer was it possible to explain constitutional conflicts solely within the constitutional context; this important lesson was finally learned. The rise in importance of this new area of study was greatly promoted by a growing 'holistic' conviction that all fields of life are interrelated and interdependent. To quote once more the *Essays on the Teaching of History*: F.W. Maitland, whose work is a highly original testimonial of this new school of thought, says in his preface that "the study of interactions and interdependences is but just beginning, and no one can foresee the end."[169]

The inquiry into the social and economic backgrounds of the old constitutional conflicts broadened the historical context to such an extent that the numerous anachronisms of an earlier generation could easily be overcome. J.E. Thorold Rogers stated in one of his lectures published as a collection called *The Economic Interpretation of History*:

What I wish you to notice is, that when we project ourselves into a bygone age, we cannot conclude invariably with those, who, however far-sighted and shrewd they are, are unable to realize, from lack of facts, these remote

---

tory of the Civil War is the history of the evolution of an efficient army out of chaos." Hardrace points out that Firth's theme has a topical value in connection with the war in South Africa and the grave defeats the British army suffered in the first phase (p. XIII). The traditional Whig fear of a standing army was one of the reasons why they had so little interest in military history. The Boer War made them change their mind; we shall discuss this later on.

[168] Cf. C. Hill, 'Recent Interpretations of the Civil War' in *Puritanism and Revolution*, pp. 3–31. See, on the rise of economic history in the Anglo-Saxon world, N.S.B. Gras, 'The Rise and Development of Economic History' in *The Economic History Review* 1 (1927–1928), pp. 12–34. Gras designates the crises of 1866 and of 1873 as important for the history of this rise (p. 21). See also H. Butterfield, 'Some Trends in Scholarship, 1868–1968, in the field of Modern History,' in *T.R.H.S.*, 5th ser. 19 (1969), pp. 159–184, pp. 171–174.

[169] *Essays on the Teaching of History*, p. XX. Cf. also Butterfield's remark: "Since 1890, in point of fact, much of our European history also has had to be reshaped, because it came to be realised that a knowledge of social structure alters the bearings of a piece of narrative." (H. Butterfield, *George III and the Historians*, p. 195). For the way in which this holistic conception spread through different sciences, see J. Romein, *Op het Breukvlak van Twee Eeuwen*, Leyden-Amsterdam 1967, vol. II.

conditions. It is a common and dangerous error to interpret the past by the present.[170]

This quantitative growth in historical scholarship doubtlessly also led to an improvement in the quality of historical interpretation in itself, especially an improved understanding of the fundamental differences between past and present and between pre-industrial and industrial society. The Whig presuppositions were thereby dealt a telling blow, although this was often in the first phase done unconsciously and indirectly.

There is to our knowledge as yet no serious book dealing with the emergence of this new subject area about 1900. Perhaps its importance is self-evident. We will therefore only very briefly deal with the situation in England at the beginning of this century, first, however, mentioning R.H. Tawney.

Tawney must be regarded as a pioneer who caused a new interpretation in the history of the 16th and 17th century through promoting social-economic history. He is as much a pioneer as Namier was when the latter applied the yardstick of his biographical (or structuralist) method to the 18th century. They are often considered the two most important innovators.[171] Namier's place has already been mentioned; Tawney's influence is undeniable, but it is difficult to determine the extent to which his writings were directly influential in the then already current anti-Whig reaction. It is this reaction that first claims our attention.

Whig historiography was never an obsession for him as it was for many of his colleagues. He had less of a dispute with previous historiography than Namier had, because his area had been in many respects yet unexplored. Perhaps even more important was that he had never in any way been closely connected with the liberal-historical Whig tradition. The decisive factor stimulating his particular historical interest was his background: neither anti-Whig nor anti-Tory, he thought more like a 19th-century Radical. His anti-capitalist moralism was visible, for instance in *The Acquisitive Society*, and was built on the foundations laid by Ruskin and Morris, and by Bishop Gore's ideal of a christian socialism.[172] Tawney wished to continue this tradition, not

---

[170] J.E.Th. Rogers, *The Economic Interpretation of History*, London, 1921, p. 304, cf. also pp. 4–6. See on J.E.Th. Rogers: N.S.B. Gras, *op. cit.*, pp. 19–20.

[171] Only cf. Gareth Jones, 'The Pathology of English History' in *New Left Review* no. 46 (1967), p. 36; W.H.B. Court, *Scarcity and Choice in History*, London, 1970, p. 17.

[172] See Raymond Williams, *Culture and Society, 1780–1960*, Harmondsworth, 1963, p. 214 ff.; T.S. Ashton, 'R.H. Tawney in *Proceedings of the British Academy* 48 (1962), pp. 461–480;

to break with the past. To what extent his historical work was either hampered or stimulated by this tradition we cannot here discuss.[173]

However, let us now consider some of Tawney's predecessors, who do plainly show an anti-Whig element, polemical and anti-liberal. J.E.T. Rogers had pointed the way as early as 1866; but the man who raised the study of economic history in England to an academic discipline was W. Cunningham.[174] One of his essays also appeared in the collection *Essays on the Teaching of History* (1901). The subject was the teaching of economic history.[175]

The most remarkable thing in this essay is that economic history has a subservient position, although not an insignificant one. It is called the means to an end, an end to which all historic research ought to be directed: the study of the development of the State.[176] Thus, economic history to Cunningham was not an end in itself, but necessary as a means "for getting a clearer view of the actual development of the State."[177] It may have been neither remarkable nor surprising that this new branch in the study of history was given a subordinate position around 1900 but, for the English tradition in any case, its involvement with the State certainly was very much so. Cunningham's scholarship, like Seeley's, was influenced by religious and church traditions, and by continental ideas, principally those of the so-called German historical school. However the first factor probably carried more weight for this Anglican divine than did the latter; Cunningham was influenced by Maurice's ideas of a christian-socialist and theocratic state.[178]

J.M. Winter, 'R.H. Tawney's Early Political Thought' in *Past and Present* no. 47 (1970), pp. 71–96; J.D. Chambers, 'The Tawney Tradition' in *The Economic History Review* 24 (1971), pp. 355–369.

[173] G.R. Elton's remark is all too simplistic: "Not a single work which Tawney wrote can be trusted. I think that in all his work he was so dominated by his preconceptions ... that everything he wrote was written to a propaganda purpose" (G.R. Elton, *The Future of the Past* Cambridge, 1968, pp. 15–16).

[174] Audrey Cunningham, *William Cunningham*, London, 1950, pp. X, 129.

[175] *Essays on the Teaching of History*, p. 40 ff.

[176] *Ibid.*, p. 42: "The development of the State is the final object of research; but the more thoroughly we apply ourselves to political and constitutional history, the more necessary will it be at every point to take account of the results obtained by the study of Economic History."

[177] *Ibid.*, p. 43.

[178] A. Cunningham, *op. cit.*, pp. 17, 21 ff., 121. "The State no less than the Church was a divine agency, bearing its witness for law and justice" (p. 21). Maurice had theocratic ideas which made him feel a sympathy for 'that lofty but much maligned doctrine of the divine rights of kings'. J.N. Figgis's revaluation of this doctrine was another significant specimen of the anti-Whig reaction in these years. See on F. Maurice: T. Christensen, 'F.D. Maurice and the Contemporary Religious World' in *Studies in Church History*, vol. III, ed. G.J. Cuming. Leyden, 1966, pp. 69–90.

It is interesting that the earliest phase of economic history in England was completely dominated by the antagonism centering around Liberal *laissez faire*; the first scholars of importance in this new field were Rogers, Cunningham and Ashley, who rejected the liberal dogma after having adhered to it in an earlier stage. While Cunningham's criticism of *laissez faire* may not have been a cause of direct damage to the political (and therefore historical) Whig tradition, indirectly it certainly was. In this sense M. Postan later wrote about Cunningham: "He believed that English thought and English politics of his time wanted rescueing from a-moral and a-national prejudices of Liberal economics and Whig history."[179] In the reprinted issues of Cunningham's first great work, *The Growth of English Industry and Commerce in Modern Times* (1882), the development from the ideology of free trade to a strong protectionism can plainly be traced.

After 1900 Cunningham apparently rejected idealistic free trade conceptions as propounded by Cobden and Bright, and became an enthusiastic supporter of a nationalistic protectionism in the manner of Chamberlain. In the fifth edition of his work, in 1910, there is not a trace left of Cobden's ideology which he once supported.[180] His nationalist feelings – which may safely be called imperialistic – inspired him with admiration for the powerful state of national unity, which in England originated with the Tudors, especially with Henry VIII's break with Rome. We have already seen that the 'nation state' was also a favourite object of study for economic historians. Cunningham's affection for the Tudors in connection with this nationalist idea bears some resemblance to Pollard's, although the latter's revaluation of the Tudors was both national and constitutional. But then Pollard remained a Liberal to the end of his life, free trade and all, as Cunningham did not.

Because he believed that the State was an important historical factor for the furtherance of a nation's economic growth, Cunningham grafted his view of economic history upon political history. On the other hand he tried, still motivated by the same beliefs in the state, to free his new subject from the harmful impact of abstract liberal political economy. He advocated an empirical-historical approach, and to him the economic laws were only hypotheses of very limited use.[181]

W. Ashley had by and large a similar development, although this

---

[179] M.M. Postan, *The Historical Method in Social Science*, Cambridge, 1939, p. 5.
[180] See, for W. Cunningham's gradual evolution: A. Cunningham, *op. cit.*, pp. 94–104; B. Semmel, *Imperialism and Social Reform*, London, 1960, pp. 188–210.

second pioneer's political faith was far less influenced by a christian tradition than was Cunningham's.[182] A liberal by birth, he became a strong supporter of a protectionist national policy after a stay in the U.S.A. His work is largely inspired by G. Schmoller, and in the end he too rallied to J. Chamberlain.

The author B. Semmel is right in stating that most of the economic historians were anti-Liberals supporting Chamberlain, with one notable exception among these early pioneers in England: George Unwin. Notwithstanding the small number of his publications, his influence – especially in later years, from Manchester – should not be under-rated.[183] His political faith, the lodestone deciding the tenor of his economic history, was the exact opposite of Cunningham's. Not only was he fervently anti-imperialist, he also retained a life-long scepticism concerning the role of the State in the social and economic field. Neither in the past nor in the present could he discern any sign of the State's creativity that had moved his colleagues to such admiration. Although he had a deep respect for G. Schmoller, who had taught him for half a year, he followed his own path. While he did not believe in 19th-century *laissez faire*, he did follow A. Smith, stating that 'the spirit of voluntary association' had been and still was the motor of social and political progression.[184] In his inaugural speech of 1908 in Edinburgh he also called A. Smith's work a magisterial model of the ideal economic historiography.

In his economic studies on the industrial organisation in the 16th and 17th century Unwin minimalised the political factors, reduced the importance of mercantilism, opposed the venerable nationalist Whig legend with Edward III as the father of English commerce and, lastly, attempted in a more general sense to separate economic history from the study of political and state history. Inclined to pacifism, he mainly fulminated against the latter branch, viz. in his criticism on Seeley's 'imperial history' although he fully acknowledged that Seeley had never been guilty of an aggressive type of imperialism.[185] Unwin was

---

[181] W. Cunningham, 'A Plea for pure Theory,' in *The Economic Review* 2 (1892), pp. 25–41; *idem*, 'The Relativity of Economic Doctrine' in *The Economic Journal* 2 (1892), pp. 1–16; *idem*, 'The Perversion of Economic History' in *The Economic Journal* 2 (1892), pp. 491–506. The latter article contained attacks on both Rogers and A. Marshall. Cf. A.W. Coats, 'The Historist Reaction in English Political Economy 1870–1890' in *Economica* 21 (1954), pp. 143–153.

[182] B. Semmel, *op. cit.*, pp. 202–215.

[183] R.H. Tawney in *Studies in Economic History. The Collected Papers of George Unwin*, ed. R.H. Tawney, London, 1927, p. XLIX.

[184] *Ibid.*, p. 33.

[185] *Ibid.*, pp. 407, 428.

fully convinced that economic history could be much more objective than political history, provided it stayed away from political historiography. He distrusted the official political records because they rationalized, because they disguised the truth and glossed over the harshness of real facts, especially in war and warfare.[186] In 1924 he was still lamenting the predominance of the 'political interpretation of history,' economic historiography with a strongly political orientation was criticized as fundamentally wrong, and Beard's *An Economic Interpretation of the Constitution* was pronounced exemplary.[187]

At first Unwin rather hesitatingly tried to join forces with sociology. Tawney, who developed along the same lines, called this Unwin's greatest merit. He wrote about Unwin: "He altered the perspective of economic history, freed it from much conventional lumber, and gave it a new objective and centre of interests. He found it strongly biased towards politics. He left it with a bias towards sociology."[188] There is no doubt that Unwin's separation of political and economic history was an important achievement; however, his interest in sociology may be slightly exaggerated by Tawney. Still these early advances towards sociology were of great importance. Tawney's own introduction of Weber into English historiography stimulated historical research and resulted in an enlargement of the traditional method; both protagonists and antagonists of this sociological approach agree on this point.[189] It also penetrated the dogmatic liberal 'politica' based on a rigidly positivist and utilitarian pattern of human political and social behaviour which had been largely unhistorical. The effects of this were felt in British thinking, even after 1900, in spite of the 'curious strength

---

[186] *Ibid.*, pp. LX, 13.

[187] *Ibid.*, p. 12. His article, 'Some Economic Factors in General History' (pp. 3–17), had been published in 1925, in *The New East and Other Essays on the Development of Civilization*. It contained essays by J.H. Breasted, H.J. Fleure and others and was edited by E.H. Carter, Oxford, 1925. Beard's pioneer study of 1913 occupies an important place in the anti-Whig reaction. In his first chapter – a program betraying strong traces of his early English medievalist training – he attacks the traditional legal thinking of Constitutional History, the 'juristic view of the Constitution,' which used to eliminate conflicts. As an alternative he proposed the biographical approach: "If it were possible to have an economic biography of all those connected with its (that is of the Constitution) framing and adoption, – perhaps about 160.000 men altogether – the materials for scientific analysis and classification would include a list of the real and personal property owned by all of these men and their families . . .," C.A. Beard, *An Economic Interpretation of the Constitution of the United States*, New York, 1913, p. 16. On Beard as the pioneer of the biographical research, see: J.E. Neale, *Essays in Elizabethan History*, London, 1958, pp. 226–227.

[188] *Collected Papers, George Unwin*, p. LXII.

[189] In his inaugural speech H.R. Trevor-Roper mentioned the 'fertile errors' of sociologists, passing a harsh judgment on his two 'professional' predecessors C.H. Firth and V.H. Galbraith; H.R. Trevor-Roper, *History: Professional and Lay*, Oxford, 1957, p. 22.

of positivism' underlined by Noël Annan.[190] A reaction against the traditional positivism was imminent, as evidenced for instance in Cunningham's rejection of liberal economy, especially on this point, and by Graham Wallas's criticism of Macaulay's simplistic psychology in his influential study *Human Nature in Politics*.[191]

Summarizing, we find that on the one hand the rise of economic history, directly as well as indirectly, undermined certain presuppositions of Whig constitutional historiography; on the other hand this statement should not be too categorical, since some at least regarded economic history more as a complement to constitutional history than as a correction. F. Seebohm, the author of *The English Village Community*, introduced his work as 'an essay in economic history,' being fully convinced that economic history would provide "secure stepping stones over what may be impassable gulfs in constitutional history."[192] N.S.B. Gras in his synopsis gave examples to prove that economic history was gradually emerging from constitutional (rather institutional) history: "the institutional approach prepared the way for the functional."[193] Finally, it should be remembered that economic history only very gradually came to achieve its present autonomous position in England. The twenties brought considerable progress: the establishment of the *Economic History Review* in 1927 and, finally, the first professorship in Cambridge, accepted in 1928 by Clapham. Three years later Oxford followed suit with G.N. Clark becoming the first Oxford professor in economic history.[194] Clark himself, however, still believed that his own subject area ought to remain subservient to institutional and constitutional history, which should continue to occupy the central place in the field of historical studies as a whole.[195]

[190] N.G. Annan, *The Curious Strength of Positivism in English Political Thought*, London, 1959.
[191] Cf. Cunningham criticizing the 'crude' psychology, the usual belief that similar economic motives decided the economic actions in all periods: *The Economic Review* 2 (1892), p. 36 and *The Economic Journal*, 2 (1892), p. 493; Graham Wallas, *Human Nature in Politics*, London, 1914, pp. 22–25. Cf. Namier's later utterances about Graham Wallas in his article of the same title: 'Human Nature in Politics,' in *Personalities and Powers*, London, 1955, pp. 1–7. See p. 2.: "Graham Wallas's criticism of the *homo sapiens* in politics won an easy victory: the time was ripe for his thrust.... By now we have travelled a great deal further along Graham Wallas's path."
[192] Frederic Seebohm, *The English Village Community, an essay in Economic History*, London, 1884, p. XIV.
[193] N.S.B. Gras, *op. cit.*, p. 21: "The institutional point of view did much to carry over the influence of history into economic history.... The free village community, the manor, the exchequer and the customs system were not only forms of institutions, but types of economic functions."
[194] J.H. Clapham's inaugural speech, *The Study of Economic History*, Cambridge, 1929. For G.N. Clark's inaugural speech, see *History* 17 (1932–1933), pp. 97–110.
[195] G.N. Clark, *Historical Scholarship and Historical Thought*, Cambridge, 1944, pp. 18–19;

3. The Rise of 'Record-History': J.H. Round and G.W. Prothero

The present age is the age of the microscope.

(A.W. Ward, 1892)

We have already dealt with the relativizing of traditional constitutional history and the emergence of economic history, but in the changing study of history in England, both before and after 1900 an important third factor is plainly visible. The historians then spoke of the transition from 'chronicle-history' to 'record-history.'[196] During the 19th century the interest in records, in systematization, in registration and in the accessibility of records had developed but slowly. During the eighties of the last century this process gained momentum, an improvement largely due to Henry Maxwell Lyte's efforts.[197] He was an archivist who was appointed chief of the Public Record Office in 1886, also the year of the first issue of the *English Historical Review*. During his tenure (until 1925) a closer bond grew up between the historical scholars working at Universities and those who had a 'first-hand'-knowledge of the national records. The old detrimental 'unhappy separation' was at last overcome and the 'archivist view of history' (as it is later referred to in the 'Confessions' of V.H. Galbraith) came to be accorded university recognition and support.[198] Medieval studies were the first to benefit from this change. Among the medievalists one historian who came especially to the fore was John Horace Round.[199] His work resulted in a thorough revision.

"But it is in public institutions that men express their will to control events, and therefore it seems to me that historians will go wrong if they try to resolve political and constitutional history into other elements.... The history of institutions must be in some sense central...."

[196] J.H. Round, *Feudal England*, London, 1909, p. VII; T.F. Tout, *The History of England, from the Accession of Henry III to the Death of Edward III*, London, 1905, p. 443.

[197] V.H. Galbraith, *An Introduction to the Use of the Public Records*, London, 1934, p. 73 ff.; R.B. Wernham, 'The Public Record Office, 1838–1938,' in *History* 23 (1938–1939), pp. 222–235, esp. p. 231 ff.; D. Knowles, 'Some Trends in Scholarship, 1868–1968, in the field of medieval history' in *T.R.H.S.* 5th ser. 19 (1969), p. 144: "The epoch of 'record-history' began in the mid-1880's and received a gentle but decisive impetus from the action of Sir Henry Maxwell Lyte in diverting funds and editors from the moribund Roll Series to the publication of public records."

[198] V.H. Galbraith, *Studies in the Public Records*, London, 1948, pp. 1–25: "Confessions of an archivist."

[199] Most of the information about the life and work of J.H. Round is to be found in *Family Origins and Other Studies by the late J.H. Round*, ed. with a memoir and bibliography by W. Page, London, 1930, pp. IX-LXXIV. A highly balanced judgment on the significance of J.H. Round for English historical scholarship is provided by J. Tait in his article, 'J.H. Round' in *E.H.R.* 43 (1928), pp. 572–577. We do not share H.G. Richardson's and G.O. Sayles' clearly unfavourable opinions. They characterise Round's method as 'amateurish' remarking: "His mind would not adapt itself to scientific processes"; actually they are badly

Round believed that the decisive changes in English medieval studies around the turn of the century were caused by the new critical way of studying and assimilating original authentic records. In his view this kind of material was more authentic, more direct and consequently more truthful than literary chronicles, usually written after the event. Round never wrote anything except analytical record-history where the record supplied addition and correction to the literary chronicle.[200] With this methodological weapon, wielded in a masterly way, (for Round had been a scholar of international repute since the publication of his book *Feudal England* in 1895[201]) he opened in the eighties the attack on E.A. Freeman, the representative of the Oxford School of History, at the very time when the latter's authority still appeared unassailable.[202] Round's studies betrayed the slightly inhuman characteristics of one possessed. They were usually so intensely polemical that more and more colleagues began to keep him at a distance, even though he was factually right in most cases. In the end even Maitland broke with him, disregarding the tendencies towards criticism and innovation which they had in common.[203]

No critic in the English historical world of the turn of the century was feared as much as Round. Whoever escaped having his work reviewed by Round, might well be thankful.[204] R.L. Poole and J. Tait admonished and even reprimanded him, but all to no avail: nothing could keep Round from crusading against everything which fell short of his high standards concerning historical criticism and historical methods; nothing could make him revert to normal proportions.[205]

---

undervaluing Round's work of critical demolition in the anti-Whig reaction. (Cf. H.G. Richardson, G.O. Sayles, *The Governance of Mediaeval England from the Conquest to Magna Carta*, Edinburgh, 1963, pp. 20, 65.

[200] J.H. Round, *Feudal England*, p. VII. The bias in the chronicle kept shifting, that of the records was much more stable; see for this, V.H. Galbraith, *Studies in the Public Records*, p. 17.

[201] Cf. Ch. Seignobos, *La méthode historique appliquée aux sciences sociales*, Paris, 1909, p. 60.

[202] J.H. Round, 'The House of Lords' in *The Antiquary*, 10 (1884); 11 (1885). Later reprinted in *Peerage and Pedigree, Studies in Peerage Law and Family History*, London, 1910, I, pp. 324–362. This early article already contains Round's view that 1066 marked a break; also his biting criticism on an unhistorical 'legal thinking' and his opinion that parliament originated in the *curia regis*. "The present constitutional crisis" made Round decide to re-publish in 1910 (*op. cit.* p. XXVII).

[203] *Selected Historical Essays of F.W. Maitland*, chosen and introduced by Helen M. Cam, Cambridge, 1957, pp. XXV–XXVI.

[204] G.M. Trevelyan, *An Autobiography and Other Essays*, p. 21: "Fortunately I escaped, perhaps I was beneath, the attentions of the terrible J.H. Round."

[205] See J. Tait's two letters to J.H. Round, dated 20-10-1910 and 5-6-1919, U.L.L., I.H.R.MS, no. 680. In the last letter Tait took the historian Ballard under his wing: "Ballard, as you say, was not always very sound in his views, he always remained more or less of an amateur in historical studies, but he did a good deal of useful spade-work, and there does not seem anyone rising up to take his place. Medieval municipal studies in this country have

The controversies caused by Round were legion. Rather than go into these we shall confine ourselves to Round's positive contribution to the study of medieval history in England. In this connection however a discussion of the quarrel with Freeman is inescapable, since it illustrates most vividly the reaction of the medievalists in the nineties against Whig historiography.

Because Round's main predilection was for record-evidence as opposed to chronicles, this predilection formed the basis for his attacks on Freeman, especially on Freeman's methods. Freeman saw himself as a specialist who practised a new and accurate form of historiography based upon original sources. It was because of the accuracy of his method that he was generally considered an authority in his field. What, however, were those original sources? They were chronicles. As Round said: 'books and ever books.' Never did he use new documents or records; and it was 'his use or rather non-use of manuscripts,' which made it impossible for Round to call Freeman a research-historian. In fact, Frederic Harrison, as a Comtean among the English historians, saw Freeman as a research historian and criticized him for it.[206]

According to Round, Freeman's historiography had always been a 'paraphrasing' of chronicles rather than a critical search for internal and external evidence in them; he seldom performed more than a 'perfunctory cross-examination.'[207] Round's attack on Freeman's ostensible accuracy hit especially hard because it was directed to the problems and new views which Freeman offered his readers as both evidence and result of his painstaking accuracy. Round was especially angered because in his opinion Freeman made occasional blunders 'in the name of accuracy.'[208] The crux of it was not just Freeman's weak points in

been singularly unfortunate in the early deaths of so many scholars; besides B. (but much above him of course) we have had to lament the loss of Maitland, Miss Bateson and Charles Gross none of whom lived to be 55." See, for Round's letters to Tait, F.M. Powicke, *Modern Historians and the Study of History*, p. 58; in his lecture 'The Garrison Theory of the Borough' (delivered for the international historical congress in London, 1913), Round had sharply attacked Ballard. (U.L.L., I.H.R., MS no. 770c). Cf. also R.L. Poole to J.H. Round, 17-10-1914, U.L.L., I.H.R., Ms. no. 664.

[206] F. Harrison, 'The Historical Method of Professor Freeman' in *Nineteenth Century* 44 (1898), pp. 791–806, esp. p. 796 ff.; Round's, 'Historical Research' in *Nineteenth Century* 44 (1898), pp. 1004–1014 was a reaction to this article.

[207] J.H. Round, *Feudal England*, pp. 454, 455: "The paraphrasing of evidence is the work of a reporter; from the historian we have a right to expect the skilled summing-up of the judge."

[208] J.H. Round, 'Professor Freeman' in *Q.R.* 175 (1892), pp. 1–37, esp. p. 11: "He was guilty not only of anachronism, but of a real wrong to geography: and in the name of accuracy, he introduced error."

historical methods and criticism, but that Freeman's historical interest was centred on a field which had become an anachronism. In 1898 Round concluded that Freeman's historiography – narrative political history – was past its prime:

Institutional, economic, social development, these are the subjects that excite the chief interests now. In these Freeman had little interest: he was a 'narrator,' a political historian on the 'drum and trumpet,' the dramatic side of history.[209]

Freeman's ostensibly accurate method and procedure had other short-comings. There was one point on which Round could agree with Harrison's objections: it was Freeman's 'multiplication of useless facts and details,' so that the forest could no longer be seen because of the trees.[210] He lacked the ability to discern the truly relevant factors in a historical event. However, perhaps the source of Round's most serious grievance was Freeman's admiration for the Anglo-Saxon woods, the Teutonic forest as cradle and protectress of true democratic freedom. "A democrat first, a historian afterwards": this was the core of Round's unceasing diatribes against Freeman's historiography. In fact, his first attack on Freeman in 1884 had been a political one, directed against Freeman's views about the origin of the House of Lords.[211] In none of his later studies was Round able to ignore Freeman's democratic beliefs.

To a conservative realist like Round Freeman's Anglo-Saxon ideas of liberty were dangerous nonsense incarnate. Freeman's tale about 1066 evinced a political moral without any sense of political reality either in that distant past or in the present day. Freeman's idealisation of Harold and his conception of an Anglo-Saxon constitution as a model for the present were part of the 'medievalist' Whig constitutional ideology of the 19th century. "Harold is for him what Dutch William was for Macaulay and the Whigs."[212] Round, however, saw these Anglo-Saxon liberties as synonymous with complete anarchy. For him the lessons of 1066 – if any – were the direct opposite of Freeman's ideas. In any case Round only very occasionally made such a direct political use of history. However, there was indeed a 'moral' for us in Hastings:

---

[209] J.H. Round, 'Historical Research' in *Nineteenth Century* 44 (1898), p. 1013.
[210] *Ibid.*
[211] See note 202. Cf. J.H. Round, *Feudal England,* p. 395.
[212] J.H. Round, 'Professor Freeman' in *Q.R.* 175 (1892), p. 35.

An almost anarchical excess of liberty, the want of a strong centralized system, the absorption in party strife, the belief that politics are statesmanship, and that oratory will save a people – these are the dangers of which it warns us, and to which the majority of Englishmen are subject now as then.[213]

The fact that England in 1066 fell a prey to the Normans was the logical outcome of the 'old-English freedom' so highly praised by Freeman and his followers. Round pointed to the work of Vinogradoff and Andrews, arguing that fortunately the reaction against this liberal myth was gaining in strength.[214]

The biggest obstacle to an understanding of the real meaning of "1066 and all that" was Freeman's 'medieval' liberalism, especially his liberal aversion to 'castles,' 'barons,' 'hereditary rule' and – last but not least – to a 'standing army.' This was a Whig theme central to all Liberal historical writings.[215] The Franco-German war had not taught Freeman anything in this respect, Round insisted.[216] And Round, being a modern Tory, saw in Freeman's concept of democracy only weakness and dissension from party strife and a lack of efficient government. "While our fathers were playing at democracy, watching the strife of rival houses, as men might now watch the contest of rival parties, the terrible Duke of the Normans was girding himself for war."[217]

This may suffice to show what Round objected to in Freeman's work. Since Round's record-history consisted mainly of analytical research, he did in this respect set the stage for the future archieve-

[213] J.H. Round, *Feudal England*, pp. 394-395.

[214] *Ibid.*, p. 396. See P. Vinogradoff, *Villainage in England*, Oxford, 1892; Ch.Mc. Andrews, *The Old English Manor. A Study in English Economic History*, Baltimore, 1892. Both books are prefaced with a still very readable historiographic introduction. See the review by Vinogradoff in *E.H.R.* 8 (1893), pp. 540-543. Cf. C.A. Beard: "It has been left to a Russian to explain to Englismen the origin of Teutonism in historical writing." (*An Economic Interpretation of the Constitution of the United States*, p. 3, note 1.)

[215] More about this in connection with Macaulay. The diminishing aversion to a standing army and the indirect meaning of this for historiography will be treated more extensively in the third chapter. See, too, note 167.

[216] J.H. Round, *Feudal England*, p. 397: "When the Franco-German war had made us look to our harness, he set himself at once, with superb blindness, to sneer at what he termed "the panic," to suggest the application of democracy to the army, and to express his characteristic aversion to the thought of 'an officer and a gentleman.' How could such a writer teach the lesson of the Norman Conquest?" On the significance of 1866 and 1870 for the growing power realism in liberal circles (not German liberalism exclusively), and particularly within liberal historiography, see P. Vinogradoff, *Villainage in England*, p. 31; Ch.Mc. Andrews, *op. cit.*, p. 4. Cf. Edward Jenks' remark: "Even the sternest repudiator of the *a priori* method could hardly distrust the suggestion that the war with Germany was, of all things, the event most likely to work a spiritual revolution in the mind of a Frenchman of the years 1870-4." (*E.H.R.* 12 (1897), p. 211).

[217] J.H. Round, *Feudal England*, p. 398.

ments of the new professional historiography. In a sense his work even provides an example for the future. In 1892 he published a book on Geoffrey de Mandeville which is a detailed case study with none of the traits of an ordinary biography. Stenton was right in stating that the book illustrated the new method which – when dealing with the history of Parliament – would be called the biographical method.[218]

Actually there is a resemblance in Round's approach to the refined research procedures of a later day, i.e. Namierism. Round's subsequent biographical work proved to be useful for a project concerning the history of Parliament begun in the twenties.[219] Powicke noted that Round, in his analytical approach to history, was driven by a fundamental conviction which he continually impressed upon his readers, "that the most obscure researches in out of the way material may throw light on the broad beaten tracks of history."[220]

But for all generalizing approaches to history this method was deadly. It was especially so for the Whig approach. However, the disadvantage in Round's as well as Namier's method was that they became more and more incapable of writing a summarizing synthesis. Round had never been able to do so; and he thus refused to write a general survey of Norman history for the well-known series edited by R.L. Poole and W. Hunt. This notwithstanding Hunt's plea for him to become a 'complete historian' by making a synthesis of his vast knowledge of the period.[221] Prior to this Round had also refused Acton's request for a chapter about Spain in the *Cambridge Modern History*, since he was convinced (and wrote so to Acton), that "the aim of your work will be wholly alien from my specialist research."[222]

[218] F.M. Stenton, 'J.H. Round' in *D.N.B.*, *1922–1930*, London, 1937. Cf. also F.M. Stenton, *The First Century of English Feudalism, 1066–1166*, Oxford, 1932, pp. 1–6; cf. a remark by G.O. Sayles, in *The Medieval Foundations of England*, London, 1966, p. 289.

[219] To this end the Committee was set up on March 22nd., 1929, after Round's death. Round's notes on the Knights of the Shire for Essex (from 1540 to 1832) were available. See: *Interim Report of the Committee on the House of Commons Personnel and Politics, 1264–1832*, London, 1932, p. 14. See, for Round's 'biographical' work, his articles in *D.N.B.* Round also zealously practiced local history, witness especially his many contributions on Colchester and Essex. Apart from the Middle Ages and the English Reformation he also had a special interest in the Civil War and in Cromwell. He saw Cromwell as a conservative statesman, in marked contrast to Gardiner's more liberal interpretation. See three lectures by Round on Cromwell and Fairfax (U.L.L., I.H.R.MS, no. 743, 744, 745) as well as his correspondence with S.R. Gardiner (U.L.L., I.H.R.MS no. 638). Cf. also Round's article 'Colchester during the Commonwealth' in *E.H.R.* 15 (1900), pp. 641–664.

[220] *E.H.R.* 26 (1911), p. 774.

[221] W. Hunt to J. Round, 13-9-1901 (U.L.L., I.H.R.MS., no. 648). Cf. R.L. Poole to F.W. Maitland in *The Cambridge Historical Journal* 10 (1952), p. 334 (letter dated 29-7-1901).

[222] J.H. Round t o Lord Acton, C.U.L., Ad. MS. 6443, letters of 15-1, 23-1, 7-2-1897. Quotation from last letter. Round was certainly not unacquainted with the history of Spain,

That Round may be considered a pioneer and a herald of the future was mainly apparent in his declared speciality, where his critical method had the fullest scope: in genealogy. His deep annoyance about the myths and legends accumulating about this subject in the course of the centuries was one reason for this genealogical-biographical interest. This interest was also motivated by the conviction that here the researcher faced a really essential aspect of English history. To his own mind the latter reflection justified his excessive interest in the history of the 'great families,' and in this he felt himself supported by Kemble, who in the 19th century had written: "The succession of the landowners and the relations arising out of these successions, are the running comment upon the events in our national history."[223]

The anti-Whig element in Round's view of English history is especially recognizable in that Round did not see the development of liberty or a paper constitution as the pivot of British political evolution; instead, he cast the development of 'authority' in that role. The focus from which he approached England's past was the structure of authority and actual power, its shifting emphasis in the course of time between alternation of 'anarchy' and 'strong rule'; in short, it was the 'pattern of authority.'[224] This view was not a mere continuation of the historiographic Tory tradition that had been relegated to the background in the second half of the 19th century, for Round lacked the Tory reverence for a sacrosanct tradition of monarchy. When this tradition could no longer stand up to the impact of historic criticism, it was attacked just as ferociously as was the liberal Whig tradition of freedom. Round distrusted all historical arguments which claimed the authority of a particular tradition. He stressed his antitraditionalism in history in very clear terms in his lecture at the international historical Congress in London in 1913: "In us the word 'tradition' excites no reverence, for the expert knows that those who appeal to it do so in default of any proof for the origin they seek to claim."[225]

A realistic conservative, he preferred periods of 'strong rule': they

see his reviews in *E.H.R. 6* (1891), p. 798; 7 (1892), p. 603. Cf. also: J.H. Round, 'Village Communities in Spain' in *Q.R.* 182 (1895), pp. 483–507.

[223] J.H. Round, *Feudal England*, p. XIV

[224] Cf. the review by E.J. Hundert of A.P. Thornton's book *The Habit of Authority* in *The Review of Politics* 29 (1967), p. 554 ff.; Thornton on Round, *op. cit.*, pp. 35, 251.

[225] J.H. Round, 'Historical Genealogy' in *Family Origins and Other Studies*, p. 12. This stinging criticism of tradition may lead to a historical misunderstanding. We refer here especially to Round's lack of understanding for the social significance of traditions in former times. Cf. J.H. Plumb's remark about Round in *The Death of the Past*, p. 28, note 15; see about the reality of traditions V.H. Galbraith, *Studies in the Public Records*, p. 28, and F.Y. Powell, *op. cit.*, vol. II, pp. 242–253.

had contributed essentially to England's national emergence and formation. The Anglo-Saxon period which had so much delighted the
preceding generation, no longer seemed fruitful, and in this respect
English medievalists sided with Round during the first twenty or thirty
years of the century. It is significant that with a few exceptions the
Anglo-Saxon period in these years suffered comparative neglect.[226]

With the term 'feudal monarchy' Round accorded more importance
to the aspect of monarchy than to feudalism. His 'monarchical' pre-
disposition regarding 1066 could be called 'centralist' or 'autocratic,'
and it made Round lose sight of the essentially 'feudal' aim of the
Domesday Book in his pioneering work about this document. In our view
it would be both confusing and wrong to speak of a 'Gladstonian view'
in this respect, as Galbraith does. The contemporary perspective in
Round's conception was the exact opposite of the 'Gladstonian' ideal
of a Teutonic state built on anti-centralist and federalist lines.[227]

Round's *geld*-theory concerning the *Domesday Book* was on the same
level as his belief in 1066 as the beginning of a new type of monarchy.
The year 1066 was a turning point, a new beginning. It gave England
a new military aristocracy and a strong monarchy. It has been said
that Round 'had an instinctive feeling that ... the political history
began in England with the Norman Conquest.''[228] His objections to
Freeman's continuity thesis, to a lesser extent also propounded by his
admired mentor Stubbs, were very plainly expressed in a series of articles about the 'introduction of the knight-service into England,' published in the *English Historical Review* of 1891–1892, and later reprinted
in his *Feudal England*. "It is the fruit of long original research," he wrote
to Maxwell Lyte in the same year, undertaken in the first instance at
the request of Walford Selby of the Public Record Office.[229] Thorough-

---

[226] Cf. F.M. Stenton, 'Early English History,' 1895–1920' in *Preparatory to Anglo-Saxon
England, Being the Collected Papers of F.M. Stenton*, D.M. Stenton, Oxford, 1970, pp. 346–356,
esp. his remark on W.H. Stevenson, p. 352: "It is particularly unfortunate that Stevenson's
Cambridge Lectures on the Old English Chancery given, as Mr. Poole used to relate, to an
audience of three-himself, Miss Mary Bateson, and Professor Maitland – were never made
available to a wider public." Cf. also V.H. Galbraith in *A.H.R.* 76 (1971), p. 1119.

[227] Cf. for this characterization V.H. Galbraith, *Studies in the Public Records*, p. 104; Cf.
C. van de Kieft, 'Domesday Book in het licht van nieuwe onderzoekingen' in *Tijdschrift voor
Geschiedenis* 75 (1965), pp. 150–178; esp. p. 158 on Round's neglect of the actual aims of the
Domesday Book.

[228] J.O. Prestwich, 'Anglo-Norman Feudalism and the Problem of Continuity' in *Past
and Present* no. 26 (1963), pp. 42–43; cf. also C.W. Hollister and J.C. Holt, 'Two Comments
on the Problem of Continuity in Anglo-Norman Feudalism' in *The Economic History Review*
16 (1963) pp. 104–118. See also: R.A. Brown, *Origins of English Feudalism*, London, 1973.

[229] J.H. Round to Sir Henry Maxwell Lyte, 7-7-1891, Public Record Office, P.R.O. 1/159.
For W.D. Selby see A.F. Pollard in *D.N.B.*, vol. 51 (1897).

ly supported by the documents, Round contended that the supposition of a gradual change from the Anglo-Saxon 'thegn' to the Norman 'knight' was mistaken. He was fully aware that his 'cataclysmic' opinion did not only go counter to current historical views, but also was contrary to the Victorian evolutionary way of thinking.[230]

In Round's view an awareness of far-reaching changes was one of the most essential elements of historical thought. He criticized the believers in continuity regarding 1066 as well as those for whom continuity existed only in the English Reformation. His conception certainly allowed for wide gaps in English history: e.g. the Norman Conquest and the Reformation. His attacks on the 'adoring believers in continuity' were sharpest in his deadly criticisms of the old genealogy. In this field his denunciation of the non-historical belief in continuity is illustrated most plainly by his confrontation with the muddle of the peerage law. We will return to Round's important contribution in freeing historical thought from noxious juridical presuppositions in a later section that deals with law and history. Here a short remark about 1066 must suffice.

Since Round's death in 1928 historiography experienced a revived emphasis on the belief of the continuity of English history before and after 1066.[231] The period before 1066 underwent a strong revaluation first because more was known about the period, and secondly, because of a growing realization that William the Conqueror was not really the strong rejuvenating figure formerly portrayed. Another interesting aspect is the re-discovery after a number of years of W.H. Stevenson's studies from about 1900, dealing with the deeper effects of the Anglo-Saxon financial organization.[232] Even Round's meagre belief in continuity in this respect was rediscovered. Thus, the year 1066 as a break, as a definite boundary, seems to be swept away much as it was in the

---

[230] Cf. his statement: "In accordance with the anticataclysmic tendencies of modern thought, the most recent students of this obscure problem have agreed to adopt the theory of gradual development and growth." in *E.H.R.* 6 (1891), p. 417. On his conception of the Reformation as a break, see his polemical exchange with Malcolm MacColl, in this respect a faithful adherent of Coke's: J.H. Round, 'As established by law' in *Contemporary Review* 75 (1899), pp. 814–822; M. MacColl in *C.R.* 76 (1899), pp. 220–230, and Round *Ibid*, pp. 231–238. See, too, *Selected Historical Essays of F.W. Maitland*, introd. by H.M. Cam, pp. XX-XXI.

[231] Cf. the literature mentioned in the article already quoted by J.O. Prestwich (note 228). Also H.G. Richardson, G.O. Sayles, *The Governance of Medieval England*, Edinburgh, 1963. Cf. also chapter 17 of G.O. Sayles, *The Medieval Foundations of England*, pp. 212–278, which still shows the influence of Round (later considered so pernicious). Cf. p. 225. See also note 233.

[232] See V.H. Galbraith, *Studies in the Public Records*, pp. 37–45. Cf. also H.G. Richardson, G.O. Sayles, *op. cit.*, p. 97, note 3.

Victorian historical writings. One representative of this revival movement is the historian R.R. Darlington, who over the course of years increasingly stressed the idea of continuity; for him the twelfth century is a legacy of the Anglo-Saxon period in every area, in social, economic, juridical, religious and architectonic respects.[233]

Yet we may state that Rounds anti-thesis in a sense created the possibilities for the present revaluation, providing it with the more realistic foundations that it had lacked in Victorian historiography. Without Round to expose the illusions behind the many mythical Victorian representations about the Anglo-Saxons, this revaluation might never even have reached its present state. But, revaluation and newly stressed continuity notwithstanding, the new view leaves some aspects unexplained. For the continuity thesis, as it were, stops short of explaining the clearly divergent political developments of the period before and that after 1066: "We must still explain the difference between the political achievements of the two societies . . ."[234] The Normans gradually and very thoroughly changed the old existing forms of government, which prevents us from viewing the events of 1066 solely as a continuous development. For a historical approach it is no less pertinent that the same things appeared in different forms before and after 1066, as that their identity remained the same.

Many of Round's colleagues shared his ideal of a record-history, aiming at the opening of the as yet numerous unused sources.[235] Of course this rapidly growing trend towards a new professionalism by means of increasing specialization gave rise to oppositional forces. The opponents were those who still preferred a clear-cut, bold survey that gave a synthesis for the common reader. (In this connection we are reminded of Frederic Harrison and his criticism of the 'research-mania.') Other opponents saw Clio become more and more unlike Clio. Here we think of George Macaulay Trevelyan, whose work,

[233] R.R. Darlington, *The Norman Conquest*, London 1963, p. 27: "The Conquest destroyed some interesting features of Anglo-Saxon civilization and led to the transformation of others, but whether we are studying the machinery of government, the law and the administration of justice, the writing of history, and other aspects of intellectual activity or the production of books and other works of art, we are impressed by the strength of the native element. The evidence, I submit, leads to the conclusion that the essential foundation of the achievement of the twelfth century is the legacy of Anglo-Saxon England." On the gradual growth of Darlington's continuity thesis see his earlier contributions: 'Ecclesiastical Reform in the late Old English Period' in *E.H.R.* 51 (1936), pp. 385–428; 'The Last Phase of Anglo-Saxon History' in *History* 22 (1937–1938), pp. 1–13; 'The Early History of English Towns' in *History* 23 (1938–1939), pp. 141–150; *Anglo-Norman Historians*, London, 1947.

[234] J.O. Prestwich, *op. cit.*, p. 53.

[235] Cf. L. Woodward's article, 'The Rise of the Professional Historian in England' in *Studies in International History*, ed. K. Bourne and D.C. Watt, London, 1967, pp. 16–34.

though it had widespread influence, did not represent the new trends in English historiography after 1900.

Moreover, neither was Round's ideal completely new. His teacher Stubbs had already shown the path, pioneering in the new direction himself. And although he showed some disappointment over the lack of results when he resigned his professorship, in Oxford his lead was certainly followed.[236] With the exception of Freeman's short term as a professor, Oxford had a number of innovating professors, among them R.L. Poole.

Poole was a specialist in the auxiliary sciences and for some decades the untiring editor of the *English Historical Review*. Other innovators were the new professors C.H. Firth and P. Vinogradoff.[237] In 1896 Poole at last saw his labours crowned with a 'readership in diplomatics,' which he hoped to turn into the beginning of a much grander attempt. "A real Ecole des Chartes would be a grand thing to establish," he wrote to Dr. Sanday after the latter's offer.[238] Poole much preferred this historical spadework to the actual writing of historical books, a task which weighed especially heavily on him. On behalf of the *Cambridge Modern History* he offered to give Acton all possible help, but he resolutely refused to contribute personally. The thought that he would be obliged shortly to write something 'on order' left him mentally paralysed.[239] In 1897 he candidly confessed to Acton: "I feel more and more that I must give up any ambition of writing and must content myself with preparing materials for others to make use of."[240] Though Oxford remained 'outstanding' after 1900, yet the emergence and growth of a more scientific way of studying history was more conspicuous in Cambridge and in the newer universities of London and Manchester. Powicke later was to speak of a 'new history school' in

---

[236] R.W. Southern, *The Shape and Substance of Academic History*, Oxford, 1961, p. 14.

[237] For R.L. Poole, see C.C.J. Webb, 'R.L. Poole' in *Proceedings of the British Academy* 25 (1939), pp. 311–320; G.N. Clark in *E.H.R.* 55 (1940), pp. 1–7. Around 1880 R.L. Poole was still seen as a 'budding theologian,' see M. Lodge, *Sir Richard Lodge*, London, 1946, p. 24. For P. Vinogradoff, see H.A.L. Fisher, *P. Vinogradoff, a Memoir*, Oxford, 1927; For C.H. Firth see E.S. de Beer, 'Sir Charles Firth' in *History* (1936–1937), pp. 1–13; E.S. Godfrey, 'C.H. Firth' in *Some Historians of Modern Europe*, ed. B.E. Schmitt, Chicago, 1942, pp. 130–151; M.B. Rex, 'C.H. Firth' in *Some Modern Historians of Britain*, ed. H. Ausubel, New York, 1951, pp. 192–214; M. Ashley, 'Sir Charles Firth: a tribute and a reassessment' in *History Today* 7 (1957), pp. 251–256.

[238] R.L. Poole to Dr. Sanday, 7-2-1896, B.L., MS, Eng. Misc. d. 125.

[239] R.L. Poole to Lord Acton, 25-10-1896; "I am the worst of all men for writing 'to order.' Any sort of writing is difficult enough to me; but when I am set a task I suffer a sort of mental paralysis" (C.U.L., Add. MS. 6443, f. 219).

[240] R.L. Poole to Lord Acton, 23-11-1897 (C.U.L. Add.MS. 6443, f. 225).

London as well as in Manchester. With this he meant Pollard and Tout, both of whom came from Oxford.[241]

In this chapter we shall first discuss Cambridge, where English historiography gained international repute principally through the work of Acton and Maitland. Especially Maitland's achievement deserves closer study. In connection with the ideal of record-history a third name should be mentioned, the name of a man who spared neither pains nor expense in order to provide English historiography with a closer knit scientific foundation: George Walter Prothero.[242] Some words about his organizing abilities are certainly in order.

For a scientifically warranted standard of higher education in history he deemed certain conditions essential and he worked for their realization until the end of his presidency of the Royal Historical Society (until 1905). His models were Stubbs and the German historiography, especially Ranke, part of whose *Weltgeschichte* he translated. Because of his many years at Cambridge, he became one of the founders of what is loosely designated as the Cambridge History School.

Only after 1870 did the study of history become an independent discipline in Cambridge, when the short-lived detrimental association of history with the study of law came to an end.[243] Notwithstanding this notable emancipation the study of history remained some what amateurish. Seeley, the Regius professor, like most of his predecessors, was not a trained historian, but a classical scholar with no professional historical experience. Early in the seventies there were two schools of historical approach in Cambridge: Prothero's friend, the co-editor of

---

[241] F.M. Powicke, *Modern Historians and the Study of History*, p. 171. Concerning the development in Oxford, see C.H. Firth, *Modern History in Oxford, 1841–1918*, Oxford, 1920, and F.M. Powicke, *op. cit.*, pp. 164–183. Cf. also E. Barker, *Age and Youth*, Oxford, 1953, pp. 25, 158 ff.

[242] On the subject of G.W. Prothero, see A. Cecil, 'Sir George Prothero' in *Q.R.* 238 (1922), pp. 213–218; D. Heatly in *The Scottish Historical Review* 20 (1922–1923), pp. 76–78; B. Williams, 'The Value of History' in *The Scottish Historical Review* 23 (1925–1926), pp. 128–129. The Royal Historical Society created the institution of a yearly Prothero-lecture only in 1968; the first of these lectures, delivered by C.W. Crawley, was devoted to him: 'Sir George Prothero and his Circle' in *T.R.H.S.*, 5th ser. 20 (1970), pp. 101–127.

[243] Cf. F.W. Maitland in *Essays on the Teaching of History*, p. XVI. Cf. A.W. Ward, 'The Study on History at Cambridge' in *The Saturday Review*, 6-7-1872, reprinted in *The Collected Papers of A.W. Ward*, Cambridge, 1921, vol. V, pp. 248–255. On Ward in general see W.H. Hutton, 'The Collected Papers of A.W. Ward' in *Q.R.* 238 (1922), pp. 314–326; S. Leathes and G.P. Gooch, 'The Editorial Methods of Sir Adolphus Ward' in *The Cambridge Historical Journal* 1 (1924), pp. 219–224.

the *Cambridge Modern History*, A.W. Ward who taught 'facts without thought'; John Seeley who taught 'thoughts without facts.'[244]

In 1885 reformers tried to find a middle path, while stressing the need to study the 'original authorities' during the educational period. Seeley was not interested in this aspect, and consequently there was some tension between him and his junior colleagues. The educational reforms were mainly carried through by Cunningham, Maitland, Gawtkin and especially Prothero (from 1879–1894 the secretary of the History Board). Their attempts to get this new educational programme accepted were supported by the ecclesiastical historian M. Creighton, who had arrived in Cambridge in 1884 and by 1886 was the first editor of the *English Historical Review*.[245] The programme drafted left space for personal initiative in historical research because it provided for a wider choice for the students. This cleared the way for more adaptability and responsibility in specialization. Prothero, tutor and fellow of King's College, acquired a very good reputation by working with this programme. King's was the first Cambridge college where History reached a level comparable to that of the other humanities. According to his colleague Oscar Browning, the great influx of students was largely the result of Prothero's efforts. Yet Browning also had many mental reservations about Prothero's scientific ideal. He favoured Acton's theory, underlining the importance of a 'broad line' ('the outline history') and would have history closely associated with 'political science' as Acton's predecessor Seeley had done.[246] For Prothero part of his programme was to continue the line of Stubbs in the publication of primary sources; his *Select Charters* ought to be continued with respect to the modern era. In his own widely known edition of the *Constitutional Documents* from the era of Elizabeth I and James I, Prothero often consulted the former Oxford-historian, Bishop Stubbs.[247]

After many years in Cambridge, Prothero was in 1894 given a new chair in Edinburgh. His inaugural speech was once again a plea for studying history 'in a scientific way.'[248] He did not deny the importance

---

[244] J.O. McLachlan, 'The Origin and Early Development of the Cambridge Historical Tripos' in *The Cambridge Historical Journal* 9 (1947), pp. 78–104, esp. p. 83 ff.; Cf. also G. Kitson Clark, 'A Hundred Years of the Teaching of History at Cambridge, 1873–1973' in *The Historical Journal* 16 (1973), pp. 535–553.

[245] *Life and Letters of Mandell Creighton by his Wife*, London, 1904, I, pp. 227–286.

[246] O. Browning on Prothero, see his *Memories of Sixty Years*, London, 1910, pp. 251–256. On Seeley: pp. 234–235, 257, 274. Browning deplored in 1910 that Seeley's ideal had become lost: "Cambridge history has now drifted away into other channels" (p. 235). Also Hedva Ben-Israel, *English Historians on the French Revolution*, p. 245.

[247] *Letters of William Stubbs*, ed. W.H. Hutton, London, 1904, pp. 358–362.

[248] G.W. Prothero, *Why Should We Learn History?*, Edinburgh, 1894.

of historical knowledge for political use, but he never had the ideal of a direct link, as propagated by Seeley and Freeman with the slogan: "history is past politics, politics is present history." He warned against misleading political analogies. A year before, he had dubbed Freeman's liberal historical writings old-fashioned and conservative: the more liberal he was *in politicis*, the more conservative *in historicis*.[249] On becoming the editor of the *Quarterly Review* (which he was to remain until his death in 1922), he took up residence in London. There he kept devoting himself to the cause of history.

As president of the Royal Historical Society (1901–1905), he mainly attempted to professionalize the Society, amateurish since its beginnings in 1868. Thanks to the work of Prothero and C.H. Firth around the turn of the century, the Society's amateurish status was overcome.[250] Prothero wanted the Society to be more than just a channel for the publication of historical records and scientific articles. His dream was for the Society to become a meeting place of national and international repute, functioning as "an armoury where all persons engaged in historical research may find the weapons necessary for starting and carrying on their work."[251]

One of the prerequisites for this, apart from an ample library, was to be a school of Advanced Historical Teaching, somewhat along the lines of the École des Chartes in Paris. As we have seen, R.L. Poole thought similarly. England had nothing of the kind in 1900, and London with its wealth of archives was a particularly suitable centre for such a training institute for specialists. A.W. Ward, the Society's president before Prothero, was the first to launch this idea of 'a school of advanced historical training' in his presidential speech of 1900. In this he ironically stated that "our English École des Chartes ... has been the school of self-help."[252] Similar complaints had been uttered by York Powell.[253] However, the realization of these plans was labori-

---

[249]   Prothero, on Freeman, in *E.H.R.* 8 (1893), p. 385. Cf. also Prothero on Seeley in his *Growth of British Policy* and his article about Seeley in *D.N.B.* 51 (1897), pp. 190–193.

[250]   C.H. Firth in these years contributed most of the articles for the Society, cf. A.T. Milne, *A Centenary Guide to the Publications of the Royal Historical Society, 1868–1968 and the Former Camden Society, 1838–1897*, London, 1968, p. 179.

[251]   *T.R.H.S.*, N.S. 19 (1905), p. 11.

[252]   *T.R.H.S.*, N.S. 14 (1900), p. 17.

[253]   F.Y. Powell, 'The École des Chartes and English Records' in *T.R.H.S.*, N.S. 11 (1897), pp. 31–40; contemporary opinion was not always favourable with regard to F.Y. Powell's significance as a historian and a Regius Professor; he had succeeded Freeman after Gardiner had refused the appointment because of the need to finish his *magnum opus*. R.L. Poole advised Acton against choosing Powell for his great project for several reasons: "an excessive hostility to all things German, an awkward archaic style, and an extreme dilatoriness in carrying out engagements" (C.U.L., Add. MS. 6443, f. 219, letter 25-10-1896). Cf.

ous work; a temporary start was made by two lecturers, H. Hall and I.S. Leadam, appointed for three years, but lack of money and the scepticism of the outside world repeatedly threatened the project.

This 'sceptical and materialistic world' was a recurrent theme in Prothero's complaints,[254] and as a matter of fact the project never really got off the ground in the years before World War I. It was Pollard who in 1921 definitely succeeded in fulfilling Ward's and Prothero's desires by founding the Institute of Historical Research for the express purpose of post-graduate study. Pollard too had in his inaugural speech of 1904 advocated such an institute, although he was to remain strangely silent about who were to be the initiators.[255] Yet he was in a sense merely the executor of the pioneers' plans, as the *Times Literary Supplement* was to write many years afterwards.[256]

We have devoted particular attention to two persons in our discussion of the process of professionalization: Round and Prothero, because their work gives the clearest view of how history became a 'science.' In this process Prothero was the organizer, whereas Round's work clearly illustrates the essential changes in historical orientation and interpretation, results of a new type of research. Most historians, including Prothero and the many others dealt with in this chapter, reacted less strongly than did Round to the historical teaching of the recent past. Nevertheless, they all realized that a new era had begun in which the demand – in the words of C.H. Firth – was for 'a historical teaching of history.'[257]

But where is the link between this process of professionalization and this ideal of record-history on the one hand, and the start of the undermining of the Whig interpretation on the other hand? Or with the emerging criticisms of Whig presuppositions? This first orientation chapter will conclude with the answer to these questions.

Poole to Round, 23-7-1904: "Powell's death was a great blow to many of us personally; but as the official head of historical learning here he left a good deal to be desired. No one rejoices more than I do that Firth has succeeded him. His knowledge and his judgment are both admirable." (U.L.L., I.H.R., MS. no. 664). Cf. also H. Hall in *Q.R.* 184 (1896), pp. 122–123.

[254] *T.R.H.S.* N.S. 19 (1905), p. 14: "Here in the richest country of the world, there is no money for such a purpose."

[255] Cf. A.F. Pollard, *Factors in Modern History*, pp. 245–247.

[256] 'The Study of History' *T.L.S.*, 5-8-1955, where we find the following passage on A. Ward: "Before the end of the century, his first presidential address to the Royal Historical Society called for the creation in London of the kind of centre which in 1921 was to take form as the Institute of Historical Research" (p. 438).

[257] C.H. Firth, *A Plea for the Historical Teaching of History*, Oxford, 1904.

One thing is clear: an existing pattern of interpretation for the history of a country or a people as such cannot be changed only by ferreting out some new facts. On the contrary, an accumulation of this kind may very well be used to prop up already existing views. In the next chapter we will find that something very like this happened in the case of Whig historiography, especially in the second half of the 19th century. Taking Thomas Kuhn's terminology about the development of science and using it in our problem structure, we could say that the 'Whig-paradigma' loses its scientific usefulness towards the end of the 19th century. More and more facts appear that cannot be accommodated within the old pattern, more and more facts are opposed to the scheme of historical development according to the old Whig-historiography.[258] In history and the humanities in general there is a tendency to explain these by means of ideological factors. However, limiting ourselves to the development within the science itself, we discover the increasing conviction that practical detailed research will be able to shed a strong, clear light on the whole of historical development.[259] This is what Round's 'facticism' meant.

From his direct experience with archives Tout also wrote in this connection: "The simple truth is that 'discoveries' in history are for the most part discoveries of detail."[260] J.S. Brewer, famed for his criticism of Green's *Short History*, wrote similarly in 1871, applying to history the following remark of F. Bacon's: "It cometh often to pass that mean and small things discover great, better than great can discover the small."[261] And what Bacon had once said about the meaning of a 'lumen siccum' is also relevant here: the poor weak light of seemingly unimportant details would in the end be able to withstand the brilliant sunshine of the Whig views, of that ever good and true line of historical development. The important thing in making English historiography scientific about 1900 was that the progress in methodology was rewarded by a new pattern of interpretation. This direct link became ever more visible, and its possibilities increased as the political

---

[258] Cf. Th.S. Kuhn, *The Structure of Scientific Revolutions*, Chicago, 1965.

[259] These were the kind of thoughts wich prompted V.H. Galbraith's characterization of Victorian anachronism as: "The attempt to replace the puzzled but authentic medieval comment upon great events by immediate out-and-dried motives is one of the commonest anachronisms of 'scientific' Victorian history" (V.H. Galbraith, *Studies in the Public Records*, p. 104).

[260] T.F. Tout, *The Place of the Reign of Edward II in English History*, Manchester, 1914, p. 28.

[261] J.S. Brewer in *Q.R.* 130 (1871), p. 393. Cf. Ch.V. Langlois, Ch. Seignobos, *Introduction aux études historiques*, p. 90.

and historical Whig tradition decreased in importance. All Gardiner's critical efforts only resulted in the correction of details of the Whig paradigm, leaving the matter itself unscathed. Around the turn of the century the growing accumulation of new facts was no longer automatically added to the existing frame of reference but (borrowing Kuhn's terminology) it led to an 'anomaly-experience.' It created a greater distance from an older pattern of interpretation, and more than that. It was – to those historians who possessed the required scientific intuition, or 'imagination,' as they preferred to call it – a nourishing substratum out of which a new interpretation could grow.

It is difficult and perhaps hazardous to try to distinguish certain common characteristics in this new view, especially in a period characterized by so much demolition. Of course the effort was made to cut loose from Victorian anachronisms, excessive finalism, and the obsession with continuity that characterized the older Whig historiography. The fact of the matter was that for a better understanding of the past (the political or Parliamentary past) a highly centralized monarchical perspective was created to take the place of the federalist constitutionalism and the anti-monarchical (or anti-tyrannical) Whig perspective. It may be seen as basically 'Norman' for the Middle Ages, and as 'Tudor' for the history of the modern period. The decisive rôle of the central government in nation-building, and the meaning of centralizing ('despotic,' said the old Whigs) tendencies and periods in England's political evolution were more stressed in the new historiography than they had been in the 19th century. This was very clear of the conservative Round. However, it is also noticeable in the structure of Maitland's *History of the English Law*. Pollard, a Liberal, stressed in all his writings the 'necessity' of the 'despotic' Tudor-phase.[262] Similarly, Tout's administrative history, most directly sprung from record-history and most closely adjusted to that ideal, was mainly concerned with the central organization of government.

This new trend towards seeing the monarchy as the most decisive historical factor had changed the perspective to something not quite constitutional in the old sense, although constitutional history as such remained an important field of study. The new monarchical bias was more realistic in that actual power was no longer relegated to the background, no longer glossed over and blurred as it had been in the

---

[262] The excellent preface by S.F.C. Milson in the latest re-issue (1968), suffices for Maitland. Round was called the 'new' Brady by D. Douglas, see D. Douglas, *English Scholars*, London, 1943, p. 157.

old liberal idealistic emphasis on freedom. Another result of the monarchical perspective was the undermining of the former insularism. On the continent there had never been a lack of monarchical and centralizing tendencies; this was interpreted by the Whigs as proof of England's uniqueness. Closer links with the continent now became easier. There was actually an interaction; a less insular interpretation strengthened the monarchical perspective. The origin and growth of the English constitutional structure proved to be less uniquely insular than had been assumed. Within this new perspective there was no longer room for some of the hitherto almost sacrosanct theories about the uniqueness of England's successful constitutional evolution. Some of these theories even involved the superior qualities of the Anglo-Saxon 'race.' The idea of race as an explanation certainly carried weight with some of the supporters of the 'Teutonic' school, but towards the end of the century it was regarded as of questionable worth by at least the leading and more professional historians, both in England and in France. 'On écartera entièrement la race' was the blunt advice of the French *Introduction* by Langlois and Seignobos, referring to J.M. Robertson's pioneering criticism in this respect.[263]

From the beginning we warned against underestimating the influence of continental historical writings on the demolition of Whig historiography. One such influence can be found in the French scientific historiography since Gabriel Monod.[264] It has already been mentioned that the École des Chartes was regarded as an example by many English innovators; there are also a number of other parallel developments extant. A realistic monarchical perspective had grown up in French medieval studies as well, usually replacing somewhat racially biased conceptions. After the romantic-literary historical writings this was a striking new phenomenon. This trend was most clearly represented first by Fustel de Coulanges and then by Achille Luchaire, whose influence on English medieval studies will be discussed further in our chapter on Tout. Imbart de la Tour wrote an excellent article summarizing the influence of Luchaire's work in the following words:

Comme Fustel, M. Luchaire réduit donc l'influence des "races" dans notre histoire; comme lui également, il va étendre celle de la royauté. Et pour la première fois, ce qui est mis en pleine lumière, c'est la permanence d'une

[263] Ch.V. Langlois, Ch. Seignobos, *Introduction aux études historiques*, p. 208.
[264] The French influence on medieval studies seems to have been greater than that of the Germans. Prothero and Ward were German-influenced. Cf. also H. Butterfield's mention of Von Ruville in *George III and the Historians*, p. 169. ff.

tradition monarchique et aussi la force d'action des premiers Capétiens qui l'ont représentée.[265]

Another parallel is visible in the deep-going influences of this monarchical bias on a number of concrete subjects. For instance: Maitland made some brilliant remarks about the origin and function of the medieval Parliament in an introduction in 1893. These remarks had their French counterpart in some studies by Langlois, published a few years earlier on the same subject (it was no coincidence that he reviewed Maitland's *Memoranda* in the *English Historical Review*). Also the recognition of the historical importance of the Royal Council by English historians (ever since Dicey's pioneering) closely resembled studies like those by Noël Valois on the 'Conseil du Roi.'[266]

No less interesting were the similarities in the reflections of a more general kind about history as such. On this too the French criticized the theory of progress, paying much more attention to accident – e.g. P. Lacombe who also rejected the racial interpretation.[267] Here again doubts about the direct use of history were evinced, and the expression 'historia magistra vitae' was declared to be an illusion. "Comme explication du présent, l'histoire se réduirait presque à l'étude de la période contemporaine."[268] Above all there was the very same desire for hard facts to make history into a real science. A very erudite Frenchman, J. Bédier, saw the coming era of historical study as largely an era of analysis, an era in which all attempts at synthesis would be premature.[269]

This cult of facts is surely worthy of note, but we should beware of the temptation to qualify (or to disqualify) it too easily as the simplistic belief of a past era in the objectivity of historiography turned into science.[270] The relativist American New History School (which was to succumb at last to its own philosophy about the 'hardness' of facts) was accustomed to dismiss the beliefs of earlier generations in this compas-

[265] Imbart de la Tour, 'Achille Luchaire' in *Revue des Deux Mondes* 52 (1909), p. 879. Cf. F.M. Powicke in *E.H.R.* 25 (1910), p. 564.

[266] Noël Valois, *Inventaire des arrêts du Conseil d'Etat*, Paris 1886, Introduction, pp. V-CLII. A.V. Dicey's *Essay on the Privy Council* appeared as early as 1869. Cf. F.W. Maitland, *The Constitutional History of England*, Cambridge, 1961, pp. 62, 199.

[267] P. Lacombe, *De l'histoire considérée comme science*, Paris, 1894, pp. 248 ff., 306 ff., 347 ff.

[268] Ch.V. Langlois, Ch. Seignobos, *Introduction*, p. 278. However, they thought it went too far to state apodictically, as did Fustel de Coulanges, that 'l'histoire ne sert à rien.'

[269] J. Bédier, 'La Société des Anciens Textes Français' in *Revue des Deux Mondes* 37 (1894), p. 932.

[270] Cf. G.N. Clark, 'General Introduction: History and the Modern Historians' in *The New Cambridge Modern History*, ed. G.R. Potter, vol. I, Cambridge, 1957, pp. XXIV ff., XXXIV.

sionate manner. What this 'cult of facts' did not imply – although often suggested – was the denial of subjectivity in historical writing or a simplistic belief in impartiality. Partiality was almost inevitable, as Langlois recognizes: "Si impartial que l'on essaie d'être quand il s'agit du passé-lointain, on juge toujours avec ses partis pris généraux et la clairvoyance qu'on a."[271] And Seignobos's final statement: "Il n'a donc pas de faits historiques par leur nature; il n'y a de faits historiques que par *position*," testifies to a perspective in the conception of truth; it is not at all a credo in the solid incontrovertible facts of history.[272]

For the English situation Bury's introduction to Gibbon's *Autobiography* is enough to cure its readers of the conviction that former generations had a simplistic belief in objectivity. Yet Bury was the same man who had a few years earlier reacted to Victorian historical writing with an inaugural speech containing a fervent plea on behalf of a more 'scientific' historiography with more attention to facts.[273] In addition we should cite C. Oman's inaugural speech in this regard; and even Round who provides a good illustration of the positive driving force of the cult of facts when he appropriates Mark Pattison's belief that each period has its own historiography.[274]

Of course there always was in English historiography a strong, somewhat exaggerated, underlying emphasis and devotion to facts which incidentally was behind the *Cambridge Modern History*.[275] The period did not make any contributions to the 'what are historical facts?' kind of problem. The 'theoretical' articles ranging from 'The Presuppositions of a Critical History' by Bradley to M. Oakeshott's *Experience and Its Modes* were not contributed by professional historians, (apart from Collingwood), and hardly even interested them.[276] Still, many historians – 'positivists' engaged in practical research – understood the need for an intuition ('imagination') in historical reconstruction.

[271] Ch.V. Langlois, 'L'histoire au XIXe siècle' in *Questions d'histoire et d'enseignement*, p. 230.

[272] Ch. Seignobos, *La méthode historique appliquée aux sciences sociales*, p. 3.

[273] Cf. N.H. Baynes, *A Bibliography of the Works of J.B. Bury*, p. 113. Cf. J.B. Bury, *The Ancient Greek Historians*, London, 1909, pp. 252–253. Cf. also his 'Letter on the writing of history' of 1926 in *Selected Essays*, pp. 70–71.

[274] Charles Oman, *Inaugural Lecture on the Study of History*, Oxford, 1906, esp. pp. 12–13. J.H. Round, 'Historical Research' in *The Nineteenth Century* 44 (1898), p. 1013. Cf. Mark Pattison, *Essays*, ed. H. Nettleship, Oxford, 1889, vol. I, p. 2.

[275] Cf. G.N. Clark, 'The Origin of the Cambridge Modern History' in *The Cambridge Historical Journal* 8 (1945), pp. 57–64. Criticism on H.G. Richardson's and G.O. Sayles's 'positivism' is found in R.L. Schuyler, 'History and Historical Criticism: recent work of Richardson and Sayles' in *Journal of British Studies* 3 (May 1964), pp. 1–23, esp. p. 7 ff.; Cf. also *T.L.S.*, 29-2-1971, pp. 195–198.

[276] More about the lukewarm reception of Croce in England in our chapter on Pollard.

Seen from this angle, the inevitable historical subjectivity is not solely a negative factor.[277]

Our concluding question is: Is there a real gap in the tradition of English historiography during the period preceding Namier? A certain continuity is noticeable in the work of some historians and in certain subjects, but we cannot agree with the view that there is no more than a slight modulation in the historical re-orientation we described, a modulation without any real shift in the approach of history. This opinion, held by G.S. Jones and others, is in our view opposed to the truth. It is too simplistic a way of perceiving the really renewing contribution of this period of *histoire événementielle*.[278]

Nevertheless, in the next chapter we shall also express some doubts about the clarity and newness of anti-Whig reaction, but our angle is not Mr. Jones' angle. A closer analysis of this period of anti-Whig criticism alone cannot do justice to the many aspects of the above question. For this, it will be necessary to go backwards; only from within the Whig historiography as such is it possible to judge the merits of these criticisms. Whether the anti-Whig reaction really caused a break, and what the size of it was, is a question that can only be answered after a review of the Wig historical writings themselves. Were there really good grounds for the many reproaches of later time?

---

[277] Only cf. J.M. Robertson, *New Essays towards a Critical Method*, London, 1897, pp. 9–10.
[278] Gareth Stedman Jones, 'The Pathology of English History' in *New Left Review* no. 46 (1967) pp. 29–43, esp. p. 36, about the 'inter-war historians': "There was still the assumption that the facts would somehow speak for themselves, and while a modest revaluation of Victorian historical interpretations was considered necessary and proper, the questions asked of the material did not radically differ."

CHAPTER II

WHIG HISTORIOGRAPHY IN THE NINETEENTH CENTURY A MYTH ABOUT A MYTH?

> ... the continued survival of the (Whig) myth
> through the times of Stubbs is one of the most in-
> teresting and significant facts in its history.
>
> (G. Kitson Clark, 1967)

A. MEDIEVAL STUDIES IN THE FIRST HALF OF THE NINETEENTH CENTURY: F. PALGRAVE, J. ALLEN AND H. HALLAM

> A fruitful source of error, in all historical enquiries,
> is found in the translation of ancient terms by
> modern ideas.
>
> (F. Palgrave, 1822)

In the preceding chapter we presented the more general objections, published since 1890, to Victorian historical writings, particularly to the constitutional Whig historical writings. We designated the first attempts towards a breakthrough: the relativization of this specific area through the emergence of other branches of history and with the initial disintegration of the Whig view by a new approach.

Our primary reason for going back to the 19th century in this chapter is to check whether the accusations of later generations are justifiable. At the same time we shall have a closer look at the most important Whig-topics in 19th-century historiography. The history of parliament will be the basis of our argument concerning the Middle Ages, and the Norman Conquest, Magna Carta and the Lancastrian constitutionalism will only be discussed in that context. As far as the modern period is concerned we shall centre our attention on the historical idealization of the opposition against George III, the exaggerated importance accorded to 1688 and, lastly, to the liberal interpretation of the Civil War, especially in the second half of the 19th century. In the discussion of these themes we will also be led into the question of the continued survival of some of the Whig views far into the 19th century, and their success as convincing explanations notwithstanding

Tory criticism and (at least since Stubbs and Gardiner) the growing tendency to treat history as a science.

The present chapter, therefore, does not pretend to offer a complete survey of English historical writings in the 19th century. From time to time we shall draw attention to the main outlines to come to a better understanding of the special themes.

We shall first deal with the beginnings of 'modern' medieval studies. Early in the forties of the last century the *Edinburgh Review* printed two articles on the development of French historiography. One of these was written by John Stuart Mill, the other by Sir Francis Palgrave. In 1844 Mill used the first five parts of Michelet's work on the history of France to discuss the progression of French historiography. Mill saw three distinct phases of development in West-European historiography: the first (and lowest) phase, was characterized by 'presentism,' an inability to think in the terms of historical periods, plainly different from one's own. Many were the examples of this in the historical writings of the 18th century. "The character of this school," he wrote, "is to transport present feelings and notions back into the past, and refer all ages and forms of human life to the standard of that in which the writer himself lives."[1]

Mill stated that anything not so translatable into present-day language was unimportant for these historians, and in this way "they antedate not only modern ideas, but the essential characters of modern mind."[2] To Tory thinkers the Greek democracy was *a priori* anathema, to Liberal thinkers Caesar and Cromwell could only be despots. Historians of the second phase, however, tried to see the past through the eyes of contemporaries, and to paint a vivid picture of historical events, 'clothed in its circumstances and peculiarities.' As the last and highest phase Mill regarded the construction of a science of history, in which thinkers would attain a scientific explanation by means of causal laws.

This division into phases served also to describe the different types of historiography in Mill's own time. He considered that Guizot had reached the last stage and that Michelet also was far advanced. Michelet's work was the ideal illustration for Mill's second phase,[3] but Mill

---

[1] J.S. Mill, 'Recent French Historians – Michelet's History of France' – *E.R.* 79 (1844), p. 5.

[2] *Ibid.*, p. 6.

[3] *Ibid.*, p. 15: "Within him (Michelet), each period has a physiognomy and a character of its own."

doubted the scientific value of Michelet's attempted explanation, because he did not believe the racial factor was a decisive explanation in
historical developments; 'circumstances' were much more conclusive.[4]

These views lead us to consider what Romanticism meant for English
historiography. In Mill's article he called the reaction to 18th-century
Enlightenment historiography, brought about by Romanticism, a great
step forward. England, however, though not unaffected by these
developments, had hardly any romantic school of historians. The only
adherents of this type of historiography in England that Mill could
mention, were Carlyle and Thomas Arnold. It has been rightly pointed
out that Romanticism in England was not nearly so influential for the
study of history as it was on the continent, especially in Germany and
France.

England's history had no deplorable gaps which might have stimulated a renewed study of its past, a going *ad fontes* in order to recreate
valuable elements that had been lost, or were in danger of getting lost.[5]
Since there was no political revolution, there was less need for a newly
created 'anti-ideology' to stress the value of tradition, of a continuous
'organic' development of the state. Actually, such a creation was superfluous, for these romantic political ideals had for centuries lain at the
base of English political practice, of English political 'philosophy' with
its hallmarks of common law tradition and its respect for precedents
and for the old constitution. Thus, Burke, rather than creating a new
conservative ideology (as his continental admirers would have it)
simply formulated in new terms a political traditionalism dating back
to ancient times.[6]

Burke's utter rejection of the French Revolution was not shared by
most 19th-century Whigs and Liberals. Yet the political philosophy of
this 18th-century Whig remained a shining example for the Liberal
Whigs of the 19th century.[7] It was hardly necessary for Romanticism
to inject a direct political and historical inspiration into an England
that already possessed ancient common-law and Whig traditions: still
these traditions were intensified (romantically intensified, if you will)
in those moments when revolution seemed inevitable. English Whig

[4] *Ibid.*, p. 19: "We think that Mr. Michelet has here carried the influence of Race too far,
and that the difference is better explained by diversity of position, than by diversity of
character in the Races."

[5] Cf. Hedva Ben-Israel, *English Historians on the French Revolution*, Cambridge, 1968, pp.
116–117; and V.H. Galbraith, *An Introduction to the Study of History*, London, 1964, pp. 7–8.

[6] See J.G.A. Pocock, 'Burke and the Ancient Constitution: a problem in the History of
Ideas' in *The Historical Journal* 3 (1960), pp. 125–143.

[7] Cf. Hedva Ben-Israel, *op. cit.*, pp. 118, 228.

historiography in its dislike of the continental revolutions tried to find an explanation for the miraculous English stability and continuity. The 19th-century Conservative historical writers on the continent did likewise in their writings on the subject of England, perhaps to an even greater extent. The explanation was found in the age-old ('immemorial') origin and development of the Anglo-Saxon constitution. At least where its broad outlines were concerned, the arguments were only an elaborated version of the historical perspective built by the early Whigs of the 17th century. This statement has an unassailable core of truth, however blunt and simplified it may prove through closer analysis.

Summarizing, the lack of political revolutions in England had two consequences for English historiography. On the one hand England missed the possible ideological stimulus of a movement *ad fontes* and of a renewed interest in a 'long-lost' past. On the other hand that unbroken past was seen as the very reason for the fortunate fact that revolutions usually by-passed England, its *causa principalis*. Both consequences strengthened that typical Whig tendency, to put emphasis on the topicality of the past as well as on the salutary effect of the continuity with the past. The more the continent was plagued by revolutions, the more plainly this trend towards actualization became manifest. In fact, 1848 'intensified' Macaulay's views concerning 1688 and Kemble's view on the political organization of the Anglo-Saxons.[8]

Still it would not do to underestimate the influence of Romanticism. This movement did not have the political-ideological overtones in England that it had on the Continent, and in comparison it also showed relatively little 'new' interest in the past as such, but in the long run some ideals of romantic historiography found their way into England as well.

In this respect there was a reaction against the so-called 'conjectural and theoretical history' of the 18th-century Scottish school, especially to its strongly deductive and generalizing properties.[9] While such characteristics could not be traced back to all Scottish Enlightenment writers, (e.g. A. Ferguson or J. Millar) they were evidenced in the work of the later utilitarian school of Bentham and James Mill. Their

---

[8] See part B1 of this chapter on Macaulay; as to J.M. Kemble, see his preface of December 1848 in *The Saxons in England*, 2 vols., London, 1876 (1849). Cf. W.B. Donne, 'The Saxons in England' in *E.R.* 89 (1849), pp. 151–184. For the significance of J.M. Kemble, see B. Dickins, 'John Mitchell Kemble and Old English Scholarship' in *Proceedings of the British Academy* 25 (1939), pp. 51–84.

[9] See J. Clive, *Scotch Reviewers. The Edinburgh Review, 1802–1815*, London, 1957, p. 166; J.W. Burrow, *Evolution and Society*, Cambridge, 1970, pp. 49–64.

historical work was a continuation of 18th-century 'philosophic history' as well as an expansion of it. James Mill's *History of British India* was not just the last, but also "the most elaborate and detailed example of Scottish philosophic history."[10]

In the period 1820–1830 Whigs such as Mackintosh and Macaulay reacted against this abstract and strongly deductive historiography. Their reaction is undoubtedly a result of Romantic influences, even though both authors retained individual historical approaches and explanations strongly reminiscent of the 18th century. Still more of the Enlightenment tradition is traceable in H. Hallam's work, and even a man like Walter Scott was not without some of the traits common to this tradition. Scott's historical works provide us with an excellent illustration of the shallowness of Romantic influences on English historiography. A surfeit of romantic imagery and picturesque details in Scott's work did not mask the rationalist presuppositions about the unchanging uniformity of human nature.[11]

However, there was a reaction. Especially after 1820 there is a noticeable turning-point. It did not lead to a revolution in history comparable to the *Monumenta Germaniae Historica* – neither the involvement nor the prerequisite organizational beginnings were present[12] – but gradually some of the ideals of romantic historiography did become accepted. The reaction was first manifest after 1820 in the continually increasing demand for better documentation, more accuracy and above all more details in historical writing. While the Whig writer, Mackintosh, emphasized this requirement, the Catholic John Lingard did so even more strongly; and the 'antiquarian', Sir Francis Palgrave, strongest of all. As the most renowned medievalist in the first half of the 19th century, his work deserves closer scrutiny.[13]

---

[10] J.W. Burrow, *op. cit.*, p. 48; see also T.P. Peardon, *The Transition in English Historical Writing, 1760–1830*, New York, 1933, p. 266 ff.

[11] Read for Scott's rationalism, D. Forbes, *The Liberal Anglican Idea of History*, Cambridge, 1952, pp. VII, 8, 137; D. Forbes, 'The Rationalism of Sir Walter Scott' in *Cambridge Journal* 7 (1953–1954), p. 20 ff.; A. Fleishman, *The English Historical Novel*, Baltimore, 1971, pp. 37–101. For Hallam, see T.P. Peardon *op. cit.*, pp. 207–212, 271–273.

[12] On the failure of the Record Commissions in the first decades of the century, see especially Edward Edwards, *Libraries and Founders of Libraries*, London, 1865, pp. 272–294. Further also: 'The Record Commission' in *E.R.* 56 (1832), pp. 177–202; T. Wright, 'Antiquarianism in England' in *E.R.* 86 (1847), p. 307–328; W.B. Donne in *E.R.* 89 (1849), p. 154; Lord Mahon, *Historical Essays*, London, 1849, p. 1. Cf. also: 'The Record Commission' in *E.R.* 58 (1837), pp. 540–597.

[13] See, on J. Lingard, D.F. Shea, *The English Ranke: John Lingard*, New York, 1969, p. 37. The Whig John Allen regarded with surprise Lingard's hardly finalistic view on The Magna Carta and the Glorious Revolution, cf. D.F. Shea, *op. cit.*, pp. 36, 58. Of great significance was the work of N.H. Nicolas, who published an edition of the *Proceedings and Ordinances of the Privy Council of England* in seven volumes between 1834 and 1837. Cf. his statement in the

Palgrave's style of writing was over-lengthy and bombastic. "He was ignorant" – as G.P. Gooch wrote more than half a century ago – "of the last and greatest art, the art to blot."[14] But it was also Gooch who pointed out the great merits of this man, whose work was almost entirely forgotten early in this century. Gooch considered it high time for a biography about Palgrave. Although it was never written, a publication in ten parts of almost all his work was issued in the twenties. Palgrave's work was indeed a surprise to the medievalists of the twentieth century. "The curious reader" – T.F. Tout wrote – "will find many shrewd anticipations of modern scholarship in Palgrave, half concealed by the verbose rigmarole in which they are sometimes embedded."[15] Palgrave was, to Tout, a pioneer mainly because he insisted that history should be written 'from records'; Tout also recognized in Palgrave's work some of the traits of his own administrative history.

Then as now Palgrave was easiest of access in the many articles he contributed to the *Quarterly Review* and the *Edinburgh Review*. Three years before Mill, in 1841, he was already writing about the progress of historical research in France.[16] It was in a review of Augustin Thierry's *Récit des Temps Mérovingiens*, to which the 'Considérations sur l'histoire de France' formed the introduction. The review gives several of Palgrave's ideas on the subject of historiography in general and medieval studies in particular. He agreed with Thierry's 'Considérations' on one point: records must be published in full. Any selection or abbreviation would reflect the compiler's subjectivity and thereby harm the historical truth.[17] The remainder of Thierry's 'Considéra-

---

preface of volume I, p. LXIX; also, N.H. Nicolas, *Observations on the State of Historical Literature* (London, 1830) and his *Refutations of Mr. Palgrave's Remarks in reply to 'Observations on the State of Historical Literature'* London, 1831. Cf. finally J. Mackintosh's protest against 'making use' of history: "As long as the events preserve the colour of the age in which they passed, the statesman is in no danger of being so misled by history as to consider the precedents of a remote antiquity as fit to be slavishly adopted in a totally dissimilar condition of society" ('Sismondi's History of France' in *E.R.* 35 (1821), p. 493).

[14] G.P. Gooch, *History and Historians in the Nineteenth Century*, London, 1920, p. 288, cf. p. 286 (note 1). Palgrave was also said to have had 'Pickwickianisms,' cf. *The Correspondence of Lord Acton and Richard Simpson*, ed. J.L. Altholz and D. McElrath, Cambridge 1971, vol. I, p. 178.

[15] See: *The Collected Historical Works of Sir Francis Palgrave*, ed. Sir R.H. Inglis Palgrave, 10 vols., Cambridge, 1919–1921 (henceforth: *C.H.W.*). Cf. T.F. Tout in *The Scottish Historical Review* 17 (1919–1920), p. 54. See also his other reviews in *The Scottish Historical Review* 19 (1921–1922), pp. 60–61, 125 and esp. 20 (1922–1923), pp. 61–62. Further, cf. R.L. Poole in *E.H.R.* 34 (1919), pp. 447–448; *E.H.R.* 37 (1922), pp. 139–140, 291–293, 610–611 and F.M. Stenton in *History* 5 (1920–1921), p. 43 and 8 (1923–1924), p. 74.

[16] F. Palgrave, 'Historical Inquiry in France' in *E.R.* 73 (1841), pp. 84–120. See also: *C.H.W.*, X, pp. 1–40.

[17] "Le pur témoignage des monuments historiques ne peut sortir que de ces monuments pris dans leur ensemble et dans leur intégrité; dès qu'il y a choix et coupure, c'est l'homme

tions' Palgrave dismissed as partisan historiography of the old style, 'part pamphlet, part history', because of Thierry's anti-aristocratic glorification of the historical importance of the 'tiers état.' Significantly, it was just Thierry's golden rule which should have protected him against reproofs of this kind.

Palgrave, like Mill, found fault with the racial undercurrent in French historical writings, which was only too plainly apparent in Thierry's tales of the Norman Conquest.[18] Thierry's black-and-white view of the oppressed Anglo-Saxons, as opposed to the cruel Norman conquerors, was inspired in part by Sir Walter Scott. Palgrave remarked that Thierry's presentation lacked that balance between 'facts and theory' so essential for historical scholarship. This shortcoming blinded Thierry from seeing exactly how the Normans had profited from 1066: "England gave more to Normandy than she borrowed... We borrowed far less than we gave," is how Palgrave succinctly described the continuity from 1066. In the second half of the century Freeman was to adopt this thesis.[19]

The effects of Romanticism on Enlightenment historiography were more praiseworthy for Palgrave than for Mill. As a Jew converted to Christianity, Palgrave could not sympathize with the lack of understanding evinced by Enlightenment figures like David Hume for the religious Middle Ages. Palgrave's criticism, although fierce, did not, however, drive him to embrace all the ideas of the romantic historiographic trend. Scott's pretended *couleur locale* never masked his basic lack of insight into the characteristics of the Middle Ages.[20]

Palgrave was first of all concerned with reorganizing the State records. He often advocated the foundation of a national Record Office and when it did come into existence he was the first deputy-keeper of

qui parle et des textes compilés disent, avant tout, ce que le compilateur a voulu dire." Cit. in *C.H.W.*, X, pp. 14, 27.

[18] Cf. Palgrave's criticism of Thierry's racism in *C.H.W.*, IV, pp. 167–168 and IX, pp. 433–439; "His theory of races, overworked, conceals the real effect and operation of the Norman Conquest" (*C.H.W.*, IX p. 439). The quotation is taken from his article, 'The Conquest and the Conqueror' (*Q.R.*, October, 1844).

[19] *C.H.W.*, IX, p. 443; see further *C.H.W.*, I, p. 58 ff.; III, pp. 332–362; IV, p. 3; VI, p. 41 ff., 195ff., 574. About the *Domesday Book* in this connection, see *C.H.W.*, IX, p. 168.

[20] Cf. his criticism of Mably in his 'Life and Works of Sismondi' (1843) in *C.H.W.*, X, pp. 41–102, and his article 'Hume and his Influence upon History' (1844) in C.H.W., IX, pp. 535–598. See also his remarks about Scott in 1851: "Historical novels are mortal enemies to history. *Ivanhoe* is all of a piece – language, characters, incidents, manners, thoughts, are out of time, out of place, out of season, out of reason, ideal or impossible" (*C.H.W.*, I, p. XXIX). He had voiced a far more favourable opinion twenty years earlier, in 1831: "Allowing for a few anachronisms in the grouping of the individual characters, which do not alter the general truth of the picture, such was the aspect of the Witenagemot, as far as it can be gathered from the documents which now exist" (*C.H.W.*, V, p. XVII cf. p. IX).

the Public Record Office. As such, he was invaluable for this new institution's future through, a.o., his *Annual Reports*.[21] All aspects of medieval history engaged him, ranging from politics to science, art, and especially architecture. This fitted in with the Gothic Revival, which was at its high-point at the time, and to which Palgrave's own publications contributed.[22] Having read for the Bar, he naturally was also fascinated by the history of Law. He was deeply convinced that such knowledge would help gain a clearer insight into certain aspects of the earliest political history. The aspect which interested him most was the origin and function of the early medieval parliament.[23]

In the first decades of the 19th century Palgrave published one very important collection of records: the 'Parliamentary Writs.' This took the major portion of his time from 1825 to 1838. After first explaining Palgrave's views we shall later on discuss the views of Stubbs, Maitland and Pollard concerning the parliament of the Middle Ages. Three key problems determine the historiography of medieval parliament. They are: the origin and functioning of parliament, its composition, and, lastly, the place held by the Commons during the first stage.

Since Palgrave never wrote a monograph specifically about the history of parliament, his views must be reconstructed from scattered paragraphs. The first relevant articles are three which were written in the 1820's; we can, in a sense, call these his 'parliament' articles.[24] In 1822 Palgrave's hypothesis that the medieval parliament was a sort of High Court was first published; he described it as a common-law court best understood as analogous to the other already existing lower courts of the common law.[25] Early medieval parliaments functioned

---

[21] For the development of the Public Record Office, cf. R.B. Wernham 'The Public Record Office, 1838–1938' in *History* 23 (1938–1939), pp. 222–235.

[22] Cf. A. Chandler, *A Dream of Order. The Medieval Ideal in Nineteenth-Century English Literature*, Lincoln, 1970, pp. 135–238.

[23] On 27th April, 1822 it was decided to publish the parliamentary writs. See also the Report of May, 1831: Report of C.W. Williams Wynn, John Allen, Sir James Mackintosh, Henry Hallam and Sir Robert Inglis, a Committee appointed by the Board on the work to be carried on by Sir F. Palgrave, Public Record Office, P.R.O. 36/46; important for these years are also the 'Historical Letters and Personal Papers of Sir Francis Palgrave,' in the possession of G.P. Barker (London). The correspondence (12 vols.), henceforth referred to as 'Palgrave's Correspondence,' covers the years 1821–1835. He had an extensive correspondence with John Allen, Hallam, Mackintosh and R. Southey. Cf. about Palgrave also Mea Allan, *Palgrave of Arabia. The life of William Gifford Palgrave, 1826–'88*, London, 1972, pp. 25–85; and J.R. Hale, *England and the Italian Renaissance*, London 1963, pp. 124–129.

[24] 'Courts of the Ancient English Common Law – The Leet – The Shire – Parliament' (*E.R.*, 1822) in *C.H.W.*, IX, pp. 187–242; 'Origin of Equitable Jurisdiction' (*Q.R.*, 1825) in *C.H.W.*, IX, pp. 243–278; 'Records and Registration' (*Q.R.*, 1829) in *C.H.W.*, IX, pp. 153–186.

[25] *C.H.W.*, IX, pp. 221, 229; only in Henry III's time did the 'remedial court' grow into a 'fiscal assembly' (cf. p. 230 ff.).

in a way which plainly betrayed their judicial origin and duty: Parliament's first task was to function as a 'remedial court,' "a High Court, in which the King and his Council were to be informed of the wrongs of the kingdom, and by whose authority such wrongs were to be redressed."[26] This central idea was everywhere in his writings.[27]

In 1822 Palgrave's view was that Parliament did not really begin life as a typical 'feudal' institution; there were no 'knights of the shire' figuring in it as representatives of the 'military tenants of the Crown'; it was much more like a higher juridical institution, in its composition comparable to a concentration of the 'juries of the shires.'[28] The primarily judicial function was supplemented by many others only gradually – especially during Edward II's reign when most of these new functions referring to finances (the levying of taxes) and the passing of laws were incorporated. Convinced that his views and approach were new by differing, at first sight, from the usual picture of Parliament as a law-giving body, he stressed the hypothetical character of his interpretation. It needed more proof, it also needed more facts, and Palgrave attempted to provide both in the coming years.

In 1825 Palgrave gave special attention to the central place of the King's Council within the functioning of Parliament as a whole.[29] Parliamentary petitions (in the first period only 'private petitions') were almost without exception sent not to Parliament as such, but to the 'Council conjointly with the King.' As their numbers increased, the 'receivers and triers of petitions' were instituted (under Edward II). They were required to make a preliminary selection of those petitions important enough to be brought to the attention of the 'Council in *parliamentis.*' Palgrave noticed a similar procedure already in 1280 in the time of Edward I.[30] Until Edward I died, the members of the

[26] *Ibid.*, p. 234; this was preceded by the remark: "Neither has the original character of the Great Council been always duly considered by historians. Parliament, according to the meaning of the ancient English Constitution, was not convened solely for the purpose of making speeches, or making laws, or granting money."

[27] Cf. *C.H.W.*, I, pp. XXVIII, 45; III, p. 347; VI, pp. 2, 90, 96–97, 103, 198, 225–226, 254–256, 473, 566; VIII, pp. 94–95, 101 ff., 114; IX, p. 470.

[28] *C.H.W.*, IX, pp. 226, 236: "Parliament, according to the hypothesis which we suggest for the consideration of our readers, has resulted from the concentration of the remedial and judicial authorities of the Kingdom. The lower House was not a representation of tenures, but of the tribunals in which the authority of the commonwealth was exercised."

[29] *Ibid.*, p. 247 ff.; "During the sitting of Parliament, the Council acted, according to the expression of Sir Matthew Hale, as a council within a council, or, in other words, it was a house or estate of Parliament....; all parliamentary petitions were addressed sometimes, though not very frequently, to the King, or to the Council alone, but in the great majority of cases, to the Council conjointly with the King" (pp. 252–253).

[30] *Ibid.*, p. 253. See for this document also: J.G. Edwards, 'Justice in early English Parliaments' in *B.I.H.R.* 27 (1954), pp. 40–41; J.G. Edwards, *Historians and the Medieval English*

council were the most important people in Parliament; only after Edward II's death did the Lords gain supremacy, and according to Palgrave, it was not until the reign of the Lancasters that the Commons had anything like real authority. In an article written in 1829, at the end of which he strongly advocated a general Public Record Office, Palgrave summarized the above, again strongly stressing the 'curia regis' as 'common centre,' as fount and origin from which so many institutions in the course of time had been derived. The real work in Parliament had been done by the Council, and not infrequently it was done after Parliament itself had been dissolved.[31]

Flashes of his parliament-thesis can be recognized in his leaflet of 1830, *Legal Right of the Dormant Parliamentary Boroughs*, in his pithy remarks in the *Report from Select Committee on Public Petitions* (1833) and above all in 1834 in his *Essay upon the original Authority of the King's Council*.[32] A similar line of thought is noticeable in his more extensive studies. Moreover, he even wrote a novel: *Truths and Fictions of the Middle Ages, The Merchant and the Friar* (1837), which was intended to popularize his ideas about the development and function of medieval Parliament. In it he warned against anticipations, against unhistorical presuppositions about an identical past and present; parliament was originally a 'remedial court' ('the poor man's court'), with the King's council as most important element ('the Crown, the first estate of Parliament'). Until well into the 14th century, the Commons – for whom representation in parliament was more of a burden than a coveted right – were nothing but a 'virtuous nullity.'[33] Palgrave's parliamentary thesis can also be found in his two best-known works, *The Rise and Progress of the English Commonwealth* (1832) and *The History of Normandy and England* (the first two parts of which were published in 1851). However, in most cases the thesis is only mentioned indirectly. His romanist treatment of the English Middle Ages was to his contemporaries a much more striking characteristic.[34]

Palgrave suggested in 1832 an answer to the important question of

Parliament, Glasgow, 1970, p. 18 ff. See also: W. Stubbs, *Constitutional History of England*, Oxford 1877, II (sec. ed.), p. 263 (note 1) (4th ed. p. 276, note 2).

[31] *C.H.W.*, IX, pp. 160, 174; ... "the law was framed by the King's Council, sometimes after the dissolution of the parliament" (p. 177).

[32] See, for the *Report* in question, *Parliamentary Papers*, XII (1833); see *Report*, pp. 19–24 on Palgrave's interrogation on the 22nd June, 1832; the conservative restorative pamphlet of 1830 was addressed to C.W. Williams Wynn. See further, Palgrave's Correspondence, vol. VI, two letters by Allen to Palgrave (28-10/30-10, 1830).

[33] Cf. *C.H.W.*, VIII, pp. 101, 110–114; cf. *C.H.W.*, VI p. 69 and IX, p. 274.

[34] Nevertheless, cf. *C.H.W.*, VI, pp. 2, 90, 96–97, 103, 198, 225–226, 473, 566; see for his romanism, *C.H.W.*, I, p. 49; VI, pp. 61, 72, 303, 347, 477–478.

why the Commons, and especially the knights, were called up for parliament during Edward I, which stressed the still very unimportant political position of the newcomers. The Commons as a 'law-giving body' was still non-existent, and Palgrave noticed that many parliamentary knights under Edward I acted as 'guardians of the peace' (*conservatores pacis*) in their districts. This pointed to a connection which he tried to prove by tabulating the known facts.[35] For the common people parliament was a court of law, for the king this emerging institution was seen as a means for acquiring more knowledge about local government and for getting the local administrations better under control.

In the preface of his study of 1851 explaining the meaning of his earlier novel, one passage occurs which finally summarizes his thesis about parliament and therefore should be quoted in full.

One principal object sought, was to depict the High Court of Parliament, during the period when service in the Upper House was deemed onerous, and the attendance in the Lower, though not altogether undesirable, was still reckoned a duty which many would shift off, just as we now endeavour to escape being put on juries, or becoming members of Parish Vestry. The attributes of medieval Parliament, moreover, require to be viewed under a different aspect to that which they now assume (the Council being an integral organ thereof), a Senate, and also a Supreme Court of Justice, to which the Subject could apply for actual redress of injuries.... It was the union of judicial and political characters in Parliament – the administration of remedial justice – which endeared that unparalleled Assembly to Old England: an attribute which has been completely ignored by foreigners and never sufficiently acknowledged by ourselves.[36]

Many details of Palgrave's thesis could well stand amplification and emendation by a 20th-century historian, but the originality of the thesis remains undeniable. Palgrave stressed the early judicial function as well as the essentially 'conciliar' character of Parliament, and this brings him very close to two prominent conceptions of the newer literature since 1890. F.M. Powicke, in the *Times Literary Supplement*, took the opportunity, when Palgrave's *Collected Works* were published in the 1920's, to draw attention to the topical meaning of his parliamentary thesis. Pollard, in 1920, also stressed Palgrave's originality in

---

[35] His table in *C.H.W.*, VII, pp. 860–861; "All that I have proposed to prove is that it was partly by means of their duties as conservators of the Peace, that the Knights of the Shire were first conducted into Parliament. The powers of conservancy are not, according to my theory, to be considered as the sole cause of Parliamentary representation, but as one of the elements which have entered into its composition" (p. 862).

[36] *C.H.W.*, I, p. XXVIII.

this respect in *The Evolution of Parliament*.[37] Remarkably enough, however, in the second half of the 19th century these two key ideas of Palgrave's vision went almost unnoticed in the leading historical writings of the day, as witness Stubbs's *Constitutional History* from which they have almost disappeared.

Was Palgrave, however, the only believer in his own ideas about medieval parliament in the first half of the 19th century? Judging from some reviews of Palgrave's work we might conclude that his views on parliamentary history did not surprise his contemporaries as much as they do us. His friend, H. Hallam, actually passed them over.[38] The reviewer of *The Merchant and the Friar*, however, was very much surprised at the ridiculously insignificant beginnings of what was destined to be the powerful English parliament.[39] There was no special mention of Palgrave's ideas on this subject, which may be the result either of some blind spot in his readers or of the fact that his ideas had certain elements in common with the current historical writings on parliament. This latter supposition seems to us to be correct. In order to prove it, we first need to analyse more closely some articles by Palgrave's friend John Allen.

A Scot by birth, Allen lived in the circle of Lord Holland since 1802; after some time he became a 'court historiographer' of sorts in the service of this influential Whig family.[40] His subject was modern as well as medieval history; and, in the area of medieval history, parliament had his special interest. Because contemporary radical groups were agitating for parliamentary reform, his interest was especially relevant. Four of Allen's articles figure in our discussion; two of them had a lasting influence on the historiography of parliament until well into the 19th century.

[37] See *T.L.S.*, 22-5-1919, p. 272; several of Palgrave's main theses were enumerated ("which have only received full justice and confirmation in the recent work of British and American scholars"), e.g., 'the significance of Parliament as a High Court,' 'the importance of the Royal Prerogative in the daily administration of justice' and 'the significance of the administrative mechanism by which the Crown controlled the Executive.' See for A.F. Pollard our 5th chapter, note 175.

[38] H. Hallam, 'Palgrave's Rise and Progress of the English Commonwealth' in *E.R.* 55 (1832), pp. 305–337.

[39] T.F. Ellis, 'Sir F. Palgrave's Merchant and Friar' in *E.R.* 66 (1838), pp. 465–476, esp. p. 468.

[40] See for John Allen: *D.N.B.*, vol. 1 (1885), pp. 309–310; Lloyd Sanders, *The Holland House Circle*, London 1908, chapter VI; In the first four decades of the 19th century Allen wrote more than 40 articles for the *Edinburgh Review*. See also, Fox Papers, British Museum, 47, 594, (Correspondence and Papers of John Allen).

In one of his first historical essays on parliamentary history Allen discussed the work of two opposing writers on parliamentary reform: the historian T.H.B. Oldfield, and the less well-known J. Jopp.[41] Oldfield was fervently in favour of a radical parliamentary reform. At first, in 1782, he had joined the Constitutional Society; later he joined Grey's Society of Friends of the People instead.[42] He had radical ideas involving annual parliaments and universal suffrage, which demands he wanted to provide with a legal base by referring them back to the old Anglo-Saxon constitution as he saw it. He typified the radical reformers who favoured a restoration of the ancient constitution lost by the 'Norman yoke.'

Oldfield was 'a historian against history,' opposing what he saw as the wrong course of the greater part of English history since 1066; despite the Magna Carta and similar brief glimpses of glory he saw things as having gone steadily downhill, and he bluntly characterized 1688 as 'the downfall of the constitution.' Since then political corruption and other parliamentary misuses had only increased. Not surprisingly, the moderate Whig Allen disregarded Oldfield's broad general outline.[43] He went deeply into the one question which he thought important in a search for early 'democratic' tracks within the constitution: who the suitors were in the county courts who elected the parliamentary representatives. He disputed the restrictive interpretations of Hume's (and Brady's), insisting rather that next to the 'tenants-in-chief' also the 'free-tenants' ('freeholders of all descriptions') must have served in the county courts.[44]

Nor did Allen spare Jopp, whose views were diametrically opposed to Oldfield's, and who defended the royal prerogative. Allen mainly

---

[41] J. Allen, 'Constitution of Parliament' in *E.R.* 26 (1816), pp. 338–383; the objects of discussion: T.H.B. Oldfield, *The Representative History of Great Britain and Ireland, being a History of the House of Commons, and of the Counties, Cities, and Boroughs of the United Kingdom, from the Earliest Period*, 6 vols. London, 1816. J. Jopp, *Historical Reflexions on the Constitution and Rrepresentative System of England, with Reference to the Popular Propositions for a Reform of Parliament*, London, 1812.

[42] About T.H.B. Oldfield, see T.P. Peardon, *op. cit.*, pp. 101–102; Lewis Namier, *The Structure of Politics at the Accession of George III*, London, 1961 pp. 74–75; E.C. Black, *The Association*, Cambridge Mass., 1963, pp. 283–288: 'Some notes on Oldfield and the Representative History of Great Britain and Ireland.' For the theory of the Norman Yoke see: C. Hill, 'The Norman Yoke' in *Puritanism and Revolution*, London, 1958, pp. 50–122.

[43] J. Allen, *op. cit.*, p. 341: "Declamatory invective, and bold assertion, are his usual substitutes for argument."

[44] *Ibid.*, pp. 343–347, 383. Cf. W. Stubbs, *op. cit.*, II (sec. ed. 1877), pp. 228–229, (note 1).

[45] J. Allen, *op. cit.*, p. 350: "He established, it is true, knight service in England and introduced some feudal incidents unknown to the Saxons. But many parts of the feudal system existed in England before his arrival." As for the moment of introduction, see p. 354 (he distrusted M. Paris for his anti-Norman feelings).

criticized Jopp's conception of the Conqueror's 'absolutist' and at the same time 'feudal' reign. Apart from the knight-service Allen admitted of nothing 'new' in 1066, and the author's term of a 'feudal absolutist' reign he called a *contradictio in terminis*; it was the decline of feudalism that had cleared the way for absolutist monarchy.[45] Where Jopp claimed that the Norman period had had an absolutist character, Allen reduced this claim by stating that the 'great councils' now and again functioned in the same way as the parliament does now, although the governmental system still was 'irregular' and even 'arbitrary.' He wrote of the 'great councils': "They were a court of appeal from inferior tribunals, and had, in certain cases, an original jurisdiction both civil and criminal."[46] This statement is the only one from 1816 mirroring even vaguely conceptions about the judicial function which Palgrave was later to formulate so clearly.

In the following year (1817), Allen himself is also more explicit about this function, but still his war against the radical reformers takes up most of the space.[47] These reformers had two repeated demands: annual parliaments and universal suffrage, neither of which he could consider to be really ancient historical constitutional popular rights. Yet the demand for an 'annual parliament' had been voiced several times in the Middle Ages. Allen could not disregard it. How, then did he parry this attack of his radical opponents?

First he moderated the importance of the demand for annual parliaments, explaining that people in past ages had not wanted newly elected parliaments once every year, but only annual sessions of possibly existing parliaments; and this great frequency of sessions was demanded "for the despatch of business and redress of grievances."[48] The demand for annual parliaments (annual sessions!) could, according to Allen, only be understood within its own medieval context: their function was "to prevent delays in the administration of justice ... to redress grievances for which no remedy can be obtained except in Parliament."[49]

By thus putting the judicial function of the early parliament in the centre, Allen robbed the radical demand for an annual parliament of its foundation. He refused to consider that the demand for an annual

---

[46] *Ibid.*, p. 363; on the rise of the *Curia Regis*, p. 365.

[47] J. Allen, 'Annual Parliaments and Universal Suffrage' in *E.R.* 28 (1817), pp. 126–150.

[48] *Ibid.*, p. 133: "They enact, not that a Parliament should be *elected* every year, but that a Parliament should be held every year, that is, that a Parliament should meet, sit and do business, or in other words, have a session."

[49] *Ibid.* Cf. also W. Stubbs *op. cit.*, II (sec. ed.) p. 614 (note 3).

parliament had a 'political' meaning; on the contrary, he interpreted the function of the medieval parliament more and more in a judicial sense precisely because in his time the question of annual parliaments was so relevant. In this roundabout way, as well as through a reconstruction also found in H. Hallam's work, Allen actually came very close to Palgrave's way of thinking.

Allen went on to argue that the duration and the frequency of parliaments had never been a matter of popular 'rights.' Until the 17th century they had been decided by the King. And the very fact of frequent short sessions pointed to other aspects peculiar to the medieval context. This context should be the guiding principle in explaining the short duration; he disclaimed references, however vague, to some old constitution.[50] Parliamentary sessions were short because the members of parliament wished them to be so. They regarded their seats in it more as a burden than as a right; and the duration of parliaments increased only after a seat in the House of Commons had become 'an object of ambition.'[51] Allen found the radical demand for annual parliaments more difficult to contest than the radicals' mythical-historical views concerning universal suffrage. In this context he simply repeated his question as to the social origin of the 'suitors of the county court.' Although he went further than Hume he still maintained that there had never been any democratic right to vote in the past.[52]

These first two contributions of Allen's already provide an important reason for us to point out that Whig historiography in the beginning of the 19th century about the early medieval parliament was stripping the mythical layers away from a historical, democratically idealized, picture of the early parliament fostered by the radical opposition.

Allen was not creating myths for Whigs; he was rather trying to dismantle radical historical myths. This work of demolition may have saved him from the temptation of projecting later situations back into earlier periods. The historians of the first half of the century wrote in a political and social context which was very different from that in the second half. The fact that the first 'Whig-medievalists' had to unveil and oppose some of the radical versions of the parliamentary past,

---

[50] J. Allen, *op. cit.*, p. 138: "We must therefore look, not to the operation of laws which did not exist, but to the situation of the country and to the circumstances of the times for an explanation, both of the short Parliaments of Edward III, and of the long Parliaments that came afterwards."

[51] *Ibid.*, pp. 139–140. He too referred to Prynne for his conviction.

[52] *Ibid.*, p. 144 ff.

made them not only more wary of some myths, but also more sensitive to certain aspects of the character of the early medieval parliament. Some subsequent professional historians had less of that quality.

Returning to Allen himself, we must still prove whether or not he shared Palgrave's belief in the judicial function of the earliest parliaments. An answer is in a way supplied by a detailed review Allen wrote in 1821 of the report which proved so important for later historiography on the subject of parliament. It was the *Report from the Lord's Committee ... for all matters touching the Dignity of a Peer of the Realm*.[53] This work, edited under the direction of Lord Redesdale, made a generally favourable first impression on Allen. It had been set up as an impartial historical research, very different from the studies he had reviewed for the *Edinburgh Review* in the preceding years. Allen was in complete agreement with the more general conclusion that the present constitution's beginnings date back no further than the 13th century, but with the restriction that many details were still 'unsettled,' and that there was but 'little similitude' between the situation then and now.

However, he had a sizable number of objections. He found it difficult to accept the unrelentingly rigorous definition of the Norman *curia regis* as a type of 'Court of Justice.' The writers of the *Report* based their arguments for the judicial function of the earliest parliaments on this very definition.[54] Allen neither denied the importance of the administration of justice nor the importance of the *curia regis* as the nucleus of the institutions called parliaments or common councils. However, he did not think that a rigorous separation between judicial and legislative powers was feasible at that early date: "... the separation of legislative from judicial business, and their allotment to distinct assemblies, are refinement of a later and more civilized age than that of our Saxon or Norman ancestors."[55]

He regretted not only the fact that the *curia regis* was reduced to a purely judicial court, but also the scant attention given by the *Report*

[53] J. Allen, 'History of the English Legislature' in *E.R.* 35 (1821), pp. 1–43.

[54] Cf. the quotation from the Report (J. Allen, *op. cit.*, p. 6). See, too, on the conceptions of the early parliament as mirrored in the *Report*, J.G. Edwards, *Historians and the Medieval English Parliament*, Glasgow, 1970, pp. 10 (the notes), 11, 42–50. Cf. also G.O. Sayles, 'The Changed Concept of History: Stubbs and Renan' in *Aberdeen University Review* 35 (1953–1954), p. 241.

[55] J. Allen, *op. cit.*, p. 9; cf. p. 7; "National councils, whether convoked for justice or advice, were indifferently termed meetings of the Curia Regis."

to the common councils in the period 1066–1215.[56] Because the *Report* saw all judicial powers as centred in the *curia regis*, the authors tended to eliminate those common councils in which judicial subjects were discussed, from the 'proper' common councils. Many of these common councils they regarded as no more than an extensive session of the 'select council of the State,' set up to advise the King. This disparaging opinion went too far for Allen's taste: it conflicted with the facts reported to posterity by contemporary historians, whom the *Report* had neglected to consult sufficiently.

Since important 'legislative' common councils were frequent in the reign of Henry I, Allen was astounded by such a large omission.[57] In his opinion the common council had become 'the highest judicature of the kingdom' after 1066, although under Henry II its power was unfortunately reduced by the *curia regis*. It regained its old privileges in 1258, under Henry III, and revolted against financial abuses of the royal administration of justice. The *Report* made much of the fact that under Edward I parliament still possessed a mainly judicial function, since the nucleus consisted of that 'upper court of justice,' the *curia regis*.

Allen saw in the period of Edward I the transition of the common council to a more modern parliament; in this connection he ventured to speak of 'the final establishment of a direct representative government,' with the restriction, however, that this splendid development was not based on any personal idealism of the King himself concerning more popular representation in government.[58] On the contrary, Edward I wanted his parliament only to consolidate his royal powers; Allen, who was well versed in the Spanish Middle Ages, thought it possible that the King had appointed some town representatives to Parliament in imitation of the situation on the Iberian peninsula.[59]

Six years afterwards Allen repeated many of the views stated above

[56] *Ibid.*, p. 15. ff.

[57] *Ibid.*, pp. 17–19; "Meetings for judicial purposes and for mixed business, partly judicial, partly legislative, and partly deliberative, occur continually in the accounts of his reign" (p. 18).

[58] *Ibid.*, p. 26: "It was no part of that Prince's character to respect the liberties of the subject, or to set up or strenghten any authority in opposition to his own."

[59] *Ibid.*, p. 26; in 1808 Allen visited Spain together with Lord Holland and John Russell. The Whigs felt a lively interest both in the national resistance to Napoleon (supported by Wellington) and in the attempted restoration of a constitutional form of government. Spain showed the earliest traces of a representative government. Cf. Allen's articles: 'Mariana on the Ancient Legislation of Spain' in *E.R.* 22 (1813) pp. 50–67, and 'Cortes of Spain' in *E.R.* 23 (1814), pp. 347–384. For an earlier visit to Spain and France (1802–1805), see J.G. Craig, 'Biographical Notices' in J. Allen, *Inquiry into the Rise and Growth of the Royal Prerogative in England*, London, 1849, pp. XII-XXIX.

in his review of the first part of Palgrave's *Parliamentary Writs*.[60] In Allen's review, it is again apparent that Allen tended to anticipate the development of the parliamentary structure. Another striking feature, however, is his continual harping on the 'unsettled state' of parliament under Edward I. We never find a 'model parliament' in his work. He warned against generalisations, and pointed out that there were many 'irregularities' and different kinds of parliaments.[61] He arrived at one very general and very important conclusion: "In all these changes and innovations, the King and his ordinary Council, from their position in the State, were the prime movers, so as apparently, to possess the right of altering and new modelling the constitution at their pleasure."[62] This process of continuously changing and 'arbitrarily' modeling made it difficult for him to think of a 'model parliament,' as Stubbs was to do.

Finally, we would draw attention to a last publication by Allen devoted exclusively to the early history of Parliament. Because of the debates about the first Reform Bill, he published in 1831 *A Short History of the House of Commons*.[63] Referring back to older authors such as Prynne and Brady, he pictured the Commons as having a very unstable position during the Middle Ages. His two main arguments were, first: that representation was a heavy personal burden for many people in the Middle Ages, and secondly that the sheriffs' powers permitted them to be enormously arbitrary and nonchalant in deciding which boroughs should send representatives. Only during the reign of Richard II did the duties of the sheriffs become revised, and only in his reign did the Commons increase in importance. That is to say, the nobility began to see that some support from factions in the Commons might be useful for them.[64]

The situation of the Commons was far from ideal under the three Edwards. Edward I pronounced the adage "quod omnes tangit ab omnibus approbetur," but the realization of this took a long time indeed.[65] Another remarkable thing is that Allen, who considered the

---

[60] J. Allen, 'Palgrave Rolls of Parliament' in *E.R.* 46 (1827), pp. 471–489. Cf. Allen's letter to Palgrave, 2-10-1827; H. Brougham congratulated Palgrave on his *magnum opus* in a letter of 15-12-1827. See Palgrave's Correspondence vol. 3.

[61] J. Allen, *op. cit.*, p. 480 ff.; cf. p. 477.

[62] *Ibid.*, p. 484.

[63] J. Allen, *A Short History of the House of Commons with reference to Reform*, London, 1831. His pamphlet was probably originally destined for publication in the *Edinburgh Review* as an article. Cf. *Wellesley Index to Victorian Periodicals, 1824–1900*, ed. W.E. Houghton, London 1966, I, p. 424.

[64] J. Allen, *op. cit.*, p. 18.

[65] *Ibid.*, p. 28, cf. pp. 20–21.

first Reform Bill too radical, was highly sceptical about the use both supporters and opponents of the Reform Bill made of history.[66]

Summarizing the aforesaid: all the authors – Palgrave, Allen and the writers of the *Report* – agreed upon the utmost importance of the monarchy, the King and his councillors, in the genesis of parliament. The council was an essential part of the composition of parliament: as to its function, both Palgrave and the authors of the *Report* were much more explicitly outspoken about it being mainly judicial than was Allen. He thought that a variety of functions during the period of emergence was much more plausible. Nevertheless, Allen too realized that the medieval demand for annual parliaments had a non-political meaning, and in his opinion this very demand was an indication of parliament's originally judicial function. It was impossible for anyone holding these opinions about the composition and function of the earliest parliament to imagine that the Commons had more than a very limited role in it.

Before going on to the work of the third important 'parliamentary' historian, Henry Hallam, we should take a closer look at two problems already mentioned: the scepticism Palgrave and Allen shared about the immediate usefulness of the past, and the romanism they had in common. Both elements indirectly resulted in the importance allotted by these historians to the monarchical element in the composition of parliament. We noticed that Allen resolutely dismissed the mythical-historical description of a 'Norman yoke,' which myth attacked the monarchical and aristocratic development of English history since 1066. Consequently it idealized the Anglo-Saxon past as a 'paradise,' where the people freely enjoyed their political rights. It is hardly surprising that the aristocratic Whigs from the first half of the 19th century rejected these elements of the 'Norman yoke' theory.

An interest in the Anglo-Saxon past for other purposes was only evinced by liberal historians much later in the 19th century. The century was half over before the 'germanist' scholars were able to accept the political ideal of an Anglo-Saxon or Teutonic tradition of freedom. It was easier for them to accept these ideas then, because after 1850 the threat of an immediate revolution had vanished. The revolutionary message, once intricately a part of the Anglo-Saxon period, had few

[66] *Ibid.*, p. 30.

supporters left after Chartism was over, and in the Anglo-Saxon past could now be located a strongly conservative-legitimizing influence instead of its old revolutionary one. In the later parts of this chapter we will see the early Anglo-Saxon past cherished as politically useful by the supporters of local self-government in their fight against increasing centralization.

This question had no topical meaning in the thirties, during the period of the first Reform Bill. Because the Anglo-Saxon age was, in a manner of speaking, the property of Radicals like Oldfield, it became automatically suspect to the Whigs. Undoubtedly Palgrave had specialized knowledge of the period, but he was interested more in 'romanized' Anglo-Saxons than in Anglo-Saxons either 'radicalized' or 'undiluted.' It is no coincidence that his work gained direct political importance only in the later discussion about political liberty needing local self-government to thrive. Only then did political activists begin to use his work.[67]

Among medievalists of the early 19th century romanists were very strong; their main representatives were Guizot, Sismondi and especially Savigny. As believers in a limited constitutional monarchy, they tried to make their political convictions fit in between the royal absolutism of the *ancien régime* and the people's sovereignty of the Revolution. Their *via media* rested on a historical foundation consisting of the two pillars or 'tendencies' on which the civilization of the Middle Ages (in their opinion) had been based. These were the Roman tradition of government-and-order and the Teutonic tradition of freedom. The reconciliation of order and freedom was a political ideal shared by English Whigs and doctrinaire French liberals, in spite of sizable differences.[68] They saw a historical example for this ideal mixture of order and freedom in the Teutonic tradition tempered and molded by Rome.

There was, however, one notable difference between Allen's and Palgrave's romanism. Allen's *Inquiry into the Rise and Growth of the Royal Prerogative in England* was an essay on political history, theoretically modeled on a limited constitutional monarchy. The effect of Roman traditions in the medieval imperial-monarchical conception was a postulate, and not something to be proven with historical facts.[69] Ac-

[67] Cf. O. Anderson, 'The Political Use of History in Mid-nineteenth Century England' in *Past and Present*, no. 36 (1967), pp. 103–104.

[68] Cf. V.E. Starzinger, *Middlingness. Juste Milieu. Political Theory in France and England, 1815–48*. Charlottesville, 1965. Cf. also L. Diez del Corral, *Doktrinärer Liberalismus. Guizot und sein Kreis*, Neuwied, 1964. Cf. also D. Johnson, *Guizot*, London, 1963, p. 339.

[69] J. Allen, *Inquiry into the Rise and Growth of the Royal Prerogative in England*, London, 1849²,

cording to Allen it was impossible for the absolutist-monarchical tendency of European history, opposed as it was to the spirit of Teutonism, to have been Teutonic in origin. His essay was by no means a song of praise for royal prerogative: as a Whig, he found that the restrictions on the royal prerogative carried more weight than did the prerogative itself.[70]

Allen believed that royal prerogatives were primarily based upon fictions created by lawyers, while Palgrave thought they had a more concrete reality.[71] The latter's romanism was based on actual historical content: like Savigny he believed in the immense importance of Roman law for medieval civilization, and he reached that conviction independent of the founder of the School of Historical Law.[72]

Nevertheless, a belief in romanism was common to both Allen and Palgrave as medievalists, and this belief also implied their rejection of the overly democratic interpretation of the Anglo-Saxon past given by some radical reformers. What is interesting here is that prior to 1824 Palgrave was not averse to such an interpretation. On the contrary, in 1819 he did not consider the radical 'doctrine of the Antiquity of the House of Commons' to be fundamentally wrong, he had some belief in the existence of an early democracy, and thought that the historical researches by radical members of Major Cartwright's Hampden Clubs were a suitable antidote to Tory historical prejudices.[73] The young Palgrave was one of those who thought that the supporters of reforms really wanted only a 'restoration of ancient rights.' Before 1824 he struck a rather radical note, although he disliked the idea of Cartwright and the 'respectable' Hampden Club members using his arguments in their demand for annual parliaments and universal suffrage. Later on he was to warn the Hampden Club members time and

p. 11: "The theory which ascribes absolute power to the Monarch, cannot have derived from the same principles that oppose constitutional checks to his prerogative. Such a government is manifestly the result of two separate, independent forces . . ." Cf. Also H. Brougham, 'Allen's Inquiry into the Rise and Growth of the Royal Prerogative inEngland' in *E.R.* 52 (1830), pp. 139–157.
[70] Cf. J. Allen, *op. cit.*, pp. XCII–XCIII; In 1834 his work was translated into French with an introduction by Berenger.
[71] Cf. J. Allen, *op. cit.*, pp. 24–26, 84, 126.
[72] See the references in note 34. *C.H.W.*, VI, pp. 477–478. Cf. also Palgrave's admiration for Dubos, see *E.R.* 73 (1841), pp. 90–93, 118.
[73] See for the Hampden Clubs, E.P. Thompson, *The Making of the English Working Class*, Harmondsworth, 1968. Cf. also N.C. Miller, 'John Cartwright and radical parliamentary reform, 1808–1819' in *E.H.R.* 83 (1968), pp. 701–728; J.W. Osborne, *John Cartwright*, Cambridge, 1972. See Palgrave's article, 'Ancient Laws and Constitution of the Frisons, in *E.R.* 32 (1819), pp. 1–27. Cf. also C. Hill, 'The Norman Yoke' in: C. Hill, *op. cit.*, p. 114 (note 3). In 1822 Palgrave repeated this argument, see *E.R.* 36 (1822), p. 332 (see also *C.H.W.*, IX, pp. 187–190 and 331–333).

again against such use of his historical work, especially when, after 1824, Palgrave's own thoughts about the early beginnings became strikingly less democratic.[74]

For all their connections with Whig circles neither Palgrave nor Allen ever actually ventured into politics. Their over-prudent antiquarianism was an obstacle to direct political participation. Palgrave is a clear example of this: he was one of the twenty members of a commission charged with the investigation of the local situation in townships, preparatory to the municipal corporation law of 1835. In this commission he was continually at odds with all (except one) of the other members, who were in favour of fast and radical reforms. When the report was published roundly condemning the existing situations, Palgrave refused to sign it, for he was convinced that the investigation, having been done hastily and inaccurately, gave an inaccurate historical picture of matters.[75] Finally Palgrave broke off relations with the commission's secretary, Parkes who, on 16th March 1835, wrote:

My notions and yours on Political Science widely differ ... You wanted to revive the decayed Parliamentary Boroughs; I agitated to obtain the creation of new ones. This is the difference between us: I want to build up new corporations, you want to patch up the old ones. We are not living in the age of Prerogative, Privy Councils and Quo Warrantos.[76]

It is remarkable that neither Palgrave nor Allen ever gave a positive historical contribution to support the Whigs' standpoint during the

[74] On this change see H. Hallam, *View of the State of Europe during the Middle Ages*, London, 1855, III, pp. 229–231. In 1832 Palgrave wrote: "... it may be doubted whether popular elections, in the modern sense of the term, ever subsisted amongst the Anglo-Saxons. I have sought, with anxiety, in the ancient records of this Kingdom, for proofs of such a custom; and when I first entered upon the study of our constitutional history, it was with the firm belief that all restrictions upon the right of suffrage were the usurpations of authority. Every year passed in inquiry has accumulated evidence tending to refute that opinion, and to show that wherever any extended right of suffrage exists, it is a victory obtained by the many over the few, and resulting from the destruction of the primitive custom, by which the legal right of election of nomination devolved either upon the chief members, the 'magnates' of the people, or upon select bodies, acting on behalf of the community ..." (*C.H.W.*, VI, pp. 103–104). Cf. for a more or less opposed development in the case of the Tory historian S. Turner, see A. Chandler, *op. cit.*, pp. 85–87.

[75] See B. Keith-Lucas, *The English Local Government Franchise*, Oxford, 1952, pp. 49–50; G.B.A.M. Finlayson, 'The Municipal Corporation Commission and Report, 1883–1835' in *B.I.H.R.* 36 (1963), pp. 36–52, esp. pp. 42, 45, 48–50. Palgrave's view and protest were welcomed by the Tory J.W. Croker; see the latter's article 'Municipal Reform' in *Q.R.* 54 (1835), pp. 231–294.

[76] See Palgrave's Correspondence, vol. 12; for Parkes, see J.K. Buckley, *Joseph Parkes of Birmingham*, London, 1926. Two years earlier, in 1833, Parkes had written about Palgrave: "a damned antiquary ... 'a Holland Householder' who wants to move centuries retrospectively. But we have put him in a trap, and restricted his voracity and set him on the City Records. Luckily also I knew him, and he is very tractable led by a certain cord – his vanity and good nature." See G.B.A.M. Finlayson, *op. cit.*, p. 49.

Reform Bill debates of 1831 and 1832. But before discussing the image of the early parliaments as it emerged during the long months of debating we must analyse H. Hallam's influential views on this subject.

Hallam's works had an incontestably greater influence on later historiography than both Allen's and Palgrave's work put together. In Hallam's case as well we will discuss only what he wrote about parliament, the constitution, in his *View of the State of Europe during the Middle Ages*, published in 1818. This was the first concise and readable survey of medieval European and English history since Hume, and it was especially praised by Whigs for its many emendations of Hume's conservative views.[77]

Hallam's eighth chapter summarizing the constitution of the Middle Ages was more or less typical of early 19th-century views on the medieval parliament. The influence of this chapter in the first half of the century may be compared with that of the fifteenth chapter in Stubbs's *Constitutional History* in the second half of the century. Rereading it, one is struck by the great attention and deep intensity with which Hallam had once more studied the *Rolls of Parliament*.[78] They were an important source on which Hallam based his conclusions concerning the great questions of Parliament's composition and function and the difficult problem of the significance of the medieval Commons. Stubbs continued in part along Hallam's path; there is a strong similarity in the argument as a whole, but there also seem to be considerable differences in interpretation between the two.

For Hallam, the summoning of Parliament by Edward I at the end of 1295 was a clear indication of the beginnings of a House of Commons. This view has been clearly formulated for the first time by Brady (and later on in the 18th century again by Hume).[79] The royalist Brady had intended to use it as a weapon against the early 'Whig' thesis about the Anglo-Saxon origins of Parliament. Although the

[77] Cf. J. Allen, 'Hallam's Middle Ages' in *E.R.* 30 (1818), pp. 140–172, esp. p. 166.
[78] *Ibid.*, pp. 165–167.
[79] See, for the 16th and 17th-century conceptions of the origin of Parliament, E. Evans, 'Of the Antiquity of Parliaments in England: Some Elizabethan and Early Stuart Opinions' in *History* 23 (1938–1939), pp. 206–221. Cf. also D. Hume, *The History of England*, London, 1825, p. 171: "This period, which is the twenty-third of his reign, seems to be the real and the true epoch of the house of commons, and the faint dawn of popular government in England." See for Hallam's associations with Spelman and Brady and his rejection of 'early' Whigs like Coke, H. Hallam, *View of the State of Europe during the Middle Ages*, III, pp. 11–15, 33–35.

year 1295 does have a place in the earliest historical writings on the subject of Parliament, it owes its almost magical overtones to Stubbs's work at the end of the 19th century. Stubbs depicts 1295 on the one hand as definitively ending and consolidating a lengthy development in the thoughts and practice of representation; on the other hand he sees 1295 as the beginning of the modern parliamentary system, providing the first clear precedent and 'model'. Hallam does not indulge in such exaggerated views. His work leaves room for other possible earlier representations of the Commons, but he warned against holding a too high opinion of the Commons during the reign of Edward I and II.[80] A recent author wrote in this connection: "Hallam is very cautious about any claims for the ancient constitution. He concedes that much before the thirteenth century was uncertain."[81]

Regarding the function of Parliament in its first phase, Hallam wrote: "The proper business of the House of Commons was to petition for redress of grievances, as much as to provide for the necessities of the Crown."[82] It was also quite clear to Hallam that in the beginning the medieval parliament was regarded as a court of justice by the people. Nevertheless, it was also a means for the King to acquire information about miscarriages of justice in the country, and about the need for him to intervene.[83] It is as a result only of this immediate interest of the subjects that Hallam comprehended the demand for annual parliaments. "The parliament was considered a high court of justice, where relief was to be given in cases where the course of law was obstructed, as well as where it was defective. Hence the intermission of parliament was looked upon as a delay of justice and their annual meeting is demanded upon that ground."[84] This demand had no connection at all with an increasing

---

[80] Cf. H. Hallam, op. cit., III, p. 37. About the problem of separation into two houses, see p. 38. Stubbs later called Hallam's opinion of the matter (the final years of Edward II's reign or the beginning of Edward III's) too 'anachronistic,' see C.H., II, p. 392, note 2. Stubbs himself later seemed prepared to place the beginning of the separation in 1295. See C.H., III, pp. 430–431.

[81] P. Clark, 'Henry Hallam reconsidered' in Q.R. 305 (1967), p. 413. He adds: "but from the reign of Edward III, he argues, the principal characteristics of the constitution were laid down." See about H. Hallam also: C.C. Weston in Some Modern Historians of Britain, ed. H. Ausubel, New York, 1951, p. 20–34 and D.M. Fahey, 'Henry Hallam – a Conservative as Whig Historian' in The Historian 28 (1966), pp. 625–647.

[82] H. Hallam, op. cit., III, p. 38.

[83] Ibid., p. 39: "In his high court of parliament a king of England was to learn where injustice had been unpunished and where right had been delayed." And then: "To parliament he (the subject) looked as the great remedial court for relief of private as well as public grievances."

[84] Ibid., p. 144. On this page he also quotes Fleta's famous text in full.

political maturity of the Commons.[85] In this connection Hallam referred with approbation to Allen's previously discussed article on annual parliaments; he agreed that the medieval demand for annual
parliaments was the clearest proof of its judicial function, whereas
Hallam's more radical contemporaries had believed it to be a revolutionary demand. Both authors reduced the 'radical' aspect of the demand by pointing to the judicial context as well as restricting annual
parliaments to annual sessions. Such frequent meetings, so conspicuous
in the beginning, could only be explained through this particular
function.[86] Yet Hallam believed that the demand for frequent meetings
was voiced only by a minority of 'activists' in the Commons; the great
majority still regarded 'representation' as a heavy burden.[87]

However, the most important part of the eighth chapter deals with
the emergence of the Commons as a more or less equally powerful
partner to the Lords. To what conclusion did Hallam come after his
intensive "perusal of the *Rolls of Parliament?*" Was he too sanguine
about the role of the Commons after Edward I's reign? Was his interpretation of the *Rolls of Parliament* biased in their favour, as Allen
seems to suggest?[88] As many others after him, Hallam too attached
great importance to the *Statute of York* (1322) as the clear proof of the
'legislative power' of the Commons.[89] He also remarked that the '11
articles' of 1309 indicated a growing independence of the Commons;
furthermore he presupposed a cooperation on the basis of equality between the so-called Lords Ordainers and the Commons in 1312.[90] Yet
Hallam did not think that the 'rights' of the Commons had been clearly defined before the period of Edward III and Richard II. Under
Edward III these rights were threefold: it was illegal to levy taxes
without the permission of Commons, for every legal change cooper-

---

[85] *Ibid.*, p. 39, note c: "Certainly the commons could not desire to have an annual parliament in order to make new statutes, much less to grant subsidies. It was, however, important
to present their petitions, and to set forth their grievances to this high court."

[86] Naturally the later frequency under Edward III was explained as a result of the King's
lack of money, see H. Hallam, *op. cit.*, III, p. 161.

[87] *Ibid.*, p. 39, note c: "We may easily reconcile the anxiety so often expressed by the
commons to have frequent sessions of parliament, with the individual reluctance of members
to attend. A few active men procured these petitions, which the majority could not with
decency oppose, since the public benefit was generally admitted. But when the writs came
down, every pretext was commonly made use of to avoid a troublesome and ill-renumerated
journey to Westminster."

[88] J. Allen, *op. cit.*, pp. 166–167.

[89] Not in the text itself, however, but in a later added note. See H. Hallam, *op. cit.*, III,
p. 233 ff. Cf. also: H. Hallam, *The Constitutional History of England*, London, 1863 (1827), I,
pp. 3–4, 10–11.

[90] H. Hallam, *View*, III, pp. 40–42. Stubbs denied that later on. Cf. W. Stubbs, *C.H.*, II
(sec. ed.), pp. 323–324, 327 (note 2), 592.

ation between Lords and Commons was imperative, and, lastly, the Commons acquired the right to impeach a councillor or a minister.[91]

Hallam thought that under Richard II the Commons experienced a highly constructive phase in the consolidation of its growth, which he saw as constitutionally "the most interesting part of our earlier history." The weapon of impeachment was again used during this period, and the Commons demanded a voice in spending the subsidies they has provided.[92]

Finally, Hallam gave a detailed account of the 'Lancastrian constitutionalism.' For this purpose he drew up seven points. Under the Lancasters the privileges acquired during the reigns of Edward III and Richard II were augmented by the first parliamentary privileges of the Commons, such as freedom of speech.[93] As proof of the Commons' independence from the Lords, Hallam pointed to the slowly growing procedure of 'intercommuning' between Commons and Lords.[94] He believed that the scarcity of information on this subject in the *Rolls of Parliament* did not necessarily indicate that the Commons had no autonomous power. There were, on the contrary, some cases where the initiative for consultation had apparently come from the Commons. In matters of taxes Commons had acquired the right to make the first proposals, not the Lords.

Hallam undoubtedly thought quite highly of the medieval Commons. Ever since Edward III they had, according to him, 'legislative power' in dealing with the recurrent royal requests for more subsidies. However: he did not idealize the position into a heroic battle for freedom: it was lack of money which forced the Crown to certain concessions and gave the country its liberty.[95]

Neither did he underestimate in the concluding chapter the position of the monarchy, which was to grow into a 'limited constitutional monarchy,' only after a period of trial and error.[96] But he clearly re-

[91] H. Hallam, *op. cit.*, III, pp. 42–57.

[92] *Ibid.*, pp. 81, 84.

[93] *Ibid.*, pp. 84–109; see for the well-known cases of Thomas Thorpe and Thomas Yonge, p. 100 ff. Cf. W. Stubbs, *C.H.*, III, pp. 489–497.

[94] H. Hallam, *op. cit.*, III, pp. 60, 66, 103–105, 107. Cf. W. Stubbs, *C.H.*, II, pp. 426, 428, 465 (note 2), 593–594; III, pp. 37, 61, 259, 457, 459.

[95] H. Hallam, *op. cit.*, III, p. 162: "It is common indeed to assert that liberties of England were bought with the blood of our forefathers ... But it is far more generally accurate to say that they were purchased by money." Cf. W. Stubbs, *C.H.*, II p. 570.

[96] H. Hallam, *op. cit.*, III, p. 153: "All seemed to grow out of the monarchy, and was referred to its advantage and honour. The voice of supplication, even in the stoutest disposition of the commons, was always humble; the prerogative was always named in large and pompous expressions."

fused to follow Hume's idea "that all limitations of royal power during the fourteenth and fifteenth centuries were as much unsettled in law and in public opinion as they were liable to be violated by force."[97]

To explain how Parliament was composed, Hallam spoke of the 'three estates,' as Stubbs was also to do. In Hallam's work there is as yet no question of a 'theory' of the three estates as far as parliament is concerned. He warned that the idea had only a very limited use for the English parliament: the Commons was not a real 'estate.' He understood the three 'estates' within parliament as the nobility, clergy and Commons, in its ordinary meaning. Palgrave's explanation, on the other hand, was clearly very different. His 'three estates' of Parliament were 'King, Lords and Commons.' This version also dated back quite a long time, being used repeatedly by several authors in the 17th and 18th centuries.[98] The difference in interpretation of the three estates is not without meaning for the way in which the two historians analyse the composition and function of the early medieval parliaments. In fact this difference will prove essential in our historiographic discussion.

Palgrave stressed the King's being an 'estate' within parliament in order to emphasize the indispensable place of the King and his Council in this body. He maintained this somewhat deviant interpretation of the three estates to underline his own 'conciliar' view of parliament. Parliament was seen as an instrument of the executive power. The 'official' element in this interpretation thus became of equal or greater importance than the 'estates.' For the composition of parliament Hallam thought that Palgrave's view of the 'three estates' for the most part contradicted the sources, although he did admit that an explication in the sense of King, Lords and Commons did occur occasionally in the *Rolls of Parliament*, e.g. in 1401.[99]

The conception of the three estates in the current sense had consequences for Hallam's view on the composition and function of Parliament as a whole. The king and his Council might belong inalienably to the administrative and executive apparatus, but they were neither essential nor necessary to Parliament, although they did perform there.

---

[97] *Ibid.*

[98] Cf. C.C. Weston, 'The Theory of Mixed Monarchy under Charles I and after' in *E.H.R.* 75 (1960), pp. 426–443, esp. p. 430 ff.; see also W.B. Gwyn, *The Meaning of the Separation of Powers*, New Orleans, 1965, pp. 25–26.

[99] H. Hallam, *op. cit.*, III, p. 106 (note). Cf. A.F. Pollard, *The Evolution of Parliament*, London, 1926, pp. 64, 70. See further G.C. Lewis, *Remarks on the Use and Abuse of Some Political Terms*, London, 1832, ch. XIX, pp. 242–246. New edition with introductory essay by C.F. Mullett, Columbia, 1970.

Hallam realized that the two bodies, Council and Parliament, cooperated under the two Edwards, but he also noted that the Council soon disappeared, as it were, in the House of Lords.[100] Since Hallam's main interest was in the 14th and 15th centuries, he viewed the royal Council and Parliament as two separate bodies, not complementing each other but rather being in opposition to one another.[101]

Depicting Parliament too exclusively as an oppositional body was, and still is, characteristic of the Whig view concerning the development of Parliament.[102] Their interest in the oppositional aspect made them underestimate the judicial function of the early parliament, and made them lose interest in periods without a clear parliamentary opposition (as, e.g., in the first Tudor phase). When the main function of parliament was seen as centred in political opposition, of course the official and administrative aspects of parliamentary history were relegated to the background. Whether the Royal Council was seen as something extraneous, (foreign to the composition of parliament as such), or whether it was thought to have melted into the Lords for the parliamentary part of its tasks (as Hallam insisted), in neither case was it possible to recognize the original important judicial function of that Council in Parliament.

Hallam, however, adhered only partly to this Whig view. For the period of the first two Edwards he certainly saw that the council occupied a central place, both before Parliament opened and during each session.[103] He made special mention of the fact that in Edward I's time parliament functioned in the first place as a High Court. This first period, however, was not his principal interest. Hallam did not think that Edward I's parliaments could be regarded as models, partly because their legislative powers were still meager, just as were their oppositional political possibilities, and partly because of the limited role of Commons.[104] Edward III's parliaments were, to Hallam, the first real Parliaments. Their prehistory and their original judicial functions appealed to him far less than they did to his friend Sir Francis Palgrave.

---

[100] H. Hallam, op. cit., III, p. 143.

[101] Cf. Ibid., pp. 249–256.

[102] Cf. G.R. Elton, The Body of the Whole Realm. Parliament and Representation in Medieval and Tudor England, Charlottesville, 1969, pp. 11, 16–17, 53–55.

[103] H. Hallam, op. cit., III, p. 143.

[104] Like Hume, Hallam nevertheless used the verb 'modeling' in referring to Edward I's acts; see H. Hallam, op. cit., III, p. 132: "Edward I, whose legislative mind was engaged in modelling the constitution on a comprehensive scheme ..."

We entered in fairly great detail into the views on medieval parliament held by three historians considered prominent in their lifetime, not only because their works are scarcely read or even consulted these days, but also because many believe that the ideas of these historians are better studied in the work of later historians, those of the second half of the century, who continued the labour of their predecessors with the help of newly discovered sources and better scientific methods. This belief represents the three earlier authors as immature precursors, doing the spadework for later more professional scholars like Stubbs and Freeman. However, it omits one very important aspect. True, much was added to the views of Hallam, Palgrave and Allen during the second half of the century, but much was also omitted – and this certainly is quite as important.

In our opinion the differences in views between the first and second halves of the century are more relevant to our theme than the similarities. But these differences are on the whole neglected in the literature. In the second half of the century we find that important aspects concerning the composition and function of early parliaments were relegated to the background. It is only towards the end of the century that they are disinterred by Maitland, who places them again in the forefront. It is our impression that these early medievalists had more understanding for some aspects of the character of medieval parliaments than had later historians such as Stubbs and Freeman – notwithstanding the fact that the latter two could consult many more sources. This is an aspect upon which we will again touch at the end of this first part.

There is no doubt that Palgrave was decisively influenced by his daily consultation of the records; for him, the 'judicial' interpretation had most importance. Hallam's views were close to those Stubbs would later hold, although there are some recorded differences. Palgrave was intensely aware of the dangers hidden in anachronistic views, in applying modern opinions to the past in order to make the past serve the present. He never wanted to be 'made use of.' The fact that the medieval parliamentary tradition could not be used in the Reform Bill, was also pointed out by Allen. In Hallam's work too the typical search for serviceable precedents was lacking.

This does not mean that the more politically motivated Whigs did not try their utmost in the case of the first Reform Bill to present their proposals as 'historically legitimate.' The parliamentarians of the years 1831/1832 provided their own picture – admittedly piecemeal – of the parliamentary past. The historical argumentation, both for and against, was a substantial part of the parliamentary debates in these two years. Examples and illustrations were dredged up out of history, as well as the final justification for the proposal. The importance of this argumentation should, however, not be exaggerated, for history soon proved to be open to so many interpretations that people thought it safer to rely on their own common sense.

The belief that history was a useful tool probably was strongest among Whigs. The small number of Radicals retained little of it, as their trust in its usefulness had suffered since 1830.[105] These debates provide us with a good idea about the then popular conception of the first parliaments. A few elements in this political-historical process of image-forming rate a closer scrutiny, because they may supply a valuable addition to the more 'antiquarian' views of the three authors mentioned.

The purport of Allen's brochure had been negative. That means that for the author the early medieval situation had been so full of changes that he could not possibly make use of this part of history for or against the proposed Reform Bill. The Whigs in Parliament, most of all Lord Russell who introduced the Bill, were inclined to borrow their more or less 'positive' proof from history, at least during the early stages. When he introduced his Bill, on the 1st of March, 1831, Russell thought history could provide him with definite proof in support of the proposal.[106] For the sake of convenience and tradition he sought a historical justification in the first 'Statute of Westminster' and the widely-famed *De Tallagio non concedendo* of 1297, in order to prove that in the first constitution the consent of all was needed for measures taken in the common interest. The authenticity of the latter document has been doubted, but not its value as a rule of law, since it was firmly

---

[105] Cf. C. Hill, *op. cit.*, pp. 109–110; O'Connell mentioned "all that rubbish and lumber of antiquity," ironically stating: "The arguments, if arguments they can be called, which have been used on this occasion against us, have all been founded on what? On charters . . ." (3 *Hansard* 3 (March 8, 1831), pp. 192, 204–205). The role of the Magna Carta was unimportant, cf. A. Pallister, *Magna Carta, The Heritage of Liberty*, Oxford, 1971, p. 73.

[106] His speech was later included in *Selections from Speeches of Earl Russell (1817 to 1841) and from Despatches (1859 to 1865)*, London, 1870, vol. I, pp. 301–336. He had long been regarded as the Whig-expert on parliamentary reform, cf. J. Mackintosh's letter of the 14th October, 1819, in *The Early Correspondence of Lord John Russell, 1805–1840*, ed. R. Russell, London 1913, vol. I, pp. 205–207; equally, the identical letter by J. Allen, of 17th October, 1819, in Spencer Walpole, *The Life of Lord John Russell*, London, 1889, vol. I, p. 116.

corroborated in the *Petition of Right* of 1628.[107] In Edward I's time 'the common assent of the realm' was demanded to be guaranteed by a truly representative House of Commons. This was what Russell wanted to achieve with his Bill, which would 'restore' the ancient constitution. Russell's argumentation in 1831 hardly differed in any essentials from the argumentation of the 'common lawyers' in 1628.

This evidential use of history was refused by the opposition in the first place because of its many naïve anachronisms. Exemplary is the reply of J. Scarlett to Russell's interpretation of the statutes of 1275 and 1297. He had an ironical comment to make about Russell's use of history: "My noble friend thought that he had found in that statute (of 1275) though, passed before the existence of any House of Commons, or any Representation of the people by election, a constitutional principle sufficient for his purpose, because he found a recital in the preamble of that statute, that it was made in Parliament by the assent of the King's Council ... and all the commonalty of the realm, thereto summoned. It must be owned, that this was a tempting passage for my noble friend to cite."[108] For what was the real meaning of the words 'the commonalty of the realm' in that early period? Scarlett's interpretation, based on the Provisions of Oxford (1258), was highly restrictive: not the 'people' were meant, but the 'barons.' He did not think the Middle Ages could be at all useful for supporting a measure like the one under discussion: "the only safe ground upon which any measure can rest, is the ground of expediency." For did it not last until Elizabeth I's time before the House of Commons achieved publicity?[109]

Scarlett's historical counter-attack hardly merited an answer by Russell, who thought it very curious to interpret 'commonalty' as 'barons.' Russell thereupon used the 'principles' of 1688 as a refuge.[110] But many Tories agreed with Scarlett's 'baronial' explanation of the medieval parliament. Sadler labelled as 'myths' any ideas that portrayed an earlier period of 'free' and 'democratic' procedures for electing the representatives of boroughs. Shrewdly he named in this connection an article of Allen's in the *Edinburgh Review*, which, however, might in his opinion be ascribed to a higher authority: to wit, to

---

[107] "Although some historical doubts have been thrown upon the authenticity of this statute, its validity in point of law is asserted in the Petition of Rights, was allowed by the Judges in the case of Hampden, and is, in fact, the foundation of the Constitution, as it has existed since the days of the Stuarts" (3 *Hansard* 2 (March 1, 1831), p. 1063).

[108] 3 *Hansard* 3 (March 22), pp. 774–775.

[109] *Ibid.*, pp. 777–778.

[110] *Ibid.*, pp. 795–796.

Russell himself.[111] The abuse that Whig reformers in Parliament made of history was termed 'machiavellian' – especially their 'restoration' ideas.[112]

The conservatives countered Russell's historical argumentation in a less 'antiquarian' way as well. Peel stated ironically that the proposal was terribly inconsistent. If Edward I's period was to be considered the justifiable norm and legal base, and if the sole purpose were to restore the ideal situation of that period with a truly representative Commons, 'free' elections, and with guaranteed consultation of the 'whole commonalty of the realm,' then why – in heaven's name – introduce in 1831 a uniform strictly limited census vote with a 10 pound sterling minimum qualification? What had become of Russell's 'whole commonalty of the realm?' Peel did not object to the fact that the measure was undemocratic: neither Whigs nor Tories had any inclination towards a more democratic franchise. What Peel was concerned with was the possible social consequences of this measure. The proposal irrevocably meant 'class'-representation. It meant that class distinctions were made explicit, it meant that the sympathy of the lower classes was relinquished.[113] There was little political wisdom in an act which made social class distinction into an inescapable political fact.

Peel's sharp analysis of the inconsistencies in Russell's historical thinking was possible because of Russell's historical eclecticism. In June 1831 Russell used history as a blank check, as it were, for deciding which boroughs should be represented in parliament and which should not. His speech of 24th June was probably inspired by the brochure written by his friend John Allen. Russell, like Allen, insisted, that during the first 250 years (until the reign of Henry VI) the history of borough representation had been largely varied and arbitrary, mainly

---

[111] 3 *Hansard* 3 (April 18), p. 1537; He quoted the following statement by Allen: "There is reason to believe that originally the right of election in boroughs was vested in the governing portion of the burgesses, and that in the progress of the House of Commons to power and importance, the tendency has been in general to render the elections more popular" (*E.R.* 28 (1817), p. 145). Allen's remark had already been commented on with some surprise by the more conservative Hallam: "Mr. Allen than whom no one of equal learning was ever less inclined to depreciate popular rights, inclined more than we should expect to the school of Brady in this point" (H. Hallam, *op. cit.*, III, p. 117 (note m)). Allen had been an admirer of the French Revolution in his youth and was originally regarded as a Radical.

[112] 3 *Hansard* 3 (April 18), p. 1537: "The motive of this strange misrepresentation of historical facts is but too obvious. Machiavelli earnestly recommends those who seeks to subvert the institutions of their country, to disguise their design as much as possible by these references to ancient privileges ... The projectors and supporters of this "sweeping measure," as they justly call it, follow his political morality." On M. Sadler see G.O. Trevelyan, *The Life and Letters of Lord Macaulay*, London, 1959, pp. 90–91, 183, 108–109.

[113] 3 *Hansard* 2 (March 3), pp. 1345–1346.

owing to the power of the sheriffs and the boroughs's unwillingness to send representatives.[114] Peel reminded Russell that the latter had spoken in praise of the ideal system of representation under Edward I in his maiden speech on the 1st of March. Evidently Russell was unconsciously undermining the very historical foundation he originally believed to be so secure. "He shows triumphantly" – as Peel said – "that it is nonsense to talk about the acknowledged principles of the Constitution ... it is the work of time and accident, and the varying circumstances of society."[115] Russell parried Peel's attack on his own 'double-bottomed history' by referring to Hume's comment on the adage used by Edward I: *quod omnes tangit ab omnibus approbetur.* Hume had commented: "a noble principle, which may seem to vindicate a liberal mind in the king, and which laid the foundation of a free and equitable government."[116]

In these unending discussions people were continually quoting authors whose opinions carried some authority for one's opponents. The Tories loved to quote the remarks of rather conservative Whig authors like Hallam and Mackintosh who, like Allen and Palgrave, thought the first Reform Bill too radical.[117] Conservatives like Peel, however, were horrified by the continual 'terror of quotations' during the endless discussions over the first Reform Bill, discussions which were the longest since 1688.[118] More 'antiquarian' Tories saw only arbitrary manipulations in these references to history made by the Whigs whenever convenient.[119] The Whigs, after the historical criticism of the opposition, became more prudent in their references to seemingly 'positive' precedents in history. A closer scrutiny often proved that their normative character for the present was doubtful.

It was far safer to refer to the general development and tendencies

---

[114] 3 *Hansard* 4 (June 24), pp. 325–326. Cf. *Selections*, vol. I, p. 336, ff.

[115] 3 *Hansard* 4 (July 6), p. 877.

[116] *Ibid.*, p. 905. Cf. D. Hume, *The History of England*, London, 1825, p. 171.

[117] Cf. Peel on Hallam (3 *Hansard* 4 (July 6), p. 879), and on Mackintosh (3 *Hansard* 5 (July 27), p. 417): "In taking a review of the institutions of the Anglo-Saxons, in the first volume of his *History of England*, Sir James Mackintosh condemns the narrow, unphilosophical spirit in which the antiquaries of the seventeenth century investigated the state of our ancient Constitution.... After blaming the prejudiced views of the Tories, he proceeds thus: 'The Whigs, with no less deviation from truth, endeavoured to prove, that the modern Constitution of King, Lords, and Commons, subsisted in the earliest times, and was then more pure and flourishing than in any succeeding age ...' "

[118] 3 *Hansard* 4 (July 6), p. 880: "I advise new members to distrust nothing more than quotations. When I hear Bacon or Burke, or any other great authority cited, I know that sometimes in the next page and more frequently in the same, a passage might be found, which, if taken separately, might be relied upon as an authority for opposite doctrines."

[119] Cf. 3 *Hansard* 4 (July 12), p. 1137.

of English history. The resulting picture was one of gradual political progress, and of a political system that was continually adapting to the changes in society. This was how Wyse, and above all, Macaulay, argued.[120] Unconnected historical facts could no longer be a norm or a legal argument within this more utilitarian thinking; now the course of history could only illustrate the need for reforms. Longer delays would mean more danger for the State; what society needed was political adaptation and in this respect it was necessary to conciliate public opinion at once. Political stability was not harmed by a conciliatory attitude, nor would it cause revolution, as the conservatives insisted. On the contrary: all history went to prove that revolutions thrived when no concessions were granted – and Mackintosh gave a long historical argument to prove how right this 'concession-theory,' beloved by Whigs, was.[121]

The one specific historical precedent in modern history, which kept recurring throughout the debates, quoted incessantly by supporters and opponents alike, was the parliamentary reorganization under Cromwell. There may not have been a 'model' parliament in the Middle Ages, but at least the Commonwealth-period provided a good example. It is hardly surprising that the Whigs began to feel admiration for Cromwell during the Reform Bill discussions, but that some Tories too were using Cromwell to support their cause needs an explanation.

The Cromwell discussion started on the very first day with that famous historical speech by R.H. Inglis. In this speech he provided a historical framework for the constitution in a way no one had ever done before: the foundation and norm for the Constitution was history and only history.[122] And according to him there was not a single link, let alone a justification, for the present proposal in all English history, with the possible single exception of Cromwell's period. The Bill consisted of "a rash and untried theory, ... founded upon no precedent

---

[120] Thomas Wyse, an Irish representative. See 3 *Hansard* 3 (March 22), p. 738 ff.; Macaulay, 3 *Hansard* 9 (Dec. 16), p. 390 ff.

[121] 3 *Hansard* 4 (July 4), pp. 693–694. This was certainly not the only 'theory' implied in this parliamentary reform. Cf. D.C. Moore, 'The Other Face of Reform' in *Victorian Studies* 5 (1961), pp. 7–34 and 'Concession or Cure: The Sociological Premises of the First Reform Act' in *The Historical Journal* 9 (1966), pp. 39–59.

[122] 3 *Hansard* 2 (March 1) pp. 1096–1097: "Our system is unwritten – it is to be extracted from our history. The King's Writs, the King's Charters, the Statutes of the Realm, and the practice of centuries, form our Constitution. We have no one formal document, to which we refer as embodying it: we have no authoritative exposition of it. Montesquieu and Delolme are not our authorities; not even Blackstone." Cf. on the speech by R.H. Inglis also S.H. Beer, *Modern British Politics*, London, 1969, pp. 18–19.

which ever existed in this country, (that model Parliament of Cromwell alone, or in part excepted) ..."[123] Never except in that period
had the 'population' principle – which Inglis wrongly regarded as the
most conspicuous trait of the Whig proposal[124] – been used in the parliamentary constitution for the purpose of allotting seats. Inglis's fellow-
Tory, Wetherell, attacked much more directly the next day by stating
in his conclusion that the Whigs were dangerous Cromwellians; it
seemed that Pride's 'Purgation' would be repeated when the first two
schedules of the law (concerning the abolition of the old boroughs,
whole or in part) would become fact.[125] Against this negative evaluation of Cromwell's reorganization Sir Thomas Denman protested
immediately. He could call on no lesser authority than the royalist
Clarendon to furnish him with a totally opposed judgment. The conservatives countered this move by pointing out that Cromwell's parliamentary experiments had all failed.[126]

Sadler, (referred to earlier), was the one man in the opposition to
bother studying more closely the nature and purpose of Cromwell's
changes in the representation of borough and county. Such a strong
sentiment coming from a royalist like Clarendon, gave rise to the
supposition that Cromwell's actions and motives must have been
other than what the Whigs at first sight supposed them to be.

Could one really identify Cromwell's measures with those of the
Whigs of 1831 simply because Cromwell had abolished a number of
'rotten boroughs'? In a very long speech Sadler demonstrated that the
Whigs had overlooked the main characteristic of Cromwell's reorganizations: he favoured the county representatives over those of the towns.
This was, in Sadler's opinion, the point in which the Whig proposal
differed from Cromwell's reorganizations. Even if Sadler's figures
quoted to support his statement were not completely accurate, his as-

---

[123] 3 *Hansard* 2 (March 1), p. 1101. In his view, too, Cromwell was still a moderate (see p.
1100, note). The term 'model parliament' apparently was first used here (in connection with
Cromwell's reorganization). Cf. also D. Hume, *The History of England*, p. 736. Stubbs and
Freeman later used the term in medieval parliamentary history in connection with 1265 and
1295. Cf. J.G. Edwards, *Historians and the Medieval English Parliament*, pp. 50–52.
[124] Cf. the two articles by D.C. Moore (note 121) and N. Gash, *Politics in the Age of Peel*,
London, 1953, ch. I.
[125] 3 *Hansard* 2 (March 2), p. 1240.
[126] Cf. *Ibid.*, pp. 1241–1242. Cf. also H. Hallam, *The Constitutional History of England*, II,
p. 246 (note y): "It is remarkable that Clarendon seems to approve this model of a parliament, saying "it was then generally looked upon as an alteration fit to be more warrantably
made, and in a better time." Cf. the reaction of W. Bankes in 3 *Hansard* 2 (March 2), pp.
1277–1278. Cf. also J. Hobhouse in 3 Hansard 2 (March 2), pp. 1287–1289.

sessment was.[127] He went into Cromwell's reorganization of county representations with great exactitude, stressing the difference from the 1831 proposal in words which held, for a conservative, a remarkably high note of praise for Cromwell's character and personality.[128] Sadler considered that Cromwell's measures had been conservative rather than revolutionary, and this explained Clarendon's laudatory comment.

Other conservatives, for the same reasons, began to claim kinship with a moderately conservative Cromwell to further their own purposes, and Sadler, henceforth, continually quoting documents from the British Museum, denied the Whigs the right to regard Cromwell's reorganization as an example worth following.[129] But to no avail. The Whigs still claimed Cromwell for their own, and Macaulay magically changed Clarendon's comment into a prophecy which should now be fulfilled: "The only circumstances which, in the opinion of Lord Clarendon, were wanting in the Reform of Cromwell, we find in the Reform of William the Fourth."[130]

Our final remark on the 'parliamentary' image of Cromwell in the years 1831–'32 concerns the one immediately visible aspect of the great debate: the past spoke a different language to each of the contesting parties. The differences between the Whig and Tory versions of history became more pointed in such a crisis atmosphere. The controversies concerning parliamentary reforms went deeper in 1831–'32 than in 1867. For our theme this contextual difference between 1832 and 1867 is not without importance. In 1867 the two parties did not disagree about the general direction the reforms should take, even though opinions differed considerably as to how far the reforms should go. However complicated and curious things were in 1866–'67, the crux of the matter was that the liberals took the initiative, and the conservatives took over after radicalizing the proposal. That the political discord was deeper and more fundamental in 1831–'32 than in

---

[127] 3 *Hansard* 3 (April 18), p. 1548 ff. Cf. V.F. Vernon, 'Parliamentary Reapportionment Proposals in the Puritan Revolution' in *E.H.R.* 74 (1959), pp. 409–442, esp. pp. 419–423. See also B. Worden, 'The Bill for a New Representation: the dissolution of the Long Parliament: April 1653' in *E.H.R.* 86 (1971), pp. 473–496. Sadler hardly differentiated between the divergent proposals put forward by different groups in this period, nor did he (like many others) sufficiently understand the lasting importance which even the reform proposal gave to the representation of the county. Cf. N. Gash, *op. cit.*, pp. 65–66; cf. however, pp. 81–82.

[128] 3 *Hansard* 3 (April 18), p. 1552.

[129] See 3 *Hansard* 5 (July 27), p. 427. Cf. 3 *Hansard* 4 (July 5), pp. 729–730.

[130] 3 *Hansard* 4 (July 4), p. 774. Cf. J. Russell in 3 *Hansard* 4 (June 24), p. 327.

'67 was doubtlessly owing to the social-economic background; the social and political disturbances of the first decades of the century form a sharp contrast to the relatively quiet mid-Victorian period, not without reason called 'the age of equipoise.' It was only after 1850, that Walter Bagehot coined the epithet 'deferential' for the whole of English society. Agreements were reached on the most fundamental political questions, and even historians allowed a more uniform (i.e. less critical) representation of the past, which favoured the Whig historiography. These differences in what, for convenience's sake, may be termed the contexts of the first and the second Reform Bill respectively, had, we think, a direct influence on historiography in a more general sense. For as political antagonisms increased, historical polemics gathered strength. The sharp Tory criticisms forced the Whigs, as it were, to be more careful; we notice this quite often during the debates of 1831–'32 in parliament. But there was another reason for this tendency towards caution.

In these first decades the Whigs opposed a historical myth about parliament, which was strongly supported by the Radicals. We must repeat that Allen's contributions about medieval parliaments can only be understood within that context. It is our opinion that this context helps to explain the fact that the three authors we mentioned earlier were better able to understand the character of early medieval parliament than were people in the later part of the century.

To prove this contention we might add a further aspect: the way in which parliament functioned at the beginning of the 19th century itself. In the course of the century a fundamental change in this respect would come about, to which we shall refer again in the third chapter. The people at the beginning of the 19th century regarded parliament in the first place as a 'Grand Inquest of the Nation,' in which quality more of its original background was visible than was to be the case in a later period. It resembled an old 'remedial court' where everybody could lodge an appeal by means of a petition. When the number of petitions increased to the point where the very task of governing was endangered – especially since each petition could unleash unlimited discussions –, this 'original popular' right of petitioning was curbed. Consequently, this direct link between parliament and people lost its meaning.[131] In the course of the second half of the century a number

---

[131] Cf. especially the radical J. Hume's protest in the debate of 7th February, 1839 (3 *Hansard* 45, pp. 156–182). See especially P. Fraser, 'Public Petitioning and Parliament Before 1832' in *History* 46 (1961), pp. 195–211. Brougham also regretted the curtailment, see *E.R.* 66 (1837), p. 215. Cf. P. Fraser, *op. cit.*, p. 210.

of ancient customs and procedures disappeared, some of them dating back (sometimes supposedly) to the Middle Ages. Thus the position of the private members became a thing of the past.[132]

Before 1832 this had not yet happened. Probably the historians of that period with their own unmodernized parliament felt a greater affinity with some characteristics of the early parliaments. This is only a general suggestion, however. Granting the possibility of a greater identity, one still must remember the deceptive aspects. When the antiquarian Palgrave in 1832 was asked about the 'public petitions,' he did not neglect the great differences between then and now. In his answers he repeatedly stressed the fact that modern petitions and the ones of the Middle Ages were not to be compared.[133] It was the Whigs themselves who had to put up a united front against radical views, and Palgrave did likewise with his remarks that some radicals, in and outside Parliament, abused the ancient right of petitioning.

If we, then, try to answer the question whether the list of complaints against Whig historiography in general is fully justified, we should begin by stating that all criticism of the historiography on the early medieval parliament, printed since 1900, ought to deal especially with the historiography of the second half of the 19th century, rather than the first half. History had been subject to controversy during the first decades of the century. It became less so in the second half. This contextual difference cannot be sufficiently stressed in its importance for the intensification of some Whig myths in the second half of the century. There were elements in the view that the Whigs held of the past which raised fewer doubts in the mind of the conservative Stubbs than they had done in conservative minds earlier in the same century.

Where political antagonism became sharper, the criticism of myths in historical representation also increased. Tories came to oppose Whig myths and Whigs those of the radicals. In such an antagonistic atmosphere it was difficult to find a historical synthesis of the constitutional history of the Middle Ages. Only when in the second half of the century the image of the Anglo-Saxon period became free of radical implications, and liberals and conservatives agreed upon the restorative ideal of Anglo-Saxon local self-government, did Stubbs provide a synthesis which bound the periods before and after 1066 into an organic whole. Undoubtedly, elements for a similar synthesis had been present in

---

[132] Cf. P. Fraser, 'The Growth of Ministerial Control in the Nineteenth-Century House of Commons' in *E.H.R.* 75 (1960), pp. 444–463.

[133] See note 32.

Palgrave's work[134]; in the twenties Guizot, the continental Whig *par excellence*, had also given a fairly clear formulation, but only Stubbs was able to provide the details for the broad outline.

Guizot also gave his view of the history of English parliament in his 1820–'22 lectures on the origin of the representative form of government in Europe. His thinking came close to that of Hallam, whose work had appeared a few years earlier.[135] For Guizot, representation was a definite, constructive aid against the tyranny of an absolute form of government in the same sense that liberty (i.c. liberties =privileges) could be seen as a definite obstacle against absolutism.[136] Representation was a form of concentration and of necessary political centralization which defended a nation against the evils of more absolutist forms of centralization. "Le but du gouvernement représentatif est d'empêcher à la fois la tyrannie et la confusion, de ramener la multitude à l'unité en la provoquant à la reconnaître et à l'accepter elle-même."[137]

Viewed from this angle, the events of 1066 acquired an inestimable significance. According to Guizot the Whigs in their historical-political orientation were too Anglo-Saxon, but the Tories too Norman. Their political quarrels over 1066 prevented a historical synthesis which Guizot as an outsider believed he could accomplish.

Cette vue des événements (of Tories and Whigs) ne me paraît point exacte ni complète. Ce ne sont pas les institutions saxonnes qui, par elles-mêmes, ont été le principe des libertés anglaises. Le rapprochement forcé des deux peuples et des deux systèmes d'institutions en est la vraie source; il y a lieu de douter que, sans la conquête, la liberté fût sortie des institutions saxonnes; [138]

The local Anglo-Saxon institutions which preserved and protected political freedom, were maintained in England not in spite of, but because of the Norman conquest.[139] However, before analysing Stubbs's work (where these thoughts will be worked out more thoroughly), we

---

[134] Cf. P. Vinogradoff, *Villainage in England*, Oxford, 1892, pp. 12–16, 23.

[135] F. Guizot, *Histoire des origines du gouvernement représentatif en Europe*, 2 vols., Paris, 1851. However, there were differences. Guizot stressed the fact the 14th and 15th-century parliaments could hardly be called 'political' parliaments in the modern sense, cf. vol. II, pp. 323–324, 337–338, 342–345.

[136] Cf. V.E. Starzinger, *op. cit.*, pp. 102–107. A uniform suffrage was also not desired, as that would cause the loss of the varieties in representation, Cf. F. Jeffrey in *E.R.* 10 (1807), p. 408, and J. Mackintosh, 'Parliamentary Reform' in *E.R.* 34 (1820), p. 471.

[137] F. Guizot, *op. cit.*, vol. I, p. 94; vol. II, pp. 129–153, 305. For the respresentation idea see also V.E. Starzinger, *op. cit.*, ch. III. Cf. also E. Kossmann in *Tijdschrift voor Geschiedenis* 64 (1951), p. 161 (note 134).

[138] F. Guizot, *op. cit.*, vol. II, p. 44. He went on to say: "C'est la conquête qui leur a imprimé une vertu nouvelle, et leur a fait produire des résultats que, livrées à elles-mêmes, elles n'auraient pas produits."

will first deal with some of the Whig themes regarding modern history, which were comparatively much more controversial than those concerning the medieval parliament.

B. THE GLORIOUS REVOLUTION AND GEORGE III; CROMWELL AND THE CIVIL WAR

1) Macaulay and the Glorious Revolution

> We said that the history of England is the history of progress; and, when we take a comprehensive view of it, it is so. But, when examined in small separate portions, it may with more propriety be called a history of actions and reactions.
>
> (Macaulay, 1835)

The three important topics of modern history which commanded the attention of 19th-century Whig historiography with ever-increasing emphasis were: the Glorious Revolution, the first years of George III's reign, the Civil War, and the personality of Cromwell. According to the most basic Whig version, the link between 1688 and 1760 was to be located in the attempt of George III, immediately after his accession, to do away with the 'principles' of 1688. James Fox undertook in his later years, while opposing George III, a study of 1688. The work was carried on by James Mackintosh, whose collection of documents on the subject proved in the end useful for Macaulay's *History*.[140]

Macaulay is still regarded as the most representative Whig historian, notwithstanding recent publications questioning the aptness of this characterization.[141] Just as in the first part we investigated the accuracy of the presentation of the early Whig medievalists, for Macaulay we shall do likewise. What is the mythical character of the English constitution, presented in Macaulay's writings? To quote a 'dissenter': H. Trevor-Roper declared that Macaulay's 'Whig-myth' is itself a

[139] F. Guizot, *op. cit.*, vol. II, pp. 55, 305.

[140] C. Firth, *A Commentary on Macaulay's History of England*, London, 1938, p. 56 ff.; J.R. Dinwiddy, 'Charles James Fox as Historian' in *The Historical Journal* 12 (1969), pp. 23–34, particularly pp. 30, 34.

[141] Cf. H. Butterfield, *George III and The Historians*, London, 1957, p. 89 ff.; A. Browning, 'Lord Macaulay, 1800–1859' in *The Historical Journal* 2 (1959), pp. 149–160, particularly p. 156; *Halifax. Complete Works*, ed. J.P. Kenyon, Harmondsworth, 1969, pp. 23–24. J. Clive, 'Macaulay, History and Historians' in *History Today* 9 (1959), pp. 830–836; J. Clive, *Thomas Babington Macaulay*, London, 1973.

myth: ". . . the Macaulay view as supposed by his modern opponents – the view that there was, in the seventeenth century, an accepted constitution which the tyrannical Stuarts broke and the virtuous Whigs defended – he never held, and one only has to read him to know it."[142]

True, Macaulay does not represent things so baldly, but do his critics? There is room for doubt in that respect. The critics' fire was drawn by different aspects in his writings and it began – his great success notwithstanding – quite soon after the first two parts had been published.[143] The very first criticism was not directed at the constitutional passages, but rather at the presentation, at the (sometimes affected) style, at the frequently black-and-white depiction of character, at the mass of detail and the self-congratulatory note pervading the whole work. A few contemporary reactions from his colleagues are in order here. Guizot wrote a short comment to H. Reeve in 1856: "Of Macaulay I will say nothing, though I might say much. In a few words, his work is a brilliant embroidery on strong material."[144] The politician and author, G.C. Lewis, praised the substance as exceptionally engrossing, but he complained: "It is too long, and it is overdone with details."[145] They both objected to the 'picturesque' aspect of Macaulay's work, an objection which, as we saw in the first chapter, was to be repeated by J.R. Seeley in much sharper terms.

The liberal W.B. Donne left much less doubt about his rejection of Macaulay. He could forgive the many mistakes in detail, but not the self-satisfaction which did not allow for any correction. "However these may and will be corrected" – he wrote in 1849 – "but nothing can correct the air of Whig self-sufficiency that pervades the book. It was begotten in Holland House in the days of Grey and Mackintosh – good days for then but not for ever."[146] It seemed as if Macaulay's mental constitution could endure neither uncertainty nor doubt: "he hurried into dogmatism to escape doubt."[147] Dogmatism and self-sufficiency – since Lytton Strachey – were epithets typical of 'Victorianism,' but even during the heyday of the so-called Victorianism Macaulay was already reproached for them. For us there remains the question of whether Macaulay's contemporary critics dealt with him

---

[142] H.R. Trevor-Roper, *Historical Essays*, London, 1957, p. 251.

[143] Cf. W.C. Abbott, 'Macaulay and The New History' in *Yale Review* 18 (1929), p. 547.

[144] *Memoirs of The Life and Correspondence of Henry Reeve*, ed. J.K. Laughton, London, 1893, I, p. 344.

[145] *Letters of Sir George Cornewall Lewis*, ed. G.F. Lewis, London, 1870, p. 310. Cf. also Lewis's sharp criticism of Macaulay's article on Bacon (1837), p. 93.

[146] C.B. Johnson, *William Bodham Donne and His Friends*, London, 1905, p. 172.

[147] A. Hayward, 'Macaulay and His School' in *Q.R.* 124 (1868), p. 288.

justly in all respects. Did the Whig self-sufficiency and dogmatism indicate a one-sided 'party history?' There were, as a matter of fact, historians in Macaulay's time who openly propagated both the inevitability and the desirability of writing history in that way.[148]

However, Macaulay, like Mackintosh before him, never stopped agitating against such abuses of history – from the very beginning in his early article 'History' (1828) until the last chapters of his *magnum opus*. He often described the process (almost a 'common-law' procedure) in which the past was misused for continual precedent-hunting by Tories and Whigs alike in the political debate. Although this method was highly regarded, Macaulay realized the fatal influence of such a political use of history on English historiography: "where history is regarded as a repository of title-deeds, on which rights of governments and nations depend, the motive to falsification becomes almost irresistible."[149] Thus the Glorious Revolution had not been solely a Whig affair; according to Macaulay, Whigs and Tories together deposed a 'tyrant,' and together they kept the 'mob' under control in 1688.[150] Neither was it rare for him to warn against judging the 17th century by 19th-century standards.[151] It is clear that he tried to keep the past and the present separated, although the result was not always satisfactory. He summarizes these attempts in the seventh chapter:

There are two opposite errors into which those who study the annals of our own country are in constant danger of falling, the error of judging the present by the past, and the error of judging the past by the present. The former is the error of minds prone to reverence whatever is old, the latter of minds readily attracted by whatever is new. The former error may perpetually be observed in the reasonings of conservative politicians on the questions of their own day. The latter error perpetually infects the speculations of writers of the liberal school when they discuss the transactions of an earlier age. The former error is the more pernicious in a statesman, and the latter in a historian. It is not easy for any person who, in our time, undertakes to treat of the revolution which overthrew the Stuarts, to preserve with steadiness the happy mean between the two extremes.[152]

---

[148] Cf. E.E. Crowe, 'Henry Martin's History of France' in *E.R.* 106 (1857), p. 384: "History to be now popular, must be written by the partisan, by one who has a creed to preach, or a strong opinion to impose. Party-spirit, which has lost its hold on the politics of the day, has taken refuge in the closet of more than one eminent historian."

[149] T.B. Macaulay, *The History of England*, London, 1906 (Everyman's Library) I, p. 27.

[150] *Ibid.*, II, p. 196: "Nothing in the history of our revolution is more deserving of admiration and of imitation than the manner in which the two parties in the Convention, at the very moment at which their dispute ran highest, joined like one man to resist the dictation of the mob of the capital" (probably written in 1848).

[151] Cf. *Ibid.*, I, p. 213; II, p. 773; III, p. 13.

[152] *Ibid.*, I, pp. 685–686.

Macaulay's ideal of writing non-partisan national history did not exclude all possibility of the direct use of the past for the present. On the contrary, the present determined what was important in the past and what was not.

What do we mean when we say that one past event is important and another insignificant? No past event has any intrinsic importance. The knowledge of it is valuable only as it leads us to form just calculations with respect to the future. A history which does not serve this purpose, though it may be filled with battles, treatises and commotions, is as useless as the series of turnpike tickets collected by Sir Matthew Mite.[153]

While the first lengthy quotation plainly indicates a Rankean trend to understand the past 'from within itself,' in the second quotation Macaulay denied the past an 'intrinsic' value of its own, determining its value by means of the present and the future. All his work shows the tension caused by an impassioned attempt to maintain an equilibrium between the two extremes, a tension between a rather 'presentist' political view on the one hand and a more historical-antiquarian view on the other, a tension, in short, caused by admiration both for the deeply respected past and for the present, so much superior to that past in many respects.[154] In the famous third chapter of his *History* he compared the situation in 1685 with that of 1848, which resulted in a song of praise for the progress made. This eulogy on the present, however, was not born of a narrow self-sufficiency nor the result of blindness to the evils of the contemporary period. The third chapter was more a reaction to prophets of evil who idealised the past because of their displeasure with their own time. What Macaulay objected to was this romantic idealisation (either of the Middle Ages or of the Stuart period), by the seekers of a 'Golden Age.'[155]

As Macaulay was a realist – which, we shall see, accounted for his 'dogmatism' – he believed an admiration of the past and tradition which was born out of a dislike of one's own period was unreasonable. Nevertheless, there was within this realism a large and worthy place for the political-constitutional 'prescriptive' tradition. This was to be expected of an admirer of aristocratic government. "Democracy does not require the support of prescription. Monarchy has often stood

[153] T.B. Macaulay, *Miscellaneous Essays*, London, 1910 (Everyman's Library), pp. 33–34. (from article 'History' of 1828).
[154] Cf. T.B. Macaulay, *Critical and Historical Essays*, London, 1907, (Everyman's Library), I, pp. 286–291.
[155] Cf. T.B. Macaulay, *The History of England*, I, p. 328. "... it is natural that, being dissatisfied with the present, we should form a too favourable estimate of the past."

without that support. But a patrician order is the work of time."[156] In this respect too the first chapter certainly is a typical paean of praise on tradition in the style of Burke.[157]

The historic survey given here made the unique quality of England's political development irresistibly clear. This aspect was to be stressed again and again in historical writings, especially since 1848: ... "no other society has yet succeeded in uniting revolution with prescription, progress with stability, the energy of youth with the majesty of immemorial antiquity."[158] Macaulay's introduction to English history up to the Restoration has several aspects characteristic for Whig historiography. Words like 'immemorial antiquity,' or 'from time immemorial' when referring to an 'old constitution' or so-called 'fundamental laws' all remind us of a 'historical' use of language dating back to the 17th and 18th century. The ideological range of this jargon has been explained by J.G.A. Pocock.[159]

The fact that Macaulay lacked interest for and was ignorant of the Middle Ages, undeniably made his introduction vague and historically uncritical. Characteristic for his Whig views is also the great importance that Macaulay saw in the circumstance that England's insular position saved it towards the end of the Middle Ages and in the beginning of the modern period from the evils of a 'standing army.'[160] This was the principal reason that there was no absolutist victory in England, with the fortunate result that the medieval parliamentary tradition could be prolonged in an adapted form. In the constitutional Whig ideology it was absolutely impossible for a regular 'standing army' to co-exist with a 'limited monarchy': the two were mutually exclusive. In the Restoration period, under the influence of the Cromwell experience, the Whigs expanded this thought into a more coherent doctrine, supported by a number of classical authors.[161] No subsequent Whig pamphlet lacked a chapter called 'standing army,' and it was this very

---

[156] *Ibid.*, I, p. 110.
[157] Cf. Macaulay on Burke: "The greatest man since Milton" in G.O. Trevelyan, *The Life and Letters of Lord Macaulay*, London, 1959, p. 613.
[158] T.B. Macaulay, *op. cit.*, I, p. 27; cf. pp. 30–32, 91.
[159] J.G.A. Pocock, *The Ancient Constitution and the Feudal Law*, Cambridge, 1957.
[160] As to a 'standing army' as the ideal instrument for the establishment of an absolute state, see T.B. Macaulay, *op. cit.*, I, pp. 39–41, 61, 74–75, 87, 161; cf. G. Davies 'The Treatment of Constitutional History in Macaulay's *History of England*' in *The Huntington Library Quarterly* 2 (1938–1939), pp. 179–204, particularly p. 180; cf. J.G.A. Pocock's remark in *Comparative Studies in Society and History* 4 (1961–1962), p. 236, note 44.
[161] About this theme of 'militia versus standing army,' see C. Robbins, *The Eighteenth Century Commonwealthman*, New York, 1968; cf. also J.W. Johnson, *The Formation of English Neo-Classical Thought*, Princeton, 1967, pp. 51–52.

aversion towards a standing army that would make itself felt, to a greater or lesser extent, until deep into the 19th century. Only towards the end of the century was the professional army incorporated constitutionally, much later than the 'harmless navy' ('powerless against civil liberty').[162] The navy had never posed a problem.

As to Macaulay's proper subject, the events of 1688 and the reign of William III, what are the most notable characteristics of his story of constitutional development? A single preliminary remark is needed: his work was not a constitutional history in the classical sense. What Macaulay wanted was to break through the narrow and traditional boundaries; he wanted a synthesis between Hallam and Scott, 'a compound of philosophy and poetry.'[163] His intention was to write a kind of history of civilization, which resulted in the now classical specimen of English 'social history' of the 'inserted' third chapter. He wished to depict a part of the past that would fire the imagination of his contemporaries; this was the purpose behind his mainly descriptive details and his many psychological and geographical digressions on persons and places. But in all this 'embroidery' (to borrow Guizot's term), he wove a thread in which a clear constitutional development was visible.[164]

Macaulay summarized England's 17th-century constitutional revolution as "the transfer of the supreme control of the executive administration from the Crown to the House of Commons."[165] Within this broad outline three different aspects can be distinguished in Macaulay's work: 1688 acquired a topical meaning because of the revolution of 1848, the Glorious Revolution was succeeded by a 'noiseless revolution,' from which emerged ministers and cabinet, and, thirdly, Macaulay deeply admired William III.

We already mentioned the first aspect. The words of praise at the end of the tenth chapter leave no doubt that in Macaulay's opinion the revolution of 1688 was vindicated by its prescriptive and conservative character. Compared with 1848 this unique character was strongly emphasized, and he considered that the answer to the question why revolutions by-passed England in the 19th century – a question for many

---

[162] Cf. T.B. Macaulay, op. cit., I, p. 231; J. Russell, An Essay on the History of the English Government and Constitution, London, 1865 (1820), p. 189 ff.; cf. also Spencer Walpole, The Life of Lord John Russell, London, 1889, I, p. 85.

[163] T.B. Macaulay, Critical and Historical Essays, I, p. 1; cf. also H.R. Trevor-Roper, The Romantic Movement and the Study of History, London, 1969, pp. 19–21.

[164] See the article (mentioned in note 160) by G. Davies and P. Danaschewski, Macaulay und Acton, München, 1960, pp. 29–36.

[165] T.B. Macaulay, The History of England, I, p. 153.

more historians after Macaulay – was to be found not in the present
but in the past, in 1688: "It is because we had a preserving revolution
in the seventeenth century that we have not had a destroying revolution in the nineteenth."[166] The failure of 1848 on the continent
reinforced the comfortable awareness of England's history as unique,
and it was easy to find an answer to the puzzling question of the origin
of Britain's successful political development: continuity and gradualness of the changes.[167] Any violent revolution was destined in advance
to fail, as it implied abandoning "that great element of all political
excellence – *stability*."[168] Thus argued Macaulay's contemporary Henry
Rogers even in 1848. Stability was not the outcome of a 'paper constitution,' but of tradition and customs, it resulted from a link with the
past: "that bond of custom, slight as it may seem, and absurd as it
often is, is a thing omnipotent in politics."[169] The revolutionary experience of 1848 raised the principle of continuity to a higher level of a
'political law of nature.' A second effect was the growing distaste on the
part of Englishmen – Macaulay especially – for political theorizing.[170]

Disregarding Macaulay's very clear eulogy on the 'restorative' and
'prescriptive' character of 1688, – "a vindication of ancient rights" –
H. Trevor-Roper stated that Macaulay saw the vindication of the revolution not in constitutional precedents, but in the constitutional consequences which become visible in the first decade after 1688.[171] There
is some truth in this statement. After 1848, when Macaulay enthusiastically turned to the period of William III, he was fascinated by the
gradual emergence of a wholly new constitutional phenomenon: the
'cabinet,' the 'ministerial government' comes into being. He speaks of
'a new era of constitutional government,' and there are remarkably
fewer passages praising constitutional precedents.[172] There seemed to be
less need of them, since the danger of a direct revolution had been exor-
cised and the support for Chartism in England was dwindling. The

---

[166] *Ibid.*, II, p. 214.
[167] Cf. H. Rogers, 'Revolution and Reform' in *E.R.* 88 (1848), p. 372: "No country . . .
has ever effected so many great changes by peaceful means, as England has done during the
last one hundred and sixty years . . . It is their gradual character, and that alone, which has
made them safe."
[168] *Ibid.*, p. 367.
[169] *Ibid.*, p. 367.
[170] *Ibid.*, p. 370: "The law of continuity . . . and the influence of time are not accidental,
but essential conditions of all political solidity."
[171] H.R. Trevor-Roper, *Historical Essays*, p. 251; cf. however, T.B. Macaulay, *op. cit.*, II,
p. 212.
[172] Cf. *Ibid.*, II, p. 241; see also Macaulay's critical remarks on the exaggerated fear of a
'standing army' among the Whigs after 1689, *Ibid.*, III, pp. 529–547.

signs of the times were hopeful, everything indicated that 1688 really had been the last revolution. The revolution which Macaulay believed he saw after 1688 he labelled 'noiseless': the contemporary observer never noticed it and there were hardly any precedents for it.[173] Thus this noiseless revolution brought something wholly new; no preceding period had known the institute of 'ministry.' There was not even a place for it in the books of classical theoreticians as De Lolme and Blackstone.[174]

The first years of William III's reign still presented the old picture of independent departments, the ministers not yet forming a team of politically like-minded persons.[175] Towards the end of 1693 a change for the better became noticeable, and after the elections of 1695 the government clearly consisted of a homogeneous cabinet. "The first English ministry was gradually formed; nor is it possible to say quite precisely when it began to exist. But on the whole, the date from which the era of ministries may most properly be reckoned is the day of the meeting of Parliament after the general election of 1695."[176] This fortunate and politically healthy situation – "liberty united with order"[177] – was to last until the elections of 1698. After this there was a new period of 'anarchy,' with an ungovernable and tyrannical House of Commons. For, "to the evil of having no ministry, to the evil of having a House of Commons permanently at war with the executive government, there is absolutely no limit."[178] Macaulay was concerned with demonstrating that 1688, as such, was not sufficient. The glory of 1688 was a relative glory; an overly autonomous or independent parliament could render the country ungovernable. After 1688 parliament still lacked 'the gravity of a Senate.'[179] To be sure, there was "parliamentary government, but there was no Ministry and, without a Ministry, the working of a parliamentary government such as ours, must always be unsteady and unsafe."[180]

A "mass" of some 500 or 600 representatives unfit for the executive power would inevitably turn into a 'mob,' and "a country of which the

---

[173] *Ibid.*, III, p. 249; cf. II, p. 224.
[174] *Ibid.*, III, pp. 248–249, 301; II, p. 224; cf. also I, pp. 166, 189, 213.
[175] *Ibid.*, II, p. 622.
[176] *Ibid.*, III, p. 616.
[177] *Ibid.*
[178] *Ibid.*, III, p. 646.
[179] *Ibid.*, III, p. 247; cf. III, p. 174 ff. and p. 281 ff. on the Place Bills; cf. also in the paragraph on Halifax the remark: "The English constitution trims between Turkish despotism and Polish anarchy" (I, p. 191). Cf. J.H. Plumb, *The Growth of Political Stability in England*, London, 1967, p. 63 and 144.
[180] T.B. Macaulay, *op. cit.*, III, p. 247.

Supreme Executive Council is a mob is surely in a perilous situation."[181] Thus the cabinet, as a 'committee of leading members of the two Houses'[182] was not just an executive organ, it was also a very necessary instrument for the prevention of governmental chaos within the walls of parliament itself. On the other hand, Parliament should be something more than purely oppositional; it should also serve the executive power. These reflections of Macaulay's, in connection with that second revolution he described, signalled a break with the very old Whig standpoint on the functioning of parliament, a standpoint clearly supported and interpreted by his colleague John Russell.[183] Only the fact that cabinet and parliament were 'attuned' to each other made it possible for a 'parliamentary government' to function well.[184]

Macaulay prided himself on being the first author to have detected the historical roots of this unique system of government, the first noticeable signs in the past that pointed in this direction.[185] At this point his description of the 'noiseless revolution' was original and topical. A fair number of constitutional pamphlets were published in the fifties and sixties describing and analysing the role and the unique importance of the cabinet. The concluding pamphlet, in a way, was Bagehot's now classical essay of 1867, which proclaimed not the 'separation,' but the 'fusion' of executive and law-giving power to be the cornerstone of the English parliamentary system. Considering the great number of 'predecessors' (including Macaulay's *History*) it has rightly been said that Bagehot's essay is less original than had formerly been thought.[186]

Reading too much of importance in these early beginnings of course was a temptation, and undoubtedly Macaulay went too far in the first flush of enthusiasm. His presentation is, on the whole, too schematic, seen simply from that single conception of modern 'cabinet government,' although his analysis had gained in subtlety since his article on Temple in 1838.[187] Macaulay also acknowledged that the second revolution would not have a permanent effect as long as the internal situation of the two parties remained uncertain because of 'factions.' But he over-estimated the unity and homogeneity of the first Whig-minis-

[181] *Ibid.*
[182] *Ibid.*, III, p. 248.
[183] Cf. D. Southgate, *The Passing of the Whigs, 1832–1886*, London, 1962, p. 212.
[184] T.B. Macaulay, *op. cit.*, III, p. 540.
[185] *Ibid.*, III, p. 249; cf. G.O. Trevelyan, *op. cit.*, p. 661.
[186] See M.J.C. Vile, *Constitutionalism and the Separation of Powers*, Oxford, 1967, pp. 212–228.
[187] J. Cotter Morison, *Macaulay*, London, 1882, p. 80; T.B. Macaulay, *Critical and Historical Essays*, I, 238 ff.; cf. also H.D. Trail, *William the Third*, London, 1888, p. 119 ff.

try, and overlooked the rise and growth of a wholly new Tory-party, which, ideologically, became truly Whig in the original sense of the word. There is no doubt that he missed much of the social background of the events around the year 1694. J.H. Plumb in his Ford Lectures refers to it in striking terms as a deep gap in party relations and political conceptions of Whigs and Tories.[188] Still, all this notwithstanding, Macaulay's theory of a 'noiseless revolution' touched upon a fundamentally vital constitutional event in the 'post-revolutionary' period: the increase of executive power necessary for administrative and political stability.

The matter of the 'cabinet' was, for Macaulay, almost automatically linked to the idea of ministerial responsibility, as well as to the idea that the King was 'bound' to compose a cabinet from the majority party in the House of Commons. Macaulay, as a Whig, paid homage to ministerial responsibility as a firm old tradition.

The doctrine that the Sovereign is not responsible is doubtless as old as any part of our constitution. The doctrine that his ministers are responsible is also of immemorial antiquity ... It may be doubted whether any real polity that ever existed has exactly corresponded to the pure idea of that polity. According to the pure idea of constitutional royalty, the prince reigns and does not govern; and constitutional royalty, as it now exists in England, comes nearer than in any other country to the pure idea. Yet it would be a great error to imagine that our princes merely reign and never govern.[189]

It is no coincidence that this remarkable passage hails from a context defending William III's high-handed foreign policy. Macaulay's deeply rooted dislike of political theoreticians is apparent in every page he wrote. He never admitted that any of them – even Locke – could have made a historical contribution to the Glorious Revolution or to that second 'noiseless revolution.' "The first Ministry was the work, partly of mere chance, and partly of wisdom, not however of that highest wisdom which is conversant with great principles of political philosophy, but of that lower wisdom which meets daily exigencies by daily expedients."[190] This absolute belief in 'lower wisdom' and its ultimate power was the basis of Macaulay's dogmatism, it supported his Whig 'self-sufficiency.' It could be called a 'dogmatism without dogma's' ...

[188] J.H. Plumb, *op. cit.*, pp. 134–135, 140–144.
[189] T.B. Macaulay, *The History of England*, II, pp. 773–774.
[190] *Ibid.*, III, p. 249. Cf. J.P. Kenyon in *Historical Perspectives. Studies in English Thought and Society in honour of J.H. Plumb*, ed. N. McKendrick, London, 1974, p. 47 (note 14).

a paradox that somewhat resembles that anti-doctrinary political stance of the French 'doctrinarians.'[191]

Because Macaulay raised the practical experience of everyday to the status of highest political wisdom, later critics like J. Cotter Morison, John Morley and Leslie Stephen declared him to be superficial, narrow-minded and anti-intellectual. Stephen's criticism of Macaulay's Whig ideology was sharpest of all.[192] Macaulay's dogmatism was also behind his admiration for William III, who to Macaulay was his political credo become flesh. He praised William as the saviour of freedom, he praised him above all for his practical qualities as expressed in his foreign policy. William was a man of action, both on the battlefield and in negotiations. He hated bootless speculations,[193] was an accomplished negotiator and was lord and master in his 'own' department, foreign affairs. In this field there was no one more capable than William in all of England.[194]

The result of Macaulay's dogmatic realism could hardly be any other than a picture of history without any idealism and almost wholly non-ideological. His work, therefore, was not inspiring and this was what the liberals reproached him with, as they desired more than Macaulay's 'superficial' Whig realism. Gladstone, who later objected to him on a number of counts, had as his main objection that Macaulay lacked idealism in his view of past and present.[195] 'Gladstonian Liberalism' needed more inspiration from historical events than what the revolution of 1688, with its paucity of ideas, could provide. It is not surprising that the Civil War, especially during the second half of the 19th century, was highly popular with non-conformist Liberals, much more so than 1688. A comparison between Macaulay and the young G.M. Trevelyan may help to illustrate this shifting historical interest.

Trevelyan's well-known conclusive survey from 1904 on the subject of the 17th century shows the evolution of Whig historiography about that time. The Civil War came in for much more attention, whereas Macaulay's 'second revolution' was merely dealt with in a footnote.[196]

[191] Cf. the books mentioned in note 68.

[192] The same qualities, however, delighted Gustave Le Bon even at the end of the 19th century. Cf. G. Le Bon, *Psychologie des Foules*, Paris, 1925, pp. 71–72; L. Stephen, *Hours in a Library*, London 1907, III, pp. 227–271, particularly pp. 234, 239, 242, 249; cf. W.C. Abbott, *op. cit.*, p. 555 ff.

[193] T.B. Macaulay, *op. cit.*, II, p. 591; cf. I, pp. 630–632.

[194] *Ibid.*, II, pp. 225, 545, 775.

[195] Cf. W.E. Gladstone, 'Lord Macaulay' in *Q.R.* 142 (1876), pp. 1–50.

[196] G.M. Trevelyan, *England under The Stuarts*, Harmondsworth, 1960, p. 440, note 1: "This principle of closer connexion between the executive and legislative, unknown to Charles II, and not laid down in the terms of the Revolution settlement, was adopted as of

Another remarkable fact – apart from the strong fascination that the Civil War held for him – is that Trevelyan insisted on characterizing it as a battle of ideas between two parties. The English Civil War was the opposite of the class war, which was to prove the ruin of the French Revolution.[197] Whosoever understood this point could count himself lucky, for he also understood the mysteries of Civil War and Glorious Revolution.[198] Macaulay has no understanding for puritanism; Trevelyan's idealistic admiration sharply contrasts with this and makes the reader realize the importance of the revolution in historiography since J. Forster and Th. Carlyle. These two were highly praised by Trevelyan for their pioneering work in this field.[199]

Macaulay's constitutional interest was roused to a degree by the emergence of the cabinet. Trevelyan considered the rise and growth of the two-party system to be much more useful as a key to understanding the English political development: "... party is the real secret of the step upwards from Cabal to Cabinet."[200] He agreed that the constitutional revolution might be summarised as a 'transfer of sovereignty' from Crown to Parliament, but the terminology in which he translated this interesting evolution unintentionally causes associations with the new liberalism which flourished around the turn of the century. We will discuss this further in the third chapter. The unique system which had come into being in seventeenth-century England, and which was to have universal importance for later ages, "was proved ... to combine freedom with efficiency, and local rights with national union. It showed the world ... how liberty could mean not weakness but strength."[201] Freedom and efficiency were two political ideals that could exist side by side; the 'old' England had learnt how to combine them, he declared in 1926.[202] But, before discussing the Civil War more deeply, we should like to explain the importance of the most controversial period in all 19th-century historiography: the early part of George III's reign.

practical utility, rather than granted as of constitutional right. In this limited sense William originated Cabinet government," cf. p. 443, note 1.

[197] *Ibid.*, p. 219: "The French Revolution was a war of two societies; the American Civil War was a war of two regions; but the Great Rebellion was a war of two parties." Cf. p. 217.

[198] *Ibid.*, pp. 187–188: "The French revolution appealed to the needs as well as to the aspirations of mankind. But in England the revolutionary passions were stirred by no class in its own material interest. Our patriots were prosperous men, enamoured of liberty, or of religion, or of loyalty, each for her own sake, not as the handmaid of class greed. This was the secret of the moral splendour of our Great Rebellion and our Civil War."

[199] *Ibid.*, pp. 507–508.

[200] G.M. Trevelyan, *The Two-Party System in English Political History*, Oxford, 1926, p. 11.

[201] G.M. Trevelyan, *England under The Stuarts*, p. XII.

[202] G.M. Trevelyan, *The Two-Party System in English Political History*, p. 10; G.M. Trevelyan, *The English Revolution*, London, 1938, pp. 65, 179.

2) The 19th-century topicality of George III

> The historical continuity of parties has a political
> as well as a sentimental value; but it is an absolute
> delusion if it is applied to measure the tendencies
> of a statesman in one age by the tendencies of another
> statesman in another age.
>
> (R. Cecil, 1861)

Beginning with the decade 1830–1840 historical attention came to be more focused on the very period that, because it was controversial, Hallam in 1827 particularly avoided: the early years of George III's reign. This change in attitude was caused by the publication of a considerable number of new sources.[203] The subject has been so extensively discussed by now, that the forest is no longer visible for trees. Despite this, there may yet be something to contribute about how the Whig myths around George III functioned in the 19th century. Sometimes the reaction to Whig historiography really gave rise to a myth about a myth, although the theoretical objections to Whig historiography, as summed up in the first chapter, are still true. There is little point in reviving old controversies; recently a tendency towards a more balanced consideration has become noticeable.[204]

Why were the early years of George III's reign so fascinating to Whig historians and politicians of the 19th century? What was the reason for the anachronistic picture they drew of that period? The basic question we have to answer is 'why' this anachronism. To put it simply: they clearly detected the first origins of the 19th-century liberal Whig party in those early years. G.O. Trevelyan stated in 1880: "The nucleus of the Liberal Party, as it has existed ever since, was formed during the turbid and discreditable period that intervened between the fall of Pitt in 1761 and the fall of Grenville in 1765."[205] Here, in this 'renovation of the party,' was the very heart of the Whig myth. They

---

[203] Cf. H. Butterfield, *George III and the Historians*, London, 1957, p. 97 ff.; O. Anderson, 'The Political Use of History in Mid-Nineteenth Century England' in *Past and Present* no. 36 (1967), p. 89 ff.

[204] The antagonism between the pro- and anti-Whig interpretation of the 18th century seems less sharp now after the political development has been evaluated again over a longer period. Cf. B.W. Hill's survey, 'Executive Monarchy and the Challenge of Parties, 1689–1832: Two Concepts of Government and two Historiographical Interpretations' in *The Historical Journal* 13 (1970), pp. 379–401. J.A.W. Gunn, 'Influence, Parties and the Constitution: Changing Attitudes, 1783–1832' in *The Historical Journal* 17 (1974), pp. 301–328. P. Kelly, 'British Parliamentary Politics, 1784–1786' in *The Historical Journal* 17 (1974), pp. 733–753.

[205] G.O. Trevelyan, *The Early History of Charles James Fox*, London, 1928, p. 124.

were convinced that this renovation began as a reaction to George III's imagined absolutism. The myth was given its ideological form by Burke in his much praised definition of a political party, and its more tangible form in the Rockingham Whig group.[206] There were, however, still further implications for the 19th century in this period. Party renewal was logically linked to the historical problem surrounding the rise and growth of the principle of ministerial responsibility as an inalienable ingredient of a 'Cabinet Government.' Finally, the picture of George III as a convicted absolutist was supported by the derogatory elements of the myth as stated by Walpole and Burke. For instance, the influence of Bolingbroke's writings, the role of the 'King's Friends,' the attitude of the Queen-Mother and Bute (both evil counsellors), and finally the uninterrupted influence of Bute's after his retirement in 1763.

But do all Whigs complacently accept Walpole and Burke as sufficiently reliable witnesses of what happened in those first years? Undeniably, they are present as such in Macaulay and in Green's bestseller of 1874. Macaulay was a classical 'throwback,' for when reviewing Hallam in 1828 he had not scrupled to dismiss the oppositional representation of affairs given by Burke as purest fiction.[207] However, only a decade afterwards he too succumbed to the lures of such a presentation. Still there was no scarcity of sceptics and critics even among liberal-thinking authors.

1845 is especially memorable in this historical discussion because of the publication of Walpole's *Memoirs of the Reign of George III*. How was this work received by the two parties? Probably the best-known reaction came from the Tory J.W. Croker, Macaulay's most fervent opponent in both political and literary matters.[208] He was *the* Walpole specialist in Tory circles, and as such he wrote seven hypercritical articles analysing Walpole's work and its use for historiography. Croker was convinced that his kind of analysis harmonized with the peculiar type of psychology Walpole used in his memoirs.[209] Walpole saw

---

[206] For his definition see G.O. Trevelyan, *op. cit.*, p. 130: "Party is a body of men united to promote the national interest by their joint endeavours, upon some particular principle in which they are all agreed."

[207] Cf. the difference between the essay on Hallam (1828) and that on The Earl of Chatham (1844). See T.B. Macaulay, *Critical and Historical Essays*, London, 1907, I, pp. 70, 416 ff., 452 ff.; John Allen believed Rockingham's party to be *sui generis*, but was not sure about Bute having any influence after 1763, see *E.R.* 58 (1834), pp. 331, 336.

[208] On J.W. Croker, see M.F. Brightfield, *John Wilson Croker*, London, 1940; H. Butterfield *op. cit.*, pp. 119–135; Hedva Ben-Israel, *op. cit.*, pp. 175–202.

[209] Cf. J.W. Croker, 'Horace Walpole' in *Q.R.* 74 (1844), pp. 395–416 and J.W. Croker, 'Memoirs of the Reign of King George III' in *Q.R.* 77 (1845), p. 258.

nothing but 'factious' self-interest in the political activities of his contemporaries and so did Croker in Walpole. He stressed only one aspect
in his analysis: Walpole's selfish motives (i.e. 'his real motives') for
writing.[210] The cynical remarks and insinuations about almost everybody in his memoirs served to hide Walpole's greed for money, his
continual hunt for lucrative jobs, his sinecures. This was the pattern
Croker repeatedly put before his readers: whoever had once thwarted
Walpole's financial greed and ambition was bound to be harshly judged
indeed. With this background, Croker could also explain the 'revisions,'
the passages that were added at some later date and the sudden changes
of opinion (sometimes turning full circle) about people. Croker no
doubt excelled in sharp analyses; in 1822 he had already pointed out
that the 'anonymous' memorial of 1752 (accusing George III's pre-
ceptors of Jacobinist leanings), had been compiled by Walpole personally in an effort to make trouble for Pelham who had refused to give
him the sinecure he coveted.[211] According to Croker, the 'lies of 1752'
came to be regarded as historical truth by that same Walpole a few
years later. Croker maintained that the 'why' and 'how' of Walpole's
writing were sufficiently explained by his desires for sinecures ('the
primum mobile of all his misanthropical feelings'). There was no
need to look further; Walpole's behaviour mirrored the spirit of the
century.[212]

Even Croker, therefore, could not find it in his heart to blame Walpole for his actions; the Victorian critic, however, could not stomach
Walpole's hypocrisy and insincerity: the discrepancy between his
actions on the one hand and his claim of unselfishness and impartiality
for himself and his historical writings on the other hand. Was not
Walpole's poem praising the new king in 1761 a thing of devilish insincerity, since he was going to slander that very king a couple of years
later in the most shameful manner in his *Memoirs?*[213] Yet, his maniacal
criticisms notwithstanding, even Croker now and then lifted a tip of
the veil to show 'another,' a 'better,' yes, even a 'converted' Walpole.

---

[210] Cf. J.W. Croker, 'Horace Walpole' in *Q.R.* 72 (1843), p. 521 ff.

[211] J.W. Croker, 'Walpole Memoirs' in *Q.R.* 27 (1822), pp. 178–215, particularly pp.
203–206; cf. R. Sedgwick, 'Horace Walpole' in *From Anne to Victoria*, ed. B. Dobrée, London,
1937, pp. 265–278, particularly p. 274 ff.; cf. *Letters from George III to Lord Bute, 1756–1766*,
ed. R. Sedgwick, London, 1939, p. XXIV ff.

[212] J.W. Croker in *Q.R.* 77 (1845), p. 256.

[213] Cf. J.W. Croker in *Q.R.* 74 (1844), pp. 415–416 and J.W. Croker, 'The Garland.
By the Hon. Horace Walpole' in *Q.R.* 90 (1852), pp. 311–313; Croker had no doubts about
the intentions of this poem: "to facilitate his comfortable arrangement of his sinecures" (p.
313).

Significant in this respect is Croker's quite moderate and even favourable review from 1848.[214] Suddenly a new Walpole appears on the scene, 'converted' by the French revolution, a 'prophet' who not only foresaw the dread misery of the revolution in France, but also that of the Reform movement in England.[215]

Not even Croker could in the last instance deny that Walpole's facts possessed a high degree of accuracy 'in themselves'; his data were, historically speaking, 'first-class' because they were first-hand. What Croker criticized was what he considered to be the imaginary 'mythical' setting of the facts: Walpole poisoned history through this mythicism. Both friends and enemies have since repeated this criticism.[216]

We shall not analyse Walpole's *Memoirs* as such – the whys and wherefores of Walpoles revisions (in 1775 and 1784) were no longer a problem for Croker. In the early years of this century C.L. Becker tried to find the right answer,[217] and in more recent times G.P. Judd also took up the subject, but gradually it has become clear that a 'definite' answer is only possible with the publication of a truly scholarly edition.[218] The crucial question is: did the Whigs after 1845 simply accept Walpole and his views? Although Macaulay, and other Whigs after him, eagerly seized upon "that part in his (Walpole's) work which is most subjective in character,"[219] concerning the 'Jacobean' education, the prince's absolutist leanings, his mother's role and Bute's unceasing influence after 1763, as with Croker, the dominant mood was one of rejection. The reasons for this are not difficult to see.

There were several Whigs who, contrary to Croker, to a great extent agreed with Walpole's unfavourable portrayal of King and Court. They rejected his denigrating judgements only when applied to their 'precursors' such as Rockingham and Fox. The disloyalty of Walpole's cousin and friend Conway to the 'Rockingham-principles,' as well as

[214] J.W. Croker, 'Horace Walpole's Letters to the Countess of Ossory' in *Q.R.* 83 (1848), 110–127, particularly p. 124.

[215] Cf. J.W. Croker in *Q.R.* 83 (1848), pp. 124–125; J.W. Croker 'Correspondence of Walpole and Masson' in *Q.R.* 89 (1851), pp. 135–169, particularly p. 169; cf. J.W. Croker in *Q.R.* 74 (1844), pp. 405–406. See also R.A. Smith, 'Walpole's Reflections on the Revolution in France' in *Horace Walpole: Writer, Politician and Connoisseur*, ed. W.H. Smith, New Haven, 1967, pp. 91–114.

[216] See on his accurate methods J.W. Croker in *Q.R.* 27 (1822), p. 179, and 77 (1845), p. 227. Cf. J. Brooke, 'Horace Walpole and the Politics of the Early Years of the Reign of George III' in *Horace Walpole: Writer, Politician and Connoisseur*, ed. W.H. Smith, pp. 3–23.

[217] C.L. Becker, 'Horace Walpole's Memoirs of the Reign of George the Third' in *A.H.R.* 16 (1910–1911), pp. 255–272, 496–507. Cf. W.S. Lewis, *Horace Walpole*, London, 1961, pp. 83–84; and *Horace Walpole. Memoirs and Portraits*, ed. M. Hodgart, London, 1963, p. XXI.

[218] G.P. Judd IV, *Horace Walpole Memoirs*, New York, 1959.

[219] J. Brooke, *op. cit.*, p. 5.

the open enmity between Walpole and Fox, made Walpole automatically suspect in the eyes of the Whigs.[220] They could depend on Walpole's historiography only in part; the Whigs of the 19th century turned for guidance and inspiration not primarily to Walpole's *Memoirs* but to the ones that Rockingham had written. Walpole's views, which were far too 'factionist' in character, lacked all those important elements which rendered the period under discussion so meaningful to the 19th century. His descriptions were far too 'debunking' to be used in the 'finalistic' Whig view.

There is little point in making a chronological summary of the many authors who took part in the discussion on George III in the course of the 19th century. H. Butterfield has already made an inventarization of this kind. Without a deeper analysis of the political context within which the discussion took place, such a summary is bound to be unsatisfactory and insufficient. The 'principle of ministerial responsibility' is essential for this political context.[221] It was this principle that proved to be so difficult in realization, retaining uncertain and experimental traits even in the 19th century. This same principle was attacked by Tories until well into the 19th century, and it was also this principle to which the period now under discussion owed its direct political importance. Constitutionally, the gradual realization of this principle implied that the monarchical ideas of the *ancien régime* were definitely discarded. Was a tendency towards this principle already evidenced in the constitutional development of the second half of the 18th century?

For convenience's sake we would divide the George III debates of the 19th century into two main themes. The differences between Tories and Whigs centred around a) whether affairs of state had been conducted in a 'constitutional' way since 1760, and b) the character of the King. The first point was by far the most important; it dominated the discussions at least until 1860.

In fact, what made this period historically relevant according to the moderate Whig G.C. Lewis, centred on this very point. He held that 'constitutional' behaviour for the King meant, concretely, that the King had to defer to majority opinion in the House of Commons. Governments had to give an account of themselves to the Commons, not to the King; should a majority in the Commons declare itself

[220] Cf. L.B. Seeley, *Horace Walpole and His World*, London, 1895, pp. 18–21; G.O. Trevelyan, *op. cit*, pp. 130–131.
[221] Cf. O. Anderson, *A Liberal State at War*, London, 1967, p. 31.

against a sitting government, such a government would have no option but to stand down on behalf of a government of the opposition.[222]

The first manifestation of these concepts were already in evidence in the latter decades of the 18th century, according to Lewis. They were to become generally accepted in the 19th century. In the fifties Lewis's historical attention was wholly taken up with this 'positive' contribution of the former century. His interest in the minor elements of the Whig myth was limited. He dismissed only the popular myth of Bute's remaining influence.[223] The one opponent with which this Whig entered into polemics was the moderate Tory historian Lord Mahon, who saw no fundamental political difference between Whigs and Tories after 1760.[224] Lewis believed that the Whig Lords, all their factions notwithstanding, gradually began to form a recognizable political unity after 1760, identifiable by their common slogan "that the King was to reign without governing."[225] There was a pretentiousness about this – in Mahon's view a serious Whig attempt to seize power – which infuriated the King so much that his dislike of the Whig Lords could be attributed to it.

Like all Whig historiography Lewis's explanation is built on a concept from a later period and might therefore be termed a characteristically Whig approach to the past. We should bear in mind, however, that Lewis never mentioned a 'Stuart-absolutism' which the King might be trying to restore. Neither was there any mention of an old principle from 1688 being damaged and renewed. Lewis was concerned with a new principle, which had first been formulated hesitantly just after 1760. In the eighties it began to gain clarity, both in word and deed. "It was not, in fact, definitely and clearly established until the year 1784, that where there is a conflict between the personal opinions of the sovereign and those of a majority of the House of Commons, the latter, and not the former, is to prevail."[226]

[222] G.C. Lewis, 'Lord John Russell's Memorials of Mr. Fox and the Buckingham Papers' in *E.R.* 99 (1854), p. 12 (on the 1779 situation); cf. pp. 46–47 on Fox's behaviour in 1783; as to G.C. Lewis, both personally and his work, see note 99; further, also E. Head, 'Sir George Cornewall Lewis on Forms of Government' in *E.R.* 118 (1863), pp. 138–166; K.E. Bock, 'History and a science of Man: an appreciation of George Cornewall Lewis' in *Journal of the History of Ideas* 12 (1951), pp. 599–608. Cf. A. Momigliano, *Studies in Historiography*, London, 1966, p. 63.

[223] G.C. Lewis in *E.R.* 99 (1854), p. 5 (note).

[224] Lord Mahon, *History of England. From the Peace of Utrecht to the Peace of Versailles, 1713–1783*, Leipzig, 1853, V, pp. 117–119; see on the significance of his work, A.F. Pollard in *D.N.B.* and H. Butterfield, *op. cit.*, pp. 93–95.

[225] G.C. Lewis, 'Modern English History' in *E.R.* 103 (1856), pp. 305–357, particularly pp. 308, 313–314.

[226] G.C. Lewis in *E.R.* 99 (1854), p. 58; cf. *E.R.* 103 (1856), p. 313 (note); '1784' lost

Lewis characterized English history from the end of the American War of Independence until the beginning of William Pitt's long supremacy as "full of instruction with respect to the working of our Parliamentary Constitution."[227] It was instructive not only to the political leaders of England, but even more so to the leaders of some continental countries. On the continent the modern parliamentary system was in danger of being discredited through ill-advised experimentation. The constitutional system, complete with hereditary monarchy and parliamentary-ministerial responsibility, was not the exclusive privilege of the Anglo-Saxon 'race' as depicted by those who tried to explain the continental failures. 'Race' did not enter into it: "the failure of the late attempts may, as it seems to us, be completely explained by the neglect of those precautions which an intelligent study of the history of England during the reign of George the Third is calculated to suggest."[228]

Actually, Lewis managed to skip the furious polemics on this subject between Whigs and Tories. He gave the period, in his historical-political reflections, a topical importance reaching far beyond the frontiers of the United Kingdom. The principle of parliamentary ministerial responsibility, so essential to modern states and to the monarchy, needed several decades to take shape in England, whereas the 'continent' had in 1848 attempted to acquire it at a moment's notice, as the mandate of a 'paper constitution.' Again the advantages of a 'naturally grown' constitution to a 'ready-made' one were plain.

Not every author around 1850 had the same non-polemical style of writing. In 1852 the *Edinburgh Review* and the *Quarterly Review* were at loggerheads about the meaning of George III's reign. Was Lewis justified in his historical and political optimism? Since 1832 the boundary line separating parties had gained in clarity, much of which it lost again after 1846. The fifties were so full of governmental changes and coalitions, that it was very hard indeed to form a majority government. Parliament found it harder to function properly under those circumstances, and Gladstone – in his analysis about the increasing 'inefficiency' of Parliament – stated that parliament sadly failed in its legis-

---

significance by the many changes of government in the early 19th century. See his later articles: 'The Addington and Pitt Administrations' in *E.R.* 107 (1858), pp. 134–172, and 'The Grenville, Portland and Perceval Administrations' in *E.R.* 108 (1858), pp. 299–343.

[227] G.C. Lewis in *E.R.* 99 (1854), p. 58.

[228] *Ibid.*, p. 60.

lative duties as well as in calling the government to account.[229] Government was far from being stable, and the lack of clarity gave the factions a new lease of life, which in turn meant that the instability forced the monarch to take matters in his own hands more than would be the case normally. Thus was the situation when the Tory Coulton described and analysed in the *Quarterly Review* the meaning of the first ten years of George III's reign.[230]

His argument is somewhat odd, even paradoxical at first sight, for this conservative author accepted several aspects of the Whig view, using them to build the most favourable image possible of George III. Again ministerial responsibility was at the heart of the argument. Because he had a deepseated dislike of 'that mischievous principle (from which France in our own day has reaped such infinite misfortune),' *le roi règne, et ne gouverne pas* – which the Whigs had made into a political dogma very early in the 18th century – his admiration for George III grew apace.[231] It was George who had tried to stop the Whigs weakening the monarchy. He saw the King as the great 'purifier' of a 'factious' and corrupt political system, the man who retrieved the monarchy from discredit, the saviour combating revolutionary anarchy. "To him, under God, we may attribute our escape from that terrible trial which France had to encounter – a trial which is yet racking every fibre and nerve of her frame – and the preservation of that Constitution under which (though since damaged) it is still our happiness to live."[232] The final passage of Coulton's 'historical' contribution leaves no doubt that it was written in order to inflict a blow on the Whigs of his time (Russell's 'small factions'), which he called 'the worst foes of the Monarchy and the Nation.'[233]

It was not long before reactions from the other side became felt. Three months afterwards W.B. Donne published an article in the *Edinburgh Review*, reviewing and recommending the *Rockingham Me-*

[229] W.E. Gladstone, 'The Declining Efficiency of Parliament' in *Q.R.* 99 (1856), pp. 521–570.

[230] D.T. Coulton, 'First Decade of George III' in *Q.R.* 90 (1852), pp. 503–543; cf. H. Butterfield, *op. cit.*, p. 136 ff.

[231] D.T. Coulton in *Q.R.* 90 (1852), p. 510, note: "This phrase though commonly ascribed to M. Thiers, and adopted as the 'dogma' of his Cabinet of 1832, is of much older date ... there can be no doubt that it originated with our Whigs, and was transplanted from this country to pave the way for the triumph of republicanism in France. It is a pity that our neighbours will borrow from our constitutional system only the evils which are incident to it."

[232] *Ibid.*, p. 543.

[233] See for the unfortunate political situation in the Whig group: D. Southgate, *op. cit.*, p. 193 ff., and N. Gash, *Reaction and Reconstruction in English Politics, 1832–1852*, Oxford, 1965, pp. 157–200, particularly p. 192 ff.

moirs as the Bible for the 19th-century Whigs.[234] True: the 18th-century Whigs were far from being politically spotless, but still the Rockingham-faction was *sui generis* – as Macaulay and others had concluded before. The author Donne described Rockingham as 'the most constitutional minister of his age.'[235] Not the King – 'the new Pharaoh' – but Rockingham was 'a purist in principle, in an age of almost universal corruption.'[236] Donne never hesitated to stress the antithesis between the 'constitutional' Rockingham and the 'unconstitutional' George III; the denigrating elements of the stories regarding the King's Jacobite education – his attempt to restore Stuart-absolutism – were therefore asserted to be true, in imitation of the earl of Albemarle, George Thomas, who had edited the publication.[237] That Donne thought 1765 (the first Rockingham ministry) important is apparent in his words: "For the first time in his life probably George the Third was confronted with a minister who set candidly before him his proper functions, his official duties, the time's abuse, and its remedies, and who met his vision of a Patriot King by the *waking reality of a Constitutional Monarch*."[238] Donne, extremism and all, in this instance only mentions the budding reality of a limited constitutional monarchy in the modern sense.

It seemed that in 1852 the gap between the Tory and Whig ways of evaluating the constitutional development after 1760 and the personality of George III was so wide, that there was no possible hope for a reconciliation, not even after the many sources published in the preceding years.

Still a somewhat milder note, surprisingly, begins to prevail in the following decades; a renewal of strife with intensified contrasts is not seen until the late seventies. First there was a tentative reconciliation: the Whig version was gaining ground as far as the constitutional aspects were concerned,[239] but what the Tories lost on this count was partly remedied by a growing liberal understanding for the King's character. Lacking the derogatory comments about his character (as for instance

[234] W.B. Donne, 'The Marquis of Rockingham and his Contemporaries' in *E.R.* 96 (1852), pp. 110–142.

[235] *Ibid.*, p. 124.

[236] *Ibid.*, p. 123.

[237] *Ibid.*, pp. 116–119; notwithstanding the fact that 'it was unsafe to put trust in Walpole' (p. 114).

[238] *Ibid.*, p. 130 (our emphasis).

[239] Cf. H. Butterfield, *op. cit.*, p. 155; G.R. Crosby, 'George III: Historians and a Royal Reputation' in *Essays in Modern English History in honour of W.C. Abbott*, Cambridge, Mass., 1941, pp. 295–313, particularly p. 303.

by J. Russell or Macaulay), even the conservatives could accept the constitutional Whig version of this period more or less, since the principle of ministerial responsibility was no longer under discussion, but generally accepted as a normal part of the constitution. The discussion on the King's character, which was our second theme, became a central topic during the sixties.

Butterfield pointed out that W.N. Massey's work was moderately Whig in character.[240] It is true that the general trend of his work is Whig, especially his representation of the King's deliberate attempt to introduce a more absolutist form of government. Yet he managed to free himself of several Whig aspects, even going so far as to criticize them sharply. In this respect his review of the first part of T.E. May's *Constitutional History*, from 1861, is enlightening.[241] Burke had, in 1770, created the myth of a 'double cabinet': Massey dismissed this categorically as a complete fiction.[242] In his characterization the government was too 'monarchical' during the first ten years, yet he would not hear of any analogy with the Stuart absolutism, this being unhistorical.[243] The King behaved in an unconstitutional way, but did not infringe the letter of the law. "His conduct was unconstitutional and productive of great calamity to his people, but it was strictly within the bounds of the law."[244] He finished with an eulogy on Prince Albert, who had died in that same year; the Prince might have definitely favoured certain political conceptions, but he had never once demeaned himself (as George III had) by using underhand methods in order to force the government to accede to his views.[245] We will have more to say about Massey and about Prince Albert in the final passages of this section. Massey's judgment of the King as a person remained unfavourable, notwithstanding all his marked criticism of the Whig version.

Another proof of the improved climate is the reaction of the *Quarterly Review* to Massey's work. The review is written by the economist H. Merivale, politically a 'staunch liberal' as Leslie Stephen was to put it

    [240] H. Butterfield, *op. cit.*, pp. 144–150.
    [241] W.N. Massey, 'May's Constitutional History of England' in *E.R.* 115 (1862), pp. 211–242; see for T.E. May also H. Butterfield, *op. cit.*, p. 151 ff.
    [242] W.N. Massey in *E.R.* 115 (1862), p. 220.
    [243] *Ibid.*, p. 223.
    [244] *Ibid.*, p. 224, cf. p. 226.
    [245] *Ibid.*, p. 241.

later on.[246] The pointedly Tory reaction, therefore, sounded improbable coming from him, but for all his liberal opinions he was not a Whig. He praised Massey for being impartial, with the single restriction that the King, as a person, had been wronged.[247] On the whole he agreed to the constitutional Whig interpretation: unfortunately the King had been mistaken when he tried both to govern and to reign. Where the extremist Whig historians had been mistaken when condemning him for this, was in not realizing how new 'the principle of Royal impersonality' still was in 1760. "We believe that George III was in this matter wholly in the wrong, and that one of the greatest blessings arising from his reign was the victory obtained in it against his own opposition, by the contrary principle under which we are now governed. But we think that those who condemn him personally, on account of it, scarcely do justice to the novelty of that principle."[248]

Next the naïve anachronism in the extreme Whig view was attacked:

There used to be a class of Whigs – there are some very respectable remnants of it still – who seemed to consider 'Revolution Principles' as something co-eval with human society and 'implanted' in it by the eternal fitness of things; who estimated all times past by this measure alone, and judged Julius Caesar, Thomas à Becket, Queen Elisabeth, and Catherine the Great, according to their several deviations from the established canon of Whiggery. But if we abandon this compendious mode of reasoning, we shall find that the principle of Royal impersonality was, as yet, in 1760, in the course of development only.[249]

The tentative beginning of this principle in the first half of the 18th century notwithstanding, the liberal Merivale made a point of stating: "At the accession of George III not only was the theory unrecognised, but the practice had fallen into disfavour."[250] The constitutional aspect no longer came first for Merivale; his chief concern was with the character of the King.

The Whigs could never understand the King's hatred of Fox. Was it just the foolish stupidity of a narrow-minded 'tyrant' towards a 'genius' like Fox, 'the friend of the people?' Merivale believed that one could understand the King's dislike being so intense, since it had no constitutional cause, but a personal one. The King, a careful man, saw the licentious Fox as the man whose dissipations had turned the King's

[246] H. Merivale, 'George III and Charles James Fox' in *Q.R.* 105 (1859), pp. 463–504; cf. L. Stephen in *D.N.B.* vol. 37 (London, 1894), pp. 280–281.

[247] H. Merivale in *Q.R.* 105 (1859), pp. 465–466, 487 ff.

[248] *Ibid.*, p. 485.

[249] *Ibid.*, pp. 485–486.

[250] *Ibid.*, p. 486.

son from the right path. Some ten years later in Merivale's review of
the just published correspondence between George III and Lord
North the same theme was again central.[251]

Undoubtedly the gradual publication after 1860 of the correspondence of the long-reviled and criticised monarch was a great help in
revaluating the King's character. The letters corrected the bad image
built up from the numerous sources published in earlier decades. The
indefatigable historian Lord Mahon had already, in his biography of
Pitt the Younger, published various important letters. Robert Cecil,
the later Lord Salisbury, when reviewing the first parts of this biography, remarked on the growing tendency to revaluate George III's
personality; the letters printed by Mahon were in this respect 'the most
interesting part' of the whole work.[252]

About the relationship between George III and Fox, Cecil and
Merivale thought alike. Cecil, however, was much more ruthless in
condemning the Whigs for extolling Fox as a 'second Hampden.' "A
political party who for the last thirty years have been powerful in politics and still more powerful in literature, being afflicted with a scarcity of heroes, have centred all their hero-worship on this single image.
This political canonization has effected transformations in history as
strange as any that were ever perpetrated by any *Acta Sanctorum.*"[253]
The conservative Cecil also accepted the principle of parliamentary
ministerial responsibility, but he thought that a historical analysis
should take the fact into account, that neither in the past (under
George III) nor in the present (under Victoria) this principle had
ever been fully realized, nor ever could have been. "Our theory, as it
stands, is that the Sovereign exerts all the power of the executive, while
his minister bears all the responsibility ... Of course in its literal sense
this never has been true, and never can be ... No minister has ever yet
succeeded in pushing this claim so far as to reduce the Sovereign to a
mere cypher."[254]

[251] *Ibid.*, p. 474 ff. and H. Merivale, 'Character of George III' in *Q.R.* 122 (1867), pp.
281–310, particularly p. 295 ff.
[252] R. Cecil, 'Lord Stanhope's Life of Pitt' in *Q.R.* 109 (1861), pp. 531–565, particularly
pp. 533–534, 553; for Cecil's political as well as historical thought see *Lord Salisbury on Politics:
A Selection from his articles in the Quarterly Review, 1860–1883*, ed. P. Smith, Cambridge, 1972.
Mahon's work on Pitt was reviewed in the *Edinburgh Review* by H. Reeve; although his review
was moderately appreciative his correspondence with Brougham reveals that he actually
agreed with the latter's sharp criticism (see *Memoirs of the Life and Correspondence of Henry
Reeve*, ed. J.K. Laughton, London, 1893, II, pp. 83–84).
[253] R. Cecil in *Q.R.* 109 (1861), p. 553.
[254] R. Cecil, 'Stanhope's Life of Pitt' in *Q.R.* 111 (1862), pp. 516–561, quotation pp.
518–519.

At last, in 1867, a sizable part of the King's correspondence was brought to light: the letters of George III to Lord North. Donne, the same author mentioned earlier, published them and wrote an introduction. He, too, had by that time lost his extremist tendencies; the views mirrored in the introduction are moderately Whig.[255] The King is still depicted as being badly brought up and behaving unconstitutionally, but theories like Bute's lasting influence after 1763 are no longer considered feasible. The opinions of the *Edinburgh Review* and the *Quarterly Review* about Donne's publication hardly differed in 1867. They both saw the unmistakably unconstitutional behaviour of the King very clearly, but they also agreed that those elements of the Whig views which had done so much to discredit the King as a person, were untrue and lying fabrications. We might say that even the Whigs could now dispense with slanderous allegations of that kind, since their constitutional version of George III's period apparently had gained general acceptance.[256]

About a decade later the new-found equilibrium between Whigs and Tories was to be unexpectedly and rudely lost by the old constitutional debate taking on a vigorous new lease of life. This happened during the last years of Disraeli's government, at the same time when G.O. Trevelyan once more propagated the Whig view in his *Early History of Charles James Fox*.[257] Once more the *Edinburgh Review* and the *Quarterly Review* were at loggerheads with one another on this subject; for the last time the period of George III was the direct inspiration for political strife. Among the many factors contributing to this renewal was the publication of Th. Martin's biography (in several parts) about Prince Albert. Another was Disraeli's 'arbitrary' foreign policy; certain liberal Whigs noticed that his relationship to the Queen seemed suspiciously like a violation of the constitution. The background to this was the Eastern question, which after 1875 had again been one of the foremost problems in foreign policy.[258] It was because of this, according to

[255] Cf. H. Butterfield, *op. cit.*, pp. 166–168. *George III's Letters to Lord North, from 1768 to 1783*, ed. W. Bodham Donne, 2 vols., London, 1867.

[256] Cf. C.J. Bayley, 'The Early Administrations of George III' in *E.R.* 126 (1867), pp. 1–43, particularly p. 7: "We shall see in the review of these letters the unconstitutional views which he held of the Royal prerogative. . . . But starting from these premises, it is unnecessary to import into the King's conduct the elements of intrigue, duplicity, or falsehood."

[257] Cf. H. Butterfield, *op. cit.*, pp. 166–168; G.M. Trevelyan, *Sir George Otto Trevelyan*, London, 1932, p. 103.

[258] For general information see R. Blake, *Disraeli*, London, 1969, p. 575 ff.; cf. W.E. Gladstone's noted reviews printed in his *Gleanings of Past Years*, London, 1879, I, pp. 23–130.

Reeve, that the third part of Martin's biography of Prince Albert became 'a political affair' upon its publication.[259] This book gave Prince
Albert's views on the Eastern question at the time of the Crimean war.
What he had thought then was what the Queen now believed. Martin's
researches proved that the allegations made against the Prince during
the Crimean War were totally unfounded.[260] The highest praise
which Reeve could give the Prince Consort in 1878, was that since
1853 he had become a typical Englishman: "He was English to the
core."[261] This was especially true for his attitude concerning the
British constitution; it was here that he had shed his German origins
and German education. He had discarded the 'absolutist' theories of
his teacher Stockmar.

The first three parts of Martin's biographical work resulted in an
article in the *Quarterly Review* called: "The Crown and the Constitution."[262] The writer was W.J. Courthope, who paid little attention to
the contents of the recent biography about the Prince Consort. The
article was mainly a protest by a conservative against the Liberal's
allegations of 'unconstitutionality' in the Disraeli government. He attacked a pamphlet, entitled *The Crown and the Constitution* and signed
with the pseudonym 'Verax.'[263] It accused Disraeli of having an 'unconstitutional' relationship with the Queen; it suggested that governmental affairs were backsliding into the situation of a 100 years ago,
the period of George III. It represented Stockmar as a second Lord
Bute and insisted that his authoritarian-absolutist theories were not
dead. Courthope did not stop at a simple denial; on the contrary, he
believed that the Crown and the Executive should have more power,
frightening as this was for the liberal Whigs. He thought it was inevitable and highly necessary, considering the growing lack of competence
in the Commons after their 'usurpation' of power. Courthope's article
was one of many articles on the 'crisis of the House of Commons' that
abounded in many periodicals towards the end of the century. (We
will see more of these in the next chapter.) He made no bones about
hating 'party-government,'[264] and was equally clear in his more con-

[259] H. Reeve, 'Third Volume of the Life of the Prince Consort' in *E.R.* 147 (1878), p. 144;
cf. also *Memoirs . . . of Henry Reeve*, II, pp. 256–257.
[260] H. Reeve in *E.R.* 147 (1878), pp. 145, 165; cf. O. Anderson, *op. cit.*, p. 154.
[261] H. Reeve in *E.R.* 147 (1878), p. 148 ff., quotation p. 150.
[262] W.J. Courthope, 'The Crown and the Constitution' in *Q.R.* 145 (1878), pp. 277–328;
cf. Gladstone's sharp reaction in the latter's *Gleanings*, I, p. 230.
[263] Cf. S. Low in 1904 about this once notorious pamphlet, in his *The Governance of England*, London, 1911, p. 271 (note).
[264] W.J. Courthope, 'Party Government' in *Q.R.* 147 (1879), pp. 264–292.

structive propositions. As parliament and people were hardly able to form an intelligent judgment about foreign affairs, it was up to the Sovereign (as outward representative of the nation) to deal with these things freely in cooperation with the Cabinet. The sacred principle of 'self-government' could only apply to home affairs.[265] Legislative initiatives were another task for the executive. Several of Courthope's colleagues supported his views, as they too wished to restore the real power of the Crown in order to solve the crisis.[266] The parliamentary crisis inspired many Tories with old-monarchical ideas.

Courthope's article, this 'Tory-manifesto' was immediately answered in the *Edinburgh Review*; not coincidentally the reply was written by an expert on George III whom we mentioned earlier, the historian W.N. Massey.[267] He was highly incensed; never since Stuart times had such misconceptions about the British constitution been publicized! Was it not very dangerous to allot an active role in foreign affairs to the Crown? Had not the period of George III taught us this very lesson? The fear for 'backsliding' into a situation like that during George III's reign was quite justified, as could be proved by the second part of Martin's biography of Albert, which had dealt with the political education and training of the Prince. With due respect for the Prince Consort "it is impossible" – Massey stated – "to disguise the fact that his Royal Highness took a more active part in public affairs than was convenient and becoming in one so highly placed."[268]

Baron Stockmar's constitutionalism was, according to Massey, a modern version of Bolingbroke's *The Idea of a Patriot King*. Massey had realized that Prince Albert had long adhered to this 'absolutism,' and now in 1878 he also realized that the conservative leader Disraeli had more in common with Stockmar than one might have thought.[269] He believed Courthope's article was significant for the constitutional way of thinking of the present government: it was a Tory manifesto. To this Courthope replied with a rather more moderate article, entitled 'The English Monarchy,' but in imitation of Prince Albert he stuck to the following description of the Sovereign: "the representative of his country, before foreign Powers, in all matters relating to war,

---

[265] W.J. Courthope in *Q.R.* 145 (1878), p. 298.
[266] Cf. A.St.J. Clerke, 'The Crown and the Army' in *Q.R.* 146 (1878), pp. 232–255.
[267] W.N. Massey, 'The Constitution and the Crown' in *E.R.* 148 (1878), pp. 262–294.
[268] *Ibid.*, p. 273.
[269] *Ibid.*, pp. 283–285, 290 ff.

peace and treaties."[270] This qualification went too far in the eyes of many, even conservatives; it was opposed to the spirit of the constitution and suggested an absolutism such as had never actually existed in modern England.[271]

Thus we see that Disraeli's governmental period, with a Whig-opposition, created a favourable climate for a revival of the myth about George III. To put it differently, the George III-myth was intensified by a similar new myth about Prince Albert. However: for the Victorian Whigs the George III-myth had not really been a myth. It had, temporarily, been actual fact, first in the person of Prince Albert and lastly in Disraeli impersonating a modern Bolingbroke. Possibly it was a 'mythical' misunderstanding on the part of the liberal Whigs who, as always, only could understand the present by means of the past. Still the romantic fuzziness and lack of clarity of Disraeli's constitutionalism (both in theory and practice) may have fostered this misunderstanding.[272]

H. Reeve, the editor of the *Edinburgh Review*, was highly pleased when the old controversy re-emerged:

Nothing is more beneficial to the two Reviews than a little controversy, especially when serious principles are concerned. This question is precisely the *crux* or test of Whig and Tory principles; it is the old fight of parliamentary power against prerogative. There has not been in England, for a hundred years, a minister so indifferent to Parliament and so subservient to the Court as Lord Beaconsfield.[273]

Reeve, a Whig, could not regard Disraeli's performance as Prime Minister in any other light: to him it was just a revival of a well-known 18th-century episode. We have often pointed out that, because of this far-sightedness about the past, Whigs suffered from short-sightedness in the present. Their anachronisms influenced their view on past and present, not the least on this matter about 1880. Clearly historical writings had to wait until this episode had lost its present-day relevance, before the 18th century could be understood in its own context, in its character of *ancien régime*. However, we must realize that the 19th century had not yet reached that point, nor could it have. Reading Bagehot's *English Constitution* – especially the chapter on the monarchy

---

[270] W.J. Courthope, 'The English Monarchy' in *Q.R.* 148 (1879), pp. 1–32, quotation p. 32.
[271] Cf. A. Hayward in *A Selection from the Correspondence of Abraham Hayward. From 1834 to 1884*, ed. H.E. Carlisle, London, 1886, II, pp. 302–303.
[272] Cf. R. Blake, *op. cit.*, pp. 547–548.
[273] *Memoirs . . . of Henry Reeve*, II, pp. 260–261.

– makes one realize that George III was very much alive to the Victorians in the sense that he embodied everything a constitutional monarch should not be. One of the critics of the Whig myth once remarked that the 19th-century Whig historians blamed George III for acting as one of the Stuarts, whereas he should have emulated Queen Victoria.[274]

However, simplifications like this are rare – even in Bagehot. Such simplifications may be didactically valuable, but they travesty a historical representation, whose reality for the 19th century should not be underrated. Without this myth the 'new' modern constitutional monarchy could not have come into being. Even under the 'ideal' Victoria the principle of 'impersonal Royalty' was still developing; even under this much extolled sovereign it had its 'ups and downs,' and it was said of the Queen that she was more prone to unconstitutional acts after her husband's death than before.[275] Was Victoria so very much an ideal? When the Whigs criticized Disraeli's 'unparliamentary and unconstitutional' ways, was not that criticism also aimed at her person? Was it just oppositional exaggeration to talk of a 'backsliding' into a George III-period, and was it really just an anachronistic delusion? It is easy to answer in the affirmative, when looking back, but in 1878–79 the *Quarterly Review* was still – under the pressure of a threatening parliamentary crisis – busily propagating a monarchical idea, completely contrary to the way the constitution had grown.

All these things have to be taken into account before speaking of 'myths' in the 19th-century conception of the 18th century. Otherwise we might well find ourselves creating our own myths, in this case concerning the 19th century. The 19th century had certain traits in common with the 18th and is farther from us than we sometimes realize.

A plea for an understanding of the particular character of earlier centuries also includes such an understanding of the 19th century. However, it is difficult to deny that 'short-sightedness' of the Whigs; their view of contemporary constitutional problems was coloured far more strongly by a traditionalist than by a truly historical consciousness. Of the principles of collective and individual ministerial respon-

---

[274] Cf. R. Sedgwick in *Letters from George III to Lord Bute*, p. VIII.

[275] Cf. C.H. Stuart, 'The Prince Consort and Ministerial Politics, 1856–1859' in *Essays in British History. Presented to Sir Keith Feiling*, ed. H.R. Trevor-Roper, London, 1964, p. 268: "The Prince was essentially rational and his influence on the Queen was always moderating. The Queen's letters became more emotional, less constitutional, perhaps also more interesting after his death in 1861."

sibility, the first became fact in the period 1830–1840, both in theory and practice. The second only became a fact around 1870. The principle of individual ministerial responsibility, at least in the second half of the century, was endangered more by an emerging Civil Service not yet politically 'neutralised' than by the monarch. The rise of the bureaucratic state was a new phenomenon threatening to disturb the tenability and feasability of the new principle. This problem, however, does not concern us here. It escaped the notice of the Whigs and many others as well. They saw only one danger to their constitutionalism: the danger that parliamentary and cabinet independence might be affected by overmuch Royal influence and prerogative. Only after the new officialdom had been made into an integral part of the State was it possible for a later administrative history to treat this problem with the attention it deserved.[276]

3) Cromwell and the Civil War

> The real corpus of thought uniting the middle class,
> or the Liberal section of it, was not a Benthamite,
> utilitarian, or natural-law view of the world, not
> American or economic principles, but something of
> a different order: a view or recollection of English
> history.
>
> (J. Vincent, 1966)

At the end of our observations on Macaulay we noticed that around 1850 there was a shift in the historical interest regarding the 17th century. In the second half of the 19th century, the period of the Puritan Revolution became much more popular; apparently its attraction surpassed that of the events in 1688 and the period of George III. The two latter subjects continued to hold the interest of the aristocratic parliamentary liberals, the increasing interest for the Civil War – culminating in a Cromwell-cult around 1900 – may partly be due to the rise of the English Liberal Party under Gladstone's leadership. The historian John Vincent has written an analysis of the rise of the Liberal Party in which he suggested that it arose as a 'community of sentiment.' 'History' is, plainly and explicitly, functioning as the ideological cornerstone of this 'party-formation' (in that phase much resembling a 'Ge-

---

[276] Cf. A.H. Birch, *Representative and Responsible Government*, London, 1964, pp. 131–149; G. Kitson Clark, 'Statesmen in Disguise: Reflexions on the History of the Neutrality of the Civil Service' in *The Historical Journal* 2 (1959), pp. 19–39.

meinschaft'), but in the main Vincent gives a more structural analysis.[277] Towards the end he summarizes the liberal wealth of ideas: for the reader a shocking confrontation with a liberalism that could hardly be more lacking in original political and economic conceptions.[278]

This poverty of ideas was veiled (or, if you will, compensated), by what later generations were to call a 'historical ballast.' Yet for the mid-Victorians the language of the past was still inspiring and useful. We should guard against the tendency to see the many 19th-century 'isms' as something abstract, in this case to reduce English liberalism to a *laissez faire* doctrine, or to identify it with a moderate utilitarianism.[279] Classic liberalism of course also contained several doctrinary elements of this kind, but support was above all looked for and found in the past. So very many different liberal groups were linked together by a historical opinion about a certain part of the past. As Vincent stated: "The really important attitudes had nothing to do with the industrial revolution, much to do with the English Civil War .... "[280] In the contemporary social and political context this use of history was not at all unimportant. In the next section, dealing with medieval studies, we shall find that it increased rather than decreased with the growth of modern state and society. The stronger the demand for change, the greater the apparent need to make history speak out as an authoritative source. The advantage of this was that many needed political adjustments could be labelled 'restorations.' The deceptive myth behind this political traditionalism was not unmasked until around 1900 when an increasing political realism began to discern the dangers, both for the past and the present, of an overly traditional view.

Before going into the historiography around Cromwell in the 19th century, we should point out that a subject like 'Cromwell and the Civil War in the 19th century' involves much more than just political liberalism. The work and personality of Thomas Carlyle provide a good example of this. 'Cromwell and the Civil War' include a great many of the problems connected with 'Victorianism' as a religious revival, especially puritanism and non-conformism, the striking hero-worship, etc. – a number of subjects in fact that we cannot do justice

[277] J. Vincent, *The Formation of the Liberal Party, 1857–1868*, London, 1966, pp. XXVIII-XXX, cf. on J. Bright, p. 163.

[278] *Ibid.*, pp. 141–253.

[279] Cf. O. Anderson's remark: "Too much attention has been paid to *laissez-faire* economics and utilitarian philosophy as sources of mid-nineteenth-century ideas about the proper function of the state, and too little to concepts of English history" (O. Anderson, *A Liberal State at War*, p. 129).

[280] J. Vincent, *op. cit.*, p. XXIX.

to here.[281] What is clear, however, is that the mid-Victorian period bears a striking resemblance to 17th-century puritanism, although interpreted in its own Victorian fashion. To quote W.B. Donne in 1860:

... it would be as incorrect to describe the present age as one of peculiar straitness in religion, as it is to impute to the Puritanism of the sixteenth and seventeenth centuries a universal spirit of gloom and ascetism. On the contrary, we are persuaded that if into any circle of respectable and intelligent English people in the year 1860 the Cavalier and Puritan of 1630 could be introduced, the former and not the latter would be out of place. A Puritan of the Miltonic stamp, a Sir Thomas Fairfax or a Colonel Hutchinson, would without much difficulty adopt the tone of modern English manners ... He would see religion affecting intimately, yet without ostentation, our daily life.[282]

As yet, to our knowledge, no exhaustive monograph has been written on the Cromwell-image in the 19th century; it is only quite recently that a more systematic approach to this subject has developed.[283] Conscious of these limitations, we attempt the following sketch. At first sight, the outlines of the picture seem clear: early in the century Cromwell was still a detested hypocrite. Through Carlyle, however, he becomes 'the most typical Englishman' in the work of S.R. Gardiner, at the end of the century. 1845, the date of *Cromwell's Letters and Speeches*, is by many authors considered to be the turning-point in this re-evaluation, yet at the end of the 19th century J.M. Robertson doubted that the effect of Carlyle's publications had been truly revolutionary. As we shall see, he was right in several respects.[284] First we must investigate what people generally thought in the first half of the 19th century about Cromwell and the Civil War.

The first decades of the century witnessed the publication of some works that were clearly written with the intention of correcting some of the unfavourable aspects attached to Cromwell- for instance, the

[281] Cf. a.o. W.E. Houghton, *The Victorian Frame of Mind*, London, 1957.

[282] W.B. Donne, 'The Youth of Milton' in *E.R.* 111 (1860), pp. 312–347, quotation p. 317; cf. on the idea of puritanism as sometimes broadly (and therefore positively) interpreted by some authors: J.G. Nelson, *The Sublime Puritan. Milton and the Victorians*, Madison, 1963, p. 95.

[283] Cf. T.W. Mason, 'Nineteenth-Century Cromwell' in *Past and Present* no. 40 (1968), pp. 187–191. Cf. P.J. van Winter, *Engeland en Cromwell*, Groningen 1939; J.P.D. Dunbabin, 'Oliver Cromwell's Popular Image in Nineteenth-Century England' in *Britain and the Netherlands*, vol. V, ed. J.S. Bromley and E.H. Kossmann, The Hague, 1975, pp. 141–163.

[284] J.M. Robertson, 'Cromwell and the Historians' in *The Reformer* (June/July 1899), pp. 334–345, 391–400, particularly p. 396.

image of him as a hypocrite, which Hume had widely propagated.[285] We already mentioned that some Whigs and Tories, during the debates on the first Reform Bill, began to think more favourably about Cromwell's politics, although their respective opinions about Cromwell still differed considerably. We shall begin by comparing two influential Whig historians.

Hallam, in his *Constitutional History of England*, clearly had reservations about the acts of the Long Parliament. Although some of their very first measures met with his approval, he strongly disapproved of the demands in the Grand Remonstrance. He characterized these as an unneccesary radicalization, sure to cause the Civil War. He sympathised not with people like Pym, but with constitutional royalists of the Falkland stamp. For Hallam the whole period of 1642–1660 could be omitted in a description of English constitutional development; none of the many experiments in this 'interim' period had any lasting effect.[286] Cromwell's personality did not in the least appeal to Hallam. The protector achieved some outward glory for the United Kingdom, but, according to Hallam, this could not be balanced with the arbitrary tyranny to which he had reduced his native country: Cromwell's despotism was worse than Charles I's absolutism.[287] In 1827 Hallam made the almost inevitable comparison with Napoleon, which was also unfavourable for Cromwell. Nor would he be convinced by the praise sometimes accorded to Cromwell because of his more swift and less partial administration of justice.[288]

His junior, Macaulay, protested against this derogatory picture. Before becoming renowned as *the* historian of 1688, Macaulay wrote a number of articles about people from the Civil War; he could hardly contain his youthful enthusiasm while writing these. In his very first essay, on Milton, he took to task the people who praised the 'Revolution' while condemning the 'Rebellion.'[289] He believed that the Long Parliament had more justification in opposing the King than had the members of the revolutionary Convention Parliament when they staged a similar opposition in 1688. The essay on Milton also has some high

[285] Cf. O. Cromwell (a descendant of the Family), *Memoirs of the Protector, Oliver Cromwell, and of his Sons, Richard and Henry*, 2 vols., London, 1829: equally R. Vaughan in the introduction of his book: *The Protectorate of Oliver Cromwell and The State of Europe during the Early Part of the Reign of Louis XIV*, 2 vols., London, 1839.

[286] H. Hallam, *The Constitutional History of England*, London, 1863, II, p. 150.

[287] *Ibid.*, II, pp. 263, 272 (note).

[288] *Ibid.*, II, pp. 253–254 (note), 264–265.

[289] T.B. Macaulay, *Critical and Historical Essays*, London, 1907, vol. I, p. 172.

praise for Cromwell.[290] Three years later Macaulay criticized especially Hallam's chapters on Cromwell and the Civil War. Hallam, like
the constitutional royalists of Charles I's time, did not fully realize how
dangerous the despotism of Charles would have been in 1641–42, if he
had had control over a standing army. For Macaulay, not only was
Cromwell to be preferred to Charles I, but compared to Napoleon,
Cromwell also emerged in a more favourable light.[291]

In his famous Hampden essay of 1831 Macaulay repeated his arguments, stressing that the Long Parliament had acted rightly, and that
Cromwell's good intentions were praiseworthy.[292] Hampden had discovered that Cromwell had considerable talents, be it 'under an ex-
terior appearance of coarseness and extravagance.' Although Macaulay had a not unfavourable opinion of Cromwell, yet most people sympathised in the years before and during the first Reform Bill far more
with Hampden's character and behaviour (witness the many Hampden
Clubs) than with Cromwell's. While Hampden was in every respect a
'legendary' person, Cromwell's legend had still to be made.[293] Hampden embodied everything one could wish for in a crisis like the Civil
War or the first Reform Bill. In Macaulay's words:

... in Hampden, and in Hampden alone, were united all the qualities
which, at such a crisis, were necessary to save the State, the valour and
energy of Cromwell, the discernment and eloquence of Vane, the humanity
and moderation of Manchester, the stern integrity of Hale, the ardent
public spirit of Sydney.[294]

Macaulay's views hardly changed at all in later years. In his *History*
too he emphasized Cromwell's honesty, administrative ability and dis-
patch. Cromwell still was 'the man of 1832'; his reign could be characterized as moderately despotic, "moderated only by the wisdom, the
sobriety, and the magnanimity of the despot."[295] Macaulay again
found himself in opposition to Hallam when remarking on two
strikingly 'liberal' aspects of Cromwell's reign: the purity of justice and
the growth of religious tolerance. Neither Milton nor Cromwell were,
in Macaulay's view, puritans in the strict sense of the word. He was

---

[290] *Ibid.*, I, pp. 175, 182–183.
[291] *Ibid.*, I, pp. 25–37, 49–54.
[292] *Ibid.*, I, pp. 142–143.
[293] Cf. Esmé Wingfield-Stratford, *Truth in Masquerade*, London, 1951, pp. 129–130. Cf.
also the Hampden-article by C.H. Firth in *D.N.B.*, vol. XXIV (London, 1890), pp. 254–
262.
[294] T.B. Macaulay, *op. cit.*, I, p. 148.
[295] T.B. Macaulay, *The History of England*, I, p. 111.

no 'warlike saint' or 'zealot,' or even 'zealous republican': "the sentiments of Cromwell were widely different."[296]

A new emphasis is found in 1848 in Macaulay's statement that Cromwell was to be regarded as a level-headed statesman, formed by practical experience, and bearing not the least resemblance to a religious dreamer.[297] Macaulay wrote comparatively little about the Civil War, but what he did write was noticeably favourable, notwithstanding his lack of understanding for religious puritanism. For Macaulay however, Cromwell was far from a religiously inspired leader and that is precisely where Macaulay and Carlyle differed.[298]

Whereas Macaulay did not allow himself to be influenced by Carlyle's views, Carlyle's friend and colleague, the historian John Forster, certainly did. Forster's first book about the Civil War period was published as early as 1839, and used terms like 'impostor' and 'traitor' to characterize Cromwell.[299] Carlyle revealed the 'true' Cromwell to him: a man, chosen by God, ". . . a man whose very thought was with the Eternal."[300] Forster's version in this respect is an apt illustration of the way in which Carlyle revolutionized the image of Cromwell for the 19th century. As early as 1840 (in his lectures on 'heroes and hero-worship') he objected to 'Hume and the mass of his followers.' But Carlyle was not the first to reject the image of Cromwell as a hypocrite, for among those who had done so earlier was Macaulay.[301] However Carlyle did more than just demolish this image, an heirloom from an unbelieving 18th century which he detested; he rescued Cromwell from narrow-minded party-historiography, for he depicted the Civil War as part of a more general worldwide struggle between Belief and Unbelief.[302]

"The view which the present generation takes of Cromwell is no longer a party view," wrote J.R. Seeley in 1868: "it seems to me that Cromwell is still the only man of the period who has fairly emerged from the mist of advocacy and abuse. He has taken his permanent

---

[296] *Ibid.*, I, p. 107, cf. p. 112.

[297] *Ibid.*, I, p. 102.

[298] Cf. J.M. Robertson's remark: "The pro-Cromwellian reaction, such as it was, was probably as much the work of Macaulay as of Carlyle, . . ." (*op. cit.*, p. 397).

[299] Cf. C.H. Firth, *Oliver Cromwell and the Rule of the Puritans in England*, Oxford, 1968 (with an introduction of G.M. Young), p. 468.

[300] J. Forster, 'The Civil Wars and Cromwell' in *E.R.* 103 (1856), pp. 1–54, quotation p. 15.

[301] Cf. also J. Allen in *E.R.* 76 (1838), pp. 415–435, especially pp. 424, 435, and in *E.R.* 67 (1838), pp. 103–122, esp. pp. 121–122.

[302] Cf. T. Carlyle, *Heroes, Hero-worship and the Heroic in History*, London, 1841 ch. 6.

place in the national imagination...."[303] Seeley rightly attributed this to Carlyle's revolution. Several of the more 'extreme' members of the Long Parliament remained subjects of strife between Whigs and Tories, but the religiously inspired Cromwell had admirers in both camps. "Cromwell himself, we firmly believe, was honest at the outset," was what W. Elwin, at the time editor of the *Quarterly Review*, wrote in 1856.[304] It was also Carlyle's Cromwell who, in the liberal camp, was to seal the 'Gladstonian Liberalism.' It was his Cromwell, not the Whig Macaulay's Cromwell, who inspired the nonconformist liberals with enthusiasm, notwithstanding the fact that some aspects of Macaulay's view retained their force until the end of the century. Trevelyan, discussing Carlyle's great efforts towards the study of the Civil War, declared in 1899 that the Whigs of 1832 had not been able to understand the Civil War in its essential character. For many of the early 19th-century Tories the puritans were only 'Jacobins,' and the Whigs thought the Civil War was not more than a constitutional-financial event: 'a matter of pounds, shillings, pence, and civil liberty,' a fight for freedom, whose favourable outcome was hindered by fanatics. "Men had not fully perceived what we all know so well today, that the Pyms and Hampdens were themselves of the 'fanatic' class; that the Protestant faith inspired and led them in all they did...."[305] Their fight against the Stuarts had been a religious fight from the very beginning.

Since Carlyle, mankind knew that Cromwell had been a far greater personality than the 'practical' man Macaulay had seen in him. The 'misconceptions' of the 18th century proved that Cromwell could be understood only by 'believers.' This was the hidden meaning of Carlyle's historical message in 1840, and even more so in 1845. In the second half of the 19th century Cromwell became a 'national hero' in the deepest sense of the word ... for believers. Carlyle had 'proved' that Cromwell could not be fitted into the existing conservative or liberal patterns.

For Carlyle, with his unconstitutional or even anti-constitutional views, it was irrelevant that Cromwell had failed on the parliamentary-constitutional level; his greatness did not lie in Westminster. Yet his greatness was to be honoured, just before the beginning of the twentieth

---

[303] J.R. Seeley, *Lectures and Essays*, London, 1895, pp. 98–99.
[304] W. Elwin, 'Causes of the Civil War' – Mr. Guizot' in *Q.R.* 99 (1856), pp. 105–159, quotation p. 113.
[305] G.M. Trevelyan, 'Carlyle as an Historian' in *Nineteenth Century* 46 (1899), pp. 493–503, quotation p. 502.

century, with a statue in Westminster though not until after endless discussion about the fitness of placing it there.[306] Already in 1845 the Frenchman A. Thiers had been surprised by the absence of such a statue; yet for a long time afterwards many conservatives as well as liberals worried whether a statue would not be too much of a good thing in the current rehabilitation of Cromwell.[307] Carlyle might have cleared Cromwell's character, but still the man's despotism could not be easily overlooked.

This very despotism would be the main subject of the first important publication after Carlyle's *Cromwell's Letters and Speeches*, i.e. F. Guizot's study of the English Civil War. The parts that deal with Cromwell were published in 1854. Thanks to a translation, published in the same year and entitled *Life of Oliver Cromwell*, many English readers could become acquainted with his views. Guizot's study of Cromwell showed his unusual talent for objectivity. His Cromwell was not a 19th-century liberal, hypocrite or zealot, but only an able dictator, a man who kept his balance on the ruins of the revolution by swift reactions to changing situations, thus not only keeping but even consolidating his position.

Guizot was, no doubt, even in his historical writings, a religious calvinist, but he was not convinced by a religiously inspired Cromwell. Carlyle's view and approach did not agree with Guizot's ideal of a historiography composed of rational explanation. "The men whom God chooses as the instruments of his great designs are full of contradiction and of mystery."[308] This is his religious-historical expression of faith. It was no obstacle to his attempt to depict Oliver Cromwell's deeds in as understandable and logical terms as he possibly could. His biographer, D. Johnson, says: "Guizot's study of the English Revolution was a study in the logic of revolutions." One might add that his study of Cromwell was a study in 'the logic of dictatorship.'[309] Guizot pictured Cromwell as a modern dictator, who never missed a chance for making political capital out of every conceivable situation. Cromwell knew when to flatter and when to strike.[310] His religious or political principles were far from fixed or unshakable: "no mind could have been less systematic than his, but he had an unerring instinct of

---

[306] Cf. G.M. Trevelyan, *An Autobiography and other Essays*, London, 1949 pp. 158–178.

[307] For A. Thiers, see *A Seclection from the Correspondence of Abraham Hayward. From 1834 to 1884*. Ed. H.E. Carlisle, London, 1886, vol. I, pp. 108–109.

[308] F. Guizot, *Life of Oliver Cromwell*, London, 1899, p. 1.

[309] D. Johnson, *Guizot. Aspects of French History, 1787–1874*, London, 1963, pp. 352–364, particularly pp. 359–364.

[310] F. Guizot, *op. cit.*, p. 31.

popular feelings and wishes; and without much caring to inquire how far they were legitimate or capable of satisfaction, he boldly became their patron, in order to make them his allies."[311] Cromwell, "always full of consideration for the opinions of the men of whom he had to make use,"[312] waited for the right moment before undertaking more severe measures; sometimes he even created this moment by allowing his opponents or not-too-willing adherents to make mistakes that furnished him with the necessary excuses for despotic intervention.[313]

Guizot's picture of Cromwell was unacceptable to many English liberals such as J. Forster. Actually Forster was deeply disappointed in Guizot's interpretation, for Cromwell's ever-present religious inspiration (so clearly evidenced in Carlyle) was here sadly absent; yet it and it alone justified Cromwell's attitude, and unified his actions. While Forster had been converted by Carlyle, Guizot had not.[314] Despite Forster's criticisms Guizot was adamant. He wrote to H. Reeve in 1856:

I persist in thinking my 'Cromwell' truer than his and I am glad that you are of my opinion. The longer I live the more I am convinced that to understand revolutions and revolutionists, one must have lived in the midst of them. Seen from afar, they are rearranged and recast at will, to suit or confirm our preconceived ideas of history or art. I have often reproached our French republicans and revolutionists with loving the republic better than liberty and revolution better than the republic. I might also say the same of Mr. Forster. He pardons everything – even actions the most illiberal and iniquitous – in the leaders of the Rump, because they were Republicans; and in Cromwell, even the destruction of the Republic, because he was the great leader of the Revolution. I wish to be more liberal and more consistent.[315]

Whatever Reeve's approval of Guizot may be worth, generally speaking English historiography about Cromwell in the second half of the 19th century preferred Carlyle's line of reasoning to Guizot's with a few isolated exceptions to be dealt with further on. Later, G.M. Young dared state that "the Cromwell of Gardiner and Firth is in all essentials the Cromwell of Carlyle."[316] The two latter historians expounded their views noticeably soberly and matter-of-factly, much more so than did the authors of second-rank literature in those years.

[311] *Ibid.*, p. 184.
[312] *Ibid.*, p. 263.
[313] *Ibid.*, p. 290. Cf. further pp. 43, 88, 90, 179, 182, 216, 244, 268, 280.
[314] Cf. J. Forster's remark: "Mr. Guizot thinks his mind was great, because it was just, perspicacious, and thoroughly practical; but of this greatness he does not find that religion formed any essential part, or contributed to it in any material way" (*op. cit.*, p. 36).
[315] *Memoirs of . . . Henry Reeve*, I, p. 343.
[316] G.M. Young in C.H. Firth, *op. cit.*, p. VII.

Yet even they found it difficult not to succumb to the lure of hero-worship and to keep a certain pathos out of their descriptions of Cromwell.

In the years just before and after 1899 (the third centenary of Cromwell's birth), all historical attention seemed to be focused upon Cromwell. There was no end to the ramifications of the subject: hardly a year passed without a new biography being announced.[317] All this new Cromwell literature had one thing in common: Cromwell was part of the English tradition, and this tradition was so multifaceted that all his biographers (for all their differences in political and religious convictions), were able to see a kindred spirit in him. R.F. Horton placed Cromwell squarely in an Anglo-Saxon tradition extolled by Freeman; neither Elizabeth I nor Charles I had brought back England's Anglo-Saxon liberties; only Cromwell did that with 'A Commonwealth or Free State.'[318]

In Horton's case a strongly idealised view of an early medieval past went hand in hand with a no less exalted interpretation of the Cromwell period. F. Harrison, whose biography was characterized as a conclusive summary in the *English Historical Review*, believed that the Cromwell period owed its importance for the present time to, among other things, the fact that it had proved the unfeasability of a 'parliamentary executive'; he praised Cromwell for having ended this.[319]

Certain aspects of Macaulay's view were still valid at the end of the 19th century, not only for F. Harrison, but also for the extremely well-informed S.R. Gardiner. The Macaulay argument would have it that Cromwell was essentially liberal and, alas, ahead of his time. This explained why he was so frequently misunderstood, as well as the failure of his judicial reforms and of his constitutional-parliamentary experiments.[320] He was thus finally forced to become a military dictator in 1655. According to this thesis Cromwell was entitled to the place at the entrance to the House of Commons. But Gardiner's conclusion had contradictory elements: he stressed Cromwell's conservatism as often

---

[317] Cf., a.o., E. Paxton Hood, *Oliver Cromwell*, London, 1882; J. A. Picton, *Oliver Cromwell. The Man and His Mission*, London, 1882; F. Harrison, *Oliver Cromwell*, London, 1888; R.F. Horton, *Oliver Cromwell. A Study in Personal Religion*, London, 1897; S.R. Gardiner, *Cromwell's Place in History*, London, 1897; A. Patterson, *Oliver Cromwell. His Life and Character*, London, 1899; J. Morley, *Oliver Cromwell*, London, 1900; S.R. Gardiner, *Oliver Cromwell*, London, 1901.

[318] R.F. Horton, *op. cit.*, pp. 97–98.

[319] F. Harrison, *op. cit.*, pp. 175–176. In the third chapter we shall discuss this matter further. Cf. *E.H.R.* 4 (1889), p. 372.

[320] Cf. S.R. Gardiner on Macaulay in his *Cromwell's Place in History*, p. 17 ff.

as he did Cromwell's modern liberalism. Also he accepted at face
value the increase in Cromwell's popularity as proof of its being well-
deserved.[321]

Yet Gardiner did not believe that Cromwell could in every respect
serve as a model. He saw him as a "mirror to ourselves where in we
may see alike our weakness and our strength."[322] Gardiner certainly
underscored Cromwell's faults, but as he had a certain comprehension
for an early Irish-Celtic nationalism (much to the annoyance of the
Edinburgh Review which had turned liberal-unionist in 1886), he tried
to explain many of Cromwell's mistakes, as in Ireland, by a lack of
information on Cromwell's part.[323] In 1897 Gardiner at last summarized the large amount of research done on the Civil War in the final
decades:

> It is beginning to be realised that many, if not all the experiments of the
> Commonwealth were but premature anticipations of the legislation of the
> nineteenth century, and it is also beginning to be realised that, whatever
> may be our opinion of some of Cromwell's isolated actions, he stands forth
> as the typical Englishman of the modern world. That he will ever be, more
> than this is not to be expected.[324]

At the end of the 19th century Cromwell was more than just accepted
in the English political tradition: he had become part of the 19th century itself.

Finally, we will discuss two figures who, although very different from
one another, both stood out as strong dissenters from this great chorus of
admirers. There was at least one Tory who tried to unmask Cromwell's 'real' persona, so much had the cultus about 'our pattern man'
disturbed him. His attempt was based on a thorough knowledge of the
original sources. This man is Reginald Palgrave, the fourth son of the
medievalist Francis Palgrave. In the first chapter we mentioned his
criticism of S.R. Gardiner, who, by the way, acknowledged Palgrave's
thorough knowledge of published and unpublished sources on 17th-
century history.[325] But Palgrave used an 'explanatory-model' rather

---

[321] S.R. Gardiner, *Oliver Cromwell*, p. 318: "Oliver's claim to greatness can be tested by
the undoubted fact that his character receives higher and wider appreciation as the centuries
pass by."

[322] S.R. Gardiner, *Cromwell's Place in History*, p. 116.

[323] *Ibid.*, p. 56; cf. W.O'C Morris, 'Gardiner's History of the Great Civil War' in *E.R.* 165
(1887), pp. 477–488, esp. pp. 451, 487.

[324] S.R. Gardiner, *Cromwell's Place in History*, p. 113; the Commonwealth period was the
cradle of modern political thought, see E. Jenks, *The Constitutional Experiments of the Commonwealth*, Cambridge, 1890.

[325] See ch. I, note 158. See, on Reginald Palgrave, W. Hunt in *D.N.B.*, Sec. Suppl., vol.
III, London, 1912, pp. 64–65. We mention the following studies: 'Pym and Shaftesbury:

full of exaggerations though not without a measure of originality. It is difficult to determine to what extent his interpretation was influenced by the growth of mass-democracy and increasing political demagogy and agitation after 1880, all of which he, as clerk of the House of Commons, was able to observe at first hand. Such an influence certainly is not improbable.[326]

In a first article of 1879, Palgrave blamed King Pym as responsible for the Civil War because of his political demagogy. For him, Pym was an unscrupulous man, not at all 'a model of moderation and constitutional observance,' and he was the one who had most to gain politically from the 'papal scare' of 1641.[327] Palgrave, obsessed by this early form of mass psychosis, repeated the same thesis in his work of 1890: "Pym intoxicated the people by a perpetual representation of the Popish Plot..."[328] What he had discovered about Pym, he also applied to Cromwell, who was for him no less 'a maker of plots' than Pym. In 1886 he published an extensive, though rather one-sided illustration, based on the Thurloe Papers, of the 'real' character of Oliver Cromwell as shown during the Royalist rising of 1655. The uprising had been engineered by Cromwell himself, through his spies. Cromwell acted behind the scene, giving his opponents plenty of opportunity to organise the conspiracy he needed. Thus Cromwell was pictured as 'the patron of the conspiracy,' which conspiracy at last served him as an excuse for setting up a military dictatorship. Furthermore, Palgrave deprived Cromwell, as a 'maker of plots,' of the last vestiges of heroism by adding another postulate: Cromwell had been a pawn of the military powers, a willing and helpless instrument of a body he had created.[329] Palgrave's much discussed article of 1886 closed with a furious tirade against the worship of Cromwell by Carlyle and his followers.

Two Popish Plots' in *Q.R.* 147 (1879), pp. 402–430; 'Fall of the Monarchy of Charles I' in *Q.R.* 154 (1882), pp. 1–32; 'Oliver Cromwell: his character illustrated by himself' in *Q.R.* 162 (1886), pp. 414–442; *Oliver Cromwell. The Protector. An Appreciation based on contemporary evidence*, London, 1890; also finally his polemics with C.H. Firth: 'Cromwell and the Insurrection of 1655. A reply to Mr. Firth' in *E.H.R.* 3 (1888), pp. 521–539, 722–751 and in *E.H.R.* 4 (1889), pp. 110–131.

326 Cf. e.g. his remarks: "The floor of the House of Commons formed, in 1640, an advertising medium quite as effective as it is now-a-days," and also: "What can convert a nothing into a something or give vitality to a hobby, more effectively than a parliamentary committee?" (*Q.R.* 147 (1879), pp. 405–406).

327 This phenomenon should not be underestimated in its social and political significance; see f.i., R. Glifton, 'The Popular Fear of Catholics during the English Revolution' in *Past and Present* nr. 52 (1971), pp. 23–55.

328 R. Palgrave, *Oliver Cromwell*, p. XXVII.

329 Cf. *Q.R.* 162 (1886), p. 439 ff.; cf. A.H. Woolrych, *Penruddock's Rising 1655*, London, 1955 (Historical Association).

Firth rebutted Palgrave's theories in the newly founded *English Historical Review*.[330] Palgrave, however, was not convinced by any of Firth's arguments. In fact, he now discerned an espionage pattern similar to that of 1655 in each and every conspiracy directed against Cromwell. His reply to Firth, directed more against F. Harrison than against Firth himself, was supported by arguments from Guizot. Much to his satisfaction, he believed to have found a sympathizer in the late Guizot.[331]

Although Guizot does indeed have a similar approach, Palgrave's attribution to Cromwell of a thoroughly logical and consistent policy of plotting made Guizot's picture of the sly dictatorial Cromwell rather less convincing than more so. Palgrave tried to create a picture of opposites: 'the pitiable Protector of 1653–1658' as opposed to the 'Grand and Good of 1845–1889.'[332] Considering the morbidly Cromwellian spirit of the later 19th century, this attempt was doomed in advance. Palgrave's obsession with one paramount principle as an all-embracing explanation also gave his opponents a useful handle for rebutting him.

Lastly, the liberal J.M. Robertson also scrutinized the copious Cromwell-literature; in the year of the great tercentenary of Cromwell's birth (1899) he published a critical summary of the situation in English historiography regarding to Cromwell.[333] His central question was whether the English Cromwell historiography had really profited by all the historical-scientific exertions since Carlyle had published his re-assessment in 1845. Had not many historians been confused by the enormous increase of sources?[334] Here, if anywhere, can Victorian moralism be said to have succeeded: in forming the image of Cromwell and the Civil War. Robertson characterized rhetoric similar to Carlyle's, permeated with moralism, as 'the bane of so much of our modern historiography.' He was quite right in calling this one of the greatest barriers to the growth of a more historical-scientific interpretation. "We have not advanced on the criticism of Hallam. With a greatly increased knowledge – thanks largely to Professor Gardiner – of the facts of the English revolution, we are still treated to ethical estimates of it

---

[330] C.H. Firth, 'Cromwell and the Insurrection of 1655' in *E.H.R.* 3 (1888), pp. 323–350 and in *E.H.R.* 4 (1889), pp. 313–338, 525–535; cf. also his article on Cromwell in *D.N.B.*, vol. 13, London, 1888, pp. 155–186, esp. p. 176.
[331] Cf. *E.H.R.* 4 (1889), p. 128, note 37, and Palgrave's *Oliver Cromwell*, pp. 106–107, 143.
[332] R. Palgrave, *Oliver Cromwell*, p. 3.
[333] See the article mentioned in note 284.
[334] J.M. Robertson, *op. cit.*, pp. 335–336.

that savour ... less of historical philosophy than of pulpit eloquence."[335] Nor did he spare Gardiner: several of Gardiner's phrases
and thoughts came in for their share of criticism because they were
inconsistent and nonsensical. Gardiner hesitated between 'Lob und
Tadel' where Cromwell was concerned, but did that serve the purposes
of historical interpretation as such?

J.H. Round agreed with Robertson in stressing the necessity of
finishing the senseless discussion about Cromwell being 'right' or
'wrong'; the historian's task was to provide more insight into the
Cromwellian system as it had functioned.[336] Robertson's reproofs were
also incidentally directed at several medievalists, and it is Victorian
medieval studies that will constitute our next subject.

C. MEDIEVAL STUDIES IN THE SECOND HALF OF
THE NINETEENTH CENTURY: THE OXFORD SCHOOL:
W. STUBBS, E.A. FREEMAN AND J.R. GREEN

> Few mid-nineteenth-century habits of thought and
> speech are more striking than the taste exhibited at
> almost every level of society for arguments from
> history.
>
> (O. Anderson, 1967)

1) Stubbs, an unwanted editor, a wanted professor

In this concluding part of our survey of English Whig historiography
we shall return to medieval studies. This field was dominated during
the second half of the 19th century by William Stubbs.[337] The better
part of this chapter will therefore deal with both him and his work,
the more so as many later critics made him a scape-goat. Stubbs is
usually thought of as belonging to the 'Oxford School,' together with

[335] *Ibid.*, p. 337.

[336] J.H. Round, 'Cromwell and The Electorate' in *Nineteenth Century* 46 (1899), pp. 947–
956, esp. p. 953. Cf. also J.M. Robertson, *op. cit.*, p. 339.

[337] Of the literature on Stubbs after 1945 we mention: H. Cam, 'Stubbs Seventy Years
After' in *The Cambridge Historical Journal* 9 (1948), pp. 129–147; J.G. Edwards, *William
Stubbs*, London, 1952 (Historical Association); G.O. Sayles, 'The Changed Concept of History: Stubbs and Renan' in *Aberdeen University Review* 35 (1953–1954) pp. 235–247; W.J.
Williams, 'Stubbs's Appointment as Regius Professor, 1866' in *B.I.H.R.* 33 (1960), pp. 121–
125; H.G. Richardson and G.O. Sayles, 'William Stubbs: The Man and the Historian' in
their *The Governance of Mediaeval England from the Conquest to Magna Carta*, Edinburgh, 1963,
pp. 1–21; R. Brentano, 'The Sound of Stubbs' in *Journal of British Studies* 6 (May, 1967), pp.
1–14.

E.A. Freeman and J.R. Green; the three were firm friends, notwithstanding some political differences, and as a matter of fact their work shows a certain similarity, even though differences in their working methods, scientific approach and point of view are not quite in keeping with the word 'school.'[338]

This was the period when the Rolls Series began, inaugurating an important development in medieval studies. This was a venture begun by Lord Romilly, Th. Duffus Hardy and J. Stevenson, in 1857. It was to have much influence on Stubbs's work both as editor and as historian. We are extensively informed about the weal and the woe (mainly the last) of this enterprise by Knowles.[339] The lack of organization and especially the lack of trained and qualified assistants has been severely attacked then and later; nevertheless, the Rolls Series – and certainly Stubbs's contributions to it – should not be underestimated as a considerable contribution to English medieval studies. However, it took people's attention away from the 'records' (Palgrave's orientation) by shifting it towards 'chronicles,' and thus determining subsequent historiography, for instance Stubbs's.

Stubbs's career had a curious beginning: only after repeated applications over five years he was hesitatingly admitted as a contributor to the Rolls Series. This indeed is in sharp contrast to his (for himself as well as for many others) unexpected nomination as a professor in Oxford in 1866. The speed with which Stubbs was nominated was mainly due to the conservative Derby, who preferred him to better-known, but politically less orthodox (and supposedly less reliable) historians like Freeman and Froude. After the political furor surrounding Goldwin Smith a 'safe political appointment' was desired.[340]

There were various reasons why the directors of the Rolls Series had subjected Stubbs's patience to such a severe test. He himself had in his applications admitted to being unknown as a historian. In his first letter he wrote:

I am afraid that my never having published anything on the subject and not being known as a student of English history may hinder my being accepted in such a position – but that I cannot help. I was a first class in classics at Oxford in 1848 and fellow of Trinity College and have for years devoted myself to this particular study.[341]

[338] Cf. G.P. Gooch, *History and Historians in the Nineteenth Century*, London, 1920, pp. 346, 351.

[339] D. Knowles, 'The Rolls Series' in his *Great Historical Enterprises*, London, 1963, pp. 101–134.

[340] W.J. Williams, *op. cit.*, p. 122.

[341] Letter by W. Stubbs to T. Hardy, dated 1-4-1857, P.R.O. (P.R.O. 37–61).

Three years afterwards he again had to admit that there was no improvement in his situation. "I cannot refer you to any work of the kind for a specimen of my powers as an editor, but can promise a careful and faithful attention to any book which you may be pleased to entrust to me."[342] Even Stubbs himself could not explain his being turned down at least three times running simply because he was too unknown. He originally mistrusted the management as a too close-knit group of friends, regarding the quality and the capacities of a number of contributors with great scepticism.[343]

Disappointed and slightly embittered he wrote to Freeman in April 1860:

It is possible they may be fettered by an uncertainty about their grant of money, but it is certain that they are determined not to go beyond their own circle of Editors, and to let them edit what they like. I cannot think that Sir J. Romilly can know much about the trash they have printed – and if Hardy inspires his communications his line has always been, as it seems to me, polite obstructiveness.[344]

Stubbs certainly was not the only one to show such mistrust, nor was he the only one who tried his utmost to get admitted. The campaign of the 'embarrassing' B. Thorpe was much more stubborn, and even ill-mannered. When he was finally admitted, he caused after the 'Hingeston affair' a second affair in connection with the publication of the *Anglo-Saxon Chronicle*.[345] Bitter because of having been refused twice, he had earlier complained to Romilly in sharp terms about Hardy's active opposition to him. He even threatened to publish a pamphlet and create a public scandal.[346] Even in 1859 Stubbs wrote about the 'clique' opposing Thorpe, but the leadership's dislike was understandable: Thorpe was feared because of his blunders.[347]

From 1862, after Stubbs had been accepted as an editor, he worked for two decades with great energy and ability at the chronicles entrusted to him. His professorship, since 1866, did not stop him in this re-

[342] Letter by W. Stubbs to T. Hardy, dated 21-12-1860. P.R.O. (P.R.O. 37–61).
[343] Cf. *Letters of William Stubbs*, ed. W.H. Hutton, London, 1904, pp. 70, 72, 79, 81.
[344] *Letters of William Stubbs*, pp. 82–83.
[345] D. Knowles, *op. cit.*, p. 115.
[346] See for all this: 'Correspondence of B. Thorpe and J. Stevenson relating to the materials for English History,' P.R.O. (P.R.O. 1–124). This collection proves that the relations between Thorpe and Hardy had already been strained for years. In the same collection we find a pamphlet from 1864 by Thorpe called 'Some correspondence from 1842 to 1862 relative to the publication of materials for British History.' See on this Thorpe affair also J.R. Green's letter to E.A. Freeman in *Letters of John Richard Green*, ed. L. Stephen, London, 1902, p. 144.
[347] Cf. *Letters of William Stubbs*, pp. 70, 90–91.

spect. In less than twenty years nineteen tomes were published (between 1864 and 1883), a consistent testimony to an inconceivable energy, especially if we remember that his *Constitutional History* (in three parts) was published during the same years. Now we must first trace the views which form the framework of his *Constitutional History*; secondly we shall attempt to analyse Stubbs's interpretation of the medieval parliament within this total vision; after that we shall compare his interpretation with the parliamentary views of the first half of the nineteenth century (as discussed in the first part of this chapter). Finally, there is the question in how far the political climate of the years around the second Reform Bill can have influenced Stubbs's view.

2) Stubbs's synthesis of medieval constitutional development

> Few dynasties in the whole history of the world, not even the Caesars or the Antonines, stand out with more distinct personal character than the Plantagenets.
>
> (W. Stubbs, 1878)

The sharp distinction sometimes made between Stubbs the editor and Stubbs the historian and writer of *The Constitutional History* seems to us to be rather exaggerated.[348] The different types of work of course differ in character: more exertion and labour are needed to write a good scholarly survey; the historian needs 'analytical' as well as 'synthesizing' powers to construct the development as a whole. The greatest challenge a *magnum opus* presents is that a hypothesis must be made to conform to reality without stretching the facts. This is a continual problem, which even Stubbs, who was well aware of the hypothetical character of some of his own conclusions, wished from time to time to be released from.[349] Moreover, as an editor Stubbs did not fear the idea of a synthesis, as evidenced by his many summarizing introductions. Some of these certainly form a first step towards the view depicted later in his *Constitutional History*. However, he preferred editing source material, which proved firm ground, compared to the slippery adventure of writing a large summary; Stubbs also thought that English historiography had more need of research than of scholarly surveys.

---

[348] Cf. also G.O. Sayles, *op. cit.*, p. 237. Ten years later (in 1963) even his opinion of Stubbs as editor has become unfavourable.

[349] Cf. *Letters of William Stubbs*, pp. 165, 175; cf. C.H. Firth, *Modern History in Oxford*, Oxford, 1920, p. 24 (note 4).

This accords with what Creighton wrote about him to Acton, in 1885: "He resented all invasions of his time as hindrances to editing MSS. That was the work he really enjoyed. He wrote his *Constitutional History* more because something was expected of him than because he enjoyed doing it."[350] Still, the expectations of an interested public could not have been the only stimulating factor to write his major work. Ever since his appointment in 1866 he had been fascinated by medieval constitutional history. At the very beginning of his professorship we hear that he is giving lectures on what was a very extensive subject: 'constitutional history from Tacitus to Henry II.'[351] Apparently his lectures had been completely written out by the beginning of 1867, and Henry II's period was, not coincidentally, to be the tentative culmination. For in the same year he published *The Chronicle of Benedict of Peterborough*, with a lengthy introduction dealing with the constitutional importance of Henry II's reign.

This introduction indicates the beginnings of the constitutional pattern, developed afterwards in Stubbs's major historical work.[352] His picture of this important Plantagenet (to which we shall have occasion to return), was built up independently of earlier authors. At the end of his argument, however, he could hardly omit Palgrave.[353] There is little information about the origin of the leading idea of Stubbs's *Constitutional History*, but one point furnishes clear proof that Stubbs since 1868 was on a less 'solipsistic' course than is sometimes thought. From that time onwards he never failed to read any of the national and the foreign publications on constitutional history. Moreover, his 'forced' lectures also made a more comparative approach inevitable. At the end of 1872, two years before the publication of the first part, he wrote to E.A. Freeman: "The subject of Comparative Politics, or as I call it Comparative Const. History is largish ... I have been lecturing on the subject, Spain, Germany, France and England, ever since 1868, and find constant new things."[354]

In 1876, after two parts of his major work had already been printed,

---

[350] M. Creighton to Lord Acton, 21-9-1885, see *Selections from the Correspondence of the First Lord Acton*, ed. J.N. Figgis and R.V. Laurence, London, 1917, vol. I, p. 309.

[351] *Letters of William Stubbs*, p. 114.

[352] See *The Chronicle of Benedict of Peterborough*, London, 1867, 2 vols.; cf. also *Letters of William Stubbs*, pp. 104–105, 108, 110. 116. He had finished this publication and its introduction in January 1867; as early as September, 1868, he wrote to Freeman about the framework of his *Constitutional History*: "the principal part is *cash*." (*Letters of William Stubbs*, p. 154.)

[353] Cf. *Letters of William Stubbs*, pp. 104–105, 150–151; *The Chronicle of Benedict of Peterborough*, I, p. CXIX ff.

[354] Cf. H. Cam, *op. cit.*, p. 131; *Letters of William Stubbs*, p. 164.

Stubbs published a concise little survey (written in less than two months), entitled *The Early Plantagenets*. This short piece contains his basic idea in highly compressed form. Here he describes the uniqueness of the period from Henry II until Edward I for European history:

The history of England under the early kings of the house of Plantagenet unfolds and traces the growth of that constitution which, far more than any other that the world has ever seen, has kept alive the forms and spirit of free government. It is scarcely too much to say that English history, during these ages, is the history of the birth of true political liberty. For, not to forget the service of the Italian republics, or of the German confederations of the middle ages, we cannot fail to see that in their actual results they fell as dead before the great monarchies of the sixteenth century, as the ancient liberties of Athens had fallen; or where the spirit survived, as in Switzerland, it took a form in which no great nationality could work. It was in England alone that the problem of national self-government was practically solved; and although under the Tudors and Stewart sovereigns Englishmen themselves ran the risk of forgetting the lesson they had learned and being robbed of the fruits for which their fathers had laboured, the men who restored political consciousness, and who discovered the endangered rights, won their victory by argumentative weapons drawn from the storehouse of medieval English history, and by the maintenance and realisation of the spirit of liberty in forms which had survived from earlier days.[355]

In this long quotation we can see important elements of the Whig view: the medieval origin of modern political liberty, the serious threat to that liberty during the period which J.R. Green called the 'New Monarchy,' and, finally, the restoration of that liberty in the 17th century with the aid of the 'great precedent' from medieval history. In other words: modern liberty was born out of medieval liberties. At the beginning of the modern era the monarchy was the most important 'adversary,' but in the 12th and 13th centuries it had played a much more positive role, even opposite to its later one. According to Stubbs both Henry II and Edward I were considered the founding fathers of the form of free political state that he concretely termed 'national self-government.' We shall see that this term became very fashionable indeed in political thinking. The core of Stubbs's view is difficult to grasp without this relatively new conception.

Earlier, in his introduction to *The Chronicle of Benedict of Peter-borough* in 1867, and in 1874 in the final chapters of the first part of his major work, Stubbs had elaborated on Henry II's contribution. Although "the notions of constitutional sovereignty and liberty were still

---

[355] W. Stubbs, *The Early Plantagenets*, London, 1889, pp. 5–6.

locked up in the libraries, or in embryo in the brains of the clergy," yet
in 1867 Stubbs stated that Henry II's reforms, both administrative and
judicial, had cleared the way for the system of 'constitutional government.'[356] "The reign of Henry II saw the end of feudalism as it had
ever prevailed in England, as a system of government."[357] This period
was one of fusion, of two peoples amalgamating – the one belonging
to the pre-Conquest time, the other post-Conquest. It was therefore
also noteworthy as the period of synthesis between the political traditions of the two peoples. Actually, it was this combination, this melting-
pot idea, which formed the strong basis for later political developments. Stubbs's view of 1066 was a moderate and original continuity-
theory: William the Conqueror only created new institutions at the
top, leaving Anglo-Saxon institutions and administrative customs intact on the local level, a view, no doubt, in which Stubbs follows Palgrave.

After 1066 the newcomers began by living alongside the autochtho-
nous population, 'doubling' local government especially in the courts
of justice (e.g., the old local courts of the hundred and the shire remained alongside the new feudal courts). This juxtaposition was to
last until Henry II. The difficulties, created by the invasion of 1066,
were solved at last under Henry II by combining the best elements of
the two existing courts of law and welding them into one. Thus, both
Anglo-Saxon and Norman elements fused within the jury system, and
here again we find the happy combination of past and present giving
birth to something completely new.[358]

More than just the courts of justice were combined; fusion was the
outstanding element of Henry's policy of centralization. Henry used
his travelling judges to promote unity in the existing local institutions,
both in matters judicial and administrative. "The visits of the itinerant
justices" – as Stubbs put it in 1874 – "form the link between the Curia
Regis and the Shire-moot, between royal and popular justice, between
the old system and the new";[359] this was the same thesis he had pithily
formulated earlier: "The Norman curia met the Anglo-Saxon gemot
in the visitations of the itinerant justices."[360]

The *justiciarii itinerantes* thus became the main executives of the

---

[356] *The Chronicle of Benedict of Peterborough* I, pp. XXVI.
[357] *Ibid.*, I, p. XXXVII.
[358] *Ibid.*, I, p. LXXXII.
[359] W. Stubbs, *The Constitutional History of England*, I, (Third edition, Oxford, 1880),
p. 605.
[360] *Ibid.*, I, p. 393.

'commixture of race and institutions': a unification of old-English and new Norman traditions, which Stubbs compared with "a chemical commixture, in which, although skilled analysis may distinguish the ingredients, they are so united both in bulk and in qualities, that the result of the commixture is something altogether distinct from the elements of which it is composed."[361] The long extant Anglo-Saxon tradition of local self-government was not only continued, it became part of the higher institutions of central government. In turn, this government accepted certain ideas and practices of local self-government, as, for instance, the idea of representation. Briefly, there was also continuity on a higher level.

The final two chapters of Stubbs's first volume mainly centred around "the interpenetration, the growing together of the local machinery and the administrative organisation"; the fusion of local Anglo-Saxon institutions and the Norman central administration.[362] The combination of the 'Norman superstructure' and 'English substructure' was really most fortunate. They supplemented each other in the most essential points: "the strongest elements of both were brought together."[363] The English system had in any case been weak on the upper administrative levels, though 'strong in the cohesion of its lower organism, the association of individuals in the township, in the hundred and in the shire,' whereas the Norman system was exactly opposite.[364] Stubbs regarded both elements as equally important. The two structures were not simply added together, they were adjusted in perfect harmony. The ancient Teutonic liberties survived intact, not in spite of, but because of the Conqueror's and his successors's harsh centralization.

Stubbs was a Germanist, but with reservations. T.F. Tout afterwards rightly called him "the soberest and most reasonable exponent" of the so-called Teutonic school.[365] For instance, Stubbs agreed with Carlyle's denigrating remark about the 'undisciplined Anglo-Saxons,' who would never have achieved anything without the Normans and the Plantagenets.[366] Stubbs's synthesis was composed of Anglo-Saxon

---

[361] *Ibid.*, I, pp. 550–551.
[362] *Ibid.*, I, p. 544.
[363] *Ibid.*, I, p. 278.
[364] *Ibid.*, I, p. 278.
[365] T.F. Tout in *D.N.B.*, Sec. Suppl., vol. III, London, 1912, pp. 444–451, quotation p. 447.
[366] W. Stubbs, *op. cit.*, I p. 216 (note 1).

liberties and Norman order: his view of the events of 1066 rendered a teutonic or a romanist approach to the Middle Ages superfluous.

This large vision, which Stubbs in the first part only now and then allows the reader to glimpse from out of the mass of details, may not have been original in all respects. We need only think of Guizot, for example. Elements of it can be traced in the tangle of Palgrave's work.[367] The latter, however, did not discern so many gradually emerging reforms under Henry II as Stubbs had. Palgrave had denied that 1066 was a turning-point; he had called Henry II's reforms a great revolution, a 'second conquest,' this time factually true. Stubbs criticized that characterization; to him the changes, ordered from above, after 1066, were far more important. Besides, he pointed out that the early beginnings of Henry II's policy had been made under Henry I.[368] The difference of opinion notwithstanding, Palgrave also thought there had been a 'concentration' of local Anglo-Saxon government after 1066. As Vinogradoff put it: the idea remained in a 'hypothetical' stage.

3) Stubbs's parliamentary thesis

> This institution of county courts in England has had greater effect on the government than has yet been distinctly pointed out by historians or traced by antiquaries.
>
> (D. Hume, 1762)

Stubbs's central idea, plainly visible in the first volume of his life's work is the indispensable background needed for understanding his later much criticized thesis about parliament. For was not the later medieval parliament the main product of that 'amalgamation' process which finally bore fruit under Henry II? It was his policy which led to "that concentration of local machinery ... out of which the representative system arose. The Parliament of the thirteenth century was the concentration of local representation in and with the national council."[369] This is how Stubbs himself phrased the essence of his parliamentary thesis. The second volume, particularly the famous fifteenth chapter about the constitution under Edward I, is thoroughly permeated by this theme. There is no more important element in the whole

---

[367] Cf. P. Vinogradoff, *Villainage in England*, Oxford, 1892, p. 23.
[368] Cf. *The Chronicle of Benedict of Peterborough*, I, pp. CXIX-CXXI.
[369] W. Stubbs, *op. cit.*, I, p. 393.

of his thesis (more even than the theories about the 'three estates' and the model parliament of 1295, although they became better known in later reviews).

At the very end of the first volume (which is to say at the end of the 12th century and the beginning of the 13th), the English nation had (according to Stubbs) already arrived at "that point of conscious unity and identity which made it necessary for it to act as a self-governing and political body, a self-reliant and self-sustained nation."[370] Of course the Magna Carta was the clearest proof of this realization of unique identity,[371] in which all ingredients of the parliamentary system were fully present. Nothing was needed but centralization, a concentration of local customs and institutions: "when the need of representative institutions made itself felt, the mere concentration and adaptation of existing machinery supplied all that was required."[372] The history of Parliament as 'a concentration of all local and provincial machinery' simply consisted of the growth and gradual realization of a system of 'self-government' by representation.[373] This principle of representation, although lacking in the Anglo-Saxon Witenagemot, was already extant in the shire-moot or county-court.[374] Stubbs argued that the Plantagenets took it to a higher level when Henry I and II enlisted the local organizations for their centralizing policy of reforms.

The system of trial by jury was (according to the famous Stubbsian argument) in many ways advantageous for the idea of representation.[375] Under Henry II the central government came down to the local level, as it were, in the form of the itinerant judges, thus training the local authorities in 'self-government.'[376] Later, during Edward I, came a concluding period ('the great period of definition,'[377] as Stubbs wrote), when the central government through the principle of representation bade the local authorities to come thither. Stubbs diligently tried to find signs foreshadowing this process, and he believed he had found a clear first 'omen of the institution of representa-

[370] *Ibid.*, I, p. 637.
[371] *Ibid.*, I, pp. 532, 543.
[372] *Ibid.*, I, p. 637.
[373] Cf. *Ibid.*, I, pp. 544, 622. Stubbs, too, considered this early representation to be a burden, a duty; see *Ibid.*, I, p. 377 (note 1) and p. 607.
[374] *Ibid.*, I, pp. 116, 121.
[375] Cf. esp. *Ibid.*, I, pp. 607–623. In 1213, Stubbs said, all the preconditions for parliament were fulfilled: "We have a system of representation, we have the practice of election, and we have a concentration of the shires in the great council" (*Ibid.*, I, p. 623).
[376] Cf. W. Stubbs, *The Early Plantagenets*, p. 82; W. Stubbs, *Constitutional History*, I, p. 393.
[377] *Ibid.*, I, p. 635.

tive parliaments' in the 'St. Alban's assembly' of 1203.[378] To put it pointedly, there was a national representative body extant (in Stubbs's view), before it was graced with the name of Parliament. In the later anti-Stubbsian version of parliamentary history the term existed long before a really representative parliament did.

In his first volume Stubbs had already drawn a broad outline directed towards the reign of king Edward I, which reign consequently appeared as an apotheosis in the second volume. In earlier literature, written in the beginning of the 19th century, this period had usually been regarded as a starting-point in parliamentary history, whereas Stubbs presented it as a final decisive phase, after which the further development of the parliamentary system did not meet with great difficulties. Stubbs's picture of parliament's prehistory no doubt was highly finalistic, intended as a glorification of the final result. He placed several events in such direct relationship to later developments, that the picture became decidedly anachronistic. Not only the generation succeeding Stubbs reproved him with this, even some (although few) of his contemporaries criticized him for it.[379]

Stubbs gave as proof of Edward I's important place in English constitutional development the fact that a parliament was summoned for the first time under his reign, a parliament that was to be a shining example for the future: the so-called 'model-parliament' of late 1295. In that year a precedent was created 'for all time to come,' although as Stubbs added, "in the early years that follow, exceptional practices may be found."[380] Stubbs introduced this term into medieval history at almost the same time as Freeman, who had used a similar term about Simon de Montfort's parliament.[381] In the first part of this chapter we observed the application of this term to Cromwell's parliaments. It is not surprising that Stubbs also applies it to Edward I's parliament, being strongly convinced of the great importance of that meeting. The terms 'model' and 'modeling' emerged at a very early stage in the historiography on Edward I. Hallam spoke of 'modeling,' and D. Hume – the first English historian to provide a more systematic survey of the constitutional development under Edward I – had characterized Edward as 'the model of a politic and warlike king.' Hume followed Brady's example in ascribing a certain importance to 1295,

[378] *Ibid.*, I, pp. 527–528; see for a second example, pp. 622–623.
[379] Cf. J.R. Green on Stubbs's view of Henry II in *Historical Studies*, London, 1903, pp. 186–187. For J. Gairdner, see below, note 406.
[380] W. Stubbs, *op. cit.*, II ,(sec. ed.) p. 224, cf. pp. 128–129.
[381] Cf. J.G. Edwards, *Historians and the Medieval English Parliament*, pp. 50–52.

although he was more circumspect than was Stubbs a century after-wards.[382]

What did Stubbs mean in referring to the 'model' parliament of 1295? He never gave a direct answer to this question, but from the context we may conclude that the parliamentary occurrences of 1295 were for him important because of 'the proper incorporation of the three estates.' The term 'model' was to indicate the manner – the 'how' – of this incorporation.[383] Knights and citizens had been summoned for meetings prior to 1295, but in most cases they had been summoned separately. Besides, the town representatives had usually been called up directly, without the sheriff as intermediary. Stubbs points out that we see knights and burgesses appear together for the first time in 1295, the sheriff having summoned also the latter group. The procedure for summoning representatives was becoming standardized.

The only new phenomenon according to Stubbs was the appearance of the *praemunientes* clause inviting also the lower clergy to the sitting. Hardly an important precedent, since the lower clergy was not des-tined to fulfil a role of any significance in parliamentary history; ac-tually they tended more and more to neglect the summons. As to the first two points it seems exaggerated to speak of a 'model parliament.' The 'modeling' consisted only in making existing practices uniform, but Stubbs firmly believed that when knights and burgesses acted to-gether, a decisive step was taken to form the Commons as such, and the formation of a third estate meant that parliament as a whole was thereby a 'concentration of the three estates.'[384] Actually there was something unique about this togetherness of knights and burgesses, and the consequences for the English parliamentary system were undeni-ably important.

What Stubbs tried to do in his fifteenth chapter was to join two elements together, two principles, the two theories of concentration (as it were), on which his view of parliament is based. He mentioned a concentration of 'local machinery' as well as a concentration of the three estates. "The thirteenth century turns the feudal council into an assembly of estates, and draws the constitution of the third estate

---

[382] Cf. D. Hume, *The History of England*, London, 1825, p. 180; cf. pp. 169–173 ('Digres-sion on the constitution of parliament'). On the historiography concerning Edward I, see G. Templeman, 'Edward I and the Historians' in *The Cambridge Historical Journal* 10 (1950), pp. 16–35. On Hume esp. pp. 20–21.

[383] Cf. W. Stubbs, *op. cit.*, III, (sec. ed.), p. 430.

[384] *Ibid.*, II, pp. 194, 306.

from the ancient local machinery which it concentrates."[385] And
Stubbs opined that the parliamentary structure still rested on these
two principles.

The parliamentary constitution of England comprises, as has been remarked
already, not only a concentration of local machinery but an assembly of estates. The parliament of the present day, and still more dearly the parliament
of Edward I, is a combination of these two theoretically distinct principles.[386]

We have discussed the first concentration-theory amply with reference
to the first volume. Here in the fifteenth chapter Stubbs repeated the
essential part of his argument from that first volume.[387] The second
type of concentration concerned the formation of the Commons into an
'estate.' For Stubbs the Commons were the third estate, but he was
fully aware of the fact that this term, with its connotation of the continental Estates-General, was far from ideal as characterization of the
English Commons. The Commons never represented just one social
group, but were the representatives of geographic unities. The crux
was that it was a 'local' representation, not a 'social' one. "The Commons are the 'communitates' or 'universitates,' the organised bodies of
freemen of the shires and towns; and the estate of the Commons is the
'communitas communitatum,' the general body into which for the
purposes of parliament those communities are combined."[388]

It was precisely this 'geographic' principle that made it difficult for
the two theories of concentration to join forces. Stubbs unwittingly
increased the difficulty by resolutely refusing to entertain the typically
English variety of the 'three-estates' theory (King, Lords, Commons),
important as it was for Palgrave's parliamentary thesis.[389] A synthesis
would not have been impossible in that version and would have made
Stubbs's view of the early Parliament more refined. We already noted
the close relationship between the view on composition and that on the
function of parliament. An important consequence of Stubbs's 'three-
estates'-theory concerning the composition, was his regarding the place
and function of the king with council as not quite essential in the
whole system. His own version of the three estates system actually

---

[385] *Ibid.*, II, p. 168.
[386] *Ibid.*, II, p. 161.
[387] Cf. *Ibid.*, II, pp. 204–217 (on the county courts); p. 220 ff. (on the idea of representation). Cf. the summarizing statement: "The primitive constitution, local, popular, self-
regulating, had received a new element from the organising power of the Normans" (II, p.
254). Thus the local administration was perfected in the 13th century (Cf. II, p. 273).
[388] *Ibid.*, II, p. 166.
[389] *Ibid.*, II, p. 168.

negated the 'conciliar' interpretation of English parliament. Of course Stubbs also laid heavy stress on the continuity of the King's personal role, and he certainly realized that the council was the nucleus of the parliamentary system, but Stubbs was like Hallam in that he regarded the 'councillors' as having been 'added' to the proper parliament as 'assistants,' not as 'essential members.'[390]

They were not representatives; they did not fit into a parliament that was a concentration of the three estates. They were an executive element, forming a *corpus alienum* in a body specialized in debates and the passing of laws. Thus it was logical for Stubbs to have assessed especially the 'council's judicial function in parliament' as less than secondary. In Stubbs's classification of the parliamentary functions the last place was reserved for the judicial function.[391] It was not really a part of the 'general parliaments,' it belonged to the sphere of the 'special parliaments,' the 'sessions of the council for judicial business.' They could well be compared with the parliament of Paris, but the work they did had no direct bearing on parliamentary history; there was more in it of interest to the lawyer and the legal historian than to the constitutional historian.[392]

Stubbs's construction left very little space for Palgrave's original thesis, both with regard to the composition and to the function of parliament. Palgrave had written, in his *Essay on the Original Authority of the King's Council*, of 1834: "During the sitting of Parliament the council ... sat as a house, branch, or estate of Parliament." Stubbs's sole comment on this was significant: "This seems to be a mere rhetorical exaggeration."[393] We know that Palgrave did not think of it as rhetorical; Stubbs's remark suggests that he was unfamiliar with Palgrave's parliamentary thesis, although other (earlier) utterances of his indicate that Stubbs was conversant with the tendencies of Palgrave's view.[394] Nevertheless he did not pursue Palgrave's central thesis.

Similarly, in Stubbs's work certain of J. Allen's and H. Hallam's constructions are also missing or adapted to Stubbs's grand vision. These two historians of the early 19th century both had regarded the 'annual parliaments' of the Middle Ages as a proof of this body's original judicial function. The frequency of the sessions had made them aware of the non-political function. Stubbs now makes the frequency

---

[390] Cf. *Ibid.*, II, p. 254, and III, p. 445, II, p. 259.
[391] Cf. *Ibid.*, II, p. 236, ff.
[392] Cf. *Ibid.*, pp. 261, 265, 573; III, p. 476.
[393] Cf. *Ibid.*, II, p. 191 (note).
[394] Particularly in the introduction of *The Chronicle of Benedict of Peterborough.*

serve as proof for an increasing political consciousness on the part of the Commons. "Accordingly when political feeling was high there was a demand for annual parliaments."[395] In the final volume of his work there is a similar argument stating that there is a greater demand for annual parliaments when the judicial work declines.

As the political functions of the national parliament became more prominently important than the judicial work of the king in his full council, it became a point of public security that regular and fairly frequent parliaments should be held; and the demand for annual parliaments accordingly emerges soon after the final admission of representatives of the Commons.[396]

Although Stubbs referred to the well-known article by John Allen on this point of the 'annual parliaments,' his view was notably different. However, he did agree with his predecessor that the representation (especially the high frequency) in the Middle Ages was felt as a heavy burden.[397] This idea had no influence on his belief in a growing political consciousness of the Commons; it removed none of the lustre from his vision.

Our remaining question concerns the rise and function of the Commons during and after Edward I. A parliament of deliberation and legislation is better supplemented by an active 'House of Commons' than by a 'high court' dispensing justice on behalf of the supplicant Commons. In this matter Stubbs's opinion accorded with that of his predecessor Hallam, but he went further. His explanation of the Commons's function was much more favourable and finalistic.[398] "Edward I had made his parliament the concentration of the three estates of his people; under Edward II, Edward III, and Richard II, the third estate claimed and won its place as the foremost of the three."[399] This was, in short, his thesis.

In our discussion of Hallam this subject was treated extensively, also referring to Stubbs; we would add a few more remarks. Stubbs acknowledged that the Commons under Edward I had next to no influence regarding the passage of laws. No advisory voice, no ideas of their own were called for; they merely had to agree, although in theory their rights extended farther.[400] Somewhat laconically Stubbs re-

---

[395] W. Stubbs, op. cit., II, p. 614; but a few lines further the old views crop up again in the words: "... Edward I observed the rule (three parliaments a year) so far as it involved annual sessions for judicial purposes."

[396] Ibid., III, p. 380.

[397] See note 373; cf. also Ibid., II, p. 613; III, pp. 407, 421.

[398] Cf. E. Miller, The Origins of Parliament, London, 1960 (Historical Association), p. 5.

[399] W. Stubbs, op. cit., II, p. 306.

[400] Cf. Ibid., II, pp. 246, 252.

marked: "it is probable that the theory of the constitution was somewhat in advance of its actual progress."[401] The insecure place of the
Commons is plainly shown in the continually varying formula of the
writs; the reasons for summoning differed, and unfortunately (for
Stubbs) the wording of the writs for the model-parliament of 1295
proves that the Commons occupied a subordinate position.[402]

According to Stubbs both the insecurity and the subordinate position were practically gone after Edward I. The Commons soon became a whole, growing into a strong close-knit body.[403] Although
Stubbs realized that a formal acknowledgment of the parliamentary
rights of the Commons was still a far cry from the 'practical enforce-
ment,'[404] his views on the power and the function of the Commons
were on the whole typically Whig, even 'Lancastrian'. The nearer he
came to the end of the medieval constitutional period, the more Stubbs
tended towards this way of thinking. To quote a letter of his to Freeman, in January 1877: "I forget whether you are a Yorkist or not;
reading Gairdner on the Paston Letters makes me more Lancastrian
than ever."[405] Ironically enough the historian J. Gairdner held a
much less glorious view than Stubbs about the medieval parliament,
since his opinions were much closer to Palgrave's.[406] As Stubbs would
have it, the Lancastrian period saw "the trial and failure of a great
constitutional experiment: a premature testing of the strength of the
parliamentary system." Whoever saw the Lancastrian period, with its
high frequency of parliamentary meetings, as a herald (be it a premature one) of the later parliamentary governmental system, could hardly
view the Yorkist period as anything but regressive, considering the
comparative infrequency of parliamentary meetings.[407]

The later chapters show Stubbs anticipating even more than he did
earlier. A clear example is his "Parliamentary Antiquities," his penul-
timate chapter. Since no sufficient information from the sources was
available, he would fall back upon the 'retrogressive' method for the

[401] Ibid., II, p. 249.
[402] Ibid., II, pp. 249–251.
[403] Cf. Ibid., II, pp. 307, 324.
[404] Ibid., II, p. 401.
[405] Letters of William Stubbs, p. 175.
[406] Cf. for Gairdner's view of parliament, especially for his conviction on the insignificance of the Commons, The Paston Letters, London, 1904, vol. I, p. 144, as well as his article
'The House of Lords. Its Functions' in The Antiquary 9 (1884), pp. 149–156, 255–259. He
referred to Palgrave (p. 150) and criticized Hallam (p. 152) and Stubbs, without mentioning
the latter's name (p. 156).
[407] Yet his judgment in this matter was cautious, see W. Stubbs, op. cit., III, pp. 5, 233–
235, 286. Cf. S.B. Chrimes, Lancastrians, Yorkists and Henry VII, London, 1964, pp. 76 ff., 115.

description of parliamentary procedures, or for the origin of the Speaker's office, or the problem of the division of Parliament into two Houses.[408] All these things were surely of very early origin; the influence of customs and parliamentary precedents seemed sufficient justification for the 'retrogressive' method.[409]

Stubbs occasionally realized the dangers of working with this anticipating, finalistic approach. He once wrote:

It is so much easier, in discussing the cause and stages of a political contest, to *generalise from the results* than to trace the growth of the principles maintained by the actors, that the historian is in some danger of substituting his own formulated conclusions for the programme of the leaders, and of giving them credit for a far more definite scheme and more conscious political sagacity than they would ever have claimed for themselves.[410]

However, Stubbs could not help regarding history as a progressive forward movement, consciously directed: "the march of constitutional progress is so steady and definite as to suggest everywhere the idea that it was guided by some great creative genius or some great directive tradition."[411] Stubbs did not exclude any historical phase or period from this great purpose; *every* event had been meaningful. Three centuries of 'preparation' had been needed to make a success of the Great Rebellion and the Revolution.[412]

Finally, it is noticeable that certain constitutional conceptions come to the fore in Stubbs's work on the medieval constitution which (as we noticed) earlier in the same century were used for highlighting important events from modern history. The ideas of a limited constitutional monarchy and even of ministerial responsibility and cabinet government were admitted to the sphere of medieval constitutional history.[413] We repeat once again that the Whig myth intensified; it also managed to penetrate into the very early medieval period. It may

---

[408] Cf. W. Stubbs, *op. cit.*, III, pp. 430–431, 453, 467.

[409] Cf. A.F. Pollard's later criticism, *The Evolution of Parliament*, London, 1926, p. 263.

[410] W. Stubbs, *op. cit.*, II, p. 511 (our emphasis).

[411] *Ibid.*, II, p. 512; he added, however: "Yet it is scarcely ever possible to distinguish the creative genius; it is impossible to assign the work to any single mind or series of minds, and scarcely easier to trace the growth of the guiding tradition in any one of the particulars which it embodies."

[412] Cf. e.g., the remark: "The failure of the house of Lancaster, the tyranny of the house of York, the statecraft of Henry VII, the apparent extinction of the constitution under the dictatorship of Henry VIII, the political re-surrection under Elizabeth, were all needed to prepare and equip England to cope successfully with the principles of Richard II, masked under legal, religious, philosophical embellishments in the theory of the Stewarts" (W. Stubbs, *op. cit.*, II, p. 622).

[413] Cf. *Ibid.*, II, p. 563 (on' the first lessons of the doctrine of ministerial responsibility'). Cf. also pp. 41, 623; on the cabinet, see III, p. 248.

not have been beneficial to the past in every respect: the Middle Ages
no longer were the Middle Ages, which is what the anti-Whig reaction
attempted to demonstrate. What, however, was the background of
this 'present-mindedness' in medieval studies which rather increased
than decreased as the century progressed? We shall attempt to find an
answer in the next section.

4) Background of Stubbs's views

> Modern thought is a little prone to eclecticism in
> history.
>
> (W. Stubbs)

Stubbs's work was valuable mainly because it was the first summarizing scholarly synthesis of the medieval constitutional development.
His *magnum opus* was a large step forward after Hallam's *View*, since
that, like many other 19th-century summaries, largely amended Hume.
Stubbs's work possessed a balance which Hallam never reached.[414]
The originality of his synthesis consisted in a well-thought-out continuity thesis which joined together the two main periods: the one before
and the one after 1066. After 1066 the Normans and the Plantagenets
renewed the Anglo-Saxon political tradition, and thereby also en-
riched their own tradition. The Anglo-Saxon parliamentary prehistory
was long and interesting, but only after the Plantagenets had finally
shaped this old tradition could the parliamentary system definitely
come into being under Edward I.

Was not the political thinking of the second half of the 19th century
also a decisive factor in Stubbs's thesis? Stubbs believed that the modern
political trends of his day were far too prone to historical eclecticism.
Contrary to his friend Freeman, he viewed with apprehension its consequences in historiography, as manifested for instance in the interpretation of Puritanism and of the Civil War.[415] Is there, however, really
none of that eclecticism in Stubbs's own original view or in his thesis
about the medieval parliament as a 'concentration of the local machinery?' Are Richardson and Sayles correct when they tell us that
Stubbs's 'illusions' about the medieval constitution are caused by a
lack of historical-critical insight instead of a political belief?[416]

---

[414] Cf. W. Stebbing, 'Canon Stubbs's *Constitutional History of England*, 1874–1878' in *E.R.*
150 (1879), p. 2.
[415] Cf. W. Stubbs, *op. cit.*, III, p. 618.
[416] Cf. H.G. Richardson and G.O. Sayles, *op. cit.*, p. 5.

While the origins of his thesis are difficult to find, we shall begin by checking which elements of his first concentration-theory might possibly have had their source in some colleague's writings. We noticed already that Stubbs, after his conception began to take shape in 1868, became more and more engrossed in what he called 'comparative constitutional history.' He consulted not only the older English historiographical tradition – embodied in the *Lords' Report* or in the works of Hallam and John Allen[417] – but also some foreigners like Waitz. These authors may have influenced his work as such, but they did not influence his central idea that parliament was a concentration of local communities.

Palgrave is the English author most likely to have influenced Stubbs. His influence in this respect however must have been negligible, as Stubbs criticized many aspects of Palgrave's work. Palgrave attached much importance to the influence of local administrative bodies on the later central parliament, but in his case the *liaison* stressed parliament's originally judicial function. Influences 'from below' had, in Palgrave's view, more consequences for the function of parliament than its composition. It was precisely this functioning that made the king and his council an indispensable 'first estate' in parliament.

Stubbs emphasized other aspects in his approach. In 1867 he acknowledged the original quality of Palgrave's approach, without going deeply into it.[418] Whatever passed from the local infrastructure to the 'national centre' of parliament, was in Stubbs's opinion mainly related to the principle of representation. The idea of representation was first developed in the infrastructure and gained national importance by means of concentration. Representation had been at the basis of the early tradition of local administration; it was also the basis of the system of national self-government. No parliament could function without this representative principle; Stubbs did not believe any parliament could exist without representation, or even without the Commons as most representative element. Only a representative parliament could lead to self-government. All of the centralising policies from Henry II until Edward I involved the safeguarding and even the consolidation of local administration, and so led to a training in 'self-government.' "The reign of Henry III and the first twenty years of Edward, prove the increasing capacity for self-government, as well as

---

[417] His parliamentary thesis as a whole cannot simply be explained with reference to the *Lords' Report*, as suggested by Richardson and Sayles (*op. cit.* p. 6).
[418] Cf. *The Chronicle of Benedict of Peterborough*, I, p. LXXXV.

the increased desire und understanding of the idea of self-government."[419] There is no doubt about it: self-government and representation stand centrally in Stubbs's view of parliament as a 'concentration
of the local machinery.' Their return happens to coincide with
Stubbs's summing-up.[420] Only one of the foreign authors consulted by
Stubbs might have been a source for the concentration idea: the
Prussian Rudolf von Gneist.[421] Notwithstanding Stubbs's objections to
Gneist's conceptions of English medieval history, there is a marked
similarity in their concentration theory. Although Gneist's work may
have had only a limited influence on Stubbs's contemporaries in England, Stubbs thought otherwise.[422] He referred to Gneist as "this great
jurist of the absolute despotism of the Norman sovereigns," and in the
Constitutional History there are a great number of references to Gneist.[423]

Was Gneist indeed so unknown in England? E.A. Freeman, for all
his dislike of German historical literature and certainly of the 'absolutist' Gneist, believed that many people in England had made use
of him. "I do not see" – he wrote to Goldwin Smith in 1888 – "why
people have run so after Gneist, who is very unintelligent and very inaccurate, when they have Hallam and Stubbs."[424] In the same year
G.W. Prothero devoted an extensive article to Gneist, whose work had
been translated at long last. Notwithstanding a long list of critical
notes, Prothero had great admiration for Gneist, insisting that it had
lasted shamefully long before Gneist had been translated and read:
"only a few students have been aware that the highest living authority,
after the bishop of Chester, on the history of English government, was
a foreigner."[425]

When Stubbs after 1868 became more and more engrossed in 'comparative constitutional history,' Gneist was undoubtedly one of those
who inspired and assisted him in his labour. Certainly more so than
French authors like Picot, Hervieu and Boutaric, who are named in

---

[419] W. Stubbs, *op. cit.*, II, pp. 292–293.

[420] See *Ibid.*, I, pp. 393, 512, 545, 595, 623; II, p. 623.

[421] See on Gneist, G. Cohn, *Gneist und Stuart Mill*, Berlin, 1869 and Ch.E. McClelland,
The German Historians and England, Cambridge, 1971, pp. 135–144; cf. on the idea of self-
government in German historical literature also pp. 269–270.

[422] Cf. J. Redlich and F.W. Hirst, *The History of Local Government in England*, sec. ed., intr.
by B. Keith-Lucas, London, 1970, pp. XIII, XV.

[423] Cf. W. Stubbs, *op. cit.*, I, pp. 356 (note 1), 358 (note 1), 377 (note 1), 388 (note 1),
436 (note 2).

[424] *The Life and Letters of E.A. Freeman*, ed. W.R.W. Stephens, London, 1895, II, p. 380.

[425] G.W. Prothero, 'Gneist on the English Constitution' in *E.H.R.* 3 (1888), pp. 1–33
(quotation p. 1); cf. also pp. 161–163.

the fifteenth chapter as experts on the subject of the French *États-Généraux*.[426] While Stubbs did not share Gneist's rather low estimate of the influence of the Anglo-Saxon tradition nor his fanatical admiration for the creative Norman kings, the line of English political developments traced by Gneist in the sixties comes very close to Stubbs's central idea.[427] Gneist had realized that both the essence and the uniqueness of the English system of self-government were based on the "Verbindung der Staatsverwaltung mit der Grafschaftsverfassung."[428]

Gneist was convinced that English constitutional history (especially as pictured by Hallam and by Macaulay) had failed to acknowledge "die entscheidende Bedeutung welche das innere Leben der Lokalverwaltung auf den Gang der englischen Geschichte ausgeübt hat."[429] This was the very essence of Gneist's perspective. The development of self-government was identical to "die innere Geschichte der Parlementsverfassung"; self-government was the very foundation of parliament.[430] It was connected with the structure of the Commons as "die Zusammenfassung der Grafschaften und Städte in der obrigen Gestalt der Verwaltungsgemeinden ... Die communae in ihrer Gesamtheit fassen sich hier als Staatskörperschaft nach denselben Grundsätzen zusammen, wie sie in den Lokalverbänden zu Amt und Steuer verbunden sind."[431] The Plantagenets had incorporated Anglo-Saxon elements of local self-government into the central administration. Both for Gneist in the sixties and for Stubbs ten years later this policy provided the frame of reference for the constitutional history of England. In 1882 Gneist perceived – rightly, we think – that in his general perspective Stubbs was influenced by his studies.[432] However, in some respects Gneist's vision of early parliamentary history differed from Stubbs's: Gneist was more realistic, his interest was centered more on the actual administration than on the constitutional theory.[433] Thus

[426] Cf. E.P. Boutaric, *Les premiers États Généraux*, Paris, 1860. See on Boutaric, *Revue Historique* 3 (1878), pp. 398–400. G. Picot, *Les élections aux États Généraux*, Paris, 1874; H. Hervieu, 'Recherches sur les premiers États Généraux et les Assemblées Représentatives' in *Revue de Législation ancienne et moderne, Française et étrangère*, année 1873, pp. 377–431, 507–520.

[427] See for Stubbs's criticism of Gneist, note 423; for Gneist's criticism of Stubbs, see R. von Gneist, *Englische Verfassungsgeschichte*, Berlin, 1882, pp. 209–210.

[428] Cf. *Ibid.*, p. 287; R. von Gneist, *Selfgovernment*, Berlin, 1871, pp. 144–204; this organic link functioned in Gneist's Hegelian conception as a 'Zwischenbau' between State and Society. See on this, J. Redlich, *Englische Lokalverwaltung*, Leipzig, 1901, pp. 746–748.

[429] R. von Gneist, *Selfgovernment*, p. 61.

[430] *Ibid.*, p. IV and p. 930 ff.

[431] *Ibid.*, p. 59.

[432] R. von Gneist, *Englische Verfassungsgeschichte*, p. 287 (note).

[433] Cf. R. von Gneist, *Das heutige englische Verfassungs- und Verwaltungsrecht*, Berlin, 1857, vol. I, pp. V-VI.

he considered the 'council' an essential part of the early parliament, fully recognizing (as did the older historiography in the first half of the 19th century) the original judicial function of this body.[434]

Gneist also brings us closer to the political atmosphere of the mid-19th century and to the problem of Stubbs's historical eclecticism. This does not mean that Stubbs's writing contained a political message; he was too good a scholar to make history serve an immediate use, as his friend Freeman was far too prone to do. However, his parliamentary thesis does have points in common with a contemporary debate. Stubbs's framework for the constitutional development of the Middle Ages gains clarity after an examination of the great constitutional debate (carried on throughout the fifties and the sixties) on central and local administration, i.e. the centralization of government. Other vital points for understanding Stubbs's main idea can be found in some theories of what the American F.H. Herrick called the 'second Reform Movement.'[435]

The fundamental problems of the relationship between central administration and local self-government are, as it were, elucidated in Stubbs's synthesis regarding 1066 as well as in the first very important concentration-theory connected to it. Following the debate on these subjects, some political activists began to put more stress on the topical meaning of the medieval constitution. A later critic of Gneist, the Austrian J. Redlich, was firmly convinced that Gneist had been inspired by 'traditionalist' defenders of the old Anglo-Saxon local self-government, such as Toulmin Smith and David Urquhart.[436]

The Whig tradition had long insisted that the greatest dangers to the constitution would come from too much 'influence' by the Crown or a 'standing army.' Apart from these dangers the fear around 1850 was of the growing tendency towards centralization. This threatened the historically evolved constitution. The past had known the glowering dangers of monarchic absolutism; the present was threatened by bureaucratic absolutism. Plainly here was a new debating-point on the

---

[434] Cf. R. von Gneist, *Englische Verfassungsgeschichte*, p. 352 (note 3); R. von Gneist, *Das englische Parlament in tausendjährigen Wandelungen*, Berlin, 1886, p. 135.

[435] F.H. Herrick, 'The Second Reform Movement in Britain 1850–1865' in *Journal of the History of Ideas* 9 (1948), pp. 174–192.

[436] J. Redlich, *Englische Lokalverwaltung*, p. 786.

subject of the British constitution, one which had been lacking – as W.J.M. Mackenzie points out – in the old Whig ideology.[437]

The matter only now acquired a topical meaning. In the thirties and forties of the last century Benthamite reformers like the theoretician Austin and E. Chadwick carried the day in their argument on behalf of the need for more centralization. This argument was coupled with a condemnation of the oligarchy and corruption in existing local self-government, in their view the greatest possible threat to democracy.[438] Around 1850 Chadwick's 'Norman' policy of centralization, together with the pernicious and 'illegal' methods of 'inquest' practised by many of the Royal Commissions, became the target of criticism. Chadwick might propagate the inevitability of a laboriously growing tendency towards centralization, but his main opponent, Toulmin Smith, still regarded it as a very serious threat to political liberty. To Smith, centralization was synonymous with unconstitutionality.[439]

The process of centralization would also cause the growth of a highly questionable 'unconstitutional' bureaucratization, for a 'standing army' of professionals and paid officials was as much to be feared in the administration as in national defence.[440] A bureaucratic centralization was in itself inimical to the spirit of the constitution; it denied the principle of representation and therefore endangered political liberty. Toulmin Smith saw centralization and representation as diametrically opposed. Liberty could only be defined from within, from the bottom up and from inside. The principle of the separation of powers was no evidence of political liberty. True liberty only flourished in countries with historically evolved traditions of local self-govern-

---

[437] W.J.M. Mackenzie, *Theories of Local Government*, London, 1961, pp. 7–9. Cf. also W.C. Lubenow, *The Politics of Government Growth. Early Victorian Attitudes toward State Intervention, 1833–1848*, Newton Abbot, 1971.

[438] Cf. E. Chadwick, 'The New Poor Law' in *E.R.* 63 (1836), pp. 487–537, esp. p. 518 ff; J. Austin, 'Centralization' in *E.R.* 85 (1847), pp. 221–258; cf. W.J.M. Mackenzie, *op. cit.*, p. 8 ff.

[439] Cf. *The Nineteenth Century Constitution. Documents and Commentary*, ed. H.J. Hanham, Cambridge, 1969, pp. 372–384. Some of J. Toulmin Smith works are: *Centralisation or Representation* (1848); *Government by Commissioners, Illegal and Pernicious* (1849): *Local Self-Government and Centralisation* (1851); *Local Self-government Un-mystified* (1857). Cf. also W.L. Burn's remark in *The Age of Equipoise*, London, 1968, p. 229, note 2; cf. also E. Moir, *The Justice of the Peace*, Harmondsworth, 1969, p. 135; cf. E. Creasy, *The Rise and Progress of the English Constitution*, London, 1886, p. 373.

[440] Cf. E. Moir, *op. cit.*, p. 135; W.R. Greg, 'French Judgments of England: Montalembert and Rémusat' in *E.R.* 103 (1856), pp. 558–590, esp. p. 575; cf. also T. Zeldin, 'English Ideals in French Politics during the Nineteenth Century' in *The Historical Journal* 2 (1959), pp. 40–58, esp. pp. 47, 52–54.

ment.[441] These ideas were not propagated solely by the 'romantic constitutionalists' and their school, although these certainly were the most prominent advocates of the idea of local self-government in the period of the Crimean war, a period regarded by many as the acid test of constitutional representative government.[442]

That the romanticists idealised their past – in their case the Anglo-Saxon tradition of local self-government – in the way of all romantic movements, was understandable as a protest against Chadwick who founded the centralizing Board of Health in 1848. Yet there were more people worrying about the tendency towards centralization, and not all were prone to idealize the old traditions. France had been confronted much earlier and more directly with the problems of centralization, and it was France which had the first – and perhaps greatest – scholar in this field: de Tocqueville. In none of his works could Tocqueville forget this problem. "He found what may be called the *culte* of corporations" Bagehot was to write later.[443]

The term self-government had only recently (about 1800) come into use in its political meaning. Because of increasing centralization, it was in the midst of the 19th century infused with a new meaning. Essential for this new meaning is the added definition 'local': no self-government without local self-government.[444] The first to use this qualification was Toulmin Smith in 1849, and many others followed suit. Some years afterwards the German-born American F. Lieber (often styled the father of American political science) wrote: "Self-government, to be of a penetrative character, requires the institutional self-government of the country or district."[445]

This early political scientist is another important promoter of the idea of local self-government. In his first major work, *Manual of Political Ethics*, published in the thirties, he pointed out its importance in what he called the unique Anglo-Saxon 'hamarchy.' He believed that

---

[441] Cf. F. Lieber's pronouncement: "... where there is only a national representative government without local self-government, there is no liberty as we understand it" in his *On Civil Liberty and Self-Government*, London, 1859, p. 172.

[442] Cf. O. Anderson, *A Liberal State at War*, pp. 129–162.

[443] W. Bagehot, *The English Constitution*, New York, 1966, (introduction R.H.S. Crossman), p. 264; cf. O. Anderson, *op. cit.*, pp. 158–159.

[444] Until the end of the 18th century self-government means self-control. Only in 1798, apparently, Jefferson interpreted self-government in a more political sense; see *Oxford Eng. Dict.*, vol. VIII, part II.

[445] F. Lieber, *op. cit.*, p. 325; cf. E. Creasy, *op. cit.*, p. 375. Cf. on Lieber: B. Crick, *The American Science of Politics*, London, 1959, pp. 15–18; for his contacts with E. Creasy see also F. Freidel, *Francis Lieber. Nineteenth-Century Liberal*, Bâton Rouge, 1947, p. 278: see also F. Lieber, *op. cit.*, p. 475 (note).

power should be mediated to prevent absolutist rule.[446] In 1853 he wrote *On Civil Liberty and Self-Government*, highly commending Toulmin Smith and extolling self-government in the sense mentioned before. 'Self-government,' to him, was 'Liberty in action'; self-government did away with political apathy, it strengthened the organic ties between the social classes, it therefore prevented social disintegration, it excluded the possibility of a bureaucracy as in Prussia, it rendered State intervention superfluous, and consequently it left room for a 'laissez faire'.[447]

Both these foreigners found increasing support in England, especially around 1850, when the 'tyranny' of centralization became threatening. It was at just this time that the popular treatise on the British Constitution by Edward Creasy was continually reprinted, with corrections and additions by Tocqueville and especially by Lieber on the very subject of centralization.[448] Looking for the word 'self-government' in the index of his book, the chance reader finds himself referred to the word 'local self-government.'

Recent studies have made clear that the victory over Chadwick, when the Board of Health was abolished in 1854 to be partly replaced by the Local Government Act Office of 1858, was in fact only a Pyrrhic victory, but everybody involved at the time believed that it meant a decisive victory for the principle of local self-government.[449] The apparent defeat of Chadwick and his followers at any rate took the wind out of the sails of the more romantically inclined opponents. The first danger seemingly being over, other voices could make themselves heard, including the voices of those realists who saw the shortcomings on the 'self-governmental level' of those vaunted traditions of local self-government. Self-government on the local level should not merely keep the central government's power in check; it was to have another, educational, function. This second function was for years to

---

[446] Cf. F. Lieber, *Manual of Political Ethics*, London, 1839, p. 358 and pp. 381–387. Cf. A. Smith, 'Lieber's Political Ethics' in *E.R.* 73 (1841), pp. 55–76.

[447] Cf. F. Lieber, *On Civil Liberty and Self-Government*, pp. 251–255.

[448] E. Creasy's book, *The Text-Book of the Constitution* was published in 1848. The third edition came out in 1855: it was wholly revised, with additions especially on the point of local self-government. See E. Creasy, *op. cit.*, pp. 201–203, 371–377. For E. Creasy, see T.F. Henderson in *D.N.B.*, vol. 13, (London, 1888), p. 64. Cf. also *The Life and Letters of E.A. Freeman*, I, pp. 172–174, 231.

[449] Cf. E. Moir, *op. cit.*, p. 147; R.M. Gutchen, 'Local Improvements and Centralisation in Nineteenth-Century England' in *The Historical Journal* 4 (1961), pp. 85–96; R. Lambert, 'Central and Local Relations in Mid-Victorian England. The Local Government Act Office, 1858–1871' in *Victorian Studies* 6 (1962), pp. 121–150; open support for Chadwick's standpoint was given by F.O. Ward, 'Sanitary Consolidation – Centralization – Local Self-government' in *Q.R.* 88 (1851), pp. 435–492.

come the theme of discussions within the so-called 'Second Reform Movement.'

In the sixties (as well as after 1867) the ideal of local-self-government was believed to have great political-educational value. While Toulmin Smith had not neglected this aspect, as '1867' approached, increasingly more attention was directed at it.[450] There was a 'dangerous' possibility that the voting rights might be extended to the lower classes, which meant that a number of future voters would have to be politically educated, and where could they be better instructed in matters political than in their own voting district?[451]

In 1861 J.S. Mill had emulated Toulmin Smith by devoting considerable space to this political-educational value and its final goal: the national concentration in Parliament. In *Considerations on Representative Government* he commended the local administrative organs as being the most useful instruments for educating the nation. They were the ideal channels along which to direct the central government's indispensable administrative know-how for the use of the inexperienced local administrators.[452] His fifteenth chapter on 'local representative bodies' has the often cited slogan: "Power may be localised, but knowledge to be most useful must be centralised."[453] A year afterwards he wrote along the same lines: "The centralisation which it (i.e. enlightened English opinion) approves is that of knowledge and experience, rather than of power."[454]

In this connection Mill desired an improvement of the representation on the local level and the introduction of representative bodies in those places (the counties) where they were still non-existent. In order to supplement the national Parliament, to form a sort of substratum for it, he insisted that 'local sub-Parliaments' should be set up.[455] These local parliaments could train political talent for the national Parliament and as such would have an importance reaching far beyond the narrow geographical boundaries of their original territory. The same idea occurs both in liberal and conservative writings

[450] Cf. H.J. Hanham, *The Reformed Electoral System in Great Britain, 1832–1914*, London, 1968 (Historical Association), p. 9.
[451] Cf. B. Keith-Lucas, *The English Local Government Franchise*, Oxford, 1952, pp. 7, 106.
[452] Cf. J.S. Mill, *Utilitarianism, Liberty and Representative Government*, ed. A.D. Lindsay, London, 1964, p. 347.
[453] *Ibid.*, p. 357.
[454] J.S. Mill, 'Centralisation' in *E.R.* 115 (1862), pp. 323–358, quotation p. 352.
[455] J.S. Mill, *Utilitarianism, Liberty and Representative Government*, p. 353.

in the second half of the 19th century: the two Local Government Acts of 1888 (creating county councils) and of 1894 are partly based on it.[456] The newly appointed representative county councils were judged by Gladstone to be "a necessary complement to democracy in the national parliament."[457] His ideal was to have 'a local parliament in every village,' which was to be justified by an appeal to the past: the Local Government Acts aimed only at the 'restoration' of the old principles of local self-government. As we saw, the first function allotted to the local bodies (checking the process of centralization) never came near the expected result. The more active task of educating the voters was also destined to fall short of what the idealistic reformers had envisaged. Never were the county councils to be 'local parliaments'; never would Gladstone's dream of a new, active and stimulating 'village democracy' come true.[458]

There is a third set of thoughts, which at that time stressed the value of the decentralization principle as expressed in the electoral system. As a matter of fact the word 'decentralization' – apparently used for the first time in England in 1822 – was not an accurate term for England, since England never in its history had known centralized government. People preferred to speak of 'localization,' this being the opposite of 'centralization.' The word originated with Creasy.[459] Another term currently used was 'the principle of locality,' or 'the localising principle,' the latter principle to be stressed continually as essential for the British constitution. It was mirrored in the national representative legislative body, which consisted of the representatives of districts. In the fifties G.C. Lewis advocated the use of this system to keep the 'tyranny of the majority' at bay, which he saw looming near with the advent of democracy. Lewis agreed with many others – J.S. Mill, Th. Hare, J.G. Marshall – that minority groups had a certain value and that their rights should be safeguarded in a representative system of government. "A minority may be the last expiring remnant of mischievous error, which survives its age; it may also be the germ of

[456] Cf. J.P.D. Dunbabin, 'The Politics of the Establishment of County Councils' in *The Historical Journal* 6 (1963), pp. 226–252 and 'Expectations of the New County Councils and their Realization' in *The Historical Journal* 8 (1965), pp. 353–379.

[457] Cf. B. Keith-Lucas, *op. cit.*, pp. 6–7.

[458] *Ibid.*, pp. 26, 42–43.

[459] Cf. E. Creasy, *op. cit.*, p. 371; see for centralization and localisation, *Oxford Eng. Dict.*, vols. II and VI.

truth and wisdom, just struggling for existence, and trying to make it-self heard. Now it is by the accidents of place that peculiarities of opin-ion and position, that limited, novel, and sectional interests, can alone obtain any representation."[460]

In the fifties Lewis was still able to formulate his thesis in this way, partly because democratization had hardly made any leeway (only 'propertied' minorities stood a chance), and partly also because his argument was based on an ideal situation in which the diversity of 'interests' was geographically similar to the diversity of constituencies. This 'sociological' way of reasoning had also influenced a number of reformers in 1831–1832 whose ideal had been socially homogeneous constituencies.[461] Lewis's idea may have had some roots in reality be-fore the third Reform Bill, which instituted more or less equal electoral constituencies, and led to the elimination of the last strongly local and traditionally defined districts. The existing district representation sys-tem, in Lewis's view, guaranteed that minorities would be represented, because the parliamentary system as such had its origin in the prin-ciple of minority representation. Wasn't every district a minority within Parliament as a whole? "Our parliamentary system is exclu-sively founded on this principle ... Every member is now elected by the majority of a minority".[462] The localising principle was an es-sential part of the British representative system, and Lewis too regarded it as the best remedy against increasing centralization. "The most effectual counteraction which a representative system can offer to an excess of the system of centralisation – the besetting sin of every active and energetic government – is to be found in the localising princi-ple."[463]

It is interesting that Lewis, in 1847 a supporter of his tutor Austin's centralization ideas, ten years afterwards was insisting on the impor-tance of local self-government.[464] His change of heart is clear evidence that the public attitude towards centralization had changed in and after 1850.

Although the second Reform Movement was relatively peaceful compared to the first Reform Movement, yet hardly a year passed

460 G.C. Lewis, 'History and Prospects of Parliamentary Reform' in *E.R.* 109 (1859), pp. 264–292, quotation p. 288.
461 Cf. H.J. Hanham, *op. cit.*, p. 29; cf. also D.C. Moore's articles, mentioned in note 121.
462 G.C. Lewis, 'Marshall on the Representation of Minorities' in *E.R.* 100 (1854), pp. 226–235, quotation p. 232.
463 G.C. Lewis in *E.R.* 109 (1859), p. 289.
464 Cf. *Letters of Sir George Cornewall Lewis*, ed. G.F. Lewis, London, 1870, pp. 152–153.

without the publication of some treatise or article on the representative principle.[465] Just as during the first Reform Bill, it was argued that not numbers should be represented in Parliament, but the interests of every class and every group. This point was stressed even stronger than in former times because the tyranny of numerical majority loomed more and more threatening with the coming electoral reform. The minority problem was now the major concern of all. To the Whig W.R. Greg it was a vital matter that the electoral districts in their diversity should continue to exist: equalizing the districts might well lead to catastrophes.

In 1857 Greg was the first Whig to hold America up as the horrifying example of a corrupt majority tyranny. Like Lewis he was of the opinion that the old English district system safeguarded minority groups simply because of the diversity and inequality of constituencies.[466] As early as 1831–1832 some early Whigs had already opposed uniformity of franchise. Now, in the fifties and sixties, many wanted to preserve the diversity in the district system as a 'guarantee' of political freedom. Ideologically the opposition against democratic majority rule was armed with theories about diversity and liberty, sometimes with mystical overtones.[467] The maintenance of the exisiting diversity meant in effect that the remaining political strongholds of the *ancien régime* were to be preserved on behalf of the reigning aristocratic élite. Now that the danger was so close, Greg was enough of a realist to acknowledge this fact.

The first Reform Bill had not caused any fundamental changes in political leadership. Because of the inequality and diversity of the electoral districts (because tiny boroughs and counties were still in existence), it was possible for the House of Commons after 1832 to

[465] During this period a Reform Bill was introduced four times: 1852, 1854, 1859 and 1860 (cf. F.H. Herrick's article). Apart from G.C. Lewis's articles we refer to the articles by W.R. Greg: 'Representative Reform' in *E.R.* 96 (1852), pp. 452–508; 'The Expected Reform bill' in *E.R.* 95 (1852), pp. 213–280; 'Representative Reform' in *E.R.* 106 (1857), pp. 254–286; in addition to the studies by J.S. Mill and Th. Hare those of G.C. Broderick also became widely known. These latter were published in his *Political Studies*, London, 1879, pp. 1–46, 452–538.

[466] Cf. D.P. Crook, *American Democracy in English Politics, 1815–1850*, Oxford, 1965, p. 87 ff.; W.R. Greg, 'Representative Reform' in *E.R.* 106 (1857), p. 281.

[467] Cf. note 136. It was believed that the English system of representation by localities, prevented the system from degenerating into class-representation, see, e.g., J.G. Dobson, 'Position and Prospects of Parties' in *E.R.* 125 (1867), pp. 269–301, esp. p. 291: "Representation in the English Parliament has always been that of localities, or, more properly, of local communities, each containing a mixture of classes and interests." The ideal of a socially homogeneous constituency was liable to foster class representation. It was later opposed by Russell and others for that very reason. See D.C. Moore in *The Historical Journal* 9 (1966), p. 43 (note 18).

continue providing the Executive Power with plainly aristocratic leaders. It was the small constituencies that had sent the future ministers to the Commons, and these same districts guaranteed greater continuity in membership for their delegates; this in turn was a guarantee of unbroken instruction in politics and in the ministerial craft. Greg could prove statistically that the new and numerically larger constituencies were in the habit of electing a changing group of representatives, with hardly a possible future minister among them.

Greg's question, therefore, was this: what was to become of the House of Commons' 'major' function? How could it go on schooling and providing new cabinet ministers if the constituencies were to be equalized and reformed only according to size of population? Parliament would lose the greater part of its 'official and ministerial purposes.'[468] But where would new ministers spring from? From the Civil Service? Could democratic reformers be planning such a change in power, such handing of power to bureaucrats? Bureaucratic rule, after all, was bound to herald the end of democracy. "Surely those democratic politicians who are bent upon abolishing small and multiplying large boroughs, and who would divide the whole country into populous and homogeneous electoral districts, can have little conception in what an anti-democratic direction their reforms are tending."[469] In this mid-Victorian period with its absence of modern organized political parties, there was something to be said for Greg's argument.

I have explained some of the ideas concerning the second Reform Movement to make it quite clear that reformist ideas on the Whig side before 1867 were rather in the 1832 tradition than an anticipation of 1867; the second Reform Movement was more of an epilogue than of a prologue. The real electoral and parliamentary reforms in 1867 and afterwards in the eighties did not come up to the expectations of the authors in the second Reform Movement, of whom Greg is an interesting if somewhat less well-known exponent.[470] His publications accorded with what other Whigs and Tories wrote in the *Edinburgh Review* and the *Quarterly Review* in 1867, who both fulminated against the Reform Bill as too radical. The combined objections amounted to one strong harangue against democracy: the recurring theme was that

---

[468] W.R. Greg, 'Representative Reform' in *E.R.* 106 (1857), p. 275.
[469] *Ibid.*, p. 276.
[470] Cf. H.J. Hanham, *op. cit.*, p. 4 ff.; G. Himmelfarb, *Victorian Minds*, New York, 1968, pp. 333–392; F.H. Herrick, *op. cit.*, pp. 174–178.

the British constitution should be 'popularized' without being 'democratized.'[471]

To return to Stubbs and his work: about 1870 the classical theory concerning the importance of local self-government in its relationship to the central administration had found, more or less its final shape.[472] There had now also been two decades of extensive discussion of the representative principle by leading political thinkers; the unique English system of 'local' representation had been stressed time and again. Stubbs himself was writing his *Constitutional History* in the seventies, between the second Reform Bill and the third one. His constitutionalism is greatly similar to many of the ideas held by the Reform Movement in the fifties and the sixties. Stubbs had no direct political message, nor was he historically eclectic. He did not admire the Anglo-Saxon tradition of local self-government too greatly, for in his inaugural speech he had warned against ancient and traditional institutions being revered simply for themselves.[473] Yet for all his caution there was a certain affinity between his important synthesis and the political atmosphere in which the second Reform Movement flourished. Among the central ideas in political thinking during the past twenty years, self-government and representation came first. The problem of centralization caused attention to be directed towards the need for the localising of political power together with the centralization of talent; similarly it had caused a demand for the institution of representative bodies on a lower level to train representatives for the national parliament.

During the seventies Stubbs stated that Queen Victoria's as well as Edward I's Parliament had been based on two principles; the 'three estates' and the concentration of 'local machinery.' The latter description denoted the House of Commons as a concentration of local communities, and as such it had some reality before the third Reform Bill was passed; as long as the constituencies were not artificially regrouped according to the number of their inhabitants, the traditional link remained between the national parliament and the old local communities of the parliamentary boroughs and counties (where people

---

[471] Cf. W.R. Greg, 'Representative Reform' in *E.R.* 106 (1857), p. 278.
[472] W.J.M. Mackenzie, *op. cit.*, p. 18.
[473] Cf. W. Stubbs, *Seventeen Lectures on the Study of Medieval and Modern History*, New York, 1967, p. 22: "To be a slave of old traditions is as great a folly as to be a slave of new quackeries."

voted more as part of a group instead of individuals).[474] Parliament, that is to say the House of Commons, was originally a concentration of these historically defined communities, the House itself being rather like a *communitas communitatum*. The conservative Gneist had been right when he complained that this very 'Gemeinschaft' character of the Commons as a concentration of local communities had disappeared after 1867, and was certainly absent after 1884.

Gneist saw that the industrial 'Gesellschaft' had made an end of the traditional political system. He was not the only one to disapprove of this. Even Freeman, 'democrat' though he was, openly condemned the 'contempt of history' responsible for 'this mangling of boundaries.' "And I cannot believe in 'one man, one vote.' It seems to upset the whole notion of the House of *Communes*," he wrote afterwards.[475] The third Reform Bill was the final farewell to a very old parliamentary past.[476]

Stubbs's synthesis 'proved' above all the miraculous success of the medieval constitutional development in integrating two political opposites: centralism and localism. Stubbs's constitutional view could not have come closer to the much-debated subject of the fifties and sixties. The ostensible conspicuous 'Teutonism' of medieval studies in the second half of the 19th century was closely connected with it. The idealization of Anglo-Saxon or Teutonic institutions meant the idealization of 'local self-government.'[477] Even in the 19th century English politics were still determined by the same two governing types: the Anglo-Saxon 'localists' and the Norman 'centralists.' In other words, people like Toulmin Smith and Chadwick. The elective affinity mentioned earlier might well indicate that the merging of the local Anglo-Saxon infrastructure and the centralist Norman suprastructure (as described by Stubbs) was reborn in the attempt to reconcile centralists and de-centralists. For that was what contemporaries thought it meant when the Local Government Act Office of 1858 was created.

Mill and his followers had a similar conciliatory attitude in mind and a similar ideal of synthesis, as witness their motto: "Power must be localised, but knowledge to be most useful, must be centralized." This had been Stubbs's aim when describing English constitutional history from Henry II to Edward I: governmental centralization while

---

[474] Cf. H.J. Hanham, *op. cit.*, pp. 25–26.
[475] *The Life and Letters of E.A. Freeman*, II, p. 441, cf. p. 314, Cf. also I, p. 210.
[476] Cf. Maitland's sharp analysis in 1888, in *The Constitutional History of England*, Cambridge, 1961, pp. 362–363; cf. R.C.K. Ensor, *England 1870–1914*, Oxford, 1936, p. 88.
[477] W.J.M. Mackenzie, *op. cit.*, p. 12.

retaining and even reinforcing local governmental bodies and traditions. This integration had been anchored institutionally, as it were, in the structure of the House of Commons, the concentration of all 'local machinery.' Never before had an English historian made such a forceful attempt to picture the central significance of the county-court as a 'local parliament.' This was how, at long last, the constitution of a county-court was defined by Stubbs; it contained all the elements necessary for a 'local parliament.'[478]

With this in mind, the hope for the revival of the good old times with the extension of the lower administrative organs of county and parish into a kind of representative parliament becomes understandable. The ideal of a 'county-council' in the sense of a 'local parliament' had the 'shire-court' as its historical precedent, as shown by Stubbs in his *Constitutional History*.

It has been remarked that English historians, (especially after 1848), when looking for an explanation of the uniqueness of the English experience of a firm and stable development of the constitutional and parliamentary governmental system, sought their answer to their question somewhere in the past. While Stubbs's predecessors had searched the 17th and 18th centuries for a solution, he turned to the Middle Ages for his proof. His work like theirs used conceptions like limited constitutional monarchy, ministerial responsibility and cabinet government. Yet what dominated his work was the idea of a national self-government, the origin and the growth of which he ascribed to the thirteenth century.[479] In this connection we should remember the significant summary in Stubbs's little publication of 1876, *The Early Plantagenets*.

Stubbs's constitutional opinions were a late continuation of a very old medieval constitutional tradition, which had had its main supporters among the chronicles of the 'school of St. Albans.'[480] Stubbs however went much farther, because of his knowledge of subsequent events, especially those of the 17th century. The Civil War, the Restoration and the Glorious Revolution partly 'repeated' and partly 'continued' the medieval struggle for a free parliamentary constitution. Certain rights that had repeatedly been demanded by the Commons in the Middle Ages became real only in the 17th century, and this led

---

[478] W. Stubbs, *op. cit.*, II, p. 205: "It contained thus all the elements of a local parliament – all the members of the body politic in as full representation as the three estates afterwards enjoyed in the general parliament."
[479] See notes 419 and 420.
[480] V.H. Galbraith, *Roger Wendover and Matthew Paris*, Glasgow, 1970, p. 20.

Stubbs to the conclusion that medieval constitutional aspirations had become fulfilled in the 17th century.[481] This long pre-history ensured the lasting success of the unique English achievement of self-government. It was a medievalist perspective also applied to the first centuries of modern history: in fact a 'Whig' perspective.

The exceptional achievements of Stubbs both as editor and historian warrant our extensive treatment of him. Never before had any English historiographer described so ingeniously and in such great detail the importance of the English Middle Ages for constitutional affairs. My aim has been to show the main trend of Stubbs's work, even at the risk of blurring the picture of his methods. Even in his very last chapter Stubbs consistently warned against an one-sided reasoning, against a 'constant accentuation of principles,' usually masking too little factual knowledge and implying 'a bias towards foregone conclusions.'[482] Stubbs was far above the common run of historians, and his concentration-theory concerning parliament far outgrew the merely contemporary significance already illustrated, at least in the general thrust of its argument. Stubbs's synthesis lost its lustre only after the mid-Victorian ideal of national self-government through local self-government had been proved hardly practicable.

5) E.A. Freeman and J.R. Green

> I do not think that you and J.R.G. mean the same thing when you talk about the unity of modern and ancient History ... I hold a religious unity, he (Green) a philosophical, and you, I suppose, an actual continuity.
>
> (W. Stubbs to E.A. Freeman, 1867)

Our discussion of the remaining two members of the Oxford-School, E.A. Freeman and J.R. Green, will be less extensive. Although Round's harsh criticism severely damaged Freeman's reputation as a historian at the end of the 19th century, he was somewhat rehabilitated afterwards by H.A. Cronne, D. Douglas and M.E. Bratchel. Also, significantly, by Stubbs's special detractors, Richardson and Sayles, who believed they had found support for their own opinions in Freeman's vision of continuity regarding 1066.[483]

---

[481] Cf. W. Stubbs, *op. cit.*, II, p. 622.
[482] *Ibid.*, III, p. 501.
[483] Cf. H.A. Cronne, 'E.A. Freeman' in *History* 28 (1943), pp. 78–92; D. Douglas, *The Norman Conquest and British Historians*, Glasgow, 1971; M.E. Bratchel, *E.A. Freeman and the*

Freeman began his writings on the Norman Conquest with two historians who held diametrically opposite views about 1066: Sir Francis Palgrave and the Frenchman, A. Thierry. Freeman devoted two articles to Palgrave's work, reviewing the final parts of Palgrave's *History of England and Normandy* in the *Edinburgh Review* of 1859 and 1865. The first article was sharp, and enumerated all the usual objections to Palgrave's historiography.[484] However, Freeman admitted that there were some 'valuable hints' in the book, and he also made it plain that he preferred Palgrave's view (continuity on the juridical-constitutional level) to Thierry's cataclysmic one, in which the occurrences of 1066 appeared as a seventeenth-century constitutional struggle for liberty. In 1865, two years before the publication of the first part of the *Norman Conquest*, Freeman's opinion about Palgrave was more favourable.[485] While Stubbs may have regarded Kemble as the foremost teacher, Freeman in some respects preferred Palgrave, especially because of 1066.[486] Engrossed in Palgrave's work at that time, and hoping for the professorship that Stubbs finally acquired, Freeman rather suddenly decided to write the history of the Norman Conquest in the hope that the subject would be popular. In any case he had already worked at it for twenty years. The main outlines of the book were clear to him as early as 1865; he needed only to commit it to paper: "there will be little more to do than write down what is already in my head."[487]

In the 1865 review he definitely rejected Thierry, to explain the real meaning of the Norman Conquest according to Palgrave's arguments. The problem of 1066 was declared no longer politically useful, as it had been in the days of Brady, Petyt and Atwood.[488] Yet Freeman's rhetoric and his political moralising pointed to a great involvement, so that the reading public was bound to draw political conclusions.[489]

Victorian Interpretation of the Norman Conquest, Ilfracombe, 1969; G.O. Sayles, *The Medieval Foundations of England*, London, 1966, p. 277; H.G. Richardson and G.O. Sayles, *op. cit.*, pp. 92–93, 117. Freeman's pronouncements on the 'conservative revolution' of 1066 are strongly reminiscent of Palgrave (cf. E.A. Freeman, *The History of the Norman Conquest of England*, Oxford, 1876, V, pp. 55, 333–334).

484 E.A. Freeman, 'Sir F. Palgrave's Normandy and England' in *E.R.* 109 (1859), pp. 486–513, esp. pp. 487, 513; cf. *The Life and Letters of E.A. Freeman*, I, pp. 205, 237.

485 E.A. Freeman, 'Sir F. Palgrave's History of England and Normandy' in *E.R.* 121 (1865), pp. 1–41; cf. *The Life and Letters of E.A. Freeman*, I, pp. 322, 327. Cf. also E.A. Freeman, *The Methods of Historical Study*, London, 1886, pp. 278–281.

486 Cf. *The Life and Letters of E.A. Freeman*, I, pp. 115–116.

487 *Ibid.*, I, pp. 334–335.

488 Cf. *E.R.* 121 (1865), p. 7 ff.

489 He fully intended to write this way. Cf. *The Life and Letters of E.A. Freeman*, I, p. 346; cf. D. Douglas, *op. cit.*, p. 21 ff.

In this way Freeman continued the old 17th-century anti-monarchical tradition, the tradition which had unceasingly stressed the continuity of the periods before and after 1066 in order to safeguard the ancient 'original' rights of the 'people.'[490] Freeman praised Palgrave, quoting him whenever the subject of continuity cropped up, only blaming Palgrave for relying too exclusively on Norman source material, which led him to a negative view of Harold and to a conviction that William was the rightful successor.[491] Incidentally in later years Freeman was reproached for too little confidence in the Norman sources.

Freeman depicted Harold as the national hero, but he began to admire William more and more for having achieved a conservative 'continuing' revolution, for being a 'far-seeing' statesman, leading the country to a prosperous future by retaining and repairing the old institutions: the only and in Freeman's opinion the ideal way of being progressive. William thus was wholly unique as a 'conqueror.'[492].

Freeman had 'archaic' ideas about progress, masking a fear for the future in the usual way by identifying progress with retrogression, a movement forward with a movement backwards. The teutonism masking his liberalism as well as his racist and anti-semitic convictions was partly the origin of these ideas.[493] Another source was a 'cyclical' view of history. Repeatedly, the expression "The cycle has come round" is used, more especially when it seemed that the ancient reputed rights of the people were being restored. The wheel had come full circle, a historical cycle was completed, the point of origin was reached again: this was what Freeman thought of Edward I's period as well as of his own period (1868–1874).[494] Regarding 1066 and its continuity Freeman was largely inspired by Palgrave, yet Thomas Arnold was the

490 Cf. Q. Skinner, 'History and Ideology in the English Revolution' in *The Historical Journal* 8 (1965), p. 177. In 1865 Freeman, however, still warned against an exaggerated modern national picture of the political reality of the 11th century, cf. *E.R.* 121 (1865), pp. 30–31; see also M.E. Bratchel, *op. cit.*, p. 10. For Freeman's idea of continuity, see also J.W. Burrow, 'The Village Community and the Uses of History in late Nineteenth-Century England' in *Historical Perspectives. Studies in English Thought and Society in honour of J.H. Plumb*, ed. N. McKendrick, London, 1974, pp. 255–284, esp. p. 267.

491 Cf. *E.R.* 121 (1865), pp. 22–25, 29, 37.

492 Cf. E.A. Freeman, *op. cit.*, V, p. 395, cf. p. 55; see also E.A. Freeman, *The Growth of the English Constitution*, London, 1872, pp. 19, 55, 105; cf. also his expression: "every modern reform is in truth a step backwards" in E.A. Freeman, *Historical Essays*. Fourth Series, London, 1892, p. 387.

493 On his hatred of Jews, cf. *The Life and Letters of E.A. Freeman*, II, p. 428; cf. also R. Blake, *Disraeli*, London 1969, p. 607.

494 Cf. E.A. Freeman, *op. cit.*, V, pp. 426, 731. The second Reform Bill was in his view more or less the ideal target; for his objections to the third Reform Bill, see note 475. Cf. also *The Life and Letters of E.A. Freeman*, II, p. 319 (Freeman on the ballot, *Ibid.*, I, pp. 210, 240).

man who converted him to the creed of continuity in a general sense. The cyclical aspect in Freeman's conception of a 'retrograde' progress also comes from Arnold, whom Freeman praised very highly in his inaugural speech of 1884.[495] He had learnt the purport of history more from Arnold than from Stubbs: how to be didactic in the political-moralising sense. The great conception of unity and continuity of history, which made him try to find similar forms of government in ancient Greece, Rome, the Middle Ages or his very own time, was taken from Arnold, who also had propagated (under the influence of the reception of Vico early in the 19th century) that the cycle of childhood-manhood-old age could be applied separately to antiquity, Middle Ages, and modern age. Arnold thought that this theory might be helpful for the comparison of certain phases in the three different epochs; he also wanted to use it to give a contemporary meaning to some of the phases of these epochs.[496]

While Freeman was writing the fifth part of his *Norman Conquest*, the two first parts of Stubbs's *Constitutional History* were published. If one compares the two *magna opera*, Stubbs is far superior to Freeman; his views are more original and his enormous accumulation of facts is better assimilated and classified. Freeman was the first to acknowledge this, calling Stubbs very 'German' indeed.[497] Freeman stated that his aim in his last volume was to translate Stubbs's main conception 'into thunder and lightning,' but the translation was only a faded, watered-down version of the original, so much so, that the very essence and originality of Stubbs's parliamentary thesis was lost.[498] It could hardly be otherwise, since, according to Freeman's 'retrograde progress,' the reign of Edward I was nothing but a return to a former situation: in this case, a revival of the old democratic witenagemot.

Thus was the historical cycle completed under Edward I. And Freeman believed that all later parliamentary achievements could be traced back to the old Anglo-Saxon witenagemot. Actually, Freeman was in this respect an adherent of the earliest school of Whig historians on the subject of parliament, a school that already at the end of the

[495] E.A. Freeman, *The Methods of Historical Study*, pp. 5–8; cf. H.A. Cronne, *op. cit.*, p. 84 ff. D. Douglas, *op. cit.*, p. 17.

[496] For an explanation of Thomas Arnold's theory of history see Duncan Forbes, *The Liberal Anglican Idea of History*, Cambridge, 1952, pp. 12–33, 43, 48–55, 66–70, 87–94, 114–116.

[497] Cf. *The Life and Letters of E.A. Freeman*, I, p. 88, cf. p. 380. See on Stubbs's work also E.A. Freeman, *op. cit.*, V, pp. 320, 333 (note 1), 652 (note 1), 719 (note 3).

[498] Cf. *The Life and Letters of E.A. Freeman*, II, p. 88.

17th century had been criticized by Spelman and Brady.[499]. Contrary to Stubbs, whose continuity thesis allowed for some really new developments in constitutional affairs, Freeman proclaimed that all historical progress was in fact only a return to and a restoration of former situations.

While Stubbs planned his constitutional history of the Middle Ages, J.R. Green decided to write the book that was to make him famous: *A Short History of the English People*. It appeared towards the end of 1874, the same year as the first volume of Stubbs's book.[500] Green's book, like Freeman's, did not contain any specific parliamentary thesis,[501] for he was not writing a narrow constitutional and political history. On the contrary he had often reproved Freeman for limiting history solely to political events. These criticisms were voiced in long reviews that contained many of the elements later to be repeated much more sharply by Round. Green followed Macaulay in his 'social history', keeping his distance from the usual form of one-sided constitutional history, and protesting against some anachronisms common to constitutional historiography on the Middle Ages. He was much more realistic than Freeman.[502] In one of his highly worthwhile essays he wrote:

So long as a word like 'Parliament' is used, in defiance of obvious facts, as a constant quantity, as an institution popular and democratic in the fifteenth century, because it is (or is not) popular and democratic in the nineteenth the whole matter must remain a riddle. So long as men regard the great Charter as directly a victory of 'English Liberty' and not (in its direct effects) as the mere substitution of an oligarchy of blood and wealth for the rule of the Crown, we must be prepared to hear the age of Edward I greeted as the opening of all that is really popular in our annals.[503]

[499] Cf. E. Evans, 'Of the Antiquity of Parliaments in England: Some Elizabethan and Early Stuart Opinions' in *History* 23 (1938–1939), pp. 206–221; cf. Freeman in *E.R.* 121 (1865), p. 25; also in *The Growth of the English Constitution*, pp. 94, 96, in his *magnum opus*, V pp. 317, 424.

[500] Cf. on J.R. Green: W.G. Addison, *J.R. Green*, London, 1956; R.L. Schuyler, 'John Richard Green and His Short History' in *Political Science Quarterly* 64 (1949), pp. 321–354; R.B. McDowell, *A. Stopford – Green*, Dublin, 1967, chapter II. Cf. for the first thoughts concerning his book: *Letters of William Stubbs*, p. 154; *Letters of John Richard Green*, pp. 239–240.

[501] It is remarkable that Green made a point of referring to Palgrave's view of the early medieval parliament, cf. J.R. Green, *A Short History of The English People*, London, 1916, pp. 169, 180–181.

[502] Cf. D. Douglas, *op. cit.*, p. 22 (note 4); Green's reviews of Freeman's work are collected in Green's *Historical Studies*, London, 1903, pp. 54–147. See for an extremely unfavourable comment on Green's historiography: C. Oman, *Memories of Victorian Oxford*, London, 1942, p. 161.

[503] J.R. Green, *Historical Studies*, p. 230 (the statement dates from 1869).

Rare utterances like the above notwithstanding, Green's *Short History* is pre-eminently a monument of English Whig historiography of the second half of the nineteenth century. All the Whig topics discussed in this second chapter are more or less present in Green's writings. Green adopted the representation of George III as an absolutist who continued to be influenced by his favourite, Bute, even after the latter had been officially dismissed.[504] Here Green differed markedly from his mentor, the older conservative Stubbs. A further point of difference was that Green viewed English puritanism much more positively, calling it the support as well as the driving force of the English 17th-century struggle for liberty. "The whole history of English progress since the Restoration" – he wrote – "on its moral and spiritual sides, has been the history of Puritanism."[505] In 1688 this puritanism was the force which gave England its freedom after failing to do so in 1642. This puritanism also contained the roots of later English liberalism which according to Green came to be more and more identified with non-conformism.[506] As the 19th century advanced, Green saw liberalism as being closer to 17th-century puritanism than to the Whig tradition of the 18th century. So profoundly did he admire the 'rebels' of the Civil War in their longing for freedom, that he refused to accept "the Ranke point of view" with its implicit understanding for the royalist opponents. Nothing could convince Green that his opinion was one-sided, neither the books of Ranke's liberal English follower, S.R. Gardiner, who plainly intended to demolish the one-sidedness of the Whig view, nor the cutting criticism of conservative historians like J.S. Brewer and J. Gairdner.[507]

"In spite of all the Gairdners and 'Rollsmen' I shall go on loving freedom and the men who won it for us to the end of the chapter."[508] Probably the clearest indication of Green's Whig views of England's past is to be found in the structure of the *Short History* (highly praised

---

[504] J.R. Green, *A Short History*, p. 757 ff.; cf. *Letters of William Stubbs*, pp. 171–172.

[505] J.R. Green, *A Short History*, p. 604; Stubbs and Freeman both were inclined to an unfavourable view of the historical significance of puritanism, cf. W. Stubbs, *op. cit.*, III, p. 618; cf. *The Life and Letters of E.A. Freeman*, II, pp. 266–267.

[506] Cf. his pronouncement of 1880: "Liberalism is becoming more and more coincident with Nonconformity; it is becoming less and less common among men of the higher social class ... I see that Liberals have an intellectual work to do as well as a directly political. I mean that they must convert the upper classes as well as organise the lower." *Letters of J.R. Green*, p. 480.

[507] Cf. *Letters of J.R. Green*, p. 476, cf. on Gardiner also p. 410. See further, Freeman on Gardiner, *The Life and Letters of E.A. Freeman*, II, pp. 266, 393, 450.

[508] *Letters of J.R. Green*, p. 477.

by Stubbs).[509] An essential element of this structure was the term 'New Monarchy.' Green was the first to use this term, and fellow-historians lost no time in adopting it, even making use of it afterwards for indicating periods other than the one for which Green had coined the term.[510] Green gave the name of New Monarchy to the period from Edward IV (its founder) to the reign of Elizabeth I. The reasoning on which this new periodization was based is significant. Green regarded the despotic phase of the Tudor monarchy as 'foreign' to England's constitutional development.[511] It denoted constitutional retrogression, and was an unwelcome break in the constitutional development. It was the Civil War which restored the ancient traditions of freedom. For the Whig Green the term New Monarchy had a pejorative meaning, indicating that the Tudor despotism was, constitutionally speaking, unnecessary and unfruitful. The liberal A.F. Pollard afterwards had a wholly opposite interpretation, which will be discussed in one of the following chapters. This reversal among English liberal historians on the subject of Tudor despotism is the clearest possible illustration of the anti-Whig reaction.

In Green's own time his theory of the New Monarchy and its consequences were mainly criticized by the historian J.S. Brewer who wrote a long destructive article about Green's *Short History* in the *Quarterly Review* of 1876.[512] Himself a conservative, he dismissed the book as leftist, revolutionary, and highly dangerous reading for younger people. Some aspects of Brewer's historical criticism, however, are quite valuable: he saw in Green's treatment of George III's period a culmination of many unjust judgments. And Green's faith, even in 1874, in Burke's *Thoughts on the Causes of the Present Discontents* as a reliable source for the legend about a secret double cabinet during the early years of George III's reign, passed his understanding.[513]

In criticizing the concept of a New Monarchy Brewer damaged several essential aspects of Green's theory. For did not the term "New

[509] Cf. *Letters of William Stubbs*, p. 171.

[510] Cf. E.A. Freeman, *Historical Essays*, Fourth Series, p. 271; F. W. Maitland, *The Constitutional History of England*, pp. 199, 237. Cf. G.O. Sayles, *The Medieval Foundations of England*, chapter 21.

[511] J.R. Green, *A Short History*, p. 290; cf., however, what a certain J.B. Brown wrote in *Nineteenth Century* 10 (1881), p. 709 (note 4): "The new monarchy, of which Mr. Green has written so ably, tyrannous, as it was, was decidedly popular, and was a great step on in the development of the national liberties."

[512] J.S. Brewer, 'Green's History of the English People' in *Q.R.* 141 (1876), pp. 285–323. Cf. also J. Rowley, 'Mr. Green's Short History of the English People: Is It Trustworthy?' in *Fraser's Magazine* 12 (1875), pp. 395–410, 710–724.

[513] J.S. Brewer, *op. cit.*, p. 321.

Monarchy" create an imaginary break in parliamentary history, a break which had never existed? Did not Green over-estimate the role of the Commons in the Middle Ages and did not he consequently highly under-estimate their importance in the New Monarchy period? And, since Green had been led astray towards this over-estimation by Coke and the other early Whig historians, was it not actually their vision that was really presented by Green, a vision that emerged from the parliamentary opposition against the Stuarts?[514] Worse for Brewer were the consequences of Green's new periodization for his opinions about the Civil War. The final result of the Great Rebellion was, for Green, that the old constitution was rehabilitated and that the political trend of the times before the New Monarchy was continued. Now this was a highly naive simplification of history, and it meant that Green did not understand the really new constitutional demands with which the Long Parliament had presented the King.[515] Nor could Brewer agree with Green's explanation of the increase in the power of the Commons on the eve of the Civil War. To the modern historian it might seem that Green was too much occupied with the 'rise of the gentry,' disregarding the decline of the aristocracy. The Tudors had 'neglected' the aristocracy, thereby making it relatively easy for the Commons in the 17th century to gain the upper hand. Brewer, inspired by Francis Bacon, laid great stress on this decline, both socially and politically, of the aristocracy.[516]

Despite such fundamental criticism Green's work was an enormous success. Evidently his own age 'needed' Green's view of the historical development. Actually, Stubbs and Freeman shared Green's idealistic view of the Middle Ages, for all their differences in opinion. More than any preceding scholars, it was these Oxford historians who proved the direct importance of the Middle Ages, the Anglo-Saxons and the Normans. The constitution of the Middle Ages was the firm foundation for modern England.

H. Thomas Buckle was much criticized by the Victorians for denying the importance of the Anglo-Saxon period in his history of English civilisation. "There and nowhere else" – as his critic J.F. Stephen

[514] *Ibid.*, pp. 305–308.
[515] *Ibid.*, p. 305, cf. p. 309; this typical restoration viewpoint is lacking in later reprints of the *Short History*.
[516] Cf. J.S. Brewer, *op. cit.*, p. 312.

wrote – "is to be found the root and foundation of those great institutions from which the laws, the liberties, and the government of Modern Europe spring."[517] Without this strong base modern history would never have been able to acquire those successes achieved in the 17th century. This idea was central, the core of the so-called Whig character of the medievalist scholars' studies. They portrayed a political picture of the medieval past, that featured the continual importance and presence of Magna Carta and parliament. In the mid-Victorian era the recurrent appeal to the past as a binding precedent was neither superfluous luxury nor empty rhetoric: it was the most trusted and dependable vehicle for politicians to justify their actions. However, with the increase of modern mass democracy, even in England it dwindled to rhetoric only. Strange as it may appear to us, Gladstone in 1878 still thought of the Magna Carta as something modern; thus, he invoked article 51 when Disraeli on his own initiative sent Indian soldiers to Malta. This, in Gladstone's view, violated the constitution, which prohibited a standing army within the United Kingdom without parliamentary consent.[518]

One of the contributors to the *Edinburgh Review* predicted in the beginning of the 19th century that constitutional precedents would come to be less valued when society was divested of its *ancien régime* characteristics. For such respect would not accord with the spirit of the times.[519] Nevertheless, it would be a long time before this came about. As Asa Briggs put it, "England did not become a business society" notwithstanding the Industrial Revolution and the increasing 'business prosperity' in the years of 1851–1867.[520] Might it not be better to say 'because of' instead of 'notwithstanding?' "It can be argued ... that the initial effects of industrialization, in conjunction with the fear of revolution in the early part of this period, were to strengthen the bonds of deference, as new capitalists looked to traditional authority as the only reliable guardian of order and property in a sea of unrest." These are F.M.L. Thompson's words.[521] Thompson perceived that the

---

[517] J.F. Stephen, 'Buckle's History of Civilization in England' in *E.R.* 107 (1858), pp. 465–512, quotation p. 499. Buckle had written: "There are few things in our history so irrational as the admiration expressed by a certain class of our writers for the institutions of our barbarous Anglo-Saxon ancestors" (*History of Civilization in England*, Leipzig, 1865; III, p. 10 (note 28).).

[518] Cf. W.E. Gladstone, 'Liberty in the East and West' in *Nineteenth Century* 3 (1878), pp. 1154–1174.

[519] A. Smith, 'Lieber's Political Ethics' in *E.R.* 73 (1841), p. 55.

[520] A. Briggs, *Victorian People*, Harmondsworth, 1965, p. 18, cf. p. 187.

[521] F.M.L. Thompson, *English Landed Society in the Nineteenth Century*, London, 1971, p. 185.

period from 1830–1850 in which desintegration of the 'structure of deference' was imminent, was followed by a period of two decades of a 'renewed social stability and revived deference.'[522]

If a 'cultural lag' existed, it must have been in this very field of English politics. New inspiration in this field was continually sought in the past, notwithstanding the great progress in commerce, industry and social life. Perhaps an exception to this is Walter Bagehot, whose realism, however, did not keep him from admiring Freeman and Stubbs.[523] Bagehot spoke of a deferential society, and such a society can have no more appropriate historiography than the Whig historiography which blossomed in the second half of the 19th century. The basis for mass democracy was unwittingly prepared by the second Reform Movement. At its peak historians and politicians sounded the praise of the powerful tradition, invisible and universal. Parliament was still regarded as consisting exclusively of 'estates' and 'communities,' even by Disraeli who finally ventured the leap in the dark. The *Edinburgh Review* published in 1866 a gleeful comment by James Moncreiff:

We are still a feudal people. The orders and gradations of society are ingrained in all our associations, bound up with our history, fixed deep in our habits and memories ... It is the influence of old tradition which gives so much stability to our constitutional mechanism; and this is the reason why it cannot be transplanted.[524]

Shortly after 1867, however, several thinkers began to be aware of the reverse side of this *reverentia antiquitatis*. As the turn of the century approached, the past was more and more regarded as so much ballast, and it was this conviction, a.o., which led to the change in liberal thinking to be discussed in our next chapter.

---

[522] *Ibid.*, p. 186.
[523] W. Bagehot, *The English Constitution*, New York, 1966, p. 252 (note 1).
[524] J. Moncreiff, 'Extension on the Franchise' if *E.R.* 123 (1866), pp. 263–296, quotation p. 288.

CHAPTER III

TRADITION DISCREDITED

If the abridgement of tradition is ideology, the criticism of tradition may be history – the ascription to the past of a relation to the present more complex than mere transmission.

(J.G.A. Pocock, 1968)

A. THE CRISIS WITHIN THE HOUSE OF COMMONS

Is the High Court of Parliament the only Court in the realm incompetent or incapable to keep order within its own Chambers?

(A. Milman, 1878)

It has often been said, that in the second half of the 19th century English historiography about the medieval parliament was highly anachronistic and finalistic; it showed an almost direct relationship with the Victorian Golden Age of the parliamentary system under Gladstone and Disraeli. This historiography extolled Parliament as something all but divine; even historical scholars studying its origins were dazzled by its glorious presence, and were unable to discern anything else. A crude simplification, yes, but nevertheless true. The English political climate at that time was ideally suited to an anachronistic perspective, the more so in comparison with countries such as France.[1]

In France, in the early years of the Third Republic, a history of the French Estates-General was published by Stubbs's contemporary, the French historian G. Picot. The prefaces both of the first (1872) and the second editions (1888) clearly indicate the enormous differences between the England of Gladstone and Disraeli on the one hand, and on the other hand the France of the early Third Republic, groping so painfully for its own identity. Picot was not the only one in France publicly to doubt the possibility of French self-government. Although

---

[1] Cf. for the cult of parliament in these years: R.C.K. Ensor, *England 1870–1914*, Oxford, 1936, p. 1; for the parliamentary debating club and the many amateur Local Houses of Commons: H.J. Hanham, *Elections and Party Management: Politics in the time of Disraeli and Gladstone*, London, 1959, pp. 104–105, and Blanchard Jerrold, 'On the manufacture of Public Opinion' in *Nineteenth Century* 13 (1883), pp. 1080–1092.

the Estates-General might not be a close-knit governing body (having only a faint resemblance to ordinary parliaments), yet their history fully merited attentive study.[2] It was a pity that previous French generations had lacked the necessary patience and courage for self-government in the face of many failures. Picot was plainly on the defensive: he was forced to preface his work with an apology for the governmental system as such, whereas his colleagues on the other side on the Channel never even dreamed of justifying their parliamentary system's existence.[3]

But these immense differences must not make us forget that after 1880 – just after the publication of Stubbs's life work – England too witnessed a parliamentary crisis, and one which mainly concerned the internal functioning of the House of Commons. All was not gold that glittered.

Although the crisis in the House of Lords early this century received much more publicity, the crisis in the House of Commons is of more fundamental importance, because the Commons are after all the most important organ of the constitution. Because of this crisis the much vaunted value of the old parliamentary traditions came to be doubted. The usefulness of the past was questioned at last, for traditional political arguments and all the historical precedents on which they were based were at last subjected to some critical scepticism. And as the tradition, once so sacred, lost face, the past could be wrested from the grasp of the present. Slowly and with difficulty, it is true, but before 1900 there were noticeable changes in the historical writing on the medieval parliaments.

A closer look at some of the aspects of this crisis is vital to our research. The crisis in the Commons became public knowledge when – around 1880 – the Irish representatives wilfully obstructed the parliamentary proceedings. A great blow to the prestige of the Commons was the ill-reputed session of 31st January–2nd February 1880, when the Speaker had to make his authority felt with the words: "The dignity, the credit and the authority of this House are seriously threatened and it is necessary they should be vindicated."[4] Many realized that the crisis of the Commons was not only the work of the Irish representa-

---

[2] G. Picot, *Histoire des États Généraux*, Paris, 1888, I, p. XV: 'Le refus d'étudier ce qui a précédé la Révolution provient d'un amour-propre désordonné.'

[3] *Ibid.*, pp. IX–X.

[4] Quoted by E. Hughes, 'The Changes in Parliamentary Procedure, 1880–1882' in *Essays presented to Sir Lewis Namier*, ed. R. Pares and A.J.P. Taylor, London, 1956, p. 305.

tives.[5] Actually the House of Commons had come a long way to reach its present dead end. A great amount of articles appeared in many periodicals; their great number itself proof that the Victorians never had that unshakable trust in their Parliament which later generations ascribed to them. All the writers attempted exhaustive background analyses of the many evils and shortcomings hampering the Commons. Some writers reduced the crisis simply to a matter of internal procedure, others placed the existing deadlock in a broad perspective, remarking on the consequences of the second Reform Bill on the composition and functioning of the House of Commons.

The Whig Henry Grey in 1890 deprecated the 1867 and 1884 Reform Bills for the very reason that none of the men who framed them had ever worried about the consequences of these measures for the functioning of the House of Commons; he called this a 'national error' for which the two main political parties were equally to blame.[6] Grey's standpoint was not a new one by any means; he had advocated it already on the eve of 1867, when that prodigious alliance between some liberals and conservatives, called the 'Adullamite Cave,' had been formed. Their leader had been the liberal renegade R. Lowe, who in later years, like Grey, stressed the correctness of their standpoint. The increasing crisis of the House of Commons was proof enough.[7]

In 1884 Grey had once more warned against a repetition of the 1867 mistake, arguing that a new reform of Parliament could only be justified if it would make the House of Commons 'a more efficient instrument for the good government of the country.'[8] Personally he doubted the success of his plea, since the matter of parliamentary reform since the fifties had, in his view, unfortunately become a political game to which the country's wider interests were sacrificed. The need for reforms was in 1867 'created' by politicians rather than demanded by the 'indifferent' nation.[9] The party leaders had been chasing popularity

---

[5] Cf. A. Milman, 'The House of Commons and the Obstructive Party' in *Q.R.* 145 (1878), p. 234; Gladstone, too, had as early as 1878 mentioned the 'brutalization of the House of Commons' as "the most remarkable and vivid change which he had witnessed in his own time." See Oscar Browning, *Memories of Sixty Years*, London, 1910, p. 274.

[6] Earl Grey, 'In Peril from Parliament' in *Nineteenth Century* 28 (1890), p. 1027; Henry George Grey (1802–1894) was the eldest son of the Grey of the first Reform Bill.

[7] See for R. Lowe: Asa Briggs, *Victorian People*, Harmondsworth, 1965, p. 240 ff.; cf. R. Lowe, 'The New Reform Bill' in *Fortnightly Review* 22 (1877), pp. 437–452.

[8] Earl Grey, 'The House of Commons' in *Nineteenth Century* 15 (1884), p. 528.

[9] *Ibid.*, pp. 515–516: "The Act of 1867 was not passed because it was really desired by the nation or because there were reasonable grounds for expecting that it would make the House of Commons more capable of efficiently discharging its duties by correcting its faults, but because an artificial necessity for some change had been created by the persevering efforts of

and had (both in 1867 and 1884) been blind to the essential question whether the House of Commons would profit in terms of increased efficiency.[10] Consequently Parliament had suffered, and had become less efficient as a law-giving and as a deliberating body. After 1867 it was literally 'swamped' by newcomers, all of them intent on their own private and local interests, as Grey put it. Of course this was damaging to the homogeneity of Parliament, and to its functioning. In 1890 Grey still regretted that the number of members had never been reduced, as proposed in 1832.[11]

F. Harrison agreed with Grey that the procedural aspects of the crisis did not really matter: it was rather the whole existing parliamentary system. He repeated his fundamental objections in the eighties:[12] "The collapse is not in this or that, but in everything."[13] Harrison believed that the Commons' tendency to usurp the power of the Executive was the deeper cause of collapse: The House of Commons had acquired an 'executive' character.[14] Yet the House of Commons was too large and heterogeneous to act as an 'executive' organ. Nor was this body the most suitable place for detailed discussions of complex laws, especially since – in Harrison's ironical words – their methods were strongly reminiscent of the Middle Ages.[15] Harrison was not alone in this belief, which can also be found in both Tory and Whig sources.[16]

Was it possible to undo the Reforms of Parliament? Apparently their damaging influence on the internal functioning of the House could only be kept within the bounds by rigorously changing the order of procedures. At the end of his article of 1881 Harrison gave quite a list of suggested improvements, amongst which we notice the introduction of the 'closure' and the system of standing committees. Such measures

speculative politicians and the rivalry of contending parties." Cf. *Nineteenth Century* 28 (1890), p. 1023.

[10] *Nineteenth Century* 28 (1890), pp. 1024, 1029.

[11] *Nineteenth Century* 15 (1884), p. 519; 28 (1890), pp. 698, 1025.

[12] Cf. F. Harrison, *Order and Reform*, London, 1875.

[13] F. Harrison, 'The Deadlock in the House of Commons' in *Nineteenth Century* 10 (1881), p. 318.

[14] *Ibid.*, p. 332: "I shall not waste words to show that an Administration, which is almost a mob, cannot in fact administer at all."

[15] *Ibid.*, p. 330: "The House of Commons persists in the medieval method of settling the drafts and amending every measure, however intricate and however technical, in floating committees of the whole House; and for no other reason but that such was the practice under the Plantagenet Kings, I suppose, by the standing orders of Simon de Montfort."

[16] Cf. A. Milman, in *Q.R.* 145 (1878), p. 234; H. Reeve, 'Earl Grey on Parliamentary Government' in *E.R.* 108 (1858), p. 280 ff.; H. Reeve, 'Todd on Parliamentary Government' in *E.R.* 125 (1867), pp. 580–581.

had already been adopted in America and France at the beginning of the 19th century; yet the oldest parliament in the world had refused even to think of introducing them: they were opposed to the ancient privileges! Similar measures however had been proposed thirty years earlier by T.E. May, a constitutional Whig historian who had long served as clerk of the House of Commons and was therefore particularly aware of the unwieldy procedures in the House of Commons. "The antiquity of our Parliamentary forms ... is a remarkable feature of our Constitution. But this reverence for custom is not without its evils," he wrote in 1854.[17] The House of Commons did not have a truly rational organization, nor were the subjects under discussion classified. The sessions were not ruled by an agenda; and the members still had unlimited opportunities for interrupting by introducing motions or amendments concerned with their own private interests or with secondary matters hardly connected to the theme under discussion. The Estimates Debates for instance provided every single member of Parliament with opportunities galore for airing in the Grand Inquest of the Nation their own desires and grievances, under the ancient constitutional rule of 'grievances before supply.'

In 1854 May denounced this rule – useful and fitting though it might have been in the Middle Ages – as an anomaly in the modern era, as a dangerous obstacle hampering any real control of government spending.[18] In this case too it was necessary to restrict the privilege of free speech, just as had happened in the thirties with the presenting of petitions and in the forties with the reading of the agenda or the debate on whether the House should go into committee after a bill had been read for the second time. In 1854 May asked for the so-called 'Rule of Progress' to be applied to the Estimates Debates, because in this case too precious time was needed for important government affairs. Parliament had to devote some time and attention to the business of governing, and May therefore wanted 'closures' on behalf of governmental affairs. May even advised the Commons in this instance to follow the example set by America and France – normally countries whose examples Victorian England sought to avoid rather than emulate.

May fully realized that 'closures' – if and when discussed in the

---

[17] T.E. May, 'The Machinery of Parliamentary Legislation' in *E.R.* 99 (1854), p. 244. See, on May's relatively moderate demands in 1882, E. Hughes 'Sir Erskine May's Views on Parliamentary Procedure in 1882' in *Public Administration* 34 (1956), pp. 419–424.

[18] *E.R.* 99 (1854), p. 262: "The only result of the present license of debate is, that less vigilance is exercised in controlling public expenditure, than is devoted to the scrutiny of a Private Bill. The voting of the supplies is postponed until the very end of the Session."

Commons – would meet with great resistance and would be regarded as an unprecedented attack on the freedom of speech – indeed, wholly unprecedented in all England's parliamentary history. He remarked ironically that, should the matter come to be discussed, there was a precedent at hand dating from the year 1604 – "what will be much more persuasive with the House of Commons than any argument."[19] In 1854 May also asked for 'standing committees' to be instituted in order to save time.[20] Parliament was far too large to be able to study all aspects of a Bill during the committee phase. In 1881 'a committee of the whole House' was described by F. Harrison also as a total anachronism: "It is nothing but the House sitting in even looser order than usual."[21]

Drastic reforms were shelved, but things were not wholly stagnant. The number of standing orders increased, though none of them was wholly effective. In the 19th century one commission after another was installed and ordered to study the internal functioning of the House of Commons.[22] Their *Reports* were the cause of some half-hearted adaptations, but never of any fundamental changes that might put an end to the loathsome practice of obstructing and hampering the government. The commissions' *Reports* were a compilation of 'useless' antiquarian information, but it took the crisis of early 1882 for this comment to be made about the *Reports*: ". . . These historical investigations are of little real assistance. We want to know, not what was done two or three centuries ago, but what should be done now to restore to the House of Commons its full efficiency and power, and to deliver it from an incubus more formidable than the ancient prerogatives of the Crown."[23] The 'Rule of Progress' was at last in 1882 applied to the Estimates Debates; two standing committees were also instituted and the notorious closure adopted. But the possibilities for obstruction were not yet exhausted. Closure was not effective enough: only the Speaker was originally empowered to take the initiative for closure. As he valued his impartiality he felt little enthusiasm for his new privilege. In

---

[19] *Ibid.*, p. 265.
[20] Before May, others had vainly advocated a better division of labour in the House of Commons, e.g. W. Wickens in *An Argument for more of the Division of Labour in Civil Life in this Country. Part First, in which the Argument is applied to Parliament.*, London, 1829. H. Brougham's reaction to his plea came very late: 'Defects of the Reform Bill – Parliamentary Business' in *E.R.* 66 (1837), pp. 208–219.
[21] *Nineteenth Century* 10 (1881), p. 331.
[22] See K. Mackenzie, *The English Parliament*, Harmondsworth, 1963, chapter 9.
[23] W.W. Manning, 'Parliamentary Procedure' in *E.R.* 155 (1882), p. 205. Cf. A. Milman in *Q.R.* 146 (1878), p. 201.

1887 the privilege was extended to all the members, but even then it was used very seldom.[24] The closure itself might even degenerate into a means for obstruction, since anyone could request it any number of times. It soon appeared much safer to institute a preventive form of closure, a procedure called 'guillotine,' which was gradually introduced after 1887. Here speaking time on certain bills was fixed in advance.

We shall not now deal with the multifarious details necessitated by the modernizing of parliamentary procedures, as our main concern is with the length of time it took England to institute these changes; in the second half of the 19th century even moderate Whigs were slow to realize that the past had become an obstacle in a modern society. The ancient parliamentary traditions were injuring the present, the so-called 'immemorial rights' such as 'grievances before supply' had never been quite so harmful as during the eighties. "Is Parliament to sacrifice its power of independent action out of a mere idolatry of precedents and traditions?" So wondered Gladstone's friend and fellow Liberal party member, J. Guinness Rogers.[25] Everywhere people demanded more 'efficiency'; J. Chamberlain mentioned the need for 'americanization' of the parliamentary rules, and many people agreed with Guinness Rogers that parliamentary inefficiency was simply due to "the supremacy of traditional ideas and the existence of obsolete forms."[26]

Some of the parliamentary traditions did not accord with the new political situations and with the new functions of the House of Commons. During the 19th century there had been a gradual but very fundamental change in the House of Commons. We already noticed F. Harrison's complaint that the House of Commons had been usurping power. He realized that the Executive's power had been weakened by a time-wasting and interfering law-giving body. What with the many chances for interrupting, the countless amendments of proposed Bills, the endless adjournments and long-winded speeches, it seemed that governmental power in the Commons had shrunk to nothing. This 'parliamentary executive' nightmare haunted Harrison's writing ever since, even his Cromwell biography in 1888. Cromwell at least had

---

[24] Nine times in more than ten years (six times by the liberals, three times by the conservatives), according to A. Milman in 'The Peril of Parliament' in *Q.R.* 178 (1894), p. 278.

[25] J.G. Rogers, 'Chatter versus Work in Parliament' in *Nineteenth Century* 16 (1884), p. 405. He continued: "That is what it is doing at present, and will continue to do, until it learns that even Parliaments must bow to the logic of facts and accommodate themselves to the changed conditions of the times."

[26] *Ibid.*, p. 406; cf. J. Chamberlain, 'Shall We Americanise our Institutions?' in *Nineteenth Century* 28 (1890), pp. 861–875.

been aware that a 'parliamentary executive' was utterly impossible; it still remained 'the great problem of our time.'[27]

Yet this 'usurping of power by the Commons' was partly a misunderstanding of Harrison's. If any usurpation was attempted, it was not done by the House of Commons as such but by some of the minority groups within the House. All through the 19th century a struggle for the possession of parliamentary time had been going on between what was called the official and the private members of the Commons.[28] This precious parliamentary time was increasingly claimed by the government, and parliament was thereby becoming a governing body in the literal sense. Almost all the private members' time was appropriated by the government. Harrison had not seen this development, struck as he was with the remarkably tenacious hold on life of some minority groups. The minorities were repeatedly guilty of disturbing the 'normal' course of affairs – disregarding government and official oppositional groups – and they abused the ancient privileges to put their own private and local demands and desires before Parliament. But in the eighties the Commons could no longer be considered a 'concentration of local communities,' which meant that there was less and less time to spare for particularism and localism. The independent members clinging to their seats by means of these traditionalist methods were old-fashioned radicals like Joseph Hume. They wanted Parliament to be a 'Grand Inquest of the Nation,' a place where everyone could come and air their griefs. Restrictions of the free discussions were regrettable to them because Parliament thus lost its original character of a 'remedial court.'

Inside Parliament the rights of all minorities had long been sacred. Because of these minorities the old rules were maintained for so long. However, with the loss of Parliament's function as a 'remedial court,' the old rules became only anachronistic obstacles. At the beginning of the 19th century private members had the same privileges as cabinet ministers. At the end of the century the private members no longer had any power; the government dominated parliament, and in parliament the majority ruled. New radicals and democrats like J. Chamberlain

---

[27] F. Harrison, 'The Transit of Power' in *Fortnightly Review* N.S. 3 (1868), pp. 374–386; cf. W.L. Burn, *The Age of Equipoise*, London, 1968, p. 320 (on H. Reeve, p. 300). Cf. also F. Harrison, *Oliver Cromwell*, London, 1912, pp. 175–176.

[28] Cf. P. Fraser, 'The Growth of Ministerial Control in the Nineteenth Century House of Commons' in *E.H.R.* 75 (1960), pp. 444–463; Valerie Cromwell, 'The Losing of the Initiative by the House of Commons' in *T.R.H.S.* 5th ser. 18 (1968), pp. 1–23.

approved this 'americanization.' The rights of the majority in parliament should take precedence over the rights of minorities.[29]

The Austrian J. Redlich placed the decline of the private members in the last quarter of the preceding century, and while P. Fraser was able to point out earlier signs, the eighties were indeniably the decisive period for their defeat. Old precedents and old procedures were discarded in the eighties, and it was then that parliament came to be regarded as primarily a law-giving body, serving the government according to the will of a majority.[30] The name 'Grand Inquest of the Nation' had long lost every connection with reality, yet it remained in use. Only in 1880 was the inadequacy of this favourite old expression generally acknowledged.[31]

Although the crisis in the English House of Commons, which came to a head in the final two decades of the 19th century, may be connected with developments elsewhere in Europe, in a certain sense it also had its own unique character. On the continent there were parliamentary crises around the turn of the century as there were in England. The continental ones however were more deep-seated and had more far-reaching consequences.[32] In most cases the English crisis did not cause the system as such to be discredited – as happened on the continent –, but it did cause the abolition of some parliamentary traditions. There was little sympathy in England for H. Belloc's anti-parliamentary ideas.

England survived the crisis in the usual way, with no noticeable fundamental changes in the political system, at least not at first sight. The next crisis concerned the House of Lords early in the 20th century: the first indication of a crisis came after 1880 with the Lords's increasing opposition to the House of Commons and their 'too liberal and democratic' Bills.[33] The existence of the parliamentary system was not then at issue, for resistance against the Lords strengthened the po-

---

[29] *Nineteenth Century* 28 (1890), p. 871.

[30] P. Fraser, *op. cit.*, pp. 444, 458.

[31] *Ibid.*, pp. 455–456. The description remained in use, however; it suggested a direct relation to the people, despite the modern party organization. Cf. P. Fraser, *op. cit.*, p. 463; and A. Milman, 'Parliamentary Procedure versus Obstruction' in *Q.R.* 178 (1894), p. 486.

[32] Cf. J. Romein, *Op Het Breukvlak Van Twee Eeuwen*, Leiden-Amsterdam, 1967, I, chapter IX.

[33] In the eighties J. Chamberlain transformed the slogan, 'The Peers against the People,' into a battle-cry. His agitation set off a ceaseless discussion on the House of Lords; a continuous stream of historical and socio-political articles on the House of Lords resulted from this. Cf. R.C.K. Ensor, *England 1870–1914*, Oxford, 1936, p. 88. See on the crisis of the House of Lords: Roy Jenkins, *Mr. Balfour's Poodle*, London, 1968.

sition of the House of Commons. The more stubborn the Lords, the more popular the Commons.

Nevertheless, the crisis did bring a definitive end to the cult of Parliament. The ideal image of a sovereign all-knowing Parliament, 'the mouthpiece of the nation,' had become irreparably maimed and was in future relegated to an imaginary constitution.[34] Parliament was now only a human institution, not averse to underhand manipulation and demagogy; it even had all the characteristics of a 'crowd': a suitable subject for analysis by mass-psychologists.[35] Nothing remained of the old lustre and even the House of Commons fell victim to a growing decadence and vulgarization. The first time it came to fisticuffs on the floor of the House, on the 27th of July 1893, is vividly described by a horrified Milman:[36] it seemed the culmination of 'the brutalization of the Commons' which Gladstone had spoken of in the seventies.[37]

A more realistic analysis of parliamentary developments resulted from the crisis, and eventually was also of benefit to historians. Sidney Low's study, *The Governance of England*, published in 1904, was a fair example of the realistic approach. W.J. Ashley called it a worthy successor to Bagehot's classic treatise of 1867.[38] Low described and analysed the changes in Parliament's position within the total governmental system towards the end of the 19th century. He referred to the myth of an unassailable parliamentary sovereignty as fostered by older constitutionalists. His essay was inspired by the forementioned crisis, of which it gave a coherent account.[39] The realism displayed by the conservative Low was a reaction to a traditionalist constitutionalism.

[34] Cf. Sidney Low, *The Governance of England*, London, 1904, esp. chapter IV.

[35] Cf. for the 'crowd-characteristics' of Parliament: M. Conway, 'Is Parliament a mere Crowd?' in *Nineteenth Century* 57 (1905), pp. 898–911.

[36] A. Milman, 'The Peril of Parliament' in *Q.R.* 178 (1894), pp. 270–271; cf. A. White, *The English Democracy*, London, 1894, p. 13.

[37] See note 5.

[38] D. Chapman-Huston, *The Lost Historian. A Memoir of Sir Sidney Low.*, London, 1936, p. 149.

[39] Cf. also Sidney Low, 'The Decline of the House of Commons' in *Nineteenth Century* 37 (1895), pp. 567–578, and 'If the House of Commons were abolished' in *Nineteenth Century* 36 (1894), pp. 846–863. Cf. the reaction of Salisbury in: S. Low, *The Governance of England*, pp. 112–113. The increasingly ('necessary') hold of the government, of the Cabinet on Parliament, fostered a strongly 'unitarist' constitutionalism of the kind seen in the historian A.F. Pollard. Leonard Courtney wrote a more 'classic' sort of treatise, *The Working Constitution of the United Kingdom*, London, 1901. E. Jenks said of it: "... the House of Commons plays too large a part, and the Cabinet too small a part, in his picture" (E. Jenks, *Parliamentary England. The Evolution of the Cabinet System.*, London, 1903, p. 399 (note 1). Low tried an approach that was neither 'formal' as a lawyer's nor 'conventional' as a constitutionalist's, but 'actual': "...the point of view ...of the practical observer, who is interested in political and social evolution, and tries to penetrate below the surface to 'the reality of things' " (S. Low, *op. cit.*, p. 14).

Later in this chapter I shall try to trace any similar realistic utterances inside the liberal movement towards the end of the century. The parliamentary crisis had far more causes and ramifications than the ones enumerated in the first part of this chapter: the modern party-organization and the increase of bureaucracy will be discussed further on. For the complaints of inefficiency and incompetence rapidly grew more numerous after 1900.

B. OLD LIBERALISM AS CONSERVATIVE REALISM

> War is the greatest test of institutions.
>
> > (R. Cecil, 1871)
>
> The cry of "efficiency," which is so often raised when the occurrence of some public disaster reveals a weakness of political machinery, expresses a feeling with which every lover of his country will sympathise.
>
> > (E. Jenks, 1903)

During the crisis of the House of Commons at the end of the 19th century, all the major parties insisted on greater efficiency inside Parliament. Efficiency became a political slogan at the turn of the century, an ideal that had to be carried through on all governmental levels. In the service of efficiency there was also a rejection of the past and of tradition, and thus concretely of certain aspects of government believed to be 'inefficient' in the modern era.

During the Crimean War some Englishmen had already been sceptical about the usefulness of a parliamentary system in time of war. The Crimean War stimulated the discussion about the use of representative bodies, even in England the supporters of a more autocratic and more efficient form of government had advocated anti-parliamentarian measures. The already mentioned W.R. Greg was a spokesman of these ideas: the positivist Richard Congreve was even more outspoken, but neither could claim much support. Even at that time the anti-parliamentarian feeling on the continent was far stronger. The parliamentary crisis occasioned by the Crimean War was short-lived, and after the surprisingly sudden end of the war the sceptical feelings disappeared.[40]

---

[40] Cf. O. Anderson, *A Liberal State at War*, London, 1967, pp. 29–93; see W.R. Greg, 'The Newspaper Press' in *E.R.* 102 (1855), pp. 470–498 and his 'French Judgements of England: Montalembert and Rémusat' in *E.R.* 103 (1856), pp. 558–590, esp. p. 573. See also W.R. Greg, *The Way Out*, (1855) and W.L. Burn, *op. cit.*, p. 144.

Less than two decades afterwards, however, there was a revival of the constitutional discussion that had been sparked off by the Crimean War. The cause was the Franco-German war. Thirty years later the South African crisis caused another very violent renewal of the discussions. In 1871 R. Cecil wrote an article called 'Political Lessons of the War' which clearly referred back to the Crimean War.[41] The most important lessons for England from the Franco-German war were again the backwardness and delays of English command and insufficient preparedness of her army; England might have been surprised by Bismarck as France was – with probably the same results. Sufficient money and capable thinkers and organizers ('organizing brains') could not make up for a fundamental lack of management. "It is our political machinery which fails."[42] Cecil complained, like many others before him, that Parliament had too much power, thus crippling the cabinet. As a conservative he blamed the 'new constitution' of 1832 for all of it. His first demand was for an immediate army reform, his second for fundamental changes in England's political structure. The past was of no use. ". . . Any reading of the future by the light of the past would be delusive."[43]

Cecil's reaction to 1870–'71 was one of many. He evidently feared for the future: the Franco-German war had definitely shattered his optimism. As a conservative, however, Cecil rather admired Germany's greater 'efficiency' and its military action against France in 1870–'71. Mingled with this of course was a growing fear of Germany's threatening hegemony.

Sympathy for Germany was on the whole wide-spread, even among Liberals, notwithstanding the fact that both English and German Liberals had in the sixties opposed Bismarck's high-handed violation of the constitution. Yet the attack on France in 1870–'71 was in their eyes justified simply because the 'tyrant,' Napoleon III, was put to flight. Combined with this was the 'historical satisfaction' for the German people, after centuries of being victimized by French expansionism. For a Gladstone-liberal like E.A. Freeman this was sufficient to decide that the Franco-German war was a fortunate and just affair. Unaware of any threatening clouds on the political horizon, Freeman was neither troubled by pessimism nor did he see any reason for panic.

[41] Q.R. 130 (1871), pp. 256–286.
[42] Ibid., p. 274, cf. p. 282.
[43] Ibid., p. 278.

He was, on the contrary, much more disturbed by panic-mongering conservatives.[44]

Not all Liberals shared Freeman's simplistic views: most of them felt that the consequences of the Franco-German war might well be very complicated. Sympathizers and supporters of the *Fortnightly Review*, sometimes styled the 'Party of Humanity,' nearly split in two as a result of the war.[45] The more enthusiastic positivists – like F. Harrison and R. Congreve – defended the country of their mentor Comte, but John Morley who started out as a fellow-positivist, was openly in favour of Prussia and Germany. Not just for 'moral' reasons, as E.A. Freeman, rejoicing because Germany had deposed a querulous tyrant; Morley went much farther, deeply admiring a Prussian Germany, serious, efficient in management and so on. The sudden display of Prussian power impressed many other English Liberals as well. J. Morley, who afterwards during the Boer War exclaimed against aggressive imperialism, was also impressed by it. His admiration for power as such crops up again and again, both in his essay on Machiavelli of 1897 and in his biography of Cromwell published in 1901. All this notwithstanding the fact that he warned against a new dangerous 'Realpolitik' in his essay.[46]

Amongst liberals the first signs of realistic power politics were noticeable in the more conservative wing, which did not agree with J.S. Mill's *On Liberty*. In this group James Fitzjames Stephen was the most important publicist and spokesman, and the general predilection was for more authoritarian politics. Curiously enough they were the first to be designated as 'New Liberals,' which critics equated with 'Bismarckianism.'[47] Actually, in comparison with 'Gladstonian Liberalism' it was more an old liberalism, very much like the conservative doctrine propagated by R. Cecil and others.

J.F. Stephen's political philosophy was formulated in *Liberty, Equality, Fraternity* (1873) based on his experiences in India.[48] In India he had seen a 'real government' at work that could reasonably boast of efficiency and achievements. There the administration was not ham-

---

[44] *The Life and Letters of E.A. Freeman*, ed. W.R.W. Stephens, London, 1895, II, pp. 1–10; F. Harrison, *Autobiographic Memoirs*, London, 1911, II, pp. 1–17.

[45] E.M. Everett, *The Party of Humanity. The Fortnightly Review and its Contributors, 1865–1874*, Chapel Hill, 1939, p. 177 ff.; D.A. Hamer, *John Morly*, Oxford, 1968, pp. 28, 360–363.

[46] D.A. Hamer, *op. cit.*, pp. 46, 54–56.

[47] Cf. J.E. Jenkins, 'Bismarckism in England' in *Contemporary Review* 22 (1873), pp. 107–125.

[48] J. Roach, 'Liberalism and the Victorian Intelligentsia' in *The Cambridge Historical Journal* 13 (1957), p. 64.

pered by the delaying and paralyzing tactics of Parliament.[49] India confirmed his deep-seated conviction that life is an unceasing struggle, that 'force' is the decisive factor everywhere, and that political freedom is not a goal in itself but is dependent upon the particular given circumstances to qualify it. His image of man was very similar to that of Hobbes: man's ineradicable egoism was central. In this he differed markedly from J.S. Mill with his pervasive optimism. The optimism entailed in the idea of the political educability of mankind was a source of continual irritation to Stephen.[50]

The political direction which Stephen took in the seventies (while Gladstone was still supreme among Liberals), was far from popular at that time; his work was only reprinted once, in 1874. Later, however, in the eighties, he had more support from liberals. Stephen's ideas clearly foreshadowed the later liberal unionists, who preferred an imperialist policy, and finally even broke with Gladstone because of his attitude on the Irish question. In those later years more support for these conservative liberals came from a new source: the historically minded anthropologist H.S. Maine. His book, *Popular Government*, published in 1885 and reprinted many times, achieved great popularity despite (or because of) its lack of originality.[51]

Maine's work was governed by the fear of growing democratization in politics and in society. He considered democracy synonymous with anarchy, bound to lead to a power vacuum. In any case it was inconsistent with efficiency in government. Democracy would put an end to progress. Maine's convictions, like Stephen's, were partly determined by his experiences in India.[52] His work as a whole can be characterized as a protest against the changing world. His political panacea for England was a constitution on the American pattern, explicitly defined and written out, combined with a reinforced House of Lords.[53] Neither Stephen nor Maine entered into practical politics, but their influence upon the more conservative Liberal politicians during the Gladstone

[49] Cf. J.F. Stephen, 'Parliamentary Government' in *Contemporary Review* 23 (1873–74), pp. 1–19, 165–181. He wrote on the fear of centralization: "I can understand the fear of centralization and bureaucracy which I have often had occasion to observe in the people of this country, though I think it is irrational" (p. 178). Cf. also his 'monarchical' ideas. (p. 179).

[50] Cf. B.E. Lippincott, *Victorian Critics of Democracy*, Minneapolis, 1938, p. 139; N.G. Annan, *Leslie Stephen*, London, 1951, pp. 202–204.

[51] J. Roach, *op. cit.*, p. 73 ff.

[52] See, however, J.W. Burrow, *Evolution and Society*, Cambridge, 1970, pp. 176–177. (His criticism of E. Stokes, *The English Utilitarians and India*, Oxford, 1959).

[53] B.E. Lippincott, *op. cit.*, p. 188 ff.

era, such as G.J. Goschen and the 'renegade' of 1867 R. Lowe, is evident. One can clearly distinguish parallel political convictions.[54]

Other adherents of this liberal intellectual group, more interested in political practice, were the historians J.R. Seeley and W. Lecky, the latter of which had written a standard work on the 18th century. Seeley's historical writings (as previously indicated) were permeated with a more realistic conservative liberalism. Lecky, however, was the one who stuck most closely to the liberal principles; his involvement with practical politics stemmed from the Home Rule-problem.[55] Like Maine, he greatly feared that democratization of the political system would lead to desintegration of society. Advocating more power for the House of Lords in order to restore political stability, Lecky shared Maine's admiration for the written American constitution.[56] Of course his conservative opinions made him detest the 'devil-begotten' socialists, although in his book *Democracy and Liberty* he condemned the excesses of 'parasitic' capitalism raging unchecked in America. This same book criticized the mock-reality of the democratic majority principle, continually violated as it was by political pressure groups.[57]

The basis of this conservative liberalism was clearly pessimistic. It feared a democratic and socialist future, and wanted to save as much as possible from the coming ruin. To this end greater efficiency and more decisive power for the executive branch of the government was demanded. These requirements were postulated on the conviction that a more democratic procedure would result in a less efficient government. Democracy was seen as the negation of all their ideals.

This emphasis on efficiency also occurs among the progressive new liberals, who differed from the 'Gladstonians' as well. Ideologically they are greatly different from the conservative liberals described before. The emphasis on efficiency among the new liberals was not primarily meant as a check on the inevitable process of democratization, but was rather a reaction to the 'administrative nihilism' of Gladstone's era. The classic liberal conception was that political liberty required a permissive government to be safely enjoyed; the new liberals had abandoned this conception.[58] Power and liberty were perceived by some later liberals as not necessarily the irreconcilable contradictions

---

[54] J. Roach, *op. cit.*, p. 79.
[55] See H. Mulvey, 'The Historian Lecky: Opponent of Irish Home Rule' in *Victorian Studies* 1 (1958), pp. 337–351.
[56] Cf. B.E. Lippincott, *op. cit.*, p. 288 (cf. p. 229).
[57] *Ibid.*, pp. 210, 233–243.
[58] *Q.R.* 130 (1871), p. 275.

that Whig ideology and classical Gladstonian liberalism had pictured. We shall take this opportunity to describe just what the Gladstonian liberalism entailed.

C. WHIGGERY VERSUS GLADSTONIAN LIBERALISM

> Whig principles . . . are based upon a study of the history of England. The man who holds them must begin by admiring that history and being proud of that country.
>
> (Lord Cowper, 1883)

The historical picture gains clarity if we divide the English Liberal movement into three types, or three main phases. Gladstonian liberalism, the classical type, is the middle phase, clearly different in its concept of liberty from the old liberalism described earlier. This concept was later criticized by the new liberalism, not because it was too utopian but because of its negative characteristics.

The meaning of the Gladstone type of liberalism has been sometimes too sharply criticized in recent historical literature. True, the ideological contribution of this liberalism was not very original, and its program could easily be summarized in a number of slogans: 'peace, retrenchment, and free trade.'[59] Progress in terms of political programmes was negligible, most of all as far as home politics were concerned, yet as John Vincent pointed out, Gladstone had imparted a peculiar vitality to these. The reason was his 'extra-parliamentary' electioneering, what his Whig opponents called his demagogy.[60] Gladstone's election campaigns swept old customs aside; he was the first liberal leader to bridge the distance between parliament and electorate.

Gladstone did not – as had his aristocratic Whig predecessors like Russell or Palmerston – confine himself to politics in the parliamentary compound. The electorate was more than ever before him, consulted in matters both national and international, which latter used to be regarded as solely parliamentary. An excellent example of this is the Bulgarian question. The aristocratic Whig liberals, hardly different

---

[59] See esp. J. Vincent, *The Formation of the Liberal Party*, London, 1966, part 3 and 4. Cf. D.M. Schreuder, 'Gladstone and Italian Unification, 1848–1870. The Making of a Liberal?' in *E.H.R.* 85 (1970), p. 475 ff.

[60] J. Vincent, *op. cit.*, pp. 143, 227, 257.

from him in political convictions and ideology, still blamed him for this sort of 'demagogy'; it made Gladstone suspect in their eyes.[61] The *Edinburgh Review*, the Whig paper that after 1867 was no longer the sole exponent and interpreter of liberal principles, never lost an opportunity for reproving Gladstone in this respect.[62] For these old Whigs there were too many indigestible elements in his political agitation. Political life suddenly became frighteningly uncertain; election results had become unpredictable, for had not both the conservative victory in 1874 and the liberal victory in 1880 been unexpected?[63] Yet it was this very political agitation that won the leadership of the liberal Party for Gladstone, although the liberal Whigs still begrudged it him in 1880.[64] Gladstone's activities also gave him a revolutionary halo, as of a man of the people, which was far from the truth.

During Gladstone's leadership the old Whig families lost their supremacy in English liberalism once and for all, even though he himself kept a fair number of seats for them in his cabinets. "His Cabinet was stuffed with Whigs," afterwards commented the critic G.W.E. Russell, writing about the cabinet of 1880.[65] Gladstone was very well-disposed towards them, partly because he intended to preserve the unity of the Liberals, partly because ideologically he had more in common with the Whigs than with radicals like J. Bright or, later, J. Chamberlain.[66]

The *Edinburgh Review*, and more especially its editor, H. Reeve, still staunchly defended the Whig political principles even during the eighties. Elsewhere these politics, so exclusively inspired by the past, began to be more and more criticized. The attack on the political position of the Whigs was also to affect their historical views. The final representative of the older view was Sir G.O. Trevelyan, who wrote a study of Fox during the height of Gladstone's agitation. It was published just before the liberal victory in the elections of 1880. As a portrayal of the origins of the 19th-century Liberal Party, it gave the conventional Whig view of these origins, glorifying the Whig oppo-

---

[61] Cf. G. Himmelfarb, *Victorian Minds*, New York, 1968, p. 207: "The Victorian definition of a demagogue was a politician who intruded conscience into politics."

[62] Cf. J.A. Hardcastle, 'Principles and Prospects of the Liberal Party' in *E.R.* 147 (1878), pp. 274–300, esp. p. 295.

[63] See G.M. Trevelyan, *Sir George Otto Trevelyan. A Memoir*, London, 1932, p. 102; cf. *Memoirs of the Life and Correspondence of Henry Reeve*, ed. J.K. Laughton, London, 1893, II, p. 277.

[64] D. Southgate, *The Passing of the Whigs*, London, 1962, p. 363.

[65] G.W.E. Russell, 'The New Liberalism: A Response' in *Nineteenth Century* 26 (1889), p. 492.

[66] J. Vincent, *op. cit.*, p. 143; D. Southgate, *op. cit.*, chapter 13: 'The Whigs and Mr. Gladstone.'

sition to George III and honouring Burke as the only true ideologue of the Liberal Party.[67]

Still, Trevelyan's historical ideology was already an anachronism, for he wrote it in a period when radical members of the National Liberal Federation (founded in 1877) had made their first successful attempt towards renewing the party by modernizing the party's organization and by clearly stating its policy in a programme. This development towards modern parties had both democratic and bureaucratic tendencies; all in all it was an unprecedented innovation, highly favoured by Chamberlain and his followers but unacceptable to right-minded Whigs. The supporters of a more classical liberalism were too individualistic to accept the new ideas. Gladstone and most of the liberal leaders who came after him were not interested in this sort of innovation, as it was too exclusively concentrated on the organizational aspects.[68] While the party had taken shape and had achieved mass membership under Gladstone, he would not change this 'community of sentiment' into a political party in the modern sense.[69]

During the eighties the old Whigs and the rising new liberalism both turned against Gladstone. Originally the new liberals opposed the aristocratic Whigs within the top levels of the Liberal Party, but later Gladstone himself became their aim. Only the *Edinburgh Review* still held on the Whig principles. Early in 1880 H. Reeve published an article called 'Plain Whig Principles,' to which more radical liberals replied. C.M. Gaskell illustrated the shaky position of the Whigs, confidently ending with the remark that the time was near when "the student of politics will search in vain for plain Whig principles except in the pages of the *Edinburgh Review*."[70] Gaskell ascribed the victory of 1880 to Gladstone's oratory on the Bulgarian question; these colourful speeches had kept the heterogeneous medley of groups in the Party together for the time being. Should the electioneering campaign have been conducted with home affairs in the centre of attention, then the result would undoubtedly have been less pleasant. In home politics, Gaskell insisted, the reforming zeal of the Whigs in the past had been minimal. Their aristocratic disdain for a more professional political party would separate them from the political mainstream of the near

---

[67] See chapter II, part B2.

[68] D. Southgate, *op. cit.*, p. 359; S.H. Beer, *Modern British Politics*, London, 1969, pp. 38, 52–61.

[69] J. Vincent, *op. cit.*, p. 257.

[70] H. Reeve, 'Plain Whig Principles' in *E.R.* 151 (1880), pp. 257–280; C.M. Gaskell, 'The Position of the Whigs' in *Nineteenth Century* 10 (1881), pp. 901–912, quote p. 912.

future and Gaskell thought that in all probability a following parliament would turn to the National Liberal Federation and offer them the chance to fulfil their programme.[71]

Gaskell was the first to say in his article what would often be repeated in the years to come: that more professional politics were both needed and desirable as a counterpart to the Whigs' traditional amateurism. "They dislike the new method in politics" – Gaskell wrote – "they have little in common with the professional politician, and rarely come into contact with them except at a general election. They do not understand the principles of agitation and preach and practice the virtue of discretion."[72] It seemed that Bagehot's 'deferential society' had definitely come to an end; mass democracy had also come to England.

H. Reeve retorted so fiercely to Gaskell's criticisms that the Whig principles at issue became vaguer than ever. His 'Retort' consisted mainly of praise for Burke's principles, combined with rejection of the Birmingham patriots, those 'revolutionaries' with their 'unliberal' demands for a stronger Executive.[73] Similar accusations made by G.W.E. Russell invited an even weaker defence by the Whig Lord Cowper.[74] Russell had in 1883 indicated what direction modern liberalism should take to retain influence in a modern society. He too saw a role for Burke, but a different one from the one Reeve had provided.

The high Whig doctrine would limit the functions of the State to the preservation of life and property. Modern Liberalism, on the other hand, regarding the State with Burke as 'the nation in its collective and corporate character,' sees in it the one sovereign agent for all moral, material, and social reforms, and recognises a special duty to deal with questions affecting the food, health, housing, amusement, and culture of the working classes.[75]

The background to this clearly formulated social idealism of the new liberal Russell deserves to be elucidated. It was proof of a shifting

---

[71] *Nineteenth Century* 10 (1881), p. 911.

[72] *Ibid.*, p. 909.

[73] H. Reeve, 'A Whig Retort' in *E.R.* 155 (1882), pp. 279–290. Cf. p. 283: "The Birmingham patriots demand a large increase of executive power – a strange perversion of Liberal principles – in order to enable them to enforce with unlimited authority what they call the "will of the people." Cf. note 16 for earlier remarks by H. Reeve with an opposite meaning.

[74] Lord Cowper, 'Desultory Reflections of a Whig' in *Nineteenth Century* 13 (1883), pp. 729–739; G.W.E. Russell, 'A Protest against Whiggery' in *Nineteenth Century* 13 (1883), pp. 920–927; Lord Cowper, 'The Whigs: A Rejoinder' in *Nineteenth Century* 14 (1883), pp. 23–30.

[75] *Nineteenth Century* 13 (1883), p. 925.

emphasis in ideology concerning the liberal doctrine, which we shall discuss later. Russell repeated his new liberal declaration of faith in 1889, at the same time definitely rejecting Gladstone's leadership.[76] According to one of Russell's political supporters, the Home Rule question was too slender a base for modern liberalism; all it did was distract liberalism from its appointed task of very necessary social reforms.[77]

D. THE NEW LIBERALISM: IDEALISM AND REALISM
EFFICIENCY USED AS AN IDEOLOGY AGAINST TRADITION

> The present can never take refuge behind the past.
> (C.F.G. Masterman, 1901)

1. Positive Liberty and Citizenship

J.S. Mill has often been regarded as the 'ideologue' of classical Gladstone liberalism, and the philosopher T.H. Green as the spiritual father of Asquith's later more socially inclined brand of liberalism. The distinction is rather too facile not to be treacherous. A few preliminary remarks are needed to throw these ostensibly opposed liberalisms into perspective. Even under Gladstone it was usual, sometimes essential, for English Liberals to trace their roots to a specific period in the past: for the Whig Liberals the 18th century of George III was essential, the other slightly more non-conformist groups had 'their' Civil War and Cromwell.

J.S. Mill, however, was different. He did not draw his inspiration from the past nor did he attach a prescriptive value to that past. In his youth Brodie's constitutionalism had caused him to remark: "It is a strange doctrine, that we are not entitled to good government, unless we can prove that our ancestors enjoyed it."[78] In his later years Mill was not so radical nor utilitarian, yet he remained critical of 'prescriptive history.' It might be said that he was not in every respect representa-

---

[76] G.W.E. Russell, 'The New Liberalism: A Response' in *Nineteenth Century* 26 (1889), pp. 492–499.

[77] L.A. Atherley-Jones, 'The New Liberalism' in *Nineteenth Century* 26 (1889), pp. 186–193. J. G. Rogers defended Gladstone against Atherley-Jones and G.W.E. Russell; see his article 'The Middle Class and the New Liberalism' in *Nineteenth Century* 26 (1889) pp. 710–720.

[78] Quoted by S.R. Letwin, *The Pursuit of Certainty*, Cambridge, 1965, p. 208; cf. also Mill's letter to Mazzini from 1858, in *The English Ruling Class*, ed. W.L. Guttsman, London, 1969, pp. 31–32.

tive of English liberalism as such. Besides, the fact that the recurrent demand for greater efficiency was a characteristic of several later Liberals does not imply that Mill could not also harbour the desire for efficiency. On the contrary, insofar as he followed his father's tradition he could not be immune to such desires. Nor did J.S. Mill follow the cult of the 'historical' parliament; like many others he considered that parliament was no longer suitable or efficient enough for legislation; a smaller body was needed for that.[79]

The most conspicuous characteristic of his political treatises, however, is not his demand for efficiency. It is his growing feeling of alarm at the danger implied in the State's accumulation of power. In the fifties and sixties he had, as we saw, taken part in the centralization debate, repeatedly stating that knowledge should be centralized but power de-centralized. If power was centralized in the hands of the national government, the freedom of the individual would be endangered. "The third and most cogent reason for restricting the interference of government is the great evil of adding unnecessarily to its power."[80] Governmental power enslaves: this is the leading thought of classical liberalism. Mill tried to reconcile decentralized power with efficiency, "the greatest dissemination of power consistent with efficiency."[81] But did not his ideal of centralized knowledge and de-centralized power rest on an increasingly utopian outlook? Knowledge is power: on the governmental level too this truth had become apparent. Could efficient government be brought about without a greater concentration of power? Was it not really the other way round and should a concentration of power not be the *sine qua non* for greater efficiency? An affirmative answer was given afterwards during the years around the turn of the century. That power and liberty were not necessarily antitheses, was gradually accepted even by liberals: power, after all, can also set free.

Even in a superficial comparison between the political ideas of J.S. Mill and those of T.H. Green we shall have to discuss both the points of difference and the points of agreement. Undoubtedly Green's influence on later Liberals was enormous, but his admirers – of which there were many among Asquith Liberals – gave a far too modern interpretation of his political philosophy. Though not so opposed to state intervention

[79] J.S. Mill, *Utilitarianism, Liberty and Representative Government*, ed. A.D. Lindsay, London, 1964 (1910), pp. 231, 233, 237, 242–256.
[80] *Ibid.*, p. 165.
[81] *Ibid.*, p. 168. Cf. p. 357.

as Mill, he neither was the prophet of the later so-called 'collectivism,' which some of his followers believed him to be.[82] Green's ideals were opposed to Mill's utilitarian principles, but in his liberalism he stuck to political individualism, just as did Mill, with the difference that Green had a more puritan and moralizing outlook.

Melvin Richter proved convincingly that some of the more essential aspects of Green's ideas are a continuation of the individualism of the classical Liberal tradition.[83] The example of Bright, the radical, was an inspiration for him and made him a champion of political activism. He shared Bright's puritanism and moralism, especially as he was an admirer of Cromwell.[84] Thus his teachings, of which 'positive liberty' and 'active citizenship' are the core, became tinged with evangelical moralistic ideas (heavily stressing the responsibility of the individual). Characteristic for this is the biased way in which he introduced Hegel to England.[85] Through Hegel's influence Green's political philosophy envisaged a greater role for the State – making it fulfil a catalytic role in reconciling social opposites – than was usual with classical Liberalism. Yet his being inspired by Hegel did not mean that he was willing to admire the Prussian state: essential was not that a state 'possessed' power, but that it had the 'duty' to promote the 'common weal.'[86]

Green's inspiratory idealism had its weak points. Because he was far too close to Gladstone and Bright, his criticism of 19th-century capitalism could not really probe deeply; in fact it was on a par with Bright's critical remarks about the monopolies of the land-owning aristocracy.[87] Green's evangelical moralism prohibited a more factual or structural criticism. Annan insists that not only Green's political and social philosophy was inhibited, but that the evil of Victorian moralism fettered all political and social science in England until a very late stage.[88]

[82] M. Richter, *The Politics of Conscience; T.H. Green and His Age*. London, 1964, p. 267 ff., p. 339 ff.; see also D. Nicholls, 'Positive Liberty, 1880–1914' in *American Political Science Review* 56 (1962), pp. 114–128.

[83] M. Richter, *op. cit.*, pp. 235, 293.

[84] *Ibid.*, p. 41. Cf. J. Vincent, *op. cit.*, pp. XXVIII–XXX, 163. On Green's admiration for Bright, see M. Richter, *op. cit.*, pp. 218, 269 ff., 283.

[85] For his reception of Hegel, see M. Richter, *op. cit.*, pp. 82, 172, 252, 260; for the idea of 'active citizenship' see *Ibid.*, pp. 110–114, 201 ff., and chapter 11.

[86] *Ibid.*, pp. 248 ff., 260.

[87] *Ibid.*, pp. 276. Cf. 362, 369.

[88] N.G. Annan, *The Curious Strength of Positivism in English Political Thought*, Oxford, 1959, p. 18: "The passion, then in this country for laying down how men ought to behave and how society ought to be reorganised in order that they may behave better has led us to neglect the new techniques for describing how in fact men do behave and how far reorganisations of

Mid-Victorian 'radicalism' was so important a component of Green's philosophy that state intervention was permitted only on behalf of temperance and education. Yet after his death in 1882 it was his philosophical beliefs which gave a new lease of life to English liberalism, and the idealistic elements within new liberalism are undoubtedly due to his influence. In the period of 1880–1914 his ideology even took pride of place before Mill's ideas. Mill's utilitarianism proved much less attractive in the long run than Green's idealism; the latter's conception of 'positive liberty' and 'active citizenship' were taken up later by theoreticians like H. Samuel and B. Bosanquet.

Liberty could no longer be defined as 'the absence of coercion'; political liberty was not only the right of every citizen, it also required individual self-fulfilment within the society. The state was to provide the most favourable conditions possible for each citizen to fulfil his calling, and what better means than education to reach that goal? Of course the first task of the schools would be to train 'active citizens.' The fulfilment of human liberty was embodied in the services to society; 'positive liberty' was to be realized in 'active citizenship.' This seemed all quite revolutionary, but for the moment it was to remain only theory. Around the turn of the century the main question was: would the practice of liberal politics be able to turn this political idealism into a concrete modern social policy?

The more idealistic components of new liberalism are mirrored in slogans such as positive liberty and active citizenship. There was also a more realistic side, however, reflected in words like efficiency and power. These latter elements were unimportant for Green. Although he had once admired efficient Prussia, his enthusiasm was for the pre-Bismarckian Prussia, and encompassed culture rather than politics.[89] All in all, Green's was a gospel of duty rather than a gospel of efficiency.

2. Power and Efficiency

During the discussions of old liberalism we noticed the great importance attached to ideas of power and efficiency. We also saw that J.F. Stephen's image of man was influenced by the ideas of Hobbes; his work can be seen as part of an 'anthropological' Hobbes revival. Afterwards a more 'political' Hobbes revival came about in the work of

society are capable of changing their behaviour." Cf. also M. Richter, *op. cit.*, p. 290. Cf. also J.A. Hobson's criticism of Green's idealism in M. Richter, *op. cit.*, pp. 282, 369.

[89] M. Richter, *op. cit.*, pp. 12, 89 (Richter's criticism of E. Halévy).

Leslie Stephen. Although a true Hobbes renaissance in English political thought did not come about until after the Second World War,[90]
around 1900 there was a great deal of renewed interest in Hobbes. A
good example of this renewed interest is Leslie Stephen's biography of
Hobbes, posthumously published in 1904.[91]

L. Stephen showed a quite remarkable understanding for Hobbes's
attitude towards the Civil War, especially for his radical opposition to
the political traditionalists such as Coke, Hampden or Eliot. Stephen
prefaced his own explanation of Hobbes's theories of the State with the
following remarks which have a certain relevance to our present theme:

The British people managed to work out a system which had, as we all believe, very great advantages and may justify some of the old panegyrics. Men
could speak more freely – if not always more wisely – in England than
elsewhere, and individual energy developed with many admirable consequences. But the success was won at a cost. The central authority of the
State was paralysed; and many observers may admit that in securing liberty
at the price of general clumsiness and inefficiency of all the central administrative functions, the cost had been considerable. It is desirable to remember
this point when we come to Hobbes' special theories.[92]

English liberty has been acquired at a not inconsiderable cost, calculated in a coin that Whigs were unfamiliar with. In describing the cost
of liberty as 'general clumsiness' and 'inefficiency' of the central
government, Stephen clearly relates Hobbes's ideas to the political context of the turn of the century.

Efficiency became an increasingly important political slogan after
1880. It found adherents among many political groups: liberal imperialists, conservatives, and even socialists. The Webbs, without doubt
the foremost promoters of the 'efficiency' ideals, influenced the leftist
liberal Haldane as well as the liberal imperialist Lord Rosebery. The
Webbs' ideal was to found a 'party of national efficiency.' It came
to nothing, although the debating club of the 'Co-efficients' flourished
for some years after its founding in 1902. Because its composition was
too heterogeneous and the political differences of the members were
too serious, the club never became a political party. In any case 1902
was too late for such an attempt. Chamberlain had lost no time in
taking the matter of Tariff Reform into the electioneering arena, thus

[90] Cf. I. Fetcher's introduction to Thomas Hobbes' *Leviathan*, (Politica, vol. 22.) Neuwied,
1966, esp. p. LXIII.
[91] Cf. G.C. Robertson, *Hobbes*, London, 1886; W.L. Courtney, 'Thomas Hobbes' in
E.R. 165 (1887), pp. 88–106. Cf. F. Pollock, *History of the Science of Politics*, London, 1911,
pp. 58–68.
[92] L. Stephen, *Hobbes*, London, 1904, p. 181; cf. pp. 180, 200–206.

giving a new lease of life to the old contrasts between liberal and conservative, just when it seemed that the Boer War had done away with
them. In those years of national crisis many leading journalists had
advocated a national efficiency coalition, to be led by Rosebery and
Chamberlain.[93]

The origins, contents and use of this conception of efficiency are
extremely significant for our present theme. Such a demand was unknown in the past, and nowhere was there any historical precedent.
The old Whig constitutionalism hardly knew the term. It might be
said that the very use of the term was a manifestation of a growing
scepticism regarding the trusted old political methods and usages. Conditions became favourable for the idea of efficiency when the past
seemed no longer relevant for the present; when efficiency eclipsed all
other political norms, the normative value of tradition was discredited.

Opposing the past in this way was more typical of the English 'Co-
efficients' than of their American counterpart, the superficially comparable 'efficiency movement' of the same period. The inspiration for
this movement came from F.W. Taylor's ideal of 'scientific management.'[94] Taylor's main work was published in 1911, too late to have
any influence on the English efficiency-movement which was already
past its prime. The progressive new liberal, J.A. Hobson, himself no
supporter of an 'efficiency' ideology, rejected Taylorism.[95] Notwithstanding identical aims, it would be difficult to compare the American
and English efficiency movements. The English movement had its own
individual origin and background in the crisis within the Empire and
in the South African failure. The political ambitions of American 'progressives' may bear some similarity to those of the English new liberals,
but that will be a point for later discussion.

The Gladstone period has been called 'administrative nihilism' both
by the Webbs and Graham Wallas. This characterization was first
used by T.H. Huxley in 1871 as a designation of political Spencerism.[96]
It was the title of a lecture in which Huxley declared himself in favour
of more State interference than liberal ideology allowed for; he insisted

[93] Cf. G.R. Searle, *The Quest for National Efficiency*, Oxford, 1971, p. 150–152 and p. 134;
see also S. Hynes, *The Edwardian Turn of Mind*, Princeton, 1968, p. 99; B. Semmel, *Imperialism
and Social Reform*, London, 1960, pp. 53–82; H.C.G. Matthew, *The Liberal Imperialists*,
Oxford, 1973; R.J. Scally, *The Origins of the Lloyd George Coalition. The Politics of Social-
Imperialism, 1900–1918*, Princeton, 1975.
[94] See S. Haber, *Efficiency and Uplift. Scientific Management in the Progressive Era, 1890–1920*,
Chicago, 1964.
[95] Cf. G.R. Searle, *op. cit.*, p. 102.
[96] T.H. Huxley, 'Administrative Nihilism' in *Fortnightly Review* 10 (1871), pp. 525–543.

that Hobbes's *Leviathan* propounded the same positive ideas.[97] His application of Spencer's biological-physiological approach to the political organism in support of his own theory, was quite original and in total contrast to Spencer's own intent. Spencer compared the development of the human nervous system to that of the modern centralized administration: Huxley concluded that this analogy actually was more an argument in favour of State intervention than a rejection of it.[98]

In the *Fabian Essays* of 1889 Sidney Webb adopted Huxley's term of 'administrative nihilism' to characterize an extreme form of *laissez faire*. Webb, however, fully realized that Huxley was wrong in supposing Spencer had been in favour of such extreme liberalism.[99] Graham Wallas used the term to design the Gladstone era; in his book, *Our Social Heritage*, he described a 'Gladstonian Liberalism' with intensely negative characteristics, very similar indeed to the picture John Vincent drew in *The Formation of the Liberal Party*. Wallas reasoned that England from 1830 to 1874 had been governed mainly by the Liberal Party. "But Liberal administration, when the first energy of the reform struggle of 1832 was spent, showed a curious combination of national complacency and national inefficiency."[100] The threefold liberal programme of 'peace, retrenchment and reform' had been empty rhetoric, with people like Chadwick and a few other Benthamites as honorable exceptions. J.S. Mill was not one of the exceptions, and came in for scathing criticism by Wallas.[101]. The latter saw the period 1895–1905 as a turning-point in many respects. Some of the causes for this were the rise of an 'industrial democracy ruling an overseas empire,' the growth of the Labour Party, the influence of Green's Hegelian theories on 'a few able Oxford politicians,' and finally the German economic, political and military pressure and competition. Together these were enough to cause 'a conscious break in the minds of the liberal leaders with the simple principle of Mill on Liberty.'[102] We shall now discuss

[97] *Ibid.*, p. 531: "... the justice of his conception of the duties of the sovereign power does not seem to me to be invalidated by his monstrous doctrines respecting the sacredness of that power." (See the beginning of chapter 30 of *Leviathan*).

[98] *Fortnightly Review* 10 (1871), pp. 534–535. Cf. Spencer's answer 'Specialized Administration' in *Fortnightly Review* 10 (1871), pp. 627–654. See also H. Spencer, *The Man versus the State*, ed. D. Macrae, Harmondsworth, 1969, pp. 26–27.

[99] S. Webb in *Fabian Essays in Socialism*, London, 1920, p. 43, cf. p. 41 (note 1).

[100] G. Wallas, *Our Social Heritage*, New Haven, 1921, p. 173; Chapter 6 was wholly devoted to settling his account with the past. See for Wallas, J. Wiener, *Between Two Worlds. The Political Thought of Graham Wallas*, Oxford, 1971, cf. also 'Socialism and Human Nature' in *T.L.S.*, 5-11-1971, p. 1391.

[101] G. Wallas, *op. cit.*, p. 176: "Only Mill, Bentham's favorite disciple, and the intellectual autocrat of British Liberalism, invented, as far as I know, nothing in the reign of politics".

[102] *Ibid.*, p. 185.

Wallas's first factor, which turned the striving for efficiency into an ideology.

3. Efficiency and Empire

Despite all the new theories about its background, modern imperialism remains the cause of many breaks in England's political tradition. It is the context in which the English efficiency movement grew and in which it acquired some concrete political meaning, even among liberals such as Lord Rosebery. A small book, written in 1901 by the journalist A. White, is significantly called *Efficiency and Empire*.[103] We noticed that the crisis in the House of Commons after 1880 lent force to the demand for more efficiency. The rise of modern imperialism and the increasing international tensions made for a military crisis which in its turn aggrevated the parliamentary crisis.[104] The peak of the military crisis was to come with the Boer War.

England proved to be increasingly ill equipped to meet the demands of the modern era; also on the military level there was nothing but the failure of old-fashioned amateurism. The need for professionalism was proclaimed loudly and repeatedly, since the critics saw only too well that the army was backward and neglected, notwithstanding the need for reorganization and modernization in the growing empire.[105] Many were the causes: strong faith in the powerful navy, and a liberal political-economic tradition which refused 'extra' expenses for military purposes because they were 'wasteful.' And lastly, a deeply rooted anti-militarism, born of an old fear of 'standing armies.'[106] Around the turn of the century this heritage of liberal constitutionalism would no longer be able to withstand contemporary criticism, although even then Campbell-Bannerman's attitude was still influenced by it.[107]

When the Boer War disclosed England's military defects, the liberal

---

[103] On Arnold White, see G.R. Searle, *op. cit.*, pp. 40, 54, 267.

[104] See particularly W.S. Hamer, *The British Army. Civil-Military Relations 1885–1905*, Oxford, 1970.

[105] Cf. J. Adye, 'Has Our Army Grown with Our Empire?' in *Nineteenth Century* 39 (1896), pp. 1012–1024; and 'The Empire and The Army' in *Fortnightly Review* 52 (1901), pp. 13–25.

[106] Cf. W.S. Hamer, *op. cit.*, p. 33; half forgotten in the middle of the century, the fear was felt again by many old liberals with the rise of modern imperialism; cf. A.V. Tucker, 'Army and Society in England 1870–1900: A Reassessment of the Cardwell Reforms' in *Journal of British Studies* 2 (1963), pp. 110–141 esp. p. 129. Cf. also T.B. Macaulay, *The History of England*, London, 1906 (Everyman's Library), III, pp. 529–530.

[107] W.S. Hamer, *op. cit.*, p. 141 (his constant opposition to instituting a General Staff), pp. 149, 153, 199; G.R. Searle, *op. cit.*, pp. 23–24, 224, 232.

constitutional tradition was fast stripped of meaning and relevance. Partly because of the anti-militarist Whig tradition, relations between military and civil authorities were strained; the liberal Whigs suspected professional armies and did their best to keep these armies small. The Cardwell reforms of 1871 aimed at an integration of these two sectors of public life, relieving the Crown of all power over the army and placing it under control of Parliament. The military authorities deplored this apparent loss of what little autonomy they had, and felt that the military apparatus was more than ever before at the mercy of an administration consisting of penny-pinching 'ignorant' civilians. Yet the coming decades improved the position of the army; the warnings of the old liberal constitutionalists came true, for the army began to have some say in financial decisions regarding military affairs.[108] The liberal measures of 1871 thus achieved the opposite of what had been intended. The last decisive step in this development was precipitated by the war in South Africa when the traditional antipathy against army men meddling in political-military decisions crumbled.[109] But it was the reorganization of 1901 which freed the army from parliamentary 'civilian management' – 'parliamentary misrule' if you will – and paved the way for a more professional 'scientific management' of army affairs. Finally, the liberal Haldane, a friend of the Webbs and like them in favour of administrative efficiency, completed this development by arranging for cooperation between the civil and military authorities.[110]

The South Africa crisis left ineffaceable traces on English constitutional thought. The Irish policy of obstruction had shown up parliamentary inefficiency, the Boer War showed that the imperium possessed a disgracefully mismanaged army. The Crimean War and the Franco-German war had raised short-lived doubts as to the usefulness of a constitutional-parliamentary system in time of war as well as of peace. Now, at the turn of the century, these doubts were intensified. Moreover the South African crisis provided a justification for the 'panic mongers' of 1870–1871: "War is the greatest test of institutions" was what Cecil had then said. Cecil himself had vanished from the political scene, but his point of view was still unchanged.[111] It might be said

[108] See C.M. Clode, *The Military Forces of the Crown*, London, 1869. Cf. W.S. Hamer, *op. cit.*, pp. 68–69; Clinton Rossiter, *Constitutional Dictatorship*, New York, 1963, p. 135 ff.

[109] W.S. Hamer, *op. cit.*, pp. 71–72, 128, 197–198.

[110] *Ibid.*, p. 260. Cf. H.O. Arnold-Forster, 'Parliamentary Misrule in Our War Services' in *Nineteenth Century* 26 (1889), pp. 523–544; see also 'Haldane Centenary Essays' in *Public Administration* 35 (1957), pp. 217–265.

[111] Cf. G.R. Searle, *op. cit.*, pp. 43, 217.

that the 'lessons' of the Boer War were learnt more diligently than the combined lessons of the Crimean and the Franco-German wars. The Boer War introduced the idea not only of the need for military efficiency but also for general and political efficiency.

The Nineteenth Century, led by J. Knowles, tried in 1900 what already had been attempted during the Crimean War: to establish an 'Administrative Reform Association' in order to have military and political affairs conducted according to 'ordinary business principles and methods.' The membership grew apace, with many prominent persons lending their support. Contemporary political scientists and historians also joined the association, e.g. A. Dicey, S. Low, J.A.R. Marriott, F. Pollock, F. York Powell, G.W. Prothero, and finally even the bishop of London, the historian Mandell Creighton.[112] Although Knowles's attempt ended in failure, political thinkers – the efficiency-thinkers most of all – carried the stamp of those ideas for years to come.

The mysterious liberal imperialist Rosebery, who had been a failure as Gladstone's successor in 1894 but whose political prospects improved because of the political events around 1900, was one of the first prominent politicians to declare himself in favour of the plan of *The Nineteenth Century*. In fact, the Boer War aided Rosebery far more than Campbell-Bannerman.[113] Rosebery's efficiency doctrine dates from this period, and the current system of 'party-government' had no place in his efficiency ideology. Weak political parties could not be expected to tackle the problems of the modern state; the people wanted 'leaders' more than the often insipid leadership offered by dim party governments.[114] Rosebery's efficiency also implied an attack on parliament as neither truly representative nor efficient; it was to be the 'rule of the fittest.' "Efficiency implies the rule of the fittest. Party means the rule of something else, not of the unfittest, but of the few fit, the accidentally not unfit, and the glaringly unfit."[115]

His preference, therefore, was for a competently efficient business

[112] See 'The Lessons of the War. A Proposed Association' in *Nineteenth Century* 48 (1900), pp. 1–3, 173–183, 859–880. Cf. in the same issue the articles: 'Ordinary Business Principles' (pp. 184–195); E. Robertson, 'Business Principles in the Public Service' (pp. 345–356); G.C. Brodrick, 'A Nation of Amateurs' (pp. 521–535); and H. Maxwell, 'Are We Really a Nation of Amateurs?' (pp. 1051–1063). See on the failure, G.R. Searle, *op. cit.*, p. 88 ff.; about an identical movement in the period of the Crimean War, see O. Anderson, *op. cit.*, p. 104 ff.
[113] Cf. J.G. Rogers' preference for Rosebery in 'Wanted a Leader' in *Nineteenth Century* 48 (1900), pp. 149–158. Cf. also M. Lodge, *Sir Richard Lodge*, London, 1946, pp. 125 ff., 153.
[114] G.R. Searle, *op. cit.*, p. 112 ff.; R.R. James, *Rosebery*, London, 1963, pp. 411, 431–433.
[115] R.R. James, *op. cit.*, p. 453 (quote from Rosebery's preface to A. Stead's study *Great Japan* (London, 1905).

cabinet to replace the existing party governments.[116] For the Glad-stonian Campbell-Bannerman there could be no worse affront to the liberal party and the liberal tradition. Rosebery, in his notorious ad-dress in Chesterfield in December 1901, used his slogan of 'efficiency' against the liberal party and its outmoded programme. Campbell-Bannerman commented acidly: "All that he said about the clean slate and efficiency was an affront to Liberalism and was pure claptrap. Efficiency as a watchword! Who is against it? This is all mere *réchauffé* of Mr. Sidney Webb, who is evidently the chief instructor of the whole faction."[117] Harcourt too interpreted Rosebery's words as an insult to 'the whole past of the Liberal Party and a betrayal of its growth in the future.'[118]

Rosebery's mania for efficiency plainly was not caused by any op-timistic view of the future, nor by a Webbs' belief in the bureaucratic expert, nor even by an American faith in the 'scientific management' of modern mass democracy. His vague doctrine of efficiency was wholly permeated by a deep distrust in the existing system of party politics. It was the same distrust which had been apparent in the old liberalism described earlier. Yet Campbell-Bannerman's reaction does not warrant the conclusion that during the Boer War only very few people shared Rosebery's disillusionment concerning 'party-govern-ment.' Several Liberals, divided as they were after 1886, did agree with Rosebery; in the nineties there was a growing belief that the system of party-government was no longer viable. The familiar and much-praised two-party system seemed to be on the wane: in 1892 Sidney Low, in his analysis of parliament, distinguished eight groups or 'factions' which made for 'the most groupified Parliament of modern times'; in his opinion it was impossible for a party-government to function properly with the handicap of this group-system.[119]

The crisis of the Boer War justified many of these pessimists. The report of the Elgin committee, after probing into the background of the Boer War, showed – as one of the many comments put it – that the South African failure was really due to the old and defective system of

[116] G.R. Searle, *op. cit.*, p. 92 ff.; cf. also 'Calchas,' 'The Test of Efficiency' in *Fortnightly Review* 72 (1902), pp. 405–418.

[117] Quoted in R.R. James, *op. cit.*, p. 433.

[118] G.R. Searle, *op. cit.*, p. 132; in September Sidney Webb had published an article in *Nineteenth Century* 50 (1901), pp. 366–386. Its title was 'Lord Rosebery's Escape from Houndsditch.' Cf. G.R. Searle, *op. cit.*, p. 126.

[119] S. Low, 'The Decline of the House of Commons' in *Nineteenth Century* 37 (1895), pp. 567–578, esp. pp. 569–571, 578.

party-government.[120] Goldwin Smith had long proclaimed similar theories, and in 1899, more secure than ever in his beliefs, he proclaimed them once more. Party-government, to him, spelled instability as well as the sacrifice of national interests to the interests of party or faction. "Constitutional Europe is strewn with the wreck of parties which have split into sections and produced total instability of government, a sufficient proof surely that the party system is not a dictate of Nature or the normal and necessary foundation of free government."[121]

The contemporary analysis of 'The Liberal Collapse' did not disregard this idea, although not everybody who either opposed or criticized the system of party-government would have it entirely abolished.[122] Most old Gladstonians took the opportunity of the crisis to vent their deep-seated distaste for modern party organization as advocated by the National Liberal Federation. A 'party machinery' to them was a demoralizing thing, as the glorified party discipline was bound to suppress originality and personal initiative. Had not one speech by Gladstone produced more and better results in the old days than years of National Liberal Federation work taken together?[123] The Gladstonian J.G. Rogers attempted in these critical times to restore some kind of unity within the divided ranks in repeatedly calling for an 'open' liberalism. By this he meant a vague and rather unprogrammed sort of liberalism according to the old pattern.[124]

Not only the coming modern party organization – in itself an indigestible morsel for the older liberal individualists – came under attack, the past itself suffered 'debunking' by those who criticized the system of party government. Disillusionment reigned everywhere: the political parties of the past became less idealized and lost some of their power and magic. In 1898 a political commentator wrote:

It will rather begin to be seen that what is known and spoken of as party government is, and has been, merely the result of a series of historical accidents, modified more or less by the sense of practical necessity and regard

[120] A. Griffiths, 'The Future of the Army' in *Fortnightly Review* 74 (1903), p. 628. Cf. W.S. Hamer, *op. cit.*, p. 212.

[121] Goldwin Smith, 'The Failure of Party Government' in *Nineteenth Century* 45 (1899), p. 731. See also E. Wallace, *Goldwin Smith. Victorian Liberal*, Toronto, 1957, pp. 140, 155, 179. Cf. T.E. Kebbel, 'Is the Party-System Breaking Up?' in *Nineteenth Century* 45 (1899), pp. 502–511. For an earlier criticism by the conservatives see W.J. Courthope, 'Party Government' in *Q.R.* 146 (1879), pp. 264–292. See chapter II, part B2.

[122] See esp. 'The Liberal Collapse' in *Nineteenth Century* 45 (1899), pp. 1–38 and 'The Future of Liberalism' in *Fortnightly Review* 63 (1898), pp. 1–21.

[123] *Fortnightly Review* 63 (1898), p. 3.

[124] *Nineteenth Century* 45 (1899), p. 8. Cf. J.G. Rogers, 'Liberalism and its Cross-currents' in *Nineteenth Century* 46 (1899), pp. 527–540.

for practical convenience. Up to the passing of the first Reform Act, certainly, party government in Great Britain was merely a struggle between rival aristocratic families to secure administrative control, with all the spoils of office and patronage resulting there from.[125]

In the decades to come, historiography was to experience a changed view of the political structures in the *ancien régime*, a revision which proved that the 'accidental view of history' was by and large right, and which also was to blur the finalist Whig view of history.[126]

During these years of crisis party government was a continual topic of discussion; it remained that even after the South African crisis was past. There was less talk about the much praised principle of cabinet government, but the old question of whether 'departmentalism' (more autonomy for each individual department) would not be more efficient than the cabinet government, again emerged.[127] This question dated from the Crimean War, when it was posed and answered affirmatively by W.R. Greg.[128] After the event it became plain that the British political system was to withstand the South African crisis reasonably well: party and cabinet government both survived, although not so matter-of-factly and inviolably as they used to do. Lloyd George's proposed coalition in 1910 made this quite clear.[129]

Around the turn of the century the Liberals, with their internal dissensions about Home Rule, imperialism, party organization and liberal leadership, had much greater problems than the Conservatives. More generally, the spate of imperialist and nationalist feeling around 1900 damaged the liberal tradition badly: there may have been no prophets of a new militarism in the liberal ranks, but for the first time in years liberal England contributed to 'scholarly' literature which depicted war as something normal, and even exalted its educational and rejuvenating qualities. There were 'Bernhardi' types in England after all: Lord Roberts (with his National Service League during the war) was one, and so were F.S. Oliver and the two later professors in military history: J.A. Cramb and the indefatigable publicist Spencer Wilkinson. One author, disillusioned after the First World War, blamed

---

[125] *Fortnightly Review* 63 (1898), p. 3.
[126] In Rosebery's historical work on the 18th century there was no trace of what was for the Whigs self-evident, a preference for Burke and the Rockingham-Whigs. Being a liberal imperialist, Rosebery favoured the old Chatham, who had plainly 'violated' Burke's 'party principles' during his last term as a minister. Cf. also G.R. Searle, *op. cit.*, p. 110.
[127] Cf. J.A.R. Marriott, 'Cabinet Government or Departmentalism?' in *Nineteenth Century* 48 (1900), pp. 685–694. See for his strongly unitarist constitutionalism, his later treatise *The Mechanism of the Modern State. A Treatise on the Science and Art of Government*, Oxford, 1927.
[128] See O. Anderson, *op. cit.*, p. 46; cf. G.C. Lewis, *Letters*, pp. 302–304.
[129] G.R. Searle, *op. cit.*, p. 171 ff.; cf. the criticism in *T.L.S.*, 15-10-1971, p. 1245.

them for having set the tone of the 'pre-war mind' in England. She was mistaken, but all the same their influence extended beyond the exclusively narrow circle of their own followers.[130]

4. Efficiency and administrative professionalism

The perilous situation around the turn of the century did not hold the liberals back for long. They put to shame all the morose prophecies of the nineties by the most impressive liberal election victory ever in 1906. Was it due to the promised social reforms? Was 1906 to be a turning-point? Had liberalism really shed the old ideology and really turned its back on the old Gladstonian tradition? We have abundant literature now that tries to prove the weak basis of the 1906 victory.[131] Today, half a century after Asquith, history's judgment of the social record of the liberals under Asquith is unfavourable rather than favourable. Once the liberals claimed to have initiated the modern welfare-state policy; modern historiography dealing with the Victorian age denies them this claim, and places the early beginnings of the welfare-state prior to 1865, in which year modern 'collectivism' was first conceived, according to A. Dicey.[132] Leaving aside any discussion of this question as well as the historically topical problem of whether or not the liberal decline had already been decided before the First World War, we wish only to indicate that although the 1906 victory had its misleading aspects, it does not diminish the liberal revival after 1900 and the great contrast between this revival and the crisis and dissensions apparent among liberals of the nineties of the preceding century. Perhaps this recovery could not guarantee the future, but it was undeniably present and the restored liberalism certainly made itself felt.

The important question for us in the matter of this recovery is whether the tradition had or had not fallen into discredit in this new social brand of liberalism. Rosebery's doctrine of efficiency aimed first at the Empire, without, however, excluding other reforms in the social

[130] C.E. Playne, *The Pre-War Mind in Britain. An Historical Review*, London, 1928, esp. chapter 3 (pp. 125–165); See on Spencer Wilkinson, p. 155 ff.; on J.A. Cramb, pp. 199 ff., pp. 273 ff.; on the popularity of romantic war literature see W.S. Hamer, *op. cit.*, pp. 214–215. See also B. Semmel, *op. cit.*, pp. 216–233; cf. also O. Anderson, 'The Growth of Christian Militarism in mid-Victorian Britain' in *E.H.R.* 86 (1971), pp. 46–72.

[131] Cf. P. Thompson, *Socialists, Liberals and Labour. The Struggle for London, 1885–1914*, London, 1967, p. 166 ff.; P. Rowland, *The Last Liberal Governments. The Promised Land, 1905–1910*, London, 1968, pp. IX ff., 30, 32, 150, 166, 215, 342 ff.

[132] See K. Woodroofe's summary, 'The Making of the Welfare State in England. A Summary of its Origin and Development' in *Journal of Social History* 1 (1968), pp. 303–324, esp. p. 308, cf. p. 316.

sector. The development of the Empire should set the pace for reforms at home, the first ones laying the groundwork for the others. The so-called 'social imperialism' made the imperialist wing of the Liberals favour social reforms at home, although they and their non-imperialist fellow Liberals held different opinions as to the means to this end.[133] Was Rosebery's mania for efficiency shared by the liberal reformers under Campbell-Bannerman, or by those later ones under Asquith? The first of these had no use for imperialism, the second was moderately imperialist. Their commitment to efficiency is doubtful: Haldane's attitude is an exception, if we remember Campbell-Bannerman's sneering remarks about Rosebery having borrowed his ideas on efficiency from the Webbs. Undoubtedly the Webbs were responsible for the magical meaning that the word 'efficiency' held for progressive reformers in England around the turn of the century, but did the Webbs – and the Fabians in general – have any influence on whatever was new in the liberal ideology? Admittedly they had discarded the (liberal) tradition; whether the liberals themselves followed suit, more or less, must still be decided.

It can no longer be denied that many people (G.B. Shaw, for instance) tended to overestimate the actual influence of the Webbs and of the Fabians in general on the political life before 1914.[134] The Fabians did not help to devise the liberal Newcastle Programme of 1891, nor did they in the eighties of the last century trigger off the 'progressive movement' in London. "Speaking politically, *Our Partnership* is a record of miscalculation, and failure" was what E.J. Hobsbawm wrote in 1949 when reviewing B. Webb's autobiography. He continued: "One after another the chosen instruments of Webb policy – the London Progressives, the Rosebery-Haldane Liberals, in the end even Churchill and Lloyd George break in their hands, or abandon them."[135]

No political failure could stop the Webbs' ideas from having a lasting influence in the early years of our century, more especially on the administrative level. Hobsbawm struck a happy mean between two extreme views in his review when he wrote:

[133] See on the young Rosebery's activity as a social reformer, R.R. James, *op. cit.*, pp. 197–199; cf. Rosebery's definition of efficiency in 1902: "a condition of national fitness equal to the demands of our Empire – administrative, naval, and military fitness – so that we could make the best of our admirable raw material." See B. Semmel, *op. cit.*, p. 63.

[134] See P. Thompson, *op. cit.*, p. 96 ff., 136 ff., 212 ff.

[135] *E.H.R.* 64 (1949), p. 258; for W. Churchill and the Webbs, see G.R. Searle, *op. cit.*, p. 248 ff.

There is at present a justified tendency to point out how little of British policy since 1906 actually derives from their plans or ideas; but this is based on a misconception. The Webbs' function was, in the main not themselves to supply ideas and suggest policies (though they had plenty of both), but to rally the scattered forces of administrators and experts, to bring them into full public service and to make them effective in politics.[136]

As a matter of fact it was the Webbs who expressed the modern state's need of professional politics, the need to have only experts in local and central government. The plea for instruction in the 'administrative sciences' came mainly (though not exclusively) from them; 'administration' came to be seen as the most important of all social sciences. 'Administration' and 'social organization' were, with 'efficiency,' part of an ideological armoury directed against a traditional amateurism; yet the Webbs insisted on regarding these arms as being purely value-free. Their central idea was that social problems could be solved by institutional means.[137]

The Webbs are the English advocates of 'scientific administration' both for politics and for government. Their socialism – from *Industrial Democracy* in 1897 until *The Constitution of a Socialist Commonwealth* in 1920 – was mainly remarkable for an unshakable faith in more and better (more scientific) administration as the sole condition for any successful reform movement. Politics should be a science: backward countries like Germany and Japan now proved their superiority by their efficiency.[138] In 1897 the Webbs in their book *Industrial Democracy* advocated forcible intervention by the state with reforms to be imposed from the top, bypassing – if need be – the ever more incompetent parliament.[139] Their ideal new democracy was 'administrative effi-

---

[136] *E.H.R.* 64 (1949), p. 259.

[137] G. Himmelfarb, 'The Intellectual in Politics: The Case of the Webbs' in *Journal of Contemporary History* 6 (1971), pp. 3–11, esp. p. 7. See for 'organization' as 'ideology': J. Romein, *Op het Breukvlak van Twee Eeuwen*, Leyden-Amsterdam, 1967, I, p. 344: the term administration came more and more to mean bureaucracy, see D. Thomson, *England in the Twentieth Century*, Harmondsworth, 1965, p. 64; See on the Webbs' 'administration ideology' also Ph. Abrams, 'The Failure of Social Reform' in *Past and Present*, no. 24 (1963), pp. 43–64, esp. pp. 59–61.

[138] In 1889, S. Webb wrote (*Fabian Essays*, p. 58): "The French nation was beaten in the last war, not because the average German was an inch and a half taller than the average Frenchman, or because he had read five more books, but because the German social organism was for the purposes of the time, superior in efficiency to the French." Cf. B. Webb in 1905 on Japan (*Our Partnership*, London, 1948, p. 300): "Japan is proving the superlative advantage of scientific methods in the international struggle for existence. How to combine the maximum of consent with the highest degree of efficiency is the problem before us in England: the average sensual man not wanting to be improved."

[139] S. and B. Webb, *Industrial Democracy*, London, 1897, II, p. 800 (note) cf. I, p. 64 (note 1). See also E. Halévy, *A History of the English People. Epilogue, 1895–1905*, Book II, Harmondsworth, 1939, p. 15.

ciency' and 'popular control' combined; in this 'New Democracy' the expert was to be the pivot.[140] That a twentieth century policy should be 'a policy of National Efficiency' was evident from the Boer War.[141]

The constitutional implications of their administrative ideology showed certain similarities with the ideals of the American progressives, such as W. Wilson, H.D. Croly, F.J. Goodnow and W. Lippmann. First, there was the preference for 'strong rule,' for an 'active State' and 'strong executive' to put the necessary social reforms through. The elitist aspects of this conception were softened – at least in the American case – by the demand for referendums and other such democratic forms. Because of its incompetence the legislative power was discredited both with the American progressives and the Webbs. For this reason there was much criticism of the separation of powers and of the too numerous legislative checks on the Executive.[142] Secondly, and following from the previous criticism, was their desire to separate politics from administration (party politics might hamper the government's work) for while the aims were to be set by the politicians, the means were to be decided by the experts.[143] The 'progressives' and the Webbs were, one might say, 'conditional' democrats; their ideology of efficiency was envisaging a modern democratic system in which experts were to fill appropriate posts.[144]

Perhaps W. Lippmann had the greatest understanding of the relationship between the Webbs and the American progressives. He had a deep admiration for the political prophecies of H.G. Wells, who began as a member of the 'Co-efficients' and a friend of the Webbs. The Webbs used him for the popularization and propagation of their own ideas, but Wells did not stay with them long; after a few years their ideas of efficiency were too narrowly technocratic for him.[145]

---

[140] *Industrial Democracy*, II, p. 845: "Whether in political or in industrial democracy though it is the Citizen who, as Elector or Consumer, ultimately gives the order, it is the Professional Expert who advises what the order shall be." Cf. S.R. Letwin, *The Pursuit of Certainty*, Cambridge, 1965, p. 369. See also the last chapter: 'The Apotheosis of Politics,' pp. 365–378.

[141] Cf. S. Webb, *Twentieth Century Politics: A Policy of National Efficiency*, London, 1901.

[142] See M.J.C. Vile, *Constitutionalism and the Separation of Powers*, Oxford, 1967, p. 265; cf. the Webbs in 1898: "What a modern democracy requires is the conduct of affairs with efficiency, integrity, and with due regard to the wishes of the whole community. This combination of efficiency with popular control is exactly what cannot be brought about by the theory of checks and balances", quote in S.R. Letwin, *op. cit.*, p. 372.

[143] Cf. F.G. Goodnow, *Politics and Administration*, New York, 1900. See for an analysis of his ideas, M.J.C. Vile, *op. cit.*, p. 277 ff.; cf. S. and B. Webb, *Industrial Democracy*, I, p. 64 (note).

[144] Cf. S. Haber, *op. cit.*, (see note 94), p. XI; for Croly and *The New Republic*, p. 85 ff.; see also D.W. Noble, *The Paradox of Progressive Thought*, Minneapolis, 1958, pp. 34–77.

[145] Cf. S. Haber, *op. cit.*, pp. 90, 94 (note 44); see for H.G. Wells and the Webbs: S. Hynes,

The political ideas of the American progressives were parallel to those of the Webbs and their supporters. But does this comparison hold good for the English new liberals? P.F. Clarke, a leading historian of new liberalism, also believes this to be a sound and justified one.[146] The new liberalism accepted the necessity of more state intervention, for the social problems about which so much was written early in the twentieth century also affected the liberals. Poverty had become a crime for which society could be held responsible, and it was seen that the past had no solution to offer. "The present can never take refuge behind the past" was what G.F.C. Masterman wrote in 1901.[147] The liberals were not the only ones to experience a feeling of what Peter Laslett in a different context called 'the world we have lost.' That feeling was beginning to affect both political and historical thinking. The work of historians in the twentieth century became increasingly characterized as an 'understanding by contrast.'[148] S. Hynes remarked that the consciousness of time in the post-Victorian period was mainly distinguished by the desire to be free of the Victorian past. "But it is also necessary to note that liberation was often the only thing that these liberating movements had in common; together they did not add up to a coherent system of beliefs or define a large common goal."[149]

The latter argument is certainly true for the new liberalism: it had social concerns, but it could not decide how to solve the social problems. Old and new liberalism both remained distinguished by a remarkable variety of views, although after 1900 the dissensions on Home Rule for Ireland and on imperialism were becoming less obtrusive than they had been.[150] The various new liberals had real ideological differences, and not just differences in emphasis. Masterman's contributions to the literature on social conditions were characterized by a moralizing about the ethics of reforms.[151] More realistic however were the analyses

op. cit., pp. 87–131; Wells's *Anticipations* (1901) and his *Mankind in the Making* (1903) both clearly voiced the ideal of 'national efficiency'; they had been published earlier in a series of articles in the *Fortnightly Review*.

[146] P.F. Clarke, *Lancashire and The New Liberalism*, Cambridge, 1971, p. 397: "It is very odd that historians should have neglected the term "progressive" which has virtually been consigned to a not dissimilar period of American history."

[147] *The Heart of the Empire*, ed. C.F.G. Masterman, London, 1901, p. V.

[148] P. Laslett, *The World We Have Lost*, London, 1968, pp. 7, 228; cf. also chapter 9, p. 200 ff.

[149] S. Hynes, op. cit., p. 9.

[150] An anthology of the different ideas (concerning politics home and abroad) of the new Liberalism in: *The Liberal Tradition. From Fox to Keynes*. ed. A. Bullock and M. Shock, Oxford, 1967, part V: 'The New Liberalism' pp. 180–253.

[151] Cf. S. Hynes, op. cit., p. 57 ff.; cf. B. Webb on C.F.G. Masterman: "in theory, he is collectivist, by instinct an anarchist individualist – above all, he is a rhetorician" (*Our Partnership*, p. 309). Cf. also Masterman on the Webbs in G.R. Searle, op. cit., p. 242.

of the economist J.A. Hobson on the social-economic and political situations. By criticizing the *laissez faire* of classic liberalism, he distanced himself from the Gladstonian past – which the 'prophet' of new liberalism, L.T. Hobhouse, never managed to do. Even in 1914 Hobson blamed the liberals for timidity and for having traditional paternalist convictions.[152]

Hobhouse's *Liberalism*, written in 1911, served the Young Liberals as a political credo, just as did H.L. Samuel's book of 1902. It certainly advocated State intervention and social laws, but it also attempted to repair the link with the Gladstonian past; new liberalism implied that old liberal principles were to be adapted to changed circumstances.[153] Among the socialist ideas that he rejected was faith in far-reaching social reforms instituted from above. His 'liberal socialism' was democratic and continued to protect the rights of the individual: "it (the reform) must come from below, not from above."[154] What he hoped and strove for was a reconciliation between his socialism and that of the more moderate Labour groups. The sharp opposition of the nineties had in his view largely disappeared.[155] Allied with his criticism of certain socialists – by which he must have meant the Webbs and their supporters – because of their ideology of extensive planning and reforms, was his own preference for relatively great autonomy for local governments. The centralizing bureaucratic tendency of the administration must be restrained by decentralization, by a 'revival of local government.'[156]

If Hobhouse's ideas are a faithful reflection of the 'average' new liberalism, the difference between this liberalism and the opinions of the American progressives, especially concerning a 'scientific' and efficient reform policy, are obvious. Words like 'efficiency' or 'strong rule' are absent from his work; he never lost his fear of 'strong rule,' centralization and an increased administrative bureaucracy necessitat-

[152] J.A. Hobson, *Traffic in Treason*, London, 1914, pp. 63–64: "Neither by temper nor by tradition is the Liberal Party alone qualified to carry forward to victory the banner of democracy. It must liberate itself from the narrowness of its outlook, the unreality of its attitude, and the timidity of its methods. It can only do so by calling in the more active assistance of the people whom it has professed to 'trust,' but has always sought to 'manage'"; see for criticism of idealism and moralism: Melvin Richter, *op. cit.*, pp. 281–282, 297, 332.

[153] L.T. Hobhouse, *Liberalism*, (1911), Reprint with introduction A.P. Grimes, Oxford, 1964, pp. 58 (on J.S. Mill), 71–72, 115, 126. P.F. Clarke (*op. cit.*, p. 173), rightly states that his work of 1911 is more truly conservative than his *Democracy and Reaction* of 1904.

[154] L.T. Hobhouse, *op. cit.*, pp. 90–91 (clearly alluding to Wells's *Samurai*).

[155] *Ibid.*, p. 109; cf. for Hobhouse's ideal of a reconciliation between liberalism and socialism: P.F. Clarke, *op. cit.*, pp. 172–173 (on Scott, p. 159 ff.).

[156] L.T. Hobhouse, *op. cit.*, pp. 116–117, 119.

ed by the welfare state. Yet in 1911 he was still enthusiastic about the American reform movement.[157] Bureaucracy caused equivocal feelings in most liberals; it was the dragon threatening the freedom of the individual, as R. Muir wrote; nevertheless the call for the bureaucratic expert became ever louder.[158]

Increasing bureaucratization led to an unintended and almost imperceptible decline in the administrative tradition, which was to have a certain impact on historiography. The wave of imperialism around the turn of the century had done away with the old anti-militarist tradition of 'no standing army,' and in the same period the new bureaucratic centralization of the administration made an end of the once highly praised Anglo-Saxon tradition of local self-government. Even on the local level an 'army of officials' gradually took the place of the traditional amateurs. From the liberals, especially, the resistance was marked against this growing New Leviathan. However, the Webbs' favourite demand for more experts (for the Webbs were 'bureaucrats by instinct') became increasingly stronger as the Leviathan of bureaucracy proceeded.[159]

The Institute of Public Administration, of which Haldane was the first President, was not founded until the twenties, but the periodical *Local Government Review* of 1909, was in a sense a forerunner of the Institute's organ, *Public Administration*. The Review had no special political bias; its purpose was to promote professionalism, and its message was directed to all affected by the coming development in local government. This development should above all promote 'a scientific adaptation to present needs,' which would make local government into "a powerful instrument in carrying forward the great work of ameliorating the social condition of the people."[160] According to the preface, the ideal of administrative and political efficiency had become very widespread:

It [the Review] will provide a common platform for all who seek to advance the cause of expert and efficient local administration; ... Local Government is now so complex and so all-embracing that there is no room in it for either the amateur administrator or the amateur writer. The former will disappear in process of time; the latter will find no place in the pages of this Review.[161]

[157] Cf. L. T. Hobhouse, 'The New Spirit in America' in *Contemporary Review* 100 (1911), pp. 1–10.
[158] Cf. J. Romein, *op. cit.*, I, p. 341.
[159] R. Muir, *How Britain is Governed*, London, 1933, p. 68.
[160] *The Local Government Review* 1 (1909–1910), p. 1.
[161] *Ibid.*

It was hardly surprising to find praise for Germany as a model of efficiency in the very first issue.[162]

The liberals however wished to retain the old tradition, although in an adapted form. L.T. Hobhouse's cousin Henry, in an address to the Brussels congress on administrative sciences in 1909, admitted that the 19th-century conception of local government was nothing but an illusion since the central government had taken over. He also pointed out that this conception had its opponents: "The bureaucratic instincts, not only of Government officials but of Members of Parliament ... have tended of recent years towards a considerable reaction against the progress of free local government in this country."[163] The advantages of a decentralized system weighed heavier than the disadvantages, a judgment he supported with the classical 19th-century arguments.

G.L. Gomme, an expert in the history of English local self-government, wavered in his largely pessimistic attitude concerning the problems of centralization and local government. The Local Government Acts, passed in the late 19th century, had missed their mark. The County Councils had no initiative of their own; they were administrative bodies in the service of the central government. The root cause of this disaster was the laws passed by the Local Government Board "with its army of officials untrained in local government," and with its unconcern for a 'local government in the historic sense.'[164] Nor was the central government alone to blame; equal blame attached to the existing local government 'with their army of badly trained officials.' The central government's interference was actually justified by local ineptness. Gomme concluded on a warning note: "Administrative science and organisation cry aloud for something better than this haphazard state of things, but the English mind, with its fatal incapacity to grasp theory and principles, will only wake up to it when it is an accomplished fact and requires a giant's effort to change it or else develop it on proper lines."[165]

The American 'progressives' were led by their administrative ideology to criticize the old *trias politica*, which had implied a too rigid separation of powers that resulted in inefficiency and political 'irre-

---

[162] W.H. Dawson, 'German Municipal Government' in *The Local Government Review* 1 (1909–1910), pp. 15–19, esp. p. 17.

[163] H. Hobhouse, 'Local Government and State Bureaucracy in Great Britain' in *The Local Government Review* 2 (1910), pp. 229–231, quote p. 230. See for H. Hobhouse, B. Webb, *Our Partnership*, pp. 128–130, 454–455.

[164] G.L. Gomme, 'Systems of English Local Government' in *The Local Government Review* 2 (1910), pp. 14–17, 119–121. (Cf. his work *Principles of Local Government* (1897)).

[165] G.L. Gomme, *op. cit.*, p. 121.

sponsibility.' In England such a rigid separation had never existed, thanks to the system of cabinet government. The increasing public control and bureaucracy led in England to a change in political and historical opinions regarding the relationship between central and local administration, both past and present.[166]

This change was apparent in the increasing scepticism towards Tocqueville's theory of local self-government as being the one and only safeguard for political freedom. It was made especially clear by H.O. Newland who opposed the *loci classici* of the ancient theorists with quotations from modern theoreticians and historians, as e.g. W. Wilson, E. Jenks and F.W. Maitland.[167] All these emphasized the monarchical or the 'Norman' perspective, which was rapidly gaining ground in English (medieval) historiography at the end of the 19th century.

Newland fully realized that this historiographical re-orientation was also a reflection of the times. With mass democracy imminent, local politics were redundant or at the most of secondary importance. The political scene was dominated by national issues such as imperialism and socialism. New conceptions had emerged: the state now had a more active role in the creation of new institutions and in the destruction of anachronistic historical traditions. These new conceptions now influenced the revision of the past.

The historian and political philosopher accordingly tend to emphasize the part which conquest and State action, either by means of monarchical tactics or parliamentary procedure have played, actively, in the creation, the revival, or the development of local governments, or, passively, in non-interference with pre-existing local practices and customs.[168]

The ideal of Anglo-Saxon local self-government – so fervently promoted in the second half of the 19th century – had become a political anachronism after 1900. But even before 1900 local self-government had (as E. Jenks explained) been more mythical than real, considering the ever increasing power of central boards, especially the Local Government Board.[169]

The process of state intervention and bureaucracy dismantled the

---

[166] Criticism of the idea of separation was plainly discernible in the work of the historian A.F. Pollard. See for Dicey's 'rule of law': M.J.C. Vile, *op. cit.*, p. 230 ff.

[167] H.O. Newland, 'Local Government and Free Institutions' in *The Local Government Review* 1 (1909–1910), pp. 264–267.

[168] *Ibid.*, p. 264.

[169] E. Jenks, 'Central and Local Government' in *The Local Government Review* 3 (1910–1911), pp. 8–11, 55–59, 103–107, 157–159.

time-honoured Anglo-Saxon ideal of local self-government. On the positive side it must be said that this special development resulted in broader historical interests. Administrative history, the history of the Civil Service, proved interesting to a growing public. The Webbs were once more pioneers in this field, since they were the first to write an extensive study about the history of English local government. This branch of history (a discussion to which we will later return) was really more than simply a continuation of traditional constitutional history.

Returning once more to the allegation that the Webbs had influenced the new liberalism: Campbell-Bannerman, (hardly a new liberal) may have disliked Rosebery's ideal of efficiency, but as Haldane (the later Labour-supporter) valued it, the average new liberal would probably have held an intermediate position. As time went on and bureaucracy increased, several elements of the Webbs' ideology of efficiency became more popular, although none were ever to be realized in totality. The liberal tradition may have been discredited, but it remained strong enough to stop the complete adaptation of these ideals.

Although the Webbs were pleased with several attempted breakthroughs in the liberal Party, they believed that the liberal leaders were too indecisive regarding the need for reorientation. Despite the Webbs' close connections with new liberals during the nineties, they refused to contribute directly towards the renewal of liberalism. From the very first they distrusted the leaders with their indistinct social programmes, the leaders who hardly listened to 'progressive' liberal-inspired proposals, let alone put them into practice. Sidney Webb wrote to H. Samuel, in the beginning of 1897: "Until it is settled *what* the Liberal Leaders mean – what reforms they have really at heart, and in what direction their intellectual convictions impel them to lead – I can only wish to see the Party weaker. There is no calamity in politics *against* which I would work harder than a return of the Liberal Leaders to office without a definite programme."[170] Liberals themselves too began to complain about the lack of a clear-cut social programme fully supported by the leadership; it was a persistent evil, the consequences of which became only too clear after the First World War. Asquith, the Liberal Leader in the pre-war period, was far from an inspiring social reformer, and as an administrator his qualities were none too im-

[170] S. Webb to H. Samuel 25–1–1897 in H. Samuel, *Memoirs*, London, 1945, p. 28. After the First World War the situation had in this respect deteriorated rather than improved; cf. Trevor Wilson, *The Downfall of the Liberal Party*, pp. 215, 287, 319, 328.

pressive either.[171] There must have been liberal 'progressives' in England, although probably they resembled their American counterparts less than did the Webbs. The London Reform Movement called itself 'progressive' as early as the eighties; and so did the short-lived magazine of the Rainbow circle, where new liberals (Hobson) and Labour leaders (R. MacDonald) used to discuss a new reform policy. The historian P.F. Clarke rightly drew attention to this sort of progressivism in Lancashire after 1900.[172]

In this chapter we have seen that progressive liberals also had many a doubt about political traditionalism. The classic of liberalism, however, Free Trade, survived for a time after 1900; in fact it was the one ideal to stimulate a regrouping of the divided liberals in a common revolt against J. Chamberlain. The great victory of 1906 had been partly due to the slogan of Free Trade. Yet even this dogma was no longer unassailable, as evidenced by the writings of the pioneers in social and economic history, discussed in the first chapter. We also mentioned in the first chapter a tendency to bring a certain professional approach to the study of history (as did the supporters of 'record-history'). This undoubtedly formed part of a much wider movement which preferred the expert to the amateur. The École des Sciences Politiques was set up as an example for politicians, and, as we have already seen, the historians decided in favour of an École des Chartes.[173] In the following chapters we shall devote more attention to the influence on English (liberal) historiography around 1900 of the combined forces of the crumbling old liberal tradition and the invigorating impulses of the new liberalism.

An ideology of efficiency and increasing professionalism harboured a criticism of tradition which might well become history, to paraphrase the words of J.G.A. Pocock with which we began this chapter. In 1928 the liberal historian and former cabinet minister H. Fisher mentioned the great damage suffered by all of 19th-century English historiography because of an exaggerated admiration and attachment to traditions.

---

[171] Cf. C. Hazlehurst, 'Asquith as Prime Minister, 1908–1916' in *E.H.R.* 85 (1970), pp. 502–531, esp. p. 514. Cf. P. Rowland, *op. cit.*, p. 150; after the World War Asquith undoubtedly returned to a 'Gladstonian orthodoxy,' cf. Trevor Wilson, *op. cit.*, pp. 212–213, 233–234, 340; he had had his fill of the term efficiency, cf. R. Kelley, 'Asquith at Paisley: the Content of British Liberalism at the End of its Era' in *Journal of British Studies* 3 (1964), pp. 133–159.

[172] See H. Samuel, *Memoirs*, p. 24 ff.

[173] G.C. Brodrick, 'A Nation of Amateurs' in *Nineteenth Century* 48 (1900), p. 532.

The same thought was expressed later by people like V.H. Galbraith and H. Butterfield. When the results of this breakthrough in the *reverentia antiquitatis* first became visible in a liberal historian's work, it was in the works of F.W. Maitland.[174]

[174] H. Fisher, 'The Whig Historians' in *Proceedings of the British Academy* 14 (1928), p. 300; V.H. Galbraith, 'Historical Research and the Preservation of the Past' in *History* 22 (1937–1938), p. 312; H. Butterfield, *The Englishman and His History*, London, 1944, p. 6.

CHAPTER IV

LAW AND HISTORY: F.W. MAITLAND

A. MAITLAND'S ROAD TO HISTORY

Now, it is but too probable that we are sadly defi-
cient in the historic sense which it is the pride of this
generation to have discovered in itself.

(F.W. Maitland, 1879)

Especially in the last two decades there has been renewed interest in
F.W. Maitland and his work. With the sole exception of Lord Acton,
no other English historian has been more studied in the post-war
years.[1] Nevertheless a discussion of Maitland in the overall treatment
of our present theme is not superfluous. We trust that we shall not be
guilty of repeating earlier assertions, as our concern is with only three
less publicized aspects of his work.

The continuing interest in Maitland is hardly surprising. Posterity
is unanimous in declaring him to have been the initiator of the movement directed against traditional historiography. In 1928 Herbert
Fisher, in his speech about Whig historians, called him the great
pioneer in this respect and G.O. Sayles declared that "Maitland
wrought the great metamorphosis."[2] Maitland's writings might well
be called an excellent illustration of the preceding chapter: the growth
of a new historical consciousness through the decline of tradition.

How did Maitland keep his historical writings free from Victorian
'presentism'? How and why was he able to understand the reality of
the Middle Ages? The existing literature usually cites three sources of

[1] Some recent literature: T.F.T. Plucknett, 'Maitland's View of Law and History' in *Law
Quarterly Review* 67 (1951), pp. 179–194; P.J. White, 'F.W. Maitland' in *Cambridge Journal* 4
(1950–1951), pp. 131–143; E. Maitland, *F.W. Maitland: A child's-eye view*, 1951; *Selected
Historical Essays of F.W. Maitland*, introduced by H.M. Cam, Cambridge, 1957; J.R. Came-
ron, *F.W. Maitland and the History of English Law*, Norman 1961; R.L. Schuyler, *F.W. Mait-
land. Historian*, Berkeley, 1960; H.E. Bell, *Maitland. A Critical Examination and Assessment*,
London, 1965; J.W. Gray, 'Canon Law in England: Some reflections on the Stubbs-
Maitland controversy,' in *Studies in Church History*, ed. G.J. Cuming, Leyden, 1966, vol. III,
pp. 48–68; Roy Stone de Montpensier, 'Maitland and the Interpretation of History' in
American Journal of Legal History 10 (1966), pp. 259–281; C.H.S. Fifoot, *Pollock and Maitland*,
Glasgow, 1971; C.H.S. Fifoot, *F.W. Maitland. A Life.*, Cambridge, Mass., 1971; *The Letters
of F.W. Maitland*, ed. C.H.S. Fifoot, Cambridge, 1965.
[2] H.A.L. Fisher, 'The Whig Historians' in *Proceedings of the British Academy* 14 (1928), p.
300; G.O. Sayles in *International Encyclopaedia of the Social Sciences*, 1968, vol. 9, p. 534.

inspiration for Maitland's ever growing penchant for history: his grandfather, S.R. Maitland, was one, the other two were W. Stubbs and P. Vinogradoff. Admiration for and indebtedness to these three occur in several of his books and letters.[3] The unassuming Maitland showed himself so grateful to Vinogradoff, that Herbert Fisher invented a story about the second meeting between Maitland and Vinogradoff having been of decisive importance for Maitland. This myth survived until the fifties, when it was exposed by T.F.T. Plucknett.[4] Actually Maitland had found the road to history and to the records well before the meeting with Vinogradoff; neither the influence of Vinogradoff nor that of the other two historians can be said to have been decisive.

Much more fundamental for his turning to history and for his historical specialization, had been his philosophical training under Sidgwick (until far into 1875). The years between 1876 and 1884, when he was a practising lawyer (conveyancer), were a second factor. Although historical methods or techniques could not be gleaned either from his philosophical training or from his practical experience, his attitude towards the past was certainly moulded by this background, and consequently also his view of history and its social tasks. Here lies the source of his great originality. He felt that he had been a success neither as a philosopher nor as a conveyancer, yet indirectly the success of his historical work is due to these two earlier failures.

In 1906 Maitland called Henry Sidgwick "one of the acutest, profoundest and most influential thinkers of our time."[5] Sidgwick's influence on Maitland is easily shown in a number of concrete instances: Sidgwick introduced Maitland to early German law and urged him to write about Law Reform as well as to translate Gierke.[6] It is more important (although far more difficult) to decide exactly what Maitland owes to Sidgwick for his intellectual and scientific education. Both were agnostics, a circumstance which lent a certain scepticism – spiced with humor and irony – to their scholarly work. Sidgwick was very critical and sceptical of the 'historical method', and undoubtedly he

---

[3] For S.R. Maitland, see *Letters*, p. 95; for Stubbs, see *Letters*, pp. 182, 225; further, *The Collected Papers of Frederic William Maitland*, Cambridge, 1911, vol. III, pp. 495–511. Cf. also: *Letters of William Stubbs*, ed. W.H. Hutton, London, 1904, pp. 275–276. In 1888, Maitland had asked Stubbs for a testimonial, see Stubbs's letter of 7-6-1888 to Maitland, C.U.L., Add. MS. 7006.

[4] Cf. H.A.L. Fisher, *F.W. Maitland*, Cambridge, 1910, p. 24; for T.F.T. Plucknett's criticism, see his article mentioned in note 1. Cf. also F.M. Powicke, *Modern Historians and the Study of History*, London, 1956, p. 10, note 1. A.L. Smith was already in 1908 very prudent in his judgment; see A.L. Smith, *F.W. Maitland*, Oxford, 1908, p. 31.

[5] *C.P.*, III, p. 540.

[6] Cf. *Letters*, pp. 7, 51, 205.

was a great help to Maitland when the latter was trying to decide what was to be expected of historical scholarship.[7] Maitland's philosophical achievements are hardly impressive; there are only a few articles in the magazine *Mind*, and a dissertation which rates a short discussion considering Maitland's later development.

The essay about liberty and equality as ideals of English political philosophy from Hobbes to Coleridge was written in 1875 in the hope of a fellowship. There was little abstract or contemplative about it; it was intended as a historical sketch only. There were two main streams in English political tradition: one the patriarchal and absolutist tradition of Filmer and Hobbes, and the other the more constitutional and conventional tradition of Locke. Both intended to justify a system of government, and were basically ethical doctrines 'disguised as pieces of history.' This resulted in an unsatisfactory admixture of ethics and history. In Maitland's opinion the historical elements of Locke's doctrine of consensus were plainly inferior to those of the patriarchal tradition.[8]

Maitland had a very clear preference for those who used a basic understanding of history in order to arrive at a more realistic and utilitarian philosophy of politics. Hence his admiration for Harrington and Hume. Harrington, unlike Hobbes, was concerned not with Man, but with human beings. Rather than using blueprints, he preferred the actual history in which the relationship between property and power was presented clearly, if somewhat simplistically. "Harrington saw the importance of consulting the history of that nation for which we are setting up an ideal."[9] Hume, the 'founder of modern utilitarianism,' praised Harrington and in a way carried on Harrington's tradition. "In Hume we see the first beginnings (if we except the remarkable work of Harrington) of a scientific use of history."[10] As history and empirical psychology were, to Maitland, essential for the study of political science, he rejected as dangerous simplifiers those theoreticians who did not believe in the value of history. In this respect James Mill's theory about general and personal interests being identical was, to Maitland, the depth of infamy. Mill's son, J.S. Mill, was cured of his father's 'geometrism' by Macaulay; this helped him to understand Coleridge's view of the values of history.[11]

[7] Cf. H. Sidgwick, 'The Historical Method' in *Mind* 11 (1886), pp. 203–219.
[8] *C.P.*, I, p. 19.
[9] *C.P.*, I, p. 22.
[10] *C.P.*, I, p. 58.
[1] *C.P.*, I, p. 136.

Maitland discussed Coleridge extensively in the final part, in conjunction with the idea of equality and property rights. Coleridge had, in his *On the Constitution of Church and State*, shown his preference for real property instead of personal property, and for the landed class as an indispensable part of an aristocratic constitution. He even propounded an argument about the distinction between classes based on this juridical distinction. The 'spiritual history of our laws' had inspired Coleridge with awe, but he had been so dazzled by his own romantic preference for what was once the law of real property in "the age which he loved," that he was unable to see the slow but inevitable judicial assimilation of real property with personal property in industrial society. His historical views were more dream than reality; the wish was father to the thought. Coleridge's view of history caused him to turn away from the present, and consequently his choice in the 19th-century contest between 'commercialism' and 'feudalism' was not difficult.[12]

This romantic sense of history, however, was rejected by Maitland. In the final part of his dissertation of 1875 he published a first attack on the existing law of real property and on the unchangingly feudal way in which the distinction between movable goods and real estate was applied, a distinction causing great social and personal injustice because of the highly complicated double law of inheritance. After a number of years conveyancing, Maitland's judgment on these matters became much sharper and more ironic.

Of course Maitland was not the only one to criticize the law of real property and the land laws in general. In 1878 the moderately liberal *Edinburgh Review* also demanded that the hereditary laws concerning real property be modernized, but Maitland evinced a much more radical attitude in his article 'The Law of Real Property,' published in 1879 in the *Westminster Review*.[13] Here he joined the ranks of those radicals and utilitarians who had throughout the 19th century been warring against the principles of entail and primogeniture and against the resulting preservation and safeguarding of aristocratic landed property. Ever since 1836 hardly a year had passed without a Bill being proposed to equalize the laws on the inheritance of real and personal property. Time and again the landed aristocracy had defended primo-

---

[12] See on Coleridge *C.P.*, I, pp. 156–161.
[13] See *C.P.*, I, pp. 162–201. Cf. J.A. Hardcastle, 'Principles and Prospects of the Liberal Party' in *E.R.* 147 (1878), pp. 274–300, esp. p. 288, proposing this legal reform as part of a political programme for a coming liberal government.

geniture as something 'inherent to English character,' as a necessary
barrier against the 'republican' tide, and finally because it enabled
them to keep up with the new industrial aristocracy with their personal
property.[14] Dividing the movement for reform of the land laws into
three phases, as F.M.L. Thompson does, we would place Maitland in the
second phase. In this period agriculture entered an era of permanent
crisis, and landlordism became the butt of extremely violent agitation
both in Ireland and in England.[15] Although after 1880 the law was
amended on several points, Maitland's 1879 proposals were not put
into practice until the twentieth century was twenty-five years old. It
was on that point, if any, that the *ancien régime* in Victorian England
died hard.[16]

Maitland's essay of 1879 has been rightly termed brilliantly destructive. For us it is important mainly because Maitland's historical
attitude already shows in the diatribes against the existing laws. He
advocated thorough changes, resolutely rejecting the usual 'patch-
work' of additions to an already 'cumbersome and clumsy system'
which would render the system even more perversely complex than it
was. 'Let all property be personal property.' In the inheritance laws,
expecially in the laws of primogeniture and the subordinate position of
women, England was clearly backward, as much as Russia or Serbia.
The English legal system was ridden by a 'misplaced antiquarianism';
Maitland pointedly called it 'the accumulated rubbish of ages' instead
of the more commonplace phrase 'accumulated wisdom of ages.' He
never supported radicalism for its own sake: historical continuity, if
salutary, should be maintained. But it was a lack of historical insight
not to realize that the law of real property had to be sacrificed on 'the
altar of historic continuity.' What Maitland found lacking was the
very historic insight for which he had striven all his life, and which may
be briefly defined as a struggle against anachronism on two fronts: the
evil of anachronism did as much damage to the present as to the past.
"Any one who really possesses what has been called the historic sense

---

[14] Cf. F.M.L. Thompson, *English Landed Society in the Nineteenth Century*, London, 1971,
pp. 65, 69, 283; *The English Ruling Class*, ed. W. L.Guttsman, London 1969, pp. 88–92; A.
Harding, *A Social History of English Law*, Harmondsworth, 1966, pp. 372–375; for real and
personal property in English common law see: C.A. Uniken Venema, *Van Common Law en
Civil Law*, Zwolle, 1971, pp. 1–95.
[15] Cf. F.M.L. Thompson, *op. cit.*, pp. 283–284; on the legislation effected before and after
1880, see G. Kitson Clark, *The Making of Victorian England*, London, 1966, pp. 248–249.
[16] On the Law of Property Act of 1925, see R.E. Megarry and H.W.R. Wade, *The Law
of Real Property*, London, 1959, ch. 19. Cf. also C.A. Uniken Venema, *op. cit.*, pp. 24, 35, 43,
66–67, 75.

must, so it seems to me, dislike to see a rule or an idea unfitly surviving in a changed environment. An anachronism should offend not only his reason, but his taste," he wrote some months before his death.[17]

It has often been said that Maitland's essay of 1879 echoed Bentham. But he never advocated a rigid utilitarianism, in which there was no place for a more historic view. Maitland rejected the lack of historical understanding in early utilitarianism just as decisively as Coleridge's romantic view of history.[18] The law of real property was rightly criticized as anachronistic, yet this very quality contributed to an easier understanding of this law as a historical phenomenon.

We can give here a concrete explanation of something discussed more theoretically in the first chapter. Maitland's 1879 essay was the direct result of his conveyancing experiences. Because he knew the existing legal system to be a useless and for the present even dangerous anachronism, he took a decisive step towards the rediscovery of the past as such. The connection between the two meanings of anachronism was pointed out in the first chapter; the later meaning of something outdated could rapidly gain ground because of the social and political development of the modern state and society. This development might be said to have made a more autonomous view of the past possible. It also was a guarantee for getting those historical aims realized which were implied in the original meaning of anachronism, as something distorting our view of the past. At first, Maitland contested anachronism as a threat to the present, but he grew to realize that anachronistic views damaged the past as well. In his later years as a legal historian he restored the Middle Ages to their rightful place, not in spite of but because of his utilitarian viewpoint. His eight years of lawyer's practice may have had no practical value, but for the wider perspective moulding his historic sense they were invaluable. "It was as a result of this work," R.W. Southern wrote, "that he became interested in the Middle Ages."[19]

Maitland's concern with the laws ruling real and personal property greatly influenced his historical perspective.[20] In his lectures of 1887–88, published after his death in 1908, the law of real property was the

[17] C.P., III, p. 486. Cf. A.L. Smith's pronouncement: "The true historic sense is that which most dislikes a survival of the unfit." (A.L. Smith, op. cit., p. 35).

[18] See on the historic way of thinking in Bentham: R. Preyer, Bentham, Coleridge and the Science of History, Bochum-Langendreer, 1958.

[19] R.W. Southern, 'The Letters of Frederic William Maitland' in History and Theory 6 (1967), p. 106. Southern's review essay ranks with Plucknett's previously mentioned article of 1951 as the best writings on Maitland's road to history.

[20] Cf. C.H.S. Fifoot, F.W. Maitland. A. Life., pp. 66, 96–97.

pivot of his *Constitutional History of England*. "It is quite impossible to speak of our medieval constitution except in terms of our medieval land law," he wrote in the beginning, concluding programmatically with: "We can make no progress whatever in the history of parliament without speaking of tenure, indeed our whole constitutional law seems at times to be but an appendix to the law of real property."[21] In his later work, *The History of English Law*, the same thought recurs; and now and then there is an echo of the 1879 radicalism, as in the final passages of the chapter on inheritance.

It is in the province of inheritance that our medieval law made its worst mistakes. They were natural mistakes. There was much to be said for the simple plan of giving all the land to the eldest son. There was much to be said for allowing the courts of the church to assume a jurisdiction, even an exclusive jurisdiction, in testamentary causes. We can hardly blame our ancestors for their dread of intestacy without attacking their religious beliefs. But the consequences have been evil. We rue them at the present day, and shall rue them so long as there is talk of real and personal property.[22]

This is the voice of the reformer-historian, which Maitland was and remained until the very end of his life.

He never lost an opportunity of combating anachronism, both where the present and where the past were concerned. Anachronism was a problem with two aspects, both of which were important for what Maitland called a historic sense. In the final pages of this chapter we shall discuss Maitland's method of contesting the anachronisms concerning the past. The intrinsic value of history as a science hung on its success. In this introductory part we have given the central place to anachronisms endangering the present; Maitland fought these as a reformer and as a historian as well, because his experience had made him familiar with the dangers. If historical scholarship had a social value and a 'liberating' force, it was in exposing such existing anachronisms. Maitland was tireless in his fight to keep alive the issue of law of real property. In 1901, he again insisted that the then current system was unworthy of a nation with any self-respect. He rejected a historical scholarship which attempted to paralyse the present by means of the past: "To-day we study the day before yesterday, in order that yesterday may not paralyse to-day, and to-day may not paralyse to-morrow."[23] In 1896 he sent a letter to Dicey in which he mentioned

[21] F.W. Maitland, *The Constitutional History of England*, Cambridge, 1961, pp. 24, 538.
[22] F. Pollock and F.W. Maitland, *The History of English Law*, Cambridge, 1968, vol. II, p. 363.
[23] *C.P.*, III, p. 439.

the 'liberating' force of legal history, with which he justified his historical labours as a radical reformer. It is a remarkable letter:

I have not for many years past believed in what calls itself historical jurisprudence. The only direct utility of legal history ... lies in the lesson that
each generation has an enormous power of shaping its own law. I don't think
that the study of legal history would make men fatalists; I doubt it would
make them conservatives. I am sure that it would free them from supersti-
tions and teach them that they have free hands. I get more and more
wrapped up in the middle ages, but the only utilitarian justification that
I ever urge in *foro conscientiae* is that, if history is to do its liberating work, it
must be as true to fact as it can possibly make itself; and true to fact it will
not be if it begins to think what lessons it can teach.[24]

The lessons of history as Maitland saw them differed greatly from
those of traditional Whig historiography. History's liberating force was
most powerful when it had no apparent direct application or 'use.'

Before entering upon a discussion of law and history, we should
mention his well-known essay 'The Shallows and Silences of Real Life,'
written when the Local Government Act of 1888 was in the making.
The Justices of the Peace were to be replaced by newly created County
Councils. Here is another striking illustration of Maitland's historical
sense. He stressed the need for a radical reform of local government:
"Taken as a whole, our local government is a weltering chaos out of
which some decent order has to be got."[25] He insisted that a longer
continuation of tradition was really dangerous. Yet this demand for
reform was accompanied by a number of brilliantly and suggestively
written pages on the unique history of the Justice of the Peace and his
function in England's past. The old unpaid official might have been
criticized for incompetence, corruption and amateurishness, but for all
that his role in history must certainly be remembered. The students
attending Maitland's lectures in that year were advised to read Lambarde's *Eirenarcha* during the holidays. Should this task be too exacting,
there always was Shakespeare: "if you cannot yet enjoy Lambarde's
Eirenarcha, you can at least enjoy Shallow and Silence, Dogberry and
Verges."[26]

[24] Quoted in: C.H.S. Fifoot, *F.W. Maitland. A Life*, p. 143
[25] *C.P.*, I, p. 472. Cf. F.W. Maitland, *The Constitutional History of England*, p. 499.
[26] F.W. Maitland, *The Constitutional History of England*, p. 236.

B. LAW AND HISTORY INCOMPATIBLE?

> A mixture of legal dogma and legal history is in
> general an unsatisfactory compound.
>
> (F.W. Maitland, 1888)

The existing law of real property had no rational justification left in
Maitland's opinion: a conclusion he drew as a conveyancer. Dating
from the Middle Ages, the law was 'out of date' and explicable only
historically. Thus might we summarize the practical experiences which
led Maitland to study legal history.

The English legal system made it extremely difficult to choose the
law or part of it as a subject of historical study. For were there not
immense problems – practical and basic – connected with the writing
of a history of Early English law? Maitland mentioned one very basic
problem in his inaugural speech of October 1888, "Why the history of
English Law is not written?"[27] Early in his career as a professor he
posed a problem which more and more began to attract people's
notice, and about which much would be written. The problem was the
relation between law and history, especially legal history. Maitland
wondered why no history of English law had yet been written. As two
main causes he named the traditional insularity of English law and
more especially the harmful influence which the historically practical
administration of justice had on the writing of history.

As to the first point: Maitland would always advocate a more comparative approach. "An isolated system cannot explain itself, still less
explain its history."[28] The second point involved the damaging influence on history of the 'legal mind.' He discussed this point very extensively emphasizing the existence of a basic contrast between the
two disciplines regarding their approach to the past. The professional
approaches to the past of lawyer and historian are basically opposed.
In this connection Maitland gave the following description of what
J.G.A. Pocock later called the 'common-law habit of thinking': "That
process by which old principles and old phrases are charged with a new
content, is from the lawyer's point of view an evolution of the true
intent and meaning of the old law; from the historian's point of view it
is almost of necessity a process of perversion and misunderstanding."[29]

[27] *C.P.*, I, pp. 480–497.
[28] *C.P.*, I, p. 489; cf. F.W. Maitland, *The Constitutional History of England*, p. 142.
[29] *C.P.*, I, p. 491; cf. F.W. Maitland, *Justice and Police*, London, 1885, p. 61.

Everyday practice forces the lawyer to bring the past 'up to date' in a way which seems gross disfigurement to the historian. The lawyer wants authority: the newer the better. The historian wants evidence: the older the better. It appears paradoxical that Maitland believed the first centuries of English law had been so little studied "because all English lawyers are expected to know something about them."[30] The practising lawyer needs only a little history to make it immediately applicable. A surfeit of history would paralyse his work. The lawyer is not interested in medieval law for its own sake, but only in its later shape "as interpreted by modern courts to suit modern facts."[31] Thus the lawyer's profession forces him to anachronistic interpretations. Maitland's conclusion was that "it is to the interest of the middle ages themselves that they be not brought into court any more."[32] In 1879 his reaction to anachronism was a desire to protect the present, now, in 1888, he was asking that the past be similarly protected.

At the end of his speech Maitland made the sharp division between the two different methods he perceived slightly less distinct. Almost as though he himself was shocked by his own statement, he afterwards excused himself in a letter to Vinogradoff on the subject of his inaugural speech: "it was meant to be heard and so I allowed myself some ex-aggerations."[33] Although there was in fact a fundamental difference in approach and interpretation of the past, no legal historian could in practice do without a thorough knowledge of the modern system of law, nor of modern legal thinking. "I do not think that an Englishman will often have the patience to study medieval procedure and conveyancing unless he has had to study modern procedure and modern conveyancing and to study them professionally."[34] Was this statement not partly hinting at his own road to legal history? Besides, Maitland continued, knowledge of the contemporary legal situation facilitated historical comparisons, which in turn yield a clearer view of the differences be-tween past and present. Maitland often used this method to avoid anachronisms. That he did make a restriction concerning the funda-mental difference between law and history, does not change his con-ception of an opposition between the two, as Plucknett later seemed to think.[35]

---

[30] *C.P.*, I, p. 490.
[31] *C.P.*, I, p. 490.
[32] *C.P.*, I, p. 493.
[33] *Letters*, p. 49.
[34] *C.P.*, I, p. 493.
[35] Cf. T.F.T. Plucknett, *op. cit.*, p. 190.

On several points a closer elucidation of the problem that Maitland posed may be useful. To do this we need a wider perspective. The subject of his inaugural speech was not new, although it had acquired a new meaning in the period around the turn of the century. Juridical-historical thought has had great influence on western historiography in general, and on English historiography in particular; to quote Alan Harding: ". . . in the West mature historiography was a by-product of the political use made of law in the sixteenth century."[36] Maitland realized that the juridical way of thinking did not only cripple legal history, but its influence was also felt on historical thought in general. In fact juridical influence is found in the very presuppositions of Whig historiography; its appearance in this section is no coincidence. For a radical demolition of Whig historiography it was first of all necessary to divorce 'history' from 'law'; the works of Maitland and of Round make this very clear.

Western historiography has seen many conflicts between law and history, especially in periods when anachronisms gave rise to problems. Renaissance historiography provided a striking example in the debates between the supporters of the so-called 'mos italicus' and their opponents who favoured the 'mos gallicus.'[37]

The old school adhered to the 'mos italicus,' basing its arguments on Bartolus and many glossarists. Their purpose was to prolong the use of Roman law for their own times by separating it as far as possible from its historical context. Those interpretations were intended only for juridical practice, and invoked the anger of lawyers with more historical-philological understanding, like Budé, Alciato and, later, Pasquier, Bodin, Cujas, and Hotman. They were what D.R. Kelley uses to call early 'historists,' striving to understand Antiquity and the Middle Ages in their proper context. Roman law was useless for them; it was nothing but a 'historical source,' a 'record.' With these historical criticisms the supporters of the 'mos gallicus' cut the bonds between past and present, at least where Roman law was concerned, thus causing a gap unacceptable to practising lawyers. Especially in France after 1550 with the increasing danger of a religious war a new link was

---

[36] A. Harding, op. cit., p. 259.

[37] See: G. Kisch, Humanismus und Jurisprudenz: Der Kampf zwischen mos italicus und mos gallicus an der Universität Basel, Basel, 1955; M.P. Gilmore, Humanists and Jurists. Six Studies in the Renaissance, Cambridge Mass., 1963; G. Huppert, The Idea of Perfect History. Historical Erudition and Historical Philosophy in Renaissance France, Chicago, 1970; D.R. Kelley, Foundations of Modern Historical Scholarship. Language, Law, and History in the French Renaissance, New York, 1970.

needed, and the reaction, sometimes called 'neo-Bartolism,' was not slow to arrive.[38] Instead of Roman law unwritten customary law with its homely *coutumes* or customs provided this link. J.G.A. Pocock writes in this respect: "one of the attractions of custom was precisely that it offered a means of escape from the divorce of past and present threatened by the criticisms of the historical school."[39] No longer did people lean on the Roman past; now they turned to their own 'national' medieval past; this was the beginning of medieval studies: born of a political-juridical need, and destined to survive in many respects until the end of the *ancien régime*.[40]

This return to the accumulation of custom, as J.G.A. Pocock pointed out, had both favourable and unfavourable consequences for historiography. The English development shows the more unfavourable aspects of what happened after customary law became idealized both juridically and historically. There were not two dissenting schools of thought in England, as there had been on the Continent, because Roman Law had never been accepted by medieval England. The comparison with the continental situation only obtains for the 'mos italicus' applied to English common law. Should Coke be styled the first Whig historian or the last medieval commentator on the 'common law'?[41] The question is superfluous, as this juridical-historical way of thinking existed very long before and even after Coke. "Common law historical thought represented," Pocock writes, "a most vigorous survival of the medieval concept of custom in English political thinking."[42] There is also much to be said for Maitland's remark of a 'marvellous resuscitation' which takes into account that the Tudor Age was in some respects a break with the pattern, even though Roman Law had never been really accepted.[43]

The historical views developed within common law have two characteristic aspects, according to Pocock. Firstly insular customary law was idealized, and secondly the origins of the custom were pronounced 'immemorial.'[44] Pocock is plainly inspired by Maitland's inaugural

[38] Cf. J.G.A. Pocock, *The Ancient Constitution and the Feudal Law*, Cambridge, 1957, p. 23 ff.
[39] *Ibid.*, p. 14.
[40] Cf. D.R. Kelley, *op. cit.*, ch. VI, VII, X; remember also that diplomatics and charter-criticism were above all juridical disciplines until far into the 18th century, cf. F.W.N. Hugenholtz, 'Adriaan Kluit en het onderwijs in de mediaevistiek' in *Forum der Letteren* 6 (1965), pp. 142–160.
[41] Cf. J.C. Holt, *Magna Carta*, Cambridge, 1969, p. 7 ff.
[42] J.G.A. Pocock, *op. cit.*, p. 51; cf. also D.R. Kelley, 'History, English Law and the Renaissance' in *Past and Present* 65 (1974), pp. 24–51.
[43] Cf. *Selected Historical Essays of F.W. Maitland*, Cambridge, 1957, p. 58.
[44] Cf. J.G.A. Pocock, *op. cit.*, p. 58.

speech in his analysis of the non-comparative insular way of thinking.[45]
Maitland did not mention the myth of 'immemorial custom' in 1888,
yet he touched upon it, as this myth was the most extreme example of
the need for a lawyer to know too little rather than too much of history
if he wanted to make use of his knowledge.

The word 'immemoriality' was generally applied to the accumulated
rights and rules called an 'ancient constitution,' dating 'from time
immemorial' or 'from immemorial antiquity.'[46] That the 'ancient constitution' dated from 'time immemorial,' implied in the 17th century
that the origins of parliament were beyond exact memory, and thus
the historical continuity of the rights and privileges of the Commons
was stressed: they could not afford any break in the pattern. Within
this continual development, from 'immemorial' origin, every change
could be explained away as either confirming some old custom or as a
return to it; the myth of the 'immemoriality' thus was wedded to 'the
myth of the confirmations.'[47] It was thought that history continued
without substantial change; real progression did not exist. "Custom
was *tam antiqua et tam nova*, always immemorial and always perfectly
up-to-date."[48] On the one hand a fundamentally non-historical aspect
was hidden inside the juridical-historical way of thinking of the common
lawyers, but on the other hand this very aspect proved to be their
greatest strength in their opposition to Stuart absolutism. Custom,
always unwritten and never fixed, was of immemorial origin, which
rendered it powerful enough to be the ideal norm for the present;
'immemorial' had become synonymous with 'prescriptive'.[49] Authority
was thus vested in an immemorial and absolutely un-knowable past
and even a little knowledge of actual historical details might destroy
the absolute assurance of its authority.

The medieval past, rooted in its mysterious origins, cannot but have
been 'productive' and 'useful.' In parliament the Stuarts saw themselves opposed by the undivided forces of lawyers and historians: Law
and History marching jointly. The historical views of these early Whigs
had for the greater part been the work of the lawyers, whose 'productive misunderstanding' of the past (a term used by Hoetink) had put its
stamp on part of the political development. And insofar as these views

[45] J.G.A. Pocock, *op. cit.*, p. 58.
[46] Maitland was fully aware of what this terminology signified in a legal context. Cf.
C.P., II, pp. 332–333; F.W. Maitland, *The Constitutional History of England*, p. 130.
[47] J.G.A. Pocock, *op. cit.*, p. 44.
[48] *Ibid.*, p. 15.
[49] A. Harding, *op. cit.*, p. 217.

were productive it was difficult to call them a 'misunderstanding.' The voices criticizing this 'misunderstanding' were heard only when the lawyers' views became less useful or less necessary for the present. Pocock shows that early Whig historiography had been criticized already in the seventeenth century. These criticisms became more fundamental afterwards when its usefulness was no longer apparent for the present. The partnership of Law and History had certainly been productive, for the past had long been useful, both politically and juridically. During the *ancien régime* it was natural for law and history to join forces; for the lawyers it was even necessary. But this meant that English constitutional and legal history could not break the fetters of a juridical-historical interpretation. The fundamental incompatibility of the two disciplines could be acknowledged only towards the end of the 19th century.

The past could render its greatest services to the practising lawyer with only 'a little history,' as Maitland phrased it in 1888. Or, keeping the myth of 'immemorial custom' in mind, the lawyer might be said to profit more if he could remember history only partially. To keep historically originated laws alive, and continually useful for the present, it is advisable to have 'no memory' of the concrete historical situation in which some juridical usages were born. Too much history was expendable ballast for the lawyer. Neglecting the concrete facts made it easier to continue the past and to commandeer authority in the present by means of that very past. The common-law tradition could only continue to exist by denying the historical context, and this same denial inevitably led to anachronistic interpretations of the past. To illustrate the unhistorical qualities of the 'common-law habit of thinking' we can adduce the system of precedents in English law characterized by *stare decisis*. In a precedent there is one binding element: the decision by law (the *ratio decidendi*), whereas the considerations (the *obiter dicta*) on which the decision was based are not binding. In *stare decisis*, the binding element of an ancient decision is not made by the decisions of the ancient judges who created the precedent, it is made by a later judge.[50] This caused a juridical-historical formalism which neglected the very historical context necessary to the (legal) historian. What the historian needs is expendable for the lawyer in order for the law to remain instrumental and to prolong the life of *stare decisis*.

---

[50] Cf. J. Drion, *Stare Decisis. Het Gezag van Precedenten*, The Hague, 1950, p. 10.

The more general characteristics of Whig historiography were discussed in the first chapter. We noted the tendency to see similarities and
continuities rather than dissimilarities and discontinuities. The example
of *stare decisis* stresses these characteristics and is a classic example of
analogical thinking.[51] Law and history always were (and still are)
closely linked within English political and constitutional traditions.
Whereas continental law has a code warranting some amount of safety
and stability, English law attempts to reach that aim by means of the
system of precedents.[52] Formally speaking, there was no break either
in the pattern of English law or in English history. This 'precluded'
a need for codification of law or a written constitution. *Stare decisis*
substituted for both. Moreover it forced the past to take on a direct and
practical role for the present. For juridical purposes the present had
to be firmly linked to the past, but as a result the emphasis on similarity
and continuity was unduly intensified; the only continuity which en-
ables the past to form any authoritative links with the present is the
sort of continuity which warrants a historical identity.

The past is highly revered in the juridical-historical interpretation of
common law - almost too highly. "A common law judge could not say, I
think the doctrine of consideration a bit of historical nonsense...."
O.W. Holmes once wrote. There could be neither distance nor irony,
nor an 'ironical view of history.'[53] The juridical-historical perception
is interested only in that part of history instrumental for present use;
that is the sort of past which provides useful precedents. Paradoxically
law (common law) needs the past more than history does. In Maitland's words legal history had the task of liberating the present from
a burdensome past; common law, if it tried to do that, would commit
suicide. Hoetink's phrase, 'productive misunderstanding,' illustrates
the non-historical aspect of the common-law habit of thinking. His
initial perception of the similarly anachronistic conceptualization by
law and history was superseded by an awareness of the more fundamental differences between the two.[54]

---

[51] Cf. R. Cross, *Precedent in English Law*, Oxford, 1961, p. 19.

[52] Cf. R. Cross, *op. cit.*, p. 9; A.L. Goodhart, 'Precedent in English and Continental Law'
in *Law Quarterly Review* 50 (1934), pp. 40–65.

[53] Cf. R. Cross, *op. cit.*, p. 27; actually the *Heterogonie der Zwecke* recurred often in the
history of English law, cf. G. Radbruch, *Der Geist des englischen Rechts*, Heidelberg, 1947, p. 91.

[54] H.R. Hoetink, *Historische Rechtsbeschouwing*, Haarlem, 1949, p. 25; cf. E. Betti, *Allgemeine Auslegungslehre als Methodik der Geisteswissenschaften*, Tübingen, 1967, pp. 438–440, 732–
739.

Maitland advocated a separation between the two disciplines in 1888 mainly as a legal historian, but it was also a welcome solution for him as a legal reformer. For, if the 'pseudo-history' of common law obstructed the development of historical scholarship, it also hampered the modernization of the legal system. The usefulness of the proven old historical interpretation of the law came to be doubted with the new social task allotted to legal history by Maitland. However, around 1900 there were not many people in England who voiced these doubts about the accepted historical interpretation within the law; most of those who criticized this approach were foreigners.

Towards the end of the 19th century the legal profession also demanded a separation between law and history under the influence of a reviving natural law thinking and the rising new sociology of law, which latter studies the aims and functions of law in society.[55] The advent of both these approaches was linked to the waning of the old Historical School of law. A legal historian like Maitland could not fail to notice that the many juridical criticisms of the historical interpretation provided a favourable climate for a further emancipation of legal history.[56]

Increasingly, doubts were raised regarding the use of this historical interpretation for the present. And inevitably, this was a vital point for the supporters of 'free justice,' once they had taken Savigny to task.[57] The past had become too burdensome; the Historical School of law had rendered law immobile.[58] Its armour of legal formalism prevented it from responding to the real needs of a modern society and nation.

Doubts were also cast upon the historical aspect of the Historical School of law: its formalism distorted the interpretation of the past as well. Saleilles reproved the Historical School in 1902 for lacking an *esprit historique*, for approaching the phenomenon of law with so much

[55] Cf. for this development, G. Gurvitch, *Sociology of Law*, London, 1947 (with a preface by R. Pound); J. Romein, *Op Het Breukvlak van Twee Eeuwen*, Leyden-Amsterdam, 1967, chapter XXVI.

[56] Cf. H.D. Hazeltine on Maitland in *E.H.R.* 38 (1923), p. 606: "His work marks indeed an advance in the history of the historical school within the domain of law. He caught the vision – a vision which is lacking in some of the most prominent legal historians from Savigny's days to our own – of the social and political forces which surrounded and modify the law from age to age in response to ever–changing needs."

[57] C. Gruys, *De Strijd over de Historische Interpretatie*, Utrecht, 1933, p. 143. He was right to doubt whether this was fair to Savigny himself. Cf. F. Wieacker, *Wandlungen im Bilde der historischen Rechtsschule*, Karlsruhe, 1967.

[58] Cf. R. Pound, *Interpretations of Legal History*, Cambridge, 1930, p. 10.

formalism that it blurred their vision of the evolution of law.[59] The evolution of law needed to be seen in a more social context and a more functional approach to be understood at all. The reduction of law to *Volksgeist* had isolated law from its highly factual social historical context and the only way to lift this curtain of isolation was to consider the social function of law. This is what R. Ihering did for law and legal history.[60] Without such an approach, the tendency towards an excessively formalist and unrealistic dogmatism was pronounced in legal history as well; numerous essays by legal historians dealt with this problem in the period around the turn of the century.[61]

The influence of continental 'modernists' could be discerned in the Anglo-Saxon world, notwithstanding the many differences between the English development on the one hand and the American development on the other. The conservative instinct was on the whole stronger in England than the urge for modernization.[62] Apparently the common-law tradition was less of a burden in America: there a stronger continental influence nourished the growth of 'realism.'[63] Thus it was possible to take a more critical view of several common-law elements, as did O.W. Holmes and R. Pound. The latter had plainly been influenced by Ihering, although he also mentioned Croce's inspiring example in his more historical-theoretical writings.[64] Pound, like Holmes, was critical about the Historical School of law with its tendencies to protect conservative values rather than stimulate progressive ideas. He too had his doubts about the 'historic qualities' of the so-called school of law: "it was not a historical school at all" in his opinion.[65] As to the formalist conception of continuity, the "continuous identity with which the historical school made us familiar," he typified that as "the fallacy of continuity of content" typical of a juridical way of

---

[59] R. Saleilles, 'École Historique et droit naturel' in *Revue trimestrielle de droit civil* 1 (1902), pp. 95–96.

[60] Cf. E.W. Böckenförde, 'Die historische Rechtsschule und das Problem der Geschichtlichkeit des Rechts' in *Collegium Philosophicum. Studien Joachim Ritter zum 60. Geburtstag*. Basel-Stuttgart, 1965, pp. 9–36. Cf. the same author in his *Die deutsche verfassungsgeschichtliche Forschung im 19. Jahrhundert*, Berlin, 1961, pp. 79–84.

[61] Cf. G. Seeliger, 'Juristische Konstruction und Geschichtsforschung' in *Historische Vierteljahrsschrift* 7 (1904), pp. 161–191; H. Mitteis, *Vom Lebenswert der Rechtsgeschichte*, Weimar, 1947, p. 44 ff.; The discussion does not seem to have got far beyond this point, see the articles by O. Brunner, H. Krause and H. Thieme in *Historische Zeitschrift* 209 (1969), pp. 1–36.

[62] "In England it may well be that the realist approach arouses distaste, if not hostility, as it seems to diminish the dignity of the law." This was said by D. Lloyd in his *The Idea of Law*, Harmondsworth, 1964, p. 349, note 18.

[63] D. Lloyd, *op. cit.*, pp. 213–217.

[64] R. Pound, *Interpretations of Legal History*, p. XVI.; cf. D. Lloyd, *op. cit.*, p. 210.

[65] R. Pound, *op. cit.*, p. 19.

thinking in which the development of the law was somewhat isolated.[66] With the doubts about the usefulness of the past as an instrument, even *stare decisis* itself came to be doubted. The principle had already come in for a good deal of attack, e.g. from the American J.H. Wigmore; like Spencer he believed it was 'the government of the living by the dead.'[67] His fellow countryman B.N. Cardozo had fewer objections, however, and in England itself objections were rare in the beginning.[68] Only later did some, like A.L. Goodhart, begin to advocate a less rigid use of precedents.[69]

Although the English legal practitioners often lacked a critical attitude, still things were happening even inside the English juridical world; legal custom became subject to systematic reflection, new ways were sought to adapt the law to the present. Part of the movement was the remarkable 'renaissance of jurisprudence' at the end of the 19th century.[70] This systematic study of law, especially of the judges' law in common law practices certainly helped to undermine the common law's 'pseudo-history.' It was more than fortuitous that this beginning of legal science coincided with the emergence of English historiography as a science; the *Law Quarterly Review* dates from 1884. In the 20th century this new science became essential for law-making; at the time jurisprudence only occasionally influenced the practice of law, as witnessed the growing importance of A.V. Dicey and F. Pollock.[71]

This jurisprudence was much more critical of the historical development of law than practical lawyers ever had been, yet it was far from being a historical science; a more critical legal history was to jurisprudence only a welcome expedient. After 1850, when law began to be taught in the university instead of only in the Inns of Court, the ties between law and history became temporarily closer. The two were brought together as allied disciplines, but this partnership survived less than twenty years in both Oxford and Cambridge, as it was considered unsatisfactory by each discipline. History first became independent in 1872 in Oxford. Three years later its emancipation was

---

[66] *Ibid.*, pp. 37–40.
[67] Cf. A.L. Goodhart, *Essays in Jurisprudence and the Common Law*, Cambridge, 1931, p. 62.
[68] *Ibid.*, pp. 50–57.
[69] Cf. J. Drion, *op. cit.*, p. 14.
[70] Cf. A. Harding, *op. cit.*, pp. 347–351.
[71] C.A. Uniken Venema, *op. cit.*, pp. 21–24; "Pollock ... was a new type of figure in English law – a jurist whose opinion was constantly sought by government and judges", as A. Harding phrased it (*op. cit.*, p. 349).

also acknowledged in Cambridge. In Cambridge the partnership had disadvantages for history, in Oxford for law.[72]

In spite of their differences history and jurisprudence had one common advantage in relation to the practice of law: neither had to be directly applicable. Jurisprudence made a different use of history in its reflections on law than did lawyers. Jurisprudence was not forced by the demands of practical life to adapt the past to the present. Still this one point of similarity was not in itself sufficient to make a complete success out of the cooperation of the jurist Pollock and the legal historian Maitland in writing their book on the history of medieval law. Pollock saw legal history as subsidiary, only a part of the current new reflections on law; for Maitland legal history became an inalienable part of history as a whole, necessary to discover the social reality of the past.[73]

To return to Maitland's inaugural speech of 1888: he blamed the unbroken continuity of legal practice for having retarded a historical-scientific study of England's laws. The greatest obstacle for legal history, however, had hardly lost its force in the 19th century; political constitutional history too was still hampered by it.[74] The past as a tool for the legal practice was a remnant of a situation in which politics habitually made use of the past. Unwittingly this fact kept people from the serious study of legal history. The oldest interpretation of the past

[72] In 1851 history in Cambridge was made a part of the moral sciences, in 1858 of the Law Tripos, and since 1870 it was known as the Law and History Tripos. See D.W. Winstanley, *Later Victorian Cambridge*, London, 1947, p. 207; F.W. Maitland in *Essays on the Teaching of History*, ed. W.A.J. Archbold, Cambridge, 1901, p. XVI; L. Woodward, 'The Rise of the Professional Historian in England' in *Studies in International History*, ed. K. Bourne and D.C. Watt, London, 1967, pp. 23–24.

[73] Cf. C.H.S. Fifoot, *Pollock and Maitland*, Glasgow, 1971, p. 16 ff.; in some respects the dogmatism of jurisprudence was a lesser obstacle than the not very reflexive non–dogmatic legal practice. Maitland insisted that the un-historic character of jurisprudence was tied to the tendency to consider historically connected events in isolation. See in this connection especially the last paragraph of his *Constitutional History of England*: "...Writers on general jurisprudence are largely concerned with the classification of legal rules. This is a very important task ... But do not get into the way of thinking of law as consisting of a number of independent compartments, one of which is labelled constitutional, another administrative, another criminal, another property, so that you can learn the contents of one compartment, and know nothing as to what is in others. No, law is a body, a living body.... Life I know is short, and law is long, very long and we cannot study everything at once; still, no good comes of refusing to see the truth, and the truth is that all parts of our law are very closely related to each other, so closely that we can set no logical limit to our labours" (*op. cit.*, p. 539). Cf. also the argument of H. van den Brink in 'Typen van Rechtshistorie' in *Lof der historie*, Rotterdam, 1973, pp. 33–46. Cf. H. v. d. Brink, *The Charm of Legal History*, Amsterdam, 1974, pp. 7–21.

[74] Cf. H. Mitteis, *op. cit.*, p. 56.

was the lawyers' historical interpretation; it was also the most common one in the *ancien régime*.[75] The tenacity of this interpretation in England is remarkable but understandable, because the *ancien régime* lost its influence only very gradually. There were no sudden breaks, no political revolutions, no codifications; a rather useful tradition simply continued.

To keep a tradition alive the past must inevitably be adapted to the present; consequently the past is depicted anachronistically and the newness of the present is denied. Maitland describes that very quality in the much-praised English legal continuity: "Its besetting sin is that of antedating the emergence of modern ideas. That is a fault into which every professional tradition is wont to fall."[76] The past cannot be viewed objectively while a living tradition still clings to it. Its real history thus remains obscure. Maitland wrote in 1886:

So long as the rules are unrepealed this rationalising process must continue; judges and text-writers find themselves compelled to work these archaisms into the system of practical intelligible law. Only when the rules are repealed, when we can put them all together and look at them from a little distance, do they begin to tell their true history.[77]

The acquisition of a detached view of the past is not only hedged around with the difficulties caused by the limitations of the human mind, equally important for detachment is the fact that the new industrialized society no longer needs to make a political or practical use of the past.

On the whole it was difficult for 19th-century Whig historiography to free itself from the legal pragmatism in which history was a tool. The Whig view of history is basically comparable to the 'common-law habit of thinking'; the similarity is especially clear in the earlier named presuppositions of Whig historiography. The objection may be raised that most of these Whigs had not been common lawyers, and that both Stubbs and Freeman had repeatedly warned against the 'lawyer's view of history.'[78] Yet they criticized only details; in the case of Freeman there was certainly no question of any criticism so radical that it

---

[75] See G. Radbruch, 'Arten der Interpretation' in *Recueil d'études sur les sources du droit en l'honneur de François Gény*, Paris, 1935, tome II, p. 219; H.G. Gadamer sees no fundamental difference regarding the juridical-historical interpretation still as an example for all other interpretations, see *Wahrheit und Methode*, Tübingen, 1960, pp. 307–323.

[76] F. Pollock and F.W. Maitland, *The History of English Law*, Cambridge, 1968, vol. I, pp. CIV–CV.

[77] *C.P.*, I, p. 383; cf. *C.P.*, II, p. 10.

[78] Cf. E.A. Freeman, *The Methods of Historical Study*, London, 1886, p. 71 ff.; *Letters of William Stubbs*, ed. W.H. Hutton, London, 1904, p. 163.

would lead to the conclusion of an incompatibility between law and history. He criticized the dogmatic Blackstone, not the 'historically' thinking lawyers of the 17th century. What Freeman desired was to restore 'the natural union of law and history' of the 17th century.[79] This was hardly surprising considering his view of history and his liberal constitutionalism, for which a useful past was a *sine qua non*. The jurist A.V. Dicey was, more than his friend Freeman, aware that the 'common law mind' still strongly influenced Freeman. There could be no better illustration of the great and lasting influence of *stare decisis* than the conception he had of 'retrogressive progress.' "The idea of retrogressive progress is merely one form of the appeal to precedent," Dicey wrote, continuing with:

This appeal has made its appearance at every crisis in the history of England, and indeed no one has stated so forcibly as my friend Mr. Freeman himself the peculiarity of all English efforts to extend the liberties of the country, namely, that these attempts at innovation have always assumed the form of an appeal to pre-existing rights. But the appeal to precedent is in the law courts merely a useful fiction by which judicial decision conceals its transformation into judicial legislation; and a fiction is none the less a fiction because it has emerged from the Courts into the field of politics or of history. Here, then, the astuteness of lawyers has imposed upon the simplicity of historians. Formalism and antiquarianism have, so to speak, joined hands; they have united to mislead students in search for the law of the constitution.[80]

Dicey did not hide his objections to Freeman's historical views: the latter's historical myths were plainly built on juridical fictions. Freeman's historiography was an obvious target. Maitland said that, because he believed 'history' was identical with 'past politics,' "he never succeeded in adding anything to our knowledge of medieval politics but spoilt everything by inept comparisons."[81]

Dicey's criticism of the pseudo-history of the 'common law mind' from a juridical point of view was mild compared to that from some historians at the turn of the century. Round, Tout and Pollard following Maitland forcefully stressed that law and history were irreconcilable. In 1888 Maitland said that although Coke was undoubtedly a fine scholar, "we are but slowly beginning to find out that he did not know everything."[82] Tout declared in 1914 that Coke's historical

[79] E.A. Freeman, *op. cit.*, p. 77.
[80] A.V. Dicey, *The Law of the Constitution*, London, 1902 (1885), pp. 18–19.
[81] *Letters*, p. 148.
[82] F.W. Maitland, *The Constitutional History of England*, p. 268; Maitland delivered a very sharp attack on the unhistoric mentality of common lawyers in his preface to W.J. Whittaker's

views were still fully alive and Butterfield, in 1944, pronounced him the first Whig historian.[83]

It is hardly surprising, though, to find that the sharpest attacks on 'non-historical' law came from J.H. Round. His specific area of contention against the lawyer was peerage law. Freeman too had warned of the fictions peddled by the 'pedigree-mongers,' but Round surpassed him, in his attack on the old 'genealogical school' and its fairy-tales. Lytton Strachey afterwards gave a humorous description of Round as "a burrower into wormholes ... gnawing at the pedigrees of the proudest families of England."[84] Later, advising the Crown in the matter of peerages, Round's inimical attitude towards law became even more pronounced.

In 1901 Round published a collection of essays called *Studies in Peerage and Family History*, which did not yet contain any open attack. He only wrote: "In view of the points of law discussed in these pages, it is perhaps desirable to mention that I am not, directly or indirectly, connected with the legal profession."[85] Nine years afterwards in his new two-volume work, *Peerage and Pedigree*, he explicated his conviction about the antithesis between law and history. Round cited Maitland as an authority, especially Maitland's inaugural speech and the *History of English Law*. Round differed from the legally trained Maitland in that he did not see the need for a pragmatic-juridical use of the past.[86] Consequently he considered law as a 'medieval fiction,' whereas history was a 'science.' The essay 'The muddle of the Law' was a straightforward attack on the juridical-historical interpretation of the past which Coke had made popular.[87] In part Round repeated Maitland's argu-

edition of *The Mirror of Justice* (London, 1895). Cf. I.S. Leadam's review in *E.H.R.* 12 (1897), pp. 148–155.

[83] T.F. Tout, *The Place of the Reign of Edward II in English History*, Manchester, 1914, p. 88; cf. also MacDonell's article on Coke in *D.N.B.*

[84] L. Strachey, *Biographical Essays*, London, 1948, p. 260. Round's work plainly shows a fear of the rising new 'money aristocracy,' of an 'americanization' of the English peerage. (See J.H. Round, *Studies in Peerage and Family History*, London, 1901, p. 33 ff.). The arrival of the east European Jews made it impossible for him to hide his anti-semitism; he spoke of "the alien inrush of to-day, the ousting of our people by the sweepings of the ghetto, the men of an outcast race" (J.H. Round, *Peerage and Pedigree*, London, 1910, vol. II, p. 129).

[85] J.H. Round, *Studies in Peerage and Family History*, p. XXX.

[86] A.F. Pollard later wrote with more understanding: "... judicial theories are as irrelevant to historical investigation as historical fact is to legal decisions" (The *Evolution of Parliament*, London, 1926, p. 83). See also, for later phases of the discussion, Sankey, 'The Historian and the Lawyer. Their aims and their methods' in *History* 21 (1936–37), pp. 97–108; W.L. Burn, 'The Historian and the Lawyer' in *History* 28 (1943), pp. 17–36. See on the 'necessity' and inevitability of 'legal fictions': L.L. Fuller, 'What motives give rise to the historical legal fiction' in *Recueil d'études sur les sources du droit en l'honneur de François Gény*, Paris, 1935, tome II, pp. 157–176.

[87] J.H. Round, *Peerage and Pedigree*, London, 1910, vol. I, pp. 103–283.

ments, but for him the main point was that the real changes in history
were neglected in favour of the pseudo-historical view of the lawyers
and their belief in the formalist continuity. The provocative tenor of
Round's argument he justified "in view of the blighting and sterilising
effect on all intelligent research of the lawyer's convenient doctrine
that the law was 'always the same.'"[88]

Round hoped for the support of his fellow historians. Wheraas the
legal historian W. Holdsworth rejected his opinions, J. Tait approved
of them. Tait could see a justification for Round's crusade against
lawyers and 'pedigree-makers,' while regretting that Round had engaged in a personal attack.[89] Tout also praised Round. Referring to
the fact that lawyers lacked an understanding for historical development, he wrote to Round: "The difficulty in arguing with the peerage
lawyers is that they see all history as a flat plain, and could not, if they
would, understand that conditions vary in different periods."[90] In his
Ford Lectures, a year afterwards, he repeated: "They look at the past
as a plane surface which has never been altered. They have imperfect
appreciation of the idea of development."[91]

Criticism of the juridical-historical interpretation of the past was an
important aspect of the anti-Whig reaction. The diatribes against the
lawyers were mainly directed at those general aspects of Whig historiography that we discussed in the first chapter. Because the English legal
system has such great reverence for the past, the lawyer's 'historical'
perception must be rather present-minded in order to book results.
Therefore, an anachronistic and teleological interpretation of the past
was inevitable.[92] In the juridical-historical interpretation a traditionalist consciousness proved to be stronger than a historical consciousness.

[88] *Ibid.*, p. 208.
[89] Cf. J. Tait in *E.H.R.* 25 (1910), pp. 798–800; W. Holdsworth, *Essays in Law and History*, Oxford, 1946, p. 24.
[90] Letter of 21-3-1912, U.L.L. I.H.R. MS. no. 683.
[91] T.F. Tout, *The Place of the Reign of Edward II in English History*, Manchester, 1914, p. 88; cf. J.H. Round, 'The House of Lords and the Model Parliament' in *E.H.R.* 30 (1915), pp. 385–397, esp. pp. 387 and 395.
[92] Cf. for this teleological 'Zu-Ende-Denken': G. Radbruch, *Einführung in die Rechtswissenschaft*, Stuttgart, 1952, pp. 242–244.

C. MAITLAND VERSUS ANACHRONISMS

> If all his theories could be overthrown, all his posi-
> tive results peptonized into textbooks, he would still
> live as a model of critical method, a model of style
> and a model of intellectual temper.
>
> (A.L. Smith on Maitland, 1908)

In this last section we will trace the innovating force of Maitland's highly individual historical work. While his style remains interesting even to the modern public, the originality of his historical approach is not merely caused by his style. An argument about Maitland's 'historical method' can hardly be based only on his (numerous) epigrammatical remarks on this subject. These remarks mirror a well thought-out (though not always explicit) theory about the way in which an historian approaches his subject.

Firstly, Maitland sought to strip away the protective layer of tradition. More than once a closer look revealed that things no longer were as self-evident as fond posterity had imagined. The more an early history appeared 'hallowed' to a later tradition, the more forebidding did the obstacles seem to be which hampered the growth of a truly historical view. Tradition thus made things appear self-evidently intelligible, but this very fact rendered historical developments in many respects unintelligible. No wonder that Maitland repeatedly warned that: "Our ancestors did not think so."[93] For the same reason he explained the direction of his lecture of 1887–1888 as: "... we are purposely choosing unusual points of view in order that we may see familiar facts in new lights...."[94] This general statement of purpose may be said to have also been a guide for his later more detailed studies; it worked as a liberating charm on all reviewers.[95]

Yet Maitland's 'abrupt onslaught upon conventional ideas' (as H.W.C. Davis put it) was not made for originality's sake; the force that drove him was a deeply-rooted knowledge of the older historiography's besetting sin of a too finalistic view.

Addressing his listeners in 1888, he said that the more we study our

---

[93] F.W. Maitland, *The Constitutional History of England*, p. 131.
[94] *Ibid.*, p. 236.
[95] Cf. J.H. Round in *E.H.R.* 5 (1890), p. 586; H.W.C. Davis in *E.H.R.* 24 (1909), pp. 341–344; cf. P. Vinogradoff in *E.H.R.* 22 (1907), p. 284: "He seems to be wandering in a strange world, crowded with fancies and shams. He is constantly on the alert against traditions kept up out of sheer indolence of mind ...."

constitution both in the present and in the past, "the less do we find it conform to any such plan as a philosopher might invent in his study."[96] Historical development had certain 'unplanned' qualities which became evident in the consequences of those very events that later generations were to think vitally important. There was a certain irony in the historical origin and development of the 'palladia' of English liberty: usually the historical result proved to be the exact opposite of the original plan. Maitland lost no time in pointing out that 'trial by jury,' for instance, had a royal origin, that the 'writ of habeas corpus' used to be a royal prerogative, that Parliament had started as an emanation of the royal power, and that representation originally was a burden.[97] This theme – of liberty being born in bondage and of parliament having an unparliamentary origin – will be further discussed in one of the following chapters. It may be called significant for the development of English historiography in the period around 1900.

The second characteristic is Maitland's attempted breakthrough of the traditional insular approach. Not only did he stress the great importance of some foreign studies on the subject of English medieval history,[98] he also insisted on a more comparative approach. There is a resemblance in this respect to Langlois, whose thoughts also showed a Comtean undercurrent.[99] Maitland's conviction was that only those historical facts could be compared which had some actual relationship in the past, through common origin, conscious imitation, or some other sort of mutual influence.

Studies of this kind were rare at that time; comparative legal history existed in name only.[100] That Maitland was so careful and sceptical in this respect was largely because of his dislike for the methods of Maine and his followers. Their belief that the laws of evolution caused all peoples to pass through the same stages, led them to use the evidence of extant primitive societies to explain the develop-

---

[96] F.W. Maitland, *The Constitutional History of England*, p. 197.

[97] *Ibid.*, pp. 130 ff.; 217 ff.; 298; 62, 87–89, 174.

[98] E.g. F. Liebermann, see *C.P.*, III, p. 447 ff.; *Letters*, p. 301; *The History of English Law*, I, p. 102 (note 1); C.H.S. Fifoot, *F.W. Maitland. A Life*, pp. 123–124.

[99] Cf. C.V. Langlois, 'The Comparative History of England and France during the Middle Ages' in *E.H.R.* 5 (1890), pp. 259–263; the remark: "If historical science does not consist solely in the critical enumeration of past phenomena, but rather in the examination of the laws which regulate the succession of such phenomena, clearly its chief agent must be the comparison of such phenomena as run parallel in different nations; for there is no surer means of knowing the *conditions* and *causes* of a particular fact than to compare it with analogous facts." (p. 259).

[100] Cf. *E.H.R.* 14 (1899), p. 137; Maitland praised H. Brunner in this respect, see *E.H.R.* 9 (1894), p. 594.

ment of medieval Europe. Maitland argued against the then current generalizations of a primitive collectivism or 'communalism' in ancient Europe. He believed the arguments based on 'survivals' to be invalid – a fundamental disagreement with his friend Vinogradoff.[101] Maitland was firmly convinced that a really comparative approach would be hampered more than aided "by theories which flit from one end of the earth to another and mix up all ages."[102] In order for a comparative approach to be fruitful it was, in Maitland's opinion, necessary to study real interactions or cases of interdependence in the past. He even insisted that this method was indispensable for historical scholarship.

The third significant characteristic of Maitland's work was his criticism of those whose historical interest in the constitution had a traditional-formalist background; he was more interested in the factual functioning of institutions. Our final chapter will show that Maitland's range of interest set an example for the near future. In 1888, in the conclusions to his *Constitutional History*, his rather enigmatic apology, difficult for several reviewers to understand, left no doubt about his views of constitutional history. He made no mention of Whigs, Tories, liberals or conservatives; he had consciously shielded his public from this 'old-fashioned and perverse view,' from what he called 'an obsolete and inadequate idea of the province of constitutional history.' "Constitutional history should ... be a history, not of parties, but of institutions, not of struggles, but of results; the struggles are evanescent, the results are permanent."[103] It was also the road which Stubbs had marked and partly travelled. Maitland hoped that Stubbs's constitutional history would be brought up to date in the coming years "as a history of institutions, a history of one great department of law, and of its actual working."[104] A year later – in his article 'The materials for English legal history,' published in the *Political Science Quarterly* – he once again criticized current constitutional history as having too often been a history

of just the showy side of the constitution, the great disputes and great catastrophes, matters about which no one can form a really sound opinion who is not thoroughly versed in the sober humdrum legal history of the time.[105]

[101] See P. Vinogradoff, 'F.W. Maitland' in *E.H.R.* 22 (1907), pp. 280–289, esp. pp. 285–286; cf. also *C.P.*, II, p. 313 ff., and F.W. Maitland, *Domesday Book and Beyond*, London, 1960, (Fontana Library), p. 398 ff.
[102] *E.H.R.* 14 (1899), p. 137. Evidently directed at Maine. See also *Letters*, p. 222.
[103] F.W. Maitland, *The Constitutional History of England*, p. 537.
[104] *Ibid.*, Maitland especially names T.E. May's work in his criticism.
[105] *C.P.*, II, p. 7.

He wished to pay more attention to documents such as Pipe Rolls and Charter Rolls, which would enable us "to study in minute detail the whole of the administrative machinery of the realm."[106]

In that same year (1889) his study of the records concerning the Parliament of February 1305 was begun. Four years later they were published together with the famous introduction. Maitland was not in the first place concerned with a new theory of the function and nature of a medieval parliament. He wrote in enthusiastic terms to Maxwell Lyte about his 'discovery,' explaining why it was important to have this one 'roll' of parliament published: it described the everyday world and the factual workings of a medieval parliament.[107] He had been motivated by a similar purpose in 1884, when preparing his first edition of source material, *Pleas of the Crown for the County of Gloucester*, a book which made him one of the founders of the 'classical manorial historiography.'[108] It was for this reason that H. Fisher later said he regarded this publication as 'an epoch in the history of history.'[109] Apart from this, Maitland, by demanding 'History from the Charter Roll,'[110] also paved the way for administrative history, which was to profit by what would become known as the biographical approach. Even a first attempt at publishing the names of witnesses on the Charter Rolls would be an inestimable service to historical scholarship.

These lists of witnesses give us week by week and almost day by day the names of those men who are in the King's presence, and I need not say that if we are to know minutely how England is being governed, it is necessary that we should know who are the persons whom the King habitually sees.[111]

In sum the three characteristic aspects of Maitland's work have a common goal: they all served Maitland's endless hunt for anachronistic representations of the past. All later historians were struck by his alertness in this respect. R.L. Schuyler called it the most significant trait of his entire historical work: "It pervades his writings."[112] Yet Schuyler doubted whether Maitland's continual alertness for every

---

[106] *C.P.*, II, p. 42; cf. also p. 55 on the Year Books.

[107] See esp.: *Letters*, pp. 70–71; the roll provided "a curious insight into the manner in which the business was conducted"; it gave a clear picture of "the connection between the different parts of the governmental machinery."

[108] Cf. J.A. Raftis, 'British Historiography Decentralizes' in *Journal of British Studies* 9 (November 1969), p. 146.

[109] H. Fisher, *F.W. Maitland*, p. 25; in his own words, Maitland envisaged "a photograph of English life as it was early in the thirteenth century, and a photograph taken from a point of view of which chronicles too seldom place themselves." Cf. A.L. Smith, *op. cit.*, p. 43.

[110] Cf. *C.P.*, II, pp. 298–309; title of an article in *E.H.R.*, April 1893.

[111] *C.P.*, II, p. 299.

[112] R.L. Schuyler, *op. cit.*, p. 34.

little anachronism was compatible with that other aspect of his work: the 'retrogressive method.' This method employed the better-known recent past to throw light on the less-known earlier periods.[113] While recent writers have suggested that this method evidences a contradiction in Maitland's work,[114] it might be better first to inquire what Maitland himself thought about the process of acquiring historical knowledge and what he did to guard against the pitfalls of anachronistic interpretations.

Of course Maitland quite realized that a certain measure of anachronism is inescapable. A statement on this subject in his *Township and Borough* became widely known: "If we speak, we must speak with words; if we think, we must think with thoughts. We are moderns and our words and thoughts cannot but be modern. Perhaps, as Mr. Gilbert once suggested, it is too late for us to be early English."[115] All knowledge – historical knowledge included – was acquired partly by induction and partly by deduction. As Maitland stated in his lecture 'The Body Politic':

The two processes, that of predicting the future and that of reconstructing the past are essentially similar, both are processes of interference and generalization. Of course when the historian tells us a single fact, for example, gives the date of a battle, interference and generalization are already at work.[116]

Maitland, as a historian, was highly gifted in that he possessed the two qualities apparently most needed for these two aspects of historical knowledge: "he combined in an extraordinary measure the gift for hypothesis with the quality of patience."[117] His hypotheses were almost always carefully thought out, according to some of his colleagues, sometimes too carefully.[118] Moreover, he was deeply convinced of the

[113] *Ibid.*, p. 37.
[114] Roy Stone de Montpensier, *op. cit.*, p. 265 ff.
[115] F.W. Maitland, *Township and Borough*, Cambridge, 1898, p. 22.
[116] *C.P.*, III, p. 285.
[117] H. Fisher, *op. cit.*, p. 56.
[118] Cf., e.g. Round's criticism of Maitland's 'garrison theory' in a lecture to the international historical congress in London (1913), later reproduced in an article, included in his (posthumously edited) *Family Origins and Other Studies*, (London, 1930), pp. 252–265; he wrote: "It is probably little realised how much conjecture and hypothesis have found their way into the work of this brilliant scholar" (p. 259). In a different context G.O. Sayles's remark is also meaningful: "This traditional account of the origin of the medieval fields, accepted by Seebohm, Vinogradoff, and surprisingly even Maitland, is now properly discredited. The problem must be approached not from the point of view of the political theorist but of the practical farmers." (G.O. Sayles, *The Medieval Foundations of England*, London, 1966, p. 117).

necessity for more detailed specialized studies where the historian's activities seemed restricted to the patient inductive labour of only gathering facts. He realized that future studies would be ever more fragmented and specialized which was why 'history as art' would not survive: "though history may be an art, it is falling out of the list of fine arts and will not be restored thereto for a long time to come," was his opinion some years before Bury's inaugural speech.[119]

The specialization desired by Maitland did not imply that historians were to confine themselves to one specialized area only. The specialization he envisioned was to time and place, not a limited 'branch-specialization.' It was impossible to achieve a good historical picture of the past in its own context without at least some insight into the interdependence of different areas of life and society. Specialist though he was, the historian Maitland remained fascinated by what he thought of as Auguste Comte's 'greatest lesson': ". . . the interdependence of human affairs, for example the interdependence of political, religious and economic phenomena."[120] He doubted whether the sociology of his own day – which appeared to have forgotten Comte's teachings in this respect – could ever be useful to history. What sociologists failed to see was not the 'uniqueness' of history, but 'the interdependence of all human affairs.' Maitland once said: "The fault . . . of the would-be scientific procedure of our sociologists lies in the too frequent attempt to obtain a set of 'laws' by the study of only one class of phenomena . . . ."[121] There is a similar reproach to be found in *Domesday Book and Beyond* some years before this:

such is the complexity of human affairs and such their interdependence, that we cannot hope for scientific laws which will formulate a sequence of stages in any one province of man's activity. We cannot, for instance, find a law which deals only with political and neglects proprietary arrangements, or a law which deals only with property and neglects religion.[122]

Earlier comparativists' thought in stages, neglecting this interdependence, was formal and unhistoric. Maitland saw the search for interdependences as necessary, especially to combat anachronism. We will return to this in our final chapter. Maitland was, however, well aware that an integrated approach, however desirable, was as yet

---

[119] *C.P.*, III, p. 294.
[120] *C.P.*, III, p. 293.
[121] *C.P.*, III, p. 294; cf. p. 293, where he dared to write: "It seems to me that the people who have learnt that lesson are not the sociologists but the historians."
[122] F.W. Maitland, *Domesday Book and Beyond*, p. 403.

more wish than reality: "The study of interactions and interdependences is but just beginning, and no one can foresee the end."[123]

However, we should ask whether the contradiction Schuyler and others noticed between the retrogressive method that Maitland had used frequently in *Domesday Book and Beyond* and the anti-anachronistic trend generally pervading his work was indeed a contradiction. Roy Stone de Montpensier insists it was, and tried to make Maitland's method more understandable by relating it to Marcel Proust. According to him, the second and doctrinaire part of Maitland's *magnum opus* betrays the 'Proustian' touch, especially where Maitland moves forwards and backwards in time.[124]

Proustian time is that conflation of the past with the present, in the case of Proust summoned from the deep recesses of the subconscious by some immediate sensory perception ... and in the case of Maitland it is the redeeming of the past by some present rule of law, use of language, or analysis of legal concepts and the intrusion from the past of some contemporaneous concept or rule into a rule or concept of law that has not then been developed.[125]

If this approach is peculiarly Proustian, then Maitland's work may indeed be characterized as Proustian. But his alertness in the matter of anachronisms is equally characteristic, and we shall find that both these salient points are closely interwoven. Maitland is continually engaging in comparisons in time, both retrogressive and progressive; he moves from later points in time back to earlier points, and from earlier points to later ones. Recurring sentences are: "The time has not yet come ..." or "Time will show what these words shall mean" or "The thirteenth century will ... supply us with the notion ..." or "... in our thirteenth century we learn ...."[126] It might be remembered that this procedure is an important, if largely unconscious constituent of all historical interpretation; the historian is a prophet after the event. But Maitland makes consciously use of this approach in his analysis. This not only because he realized the great danger of this method if used unthinkingly in historical interpretation. Like Vinogradoff he had often warned of these dangers – moreover, he published

---

[123] *Essays on the Teaching of History*, ed. W.A.J. Archbold, Cambridge, 1901, p. XX.

[124] Roy Stone de Montpensier, *op. cit.*, p. 277. "There is room for hindsight, déjà vue, foresight, insight and so on."

[125] *Ibid.*, p. 279. This description neglects Maitland's aims.

[126] Cf. F.W. Maitland, *Domesday and Beyond*, pp. 31, 69–70, 110, 122; cf. *The History of English Law*, I, p. 525.

these warnings whenever he perceived conclusions emphasizing the similarity or resemblances between different periods.[127]

What was Maitland's aim with this procedure? Some of his motives were practical: when the subject of his study was a period about which only few records were extant, sources from a later period dealing with similar events could prove revealing. True, they were used for want of better, which was far from ideal and which might stimulate an anachronistic interpretation.[128] But Maitland used the retrogressive method not only for want of sources, but more because in some respects it provided an ideal safeguard against anachronistic interpretations. It was precisely this latter reason that accounts for the consciousness with which Maitland sought to employ this method.

Some attention should be paid to the famous final passage of Maitland's essay on the 'village community' in *Domesday Book and Beyond*, which contained a warning against anachronisms. Yet the very last sentence of the passage has been seldom noticed by authors dealing with Maitland.

Against many kinds of anachronism we now guard ourselves. We are careful of costume, of armour and architecture, of words and forms of speech. But it is far easier to be careful of these things than to prevent the intrusion of untimely ideas. In particular there lies a besetting danger for us in the barbarian's use of a language which is too good for his thought. Mistakes then are easy, and when committed they will be fatal and fundamental mistakes. If, for example, we introduce the *persona ficta* too soon, we shall be doing worse than if we armed Hengest and Horsa with machine guns or pictured the venerable Bede correcting proofs for the press; we shall have built upon a crumbling foundation. *The most efficient method of protecting ourselves against such errors is that of reading our history backwards as well as forwards,* of making sure of our middle ages before we talk about the 'archaic,' of accustoming our eyes to the twilight before we go out into the night.[129]

These comparisons in time moving backwards and forwards were essentially helpful in Maitland's unending battle against anachronisms. They should not lead to a 'conflation of the past with the present,' but rather help to disentangle the past, present and future. Furthermore, the method was ideally suited to show the continuous and the dis-

---

[127] Cf. *C.P.* II, p. 314, and Vinogradoff's pronouncement: "The investigation from the known to the unknown has its definite dangers against which one has to be constantly on one's guard; its obvious danger is to destroy perspective and ignore development by carrying into the 'unknown' of earlier times that which is known of later conditions." (P. Vinogradoff, *Villainage in England*, Oxford, 1892, p. 38).

[128] Cf. R.L. Schuyler, *op. cit., p.* 38.

[129] F.W. Maitland, *Domesday Book and Beyond*, p. 415 (our emphasis); cf. also the 'last words' in *The History of English Law*, II, p. 672 ff.

continuous elements in historical development. The back and forth alternations in time were intended more as a purification with regard to later and modern ideas. This is the decisive factor in Maitland's method, and accounts for the principal difference between his approach and the older 'retrogressive method' proclaimed by F. Seebohm and used by other (mostly older) historians.[130]

While we cannot here enter into the question of whether Maitland was always successful with this method, the existence of a large amount of already published studies viewing the lasting value of Maitland's views in the light of the results of modern research should be noticed. In some cases even Maitland has been found guilty of antedating.[131]

Finally, there is one study of Maitland's which must be briefly discussed: *Memoranda de Parliamento*, Maitland's edition of records concerning the parliament of February 1305.[132] This will not only bring us back to that very first phase of English medieval studies in the 19th century, it will also provide an introduction to the subject of the next chapter.

To this edition Maitland added a lengthy and highly interesting Introduction, which modern historiography generally regards as a turning-point, as the beginning of a new approach for studying and interpreting the medieval Parliament.[133] Maitland's work on this publication lasted from 1889 to 1893. During that period he gradually evolved a theory about the function and composition of the medieval Parliament which posterity (if not Maitland) has since qualified as thoroughly new. He concludes his introduction with the following summary:

Perhaps more than enough has already been said about these controverted matters; but it seemed necessary to remind readers, who are conversant with the 'parliaments' of later days, that about the parliaments of Edward I's time there is still much to be discovered and that should they come to the opinion that a session of the king's council is the core and essence of every *parliamentum*, that the documents usually called 'parliamentary petitions' are petitions to the king and his council, that the auditors of petitions are committees of the council, that the rolls of parliament are the records of the

---

[130] Cf. also W.J. Ashley, *Surveys, Historic and Economic*, London, 1900, pp. 39–91, particularly pp. 45, 89–90.

[131] Cf. E. Miller in his preface to *Domesday Book and Beyond*, p. 19.

[132] Reviewed in *E.H.R.* by the French specialist in medieval parliamentary history C.V. Langlois, see *E.H.R.* 9 (1894), pp. 755–758.

[133] See, however, H.E. Bell, *op. cit.*, pp. 91–92.

business done by the council – sometimes with, but much more often without, the concurrence of the estates of the realm – that the highest tribunal in England is not a general assembly of barons and prelates, but the king's council, they will not be departing very far from the path marked out by books that are already classical.[134]

The last sentence seems strange and difficult to reconcile with the idea that Maitland's *Memoranda* marked a new beginning. Perhaps it is to be thought of as an 'understatement.' Or, since Maitland expressly speaks of books, it might be worthwhile to try and find out to which books Maitland referred with the adjective 'classical.' This was how J.G. Edwards solved the problem. What he found was the Lords' *Report*, mentioned in our second chapter, from the beginning of the 19th century (published in four different versions).[135] Edwards's suggestion certainly points in the right direction as to time. But nowhere in Maitland's work is this *Report* mentioned. The enigmatic conclusions of his introduction can probably be more easily clarified by closer scrutiny of the first part, a section later neglected, and not even considered worth reprinting in a subsequent edition of some of Maitland's important essays.[136]

We believe the key to this obscure passage can be found in the first part. Here Maitland reported his research of the years 1889–1893. It also contained a somewhat imperfect historiographical survey of what he called 'the modern history of the bundles of Ancient Petitions.'[137] With growing interest he continued to look for printed and unprinted reports on the subject by the Record Commissioners in the early years of the 19th century. In this 'campaign against the Petitions in Parliament' (as he called it) he inevitably came across the one person whose work – both in quantity and in quality – outshone all the early 19th-century pioneers in parliamentary history, a man who Maitland increasingly admired: Sir Francis Palgrave. Was it not Palgrave's plan to publish a new 'critical' edition of the 'rolls of Parliament' with all the 'ancient parliamentary petitions'? For, as Maitland saw it, Palgrave's publication of the 'parliamentary writs' had been intended as an in-

---

[134] *Memoranda de Parliamento*, ed. F.W. Maitland, London 1893, p. LXXXVIII. See on the subordinate place of the Commons, pp. LXXV–LXXVI.
[135] J.G. Edwards, *Historians and the Medieval English Parliament*, Glasgow, 1970, pp. 10–11, 42–50; see also H.E. Bell, *op. cit.*, p. 92. Cf. G.O. Sayles, *The King's Parliament of England*, London, 1975, p. 14.
[136] Cf. *Selected Historical Essays of F.W. Maitland*, introduced by H. Cam, Cambridge, 1957.
[137] See *Letters*, pp. 110 and 99; *Memoranda*, p. XXIX.

troduction.[138] Maitland pointed out that it had taken Palgrave years
to transcribe these old petitions: an immense labour to which 66
volumes in the Public Record Office still testified. That Palgrave had
not known about the roll of Parliament of February 1305 was for
Maitland sufficient evidence of its obscurity: "when we have said it
was unknown to Palgrave, we have said it was unknown to anybody."[139]
When Maitland had finished the first part of his own introduction, he
wrote to Maxwell Lyte: "Such is my admiration for Palgrave that I do
not like saying anything that anybody, however perverse, could twist
into blame."[140]

Both Maitland's correspondence with Maxwell Lyte and the first
part of his introduction point to an interpretation of "the path marked
out by books that are already classical" as the trail blazed by Palgrave's
works.[141] It was very clear that Maitland in 1893 advocated something
like a return to an interpretation along the lines laid out by Palgrave
(and others) in the first half of the 19th century. Maitland intentionally
linked his views to this earlier tradition, because it – apart from the
pioneering work in the archives – had been of great importance for the
interpretation of the medieval Parliament. There is no doubt that the
Memoranda marked a turning-point; Maitland caused a revival of
interest in an old half-forgotten historiographical tradition. Consequently, several of the elements of Stubbs's views became subject to
doubt.[142] Maitland would not in his research openly attack Stubbs on
this point, for he had too much admiration for Stubbs; Stubbs's view
of Parliament still contained a great number of valuable elements. In
the next chapter we will see that it was only in a later phase that some
historians felt obliged to attack Stubbs openly.

[138] *Memoranda*, p. XXVIII. Maitland, too, had originally had more elaborate plans, see
H.E. Bell, *op. cit.*, p. 88 ff.
[139] *Memoranda*, pp. XII–XIII. The often great deficiencies in his predecessors' work notwithstanding, Maitland's judgment was remarkably mild. H.E. Bell 'explains' his attitude in
this respect with the remark: "Maitland was a remarkably generous man" (*op. cit.*, p. 89).
In our opinion there was more to this rather positive judgment: he must have been aware
how original Palgrave's views were.
[140] *Letters*, p. 110.
[141] See 16 letters to Maxwell Lyte, in *Letters*, numbered: 70, 71, 73, 77, 100, 101, 102, 103,
105, 107, 108, 110, 115, 117, 119, 120. For Maitland's knowledge of one of Palgrave's early
'parliamentary' articles in the *Quarterly Review*, see *Letters*, p. 69 and *Memoranda*, p. XXXI
(note 1); In order to go back into time even further regarding the term 'classical' (it says,
however, 'already classical'), it might be advisable to refer to M. Hale. Both Palgrave and
Maitland refer to his *Jurisdiction of the House of Lords* remarkably often. See *Memoranda*, pp.
LXV (note 2), LXVI (note), LXVIII, LXIX, LXXX (note 1), LXXXVII; see also *History
of English Law*, I, p. 200, and *C.P.*, II, p. 5.
[142] For all the innovations in his work, Maitland remained convinced of the great continuity within historical scholarship. "No historian dreams of beginning the work all over
again. Even if he has a taste for paradox and a quarrelsome temper he accepts what is after
all the great bulk of his predecessor's results" (*C.P.*, III, p. 287).

CHAPTER V

A LIBERAL REVALUATION OF THE TUDOR
MONARCHY: A. F. POLLARD

> It was an education to me ... to watch Professor
> Pollard's mind at work, to see the march of his ideas
> as question succeeded question, and to admire the
> lucidity and logic with which they were deployed.
> (E. Barker, 1953)

A. A. F. POLLARD AND ENGLISH HISTORIOGRAPHY

A.F. Pollard's position is different from that of F.W. Maitland's:
whereas the latter is now generally revered, posterity had more criticism
than admiration for Pollard. What admiration there was was never
without a certain reserve. Unlike Maitland, Pollard is not one of the
'immortals'; nor was Pollard the kind of person to attract much
sympathy or admiration. Because of his authoritarian personality his
many colleagues seldom became friends. Moreover, in his critical
reviews he sometimes showed a lack of understanding of other people's
viewpoints; once he had become convinced of the correctness of his
own point of view, he found it hard to give an unbiased judgment of
other people's views.[1] In this respect his reviews resemble those of
J.H. Round, for whose highly critical way of thinking Pollard (unlike
many others) had great admiration. He defended Round's view as
indispensable to post-Victorian revisionist historiography: "Since history, particularly medieval history, has consisted so largely of hypothesis and fable, historical research has had to devote itself largely to
demolition."[2]

The tribute deservedly paid to Pollard during his lifetime was
noticeably less than that given to others. Might his impact on English
historiography during the first decades of the 20th century not have
been fully appreciated? Although he had been presented with a *Festschrift* in 1924, he was never awarded the honour of having his numer-

---

[1] Cf. G.P. Gooch in *The Historical Association, 1906–1956*, London, 1957, p. 141; G.R.
Elton, *The Practice of History*, London, 1967, p. 120, note 1; A.G. Dickens in A.F. Pollard,
Henry VIII, New York, 1966 (Harper Torchbook), p. X.
[2] *History* 16 (1931–1932), p. 280.

ous scattered articles published together in a volume of 'Collected Papers' as had Maitland, Vinogradoff and Tout. G.N. Clark later regretted this.[3] It is true that upon his death Pollard was accorded many appreciative commemorative articles: by his pupil J.E. Neale in the *English Historical Review*, by C.H. Williams in the *Bulletin* of 'his own' Institute, and finally in a lecture by the medievalist V.H. Galbraith for the British Academy. Nevertheless only a few pages could be spared for his person and work in *History*, although he had been instrumental in founding it, and had contributed to it regularly.[4] Nor has anyone yet troubled to compose a bibliography of his many writings and articles.

However, before analysing his main publications, some of Pollard's organizational merits should be given due attention because these qualities provide a valuable clue to understanding him. Pollard was a splendid organizer with a great 'bias for efficiency'; his qualities in this respect are beyond dispute.[5] After the First World War he took part in setting up the Institute of International Affairs; furthermore, English historiography profited by his activities on behalf of the foundation of a national and international centre for the study of history in London, which resulted in the establishment of the Institute of Historical Research in 1921.

In 1906 Pollard, together with T.F. Tout and C.H. Firth, founded the Historical Association. Historians from the older universities, like R.L. Poole and J.B. Bury, were unenthusiastic at first, but the firm support of Firth and Tout guaranteed a good beginning. Pollard in part determined the direction the Association would follow. The original idea – a union of history teachers concerned principally with educational matters – was abandoned in favour of a much wider conception in which the universities had a leading part. Pollard was convinced that only a university education in history could guarantee a sufficiently high level of instruction in the secondary school. The Association's first task was to pay attention to the study of history in the University. Pollard voiced the Association's double aim: "That history should be properly recognised by universities and that history should be properly taught in schools."[6] Tout approved: on 25th April 1906,

[3] G.N. Clark, *D.N.B.*, 1941–1950, London, 1950, p. 680.

[4] Cf. *History* 33 (1948), pp. 251–253; J.E. Neale, 'A.F. Pollard' in *E.H.R.* 64 (1949), pp. 198–205; C.H. Williams, 'A.F. Pollard' in *B.I.H.R.* 22 (1949), pp. 1–10; V.H. Galbraith, 'A.F. Pollard' in *Proceedings of the British Academy* 35 (1949), pp. 257–274.

[5] Cf. G. Parsloe, 'Recollections of the Institute, 1922–1943' in *B.I.H.R.* 44 (1971), p. 280.

[6] Quoting Pollard in an official letter of 9-1-1906, according to A.T. Milne in his article, 'The Historical Association and Its Founders' in *History Today* 16 (1966), p. 279.

he wrote to Pollard: "I'm getting rather sick of pedagogics"; in 1911, he again stressed that educational and pedagogic matters should not be the Association's only concern. Continuing special attention ought to be afforded to advanced and post-graduate history students.[7]

In 1917 the Association took over the periodical *History* from F.B. Wheeler, who had originally founded the periodical with his private means, but now had to appeal to the Association because of financial difficulties. Pollard became the first editor, and wrote a preface to the first issue in which, as was only natural during these war years his political convictions came to the surface. He stated that the main reason for continuing Wheeler's enterprise was that the war had created problems "which can only be solved in the light of History, and some of them are discussed in the passages that follow."[8]

Such a statement would have been totally uncharacteristic for the highly specialized *English Historical Review*, but for Pollard this programme was more than mere rhetorics.

The general significance of *History* for English historical studies must not be underestimated. As early as 1917 the periodical started the famous series 'Historical Revisions.' The first of these was of course (written by Pollard) on the Magna Carta; other subjects were those "which modern research has shown to be most widely misunderstood."[9] Future issues of *History* also differed from the *English Historical Review* in that it contained theoretical discussions on history and its relationship to other disciplines. The most important result of Pollard's organizational ability was the creation of the Institute of Historical Research, called by Neale 'his greatest act of academic statesmanship.'[10] That London became a centre for historical research after 1900 was largely due to Pollard. According to R.W. Seton-Watson, he caused "a complete revolution in the study of history in the metropolis."[11] This institute and its beginnings have been discussed in the first chapter. The idea was mentioned by Pollard in 1904, in his inaugural lecture – as a (for the time) unsalaried professor in constitutional history –, without referring to the earlier initiatives by Ward or Prothero.[12] The first years after the war were far from favourable for

[7] Cf. A.T. Milne, *op. cit.*, p. 281; *The Historical Association, 1906–1956*, p. 10.
[8] *History* 1 (1916–1917), p. 2.
[9] *History* 2 (1917–1918), p. 170.
[10] J.E. Neale, *op. cit.*, p. 201.
[11] *Tudor Studies*, ed. R.W. Seton-Watson, London, 1924, p. V; cf. H. Fisher in *History* 10 (1925–1926), p. 165.
[12] Cf. also R.A. Humphreys, *The Royal Historical Society, 1868–1968*, London, 1969, p. 28 ff.

this kind of project, and it took the financial support of Cecil Power, with whom Pollard had become friendly during the war, to get the institute finally started in 1921.[13]

In 1926 Pollard could proudly record that the Institute was fulfilling all expectations: it was a 'historical laboratory' training historians for research work on London records, and to Pollard's great joy it had developed into an international centre and meeting place for historians; the Institute organized historical conferences for English and American historians. Other sources of pride were letters from all parts of the Empire manifesting interest and approval, and finally, the fact that the League of Nations – which Pollard had supported in England – had requested its assistance as well.[14]

These facts are evidence of Pollard's political involvement: he never began a historical project without pointing out its direct and indirect political usefulness. Part of his attitude was tactical, part was based on conviction, as evidenced in the preface to *History*. This same tendency was apparent in the founding of a research institute.[15] Perhaps it was paradoxical that Pollard should be the founder of a research institute, although never (or hardly ever) coming to the archives and accused by his colleagues for wasting his time by writing 'journalistic' articles in *The Times*.[16] Neale would say that Pollard lacked the right temperament for the long drawn-out labour of endless patient research. However, he certainly realized the need for such research, and he had great admiration for the results of fellow-historians in this field.[17] To us, comfortable in the present historiographical situation, A.G. Dickens's opinion may be well worth endorsing. He states that Pollard's great books of the pre-war period represent an interim phase "between the spacious days of pre-professional, big-scale historiography and the era of the painstaking and specialised researcher."[18]

Yet Pollard was a 'professional' historian for all that and we need to know what he thought about history as such in order to understand his attitude towards the function of historical research. Being English to the core, he did not greatly pursue theoretical studies; yet several of his remarks invite appropriate reflections. There are only two essays

[13] Cf. G. Parsloe, *op. cit.*, p. 275; J.G. Edwards, 'Sir John Cecil Power' in *B.I.H.R.* 23 (1950), pp. 139–146.
[14] Cf. A.F. Pollard, *Factors in Modern History*, London, 1948, p. 268; H.R. Winkler, *The League of Nations Movement in Great Britain, 1914–1919*, Kingsport (Tennessee), 1952, p. 234 ff.
[15] Cf. J.G. Edwards, *op. cit.*, p. 141.
[16] Cf. V.H. Galbraith, *op. cit.*, p. 264.
[17] Cf. Cf. C.H. Williams, *op. cit.*, p. 4; J.E. Neale, *op. cit.*, p. 203.
[18] A.G. Dickens, *op. cit.*, p. XIII.

treating of general matters in his frequently reprinted book *Factors in Modern History*: 'The value of history,' written in 1911, and 'History and citizenship' from 1930, both abound in stereotypes. His numerous leading articles in the *Times Literary Supplement*, published mainly in the twenties and the thirties, are much more original and have an identity of their own.[19] In these years England felt the influence of Croce, though less so than other countries. The 'bias in history' posed by Croce engaged Pollard's attention too, but his chief interest remained firmly focused on the more 'technical' aspects of historical research in its narrowest sense.[20]

Early in his career, in 1899, Pollard designated the two essential qualities for a good historian: 'patient research' and 'mature reflection.' Historical reflection should be centred upon commonly unnoticed facts and conditions which had been taken for granted by contemporary observers. The ideal context for a correct interpretation is built from this material.[21] While Pollard puts great value on the indispensable document, he does not hold it sacred, for he was firmly convinced that the value of the historical document as such was only relative.

When we have all our documents collected, collated, sifted and arranged we still need the intuition and imagination to discover behind the parchment the play of human minds. For in all ages the most valid and intimate decisions are reached by unrecorded discussions and arranged by word of mouth, and even the spoken word often conceals the real intention.[22]

He wrote this in 1919. In his opinion the end of historical labour sometimes was not even in sight after the historical research in the strict sense had been completed. Thus it was that his laudatory review of Gairdner's great work, (the publication of *The Letters and Papers of Henry VIII*, immensely useful to Pollard's Tudor biographies) ended with the irritatingly sober words: "History, even when based upon all the extant materials, is bound to be largely a matter of surmise and deduction."[23]

[19] See bibliography. As for Pollard's authorship, see: A.F. Pollard, College Collection D 77: A collection of press-cutting mainly of the 1930's, in pamphlet box (together with articles in *The Listener* 1934). Library, University College, London.

[20] Cf. his article, 'The Use and Abuse of Capital Letters' in *B.I.H.R.* 5 (1927–1928), pp. 1–12. See bibliography for other articles of this kind. For the reception of Croce in England, see: W.M. Johnston, *The Formative Years of R.G. Collingwood*, The Hague, 1967, p. 76 ff.; cf. also A.S. Turberville, 'History objective and subjective' in *History* 17 (1932–1933), pp. 289–302.

[21] "Facts that are not categorically stated in documents escape his notice, and it is precisely those facts, those conditions taken for granted by contemporaries, that most need explanation to students in a later age." *E.H.R.* 14 (1899), p. 164.

[22] 'Lord Morley on History' in *History* 3 (1918–1919), p. 217.

[23] 'The Letters and Papers of Henry VIII' in *E.H.R.* 26 (1911), p. 261; cf. also the review in the same volume, p. 785.

In the famous debate on whether 'history' was a 'science' or an 'art' he reserved his judgment (as did many others, including J.B. Bury), declaring that history was both.[24] He defended the scientific character of history against those who would submerge history in literature, but he never tired of holding up the literary aspects of history to those who would make it a social science. In this he was adamant: history was, and always would be, a literary discipline.[25]

Pollard had an unshakeable belief in history's political values, however difficult they might be to define. Was not a healthy scepticism and relativism the most worthwhile result of historical training and thinking? Could there be a better correction to absolutist and pseudo-scientific pronouncements and opinions? In 1911 he wrote sharply against the practice of using history for ethical and moral purposes: "all values depend upon environment."[26] Pollard was a relativist and a sceptic, but he never permitted his scepticism to undermine his faith in the fundamental value of his science, notwithstanding the emergence in the twenties of Croce's theory of subjectivity in history. How did Pollard react to this?

Like very many leading historians of that time, Pollard believed that the scholarly character of the study of history was greatly endangered as well as damaged by Croce's strong emphasis on subjectivity. 'Croceanism' was, in their opinion, a step backwards on the path travelled since 1890. Time and again they had pleaded in favour of the research work that England so badly needed to catch up with the Continent, but Croce's adage that 'all history is contemporary history' was a statement of faith in an inevitable presentism, negating all their efforts for more 'facts' and better research to combat this very present-mindedness.

In his lecture 'History and Philosophy' E. Barker called historians to account in the tribunal of philosophy. He praised Croce's views which would deliver history from the continually growing chaos of ever more irrelevant facts; he waxed ironic on 'the magic about unprinted material and new facts.'[27] It was clear to all, that Barker's critical remarks about 'facticity' were an unmistakable attack on Tout's great work on the administrative history of the Middle Ages, the first parts of which had only just been published. Pollard was the first to parry

---

[24] Cf. *Encyclopaedia Britannica*, vol. IX, Cambridge, 1910, p. 587.
[25] Cf. C.H. Williams, *op. cit.*, p. 8; cf. *History* 25 (1940–1941), p. 207.
[26] *Factors*, p. 5.
[27] E. Barker, 'History and Philosophy' in *History* 7 (1922–1923), p. 89; cf. A.F. Pollard, 'An Apology for Historical Research' in *History* 7 (1922–1923), pp. 161–177.

Barker's attacks. In his 'apology of historical research' he made it very clear that there was a fundamental difference between abstract philosophical thought and concrete historical thought; he also blamed Barker for having given a one-sided, simple and very wrong interpretation of Croce: if we write a history of the past it is contemporaneous historiography, *not* 'contemporary history.'[28]

Barker's actualism, in which history could see the past only as the origin of the present, was the exact opposite of what Pollard believed historical thought should be. To him, nothing could be simpler than Croce's slogan that 'all history is contemporary history': it was a commonplace truth, since all history can only exist in the mind, and "the thought must be contemporary with the thinker."[29] Perhaps much so-called history was only a reflection of the present, but in Pollard's view the real scientifically justified historiography was anything but 'a mirror of the moment.' He believed that it was typical for historical thought to draw comparisons, showing the links as well as the contrasts between past and present. The past might be the origin of the present, but the historian could never permit himself to overlook the difference between the roots and the tree.[30]

The German *Weltanschauung-Forschung* as manifested in the continental approach of the history of historiography only elicited scepticism from Pollard: "If Mahan or Maitland had a view of the world, it did not obtrude upon their historical research."[31] For him the question 'What is history?' derived from the practical context of his work.[32] His conviction that it was possible and desirable for a historian to detach himself occasionally from the present, made him repeatedly aware of the problems of anachronism in history. "Anachronism is the historian's evil spirit and he cannot help its dogging his steps because he is seeking to tell the truth about earlier times, when he can only think in the terms of the present and write in a language clogged with later accretions."[33] It is not coincidental that these words occur in an article on the familiar theme of history and law.

On the one hand Pollard stressed the absolute need for a 'freedom of the present,' on the other hand his scepticism and realism made him

[28] Cf. A.F. Pollard, 'What is History'? in *T.L.S.*, 16-12-1926, p. 921; and A.F. Pollard, 'History and Progress' in *History* 8 (1923–1924), pp. 81–97.

[29] *T.L.S.*, 16-12-1926, p. 921.

[30] *Ibid.*, p. 922.

[31] *Ibid.*

[32] A.F. Pollard, 'History and The Law' in *History* 10 (1925–1926), p. 203.

[33] *History* 10 (1925–1926), p. 208; cf. also *E.H.R.* 12 (1897), p. 591 and *History* 8 (1923–1924), p. 135.

doubt if this was at all feasible. "Can we really be fair to men of the past, knowing what they could not know? Can we indeed understand them at all ... with our minds prepossessed by a knowledge of the result?"[34] Knowledge of later events could adversely affect knowledge of earlier events; yet Pollard believed that knowledge of later events was necessary for a thorough understanding of what had happened earlier. "We cannot really know what was in the parent unless we know what has come out in the children."[35] To know modern history a sound knowledge of the Middle Ages was essential. Conversely, in order to have a 'full understanding' of the Middle Ages a knowledge of Modern History was a prerequisite. Pollard's opinion of the Middle Ages was, as we shall see, determined by his view of the Tudor monarchy; it is doubtful whether this could result in a better and more complete understanding of the Middle Ages. Numerous medievalists disputed his approach.

Summarizing, it may be stated that Pollard retained a favourable attitude towards historical research, which determined the character of the historical discipline.[36] Being strongly aware of the subjective and deductive character of all historical interpretation, he insisted that the document itself only had a relative importance. For facts are not history, they are the raw materials: 'the quality of history is the logic of events.'[37] Later he judged the seemingly unending process of specialization in the same spirit. Thorough specialization was useful in undermining a great number of unpardonable generalizations, but its growth also had noticeable drawbacks. Pollard quoted Croce's familiar lecture of 1932 about the growth of an 'anti-historicism' to prove that 'Clio's Recessional' was related to this very process.[38] Whereas Croce explained Clio's decline by pointing an accusing finger at people's passion for the Absolute or their worship of violence, Pollard blamed specialization. He did not really regret that Clio no longer was Clio, but he did see a serious threat in a specialization that went too far, reducing the study of history to a purely antiquarian matter and often hindering the historian from seeking the interdependent relationship of the many details, the 'logic of events.' In that case he feared specialization would reach the point 'at which scholarship ceases to be such.'[39] When his

---

[34] A.F. Pollard, 'Historical Criticism' in *History* 5 (1920–1921), p. 29.
[35] A.F. Pollard, *Factors in American History*, Cambridge, 1925, p. 304.
[36] *T.L.S.*, 16-12-1926, p. 922.
[37] *Ibid.*
[38] A.F. Pollard, 'Clio's Recessional' in *T.L.S.*, 3-3-1932, pp. 141–142.
[39] *Ibid.*, p. 142.

friend W. Notestein published an edition of records in seven volumes he had the courage to write, in 1936: "Clio becomes a mummy in a museum."[40]

As an organizer Pollard made London a centre for the study of history. As a professional historian with all its restrictions he was no longer part of the 'Macaulay-tradition,' although some critics still place him there. Moreover, Pollard's books on the Tudor period also herald a breach with the 19th-century tradition of English historiography. Pollard also helped to demolish the Whig views. J.H. Hexter writes: "For his holocaust of historical idols we are all still indebted to A.F. Pollard."[41] He represents Pollard as demolishing old myths with one hand while creating new ones with the other. For him, Pollard was still ridden by a number of "inexplicit assumptions, dear to the hearts of practitioners of the sociology of knowledge."[42] These assumptions will be discussed below; however, in our opinion they were not identical to Hexter's facile generalizations on this subject.

B. A LIBERAL REVALUATION OF THE NEW MONARCHY: ENGLISH FREEDOM AND ITS FETTERED BIRTH

1. Somerset and Henry VIII

> The contrast between morals and politics, which comes out in Henry's reign as a terrible contradiction, is inherent in all forms of human society.
>
> (A.F. Pollard, 1902)

What made Pollard choose the Tudors? He had read history in Oxford, at Jesus College where R.L. Poole had been one of his tutors. Early in

---

[40] Cf. V.H. Galbraith, *op. cit.*, p. 264; cf. also the almost identical ending in the review of the *'Commons Debates'* (in 7 vols.) in *T.L.S.*, 1936, p. 370: "The editors are concerned only with the materials; the history is left for the reader himself to discover. That is the latest and highest doctrine of the infallible church of historical research. It springs from the deepest humility and a profound sense of the categorical sanctity of original documents; if not untouchable, they must at least remain intact. These 'Debates' are a mine of wealth indispensable for every historical library and every individual specialist in any aspect of the period, and their editors are the miners of history. As such they perform an essential and arduous task. They bring their coal to the surface, and there they dump it, agreeing, it seems, with Mark Pattison that history cannot be written from manuscripts. 'From them,' they say (I, 101) 'we could piece together a pretty complete account of the Commons'. But they refrain; they have too fine a regard for the original form to convert the mineral into electric light or power – or gas for the cooker of history."

[41] J.H. Hexter, *Reappraisals in History*, London, 1961, p. 28.

[42] *Ibid.*, p. 37 ff.

the nineties he graduated very successfully, taking a First in History. His study on the Polish Jesuits earned him the Lothian Prize, and this success encouraged him to hope for a job in his beloved University town. However, Oxford at that time had no place for him; after 1891 he had to find employment outside Oxford, and in 1892 he became the assistant-editor of the *Dictionary of National Biography*, under the leadership of Sidney Lee, editor-in-chief as successor to Leslie Stephen. Thus Pollard had a regular income until the *D.N.B.* was completed in 1901. This left him 'stranded' again, as he expressed it in a letter of 1903 to Maitland, asking for a testimonial because he had applied for a London professorship.[43]

The period at the *D.N.B.* was of decisive importance for Pollard. His general historical knowledge was enormously enlarged and the work also provided training in research and precision; here it was that he became fascinated with the Tudor period, becoming England's foremost authority on this subject for years to come. Pollard said that, just as J.R. Green's *Short History* had in his youth fired him with enthusiasm for the study of history, the *D.N.B.* played an equal part in introducing him to his specialization.[44] There is no doubt that the best of his more than 500 articles dealt with the Tudor period. In 1893 his first 'biographies' appeared; among them the ones on Thomas Lydiat and the Tudor diplomat John Mason. Around 1900 he had definitely chosen the period as well as the direction of his future research. His approach was to be a revision of H. Hallam's work, which was too constitutional in the old sense of the word. When Pollard wrote to thank Maitland for his testimonial he also said: "I should endeavour to write something on the constitutional, administrative, and parliamentary history of England in the 16th century. Hallam is merely a sketch which gives but the vaguest indication of the real working of the government machine."[45]

In the nineties Pollard also wrote his first reviews for the *English Historical Review*. He became better known after unmasking two falsified historical documents about the French Revolution. His best known review deals with the work of a certain Raoul Hesdin, entitled *The Journal of a Spy in Paris during the Reign of Terror*, published in London in

[43] A.F. Pollard to F.W. Maitland, 29-4-1903: "I am applying for the professorship of 'constitutional law and history' at University College, London, a post which will carry with it but slender and precarious emoluments, but is not to be despised by one who has been stranded by the completion of the D.N.B." C.U.L., Add. MS. 7007.

[44] A.F. Pollard, *Why We Study History*, Historical Association Pamphlet, no. 131, 1944, p. 13.

[45] A.F. Pollard to F.W. Maitland, 1-5-1903, C.U.L. Add. MS. 7007.

1895 and hailed week after week by reviewers as a valuable contribution to the history of the French Revolution. Pollard was the first to expose the cleverly constructed document as a literary falsification, and even to detect the editor as the author of the diary.[46] The real author proved to be no less a person than a well-known scholar of that time, Charles Fletcher of Magdalen College, author and historian, and gifted with "a strong appreciation of the humorous side of history that he was teaching."[47] Referring to this event C. Oman later spoke of Pollard (without mentioning his name) as a 'deadly specialist.' An ironical note is that Pollard owed much of his knowledge of the French Revolution to this same Fletcher, which may account for his recognition of him.[48]

Pollard's fame began with his first major book, published in 1900 under the title *England under Protector Somerset*. Maitland mentioned this book with great satisfaction in a letter to R.L. Poole, although he refused to comply with Poole's request to write a review about it for the *English Historical Review*.[49] In the years after 1900 Pollard was also accepted as a contributor to the *Cambridge Modern History*, originally at the suggestion of G.W. Prothero that he write all the sections on German history.[50]

Both the book about Somerset and his biography of Henry VIII (published in 1902) made Pollard a respected historian. He called the first book an essay, because of its clearly revisionist tendencies.

First, Pollard generally attempted to free the period of the Reformation from the shackles of theological-political historiography. He believed the important social and political events of the period had been either neglected or not dealt with at all.[51] This tendency is evident

---

[46] See *E.H.R.* 11 (1896), pp. 594–597; cf. Ch. Oman, *Memories of Victorian Oxford*, London, 1941, p. 125; Hedva Ben-Israel, *English Historians and the French Revolution*, Cambridge, 1968, p. 65.

[47] Ch. Oman, *op. cit.*, p. 125.

[48] See: A.F. Pollard, Notebooks (2) for lectures taken down at Oxford University, Library University College, London, Add.MS. 80, including notes on Fletcher's 'Lectures on the French Revolution' of October 1890.

[49] F.W. Maitland to R.L. Poole, 17-10-1900, included in A.L. Poole, 'F.W. Maitland to R.L. Poole,' in *The Cambridge Historical Journal* 10 (1952), p. 330; cf. also the letter of 6-5-1901, p. 332.

[50] G.W. Prothero asked S. Lee for confidential information about Pollard's qualities: "I am looking for a man to write a History of Germany (from about 1500–1789) for the Cambridge Historical series of which I am editor now." See G.W. Prothero's letter of 23-12-1900 to S. Lee, MS. Eng. Misc. d. 179, B.L. Oxford. Pollard may have been recommended by R.L. Poole.

[51] A.F. Pollard, *England under Protector Somerset. An Essay*, London, 1900, pp. 91, 257 (henceforth referred to as *Somerset*); cf. also *E.H.R.* 13 (1898), p. 464 and in *Henry VIII*, p. 344: "It is called a theological age, but it was also irreligious, and its principal feature was secularisation."

in all his work, as it is also in the writings of Maitland on the 16th century. Pollard's more specific revisionism was applied to the period of Edward VI, which he saw as divided into two separate contradictory phases: that of the freedom-loving Somerset and the succeeding phase of Warwick, an unscrupulous Machiavellian, whose short reign marked a return to an old despotism. Warwick's seeming continuation of his predecessor's religious policy was belied, Pollard insisted, by the intentions underlying that policy; this was evidenced in its implementation, which was quite different after Somerset's fall.[52]

Pollard's (re)-valuation of Somerset undoubtedly centred around the latter's 'experiment in Liberty' which appealed to Pollard's liberal feelings.[53] Unlike the church historian N. Pocock, he did not view Somerset as a 'rank Calvinist,' but rather as a 'Calvinist Erastian' for whom the State had to be supreme over the Church.[54] Somerset's liberal reign abolished the six articles and did not engage in religious persecution or executions; in many respects it was a foreshadowing of the coming century when English freedom would be fought out in the Great Rebellion and the Glorious Revolution.[55] Pollard's ideas superficially resemble the traditional historical interest of 19th-century liberals. The description of Somerset's reign had much in common with the old Whig topics, but can Pollard's rehabilitation of Henry VIII two years later be reconciled with his rehabilitation of Somerset, especially since the comparison between the Protector and the King in Pollard's *Somerset* are not at all favourable to Henry? The inheritance Somerset was confronted with upon Henry's death was hardly praiseworthy: while Henry VIII had inherited from his father a stable throne, a well-filled treasury and the goodwill of the people, "he undermined the first, he emptied the second and alienated the third."[56]

Later reviewers actually believed that Pollard had completely changed his mind about Henry VIII.[57] It should be remembered, however, that Pollard – for all his enthusiasm over Somerset's political aims and methods – never ceased to point out the causes that led to his downfall. His reign was not what J.A. Froude had supposed it to be:

[52] *Somerset*, pp. 105, 257, 264.
[53] *Somerset*, pp. 58, 258. Cf. *Factors*, p. 132. Cf. also S.T. Bindoff, *Tudor England*, Harmondsworth, 1950, p. 157.
[54] *Somerset*, pp. 95, 110, 321; *D.N.B.*, vol. 51, 1987, p. 303. Cf. Pollard on N. Pocock in the *D.N.B.*
[55] *Somerset*, pp. 67, 313.
[56] *Somerset*, p. 40; see further pp. 53, 73, 130, 338. The only thing praised by Pollard was Henry's naval policy, p. 266.
[57] Cf. the review of the *Factors* in *T.L.S.*, 16-8-1907, p. 251: "We are not sure that second thoughts are always best or that Mr. Pollard has escaped the *lues biographica*."

one with the 'spirit of the time.' His belief in constitutional freedom and his dislike of coercion and religious persecution made Somerset an exception in the governing circles of his time. His very love of freedom gave the opposition a chance to wax strong, and so 'liberty' was quite as much the cause of his downfall as was his social agrarian policy, which had been intended as an appeasing gesture towards the 'Commonwealth-men' of the period.[58] "He was too little of an opportunist to be a successful ruler," had Pollard written as early as 1897.[59] Somerset's Scottish policy, envisaging the possibility of incorporating Scotland, possessed a visionary quality, which Pollard believed was precisely what characterized his lack of statesmanship: "He was a man of ideas rather than a statesman."[60] Two years later Pollard equally enthusiastically contrasted the realistic policy of Henry VIII to Somerset's liberal idealism. That a liberal historian like Pollard could have been such a great admirer of this authoritarian Tudor monarch calls for an explanation.

His *Henry VIII* was first published in 1902 as a commentary companion volume to a luxury edition of some Tudor portraits, mainly painted by Holbein. In 1905 this was succeeded by a scholarly edition with extensive notes. Pollard's conviction was that good historical biography should be more than a study of character: the main component should be an analysis of the background, the environment and the circumstances which made the appearance of the person in question possible, and what enabled the later historian in turn to find the right context for his historical interpretation. Pollard plainly disavowed Carlyle's biographical interpretation of history in which the strong personality stood over and above his environment.

The miraculous interpretation of history is as obsolete as the catastrophic theory of geology, and the explanation of Henry's career must be sought not so much in the study of his character as in the study of his environment, of the conditions which made things possible to him that were not possible before or since and are not likely to be so again.[61]

For Pollard Henry VIII embodied an inevitable political development separating the Middle Ages from the modern period.[62] Through a

---

[58] See *Somerset*, ch. VIII; *Factors*, ch. VII.
[59] *D.N.B.*, vol. 51, 1897, p. 308.
[60] *Somerset*, p. 317; cf. *Henry VIII*, pp. 346–347.
[61] *Henry VIII*, p. 3; Pollard had the same views regarding historical biographies as Lord Morley, see: Basil Willey, *More Nineteenth Century Studies*, London, 1956, p. 290 ff.; D.A. Hamer, *John Morley*, Oxford, 1968, p. 46.
[62] *Henry VIII*, p. 351.

description of his principal figure, Pollard illustrated his view of the 'historical necessity' of the Tudor despotism, as well as explaining the 'sounder views' regarding the Tudors, views which he had already advocated in a review of 1900.[63]

A 'sounder' judgment could not be arrived at until some constitutional misunderstandings were first cleared away. These misunderstandings dated from the 17th and, more especially, the 19th century, and were centred upon the Whig preference for 'Lancastrian constitutionalism.' For Pollard the late medieval parliamentarianism was only an empty husk as it was characterized by an 'irresponsible parliament' antagonistic to the executive. The only result was what Fortescue called 'a lack of government.' In Pollard's more modern terminology the result was 'administrative anarchy.'[64] In the early parts of his *Henry VIII* Pollard did his best to demolish several of the myths current in the ostensibly democratic 19th century: that freedom and 'strong government' were mutually exclusive, that the executive power was the natural enemy of the legislative power and, finally, that Englishmen from 'time immemorial' had had a predilection for parliamentary government.

Our third chapter argued that this Whig constitutionalism was already past its prime in the political climate of the late 19th century, and criticism of this constitutionalism in part provided the basis for Pollard's re-discovery of the political importance of the Tudor period. He was the first liberal historian to give a favourable interpretation of the concept of the New Monarchy introduced by J.R. Green. This New Monarchy was not a 'strange and isolated' episode; for Pollard this period was wholly integrated within the context of English parliamentary development. Pollard cautioned against 'anticipation,' but he placed Edward IV as a 'new monarch' and the inaugurator of the necessary constitutional innovations that were to achieve completion under Henry VIII. Edward IV restored the bonds and mutual trust between crown and parliament. In a lecture on Parliament during the Wars of the Roses, Pollard said that the discredit into which the 'diarchic' character of Lancastrian constitutionalism had fallen, put an end to the detestable 'heresy' of the separation of powers.[65] Edward IV's protracted parliaments may have been few in number, but they were certainly much more salutary and had a more lasting effect than the

[63] *E.H.R.* 15 (1900), pp. 168–170 and 581–585.
[64] *Henry VIII*, p. 26; *Factors*, pp. 67–68.
[65] A.F. Pollard, *Parliament in the Wars of the Roses*, Glasgow, 1936, p. 28; see also the review in *E.H.R.* 53 (1938), pp. 159–160.

numerous short-lived parliaments under the House of Lancaster, thanks to the 'necessary' legislative initiative of the Crown.[66]

The first condition for a historical understanding of the Tudor despotism and its true nature, was to understand why the 'Lancastrian experiment' had failed. Pollard was to mention that failure in every one of his books. He believed that, apart from a return to the anarchy and chaos of the Wars of the Roses, there had been no alternative to Tudor despotism (and contemporary Tudor authors could be quoted in support of this belief).[67] However, Pollard pleaded for more than simply an understanding of the Tudors as part of a situation in which there was no alternative. Squarely opposing the Whig view, he claimed that parliament survived the 16th century not *in spite of* Tudor policy, but *because* of it.[68] Parliament owed much more to the Tudor monarchy than a 'democratic century' was willing to concede. Pollard saw Henry VIII as the architect of Parliament, as the champion of parliamentary privileges, and as the pioneer of the sound constitutional doctrine of the indivisible sovereignty of 'the king in Parliament.'[69]

A number of objections to Henry's parliamentary policy had been raised in the past, and as they presented an obstacle to positive revaluation, the first need was to determine whether they were historically correct: to wit, unfree Parliamentary elections led to 'packed' parliaments, which fact explained their 'servility.'

In an attempt to discredit these old reproaches Pollard first of all claimed that there was no incontrovertible proof, for the available records were insufficient.[70] Besides, how could one determine the extent of 'packing' or 'servility' in a parliament? The democratic criticism which spawned these reproaches was hardly appropriate for a *historical* view of Tudor despotism. As for the royal appointments, Pollard pointed out that even in the early phases of the Tudor monarchy serving in Parliament was still an unpleasant and time-wasting burden for many.[71] In his opinion the reproach of 'servility' had its roots in the popular belief that Parliament could only be called a true Parliament if the nation's legislation was entirely a result of parliamentary initiatives. But this was not the case then, nor now, nor had it ever been, as Pollard stated. "Parliament had generally been the

[66] *Ibid.*, pp. 21–22; under Lancastrian rule parliament "was a spoke in the wheel rather than a means of government ..." (p. 16); cf. *Factors*, p. 67.

[67] Cf. *Henry VIII*, pp. 206, 252, 345.

[68] *Factors*, p. 97.

[69] *Henry VIII*, pp. 207, 228, 345.

[70] *Henry VIII*, pp. 202, 210 (criticism on J.S. Brewer), *Factors*, p. 103.

[71] *Henry VIII*, p. 213 (note 1); *Factors*, p. 95.

instrument of Government, a condition essential to strong and successful administration.''[72] Both Pollard's criticism of the Lancastrian experiment and his admiration for the New Monarchy, including Tudor
despotism, sprang from his 'unitarist' constitutionalism, which characterized his realistic liberalism as well.

After having discredited the traditional objections as nothing but
obstacles in the way of 'rational explanation', Pollard believed it would
now be possible to evaluate more favourably the political aspects of the
Reformation.[73] Packed parliaments and servility were replaced by a
harmonious relationship between king and parliament, originating in
and based upon a fundamental similarity of interests.[74] Because the
Commons wanted peace and order above all and feared nothing so
much as the return of anarchy and civil war, they willingly supported
the King's anti-Roman policy. Contrary to his enemies' representation
of Henry's power as shaky, he had in fact broad 'national' support. The
growth of the national consciousness, together with the growth of the
middle class, was an important aspect of Pollard's perception of the
Reformation period. It coloured his favourable judgment of the Tudor
phase, and in the same measure did it colour his unfavourable view of
the preceding medieval period. These national feelings in the 16th
century had nothing to do with 'race' or with an inborn Anglo-Saxon
disposition but were rather the result of a historical process, which at
the very beginning of the modern period was already so developed
that it became a factor in European history.[75]

In his *Evolution of Parliament* Pollard tried to explain in a more
original manner how England's growth into a nation had been a
'parliamentary' process, the early nationalism was not merely a matter
of dynastic developments. It was a victory over the church's universalist
tendencies and over the feudal and local particularism of the Middle
Ages as well. Under Henry VIII there was great approval for the
nationalization of the Church, but this occurred only after the demolition of feudal particularism had already contributed to the enrichment
of national political life. The conception of a national state as the hallmark of a new age was not, according to Pollard, propagated only
through a dynasty, but also through a rising middle class. This class
might be small to start with, but he was firmly convinced that it

---

[72] *Henry VIII*, p. 212.
[73] Cf. *Factors*, pp. 75, 101.
[74] *Henry VIII*, p. 211; *Factors*, p. 102 ff.
[75] Cf. *Factors*, pp. 25, 31.

dominated the whole century.[76] Its open structure enabled it to provide
for the assimilation of burgesses and landed gentry, thus giving it a
better claim to represent the nation than that of any other medieval
class. The mobility between burgesses and gentry was the secret of the
'national' power of the Commons in the Tudor period.[77]

Pollard's interest in the non-religious aspects of the Reformation
period made him underrate the deep-rooted religious forces within the
English Reformation. The religious aspect of the Reformation was in
his view non-doctrinarian, typically English, and preferred improved
religious practice to the reorientation of theological dogma's.[78] In a way
it was an insular movement: impregnated more with Wycliffe's ideas
than with those of continental reformers.[79] As Pollard said, Wycliffe
had already remarked that only the State could efficiently put the reformers' ideas into practice. The Church was inwardedly weakened
and corrupt and absolutely unable to reform itself. Any reform movement that did not have the support of the State was bound to lead to
civil war. Pollard concluded sceptically: "It is doubtful whether religion
has fashioned nationality so much as nationality has moulded religion."[80]

J.H. Hexter too facilely dismisses Pollard's thesis concerning the
middle class and the growing national consciousness as a myth. Pollard's
characterization of the English Reformation as mainly political had
sufficient basis in these two phenomena. Constitutionally, he saw the
Reformation as 'the last and greatest conquest of the State,' as a
translatio imperii, the replacement of universal Papal despotism by a
'national' royal despotism.[81] Pollard agreed in part with J.N. Figgis
that the modern state might be considered the greatest achievement of
the Reformation. But he also believed the statement could be interpreted the other way round: the Reformation might be called the
greatest achievement of the modern state in the 16th century.[82] Essentially the Reformation was an act of the State, a royal act, but
approved by Parliament and supported by an ever-growing sense of

[76] *Henry VIII*, pp. 240, 250–251.
[77] *Factors*, pp. 30, 46.
[78] A.F. Pollard, *Thomas Cranmer and the English Reformation*, London, 1904, pp. 104, 188;
Henry VIII, p. 218.
[79] *Cranmer*, p. 270 (note 1); *Factors*, p. 92.
[80] *Cranmer*, p. 224.
[81] *Factors*, p. 87; *Henry VIII*, pp. 215, 261 ff.; cf. also A.F. Pollard, *The Political History of
England from the Accession of Edward VI to the Death of Elizabeth, 1547–1603*, London, 1910, p.
355.
[82] *The Political History*, p. 209; cf. A.F. Pollard, *The Evolution of Parliament*, London, 1926,
p. 216.

national unity, which was strengthened by the nationalization of the Church. The break with Rome definitely made an end of the last great medieval stronghold that still opposed national unity.

In Pollard's constitutional view this political Reformation was the opposite to feudalism, which he described as the negation of the State. He believed that Tudor despotism had a historical mission to destroy the feudal past; the most striking characteristic of his theory was his belief in the need and inevitability of the despotic Tudor phase. England had to pass through the Tudor phase in order to arrive at a state of modern liberty and a more modern society. He did not use the term 'historical necessity' in a causal way; implicit in his view of inevitability was the condition that if there had been no despotism, English liberty would never have become what it had become – i.e. the despotism had actually paved the way for liberty. This conception occurs repeatedly in the books published after *Henry VIII*. In *Factors* Pollard wrote about the New Monarchy:

it was strong, unprincipled, and efficient. But its greatest achievement was that its success made the reception of such an experiment superfluous for the future. Order is Heaven's first law; on earth it must always go before liberty. England could not have done without the Tudors and all their works; for they gave us law and order. They prepared the way of liberty.[83]

This was clearly quite different from the dominant Whig historiography of the 19th century. As well as looking further into the elaboration of this conception in Pollard's later work, the next section will deal with some aspects of his theory in the light of his liberalism. The inevitability he ascribed to Tudor despotism can also be found in his biography of Henry VIII; no doubt it caused him to exculpate Henry in many instances. A reviewer in the first volume of the *Times Literary Supplement* wrote in praise of the book:

Mr. Pollard has produced by far the most convincing defence of the policy of Henry VIII that has yet appeared. Its ultimate defence consists in its success; Mr. Pollard has found a way of combining this frankly non-moral view with a vigorous appeal to a somewhat higher ground; he has taken the moral responsibility off the broad shoulders alike of the king and the historian, and has placed it on the broader shoulders of an inevitable destiny, of whose 16th century agents Henry was the most benevolent.[84]

---

[83] *Factors*, pp. 71–72.
[84] *T.L.S.*, 11-7-1902, p. 202.

2. *Pollard's Liberalism and Tudor Efficiency*

> The interpretation of history, like that of the Scriptures, varies from age to age; and present political theories colour our views of the past.
>
> (A.F. Pollard, 1902)

An explanation for Pollard's way of thinking may be found in what J.E. Neale called 'the constitutional trend of his mind.'[85] In some respects, of course, his constitutionalism was similar to the new liberalism described in our third chapter. It enabled him to formulate new questions about the Tudors, as well as a more 'rational view' regarding their despotism, which no previous liberal historian had achieved. Pollard is the first English historian to explain the Tudor period – especially the reign of Henry VIII – as fundamental to and indispensable within the constitutional development of England as a whole. The first Tudor phase was not one of the topics of Whig historiography; on the contrary, its return to tyranny illustrated nothing so plainly as what should not have been. Henry VIII had only his anti-Roman policy to his credit, for the rest, his behaviour met with disapproval.[86] In the 19th century only two historians had attempted to paint this King in brighter colours: Sharon Turner in the beginning of the century, and later the famous historian J.A. Froude, apparently influenced by Turner.[87] However, Froude was not a liberal. His rehabilitation of the King had heroic overtones and was meant to restore the Reformation and its followers to their unique central place in English history, from which they had been ousted, in Froude's opinion regrettably, by the Oxford Movement.[88]

---

[85] J.E. Neale, *op. cit.*, p. 202.

[86] See on the 19th-century image of Henry VIII: Esmé Wingfield-Stratford, *Truth in Masquerade*, London, 1951, ch. VIII; cf. H. Hallam, *The Constitutional History of England*, London, 1863, I, p. 36; cf. also H. Brougham, *The British Constitution*, London, 1861, p. 200 ff.; Goldwin Smith, *The United Kingdom. A Political History*, London, 1899, vol. I, p. 301 ff. (cf. S.R. Gardiner's review in *E.H.R.* 15 (1900), pp. 348–350); undoubtedly J. Russell gave a much more balanced judgment of the constitutional development: "The reign of Henry the eighth is justly esteemed the most arbitrary in our annals. Yet it affords many curious precedents of the authority of Parliament," see J. Russell, *An Essay on the History of the English Government and Constitution*, London, 1865, p. 16.

[87] Th. P. Peardon, *The Transition in English Historical Writing, 1760–1830*, New York, 1933, p. 228 ff.; cf. Hallam's denunciation of Turner: in Hallam, *op. cit.*, I, p. 32, (note 1).

[88] Cf. Basil Willey, *More Nineteenth Century Studies*, pp. 132–133; cf. Froude's early remark (around 1850): "We had been told at Oxford that it (The Reformation) was the most unfortunate incident which had destroyed the unity of the Church, that it had been a rebellion against divinely given authority, that it was schism promoted by corrupt and tyrannical princes, carried out by unprincipled and priestly renegades," quoted by W.H. Dunn, *J.A. Froude. A Biography.*, Oxford, 1961, p. 170.

Pollard, on the other hand, was much more interested in the constitutional aspects of the period, although he did value Froude's work which had come in for rather harsh criticism from 19-thcentury liberals. As a liberal, Pollard of course rejected a heroic type of history. What he did admire in Froude's major work was its literary quality and its historical method. "Though I have compared a considerable number of his quotations with the originals, I cannot say that these abridgments are unfair representations of them," Pollard wrote at the end of his *Somerset*.[89] They apparently had a common admiration for Henry VIII, but the basis for this admiration was different for both. Pollard had a liberal background, though unrelated to the Gladstone-tradition. And while we are not suggesting that Pollard grew to admire Henry VIII despite his liberalism (as does G.R. Elton), yet it was the one quality that enabled him to achieve a more positive interpretation, precisely because it was *not* of a Whiggish or Gladstonian bent.[90] Nor is it correct to suggest that Pollard's conception of Henry VIII as a constitutional and parliamentary monarch grew from a Victorian glorification of the parliamentary tradition.[91] Henry VIII was not really part of the Victorian admiration of the parliamentary past. Pollard's interpretation was a new one, which undermined a long-standing historiographical tradition.

By now the two main characteristics of Pollard's liberal constitutionalism are plainly visible: power and efficiency. These two conceptions, more than 'positive liberty' or 'citizenship,' set their stamp on his political credo. Yet it remained liberal. Power and efficiency could also be used for liberal purposes; they could help to defend a free society and the liberty of the individual. Pollard was not advocating efficiency as such, and he often warned against efficiency for efficiency's sake.[92] Ideas which had been mutually exclusive within classic liberalism, had become unified in his view; to many people this seemed a paradox. Liberty and despotism, which Pollard brought together, actually had more in common than classic liberalism had ever admitted. This close relationship, offered even by Pollard as a paradox, was yet essential to

---

[89] *Somerset*, p. 338; cf. other comments about Froude: *D.N.B.*, Suppl. vol. II, London, 1901, pp. 254–262; *Henry VIII*, p. XXVII ff.; *Cranmer*, p. VIII; *Factors*, pp. 73, 238.

[90] G.R. Elton in A.F. Pollard, *Wolsey*, London, 1965 (Fontana Library), p. XIII ff.; G.R. Elton, 'Fifty Years of Tudor Studies at London Universities' in *T.L.S.*, 6-1-1956, p. VIII; G.R. Elton, *Henry VIII*, London, 1967 (Historical Association Pamphlet, no. 51), p. 4.

[91] Cf. A.G. Dickens in A.F. Pollard, *Henry VIII*, New York, 1966 (Harper Torchbook), p. XIV.

[92] Cf. A.F. Pollard, 'History and Science: a Rejoinder' in History 1 (1916–1917), p. 27; A.F. Pollard, *The League of Nations*, Oxford, 1918, p. 23.

the growth of the modern state and society. The connection could be 'proved' historically: the liberal principles of liberty and toleration could only become facts through, and because of, absolutism. "Toleration has been achieved by methods of persecution, and liberty by coercion."[93] The absolute power of the state had to destroy feudal and intermediary powers which had hamstrung it; on the foundations of the new absolute state individual freedom and religious toleration could develop. They both had to be enforced and guaranteed by the indivisible sovereign power of the state. "So long as the state was weak, it was cruel ... Political liberty and religious freedom depend upon the power of the state."[94]

Pollard's much praised small study, written for the Home University Library, and published in 1912 under the title *The History of England, A Study in Political Evolution*, closed with the above lines. It contained, in very compact form, what Neale had called 'the constitutional trend of his mind.' In 1912 Pollard no longer seemed to fear the traditionally distrusted power of the state as a threat to liberty. In Pollard's work, this power was turned into 'an indispensable weapon of progress.'[95] The two main articles of faith in 19th-century liberalism had been: national independence and popular self-government, each quite different from the other. Popular self-government could only succeed after national independence had been achieved.[96] The growth of England into a single nation-state had its medieval foundations, not, however, in the Anglo-Saxon period, which had no place in Pollard's scheme, but in the 'efficient despotism' of the Norman and Angevin kings: the foundations of the national monarchy had been laid by Henry II, and Pollard therefore considered him the precursor of Henry VIII.[97] In 1909 he wrote in a survey: "the aims of Henry II were not achieved till the reign of Henry VIII."[98] He thought that the ideal of self-government could only be partly achieved; but in any case a state of national unity was an absolute condition. In Pollard's conception nothing remained of the 'Anglo-Saxon local liberties' which the 19th century had extolled as a guarantee for self-government.

In this little study from 1912, and in all his work on the Tudors,

---

[93] *E.H.R.* 21 (1906), p. 164.
[94] A.F. Pollard, *The History of England. A Study in Political Evolution*, London, 1912, p. 246.
[95] *Ibid.*, pp. 245–246.
[96] *Ibid.*, chapters IV and V.
[97] *Ibid.*, pp. 51, 101.
[98] A.F. Pollard (ed.), *The British Empire*, London, 1909, p. 27.

Pollard characteristically uses Hobbes to support his views on the meaning and function of the Tudor monarchy. Generally Pollard had little interest in political theoreticians. And indeed political science owed more to the British colonies than to "all the armchair philosophers from Aristotle downwards."[99] Hobbes, however, is often referred to, for Pollard, though a Liberal, could wholly enter into Hobbes's absolutist way of thinking; and this fact in itself illustrates the shifting values within Liberal ideology around the turn of the century. Pollard used Hobbes to explain his views on the Tudor monarchy, which the Whigs had 'left out,' as it were, of their historical constitutionalism. Already in his *Henry VIII* Pollard had written: "*The Leviathan* is the best philosophical commentary on the Tudor system; Hobbes was Tudor and not Stuart in all his ideas ...."[100] The indivisible sovereign power of the state might have been abolished in the 18th century 'by the rights of man' (as Pollard said), but it had regained recognition in the modern age and lent an incomparable modernity – for Pollard – to the Tudor period.[101]

Under the Tudors even England had known a centralizing and 'equalizing' absolute monarchy; it had been the precondition for definitively ending the feudal past, which never could have been the immediate precursor of modern liberty. Pollard centered his attention upon the indispensability of the transition period between the feudal and modern eras. While former Liberals had been inspired by the Civil War or by the Glorious Revolution, Pollard emphasized rather the modernity of the Tudor period.

Consciously or not, the idea of efficiency, popular around 1900, influenced Pollard's work on the Tudors. He believed that an increased administrative efficiency proved the usefulness and the necessity of Tudor despotism; in a bout of pre-war optimism he even stated that a highly perfected efficiency would render a despotism superfluous: "The more efficient a despotism, the more certain is its supersession."[102] In any case, efficiency was a hallmark of the New Monarchy and it was this quality for which Henry VIII was praised.[103] When Pollard applied efficiency to constitutional doctrines, he would sometimes be in sharp disagreement with the theory of separation of powers. In this respect his ideas resembled those of the American progressives.

[99] *The History of England*, p. 215.
[100] *Henry VIII*, p. 348 (note 1); *Factors*, pp. 54, 57, 147–150; *Wolsey*, p. 371.
[101] Cf. *E.H.R.* 27 (1912), p. 577; *Henry VIII*, p. 273 (note 1); *The History of England*, p. 229.
[102] *The History of England*, p. 206, cf. pp. 33, 52, 129.
[103] Cf. *Henry VIII*, p. 295; *Factors*, p. 72.

He described, in 1910, the Tudor monarchy's greatest achievement as "the permanent transference of the initiative in legislation which had been excercised intermittently by barons and knights of the shire from the thirteenth to the fifteenth century, to the crown and its ministers." This was a necessary revolution, for Lancastrian constitutionalism's separation of powers "had been disastrous to the efficiency of government and dangerous to the existence of the State."[104] Pollard declared that Tudor England "grasped the practical bearings of the indivisibility of sovereignty, which had been Henry VIII's chief contribution to the body of modern constitutional law and theory."[105] Later on Pollard called this 'dangerous' theory of separation a myth when applied to English constitutional history. With his bias in favour of efficiency, Pollard saw this theory only as an obstacle to strong government. In the articles on Tudor history that Pollard wrote in the first decade of the twentieth century for the eleventh volume of the *Encyclopaedia Britannica*, the incidence of the term efficiency is remarkable. This rather vague contemporary political slogan became at times an equally vague, and not sufficiently specified, description of Tudor policy. Henry VIII "cared little for principle. But he had a passion for efficiency ..." And about Cecil: "To say that he was Machiavellian is meaningless, for every statesman is so more or less; especially the 16th century preferred efficiency to principle."[106] "Even when all conscious bias is eliminated, the unconscious bias remains ...," was Pollard's conclusion about historical writing in general (in the same encyclopaedia).[107]

The ideas that Pollard maintained about the Tudor period are not traceable to a single influence, even though the medievalist P. Williams believes that J.N. Figgis did have such a decisive influence on Pollard.[108] It is, however, evident that his ideas took shape in a period when classic liberalism was past its prime. Significant in this respect is Pollard's sympathy for power (at least in the years before the First World War). In fact, his attitude could be compared to Lord Morley's,

---

[104] *The Political History*, p. 149.
[105] *Ibid.*, p. 212.
[106] *Encyclopaedia Britannica*, vol. IV, p. 817, vol. VIII, p. 290.
[107] *Ibid.*, vol. IX, p. 586.
[108] P. Williams, 'Dr. Elton's Interpretation of the Age' in *Past and Present* 25 (1963), p. 7, note 2; cf. Pollard on J.N. Figgis in *The Evolution of Parliament*, pp. 14, 198 (note 1), 216; A.F. Pollard, 'Some Causes of the Reformation' in *The Churchman* 40 (1926), p. 12. There are undeniable differences of stress, but Pollard's more secular conception of sovereignty (inspired by Hobbes) is largely identical with Figgis's idea, at least where the Tudor monarchy is concerned. For the significance of Figgis's work see G.R. Elton in: J.N. Figgis, *The Divine Right of Kings*, New York, 1965 (Harper Torchbook), pp. VII–XXXI.

whose Cromwell-biography and lectures on Machiavelli in 1897 were admired by Pollard.[109] In these lectures Morley indubitably fulminated against 'the Bismarckian gospel of Force,' and against a revived *Realpolitik* under imperialism. Yet a note of admiration can be discerned for the hard realist, Machiavelli, who had discarded all fruitless speculations about the 'ideal state' to proclaim the theory of the *raison d'état*. "If we were to try to put the case for the Machiavellian philosophy in a modern way, it would, I suppose, be something of this kind: Nature does not work by moral rules," Morley said in 1897.[110]

For all his mental reserves and all liberal criticism notwithstanding, Morley was fascinated by 'the men of iron' in politics, by Cromwell, Strafford, Bismarck. He, too, came to see power as a quality in itself and he "looked upon the exercise of power as in itself an admirable quality no matter what might be the end to which power was being applied."[111] Pollard held a similar attitude towards power, describing Henry VIII often as 'Machiavelli's *Prince* in action.'[112] In *Henry VIII* he represented the contrast between 'morals' and 'politics' as a 'terrible contradiction' inherent to state and society.[113] "Politics ... are akin to the operation of natural forces; and, as such, they are neither moral nor immoral; they are simply non-moral."[114] This sounds like an echo of Morley's argument about Machiavelli. Pollard did not share Acton's enthusiasm for a stringently moral view in historical writing; he dismissed the idea as being unhistorical.[115]

Somerset had demonstrated that the political situation was not yet ripe for the liberal ideal of freedom to be put into practice; his 'experiment' had come to an untimely end because of lack of realism, opportunism and expediency. But whatever realism Somerset lacked Henry VIII possessed in abundance, and it made him a successful statesman. What had caused former Liberals to cringe – the factor of power – was realistically acknowledged by Pollard's liberal and historical argument. This factor occupies an important place in Pollard's interpretation of the evolution of political liberties. The central theme

---

[109] Cf. A.F. Pollard, 'Lord Morley on History' in *History* 3 (1918–1919), pp. 210–221; A.F. Pollard, 'Biographers and Historians' in *History* 13 (1928–1929), pp. 315–324; Pollard repeatedly declared his approval of Morley's criticism of Macaulay, see: *Cranmer*, pp. 304–305, and A.F. Pollard, *The League of Nations*, Oxford, 1918, pp. 45–46.
[110] *The Works of Lord Morley*, London, 1924, vol. IV, p. 134; p. 243 refers to Pollard's *Somerset* (Cf. *Somerset*, p. 284).
[111] D.A. Hamer, *op. cit.*, p. 53.
[112] *Henry VIII*, p. 353, cf. p. 222; *Factors*, pp. 78, 136–137.
[113] *Henry VIII*, pp. XXVI, 351.
[114] *Ibid.*, p. 351.
[115] *Factors*, p. 137; *E.H.R.* 21 (1906), p. 164.

of his work on the Tudors is the dialectical argument about modern freedom being born of constraint. The Whigs had not noticed this paradox because of their linear historical and constitutional thinking, which used to project the result straight back to an origin wholly identical with that result.

Pollard considered that, viewed historically, an ideal often came about by ways and means whose apparent purpose seemed far removed from the stated aim. Often enough an ideal became realized unintentionally, or even as a consequence of an act having an opposed purpose. It was precisely the tensions between aims and means, between ethics and politics, that made Pollard sharply aware of incongruous situations and unexpected developments; more often than not his conclusion was an unmistakable paradox, formulated in that rocky style which so greatly puzzled his critics. Though Pollard's *The Evolution of Parliament* is the best example of his 'paradoxical' interpretation of history, earlier works carry the same stamp.

J.A. Gairdner wrote two reviews of Pollard's *Henry VIII*[116]; in the first review, in 1902, Pollard's theories about the constitutionalism of Henry were classified as "mere paradoxes, not only without apparent warrants, but sometimes with comments and arguments which seem to carry with them their own refutation."[117] In his review of the scientific edition of 1905, he objected again to a too favourable interpretation of Henry's (political) behaviour. Gairdner particularly disliked the passages in the first part dealing with the King's conscience. Pollard explained Henry's conscience as a curious mixture of ethical norms and political necessities, with a predominance of the latter. He called Henry's conscience 'convenient' and 'skillful'; it equalled the sharp practices of Machiavelli's Prince in political affairs. Pollard pointed out that this conscience had an unscrupulous background, that it committed criminal self-deception, and that it rationalized self-interest.[118] In 1904, Pollard wrote of Henry VIII: "he is not the only figure in history who has possessed the useful faculty of really convincing his conscience that what is personally desirable and politically

---

[116] Cf. *Atheneum*, 6-7-1902, p. 115: *E.H.R.* 21 (1906), pp. 155–157. See also Gairdner's review of Pollard's *Somerset* in *E.H.R.* 16 (1901), pp. 151–153. Gairdner on 1-12-1896 wrote to Acton in modest terms: "I am not a born historian myself, but history has grown upon me as an official duty and all I have hitherto written *apart* from official duty has really been a good deal in the nature of exercitations to enlarge my own field of view which I always felt very much needed enlargement." C.U.L., Add.MS. 6443.

[117] *Atheneum*, 6-7-1902, p. 115.

[118] Cf. *Henry VIII*, pp. 156, 168, 195.

expedient must therefore be morally right."[119] His psycho-political approach to the King's conscience slightly resembles the psycho-political realism of his friend Graham Walles.[120] "Conscience ... often moves men in directions indicated by other than conscientious motives," wrote Pollard in 1902.[121] The unassuming Gairdner had no other option than to capitulate humbly in the face of such paradoxes: "This is very refined metaphysics and for my part I give it up."[122] Much as Pollard stressed the fact, Gairdner could not see that Henry VIII's constitutionalism was really necessary; Henry's behaviour remained unconstitutional to him. "Such criticism makes all our government prior to 1832 unconstitutional ..." Pollard afterwards noted with regard to this criticism.[123]

In the Roman Catholic camp many blamed Pollard for having denied the significance of men like More and Fisher, in order to promote Henry VIII.[124] For had not these two defended individual conscience? Pollard doubted this: as he saw it, they had refused to follow the King more because of the authority of their Church than because of the dictates of their own individual conscience.[125] "The dispute ... passes the wit of man to decide." We cannot avoid being reminded of the twenty-ninth chapter of Hobbes's *Leviathan*, commended by Pollard for its relevance to Tudor despotism. Pollard writes: "If conscience must reign supreme, all government is a *pis aller*, and in anarchy the true millennium must be found."[126]

His paradoxes were not confined only to human behaviour, with or without the veils of rationalization: the progress of history itself was also permeated by paradoxes. The historian cannot ignore these, or he risks lack of understanding for historical developments. Henry VIII contributed to the development of parliament; he respected its privileges, he acknowledged its authority, and by means of this body he created a firm foundation for his own reign. The Reformation parliament differed from all medieval parliaments in expressing a 'national' feeling; its long duration fostered a fellow-feeling among the members, which in turn strengthened the parliamentary structure. Innocently, unintentionally

---

[119] *Cranmer*, p. 33.
[120] *Ibid.*, p. X.
[121] *Henry VIII*, p. 144.
[122] *E.H.R.* 21 (1906), p. 156.
[123] See Pollard's Notebook, entry of 12-7-1911. MS. top.oxon.d. 442. B.L. Oxford.
[124] J. Gerard, 'An Apologist for Henry VIII' in *The Month, A Catholic Magazine* 106 (1905), pp. 474–487.
[125] *Henry VIII*, p. 266 (note 3).
[126] *Henry VIII*, p. 267; cf. *Cranmer*, p. 363; cf. *The Political History*, p. 132.

did Henry VIII personally forge the weapon which was in the end to take away monarchy's real power. Being the 'architect of parliament,' he played his part in contributing to the final development and the growth of the free parliamentary form of government.[127] If the end result had even in part been known to Henry, he would doubtlessly have pursued an opposite course.

An important element of Pollard's evolutionism was his emphasis on the *Heterogonie der Zwecke* – the irony and accident of historical development. This emphasis of Pollard's evolutionism was largely a reaction against a too finalist view of the historical development, a picture in which the quality of the final results was far too easily identified with the cause. While contemporaries might try to direct such development, actual history never progressed according to those directives. Thus could the awareness of later results obscure the historian's understanding of earlier events; finalism, or thinking in terms of a linear development might, if carried to extremes, render historiography a sterile waste of time.[128]

Pollard was not at all averse to broad outlines, to that finalism which is indispensable for historical interpretation. Indeed his theory of the Tudor despotism had finalist features. His evolutionism, however, was dialectical, giving full scope to chance and to the unplanned aspects of the entire historical development. He differed from the 19th-century historiographers in stressing that history was unintentionally purposeful.

While discussing the revaluation of the Tudor despotism we have focused on Pollard's underlying theory, defined by the historian P. Williams as "the establishment of national sovereignty which freed men from the restrictions of the Middle Ages by establishing the order that was essential to liberty."[129] Seen against the background of 19th-century Whig historiography, Pollard's conception certainly is an important innovation. We attempted to indicate the role a changed liberalism played in clearing the road for this innovation. Pollard's historical research was not hampered by his liberal convictions; on the contrary, he found them advantageous in the rediscovery of a significant 'forgotten' constitutional aspect of the 16th century. He was also

---

[127] *Factors*, pp. 97, 110.
[128] Cf. *Cranmer*, pp. 307–308.
[129] P. Williams, *op. cit.*, p. 3.

guided by them in arranging the almost innumerable facts; "selection is inevitable, and arrangement essential. The historian has no option if he wishes to be intelligible."[130]

Pollard's work made English historians familiar with the idea that 'true liberty can only be brought about by exterminating medieval liberties.' C.H. Firth wrote: "This is the general principle which while far from exhausting its significance is essential to the understanding of that complicated series of movements known as the English Reforma-ation."[131] And in 1926 the 'Whig' Trevelyan could write:

The judicial and political "liberties" of the medieval clergy and aristocracy, slices of sovereignty held in private or corporate hands, were abolished in favour of the liberty of the ordinary English subject, sheltered behind the power of the State.[132]

For Pollard this general principle was like a working hypothesis; it provided his research with a perspective. Some medievalists have doubted the utility and relevance of Pollard's Tudor theories for the 16th-century constitutional and administrative development.[133] A rigid notion of sovereignty provides little information about a State's labo-rious growth to power, which Pollard fully realized. The establishment of the absolute sovereignty of the state was a slow process and its realiza-tion was beset with difficulties, partly because the central government still lacked sufficient power and partly because the Tudor centralism was stubbornly resisted by some of the feudal and local powers.[134]

Although Pollard's general interpretation of the Tudor period has not lost its value despite many later refinements and corrections of details, it has largely been stripped of its 'character of necessity,' a trait necessitated by his historical evolutionism, and emphasized in reaction to the earlier historiographical tradition. We have already referred to Pollard's lack of interest in the religious Reformation, for which he was criticized by contemporary and subsequent historians.[135] Pollard's 'one-sidedness' deliberately emphasized the political aspects of the Reformation. His picture of the importance of the Statesman-King has been essentially corrected by G.R. Elton's studies showing Thomas Cromwell's central part in administrative innovations. Pollard was of

---

[130] *Henry VIII*, p. XXVIII.
[131] *E.H.R.* 32 (1917), p. 175.
[132] *History* 11 (1926–1927), p. 12.
[133] P. Williams, 'The Tudor State' in *Past and Present* no. 25 (1963), p. 44.
[134] Cf. on the feudal rising of 1569, *The Political History*, p. 278 ff; cf. *Evolution*, p. 227.
[135] Cf. E.W. Watson in *E.H.R.* 19 (1904), pp. 777–780; A. Marshal in *The Scottish Historical Review* 9 (1911), pp. 294–296; S.L. Ollard in *E.H.R.* 27 (1912), pp. 780–783.

course acquainted with the first few studies early in the century dealing with Thomas Cromwell: Thomas Cromwell's letters were published in 1902 by R.B. Merriman, Pollard's American critic.[136]

But Pollard warned against overrating Thomas Cromwell. Tradition (the inimical Catholic tradition, above all) had regarded him too much as the 'maker' of the Reformation and as the real leader of government after 1530. "Cromwell ... was not the author of that policy, but he was the most efficient instrument in its execution."[137] Pollard's own overestimation of Henry VIII's statesmanship scarcely left room for Cromwell's creative abilities in governmental affairs. The fourteenth chapter of *Henry VIII* testifies most plainly to the contemporary nature of Pollard's writing: Henry is *rex et imperator*, the father of modern imperialism. As Pollard saw it, the king's policy of integrating Wales and Scotland was the result of his striving for efficiency combined with an 'imperial vision.'[138] A liberal imperialist, Pollard exaggerated Henry's imperialism, for which he has been corrected by J.J. Scarisbrick.[139]

We are not here concerned with enumerating the points on which Pollard's works on the Tudors are criticized by modern historiographers. His Wolsey biography will be dealt with later; here we should decide the extent to which his view of the Tudors influenced his view of English parliamentary developments.

C. PARLIAMENT'S UNPARLIAMENTARY ORIGIN AND EVOLUTION

1. *In the steps of F.W. Maitland*

It had been thought that the First World War had influenced Pollard's most contested work, which appeared in 1920.[140] However, most of the essays in *The Evolution of Parliament* had already been written before

[136] R.B. Merriman, *The Life and Letters of Thomas Cromwell*, Oxford, 1902. See R.B. Merriman's reviews of Pollard's works in *A.H.R.* 10 (1904–1905), pp. 861–863; 11 (1905–1906), pp. 650–651; 13 (1907–1908), pp. 571–572; 16 (1910–1911), pp. 600–602. Cf. on Henry VIII's independent policy the very carefully worded observation by J.J. Scarisbrick in his *Henry VIII*, London, 1968, pp. 396–397, 408 ff., 551.

[137] Cf. *Encyclopaedia Britannica*, vol. VII, 1910, p. 500; cf. *Henry VIII*, p. 259; *Evolution*, pp. 266–269.

[138] *Henry VIII*, p. 290 ff.

[139] J.J. Scarisbrick, *Henry VIII*, London, 1968, p. 424 ff.

[140] Cf. H.J. Randall, *The Creative Centuries. A Study in Historical Development*, London, 1944, p. 238.

1914. Any possible ideological influence is far more likely to be connected with the crisis symptoms mentioned in our third chapter, dealing with discredited traditions. The turn-of-the-century political climate gave rise to a new historiography concerning parliament, which has been commonly called a 'Copernican revolution.'[141] This ideological factor enabled modern historians to take up a less involved attitude towards the past. In the words of J.G. Edwards, this factor may be described as "the general spirit of the Age, which no longer regards representative government as being axiomatically 'a good thing.'"[142] Pollard was writing under the pressure of a very mixed company of critics of the parliamentary system, consisting of bureaucrats, syndicalists, upholders of the referendum system, and 'believers in the sovereignty of force'; now it was more difficult to defend the parliament's right to exist, but contemporary criticism also made it easier to have a more historical view: "if it were true that parliament has run its course of public utility, that fact would make it all the easier to determine its place in history."[143]

The one historian of far-reaching importance for the preparatory stages of Pollard's work was undoubtedly F.W. Maitland. His *Memoranda* became the point of departure for Pollard's labour, and Pollard chose to follow Maitland when, in 1908, he was offered a fellowship of All Souls' College "on condition of pursuing researches, suggested by the late F.W. Maitland."[144] Pollard claimed that Maitland's original essay of 1893 had not received its due share of attention; it had not even been included in Maitland's *Collected Papers* of 1911.[145] Pollard was also well aware of the fact that after 1890 the innovation in English historical scholarship had been due to medievalists like Maitland, and he regretted that especially their exertions were neglected in general historiographical surveys.[146] Yet Pollard was not a medievalist, nor did he become one while preparing his *Evolution*. As he explained, he did not possess the necessary 'technical' knowledge of many details. Another weakness was that he had missed reading some significant recent literature; in later years he openly admitted being unacquainted with the early pioneering work of the German L. Riess,

[141] G. Templeman, 'The History of Parliament to 1499 in the Light of Modern Research' in *University of Birmingham Historical Journal* 1 (1947–1948), p. 205.

[142] J.G. Edwards, *Historians and the Medieval English Parliament*, Glasgow, 1970, p. 27.

[143] *Evolution*, p. 2.

[144] *Evolution*, p. V; *E.H.R.* 23 (1908), p. 789.

[145] *Evolution*, p. VI; Cf. G.O. Sayles, *The King's Parliament of England*, London, 1975, p. 14.

[146] Cf. *E.H.R.* 22 (1907), p. 393 and *E.H.R.* 28 (1913), p. 754.

a man well-known both to Maitland and Stubbs.[147] Nevertheless Pollard, a Tudor historian, ventured back into medieval history precisely to widen his understanding of the Tudor constitution.

Only occasionally do scattered reviews and articles give us more than a glimpse of the direction in which Pollard travelled during these preparatory years. Sometimes he appeared to oppose Stubbs when he spoke of the need for expunging from people's minds 'the familiar notions of Parliament.' According to Pollard, most historians placed the completion of the constitution too early, at the end of the Middle Ages and before the modern Tudor phase, simply because the greatest of English constitutional historians, Stubbs, had not proceeded further than the Middle Ages.[148] Pollard also opposed the traditional narrative style of constitutional historiography: he wanted a more 'analytical' approach. This criticism was already evidenced in the review in which he rejected E. Barker's study *The Dominican Order and Convocation. A Study of the Growth of Representation in the Church during the Thirteenth Century.*[149] Barker's thesis was that the growth of the representative parliament was the result of the democratic principle of representation, whose origins he believed were to be found in the constitution of the Dominican order.

Pollard declared that this too idealistic explanation of Barker's reckoned without the feudal reality of the Middle Ages. Barker did not follow Maitland: "He ... ignores the idea of suit and service as a factor in the high court of parliament, and the feudal conditions from which it sprang."[150] Original representation was 'more like an incident of feudal tenure' than a modern democratic principle. "Mr. Barker is too much of an idealist for this political materialism; in spite of his admission of the importance of the local life of the shire, he will not admit the importance of local representation in the shire court as a basis for national representation in parliament."[151]

So Pollard criticized Barker for not paying sufficient attention to

---

[147] *Evolution*, p. X. C.H. McIlwain's work of 1910, *The High Court of Parliament and its Supremacy* was consulted. At the time Riess's work had been extensively reviewed by G.W. Prothero in *E.H.R.* 5 (1890), pp. 146–156; his *Geschichte des Wahlrechts zum Englischen Parlament im Mittelalter* (1885) was translated in 1940 under the title *The History of English Electoral Law in the Middle Ages*. See H.G. Richardson in *E.H.R.* 56 (1941) pp. 339–340. Cf. also G. Lapsley in *E.H.R.* 28 (1913), p. 120.

[148] A.F. Pollard (ed.), *The Reign of Henry VII*, London, 1913–1914, I, pp. XXVIII–XXIX en p. XXXII; cf. *E.H.R.* 27 (1912), p. 576 ff.

[149] *E.H.R.* 29 (1914), pp. 146–148.

[150] *E.H.R.* 29 (1914), p. 147.

[151] *E.H.R.* 29 (1914), pp. 147–148; Pollard had many a dispute with Barker, see on the conception of 'state,' *T.L.S.*, 23-9-1920, p. 618.

Maitland in his approach, and in the last quotation he also blamed Barker for not giving Stubbs's so-called (first) concentration theory its proper due.[152] For Pollard might be following Maitland, but it is later often forgotten that his *Evolution* also refers to Stubbs's ideas. But he did disagree with Stubbs on several other points, dismissing Stubbs's notion of a 'model parliament' in 1295. While he perceived a 'model parliament' under Edward I, it was in a different and a wider sense than Stubbs had done. "One of the chief causes of differentiation between English and French constitutional history is that *parlement* and *états* were amalgamated in England, but kept distinct in France. This amalgamation was Edward I's real contribution to 'a model parliament,'" Pollard wrote in 1915, anticipating the third chapter of his *Evolution*.[153]

In the first months of 1914 Pollard delivered six lectures on the parliament under the Tudors, and later came fifteen lectures in the United States on the evolution of parliament.[154] The two series of lectures may be regarded as an important first outline of his work of 1920, the manuscript of which was finished in August 1915. In the introductory lecture of the first series he proposed a number of essential themes: parliament as a 'high court', the judicial origin of parliament as something 'fatal' to the theory of the 'three estates'; representation as a burden, the gradual change 'from law to politics' when individual petitions were replaced by common ones; the fundamental unity of the constitution, allowing for a specialization of functions, not for a separation of powers, and as final theme 'Henry VIII and the foundation of constitutional government.'[155]

Each of these themes was further elaborated upon in lectures with the following titles: 'the Crown in Parliament,' 'the Lords in Parliament,' 'the Commons in Parliament,' 'Parliament and the Church,' and finally, 'Parliament and the State.' In his lecture about the Lords as well as in that on the Commons Pollard repeatedly drew attention to the many unplanned, unexpected and even accidental aspects of the history of parliament. "No party or dynasty has ever achieved what it set out to do: the ultimate results of policies have been far different from the designs of their originations."[156]

[152] *E.H.R.* 29 (1914), p. 148: "Mr. Barker has left the law out of his account of the genesis of English representative institutions."
[153] *E.H.R.* 30 (1915), p. 662 (note 12).
[154] Delivered on January 29th, February 5, 12, 19 and 26, and March 5, 1914.
[155] See 'Notes taken by Miss E.J. Davis on various matters, including some of A.F. Pollard's lectures,' Add. MS. 19, Library University College.
[156] See 'Notes' by Miss E.J. Davis, p. 39 ff.

Pollard's conviction that much in the course of history is unexpected and accidental, is especially clear in his work of 1920. His accidentalism differed from the later accidentalism of Bury in that it was far less extreme.[157] It did not deny that there might be a fundamental causality, actually, it was a reflection of Wundt's theory of the *Heterogonie der Zwecke*. In October 1916, he gave a detailed explanation of his accidentalist theories in the rather notorious Creighton-lecture about the growth of an 'Imperial Parliament.' This matter had become of current interest since the war, the financial burdens of the war being incumbent upon the Dominions also. If a new Imperial Parliament were created it could well be expected to guarantee that all Commonwealth members should have more immediate influence on all matters pertaining to international politics. The likelihood of this development was slender in Pollard's sceptical opinion: with historical arguments, he warned his listeners to be cautious. As he expressed it, his 'whole conception of history' was present in his argument; it contained a sharp rejection of a political utopism based on overrating the capacities of Man as a 'conscious creator'.[158] He had different ideas of 'human nature in politics', basing his opinions on his understanding of the development of parliament. He rejected the myth that the English were born with a genius for parliamentary democracy, and stated that no single part of the constitution showed signs of having originated in a conscious plan or design: the constitution, such as it was, was the result of material and ideological conflicts. The history of parliament could thus be defined as "the record of a development in which human design has played an almost insignificant part."[159]

This definition is the core of Pollard's lyrical praise for 'historical growth,' a recurrent topic in his *Evolution* of 1920.[160] It seemed as if the consequences of these opinions for the present were a return to a *laissez faire* mentality, but nothing was farther from Pollard's mind: if he exaggerated, it was because he wanted to warn against political utopism and extremism, two qualities often found in the designers of constitutions. Still it is (and was) remarkable, at first sight, that Pollard, a great believer in efficient organizing, should have stressed the im-

---

[157] Cf. Pollard's criticism of Bury in *The Churchman* 40 (1926), p. 93 and *T.L.S.* 3-3-1932, p. 141.

[158] A.F. Pollard, 'The Growth of an Imperial Parliament' in *History* 1 (1916–1917), pp. 129–130.

[159] *History* 1 (1916–1917), p. 133.

[160] *Evolution*, pp. 29, 45, 120, 216–217, 239; cf. *History* 1 (1916–1917), p. 132: "The sovereignty of Parliament is itself a growth; that is why it exists, for a sovereignty that is created is a contradiction in terms."

portance of the non-planned aspects of the historical development. Pollard's theory of evolution, with so little apparent space for a self-assured and creative mankind, was a source of great irritation for quite a number of people. R. Muir, a liberal politician and historian, declared that it baffled him to find an eminent historian utter such an opinion; as for the antithesis between 'human design' and 'human evolution,' he thought it was insufferable exaggeration: "as a sound Tory, he is all for evolution."[161]

Pollard's views gave the impression that the entire British constitution had come about 'almost by accident.' It was a paradox which did not appeal to Pollard's fellow historian, T.F. Tout.[162] And finally, there was the critic, D.O. Malcolm, who supposed that Pollard had been trying indirectly to contradict the ideas of Lionel Curtis, who had put it so much more optimistically and hopefully in his *Problem of the Commonwealth*, writing: "Human institutions do not grow; they are made by human will for the realisation of human purposes."[163] Curtis' view seemed to be the exact opposite of Pollard's paradoxes.

Replying to his critics, Pollard later explained that his Creighton-lecture had been "a brief indication of a view of the development of the British Constitution which I worked out more fully in a book, written two years ago but still unpublished owing to the war."[164] He denied having attacked Curtis in his lecture; he had not meant that 'growth' and 'design' were irreconcilable opposites. He had merely intended to show that the evolution of an institution had countless times in history made a mockery of the original plan. He had acquired this knowledge by scientific research; it had no connection with old Liberal ideology. All it did was advocate caution. For the rest, Pollard had no faith as yet in a coming constitution for the Commonwealth: it would be little else than another piece of paper. "If I am tainted with historical fatalism in Imperial politics, it is a fatalism of faith, and not of fear."[165]

Pollard's own exaggeration was largely the cause of the misunderstandings. His adage that 'institutions are not made but grow' was quite ancient, but he did not seem aware of its historical origin. He was afterwards surprised to come across it, in the same words, in Morley's work; his surprise seems rather naïve,[166] as this motto had

[161] *History* 1 (1916–1917), pp. 194–195.
[162] T.F. Tout, *Collected Papers*, Manchester, 1934, vol. III, p. 65.
[163] *History* 1 (1916–1917), p. 199.
[164] A.F. Pollard, 'The Growth of an Imperial Parliament: a Rejoinder' in *History* 2 (1917–1918), p. 3.
[165] *Ibid.*, p. 11.
[166] Cf. *History* 3 (1918–1919), p. 221.

occupied a central place in political romanticism, as well as being used in the old Whig literature of Burke and Mackintosh.[167] However, Pollard was using this old adage not as a weapon against the revolution, but as evidence of the 'irony of history,' in a way recalling Spencer's thoughts on the same subject. Thus did the adage make its way into the pages of *The Evolution of Parliament*, a book that in the months preceding its publication had been announced as the final breakthrough in parliamentary historiography after its age-old bondage to 'myths' and 'fictions.'[168] But was it?

2. *Pollard's confusing abundance*

> Parliament in the middle ages was ... a set of conditions under which men acted rather than itself the agent ... Under the Tudors it became an entity and an authority, active and independent ...
>
> (A.F. Pollard, 1920)

A work which the author intended solely as a broad outline for the model of parliamentary history in the future is difficult to summarize; such a summary may degenerate into a dry synopsis of Pollard's 'shrewd generalisations' (Notestein). It consists of 18 essays, in which neither the sequence nor the interrelationship are always very clear; trains of thought are sometimes annoyingly repeated. Still, we shall attempt a brief summary. Following the plan of our second chapter, there will again be three central questions to our argument: the function of parliament, its composition, and the place of the Commons.

First, however, we must emphasize that Pollard took a wider view of 'function' than may have been usual in parliamentary historiography. He was especially fascinated by parliament's historical function in the forging of England into a nation; unintentional as it was, this function served as background for all his observations. The process of 'nation-building' was for Pollard more than a simple dynastic matter: mon-

---

[167] Cf. Hedva Ben-Israel, *op. cit.*, p. 38; J.S. Mill, *Utilitarianism, Liberty and Representative Government*, ed. A.D. Lindsay, London, 1964, p. 176. Pollard's thoughts in this respect greatly resemble H. Spencer's. See H. Spencer, *The Man versus the State*, ed. D.Macrae, Harmondsworth, 1969, pp. 33 ff., 195–198.

[168] *T.L.S.*, 26-2-1920, p. 134: "Professor A.F. Pollard had a new work in the press ... entitled *The Evolution of Parliament*, the object of which is to clean away the fictions of the seventeenth and later centuries relating to the origins and development of Parliamentary institutions. Similar fictions with regard to feudalism have been exposed by Maitland and other scholars, but it is urged that conceptions of Parliament which were framed to meet the controversial needs of the seventeenth century still persist and dominate current constitutional history."

archy did have a central place, but parliament was still the most important instrument. "Parliament has ... been the peculiar means through which the English people achieved their unity and nationality ...."[169]

England had grown to nationhood through a gradual (parliamentary) process; in this respect Stubbs's idea concerning parliament as a concentration of local communities is repeated in Pollard's work.[170] "Insufficient meaning has sometimes been attached to Stubbs' remark that the medieval house of Commons was a concentration of county-courts," Pollard remarked in 1926.[171] Stubbs's concentration theory occupied a special place in Pollard's argument, but only after Pollard had stripped it of the classical 19th-century idea of self-government. As he saw it, the concentration of shire and borough communities in one single parliament, that one single House of Commons which was a *communitas communitatum*, had finally tamed medieval localism and provincialism, and thereby prevented the continental development of local and provincial representative bodies. Now that the Crown had united the shires in parliament, a foundation was laid for a national feeling: shire joined shire, borough joined borough.

The innovation was stimulated from 'above,' *viz.* by the central government. Self-government was only possible after this national consciousness had come into being by means of this parliamentary organization. The development of parliament and the growth into a national state went hand in hand. "It is really co-eval with them both"; parliament partly 'created' national consciousness and was partly 'created' by it.[172] Pollard devoted a whole chapter in his *Evolution* to this unintended yet highly significant result. Later in his career he again dealt explicitly with this theme in his discussion of the Reformation parliament.[173]

Did Pollard in his second essay on 'The High Court of Parliament' go any further than Maitland in his discussion of the original judicial function of parliament and the essential place of the council? Hardly. Pollard too made Fleta's familiar text his starting point, although he did use more material to illustrate and justify his opinion. However, he never denied that this original function did not exclude divers other

[169] *Evolution*, p. 9, cf. p. 4 and p. 132 ff.; the later reviewers paid hardly any attention to Pollard's wide perspective.
[170] *Ibid.*, pp. 67, 80, 107–114, 140–142.
[171] *Ibid.*, p. 422.
[172] *Ibid.*, pp. 4, 148.
[173] A.F. Pollard, 'The Reformation Parliament as a Matrimonial Agency and its National Effects' in *History* 21 (1936–1937), pp. 219–229.

functions.[174] The end of his essay, where he dealt with the remarkable frequency of early parliaments, is especially interesting. Pollard, unwittingly following Allen and Hallam's explanation of a hundred years ago, equally explained this early frequency as a result of the judicial function.[175]

In the next chapter, dealing with the moulding of Parliament under Edward I, Pollard went further. The meaning of this period, according to him, was to be found in the concurrence of two different types of sittings: the regular periodical sessions of the Royal Council 'inside' parliament as a judicial court, and the irregular gatherings of this council with the estates 'inside' a parliament which was an assembly of estates. In his view there was a complete discrepancy between the Parliamentary Writs summoning the latter type of sitting, and the Rolls of Parliament, which contained the reports of the earlier type of meetings; these could be compared to the parliament of Paris, and Pollard, unlike Stubbs, considered them to be the original type of parliament.[176]

His later critics, Richardson and Sayles, on the one hand regarded the stated discrepancy as proof that Pollard's research had been rather shallow; on the other hand, they welcomed Pollard's explanation as a vague, tentative beginning of their own highly explicit views: "He (Pollard) seems to have been on the verge of accepting 'regular sessions' of the records as the true parliaments, scouting the idea that there could be anything vague and uncertain about a scheme which involved adjournments from one parliament to the next parliament."[177] Like Maitland before him, Pollard too pointed out that parliament under Edward I could hardly be called an 'institution' ("Parliament is *vox et praeterea nihil*"). The fact that it was frequent and occurred periodically, indicated a judicial function, but did not lead him to conclude that there was at that period an institutionalized parliament *sui generis* with an exclusively judicial function, as did later the two medievalists we mentioned.[178]

His essay in *The Evolution* dealing with 'the myth of the three estates'

[174] *Evolution*, p. 35.
[175] Cf. *Evolution*, pp. 42–43 and 130–131; Pollard was quite familiar with Palgrave's work. For Palgrave, see pp. 99 (note 1), 117 (note 2), 242 (note 2), 251 (note 2), 270 (note 2); see also *Factors*, pp. 301–302.
[176] *Evolution*, pp. 47–51. "The gatherings convoked by these so-called "parliamentary" writs were not parliaments; and the meetings called parliaments in the rolls were not summoned by the writs to which the name has since been given" (p. 47).
[177] H.G. Richardson, G.O. Sayles, *Parliaments and Great Councils in Medieval England*, London, 1961, pp. 5–6, 47; cf. *B.I.H.R.* 5 (1927–1928), pp. 133–134, 143–144.
[178] Cf. *Evolution*, p. 46. More of their opinions later.

has probably been most widely discussed. The theory of the three estates disregarded medieval parliament in its origin and function, and this was the point Pollard attacked: "... in a system of three estates there is no natural or logical place for the large official and legal element which we find throughout in the high court of parliament."[179] Our second chapter showed that this theory accounted hardly (if at all) for the judicial function and the 'conciliar' character in its composition. To Pollard it was no less important that this theory denied the quintessence of the House of Commons as 'a concentration of all the communities of England.' For did not a system of estates mean that separate groups had to be represented? If that myth had ever been a political reality in England, parliament could not have been instrumental in bringing national unity about, and yet that was for Pollard the most important aspect of parliamentary history.[180]

We shall omit Pollard's discussion of 'the fiction of the peerage,' preceded by a short argument about the damage done by the 'legal mind' to historical thought. Subsequent medievalists were to criticize this chapter sharply.[181] Evidently, Pollard's survey was inimical to the Lords; whether the crisis of the House of Lords was an additional (be it subconscious) cause of this, as Huizinga suggested, is hard to prove.[182]

The Commons, unlike the Lords, were not alienated from their historical origin. As to that, the argument in Pollard's sixth chapter (dealing with the growth of the House of Commons) was clearly influenced by Stubbs ('the county court is the foundation of the house of commons'), but he had no patience with Stubbs's exaggerated ideas when the function, the place and the position of the Commons in the medieval parliament were in question.[183] The Commons gained in significance when, in the fourteenth century, 'law' had turned into 'politics,' and after common petitions had become more numerous than individual ones; but still their legislative authority was not acknowledged.[184] Another sign of a growing political sense of unity in

---

[179] *Ibid.*, p. 67.

[180] *Ibid.*, pp. 67, 77.

[181] *Ibid.*, p. 83. Cf. also 'The Nature of History' in *T.L.S.* 25-9-1919, pp. 505–506 (presumably by Pollard). See for criticism, T.F. Tout, *Chapters in the Administrative History of Medieval England*, 6 vols., Manchester, 1920–1933, III, pp. 137–138. See also J. Tait in a more favourable review in *E.H.R.* 36 (1921), pp. 256–257.

[182] J. Huizinga, *Verzamelde Werken*, Haarlem, 1949, vol. IX, p. 176. Of course Pollard was in favour of having the 'inefficient' House of Lords abolished or radically reformed. He often referred to the medieval 'peers' as 'a clique of barons' (*Evolution*, p. 114).

[183] *Evolution*, p. 115 ff.

[184] Cf. also the later much discussed Statute of York of 1322, *Evolution*, pp. 129, 241–242; cf. G. Lapsley, 'The Interpretation of the Statute of York' in *E.H.R.* 56 (1941), pp. 22–51; 411–446. See for the change of 'law' to 'politics': *Evolution*, pp. 60, 118–120, 127 ff.

the Commons, apart from the common petitions, was the emergence of an internal organization (the function of the Speaker). Yet Pollard maintained that it was dangerous to believe too much in the significance of all this. The ruling idea behind his denials, almost an obsession in his work, was the old conception that representation during the Middle Ages had been a burden from which people tried to escape. Pollard felt that this view was justified when, in 1920, he compared the parliamentary writs with the writs *de expensis*; in other words, he compared the number of people summoned with the number obeying the summons. The great discrepancy between the two he showed in a subsequent chapter dealing with the Commons.[185]

This was one more cause for the black-and-white picture of a passive medieval Commons, as contrasted to the more active Commons under the Tudors. Allied to this are numerous typical Pollardian conceptions interspersed throughout his work. To his mind, infrequently summoned parliaments with more sessions and of a longer duration (as under the Tudors) were more important than frequent short-lived parliaments of mostly only one session (as during the Middle Ages).[186] The duration of the medieval parliaments was too short to foster the necessary firm solidarity between the members of the Commons. The frequency of the medieval parliaments did not make for continuity; there was no such thing as a 'continued membership' or of re-election in the medieval phase, as Pollard argued in his chapter on the growth of representation, where he repeated his criticism of Barker's thesis.[187]

The medieval parliament was an affair of weeks; it seldom had more than one session, and members rarely sought re-election. Every house was, therefore, a body of strangers, speaking perhaps incomprehensible dialects distrustful of one another, here to-day and gone to-morrow, never, in most cases, to meet again, and utterly unable, on account of their transitory existence, to acquire confidence in one another or to develop leadership and parliamentary skill.[188]

Compared with this, the Reformation Parliament (1529–1536) was

---

[185] *Evolution*, pp. 116, 317 ff.

[186] Pollard's essential meaning was rendered by F.W. Maitland in 1887–88: "The long parliaments of Henry VIII, Elizabeth and James, no doubt had very important results – not only did they educate the commons to act together, but they familiarized the nation with the notion of parliament as a permanent entity, in which the sovereignty of the realm might be vested: it is difficult to think of sovereignty being vested in so fleeting an affair as a medieval parliament, which exists for a month or two and disappears". F.W. Maitland, *The Constitutional History of England*, Cambridge, 1961, p. 250. See also for frequency and duration: F.W. Maitland, *op. cit.*, pp. 177–178, 248–251, 292–297.

[187] *Evolution*, pp. 137, 150–151.

[188] *Ibid.*, p. 161; cf. pp. 286–287.

especially significant with its eight long sessions.[189] Pollard saw the
16th century as the period of consolidation for the House of Commons:
the membership increased considerably, the attendance was quite good,
representation became an honour, and the Commons, having gained in
self-confidence, now had a *Journal* of their own. The link with the 17th
century now became apparent: for the struggle in Stuart times would
have been unsuccessful without this preparation under the Tudors.
"Without that consolidation the house would have been incapable of
the work it achieved in the seventeenth."[190] This view made short
work of the so-called servility of Tudor parliaments: "If Tudor parliaments had been servile, Stuart parliaments would not have achieved
their independence."[191]

Pollard stressed the importance of this parliamentary development
in the 16th century mainly by repeating his views of the historical
rôle of the Tudor despotism. His conception that the Tudor period laid
the foundation for the modern state recurred in the chapters dealing
with parliament and liberty, parliament and the church, and parliament and the growth of sovereignty in parliament. Connected with
this was his unitarist view of the constitution; it was the cornerstone
both of his general discussions about the separation of powers, and of
his historical essays concerning the Crown in Parliament and the
Council in Parliament. In the 16th century liberty became "a national
matter rather than the privilege of a class or a locality."[192] The Tudors
destroyed the medieval conception in which liberties were 'exceptions
to the rule.'

The destruction of these liberties was the great service rendered by the
Tudors to the cause of English liberty. Parliament in the middle ages had
failed to nationalize liberty: with the help of the crown that nationalization
was achieved in the sixteenth century.[193]

This destruction of medieval liberties was, Pollard said, comparable to
the many emancipation movements in history: it was brought about
by despotic means and centralization of power. "By centralizing power
the Tudors expanded English liberties and converted local privileges
into a common national right."[194]

[189] *Ibid.*, p. 325.
[190] *Ibid.*, p. 160.
[191] *Ibid.*, pp. 335–336.
[192] *Ibid.*, p. 177.
[193] *Ibid.*, p. 173.
[194] *Ibid.*, p. 175; as before, he described the Tudor-age as an 'age of liberation', see
Evolution, p. 77 and *The Political History*, pp. 456–457.

Pollard repeatedly cautioned against the view that increased individual liberty automatically implied a weakening of sovereignty. "Freedom without sovereignty is the idle dream of anarchists; and sovereignty without freedom is the aim of bureaucratic despots" was his liberal standpoint.[195] The Lancastrian experiment and the Wars of the Roses were both necessary to convince England that sovereignty was an indispensable complement of freedom; an indivisible sovereign State power was a necessary condition for modern freedom and for tolerance. In Pollard's words: "The weakness of the state was the parent of its cruelty."[196] Notwithstanding the fact that the establishment of the sovereign state had come about by 'growth' (it had not been 'created'), the 16th-century sovereign state power had a new appearance, totally different from that of the Middle Ages: "There was little of it in the middle ages, but only suzerainty of many sorts."[197] The paramount constitutional question in the new era was how to curb this new sovereignty and force it to responsibility. America chose to split the sovereign power into separated powers; "England decided for unity of powers combined with responsibility for their exercise; it hitched a democratic wagon to *le roi soleil*."[198] This 'choice' could finally be explained by the history of parliament, which had 'taken over' the sovereignty of the crown without dividing it.

In this kind of survey Pollard hardly could omit a chapter on the separation of powers; in his constitutionalism the criticism of this theory occupied a central place. He attacked this political conception because it was, he said, quite as inapplicable to English history as that other myth of the 'three estates.' This chapter is highly significant for his constitutionalism, yet its arguments are far from strong. Pollard attacked without a thorough investigation of the earlier origins or use of the theory. This negligence made it easier for him to present a caricature of it.[199] Another weak point was his neglecting the many earlier scholars, who had already criticized this theory. He did not even mention Bagehot.[200] Pollard's argument was related to the many criticisms (mainly American) of a federalist or 'separatist' constitution-

195 *Evolution*, p. 218.
196 *Ibid.*, p. 221; cf. on the 'Lancastrian experiment,' *Ibid.*, pp. 133, 172, 217, 224.
197 *Ibid.*, p. 227.
198 *Ibid.*, p. 229.
199 Cf. W.B. Gwyn, *The Meaning of the Separation of Powers*, New Orleans, 1965, p. 68, note 2: "Pollard was so intent on freeing his own country from any responsibility for what he considered to be an erroneous doctrine that he failed even to mention Locke in his chapter on the separation of powers." Pollard consulted one book only: W. Bondy, *The Separation of Governmental Powers*, 1896. Cf. W.B. Gwyn's criticism of this work, *op. cit.*, p. 4.
200 Cf. M.J.C. Vile, *Constitutionalism and the Separation of Powers*, Oxford, 1967, pp. 212–238.

alism, which, as our third chapter showed, was regarded as a barrier to more efficient government. It is an irony of history that the separation theory, when presented for the first time, was advocated in order to gain greater efficiency.[201] Pollard gave historical arguments for the unitarist character of the British constitution both on the local and on the central level. In his final observations he compared the British and the American constitutions: he argued that the British system was characterized by a 'mutual responsibility,' whereas in America the relationship between the powers was mainly one of distrust. The loose and essentially negative link of 'checks and balances' made for arbitrariness and irresponsibility; the result was inefficiency in governmental administration, starkly contrasting with the typical American expertise in private matters.

In the chapters on the 'Crown in Parliament' and the 'Council in Parliament' Pollard 'proved' the advantages of a 'fusion' between the executive and legislative powers. Parliament was originally an emanation of the Crown, and it had never lost sight of its royal background. The 16th-century picture of harmony, with the crown in council representing the executive power and the crown in parliament representing the legislative power,[202] was the sequel to a medieval anarchy, when the power of the monarch had been paralysed both by parliament and by a 'great council' of factions in an irresponsible 'baronial opposition.' In Tudor times the struggle between the great council and the secret council (the later privy council) ended in the latter's favour. The rise of the privy council heightened the prestige of the Commons when privy councillors became members.[203] The presence of the councillors created a link between legislature and executive, and parliament began to share responsibility for governmental affairs. Pollard denied that these facts were equal to 'the packing of parliament': councillors in parliament were elected representatives, not royal appointees.[204]

In putting forward these unitarist views Pollard intentionally broke away from the preceding generation of historians and their starry-eyed admiration for Anglo-Saxon localism or Swiss federalism.[205] In *The*

---

[201] W.B. Gwyn, *op. cit.*, p. 34.

[202] *Evolution*, p. 276.

[203] *Ibid.*, pp. 296–297; see on the difference between 'parliaments' and 'great councils': *Ibid.*, pp. 242, 278–283 cf. T.F.T. Plucknett, 'The Place of the Council in the Fifteenth Century' in *T.R.H.S.*, 4th ser. 1 (1918), pp. 157–189, particularly pp. 165, 171–172, cf. also *Evolution*, p. 98.

[204] *Evolution*, p. 295 ff.

[205] *Ibid.*, p. 261.

Evolution Pollard attacked several parliamentary myths and legends belonging to the parliamentary tradition of the 17th century and later accepted by Whig historians. Only rarely did he mention them by name; what he did was provide a new monarchical perspective, by which he tried to correct a historical self-deception of later democratic times. "It is a late development of self-consciousness when the creature comes to regard itself as its own creator."[206] To this, Pollard opposed his 'growth-theory'. Did his attack succeed?

3. Pollard and his critics

> We have no constants in history. It is far safer to assume discrepancy than identity ...
>
> (A.F. Pollard, 1920)

The Evolution of Parliament was the highlight of Pollard's career. For some time already he had been an undisputed Tudor specialist: and in political affairs he was far from unknown, partly because of the First World War. During the war he was a very active political publicist, and as a member of the Phillimore commission he was a fervent advocate of the League of Nations. These activities seemed to indicate that Pollard was bound for a political career and he did actually run for Parliament three times during the twenties, as a Liberal candidate, but without success.[207]

Pollard's historical studies about the evolution of parliament were additional evidence of his political engagement, for the final two chapters dealt with current political questions rather than with historical ones. He also raised the issue of parliament's place in a changed social bureaucratic system: the relationship between parliamentarians and 'bureaucratic experts.' He too had come to believe that government was largely "a technical matter with which only experts are fitted to deal."[208] Still, he consistently preferred a parliamentary form of government to a 'scientific despotism' of whatever description. He thought that within the highly complicated structure of modern society the direct democracy of a referendum was unreasonable.

The Evolution was a defence of the parliamentary system, but it did not give any precepts for the present; its aim was not to link the present to the past, but to set the present free. "We are not obliged to fix our

[206] *Ibid.*, p. 289.
[207] Cf. V.H. Galbraith, *op. cit.*, pp. 266–269; cf. for a number of election pamphlets, College Collection, D.P. 77.9 and College Collection D.P. 77, Library University College.
[208] *Evolution*, p. 346.

vision on the depths from which we have risen, and the future may lie in aversion from the past."[209] This was the lesson of parliament's unparliamentary origins and of its unforeseen and unintended growth. Pollard was considered an authority in constitutional affairs because of his knowledge of parliament; consequently, after the coalition government had been defeated in the elections of 1922, Lord Stamfordham, secretary to the King, turned to Pollard for advice.[210] The present question is whether his studies enhanced his prestige as a historian with his fellow historians.

At first even the specialists were favourably impressed. With regard to Pollard's publication Sir Henry Maxwell Lyte wrote to Round: "It is very interesting and, from a literary standpoint, brilliant, but incorrect in several points of detail."[211] Criticism came next, both concerning several general characteristics of the book and about many detailed points. Pollard's argument characteristically stressed the discrepancy between present and past at the expense of an identity which had been of paramount importance in older historical writings. While English historiography in the first decades of our century was generally prone to stress this discrepancy (as we pointed out in our first chapter), Pollard's style of writing makes this even more pronounced. The medievalist C.G. Crump amusingly described his reactions during Pollard's *The Evolution* lecture: "like a plain Englishman reading a description of his own country written by a Japanese traveller of genius: ... everything looks a little odd."[212]

No doubt Pollard's approach stimulated historical researchers, but some critics began to wonder whether Pollard's revisionism was all that necessary in 1920. Which historians would support theories distorted and ridiculed by Pollard? Pollard himself had said he only attacked some conceptions of the 'popular mind'.[213] Apart from this, he was convinced that for several decades Maitland's 'Introduction' of 1893 had been ignored by teachers of history, which Helen Cam many years later was also to maintain.[214] As far as Oxford was con-

---

[209] *Ibid.*, p. 352; on expert and bureaucracy, cf. *Ibid.*, pp. 18, 255, 346–348, 360; *Factors*, p. 226.

[210] Mr. Graham Pollard's information.

[211] H. Maxwell Lyte to J.H. Round, 15–1–1921, U.L.L., I.H.R. MS. no. 658.

[212] *History* 6 (1921–1922), p. 46.

[213] *Evolution*, p. 20.

[214] "It was not till 1920 that Pollard's lively and readable sketch sent his reader back to the *Memoranda* ..." H. Cam in *Selected Historical Essays of F.W. Maitland*, Cambridge, 1957, p. XVII.

cerned, E. Barker contradicted Pollard's statement as did G. Lapsley in Cambridge.[215]

Abroad too historians showed their scepsis: F. Lieberman had some sympathy for Pollard's style, but the American J.F. Baldwin minced no words in a review he wrote: "For the sake of argument ... there is an inclination to set forth obsolete theories as though they were still prepossessions of the public mind."[216] The Cambridge specialist in parliamentary history, Lapsley, an immigrant from America, was later to reproach Pollard with having shot nothing but clay pigeons. "He (Pollard) dismisses as mythology much that had long ago been quietly set aside by those who were investigating and teaching the subject."[217] There was some justice in this reproach; Pollard's criticism appears to have been less vital than he thought.

Pollard's approach was also criticized for according a central place to the Tudor period, although this was hardly surprising in a Tudor specialist. In Lapsley's explanation Pollard had adopted the views of Maitland (and McIlwain) "to construct a system in which the importance of the medieval parliament lay not in what it was but in what it was destined to become in Protestant and Tudor England."[218] Pollard was aware of his 'Tudor' interpretation, and it is true that this interpretation gave rise to new and fruitful discussions among medievalists of Pollard's own time. Yet in *The Evolution* the inevitable result of the Tudor perspective was a starkly black-and-white picture of the medieval and the Tudor phases of Parliament. In the 'high court' theory a tendency to play down the 'political' significance of parliament and Commons could already be noted. Pollard's observations 'from the Tudor vantage point' only strengthened that tendency. E. Barker believed that the medieval period had intentionally been represented as unfavourably as possible for the purpose of 'glorifying'

[215] E. Barker, 'The Origin and Future of Parliament' in *E.R.* 234 (1921), p. 62; G. Lapsley in *Cambridge Review*, 28-5-1926, p. 442: "It is a pity he did not omit ... the passage with regard to Maitland's Introduction to the *Memoranda de Parliamento* which he describes as "buried in the Rolls Series ... and generally ignored by English instructors of youth for nearly a generation." In Cambridge libraries at least the copies of that well-known work bear the marks of many an observant undergraduate thumb."

[216] *A.H.R.* 27 (1921), p. 108; cf. also F. Lieberman on Pollard: "He considers it still necessary, doubtless with good reason, to refute again popular errors though long exploded." in *Q.R.* 236 (1921), p. 364.

[217] G. Lapsley, 'Some Recent Advance in English Constitutional History' in *The Cambridge Historical Journal* 5 (1936), p. 134.; Cf. G. Templeman, *op. cit.*, pp. 211–212; G. Lapsley's many articles on the history of parliament are collected in G. Lapsley, *Crown, Community and Parliament in the Middle Ages*, ed. H. Cam and G. Barraclough, Oxford, 1951.

[218] G. Lapsley, *op. cit.*, p. 134.

the Tudors.[219] Pollard had purposely exaggerated the discrepancy between the medieval phase and the Tudor one, thus creating a new anachronism concerning the medieval parliamentary system; later on the medievalist J.G. Edwards was to take him to task for this.

Barker had still more objections: he thought Pollard's approach not comparative enough. His few comparisons with the parliamentary developments elsewhere merely served to stress the unique aspects of the English development. Comparisons with medieval France as well as with modern America all resulted in a contrast. Barker insisted that a broad European framework was needed to provide scope for the study of the institutional and constitutional history of the middle ages; his own opinions – much berated by Pollard – that the representative idea had its origin in ecclesiastical organization came from this broader background.[220] Finally, Barker scrutinized Pollard's evolutionism; he too believed that the growth theory implied an old liberal *laissez faire*, which neglected the sense of political-social responsibility.[221]

To our mind Pollard's growth theory, (an almost mystic differentiation between things 'grown' and things 'made'), served him in the first place as an argument against the legend that parliament could have been the 'creator' of its own greatness. Not only we have attempted to find the true meaning of his evolutionism in the idea of the *Heterogonie der Zwecke*; Crump too had felt that this was the essence of Pollard's ideas, and when Romein wrote his essay on the dialectics of progress he used Pollard's 'confusing abundance' (a term he had coined) as illustrative of that new historiography which differed so clearly from the old genetic and linear types. There, all evolution had been gradual and straightforward, without any sudden transformation.[222]

Pollard did not perceive any straight line in the continuity of the parliamentary development to justify projecting the present back into the past, in other words to project the result back to its origin. Pollard's evolutionism was far too 'accidental' for this; in his view the 'accidental' occurrences, far from having been a hindrance, had actually been the root cause of the parliamentary development. In our judgment J.H. Hexter missed essential aspects of Pollard's developmental thinking, since he simply called it 'linear' and believed that it

---

[219] E. Barker, *op. cit.*, p. 66.
[220] *Ibid.*, pp. 63–66; cf. A. Marongiu, *Medieval Parliaments: A Comparative Study*, London, 1968.
[221] E. Barker, *op. cit.*, pp. 70–71.
[222] J. Romein, *Het Onvoltooid Verleden*, Amsterdam, 1937, p. 55.

could be traced back to an idea of progress.[223] While granting the occasional Darwinism of Pollard's evolutionary view, we must note that this 'quality' results more in a denial of that linear thinking noticed by Hexter than in a confirmation of it.[224]

The Evolution of Parliament was the occasion not only for general criticism but equally for criticism on points of details. We shall mainly discuss those historians who reacted to Pollard's study.

There are two main trends discernable in modern parliamentary historiography: the first extended the 'Maitland thesis' of 1893 so rigidly in the administrative direction that there was hardly any room left for Stubbs's high-flown political views. The second adopted the essential aspects of Maitland's argument, though not to the exclusion of the Stubbsian tradition. In fact, H. Cam thought that during the thirties there was a remarkable 'revival of older views,' even a 'swing-back to Stubbs.'[225]

The historians of the first group reacted differently – consciously or not – to the traditional views. Pollard himself did not really 'discard' Stubbs, as we saw. He tried to infuse a new meaning into Stubbs's highly important 'concentration idea,' by means of his own conception of England's growth to nationhood. Pollard's 'forgotten' American, A.B. White, did something similar: he studies Stubbs's ideas in connection with the notion of self-government. However, the dominant monarchical perspective in his final results was so strong that he may be said to have revised Stubbs, with a significant shift of emphasis. His book, *Self-Government at the King's Command*, was published in 1933.[226] The Frenchman, D. Pasquet, another revisionist, had published a book in 1914, which had also escaped Pollard's attention notwithstanding

[223] J.H. Hexter, *Reappraisals in History*, pp. 38–39.
[224] Cf. *Somerset*, p. 201; *Evolution*, pp. 25, 120, 239.
[225] *E.H.R.* 51 (1936), p. 701: "Pasquet's brilliant study enforced the thesis that royal administrative policy rather than any democratic theory explained the rise of the house of commons. But of recent years signs of a revival of older views have appeared: evidence has been adduced of a desire to represent or to be represented in parliament, as well as evidence that consent by representatives to taxation was not merely formal. Miss Clarke's book is the most conspicuous sign that has yet appeared of this swing-back to Stubbs, but her views are to be regarded not as a substitute for but as a complement to those of Pasquet and Richardson." Review of M.V. Clarke, *Medieval Representation and Consent*, London, 1936. Cf. H.G. Richardson in *History* 22 (1937–1938), pp. 66–67.
[226] Cf. G. Lapsley, *op. cit.*, p. 126 (note 21); and *E.H.R.* 50 (1935), p. 166. See also F.M. Powicke in *History* 19 (1934–1935), pp. 261–263. For previous studies by A.B. White, see his articles 'The First Concentration of Juries: The Writ of July 21, 1213' in *A.H.R.* 17 (1911–1912), pp. 12–16 and 'Some early instances of concentration of representatives in England' in *A.H.R.* 19 (1913–1914), pp. 735–750.

the extensive and critical review by J. Tait in the *English Historical Review* of that year.[227] Tait believed that Pasquet had gone too far in his reaction to Stubbs, and had made too much of people's 'aversion' to serving in the yet insignificant Commons. The American G.L. Haskins shone as an anti-Stubbs champion, conducting his research in the firm belief that the modern 'crisis of democracy' initiated the need to re-write a large part of the medieval parliamentary past; he criticized the Victorians' 'wishful thinking,' continually singling out Stubbs, and therefore highly displeasing Stubbs's supporters among historians: H. Cam and M. McKisack.[228]

The most important medievalists of this first group are still two well-known critics of Stubbs: H.G. Richardson and G.O. Sayles. In the late twenties they published the first of a series of interesting studies on the early medieval parliament. The series was rounded off, for the time being, in 1961 with their 'last words.' These scholars acquired more first hand knowledge than anybody else. Their constant message was that interpretations had to be based only on the records but remarkably enough their interpretation remained essentially unchanged since their very first publications.[229] They wanted to do away once and for all with Stubbs's influence, and to erase the notion of self-government from studies dealing with the early history of parliament.[230] Stubbs came under attack on three main points: he had pictured parliament as a 'national council' characterized by the 'three estates' in its composition, thus obscuring the role of the King's council. Further, he had considered the judicial function the least important, and finally, he had believed that under Edward II and III the Commons had been the most important part of Parliament.[231]

Concerning the composition and function of Parliament, these two historians agreed with Maitland, but they went much further, laying extra stress on the aspects of 'law' and 'administration.'[232] The essential

---

[227] D. Pasquet, *Essai sur les origines de la Chambre des Communes*, Paris, 1914. See J. Tait in *E.H.R.* 29 (1914), pp. 750–754. The book was translated with a brief preface by G. Lapsley in 1925. See J. Tait in *E.H.R.* 41 (1926), pp. 464–465.

[228] G.L. Haskins, *The Statute of York and The Interest of the Commons*, Cambridge Mass., 1935. Reviewed by H. Cam in *E.H.R.* 52 (1937), pp. 319–321; G.L. Haskins, *The Growth of English Representative Government*, Oxford, 1948. Reviewed by M. McKisack in *E.H.R.* 64 (1949), pp. 394–395: "It is ... unfortunate that the cogent arguments for a more conservative interpretation should be passed over in silence."

[229] Cf. H.G. Richardson, G.O. Sayles, 'The Early Records of the English Parliaments' in *B.I.H.R.* 5 (1927–1928), pp. 129–130.

[230] G.O. Sayles, *The Medieval Foundations of England*, London, 1966, p. 438.

[231] H.G. Richardson, G.O. Sayles, *Parliaments and Great Councils in Medieval England*, London, 1961, pp. 31–32.

[232] *B.I.H.R.* 5 (1927–1928), p. 132.

function of the early parliament (in the period 1272–1327) was 'the dispensing of justice'; to this core were later added non-essential elements such as representation, legislature and taxation.[233] From the administration's vantage point 'the official element' was the most neglected part of early parliamentary history.[234] In this perspective parliamentary historiography must largely become a "history of procedure, and details of procedure are apt to be dull. But the evolution of any organ of government cannot be without interest, and the story of the origin and the growth of the English parliament with so tremendous a destiny, beyond any dream of its unknown architects, must be of the highest interest. And yet, as it seems to us, it has hardly begun to be written." This was what Richardson and Sayles wrote in 1928.[235] Their favourite administrative history of the early parliament predictably became a razor-edged weapon against the old constitutional history. It was much more than simply a new field of research, it provided a new perspective of the parliamentary past. In the 'official view' parliament was an apparatus of royal officials which allowed hardly any role for the more politically active Commons. "The Commons represented a mode of procedure", G.O. Sayles was significantly to write.[236]

This changing perspective carries the most weight for the student of historiography; the factual elaboration concerns us less. As we said, Richardson and Sayles went further than Maitland had gone, in their insistence that the early 13th-century 'royal' and 'judicial' parliament was largely institutionalized. Contemporaries knew 'exactly' what parliament meant; to them it did not seem a Pollardian *vox et praeterea nihil.*[237] Richardson and Sayles emphasized that the early 13th-century parliament – a judicial organ *sui generis* – was fundamentally different from the 14th-century more 'political' parliaments, which came into being because of the 'feudal reaction' under Edward II. "The modern parliament is the consequence of the feudal reaction of the fourteenth century. If this sounds paradoxical, let us emphasize that we are discussing the history of an institution, of the machinery of administration: we are not attempting to explain the triumph of modern democracy."[238] This feudal reaction marked the change from 'law to

---

[233] *Ibid.*, p. 133.
[234] *B.I.H.R.* 6 (1928–1929), p. 145.
[235] *Ibid.*
[236] G.O. Sayles, *The Medieval Foundations of England*, p. 464.
[237] *B.I.H.R.* 5 (1927–1928), p. 133. Cf. G.O. Sayles, *The King's Parliament of England*, London, 1975, p. 16.
[238] H.G. Richardson, G.O. Sayles, 'The King's ministers in Parliament' in *E.H.R.* 47 (1932), p. 397.

politics,' which Pollard had believed to illustrate by the rise of the common petitions in that very period.

Central to their conception of the already institutionalized character of 13th-century parliament was a 'bureaucratic' refinement of an old idea concerning the remarkable frequency and periodicity of parliaments in their first phase. It was this very phenomenon which early in the 19th century had led the historians Allen and Hallam to suppose that parliament's original function must have been judicial, and Pollard had unwittingly adopted their construction. Richardson and Sayles had created a 'bureaucratic' interpretation, in which the medieval demand for frequency and periodicity ('annual parliaments' and the request for summoning parliament three times a year) acquired a deeper meaning: "... periodicity implies definition: there cannot be a periodical occurrence of something that is not defined."[239]

As far as we know, Pollard never replied to the detailed criticism Richardson and Sayles of his work of 1920. Evidently, Pollard's general outline was confirmed rather than denied in their approach to the medieval parliamentary past and in their 'administrative' additions to Maitland's thesis. Actually, through using 'the records alone', without the Tudor perspective, these two medievalists succeeded in 'debunking' the image of the medieval Commons as politically significant. "Messrs. Richardson and Sayles have added a good deal to Maitland and it may be hoped that their contributions will some day be available in a collected form", Pollard wrote appreciatively in 1942.[240]

When Pollard did enter into a discussion it was with the representatives of the second group, who re-animated a somewhat dated interpretation without dismissing Maitland. The critical remarks of these 'traditionalists' about *The Evolution* were too sound to be left unanswered. First M. McKisack published, in 1924, an article on borough representation in the time of Richard II, a year later it was J.G. Edwards who contributed an article to the *Festschrift* for T.F. Tout dealing with the phenomenon of re-election to the Commons under Edward I and Edward II.[241]

239 *B.I.H.R.* 5 (1927–1928), p. 130; H.G. Richardson, G.O. Sayles, *Parliaments and Great Councils*, p. 9.
240 *E.H.R.* 57 (1942), p. 204, note 2.
241 M. McKisack, 'Borough Representation in Richard II's Reign' in *E.H.R.* 39 (1924), pp. 511–522; J.G. Edwards, 'The Personnel of the Commons in Parliament under Edward I and Edward II' in *Essays in Medieval History presented to T.F. Tout*, ed. A.G. Little and F.M. Powicke, Manchester, 1925, pp. 197–214. J.G. Edwards's article is also printed in *Historical Studies of the English Parliament*, ed. E.B. Fryde and E. Miller, Cambridge, 1970, vol. I, p. 150 ff.

McKisack criticized some of Pollard's essential opinions, with their tedious insistence that representation in Parliament was unpopular and burdensome, that the choice of representatives did not interest the citizens, and that parliamentary membership had no continuity and little frequency. McKisack first attacked Pollard for suggesting that the writs *de expensis* could accurately indicate the size of the medieval House of Commons. She did not think that these writs, which settled the payment for the rendering of representative services, were actual proof; her investigation of borough records had made it clear that for several reasons the writs had not been received by every representative, despite their clear presence in parliament.

Pollard agreed that local records might well provide additional and corrective material for his theory: "it is only from local sources that the problem of the actual attendance in medieval parliaments can be solved."[242] Yet the critical remarks did not convince him that his low opinion of the medieval Commons was mistaken. In 1926 he defended himself in the circumstantial appendix to the second edition of *The Evolution*. He appealed to an old historiographical tradition, e.g. Prynne, with whose work he had undoubtedly become very well acquainted during his preparatory studies on parliament. Pollard regarded Prynne as a pioneer in historical research for providing a far less unhistorical interpretation than the 19th-century 'votaries of parliamentary legends.'[243] Prynne had argued that representation used to be an arbitrary power of the sheriffs: "Sheriffs ... made and unmade, continued, discontinued, and revived boroughs at their wills."[244] Here is a noticeable connection with early 19th-century historiography. Pollard unwittingly adopted in his appendix of 1926 the main theme of Allen's treatise on the history of the House of Commons, published in 1831. Not only Prynne, but also Riess and Pasquet insisted that the correct way to interpret medieval parliamentary representation was to see in it an enforced *servitium*. Ironically enough Pollard could even find support for this opinion in some passages by Stubbs, since the latter, for all his Victorian optimism, had been quite outspoken about the medieval distaste for representation.[245]

It is indeed ironic that Pollard should reply to McKisack's criticisms

[242] *Evolution*, p. 424; cf. A.F. Pollard, 'Local History' in *T.L.S.* 11-3-1920, p. 161: "We shall never really know how the House of Commons grew until we have printed and digested our borough records."
[243] *Evolution*, p. 392; cf. *B.I.H.R.* 16 (1938–1939), p. 19.
[244] *Evolution*, p. 396.
[245] *Evolution*, pp. 397, 406, 429; For Stubbs's later corrections, however, see J.G. Edwards, *Historians and the Medieval English Parliament*, Glasgow, 1970, p. 28 (note 1).

by referring to Stubbs. Pollard retained his unfavourable view of the
medieval Commons, for instance in his characterization of 'election' as
'nomination,' and his emphasis on the infrequency of re-election. In
the thirties, when he reviewed books with a far more positive bias – f.i.
by H.L. Gray and S.B. Chrimes – many of the main arguments of *The
Evolution* were endlessly repeated.[246] In her book of 1932, reviewed by
Pollard in *History*, McKisack once more discussed the familiar problems.[247] On questions like attendance or election and re-election, the
old contrasting positions remained unchanged, yet the many differences
of opinion did not rule out a reciprocal appreciation. While Pollard
praised his adversary for her passages on the electoral methods in the
boroughs, McKisack may possibly have been ironical when referring
to some of Pollard's early *D.N.B.* articles in support of her own more
positive interpretation. Later she called *The Evolution* a brilliant work,
with the reservation, however, that the parts dealing with the Middle
Ages had to be read with some caution as "the author was insufficiently
appreciative of the genius of Stubbs."[248] Actually, as already stated,
Stubbs had not been completely forgotten in *The Evolution* and in later
years, too, Pollard was wont to mention Stubbs's 'usual caution'.[249]

McKisack's criticism of Pollard on the infrequency of re-election
followed J.G. Edwards's lead in a certain sense. For Pollard it was
proof of the lack of parliamentary experience in the Middle Ages,
which in itself served as proof of the small political relevance of the
House of Commons. J.G. Edwards belongs to our 'second group,' together with H. Cam, T.F.T. Plucknett, J.E.A. Jolliffe, R.F. Treharne
and B. Wilkinson. In the historiography on the medieval parliament
after 1920, Edwards is a significant figure,[250] and a brief discussion of
his work is necessary, because he clearly contradicted some of the
interpretations of the first group in his criticism both of Pollard and of
Richardson and Sayles. In his essay of 1925 he undermined Pollard's

[246] Cf. H.L. Gray, *The Influence of the Commons on Early Legislation: A Study of the Fourteenth
and Fifteenth Centuries*, Cambridge, Mass., 1932, reviewed in *History* 18 (1933–1934), pp.
262–263; and S.B. Chrimes, *English Constitutional Ideas in the Fifteenth Century*, Cambridge, 1936,
reviewed in *History* 22 (1937–1938), pp. 162–165.

[247] M. McKisack, *The Parliamentary Representation of the English Boroughs during the Middle
Ages*, Oxford, 1932, reviewed in *History* 17 (1932–1933), pp. 257–259.

[248] M. McKisack, *The Fourteenth Century*, Oxford, 1959, pp. 555–556; cf. the reference to
Thomas Yonge in *D.N.B.*, in her book of 1932, pp. 117, 125 Cf. A.F. Pollard in *D.N.B.*,
vol. 63, 1900; cf. also, on John Tiptoft (*D.N.B.* vol. 56, 1898, p. 409), Thomas and William
Tresham (*D.N.B.*, vol. 57, 1899, p. 203 ff.) and Thomas Walton (*D.N.B.*, vol. 60, 1899,
p. 279). All of them were clearly medieval parliamentarians with years of experience.

[249] *E.H.R.* 53 (1938), p. 597.

[250] Several articles by the authors referred to here are to be found in the previously
mentioned volume of E.B. Fryde and E. Miller, *Historical Studies of the English Parliament*.

provocative theory concerning the infrequency of re-elections. He translated this problem into statistics covering the entire period of 1290–1327, and finally concluded that quite a few representatives were re-elected. Admittedly, the majority was not, and moreover, some members represented different districts in different elections. As to re-election in the strictest sense (that is, for two or more successive parliaments), Edwards largely agreed with Pollard's beliefs, although in a number of cases even this intensive form of re-election had occurred. And he, too, finally concurred with McKisack's argument of a year before when she urged that the writs *de expensis* were not sufficiently indicative of real attendance and actual presence of the borough representatives in Parliament.

It was difficult to contradict Edwards's statistical argumentation. Pollard replied that the infrequency of re-elections characterized medieval parliamentary life, especially considering the membership of modern parliaments which consists for three-quarters of re-elected representatives. He had made this rarity the yardstick for the medieval past by an (implicit) comparison with the present; in his view such a comparison was justified, and even inevitable, in a survey like *The Evolution*: "when one talks about the rarity of medieval re-elections, especially in the opening chapters of a general treatise, one necessarily means their rarity compared with modern custom."[251] The purpose of the comparison had merely been to illustrate how short-lived a parliamentary career must have been in the Middle Ages: there simply was no continuous parliamentary experience.

Edwards reacted in the same year. He granted that Pollard was right in supposing that changing membership and brief sessions could not lead to much continuity in parliamentary life. But was a continued membership within the much less complicated medieval constellation vital for acquiring the experience Pollard had in mind? He believed that this precondition was necessary only after parliament had become an established part of the constitution. Repeated membership in the Middle Ages would give quite as much experience as would a continuous membership to-day. The criteria used in Pollard's view of the Middle Ages were far too anachronistic – surely a remarkable circumstance in a historian of Pollard's stature: "That fallacy Mr. Pollard has often and rightly denounced."[252]

[251] A.F. Pollard, 'History, English and Statistics' in *History* 11 (1926–1927), p. 23.
[252] J.G. Edwards, 'Re-election and the Medieval Parliament' in *History* 11 (1926–1927), p. 206.

The great difference between Pollard's 'presentism' and that of his predecessors in the 19th century was that Pollard used it for stressing the differences from the past rather than the similarities with that past. It was in fact essential for the reaction to 19th-century Whig historiography to accentuate differences. Nevertheless, even this salutary reaction was no guarantee against anachronism, be it of a different quality. It remained a lurking evil, threatening even those who had made 'difference' the guiding principle of their argument; that led one only half way. The historical context still needed a reconstruction of its own. Was this feasible?

Edwards certainly made a gallant attempt in this direction, not only when offering criticism of Pollard, but equally in his criticism of Richardson and Sayles. In his judgment parliament's function was in the first phase of its history largely a judicial one; at least it must have seemed so to the subjects of that time. Yet the 13th-century sources are open to more than one interpretation of the function of parliament; the king and his close collaborators wanted more than just a judicial court: the parliament they envisaged would also be an advisory body. According to Edwards, the 19th century might have interpreted the records too generously in this respect, but Richardson and Sayles certainly interpreted them too narrowly.[253]

In Pollard's judgment matters like attendance, election and re-election were clear proof of the insignificant position of the medieval Commons. In a later stage Richardson and Sayles proved the Commons' subservience to the Lords also by the parliamentary procedures.[254] In 1958 Edwards, in a sharp and lucid lecture on the usual 'parliamentary intercommuning' between Lords and Commons, analysed the extremely hypothetical character of their construction, and argued quite convincingly that available records provided more proof of a favourable place for the Commons than of the opposite.[255] In this way Edwards came very close to a refined Stubbsian view. Finally, we should mention that the importance and the originality of Stubbs's first concentration-thesis were again stressed by H. Cam in a number of surveys.[256]

---

[253] See on the function, esp. J.G. Edwards, 'Justice in Early Parliaments' in *B.I.H.R.* 27 (1954), pp. 35–53. See also *Historical Studies*, ed. E.B. Fryde and E. Miller, I.
[254] H.G. Richardson, 'The Commons and Medieval Politics' in *T.R.H.S.* 4th ser. 28 (1946), pp. 21–45; G.O. Sayles, *The Medieval Foundations of England*, p. 460 ff.
[255] J.G. Edwards, *The Commons in Medieval English Parliament*, London, 1958.
[256] Cf. H. Cam, 'The Theory and Practice of Representation in Medieval England' in *History* 38 (1953), pp. 11–26; see also *Historical Studies*, ed. E.B. Fryde and E. Miller.

That Pollard's *The Evolution* had, in the decades following 1920, a revitalizing effect in the debates on the significance of medieval parliament, can hardly be denied. Now, forty years afterwards, these debates seem to have reached the saturation point. Are the differences of opinion between the two groups of historians really so great as to exclude reconciliation? Cannot the points of discord be reduced to differences in emphasis, and are not the two view-points much nearer than was immediately apparent because of their origins in differing perspectives?[257] In 1961 the 'last words' of Richardson and Sayles were: "The discussion of the nature and characteristics of parliament under Henry III and the first three Edwards threatens to become a vain dispute about the niceties of language. In such disputes we have no interest."[258] But who has? The debates concerning the medieval parliament have continued for several decades, and resemble the endless discussions about the 18th-century constitution, of which A.L. Rowse hoped the last word had finally been said.[259]

Let us return once more to Pollard during the last years of his life. His study of 1920 about parliament also raised questions pertaining to its development in the modern period. Had not the constitutional meaning of the 17th century been relegated to the background in Pollard's *The Evolution*, when the Tudor period was pictured as the turning-point within the whole parliamentary development?

D. 'POLLARDISM'. THE REFORMATION PARLIAMENT

> A Parliament with so long a life was a very new thing.
>
> (F.W. Maitland, 1888)

The First World War and the succeeding years had taken Pollard away from his proper field of specialized historical labour to an unusual extent; he himself said that even the preparation and the completion of his *Evolution* had suffered from them.[260] Not only did the political situation demand attention, after 1918, as a historian, he faced a period full of uncertainty and confusion because of the various discussions about the philosophy of history by Spengler and Croce. However,

---

[257] See for a concise summary of the present debate, E. Miller, *The Origins of Parliament*, London, 1960 (Historical Association).
[258] H.G. Richardson, G.O. Sayles, *Parliaments and Great Councils*, p. 49.
[259] Cf. A.L. Rowse, 'Richard Pares' in *Proceedings of the British Academy* 48 (1958), p. 353.
[260] *Evolution*, p. X.

towards the late twenties he regained his confidence, and continued his historical studies on the familiar subject of the Tudor period.[261] "History that is real and sober is not easy to define. But it is nothing without authenticated evidence and patient investigation," said Pollard in his lecture 'History à la Mode.'[262] Most of the work done by Pollard during the last two decades of his life consists of highly specialized articles written for publication in historical periodicals. He wrote only one more biography, on Wolsey, in 1929; it purported to be a sequel to his *Henry VIII*, and was the best thing he ever wrote. His journalistic contributions were still numerous; two of them dealt, once more, with the statesman Henry VIII, whom Pollard in the thirties unfortunately described as 'the father of all the Fascists,' with the one great difference that Henry was not the rapist, but the 'foster father' of parliament.[263]

Pollard's last great Tudor biography was remarkably for its thesis about the driving force behind Wolsey's foreign policy. Pollard believed Wolsey's 'un-English activities' were determined by Wolsey's personal aspirations to the Papacy. The mirage of the papal tiara prompted his diplomatic actions and explained why England showed so much good will and forbearance towards the European policy of the Church of Rome.[264] In the words of the historian Philip Hughes: "Ubi Petrus, ibi Anglia."[265]

Pollard's conception dated from 1913 when he had contrasted Wolsey's policy with Henry VII's foreign policy. "Wolsey's diplomacy was tainted by private un-English ends. England for him was a stepping-stone to Rome; and to achieve the papal tiara he must dazzle the eyes of the Western world and play a great part on the stage of Europe."[266] In 1929, moreover, Pollard discerned the very antithesis to Henry VIII's rather 'national' policy in Wolsey's.[267] Thinking in contrasts was always characteristic for Pollard: his first study, on Somerset, was remarkable for its black-and-white portrayal. Thus, the perspective as well as the argument became clearer. However, viewpoints of this sort lead to an extremism which in its turn implies a

---

[261] C.H. Williams, *op. cit.*, p. 8.

[262] A.F. Pollard, 'History à la Mode' in *Proceedings of the Royal Institution of Great Britain* 26 (1929–1931), p. 198.

[263] A.F. Pollard, 'Henry VIII' in *The Great Tudors*, ed. K. Garvin, New York, 1935, p. 27. Cf. R. Mortimer in *The New Statesman and the Nation*, 9-3-1935.

[264] A.F. Pollard, *Wolsey* (Fontana Library, 1965), pp. 16, 25 (note 2), 121–122, 161–165, 229 ff. Cf. the reviews in *E.H.R.* 45 (1930), pp. 304–307; in *T.L.S.* 30-5-1929, and T. Dibdin, 'Wolsey' in *History* 15 (1930–1931), pp. 18–26.

[265] Ph. Hughes, *The Reformation in England*. London, 1954, vol. I, p. 113.

[266] A.F. Pollard (ed.), *The Reign of Henry VII*, London, 1913–1914, Vol. I, p. LI.

[267] *Wolsey*, pp. 332, 369.

simplification of the historical truth. Thus later historiographers found it easy to detract from the value of Pollard's theories; ironically enough the modern interpretation makes Wolsey's policy nearly identical to the views of Henry VII: the historian J. Scarisbrick calls Wolsey "a disciple of that king's school of thrift."[268]

Pollard's *Wolsey* also pays attention to administrative history; the main point of interest to us is the typical Pollardian approach and interest in the actual working of the Tudor constitution. Nor were this approach and interest restricted to the later Pollard: they are present in his earliest works, and he mentioned them already in 1903 in a letter to Maitland. As a matter of fact, they had formed a part of the general pattern of interpretation of his great Tudor books. Maitland had in an early stage referred to the Tudor period as 'the golden age of council.' Pollard wrote in 1900: "The privy council was the pivot of Tudor administration, and though the records of its everyday working may not provide sensational reading it is only by its everyday working than an institution can be judged."[269] Judging the everyday working of any institution, be it council or parliament, requires an analysis of procedures and internal organization, as well as a biographical study to highlight the role of those civil servants and administrators who were not in the public eye. The elements of the 'biographical method' were present within the framework of the Pollardian perspective; they came more to the fore, however, in his specialized later articles.

Pollard's most important pupil, J.E. Neale, spoke in this respect of 'Namierism'; 'Pollardism' might be equally suitable. "Pollard himself in his last years (*sic*) started what I may call the Namier method in dealing with the Reformation Parliament," wrote Neale in 1958.[270] But Neale had earlier insisted that Pollard's later work, dealing with the Reformation Parliament, actually heralded a return to his 'Dictionary Days.'[271] He was not even contradicting himself, for it is quite possible to regard the *Dictionary of National Biography* as a not insignificant beginning of the biographical method, later so much *en vogue*.

That the years of *Dictionary of National Biography* had a great significance for Pollard himself has already been pointed out; the *D.N.B.* was of great importance for others as well. Some ardent and valuable contributors were older historians like S.R. Gardiner and J. Gairdner,

[268]   J.J. Scarisbrick, *Henry VIII*, London, 1968, p. 48; cf. also D.S. Chambers, 'Cardinal Wolsey and the Papal Tiara' in *B.I.H.R.* 38 (1965),p. 20.
[269]   *E.H.R.* 15 (1900), p. 583.
[270]   J.E. Neale, *Essays in Elizabethan History*, London, 1958, p. 227.
[271]   *E.H.R.* 64 (1949), p. 204.

but also the younger J. Tait, C.H. Firth, T.F. Tout and Pollard himself. The number of biographies contributed by each of the last-named three could fill a whole volume.[272] Speaking historiographical-ly, it may be even more important that the perspective on English history shifted almost imperceptibly for the readers of these many biographies about persons of greater and lesser importance from by-gone ages and from a more recent past. This gradual shift was already favourably commented upon as early as 1890 by the *English Historical Review*, which saw it as a welcome broadening of the historical percep-tion after its long one-sided concern with kings and leading statesmen. The same reviewer commented about the first 22 volumes: "What a new sense of the meaning of an age comes to anyone who follows out the fortunes of a few families who never rose to any commanding position."[273]

As we said, the most important theme of Pollard's later publica-tions was the development of parliament under the Tudors, the main outlines of which had already been drawn in *The Evolution*. The sweeping outline of 1920 needed more factual details, and to this end Pollard himself concentrated on the Reformation Parliament; his pupil Neale in the twenties began his study on the ten parliaments of Elizabeth, and Pollard's friend Notestein, an American who saw Firth as his English 'master', decided in favour of the early Stuart years, the transitionnal period between Tudor and Stuart.[274] In 1924, Notestein delivered a magisterial lecture in which he dotted the i's:

Professor Pollard, with his gift of swift and shrewd generalization, has re-marked that in the sixteenth century the Crown in Council was the Govern-ment and the Crown in Parliament was the maker of the laws. I have only been dotting the i's and crossing the t's to that sentence.[275]

He added that his rather elaborate discourses needed still further details, and in a later stage both he and Neale devoted their best efforts to this. Pollard did not progress beyond some preliminary studies in this field. Was he hampered in his biographical work by his too evolutionary way of thinking, as Neale supposes? Or could it be the fear he himself mentioned that a 'too extreme concentration on the detail at the ex-

---

[272] See 'A Statistical Account' in *D.N.B.* vol. 63, 1900, pp. XVIII–XIX.

[273] *E.H.R.* 5 (1890), p. 784; his conclusion also was: "The *D.N.B.* has become a training school of historical research . . ." (p. 788). Cf. also 'George Smith and the *D.N.B.*' in *T.L.S.*, 24-12-1971, pp. 1593–1595.

[274] Cf. *Studies in History. British Academy Lectures*, selected and introduced by L.S. Suther-land, London, 1966, p. 7 (note 11).

[275] W. Notestein, *The Winning of the Initiative by the House of Commons*, London, 1924, p. 24.

pense of the whole' might lead to a 'pulverisation' of history?[276] Both factors may have formed an obstacle.

Pollard made some of the results of his investigation public in an address on the occasion of the Anglo-American historical conference of 1936. Its title was: 'The Reformation Parliament as a matrimonial agency and its national effects.'[277] The original quality of this speech was evidence of Pollard's strongest point; his gift for general outlines, vividly drawn, and for making a situation understandable by placing it in a broad perspective. In fact, he elaborated in this speech his well-worn conception of England's process of (parliamentary) nationalization. What he was concerned with was not in the first place the religious and political affairs discussed by this parliament, but the unrehearsed and undesigned effects of the duration of the sessions in this 16th-century long parliament. "We are here concerned with the human nature in history, which man did not plan and the parchment school of history is only too apt to ignore, and the effects upon men of a changing environment which itself was undesigned."[278] This was the voice of the Pollard who wrote *The Evolution*. The effects in question were the increasing social intercourse between members, strengthened and confirmed by marriage ties, and resulting in a growing 'national' consciousness of the Commons, who hailed from different parts of the country but had become more or less permanent residents of London for a period of seven years. It was difficult to provide a reliable and exact estimation of the 'colonization of London by the provinces'; the records of this early Tudor period are much scarcer than those of the next period. There were practically no sheriff's returns for the period 1478–1542, and the only way of tracing some of the members was with the aid of Thomas Cromwell's parliamentary lists and other such notes, only too rarely preserved.[279] Consequently, Pollard could not do more than advance some suggestions supported by only a few examples.

One of those who joined in the discussion following the lecture was Namier whose intellectual capacities Pollard had noticed as early as 1911.[280] Neale mooted the subject of the 1929 commission, headed by

[276] A.F. Pollard, 'History à la Mode,' p. 198; cf. J.E. Neale, *Essays in Elizabethan History*, London, 1958, p. 227.

[277] Published in *History* 21 (1936–1937), pp. 219–229.

[278] *History* 21 (1936–1937), p. 221.

[279] A.F. Pollard, 'Thomas Cromwell's Parliamentary Lists' in *B.I.H.R.* 9 (1931–1932), pp. 31–43.

[280] See *B.I.H.R.* 14 (1936–1937), pp. 80–81; Pollard's opinion of Namier as a student in 1911 is to be found in a letter to his parents, 5-11-1911, quoted by Julia Namier in *Lewis*

Colonel J. Wedgwood, for the preparation of a 'biographical history' of Parliament, and this commission's subsequent failure. As Pollard was one of the expert members of this commission, an explanatory note about this first and partially unsuccessful attempt to write a biographical history of parliament may be in order. The inspiring initiator was the independent radical J. Wedgwood, M.P. since 1906.[281] The dominant factor in his political activities was the fight for more humanity and more justice. It did not, however, keep him from trying his hand at history.[282] It was his political fervour combined with a fear of the dangers besetting democracy, which during the twenties gave impetus to the idea of writing a major history of parliament. "Political development in Europe was a major incentive," his niece afterwards wrote in her excellent biography, "to his growing ambition to sponsor a Parliamentary history on the lines of the *Dictionary of National Biography*."[283] Both this ideological background and the increasing financial straits during the great Depression seriously hampered progress and occasioned a serious conflict between him and the expert historians he had invited.

Wedgwood envisaged a parliamentary history that would be an enduring and inspiring monument to an age-old parliamentary democracy. He distrusted the iconoclastic attitude with which his chief advisors Namier and Neale and other professional historians approached Whig interpretations.[284] "The new history blackens England's past in an endeavour to belittle liberalism and exalt authority ..." he later wrote.[285] In the first decades of the 20th century English historiography had undergone much too fundamental a change to allow a reconciliation between his conception and that of the experts.[286] In Wedgwood's judgment, history still had a special function which the 'professional' party would no longer accord to it. That may have been the price of professionalism. Pollard later wrote that the trend towards 'scientific' history resulted in an increasing estrangement.[287]

Namier, London, 1971, p. 101: "The best man by far in sheer intellect was a Balliol man of Polish-Jewish origin and I did my best for him, but the Warden and majority of Fellows shied at his race, and eventually we elected the two next best."

[281] See C.V. Wedgwood, *The Last of the Radicals. Josiah Wedgwood, M.P.*, London, 1951. Until 1919 he was a Liberal M.P., after that a Labour representative.

[282] C.V. Wedgwood, *op. cit.*, p. 163 ff.

[283] *Ibid.*, p. 168.

[284] *Ibid.*, pp. 171, 174 ff.

[285] J. Wedgwood, *Forever Freedom*, Harmondsworth, 1940, Introduction, quoted by C.V. Wedgwood, *op. cit.*, p. 175.

[286] See also Julia Namier, *op. cit.*, pp. 199–200, 282–285.

[287] A.F. Pollard in *The Times*, 7-11-1938.

The tragic aspect of this gulf was that the international situation in the thirties brought Wedgwood, a Labour man, closer than ever to the the Tory Namier and the Liberal Pollard especially in his struggle against fascism and his warnings against the 'appeasers.' Namier and Pollard were very aware of this; Pollard, at any rate, did not consider himself too much estranged from Wedgwood .[288] Towards the end of the thirties Wedgwood wrote:

I am back at work fighting Papists, Fascists and historians. I am becoming speechless over Spain, Palestine, Irak and Germany. Everybody is very kind to me and pays not the slightest attention. Pollard and I have sworn alliance because we are both so old and helpless.[289]

At least twice in these years Pollard published his wishes concerning the great undertaking in the *Times*.[290] He joined the protest against the expansion of the project to include the 'Peers' and the period after 1832 in order to gain more money for the project. He wanted an expert editor for every period, and to formulate the aims of the biographical method more strictly. The important thing for Namier was the 'interests' of the members and their social relationship. Pollard wanted a rather wider perspective: he asked for 'sections on Parliament as a matrimonial agency' because he considered them relevant to the growth of the national consciousness.[291]

Before it came to an open split the commission had met for seventeen sessions, and published an interesting *Interim Report* in 1932, which contained also a notable contribution by Richardson and Sayles.[292] The document first gave a list of existing source editions and literature from Prynne to, among others, W.D. Pink, who, in Namier's judgment of 1928, was 'one of the greatest antiquaries of our time.'[293] The sections dealing with the interpretation and explanation of English parliamentary development gave the overall impression that in many respects the innovation after 1893 and the views of the previously mentioned 'first group' of historians had finally triumphed. The docu-

---

[288] See L. Namier on J. Wedgwood in *Avenues of History*, London, 1952, p. 171.

[289] C.V. Wedgwood, *op. cit.*, p. 219; J. Wedgwood's fussy reaction to the publication of W.H. Dunham's *The Fane Fragment of the 1461 Lord's Journal*, (New Haven, Conn. 1935) had caused a certain alienation. Cf. C.V. Wedgwood *op. cit.*, p. 173. See also Pollard's review in *T.L.S.*, 5-9-1935.

[290] See A.F. Pollard, 'Documents Astray. The Problem of Ownership' in *The Times*, 1-9-1934, and 'The History of Parliament. An Editor for each Period' in *The Times*, 7-11-1938. Cf. also F.M. Powicke in *The Times*, 2-11-1938.

[291] *The Times*, 1-9- 1934.

[292] *Interim Report of the Committee on House of Commons Personnel and Politics, 1264–1832*, London, 1932. Reviewed in *T.L.S.*, 13-10-1932, pp. 717–718 (presumably by Pollard).

[293] L. Namier, *Crossroads of Power*, London, 1962, p. 5.

ment summarized the theories developed by Maitland and his successors: the very first parliament was seen as 'an afforced meeting of the
king's council' mainly remarkable for 'the dispensing of justice.' The
Commons had been less than necessary in that court of justice.[294] Nor
was the theory omitted concerning the passive attitude of the members
of the House of Commons.[295] The purpose of the work was to raise a
series of historical and even sociological questions concerning the
background and motivations of the representatives. Other questions
were e.g., the packing of parliament, the development of the system of
patronage, and the gradual party formation for the reasons of principle
as well as of private interest.[296] Underlining the topical significance of
the whole project, the writers pointed to the crisis of European parliamentary democracy: 'even in our own country' parliament was respected less.[297]

Not before 1950 did L. Namier and F.M. Stenton start a scholarly
attempt to elaborate the aims of this *Interim Report*: in Pollard's words
'the indispensable first aid to every student of Parliamentary history.'[298]
In a survey of 1956, Stenton gave a not unfavourable opinion of the
two pre-war volumes dealing with the period 1439–1509, which were
supervised by J. Wedgwood.[299] Pollard's work on the Tudor period
was described in the following terms: "it is unlikely that future work
will affect the essential pattern of his reconstruction."[300]

Stenton was right. In later books on the Elizabethan parliaments,
written by that much more specialized scholar J.E. Neale, the main
outline is almost swamped by the mass of details; but whenever a more
general evaluation is discernible one is reminded of Neale's teacher
Pollard. In his work, too, the Tudor phase is seen as the consolidation
of the House of Commons and preliminary to the parliamentary strife
under the Stuarts. He ended his discussion of the 'quality' of the House
of Commons under Elizabeth with the words:

The House of Commons reached maturity in Elizabeth's reign. The instrument was tempered with which the Crown was to be resisted and conquered.
It was not from the Stygian darkness of Tudor despotism that early Stuart

[294] *Interim Report*, p. 15.
[295] *Ibid.*, p. 32.
[296] *Ibid.*, p. 54.
[297] *Ibidem.*, p. 52; cf. C.V. Wedgwood, *op. cit.*, p. 169.
[298] See Julia Namier, *op. cit.*, p. 282 ff.
[299] F.M. Stenton, 'The History of Parliament' in *T.L.S.*, 6-1-1956, p. XII.
[300] *Ibid.*, p. XII.

parliaments emerged. They succeeded to a rich heritage, to great traditions.[301]

In this connection we no longer find Pollard's adjective 'necessary.' Now that Pollard had won, now that the phase which earlier historiography had dismissed as 'strange and isolated' was constitutionally and parliamentarily integrated, the word 'necessary' may have been viewed as superfluous. Consolidation was an important factor for Neale also: the 16th-century Commons acquired power over their own members, and as they acquired parliamentary privileges, their independence grew.[302] Later still, they began publicly to claim the right to initiatives, and they became a powerful oppositional force.[303] Parliament had in the 16th century become "a political force with which the Crown and government had to reckon."[304] Like Pollard and Notestein, Neale also stressed that the privy councillors were a link between government and parliament; he gave concrete examples of this fact, which would lose most of its importance later under the reign of James I.[305]

As a 16th-century specialist, Neale very rarely dealt with the preceding medieval phase. The one time that he did, in the *Festschrift* for Pollard in 1924, deserves to be mentioned.[306] His contribution was a careful essay on the privilege of freedom of speech. The essay compared the medieval development with the Tudor period, and ended by extolling the Tudors: the Middle Ages had not much more to offer than a vague 'customary right,' whereas in Tudor times the Commons demanded this right as their parliamentary privilege.[307]

Although behaving like a Tudor historian reading history backwards, Neale retained a balanced judgment even with regard to Stubbs. The essay left no doubt that there was a 'fundamental distinction' between the Middle Ages and the Tudor period, when the Commons had finally acquired a rather independent position. Stubbs must have

---

[301] J.E. Neale, *The Elizabethan House of Commons*, Harmondsworth, 1963, p. 307.

[302] J.E. Neale, *Elizabeth I and Her Parliaments*, London, 1965, I, p. 19: "Thus, between 1515 and 1558 the House of Commons had acquired the rights – not the exclusive right – to control the attendance of its members; it had created for itself the right to enforce its privilege of freedom from arrest; it had invented a power to imprison offenders against its privileges and its dignity; it had converted an uncertain prescriptive enjoyment of free speech into a formal privilege possessing revolutionary possibilities."

[303] *Ibid.*, I, pp. 176, 420–421; II, p. 436.

[304] *Ibid.*, I, p. 16.

[305] *Ibid.*, I, pp. 136 ff., 203, 244; II, pp. 243–244; J.E. Neale, *The Elizabethan House of Commons*, pp. 295–296, 341–344.

[306] J.E. Neale, 'The Commons' Privilege of Free Speech in Parliament' in *Tudor Studies*, ed. R.W. Seton-Watson, London, 1924, pp. 257–286. (Also included in *Historical Studies*, ed. E.B. Fryde and E. Miller, vol. II).

[307] *Ibid.*, pp. 265, 258.

been so captivated by the splendour of the historical vision which the 17th-century parliamentary antiquarians had of the Lancastrian Commons that he had even put new life into it.

And yet it was difficult for Neale, after perusing the rolls of parliament, to give up Stubbs altogether: "Few people reading through the rolls of parliament would escape thinking of the constitutional struggle under Henry IV as Stubbs thought of it, for the attacks upon the crown in that, and to some extent in Richard II's reign were seemingly launched by the Commons."[308] Neale, interpreting this inescapable fact in the light of the 'new school of administrative history,' explained it as an episode in the medieval struggle between king and aristocracy for control of the government, not as a premature rehearsal of the seventeenth century.[309] He agreed that the Commons were in a subordinate position, being simply one of the weapons in this struggle: "They were used by the lords as a body ... to initiate their requests ...."[310] Thus, when they took an initiative, it had no real value, it was a formal, procedural matter. Still, even Neale's thinking was bounded by a conditional "and yet ...", since in his judgment there was nothing in the records to justify a too negative view of the relationship between Lords and Commons and of their mutual 'intercommuning.' Neale, as it were, anticipated the essential meaning of J.G. Edwards's argument of 1958: "It would be a hasty conclusion, and one palpably untrue, to imagine in the light of this practice that the commons were no more than instruments of the lords."[311]

There now remains the question of the place Neale and other historians accorded to the Tudor period within the entire parliamentary development. However much Neale may have believed in the improved position of the Commons after the medieval period, he still placed the final victory definitely in the seventeenth century: "parliamentary sovereignty was born only in the seventeenth century – though in the womb, no doubt, in the sixteenth ...."[312] We have already said that Neale did not trace a clear line across the centuries, contrary to his teacher Pollard, who had explicitly devoted some research to the preceding medieval period. However, not even Pollard had made the 17th century

[308] *Ibid.*, p. 261.
[309] *Ibid.*, p. 261.
[310] *Ibid.*, p. 262.
[311] *Ibid.*, p. 263.
[312] *Ibid.*, pp. 273, 278.

an integral part of his argument; 1688 occurred in his work usually in a derogatory sense, as he liked to point out the defects of the Glorious Revolution.[313]

In the twenties the historian J.R. Tanner made a more detailed comparison of the constitutional development under the Tudors with that of the following century. Although he was a 17th-century expert, he was thoroughly familiar with the preceding Tudor period. In 1922 Tanner published *Tudor Constitutional Documents* with an accompanying commentary, where he gave his own interpretation of the constitutional development, partly following Pollard's argument. In the 16th century the Commons acquired 'a new sense of its own dignity,' which amounted to a useful training for the next century. The number of parliamentary privileges was notably increased.[314] Tanner had a highly remarkable (even contradictory) comment on the frequency and duration of the Tudor parliaments; first he spoke of an increase in length and then, five pages later, stated that all parliamentary sessions were short, even those of the Reformation Parliament. For all its significance, this 'long' parliament "stands alone in the 16th century. The striking fact about the sessions of Parliament taken over the whole period is that they were so short and were separated by such long intervals."[315] The remarkably low frequency and short duration of parliament retarded the growth of an organized opposition and hindered its control of the executive power. Tanner's 'balanced bookkeeping,' his counting of the 'parliamentary' years and months, clearly invalidated the revaluation Pollard had so actively promoted.[316]

Six years later Tanner published an often reprinted and still highly useful survey on the constitutional development in the 17th century. The survey admittedly mentioned a significant development under the Tudors, but without referring to Pollard. What it did quote was a statement from 1900 by G.W. Prothero, anticipating the Tudor historians who were to raise this idea to a position of such prominence. Now it was Tanner's turn to write: "One of the great achievements of the Tudor period on the constitutional side was the consolidation of

---

[313] Cf. *Evolution*, pp. 179 ff.; *The History of England*, p. 136 ff.

[314] J.R. Tanner, *Tudor Constitutional Documents*, 1485–1603, Cambridge, 1930, p. 512.

[315] *Ibid.*, p. 515 (cf. p. 512).

[316] *Ibid.*, p. 550: "It is remarkable that in the Tudor period ... there should have been steady progress in the development and definition of the privilege of Parliament. The explanation is to be found not in the strength of Parliament but in its weakness. It was the Tudor policy to rule by means of Parliament because the Tudor sovereigns were not afraid of Parliament. They were too strong to be threatened by their assemblies ...."

Parliamentary institutions."[317] There followed, however, the significant restriction that the Tudor parliaments were few and short-lived.[318] Plainly he believed that the 17th century had been decisive for the development of parliament into an indispensable, active and powerful part of the constitution. Yet in which period of that century did the decisive moment occur?

Notestein had in his lecture of 1924 outlined the essential role of the privy councillors in Parliament under the Tudors, "in order to point the contrast to the time that follows."[319] After Elizabeth their importance dwindled for a number of reasons; the initiative passed to the leaders of the Commons, which was exactly what Notestein was trying to prove. The decisive point, according to Notestein, occurred in the twenties. "The Bill of Rights is said to mark the point at which the legislative supremacy of Parliament was established. Was not the Bill of Rights immanent in the leadership of Coke, Sandys and Phelips in the twenties?"[320] Nor did Tanner see the Bill of Rights as decisive; in fact, he was remarkably silent about 1688, much more so than about the Civil War and its consequences. For him the point of decision occurred in the Restoration period: he judged the Restoration's long parliament – the so-called 'Pension Parliament' – worthy of terms like 'strong,' 'independent' and 'powerful,' all of them terms which the Tudor historians occasionally used for 'their' parliaments. "In the growth of this immensely strong and successful Opposition in the Pension Parliament, the Revolution of 1688 may be seen casting its shadow before it."[321] Tanner's view was evidently inspired by W.C. Abbott's study of 1906; moreover, his interpretation bore the imprint of an old idea from his teacher Seeley.[322] While not explicitly critical, Tanner's view weakened the effect of some statements by Tudor historians who at first sight seem to have gone too far in their sanguine views of the Tudor Commons, or unwittingly lost sight of the 17th-century sequel.

A more explicit criticism of some Tudor historians' view of Parliament was published only much later by the medievalist J.S. Roskell.

[317] J.R. Tanner, *English Constitutional Conflicts of the Seventeenth Century*, 1603–1689, Cambridge, 1966, pp. 5–6.
[318] *Ibid.*, p. 9.
[319] W. Notestein, *The Winning of the Initiative by the House of Commons*, p. 24.
[320] *Ibid.*, p. 53.
[321] J.R. Tanner, *op. cit.*, p. 241. Cf. pp. 217–232 and 236–237.
[322] W.C. Abbott, 'The Long Parliament of Charles II' in *E.H.R.* 21 (1906), pp. 21 ff., 254 ff.: cf. J.R. Seeley, *Introduction to Political Science*, Cambridge, 1923, pp. 236 ff., 262 ff.; J.R. Seeley, *The Growth of British Policy. An Historical Essay*, Cambridge, 1895, vol. II, pp. 171–172.

Again, the Tudor phase is depicted as a relatively unfruitful interval, an opinion mainly based on a comparison of the medieval parliament with the 17th-century development.[323] His survey of 1964 chiefly denied "the unreal distinction in the treatment of the history of parliament between the medieval and modern periods", the stress on the gap between the late medieval phase and the early 'modern' Tudor phase. He also repeated the reproach which G. Lapsley and others long ago levelled against Pollard's *The Evolution*, be it in the form of a question: "To help substantiate the responsibility of the Tudors for the emergence of parliament in the modern, say 'historic' phase, may they not have run the risk of depreciating the significance of parliament, especially its Lower House, in the medieval, say, 'prehistoric' phase?"[324]

Roskell's enumeration of the frequency and duration of the parliaments in the late medieval and Tudor phase greatly invalidated the probability of a gap. Pollard had not considered the lessening frequency under the Tudors as inconvenient; in his argument the more or less pre-supposed longer duration of the sessions was of far greater importance for the internal development of parliament. Now Roskell calculated that there were hardly any differences between the duration in the second half of the 15th century and the later Tudor period. He concluded like Tanner had done, that the duration of the Reformation Parliament was an exception.[325] The remarkable thing about the Tudor period was again that there had been such long intervals without any Parliament whatever. In Roskell's survey the only true gap in parliamentary history occurred late in the seventeenth century; parliament then entered a new and modern phase, as an independent, powerful and firmly established part of the constitution. Parliament earned the appellation of 'standing' parliament only after the decisions on frequency and duration had come into its own hands and, after the king had been forced (by a 'Triennial Bill') to summon Parliament at regular intervals, and was bereft of the power to dissolve it at his pleasure. Then and only then was it possible for parliament effectively to control the government.[326] Such was, in brief, Roskell's definition of the decisive importance of the 17th century in this respect.

What had meanwhile become of Tudor despotism's role in the de-

---

[323] J.S. Roskell, 'Perspectives in English Parliamentary History' in *Bulletin of the John Rylands Library* 46 (1963-1964), pp. 448-475. (also included in *Historical Studies*, ed. B.R. Fryde and E. Miller, vol. II).
[324] *Ibid.*, p. 455, cf. p. 452.
[325] *Ibid.*, p. 456-457.
[326] *Ibid.*, p. 453-455.

struction of medieval 'liberties' on behalf of 'Liberty'? To found a 'New Leviathan' by sweeping away all feudal medieval disintegration? And what, above all had become of the characteristic features distinguishing the Tudor period as 'preparatory' phase for the 17th-century struggle? Evidently the 'partnership,' so highly valued by Pollard, had no meaning in Roskell's evaluation; Roskell was concerned with the function of Parliament only as a controlling organ; not with its partnership in government affairs.[327] Roskell, while not unaware of that typical Pollardian treasury of ideas – a proudly self-conscious Tudor Commons with their own *Journal* and their own privileges – attached no special value to it either; these Commons had never more than a potential power.[328] Nor did he see a new potency in the Tudor situation; it was simply a continuation of the Middle Ages, and in some respects – concerning control of and the right to speak about taxation – it was even a step backwards.

What reduced the importance of the Tudor period was not only the gap which Roskell saw at the end of the 17th century. Also the Tudor 'preparation' appeared less significant compared with Roskell's favourite picture of the (late) medieval Commons. Roskell referred to the weapon of impeachment and to the agreement of the Commons as essential for direct taxation.[329] The Stuart period witnessed a noticeable revival of impeachment, and the oppositional Stuart parliaments were busy gathering still other medieval precedents. Whereas modern Tudor historians dismissed this as 'wishful thinking,' in Roskell's survey it regained more than strategic value:

The seventeenth-century lawyers, searching for precedents in the parliamentary records of the fourteenth and fifteenth centuries appropriate and apposite to their own situation, mistakes of interpretation though they committed from time to time, suffered from no delusions as to the importance and relevance of the work of their medieval forebears.[330]

He appreciated the salutary anti-Whig reaction shown by people like Pollard, Richardson and Sayles when stressing the influence of monarchical, legal and official elements in the development of parliament. Yet in his main outline the return of some elements of the old Whig interpretation were evident.

[327] It must be emphasized that this applies only to his *evaluation*: of course Roskell, too, mentioned this perspective in his criticism of G.R. Elton (see J.S. Roskell, *op. cit.*, pp. 457–458).

[328] *Ibid.*, p. 474.

[329] *Ibid.*, pp. 466–472.

[330] *Ibid.*, p. 474; cf. J.E. Neale, *Elizabeth I and Her Parliaments*, I, pp. 155 ff., 407 ff., 420.

When Roskell criticized J.E. Neale he made much of the failure of Peter Wentworth's efforts with regard to the development of free speech; again there was no more than a 'potentiality' of power, there was merely a desire to form an opposition and to take an initiative, but under the Tudors this could never come true. But had Neale ever denied this, we wonder?

He may have been guilty of occasional exaggeration when referring to the Commons as a 'powerful force,' yet Roskell himself had to acknowledge that the backbone of all Neale's work was his theory that the royal prerogative strongly dominated the whole sixteenth century and had never been seriously threatened.[331] As to 'preparation': J.E. Neale believed that it was preparation in itself just to learn how to conduct an opposition. On the other hand, he insisted, just as Tanner before him and Roskell afterwards, that the parliamentary sessions suffered from too little frequency and too short duration.[332] Borrowing the terminology of Richardson and Sayles, we might say that Roskell's criticism of Neale occasionally appears like a vain dispute about the niceties of language.

The substance of Roskell's criticism was aimed at the overvalued 'preparation' and 'consolidation' under the Tudors. The word 'preparation' implies that even Tudor historians still awaited the result, in this case, the unfurling of the real power of the Commons. Roskell's 'perspectives' can be reduced to one dominating perspective on the function of parliament in controlling the executive power; parliament possesses power only when strongly oppositional. That viewpoint makes the 'oppositional' periods the most important in the development of parliament; and seen from that angle, Roskell's evaluation of the different periods becomes understandable. The Whig historians shared the essential aspects of this opinion, but Pollard had tried to do something else in his work: he had tried to break through this perspective in order to see parliament as an extension and an instrument of government: that was his monarchical and administrative perspective. Of course, when parliament was an oppositional organ, its power was more in evidence, but that did not mean that as a governmental organ it could only be helplessly 'servile'. In this connection we should like to refer once more to a pronouncement of Pollard's, in which he described the constitutional Tudor revolution as a permanent transference of the initiative in legislation from the Commons to the 'Crown

331 J.E. Neale, *Elizabeth I and Her Parliaments*, II, p. 437; cf. J.S. Roskell, *op. cit.*, p. 463.
332 Cf. J.E. Neale, *The Elizabethan House of Commons*, pp. 296, 367.

and its ministers.'[333] In this transference Pollard saw the newness and modernity of the Tudors.

It will be clear that in this constitutional thinking the 'initiative' of the Commons was not so important. The English system, with its unique partnership between Crown and parliament, differed greatly from the continent. The continental Estates-General remained a weak organ of protest and opposition, which was shunted aside in the absolutist periods. The oppositional element of the English parliament was strong during the Lancastrian period; according to Pollard it had been an irresponsible opposition, hampering a more efficient system of government. Edward IV was the first to put an end to this separation, and it was made definitive by the Tudors in the union of the crown in parliament. A 'necessary' link was restored. This was Pollard's basic argument; in all essential points it still is Elton's. He was the Tudor historian to take up Roskell's challenge with a survey of his own, and the gist of Elton's reply can be termed 'Pollardian.'[334] Are the two views indeed fundamentally opposed? In our opinion a careful look at the different perspectives and the variety of parliamentary functions will lead to the conclusion that the views supplement each other.

Seen as a return to an old Whig pattern, Roskell's great outline may seem a somewhat peculiar ending to our survey of anti-Whig historiography on the subject of parliament in the first decades of the present century. However, we have also noticed that not even Stubbs had become totally submerged in this reaction, for there was a Stubbsian 'revival' in the thirties. We have attempted to make the work of the historian Pollard, especially his book *The Evolution*, the focus of the development of this historiography, without neglecting the two 19th-century 'phases' of our second chapter. The first phase was given something of a revival in the beginning of the 20th century. In the first half of the 19th century Whigs like Allen kept a distant and early parliamentary past at arm's length because of their fear of the coming democracy, but at the beginning of the 20th century the distance from the parliamentary past was the result of a crisis of parliamentary democracy itself. Still, in both cases the earliest parliamentary context was evoked both for Palgrave and Maitland by the 'records' themselves

[333] See note 104 of this chapter; see on the 'partnership' between crown and parliament under Henry VIII, S.E. Lehmberg's study, *The Reformation Parliament*, Cambridge, 1970, p. 255.

[334] G.R. Elton, *The Body of the Whole Realm. Parliament and Representation in Medieval and Tudor England*, Charlottesville, 1969, see esp. pp. 11, 16, 17, 53–55.

which were relegated to the background in the second half of the 19th century.

Pollard's work occupies the central place here. However indigestible for the present specialist, his work and his *Evolution* remain a monument for the development of historiography; we owe it to him that progress was made in the study of parliament both in its medieval and in its Tudor phases. In a more general sense Pollard's historical work of half a century is indissolubly welded within the development of English historiography in the first decades of the 20th century. Partly because of his efforts English historiography arrived at a turning-point. Then, too, he promoted historical scholarship and specialization, though not, especially during his last years, without misgivings. Was his anxiety wholly unfounded? The work of T.F. Tout and administrative history in general were soon to make the growing irrelevance of history even more plainly manifest to some people.

CHAPTER VI

ADMINISTRATIVE HISTORY: T. F. TOUT

> ... it would be a mistake to conclude that the
> history of institutions, lay and ecclesiastical, will
> continue indefinitely to absorb the attention of
> young men and women who want to know, in the
> current phrase, what the medieval world was all
> about ...
>
> (F.M. Powicke, 1947)

A. ADMINISTRATIVE HISTORY AS A REACTION TO WHIG HISTORIOGRAPHY

While analysing A.F. Pollard's work in the preceding chapter, we discussed the rise of a historical trend which had the avowed purpose of 'debunking' medieval parliamentary history by severely criticizing some parts of it. By stressing the judicial function, the 'conciliar' composition and the political insignificance of the medieval Commons some historians undermined the 'parliamentary myth' of the 19th century about medieval parliament.

Another way to reach the same goal is illustrated in the work of T.F. Tout. The history of administration and administrative offices gradually became a separate discipline in Tout's work. In the earliest phase there was no question of purposely striving for the formation of a new field of research. It only grew out of the reactions to the constitutional historiography of the 19th century, and it did so because people hoped that a more truthful historical reconstruction of medieval society might result from it. Here we may quote Tout, who in 1920 wrote in connection with the 19th-century anachronisms in historic representations: "... our natural absorption in the present had led us to study the past with minds too much set on present presuppositions. We seek in the middle ages what seems important to ourselves, not what was important to them."[1]

By way of this administrative history Tout hoped to penetrate into the true setting and factual context of medieval politics. Former con-

---

[1] T.F. Tout, *Chapters in the Administrative History of Medieval England*, Manchester, 1920–1929, I, p. 2.

stitutional historians had built their historical representations on the cornerstone of parliament, which had been banished to the periphery in administrative history. Tout did not characterize the traditional views of constitutional development as untrue or wrong; in his judgment they were simply 'out of focus'. His remedy for the overvaluation of the medieval parliamentary system was "the study of the machinery and daily routine of medieval executive government."[2] The medieval parliaments had never been part of the national routine, parliaments were of short duration, occurred only occasionally and owed their existence to exceptional rather than normal conditions. Tout made a fresh start stating that "administrative machinery was always in operation."[3] This made Tout's work part of the anti-Whig reaction to Victorian historiography; it might be said that, having finally located the true focus, he insisted on doing without the support of dogma's like the 'High Court' thesis and the belief in the conciliar character of Parliament's composition. In a way he criticized the old historiography less directly, but that made his critical remarks no less fundamental, despite his having several times dismissed an extreme High Court thesis. Parliament and the royal council were no part of the real executive power and continuous government; they formed no part of Tout's true focus.[4]

Tout had much praise for his teacher, Stubbs, and the latter's explanation of the administrative development under Henry I and II. An objection was that Stubbs had been too exclusively interested in the later parliamentary development. "Stubbs studied sheriffs and justices, juries and inquests, the exchequer and the *curia regis*, because he recognised in the routine fashioned at the will of a despot, the beginnings of our representative institutions, the House of Commons, and the constitutional monarchy of a later age."[5] Tout's intention was to add something qualitative to Stubbs's work, which would lead to re-orientation and re-interpretation.[6]

In Tout's view the reactions to the 19th-century parliamentary historiography amounted simply to replacing old generalizations by new ones; old extremist views were discarded in favour of new extremes.

---

[2] *Ibid.*, I, p. 7.
[3] *Ibid.*, I, p. 5.
[4] *Ibid.*, I, p. 11; II, pp. 146–148; III, p. 62 (note 3); V, p. 61.
[5] *Ibid.*, I, p. 2.
[6] *Ibid.*, p. 4. Cf. what A. Steel wrote in 1927: "Administrative history, which is to-day only in its infancy, is doing a great work, not so much in correcting Stubbs – for that is a comparatively small one – as in supplying something towards our knowledge of those elements in later medieval life which Stubbs ignored." in *History* 12 (1927–1928), p. 308.

To combat both, he wanted a new method, and administrative history lent itself admirably to this purpose. Essential for this method was a conscientious and detailed inquiry into the records. In Tout's case it was partly biographical investigation, following his early training acquired in the *Dictionary of National Biography*.[7]

His new approach was justified because the new method seemed to bring the result within reach. The approach was based on the one presupposition which was to be Tout's lifelong guideline:

> To imagine the past correctly we must picture it in its minutest details, because it is only by studying it in such a fashion that we can rightly obtain a sound conception of the structure and functions of bygone human society as a whole.[8]

A highly specialized and detailed investigation should lead to the nearest truthful picture of a past reality; to this end all means were justified. Tout himself fully realized how dull his approach could be, and how trivial some details must at first sight seem to the investigator, but he was deeply convinced "not only that the most trivial of historical details may be used to illustrate a principle of general importance, but also that the work most specially needed in English medieval history is just the patient and plodding working out of apparently unimportant detail."[9] Later in this chapter we shall discuss whether the hoped-for result was actually reached and whether it was at all possible to reach such results in that way.

B. ADMINISTRATIVE HISTORY: A MIRROR OF THE TIMES

It is easy to see Tout's administrative history as part of the reaction to Whig historiography. Tout forced the English medievalists to have a new range of interests, plainly characteristic of the period around the turn of the century. Thus, administrative history has also been designated as a reflection of that time.[10] A growing bureaucratization and the increasing power of the Civil Service caused a noticeable shift in historic interests: "Administration is more important than legislation, even in modern times", as Tout would have it.[11] In the earlier

[7] About the *D.N.B.*, cf. T.F. Tout, *op. cit.*, I, pp. 28, 64; II, p. 18. Cf. A.T. Milne on Tout as the 'precursor' of the biographical method, in *Historical Study in the West*, introd. B.C. Shafer, New York, 1968, p. 166.

[8] T.F. Tout, *op. cit.*, I, p. 26.

[9] *Ibid.*, I, p. 27.

[10] Cf. G. Barraclough, *History in a Changing World*, Oxford, 1957, p. 22 ff.

[11] T.F. Tout, *op. cit.*, I, pp. 4–5.

constitutional history increasing or decreasing political liberties had been the yardstick for a historical evaluation. In administrative history that yardstick was, in a sense, efficiency: periods were labelled according to their administrative efficiency. Thus did one period become far more relevant than others, and thus did Edward II's period in Tout's work easily outrank the reign of his great constitutional predecessor.

It was natural for this new branch of history, as a mirror of the times, not to limit itself to the medieval period. H.W.C. Davis, in an extensive review of Tout's work, mentioned analogous tendencies in the historiography on Greek and Roman antiquity. He wondered whether this new trend was something more than just a symptom of a 'sceptical reaction to 19th-century liberalism.'[12] And F.M. Powicke, enumerating the initiators of administrative history in England, ranged medievalists like Tout and C.J. Davies next to the Webbs and the economic historian G. Unwin. Powicke later wrote that, for all their political differences "all good administrative historians seem to hold one conviction in common: a belief in the importance of deliberate efficiency, whether in civil service, or in the members of a trade union."[13]

Until the end of the 19th century the Anglo-Saxon world had never shown much interest in the professional art of government, in any case much less than France and Germany. Woodrow Wilson stated this fact in 1886, in a lecture entitled 'The Study of Administration.'[14] As a political scientist, he felt that this particular field of study was of great importance; as a historian, he tried to explain why the English lagged behind in this respect.

The English race ... has long and successfully studied the art of curbing executive power to the constant neglect of the art of perfecting executive methods. It has exercised itself much more in controlling than in energizing government. It has been more concerned to render government just and moderate than to make it facile, well-ordered and effective.[15]

[12] Cf. his words: "Whether it is merely one more symptom of a sceptical reaction against nineteenth-century liberalism, or whether it is really based upon a new and deeper conception of the nature of civilized government, time alone can show." in E.H.R. 36 (1921), p. 108. Cf. J.B. Bury, The Imperial Administrative System in the Ninth Century, London, 1911; cf. C.J. Davies, The Baronial Opposition to Edward II, its Character and Policy: A Study in Administrative History. Cambridge, 1918. See also the anonymous review of this book in History 5 (1920–21), pp. 178–179.

[13] F.M Powicke, 'Administrative History' in T.L.S., 6-1-1956, pp. XXVI–XXVII.

[14] See The Papers of Woodrow Wilson, ed. A.S. Link, Princeton, 1968, V, pp. 357–380.

[15] Ibid., V, p. 367.

In 1920 Tout construed a similar argument to explain why adminis-trative history had lagged behind in British historiography.[16]

Wilson went on to say that attention had been focused on the triumph of the much-extolled Anglo-Saxon constitutional system to the neglect of an efficient and orderly government. After the period of absolutism and a more constitutional phase, European history now seemed to be entering into a third period; the day of a new adminis-trative science had dawned which was going to render government less 'unbusinesslike.' Now was the time to conquer the old fear of cen-tralized power and the fear that bureaucracy would pose a threat to liberty. Deeply rooted though this distrust was, Wilson, as a new liberal, proved it to be wrong and unreasonable. He insisted that politics and administration should be kept separate; politicians might state the aims, but the officials had to provide the most efficient means for attaining these aims. With too much separation of powers the situation would become so impenetrable that political abuse of power and irresponsibility were bound to follow. A.F. Pollard used to reason along similar lines, and the same general trend became discernible in English administrative history without any direct or conscious influence from the American new liberalism.

In the young political science a new discipline, administrative science, was developing along with a rising interest within the historical world for the role of administration in the past. This subject was not entirely new, since there already existed a tradition in Germany of *Verwaltungsgeschichte* (administrative history), and the mention of Tocqueville should be sufficient for France.[17] There were also some pioneers in England, among them Th. Madox early in the 18th century and, in a sense, Francis Palgrave a century afterwards. They, however, stood alone. A new phenomenon occurred around the turn of the century when administrative history became a separate discipline, fascinating medievalists like Round, Poole and, above all, Tout. The latter was certainly not influenced by America or Germany, but he was undeniably influenced by that branch of French historiography around the turn of the century which would become known under the slightly misleading name of *l'histoire événementielle*.

---

[16] T.F. Tout. *op. cit.*, I, pp. 1–2.
[17] Cf. E. Fueter, *Geschichte der neueren Historiographie*, München, 1911, p. 557.

C. T. F. TOUT AND THE FRENCH HISTOIRE ÉVÉNEMENTIELLE

La science approfondie des institutions.

(A. Luchaire)

Tout's work makes it abundantly clear that nothing could have been more wrong than the belief that before the First World War only the Germans had any noticeable influence on English historiography.[18] As early as 1889 Tout mentioned 'the admirable school of historians that is now growing up in France,' in his review of C.V. Langlois's *Le Règne de Philippe III le Hardi*. In his opinion this school was initiating new methods and new interpretations, and Tout proved his point by writing that the historians of this school were too well-informed ever to believe

that the importance of a period rests upon the personal character of the prince. The slow development of the administrative institution of the monarchy went on just the same whether a saint or a hero or a common-place mediocrity sat upon the throne.[19]

To explain that the developing administrative tradition had a mechanism of its own he wrote:

To assume . . . that the regular development of . . . institutions supposes the single directive hand of a monarch is an unverifiable hypothesis. The existence of a regular tradition of government among the clerks and knights of the royal court is *the only true explanation of the facts*. French history is no more a series of biographies of famous kings and ministers. It owes its real interest and importance to the development of institutions.[20]

Although 1889 was an early date, the creed then stated already implied several of the more important presuppositions of administrative history; an amplification is in order, for which some of those French historians admired by Tout may prove useful. It is not quite clear which ones were part of the new school, but we can state with certainty that, for Tout, Langlois, the elder Achille Luchaire and the legal historian Paul Viollet were exponents of the new trend.[21]

A. Luchaire (1846–1908) has already been mentioned at some length in our first chapter. Medievalists like him and Fustel de Coulanges did away with the romantic visions of the Middle Ages in the second half of the 19th century. In 1910, F.M. Powicke wrote about Luchaire:

---

[18] Cf. G. Lefebvre, *La naissance de l'historiographie moderne*, Paris, 1971, p. 282.

[19] *E.H.R.* 4 (1889), p. 364.

[20] *Ibid.*, Our emphasis.

[21] Tout reviewed a great number of books by French medievalists; cf. *E.H.R.* 16 (1901), pp. 355–358; *E.H.R.* 18 (1903), p. 143 ff. (on A. Luchaire); *E.H.R.* 19 (1904), pp. 347–349, 754–757. Cf. also J.B. Mullinger in *E.H.R.* 14 (1899), p. 134 ff.

"he was one of the best representatives of the second generation of French scholars which has sought to throw off the prejudices of race and the influence of romanticism."[22] In 1883 he published the first of his major works, the *Histoire des institutions monarchiques de la France sous les Premiers Capétiens*, in which he broke away definitively from the romantic nationalist view – often racially tinged – of the early French monarchy. The central fact in Luchaire's work is the gradual and painstaking growth of a monarchical administrative tradition, which to his mind constituted the one and only real and lasting base for a future French state. This administrative development was what gave the Middle Ages their relevance; from this growing administrative tradition had emanated a powerful formative influence, which in his opinion had decided the course of history, at least to a greater extent than had such vague factors as 'national feeling' or 'strong personality.' Their explanatory value began to be increasingly doubted. Luchaire presented his administrative history as a new historical approach whose quality far outranked narrative political history.[23]

Our first chapter mentioned the dawn of a monarchical perspective in medieval studies, especially in the history of administration. This new perspective should not be regarded as the extension of a romantic-heroic and highly moralising conception of history. On the contrary, it was a reaction to that conception: Tout's review of 1889 made this quite clear. The adherents of this new branch of history were not concerned with the king as a person; for them, he was a functionary or official. Their concern was with the monarchy not as an ideal form of government but as a useful tool for unification of the state. Thus, the king and his court were seen as the administrative centre from which even more organs sprang in the same proportion as administrative functions increased under the stress of circumstances. In this institutional approach the growing division in administrative labour was the chief trait of the historic evolution as such, which finally made the royal councillors and officials more important than the king in his own person. The evolution of the *curia regis* did not run parallel to an increase in personal power of the monarch; what increased was the administrative apparatus which sprang up around the person of the monarch.[24] As this 'bureaucratic' image of the medieval kings became accepted, the old image was robbed of its idealized religious aspects.

[22] *E.H.R.* 25 (1910), p. 564.
[23] A. Luchaire, *Histoire des institutions monarchiques de la France sous les Premiers Capétiens*, Paris, 1891, I, p. V.
[24] Cf. C.V. Langlois, *Le Règne de Philippe III le Hardi*, Paris, 1887, pp. 12 ff., 304.

This change gave to many medievalists a more truthful reflection of medieval reality. Luchaire is a very good example of this: his work may be said to have a strongly secular trend. It was only to the political and institutional aspects of medieval catholicism that he gave his historian's interest, as can be seen by his later great book on Innocent III.[25] He dismissed medieval religion with the famous expression – later with much approval quoted by G.G. Coulton: "La vraie religion du moyen âge, il ne faut pas s'y tromper, c'est le culte des reliques."[26]

Apart from his interest in Luchaire and other French medievalists, Tout was much attracted to the work of the historian Paul Viollet, with a special preference for the *Histoire des institutions politiques et administratives de la France*.[27] Viollet, unlike Luchaire, was a devout Catholic, but there was hardly any difference between his historic-institutional approach to the Middle Ages and that of Luchaire's. We will only give a short discussion of some of Viollet's *idées maîtresses*; with some changes they recur in Tout's work as well as in the work of numerous other administrative historians.

In the introduction to the first volume of his major work, dating from 1890, Viollet insisted that the development of history (and administration) was largely unplanned. The laws deciding the course of history were "indépendantes de la volonté de l'homme et supérieures à cette volonté."[28] A historical evolution was taking place through the centuries; contemporaries might look on, but they were unable to discern its direction, let alone its final target. All too often history seemed to set its own course without any interference from a human agency.[29] Viollet repeatedly quoted that 'man proposes but God disposes.' There is an undercurrent of meaning in this saying echoing the fatalist *Heterogonie der Zwecke* – somewhat softened by Christianity.[30] An important characteristic of this conception of history is that it leaves little scope for individual actions. "L'histoire sociale et constitutionelle, telle que nous la comprenons, laisse peu de place à

---

[25] Cf. Imbart de la Tour, 'Achille Luchaire' in *Revue des Deux Mondes* 52 (109), pp. 876–901, particularly p. 886 ff.

[26] A. Luchaire, *La Société Française au temps de Philippe Auguste*, Paris, 1909, p. 30. Cf. G.G. Coulton in *History* 9 (1924–1925), p. 11.

[27] The first volume of his work had been reviewed by H.A.L. Fisher, see *E.H.R.* 6 (1891), p. 165. Tout reviewed the next two volumes, see *E.H.R.* 21 (1906), pp. 768–772. Cf. F.M. Powicke, *Modern Historians and The Study of History*, London, 1956, p. 33.

[28] P. Viollet, *Histoire des institutions politiques et administratives de la France*, Paris, 1890–1903, I, p. 11.

[29] *Ibid.*, I, p. 256. Cf. II, p. 188.

[30] See F. Delaborde, 'Notice sur la vie et les travaux de M. Paul Viollet' in *Bibliothèque de L'École des Chartes'* 79 (1918), pp. 153–154, 164–165; P. Fournier, 'Paul Viollet' in *Nouvelle Revue Historique de droit français et étranger* 38 (1914–1915), pp. 816–827.

l'action individuelle; que pèsent les 'grands hommes,' en face de ces forces mal connues qui les poussent et dont il ne sont, la plupart du temps, que les agents?"[31]

The course of history may owe very little to any direct actions of mankind, yet from an administrative point of view it was firmly governed by two laws: "la loi de division progressive du travail et des fonctions et la loi de centralisation progressive."[32] Thus the division of labour becomes at once the cause and the result of an increasing centralization. The reverse side of the coin was an increasing loss of 'self-government' in its most autarchic sense. Viollet believed that the historical facts permitted only of one single generalization: the division of labour and the separation of functions. He referred repeatedly to it in his argument.[33] Personally, he was critical of this centralization, but as a historian he believed that it was unavoidable.[34] The bureaucratic process through which the state turned into a 'gigantesque usine' was more frightening than desirable; yet he sought to investigate its origin and growth both in the Middle Ages and the modern period. What he did perceive was a sort of mechanism peculiar to the origin and growth of institutions, which he found difficult to explain except through comparison with physical and biological laws. The analogy with the physical world was not only to be found in Viollet's arguments, for it is also in Luchaire, Langlois and other administrative historians.[35] The entire social and administrative context was, for them, governed by its own laws, irrespective of whether kings were weak or strong.

This mechanism was active from the very beginnings of any system or institution. Discussing the origin of feudalism, Viollet states emphatically that no single system can be called the direct product of the human intellect or the human will. "... toute organisation, au lieu d'être un jour inventée par quelque homme de génie, se fait d'elle-même, se fait lentement."[36] Because of his realism he rejected the ideational historical explanation of the origin of feudalism; feudalism was not a product of ideas – neither roman nor germanic – but the outcome of "lois de la necessité présente, cette souveraine jamais détrônée."[37] Not only Viollet's work bears the stamp of this intentional-

[31] P. Viollet, *op. cit.*, I, p. VII, cf. p. 257.
[32] *Ibid.*, I, p. IV.
[33] *Ibid.*, I, p. 217; II, pp. 104, 138; III, p. 524.
[34] *Ibid.*, II, p. 141. Cf. P. Fournier, *op. cit.*, p. 824.
[35] Cf. P. Viollet, *op. cit.*, I, p. VII, cf. p. 257.
[36] *Ibid.*, p. 419.
[37] *Ibid.*, pp. 459–460; cf. also P. Fournier, *op. cit.*, p. 821.

ly non-ideological approach; it is characteristic for administrative history as such.[38]

He had similar thoughts about the further development of administrative institutions. Again the stress on the spontaneous, non-planned and unexpected aspects of the development, pointing out that the development occurred willy-nilly: "Les institutions se font avec le temps; mais, à proprement parler, on ne les fait pas ...."[39] At the end of the third volume the text ran as follows: "... Les institutions se faisaient, comme dira Portalis, par une sorte de végétations et de croissance spontanée; on ne les faisait pas, aucune loi écrite ... ne présidait à ce développement naturel."[40] Yet Viollet expressly kept his evolutionist theory free from Darwinist influences; what he desired was an anti-finalism in historical matters, which was later also propagated in England by Pollard, as we noticed. It was a theory of growth, not directly related to the romantic historiography then under such sharp attack, but resembling rather some of H. Spencer's sociological thoughts. Viollet even quoted him.[41]

Briefly, what was central to Viollet's administrative history was the making of the state as a constant and permanent regulating factor, of whatever form or shape. Reading his paragraphs about the state in the making, it is difficult to escape the conclusion that he could not withstand the temptation to trace this modern Leviathan to its earliest possible stage. In the first volume he wrote:

L'État se ressemble toujours à lui-même ... Qu'il préside, comme aux VIIIe et IXe siècles, au salut des âmes, comme aux XVIIe et XVIIIe, au commerce et à l'industrie, comme au XIXe, à l'instruction publique, il légifère, il réglemente, non seulement avec la même conviction, mais avec la même abondance, avec le même luxe de détails.[42]

Where Tocqueville had proved that there was an administrative continuity between the period of the revolution and that of the *ancien régime*, Viollet had a less brilliant but much more all-embracing view: even the medieval period was part of one and the same evolution. He saw the rise of the modern state within the context of the growing

[38] On the 'relationship' between administrative history and 'Realpolitik,' cf. W.H. Dunham in *Speculum* 39 (1964), p. 563. See also J. Hart, 'Nineteenth-Century Social Reform: A Tory Interpretation of History' in *Past and Present* no. 31 (1965), pp. 39–61. We think it confusing to use the term 'Tory' interpretation here.

[39] P. Viollet, *op. cit.*, II, p. 17.

[40] *Ibid.*, III, p. 523.

[41] *Ibid.*, I, p. II; II. p. 16 (note 1), Cf. for Pollard's Spencerian evolutionism, ch. V, note 167.

[42] P. Viollet, *op. cit.*, I, p. 369.

medieval monarchy. The triumph of the latter laid the foundation for the triumph of the modern state: "Ce fut longtemps le secret de notre force. C'est aujourd'hui le secret de notre maturité."[43] Monarchy in France made its exit towards the end of the 18th century, (only to make a brief reappearance during the 19th century). The state itself, however, survived to continue the work of ages.[44]

Viollet and other administrative historians of the period around 1900 gave facts rather than views in their writings. But the facts collected and selected by these erudite persons were based on one view which partly decided their selection and interpretation. It was: that all states shared the same mechanism of growth, that the central administration in the rising Western European states possessed an impersonal and coercive power. The *histoire événementielle*, coinciding as it did with this administrative history, undoubtedly gave more scope and more depth to the understanding of history. An interpretative innovation from this new branch of history was valued even by the sociologist Norbert Elias, not ordinarily a believer in the 'scientific' standards of history.[45] At last historical scholarship seemed to be on the right road. We will return to this point later in connection with our discussion of the deficiencies of administrative history.

D. T. F. TOUT AND HIS ADMINISTRATIVE HISTORY

> Our real masters are not the voters, still less are they the vote-hunting politicians who flit from office to office, either singly or in whole packs. Our masters are the demure and obscure gentlemen in neat black coats and tall hats who are seen every morning flocking to the government offices in Western London at hours varying according to their dignity.
>
> (T.F. Tout, 1915).

The statement that Tout had already at an early stage been attracted to the new French administrative history, should be qualified in two ways. The first is that theoretically Tout was not inclined to regard this branch of history as the only valid approach. He was especially enthusiastic for the few pages in which Viollet ventured outside his narrow framework to place the medieval period in a much wider

---

[43] *Ibid.*, II, p. 20.
[44] *Ibid.*, II, p. 185; III, p. 12; Cf. also P. Viollet, *Le Roi et ses ministres*, Paris, 1912, p. VIII.
[45] N. Elias, *Über den Prozess der Zivilisation*, Bern-München, 1969, II, pp. 37–38.

cultural perspective. The famous high-flown introduction to Viollet's second volume, entitled "Le Moyen Age au point de vue de nos origines" went straight to his heart; two years before his death, in 1927, he once more praised this particular passage.[46]

In the second place, Tout's ideas around 1900 may have foreshadowed his coming specialization, but it would still be some time before he found that he could use the French approach in English medieval history. The delay had a number of causes, both practical and ideological. His many encyclopedia articles and general surveys took up the time which he would have needed for more thorough research; yet he did manage to publish in this first phase a number of original studies on the subject of medieval military history and the history of Wales.[47] Apart from these practical considerations, he was also still influenced by the tradition of his teacher, Stubbs. There was, for instance, Tout's concise monograph on Edward I, published in 1893, which certainly mirrored Stubbs's ideas on constitution and parliament. G. Templeman is undoubtedly right in stating that it took Tout a quarter of a century completely to revise his ideas on Edward I.[48] Nevertheless, even this early book foreshadows something of that 'unpersonal' view of administration that later became the most dominating feature of Tout's work. And this did not escape G.W. Prothero's critical eye: he believed that Tout, in *Edward I*, had mistakenly belittled the King's personal share in the important legislation of that period: "He (Tout) refuses to credit him with the 'initiative,' or with 'any great originality or insight.' The chief praise for judicial and other reforms, he thinks, belongs to the king's ministers and advisers."[49]

What brought Tout to the writing of his major work was E. Déprez' study, *Études de diplomatique anglaise, 1272–1485*, which carried the subtitle of 'Le sceau privé. Le sceau secret. Le signet.' Tout reviewed this book extensively in the *English Historical Review*, two years after reviewing Viollet's work.[50] However, his investigations into the privy seal and its history soon developed within a much wider scope than the purely diplomatic framework of Eugène Déprez. In 1913, Tout de-

[46] Cf. *E.H.R.* 21 (1906), p. 772 and *History* 12 (1927–1928), p. 69.

[47] See especially the articles in the second volume of his *Collected Papers*, Manchester, 1934; see for Tout, both personally and for his work as a historian, the articles by Mary Tout and S. Alexander, published in vol. I of the *Collected Papers*. See further J. Tait, 'T.F. Tout' in *E.H.R.* 45 (1930), pp. 78–85; A.G. Little, 'Professor Tout' in *History* 14 (1929–1930), pp. 313–324 and F.M. Powicke, *Modern Historians and the Study of History*, pp. 21–44.

[48] G. Templeman, 'Edward I and the Historians' in *The Cambridge Historical Journal* 10 (1950), pp. 24–25.

[49] *E.H.R.* 9 (1894), p. 566.

[50] *E.H.R.* 23 (1908), pp. 556–559.

livered the Ford Lectures, and during the war there were a few other lectures and articles, all preliminary studies for his major work, the first two volumes of which were published in 1920.[51]

In December, 1915, Tout delivered a lecture called 'The English Civil Service in the Fourteenth Century.' In it, he elucidated some special aspects for research within his administrative history, e.g. the growth of offices which had become independent from the Court, the background and status of officials, and the various appointment procedures. He also explained how the recent bureaucratization of state and society had influenced his approach. The lecture touched briefly but very vividly on a wide range of subjects: the political changes mentioned in our third chapter, the state's responsibilities, the high status of the professional civil service, the acknowledgment that a more permanent bureaucracy wielded greater power than political systems subject to change. Only after this did Tout start on his proper medieval subject, stating that the 'Civil Service' had actually existed before it acquired its 19th-century name.[52]

Tout could afford a large measure of schematization in lectures like these, but in the six volumes of his major work he stuck to details. Many readers complained, and rightly so, that the highly detailed analyses of administrative organs and functions were rarely placed in the framework of a wider social-political development. The true importance of this administrative history might thus have been shown to better advantage.[53] However, attentive and persevering readers were able to discern a number of outlines.[54]

The more conspicuous and frequently studied offices of the Chancellor and the Exchequer were not Tout's main concern; his favourite subjects were 'wardrobe' and 'camera': tiny beginnings growing into administrative bodies of the royal household. The fact that this was practically virgin territory was not the only reason for his choice; nor had he selected the development and functioning of these bodies in themselves, however much this mistaken impression may have been fostered by his painstaking attention to detail. He investigated everything pertaining to the 'privy seal' and the later 'small seals,' not because of their antiquarian value, his concern was how they func-

---

[51] F.T. Tout, *The Place of the Reign of Edward II in English History*, Manchester, 1914.

[52] See *Collected Papers*, III, pp. 191–221, esp. 191–194.

[53] Cf. the criticism in *T.L.S.*, 19-8-1920.

[54] Cf. also Tout's own summary in a lecture given in 1923, called 'Some conflicting tendencies in English administrative history during the fourteenth century,' see *Collected Papers*, III, p. 223 ff.; cf. also G. Lapsley, 'Some Recent Advance in English Constitutional History' in *The Cambridge Historical Journal* 5 (1936), pp. 121–122.

tioned as instruments of power under kings concerned with enforcing their own authority against an aristocratic opposition, which tried itself to increase its own hold on the central administration.[55] Wardrobe and camera, administrative bodies connected with the king's personal power, functioned until the 13th century as a counter-balance to the more 'public' and 'national' offices of Chancellor and Exchequer. These were relatively independent of the Court, since they had for some time been made 'official.' Wardrobe and camera would develop in a similar way which finally was to depersonalize the monarchy; in Tout's words it was then entirely 'officialised'.

When the privy seal, the secret seal and the signet were 'officialised', the king had no longer any personal power. He, too, became an official, part of an administrative routine which largely determined his power relationship with his counselors. That the monarchy finally acquired its present shape, was due more to this administrative routine than to any constitutional idea. Admittedly, the process had taken centuries. "There is the perpetual effort to distinguish by a visible token between the king as an official and the king in his personal capacity", Tout wrote in the last volume. He proceeded with:

There are the equally unending struggles of the king to extricate himself from the network of red tapes which choked his personal initiative and hedged his authority by forms and routine which destroyed his individual will. But the office was greater than the man, and the strongest king could not success-fully distinguish between the two. Even in the age of Angevin despotism, routine stayed the hand of the autocrat.[56]

The rise of this medieval administrative routine as one of the factors deciding the power relationship between the king and the 'barons' had a constitutional importance as well. Tout may be said to have attempted a clarification, sometimes even an explanation, of the permanent political tension between king and barons. At any rate, he analysed the institutional aspects of this struggle: "In the failure of the sovereign to preserve a personal seal we see the whole process of our constitutional development."[57] On the one hand, Tout elucidated the king's attempts at personal government, on the other hand, he signalled the resistance of the aristocracy with their continuous efforts to control the royal household by turning the 'court officials' into 'state officials'.[58]

[55] Cf. T.F. Tout, *Chapters in the Administrative History of Medieval England*, I, p. 26; cf. V, p. 161 ff. (chapter 'The reduplications of the privy seal').
[56] *Ibid.*, V, p. 229.
[57] *Ibid.*, V, p. 229.
[58] *Ibid.*, I, p. 219 ff.; II, p. 10 ff.; V, p. 207.

These self-seeking barons, while gradually enlarging their own power, unwittingly and unintentionally caused the final victory of the State. Tout, contrary to his French colleagues, stressed the aristocracy's important contribution towards the formation of the State. Was it not the direct aim of their resistance to have the government of the country taken out from the King's personal influence and to make it independent of his personal environment, the Court? Indeed, their aim was to make government into a 'public' affair in the medieval-aristocratic meaning of the word. Tout wrote in his first volume:

The separation between the state and the household was due to inherent political necessity. It was, however, brought about much more quickly in England, because of the strength of the baronial power at the critical time of the process.[59]

This development had first started under Henry III, and Edward I was called a conservative because he tried to curtail this early differentiation between private and public affairs. Yet this division was consolidated during the reign of Edward II, and Tout therefore located a turning-point in medieval history with Edward II. It was then that *hospicium* and *regnum* became separated, and the differences between 'offices of the royal household' and 'offices of the state' became definitely clear: the Wardrobe (with privy seal) was separated from the Court (became 'out of Court') as an 'office of the State,' whereas the King retreated into his 'camera,' keeping his 'secret seal' as – provisionally – a last line of defence for the royal prerogative.[60]

Tout's general conclusion was that "the machine of the State, as left by Edward II, retained its general shape for the rest of the middle ages."[61] After Edward II a non-political corps of civil servants sprang up; an administrative tradition was consolidated which lasted all through the middle ages despite 'political' revolutions. Tout never wearied of insisting that 'politics' and 'administration' were two separate entities after this time.[62] This separation – a common enough thesis around 1900 – made his historical view clearly non-ideological. For did not this conception minimalise the significance of ideological party politics? Such politics were reduced to a mere facade hiding the existence of a permanent administration. Politics might bring reaction or revolution, but the administrative structure remained unchanged.

[59] *Ibid.*, I, p. 182, cf. also pp. 212–213.
[60] *Ibid.*, II, pp. 60, 188 ff., 222–223, 312–313; V, p. 143 ff.
[61] *Ibid.*, II, p. 189.
[62] Cf. C.G. Crump's review in *E.H.R.* 44 (1929), pp. 130–131. Cf. T.F. Tout, *op. cit.*, II, pp. 218, 281; IV, p. 187.

The recurring conclusion of Tout's research, therefore, points to a continuity in the administration since Edward II.[63]

Summarizing, Tout's *Administrative History* may be said to have attempted an elucidation of the constitutional development, but he differed greatly from his predecessors in the way he approached it. Rather than dealing with this development as part of a constitutional history of ideas, he gleaned his interpretation from a close study of the facts of the developing central administration. In this sense his work was a landmark, which was why G. Lapsley considered it a significant re-interpretation – perhaps the most important one in English medieval studies during the first decades of the twentieth century.[64] The administration was of paramount importance in Tout's thesis, because he believed in the powerful influence of the administrative routine and in the increasing separation between politics and administration.

This idea of a growing independence of the administration was responsible for the dwindling of his historical interpretation. As a specialist, he had intended to restrict his activities to one area, which was justified by his conviction that this particular field of inquiry enabled one to gain a better insight into the structure of a past society. The vision prompting Tout's choice was concisely expressed in 1889 in a kind of 'credo,' which was to be elaborated in his major work. Tout's firm belief that the administration had become a world of its own, and was regulated by its own mechanism, made him look only in this world for an explanation; he disregarded 'external' factors originating outside the administrative enclosure.[65] Thus his specialization lacked all connection with other fields of life, although after the third volume Tout himself abandoned the strictly thematic treatment and presented his administrative history in the chronological framework of the political development. His interpretation did not allow for any further relationship: his conception of the relation between politics and administration was based on the view that "the existence of a regular tradition of government ... is the only true explanation of the facts."

Tout's administrative history, like other administrative studies of that period, questioned only the way in which the institutions functioned. A quarter of a century ago W.H. Dunham wrote:

Medievalists, like so many other historians in 1930, were most concerned

---

[63] *Ibid.*, II, pp. 217–218; III, pp. 10, 20, 385; IV, pp. 64–65, 187.
[64] G. Lapsley, *op. cit.*, p. 212.
[65] Cf. e.g., E. Perroy's criticism in *Le Moyen Age*, 30 (1929), p. 110.

with finding out the nature of past institutions, what they were like, and how they worked. So when they wrote about what happened, what the English government did, they concentrated less upon the causes than upon the means, upon how men governed more than upon the purposes of government.[66]

Attention shifted from aims to means, from 'why' to 'how'; it was a chief characteristic of the historiography in the period we are concerned with, a historiography plainly reacting to some of the presuppositions of the 19th-century Whig historiography. For all their great differences Tout and the Webbs shared a dominating interest in organizational matters.[67] Tout intentionally restricted the scope of his research, and explicitly rejected a search for motives. He believed this would lead the historian astray from the firm ground of administrative history and into the swamp of guesswork. "... As always in medieval history, though we can carefully record the acts of the period, we at once fall back into vain conjecture when we begin to investigate the motives which inspired those acts."[68] Nevertheless, in his reviews of the books of his fellow historians, Tout repeatedly exhorted them to reproduce the right 'historical atmosphere.'[69] Had not his own administrative history meant to achieve just that? And finally, did he indeed succeed with his specialization?

E. THE REACTION: THE LIMITS OF ADMINISTRATIVE
HISTORY AND THE ILLUSIONS OF SPECIALIZATION

> It has been fashionable of late years to lay emphasis upon the bureaucratic element in medieval England, just as French scholars trace the connection between bureaucratic development in medieval France and the later French autocracy. Yet if we compare medieval and modern conditions, we find that the bureaucrat plays a comparatively small part in the administration of daily affairs.
>
> (F.M. Powicke, 1931)

[66] W.H. Dunham in *The English Government at Work, 1327–1336*, ed. J.F. Willard, W.A. Morris, W.H. Dunham, vol. III: *Local Administration and Justice*, Cambridge Mass., 1950, p. XVI.

[67] Cf. for the Webbs, V.L. Allen, 'Valuations and Historical Interpretation: A Case Study' in *British Journal of Sociology* 14 (1963), pp. 48–58.

[68] *E.H.R.* 34 (1919), p. 601; cf. T.F. Tout, *op. cit.*, II, p. 314; III, p. 264.

[69] Cf. *E.H.R.* 28 (1913), p. 803; *E.H.R.* 29 (1914), p. 756; *The Scottish Historical Review* 22 (1924–1925), p. 96; cf. also his sharp criticism of G.M. Trevelyan's *A History of England*, in *History* 11 (1926–1927), pp. 235–237.

At least two trends are observable in the criticism occasioned by Tout's work. The immediate critical reaction exhibited an emotional aversion, not only because of the book's dullish and dry presentation, but also because of the mass of irrelevant details. E. Barker's reaction mentioned in the preceding chapter was one such. Tout replied to Barker after a year that history had little direct use, at the same time emphasizing the full relevance of his administrative history considering recent developments.[70] He repeated: "In the fourteenth century we had already a permanent, specialised, highly trained and reasonably efficient service of officials, the predecessors of our civil servants of to-day."[71] Like Barker, the American medievalist N.F. Cantor recently wrote of Tout:

It is not accidental that the golden age of administrative history came in the 1920's and 1930's – a period not distinguished in England for the vitality of either its political or its intellectual life. The drabness of Stanley Baldwin has its parallel in English historical writing.[72]

This emotionally coloured picture of administrative history as a form of cultural decadence clearly omits the many positive aspects of it as a corrective to 19th-century historiography. Furthermore, by linking Tout's work to his own time in an arbitrary and strongly impressionistic way such criticism does not really explain anything. It merely gives historiography a bad name.

Much more significant is another kind of criticism which shows the failings and biases of the increasingly popular administrative history. Neither discussing the dullness nor the direct relevance of administrative history, it is centred rather on the crucial question of whether administrative history fulfilled its promise to make medieval society more accessible. Without denying the growing emotional dislike felt by the historian F.M. Powicke, the latter's objections retain their scholarly quality.[73] For the remainder of this chapter we intend to discuss some of these objections.

In our first chapter we touched upon the fact that for F.M. Powicke

---

[70] Cf. E. Barker, 'History and Philosophy' in *History* 7 (1922–1923), pp. 81–91; F.T. Tout, 'The Place of the Middle Ages in the Teaching of History' in *History* 8 (1923–1924), pp. 1–18.
[71] *History* 8 (1923–1924), p. 15.
[72] N.F. Cantor, 'Medieval Historiography as Modern Political and Social Thought' in *Journal of Contemporary History* 3 (1968), p. 68.
[73] See, about F.M. Powicke, W.A. Pantin, 'F.M. Powicke' in *E.H.R.* 80 (1965), pp. 1–9.
[74] Cf. ch. I, note 89.

the Magna Carta was a political-constitutional document whose significance could not be simply reduced to that of a feudal charter of
'reactionary barons' – as some historians had tried to do in a reaction
to the Victorian views.[74] But there was more to Powicke's revaluation
than just this one point. It would not be an exaggeration to state that
in the reaction against 19th-century historiography he – as a medievalist – went his own way; he neither accepted Victorian excesses nor the
equally excessive reactions to them. Thus his later work is in a sense a
reaction to a reaction. It was only around 1930 that his position became
clear, in part because he began to have misgivings about the growing
complacent professionalism, which Pollard also protested against. As
to Powicke, he closed a lecture in 1931 with the clear statement:

Dangers beset the new historical learning: the arid professionalism which
regards history as made for the historian, the absence of vision which can
make historical research 'a pedantic chase after the insignificant,' the
generalisations which disregard the inner significances of human experience
and do violence to history. We must find a way of escape.[75]

In the same year, 1931, Powicke published *Medieval England, 1066–1485*.
This concise book was more thematic than chronological in organization. Each theme was presented together with, first, the old traditional
view and then with the new modern post-1900 views. Powicke had
already showed his scepticism concerning too much 'debunking' of the
Magna Carta; now he objected to the new trend in modern historiography regarding the medieval parliament.[76]

Although Powicke had been originally trained as an administrative
historian, in 1931 he emphasized the dangers of an exclusively administrative approach to the history of medieval society. He did not
complain of the many details nor of the painstakingly accurate record-
criticism; his target was the new perspective on medieval society
created by a purely administrative approach. Like other perspectives,
this one was incomplete and fragmentary; but also it was basically
wrong and misleading, as it distracted people's attention from the
medieval context and the thoughts and emotions of that period. As a
result, the bureaucratic development during the Middle Ages was
overrated, although in actual fact it had hardly existed in England.
Granted the tendency towards more bureaucratic apparatus of govern-

[75] F.M. Powicke, 'The Collection and Criticism of Original Texts' in *History* 17 (1932–
1933), p. 8. Cf. F.M. Powicke, *Modern Historians and The Study of History*, p. 192.
[76] Cf. F.M. Powicke, *Medieval England, 1066–1485*, London, 1931, pp. 48–49, 193–194,
222 ff., 243 ff.; cf. F.M. Powicke, *Modern Historians and the Study of History*, pp. 217–244. Cf.
H.G. Richardson in *E.H.R.* 56 (1941), p. 124.

ment since Henry III, the differences with the present situation were still so vast that a term like civil service was bound to create a tangle of misunderstandings.[77] Civil service was not to be confused with the feudal concept of 'servitium.'[78] Moreover, all this focusing on the rise of a central 'official' class led to misrepresentation of an essential element in England's political history. In the past England's 'officials' had been the very opposite of an official class; certainly on the local level amateurs had retained a firm hold on administrative affairs.[79]

We need no fully detailed enumeration of Powicke's objections to see that they hit administrative history in the heart. For had not this history in its reaction to the 19-century Whig historiography tried to represent matters less anachronistically, and had not Tout directed all his efforts towards an exactly right 'setting'? Unfortunately, without success. Essentially Powicke's objections were the same as Huizinga's. In *The Waning of the Middle Ages* Huizinga had similarly criticized both record-history and administrative history which had had such decisive influence on medieval studies after 1900. In 1919 Huizinga wrote: "It is possible with the aid of the official documents to draw a picture of a medieval history which looks exactly like the eighteenth century with its policy-making ministers and ambassadors."[80] He warned that administrative history as a specialization brought fragmentation in its wake, with all the inherent dangers for interpretation. In his own words:

A scientific historian of the Middle Ages, relying first and foremost on official documents, which rarely refer to the passions, except violence and cupidity, occasionally runs the risk of neglecting the difference of tone between the life of the expiring Middle Ages and that of our own days. Such documents would sometimes make us forget the vehement pathos of medieval life, of which the chronicles, however defective as to material facts, always keep us in mind.[81]

Huizinga's fundamental criticism, delivered half a century ago, is still valid. The historian Dunham's marginal notes on Richardson's and Sayles's administrative history point in the same direction.[82]

Let it however not be forgotten that Powicke hardly ever named one of the modern historians whose views he discussed in 1931. While

[77] F.M. Powicke, *Medieval England, 1066–1485*, pp. 165, 195–196, 201–202, 205–207.
[78] *Ibid.*, p. 191 ff.
[79] *Ibid.*, p. 207 ff.
[80] J. Huizinga, *Herfsttij der Middeleeuwen*, Haarlem, 1919, p. 19.
[81] J. Huizinga, *The Waning of the Middle Ages*, Harmondsworth, 1955, p. 15, cf. pp. 20, 56 ff.; cf. also Huizinga's words as quoted by J. Le Goff, 'Is Politics Still the Backbone of History?' in *Daedalus* (Winter 1971), p. 14 (note 8).
[82] Cf. *Speculum* 39 (1964), p. 563.

blaming a number of them for believing that the past could only be made visible by means of this administrative and institutionalist approach, he certainly did not want to have his teacher and colleague, Tout, tarred with that brush: "he was far too sagacious and comprehensive a scholar to seek in the development of medieval institutions, in any specialized sense, an interpretation of English history, to give an unduly bureaucratic twist to classic interpretations," he said of Tout in 1938.[83]

It is undoubtedly true that in Tout's mind the Middle Ages had a much wider significance, reaching far beyond its own institutional development. For all that, Powicke's appreciative words seem incompatible with Tout's works and way of thinking. Powicke's later objections were directed mainly against Tout's early thesis (restated several times in Tout's later work) that the existence of a well-regulated administrative tradition was 'the only true explanation of the facts.' The 'way of escape' Powicke desired to find in 1931 could be called traditional, and in his 1931 lecture he demanded that the literary tradition in historical writings should be reinstated. In his own work he showed a growing interest in the history of ideas; it was as if the mistakes of the one branch – administrative history – must be corrected with the aid of that other branch, the history of ideas. Yet, Powicke was unable to integrate these two sufficiently. It may not be accidental that his interest in history took this direction just when he felt himself increasingly attracted to Collingwood's idealistic philosophy of history, including Collingwood's description of the historical object as 'actions of thinking beings.'[84]

Was Powicke's 'escape' into the history of ideas a solution? Could it correct the one-sided perspective of administrative history? Could it bring about the right historical atmosphere everybody desired so much? During the twenties there was certainly no unanimity in this branch of history. Powicke and G.G. Coulton had a short debate on the subject, resulting in fundamental differences of opinion, and neither could explain himself in other than intuitive terms.[85] There was a

---

[83] F.M. Powicke, *Modern Historians and the Study of History*, p. 219.

[84] Cf. F.M. Powicke, *History, Freedom and Religion*, London, 1938, and C.C.J. Webb's review of it in *E.H.R.* 54 (1939), pp. 520–521; cf. F.M. Powicke, *Three Lecturers*, Oxford, 1947, and F.M. Powicke, *Modern Historians and the Study of History*, p. 191 (note).

[85] Cf. F.M. Powicke, 'The Historical Method of Mr. Coulton' in *History* 8 (1923–1924), pp. 256–268; G.G. Coulton, 'Two Ways of History' in *History* 9 (1924–1925), pp. 1–13. Cf. also G.G. Coulton, 'An Episode in Canon Law' in *History* 6 (1921–1922), pp. 67–76 and G.G. Coulton, 'Monastic History' in *The Scottish Historical Review* 25 (1927–1928), pp. 318–326.

certain similarity between Coulton's assumptions and aims and those of his fellow medievalists: like them he favoured a 'realistic' approach within his field of research to bring out the great differences between the theory (mainly theology) and practice of medieval religion. His vast and erudite labour often led to nothing but a vast accumulation of material, but whenever his investigation into the religious attitudes of mind resulted in a clear picture, that picture differed greatly from Powicke's and Tout's. Coulton himself rightly stated that such a difference was more than just a difference in historical method.[86]

Coulton admitted that he was prone to do too often what other historians never did at all: to found his historical explanations on very base human motives.[87] As a convinced Voltairian anti-clericalist he could hardly do otherwise: he had to take sides in this respect, which led to Powicke's accusation that he used a far too modern and ana-chronistic frame of reference. Nobody denied Coulton's wide knowledge, not even Tout whose specialist's conscience prompted his condemnation of Coulton's *Five Centuries of Religion*: he labelled it an 'eloquent anti-clerical pamphlet on a colossal scale.'[88] History demanded a capacity for 'understanding and sympathy,' which was exactly what Coulton lacked.

Not even Tout could explain the exact implications of the latter demand; his objections were not essentially different from Powicke's reproof of Coulton's modern anti-clerical frame of reference. We already noticed that all administrative history in a narrower sense was equally blamed by Powicke for having a too modern frame of reference. Huizinga shared this fundamental objection; in his judgment administrative history failed to take into account that medieval man had an essentially different emotional life from modern man. Coulton was plainly and directly involved, which largely explained his anachronisms. Administrative history, being less involved, had achieved a more objective approach; with the aid of an impersonal administrative view it had managed to shed the naive unscientific moralism of the Victorian historical writings. Yet the initial purpose of this new specialization was not achieved: somehow both the right point of view and the right frame of reference had been missed. What precisely had gone wrong?

[86] *History* 9 (1924–1925), p. 11.
[87] *Ibid.*, p. 9.
[88] Cf. *The Scottish Historical Review* 20 (1922–1923), p. 319; see also *The Scottish Historical Review* 25 (1927–1928), pp. 205–206. Cf. also G.G. Coulton, *Fourscore Years*, Cambridge, 1944, p. 349.

New branches of historical scholarship always result in more fragmentation of historical truth. Such fragmentation was not felt as an impoverishment, because it was believed that a more scientifically based knowledge of a past reality would benefit by such further splitting up into branches of history. Some historians may have regretted the loss of history as literature, but even they agreed that specialization meant a scientific enrichment. How else could the many new facts, brought to the surface by record-history, be judged? Yet Powicke's criticism of administrative history suddenly made it very clear that the mass of new facts might lead to a warped perspective. Only too often were these new facts interpreted in a modern rather than a medieval context. Administrative history could not, of itself, create the precise setting to which Tout had aspired.

This specialization, despite its careful attention to details, was beset with fundamental dangers which had been insufficiently noticed. We are not concerned with the common complaint that historical studies suffered a loss in literary quality as they became more specialized. It is not the presentation, but the interpretation with which we are concerned here. 'Branch-specialization' may hinder historical insight into the interdependence between different fields, an insight that is a *sine qua non* for the greatest possible autonomous evaluation of any historical phenomenon. What happens is that these specializations unwittingly deprived themselves of a much needed expedient for the exexplanation of those very phenomena they were investigating. The more such a specialization remains within itself, without seeking an integrated insight, the greater the danger that heteronomous and even anachronistic conceptions may determine an interpretation.

We have already stated that as a specialization administrative history is relatively autonomous, partly because of its subject matter and peculiar sources, but also because of its own individual approach and interpretation. Huizinga understood the close ties between administrative history and record-history. Records were better suited to inform later generations about the technical details of administration than were chronicles. The particular question as to 'how' an organization functions is best answered by records. Many questions were, however, limited to external organizational details because of the firm belief that administration was relatively autonomous and independent from politics. Consequently, the distance increased from that specific context which provided the means for understanding its functioning. Such questioning led to an unwanted modernization of the frame of reference.

Actually, Viollet and Tout in their administrative history initially refused even to take the history of the court ceremonies into account; they did not think them important for institutional history.[89] It did not occur to them that the rich symbolic pageantry might in its time have been functional and meaningful; they missed seeing its relevancy.

It seems that these specialists often felt safer by narrowing down their object of study. Their interpretation could be more exact (less anachronistic) when the object was more limited and the focus narrower. Not only was this a mistake; it has also proved to be an illusion. Such specialization did not provide a higher scientific standard for historical interpretations. Specialization may have been the driving force necessary for the demolition of Whig historiography, and specialization to time and place may even be indispensable, but the fact remains that specialization in one branch or field of history offered no safeguard against anachronisms. Dangers lurked in the fragmentation: what originally appeared as the strong point of administrative history became its greatest weakness.

Many a contemporary administrative historian may call this picture of administrative history as a specialization a mere caricature. Elton insists that administrative history is just as much part of the science of history as any other branch. It covers a wider field than just the machinery of government, for it should include the history of political ideas in the broadest sense.[90] Yet in the sixties of the twentieth century it was Elton who wrote: "For an understanding of institutions it is necessary that they should be discussed by themselves, but this unquestionably hides some of the realities of government which involve interacting institutions used differently from time to time."[91] There is no denying that many administrative historians have moved outside their own specialization, yet we are concerned with the degree of integration achieved between the specialized area and other fields. For only thus can a coherent context be construed, only thus can the frame of reference be found which we need to map our historical interpretation. A specialization concerned with only one field of life is a temptation. It tends to refer to the present rather than to the past, hiding indispensable historical data from other branches of history. The more historians strive to discover interdependencies, by an integrated historical approach (within a specialization), the greater are

---

[89] Cf. P. Viollet, *op. cit.*, I, p. 239; T.F. Tout, *op. cit.*, I, p. 18. Modern medieval historiography has changed from this point of view, see J. Le Goff, 'Is Politics Still the Backbone of History?,' in *Deadalus* (Winter 1971), pp. 1–19.

the possibilities of a more autonomous evaluation. Maitland argued along similar lines when referring to the importance of Comte's 'greatest lesson' for historians. Hurstfield's criticism of Elton's work still holds a meaning for us:

What seems without doubt is that we have passed beyond recall the stage where the machinery alone, however intimately understood, can answer the questions of the period ... we have reached a stage in historiography in which we badly need some hybrid subject which is neither economic history alone, nor constitutional history alone, but assimilates both in order to investigate the government in depth. This does not exclude the study of administrative history in its most technical sense; but it would become the handmaiden of a larger discipline. This discipline would reflect ... that the forms of government owe much, but by no means all, of their character to the economic, social and religious content of the society which fashions them. The most important part of the constitutional iceberg is below the water-line.[92]

Recently the historian J.H. Plumb forwarded a similar argument, while emphasizing that continuation of a too rigorous specialization would be hazardous for historical scholarship.[93]

The reaction to 19th-century Whig historiography was characterized by its battle against anachronisms. However, our final recommendation of an integral history as a guarantee against the hazards of anachronisms should not be misunderstood. In the first place, our recommendation is not intended to prevent what Romein called the 'atomization' of the historical image and which he tried to cure by creating a new specialization (integral history) for restoring the ties between professional historiography and the reading public. Our aim is rather to intensify the scientific quality of historiography, in other words to ensure to the greatest possible extent an autonomous evaluation of historical events and phenomena. Integration is needed in order to provide the historian with the widest possible and most varied context. Without it

[90] G.R. Elton, 'The Problems and Significance of Administrative History in the Tudor Period' in *Journal of British Studies* 4 (May 1965), pp. 18–28.

[91] *The Tudor Constitution. Documents and Commentary*, ed. G.R. Elton, Cambridge, 1960, p. VI.

[92] *E.H.R.* 77 (1962), p. 730.

[93] Cf. J.H. Plumb, 'The Function of History' in *Encounter* (June 1971), pp. 71–78, esp. p. 76, and J.H. Plumb, 'The World Beyond Westminster' in *The New Statesman*, 16-2-1973, pp. 234–235. For Plumb, the heart of the matter is not only a correct interpretation, it is also important that the social function of historiography be restored. In our view, the realization of the first aspect is essential for the realization of the second one. The two should initially be considered independent from each other.

there is no reliable frame of reference for selection and interpretation. The construction of such a context requires a mass of data, some easily incorporable, some more difficult. But as more pieces are provided to fit into the jigsaw puzzle of the past, the outlines of the entire picture become clearer. The resulting improvement in the frame of reference makes it possible to discard the pieces belonging to the puzzle of the present. Comparisons in time, so important in Maitland's work, are a necessity for such a reconstruction of the historical context.

Secondly, we do not pretend that our demand for integration is new. On the contrary, the words 'context' and 'coherence' imply a need for an integrated approach, and are quite as old as the study of history itself, for the roots of this demand go back to the very philological origins of history. The golden rule of hermeneutics only counts those interpretations correct that remain within their subject's context. The rule is still valid, even for history, notwithstanding all discussions about the possibility or impossibility of such reconstructions. It still binds every historian, whether he is carrying out his research in the time-honoured way of philology or whether he starts enumerating or quantifying.

A glance at the history of historiography seems to reveal the truth of the ancient saying that every period has its own historiography. Its acceptance as a matter of fact is not without danger. Yet many historians, especially the active opponents of the Whig view, set out to produce as autonomous an interpretation of past reality as they possibly could; we believe this is the only really scientific attitude. During the period 1890–1930 progress was made in this respect.

The English historians of that period were deeply aware of the fact that it would do historical scholarship more harm than good if the historian's involvement was fed by a belief in a directly useful past. Such beliefs hampered an autonomous evaluation, but they were largely neutralized by a reaction consisting of a historical way of thinking which focused more on the differences between past and present than on the similarities. We found this in Maitland, Pollard and to a lesser extent in Tout. This was a first and very significant step towards a less anachronistic interpretation of the past, but this first step often led to a negative result: when comparing the past with the present, it was plainly understood how *not* to view the interrelationship of past occurrences, but it was not always equally plain how they *should* be viewed. It was possible never to go beyond this merely negative result, which meant that the past would again be hampered by an inadmissibly modern yardstick. The discussion between Pollard and Edwards is a case in point.

To our mind there was also progress in the thinking about historical development itself. The *Heterogonie der Zwecke* did away with the idea of a consciously planned historical development; no longer was it a tale of personal actions, it became the story of a structural process. Historical developments came to be regarded with less involvement, and the depersonalized view of the origin and development of institutions could gain in depth.[94] The linear finalistic way of thinking was undermined as the unintended results of human actions were also taken into account. Also the realization grew that a historical development once begun is relatively autonomous, independent of man's intentions or motivations. The principle of causality might be said to be de-finalized, because the way in which an organization functioned was considered more important that its stated aims. 'Efficient' causes weighed more heavily than did 'final' ones. All this has been discussed extensively in the chapter on Maitland, in connection with Pollard's theory of growth and in this chapter in connection with several French and English administrative historians.[95] We discussed these general trends at far greater length in our first chapter, and we now return to them, not only to correct some misapprehensions as to the significance of the so-called *histoire événementielle*, but equally in order to oppose the belief that historical scholarship has known hardly any progress in more scientifically based historical explanations.

The sociologist Norbert Elias seems to hold the latter opinion, but his caricature of history suggests that his knowledge of historical studies during the last fifty years must be very scanty indeed.[96] However, there is a remarkable resemblance between some of his main ideas on developmental sociology and the above-named general trends, so very plainly apparent in the reaction to Whig historiography. Had not Elias himself in his important study of 1939 mentioned a kind of breakthrough in historical scholarship, and had he not openly expressed his appreciation of some of the historians we have discussed?[97]

[94] Cf. N. Elias, *Wat Is Sociologie?*, Utrecht-Antwerpen, 1971, p. 162 ff.

[95] O. Hintze may be referred to regarding Germany, see J. Kocka, 'Otto Hintze' in *Deutsche Historiker*, Hrsg. H.U. Wehler, Göttingen, 1972, Band III, pp. 41–64, esp. p. 57, cf. p. 64, note 44 (for the idea of the *Heterogonie der Zwecke* in his work).

[96] Cf. N. Elias, *Die höfische Gesellschaft*, Neuwied, 1969, pp. 9–58.

[97] N. Elias, *Über den Prozess der Zivilisation*, Bern-München, 1969, II, pp. 37–38, cf. pp. 88–89. See on Achille Luchaire, pp. 94, 106, 124. Cf. also Elias on the *Heterogonie der Zwecke*, pp. 219–221, 242, 250, 287, 313–315. Also see for J. Calmette the articles in *Annales du Midi* 65 (1953), pp. 241–268.

Nevertheless, there was great difference in historical approach and interpretation, caused in part by the extent to which Elias succeeded in achieving an integration of historical data. For Elias, the most serious shortcoming of all historical studies is still that most historical interpretations are continually saddled with anachronisms – heteronomous evaluations, as Elias calls them. Yet all the tendencies named above were aimed at the abolition of these defects. The reproach is still valid, for despite the continuous struggles against the anachronisms of 19th-century historiography, this very defect made an unexpected reappearance by way of specialization in branches. While it was fully acknowledged that the past reality had a totally different character and that the immediate lessons of history had only a very limited usefulness, a more autonomous and more correct interpretation was still far from guaranteed.

This specialization (we called it an illusion) did not guarantee a more autonomous interpretation, as some record-historians supposed. On the contrary, administrative history was our example of a branch of history grown to such independence that many a specialist began to feel that the search for interdependencies was a dangerous luxury instead of an indispensable and firm aid to interpretation. Lacking this support, contemporary ideas and presuppositions were again given an opportunity for determining interpretation. This has not been sufficiently acknowledged. Thus, our central problem of anachronism still offers a challenge, and this is what makes Elias's analysis of history's incomplete questioning and method such an incontestable truth: "Die Lücken des Wissens von den Zusammenhängen gut dokumentierter Einzelheiten werden immer von neuen mit Hilfe von Interpretationen gefüllt, die durch kurzfristige Wertungen und Ideale der Forscher bestimmt sind."[98] An interpretation within the boundaries of a subject's proper context was rarely accomplished not in spite of, but because of specialization.

The work of Elias may be criticized on many points, but to our mind he has great merit in having pointed out a well-defined road towards the realization of an old ideal. He provided the originally philological rule of hermeneutics with a sociological extension. The necessary integrated approach which we have in mind finds its best example in Elias's concept of 'figuration' analysis.[99]

We have noticed that also within the new administrative history the

[98] N. Elias, *Die höfische Gesellschaft*, p. 58.
[99] *Ibid.*, pp. 34–35, 215, 317–318.

'principle' of an increased division of functions and labour was a constant law of history. Unlike Elias, those historians did not ask questions as to the wider social context of the developing medieval and early-modern institutions of government or about this development's influence on the regulation of behaviour, on the social standing and on ethical conceptions of elitist groups. Those questions were hardly regarded in a specialized research concerned only with the 'factual' workings of the administration and its organs. Such research desired above all to find the origins of the modern state and of its civil service. Moreover, this 'branch-specialization' caused ever wider gaps between the various subject areas, leaving a too heteronomous way of posing historical problems: the questions concerned more the present-day problems than those of the past. Huizinga and Powicke intuitively and with only a partial effect criticized administrative history. The systematic approach of Elias in *Die höfische Gesellschaft* has a more permanent value. Elias, like many historians, used a continuous comparison with the present for the purpose of painting a lifelike picture of the *ancien régime* in its proper context and with all its peculiarities. Elias, by having discovered that a varied mass of historical data differing in quality and character and seemingly insignificant to modern perceptions, were yet functionally interrelated, created a historical frame of reference which was the final aim of all his circumstantial explanations about housing, etiquette and ceremony. Only when we realize the significance of this courtly background can we also understand how misleading the modern term 'efficiency' can be in an administrative history dealing with the medieval and early modern periods.[100]

[100] Viewing the matter from the vantage point of his attempted theory of civilization, we fully understand the anachronism inherent in applying terms such as 'self-government' to the medieval and early-modern periods.

BIBLIOGRAPHY OF A.F. POLLARD'S WRITINGS

This bibliography is not quite complete: we omitted mention of very short book reviews, and we have not been able to trace every one of Pollard's contributions to the *T.L.S.* As to his letters to the Editor of *The Times*, we only mentioned the ones consulted on behalf of our research. There has been no separate mention of Pollard's essays from the years 1915–1917, collectedly published in *The Commonwealth at War* (1917).

1892

The Jesuits in Poland, Oxford, 1892.

1893

D.N.B. vol. 34: Lucas, Ch. (1769–1854); Luckombe, Ph. (d. 1803); Lydiat, Th. (1572–1646).

  vol. 35: Macdonald, A. (1834–1886); Macdonell, A. (1762–1840); Macegan, O. (d. 1603); Macfarlan, W. (d. 1767); Machado, R. (d. 1511?); Mackenzie, W.B. (1806–1870); Maclean, Ch. (1788–1824); Magauran, E. (1548–1593); Maguire, H. (d. 1600); Maguire, N. (1460–1512).

  vol. 36: Manderstown, W. (1515–1540); Mansell, F. (1579–1665); Marshall, W. (d. 1535); Martin, Fr. (1652–1722); Martyn, R. (d. 1483); Mascall, R. (d. 1416); Mason, J. (1503–1566); Mason, R. (1571–1635).

Review: J.B. Perkins, *France under the Regency*, London, 1892. *E.H.R.* 8 (1893), pp. 791–793.

1894

'Sir Edward Kelley' in *Lives of Twelve Bad Men*, ed. Th. Seccombe, London, 1894, pp. 34–54.

D.N.B. vol. 37: Matcham, G. (1753–1833); Maunsfield, H. (d. 1328); Maurice, Th. (1754–1824); Maxfield, Th. (d. 1616); May, W. (d. 1560); Mayart, S. (d. 1660?); Mayers, W.F. (1831–1878); Melton, J. (d. 1640); Melton, W. (d. 1528); Meredith, R. (1550–1597); Merrifield, C.W. (1827–1884); Metcalfe, F. (1815–1885); Mey, J. (d. 1456); Meyrick, J. (1538–1599); Michell, H. (1714–1789).

vol. 38: Milne, W. (1785–1822); Mitchell, J. (d. 1768); Mogridge, G. (1787–1854); Moir, G. (1800–1870); Molines, J. (d. 1362); Molyneux, R. (d. 1459); Monmouth, J. (1182?–1247?); Montacute, S. (d. 1317); Montacute, W. (d. 1319); Montacute, W. (1301–1344); More, S. (1594–1662).

vol. 39: Morison, Th. (1558?–1603?); Morley, D. (fl. 1170–1190); Morley, R. (1296?–1360); Morris, Ch. (1490?–1544); Morris, Th. (1660–1748); Mozley, A. (1809–1891); Mozley, Th. (1806–1893); Muir, W. (1787–1869); Mulholland, A. (1791–1866); Murray, G. (1761–1803); Murray, Th. (1564–1623).

vol. 40: Nairne, E. (1726–1806); Nangle, R. (d. 1541?); Napier, R. (d. 1615); Napier, R. (1791–1876); Nassyngton, W. (fl. 1375); Nathalan (d. 452?); Needham, J. (d. 1480); Neele, R. (d. 1486); Neville, G. (d. 1225); Neville, G. (d. 1285); Neville, H. (d. 1222); Neville, J. (d. 1246); Neville, R. (d. 1282); Neville, W. (d. 1389?); Newbald, G. (d. 1283); Newenham, J. (d. 1382?); Newland, J. (d. 1515); Nicholas de Wallington (fl. 1193?); Nicholas, R. (1597–1665?).

1895

D.N.B. vol. 41: Nicolls, B. (d. 1433); Normanville, Th. (1256–1295); Northwell, W. (d. 1363); Norwich, R. (d. 1535); Notten, W. (fl. 1346–1363); O'Brien, B. (d. 1657); O'Brien, D. (1577–1663); O'Brien, D. (d. 1624); O'Brien, L.H. (d. 1795); O'Cahan, D.B. (d. 1617?).

vol. 42: O'Hely, P. (d. 1578); O'Neill, D. (1612?–1664); O'Neill, N. (1658?–1690); O'Neill, O. (1380?–1456); O'Reilly, E. (1606–1669); O'Reilly, Ph.M.H. (d. 1657?); O'Rourke, B. (d. 1591); O'Shaughnessy, W.B. (1809–1889); Owen, L. (1572–1633); Owen, N. (d. 1606); Owen, N. (1752–1811).

vol. 43: Palmer, J. (d. 1556); Parfitt, E. (1820–1893); Parker, H. (d. 1470); Parry, W. (d. 1585); Partridge, M. (d. 1552); Partridge, P. (d. 1451); Partridge, S. (1603–1686).

vol. 44: Paul, W. (d. 1349); Paynell, Th. (fl. 1528–1567); Pearse, E (1633?–1674?); Pease, E. (1767–1858); Peat, Th. (1708–1780); Peeris, W. (fl. 1520); Peers, R. (1645–1690); Peerson, A. (d. 1594; Peeters, G. (fl. 1582–1592); Pelham, E. (d. 1606); Pemberton, Ch.R. (1790–1840); Pendleton, H. (d. 1557); Perceval, A.Ph. (1799–1853).

Review: *Secret Memoirs of the Royal Family of France during the Revolution; published from the Journal, Letters and Conversation of the Princess Lamballe.* By a Lady of Rank. 2 vols., London, 1895, *E.H.R.* 10 (1895), pp. 588–591.

1896

D.N.B. vol. 45: Peryn, W. (d. 1558); Petre, W. (1505?–1572); Petrie, H. (1768–1842); Phelips, E. (1560?–1614); Phelips, R. (1586?–1638); Philips, G.S. (1815–1889); Phiston, W. (1570–1609); Pickering, W. (1516–1575); Plough, J. (d. 1562); Plumptre, H. (d. 1746).

vol. 46: Pole, A. (1531–1570?); Pole, W. (1561–1635); Pollard, H. (d. 1666); Port, J. (1480?–1541); Potts, Th. (fl. 1612–1618); Powell, E. (1478?–1540); Powell, H. (fl. 1548–1556); Powell, Th. (1572?–1635?); Poynings, E. (1459–1521); Poyntz, F. (d. 1528); Price, F. (d. 1753); Price, H. (1495?–1574); Price, J. (1734–1813).

vol. 47: Puller, T. (1638?–1693); Rainsford, Ch. (1728–1809); Ralston, J. (d. 1452); Ravenser, R. (d. 1386); Rawson, J. (1470?–1547); Rayman, J. (fl. 1620–1650); Redford, H. (d. 1404?); Redman, R. (d. 1426); Reid, A. (d. 1767?).

vol. 48: Rempston, Th. (d. 1406); Rich, R. (1496?–1567); Richard de Abyndon (d. 1327?); Richards, W.U. (1811–1873); Richey, A.G. (1830–1883); Rider, W. (1723–1785); Ringstead, Th. (d. 1366); Robert (d. 1139); Robins, S. (1801–1862).

Review: P. Bondois, *Napoléon et la société de son temps, 1793–1821*, Paris, 1895. *E.H.R.* 11 (1896), pp. 388–389.

Review: R. Hesdin, *The Journal of a Spy in Paris during the Reign of Terror, January–July* 1794, London, 1895. *E.H.R.* 11 (1896), pp. 594–597.

Review: E.A. Vizetelly, *The True Story of the Chevalier d'Eon*, London, 1895. *E.H.R.* 11 (1896), pp. 801–802.

1897

Political Pamphlets. Selected and arranged by A.F. Pollard. London, 1897.

D.N.B. vol. 49: Robinson, A. (1762–1827); Robinson, Th. (1790–1873); Rochester, R. (1494?–1557); Rochester, S. (d. 1294); Rochford, J. (fl. 1390–1410); Rodes, F. (1530?–1588);

Rodington, J. (d. 1348); Rogers, R. (1532?–1597); Rokeby, R. (1527?–1596); Rokeby, W. (d. 1521); Rookwood, A. (1578–1606); Roucliffe, B. (d. 1494); Rush, A. (1537–1577).

vol. 50: Ruthven, E.S. (1772–1836); Ryerson, E. (1803–1882); Ryves, Th. (1583?–1652); St. John, O. (155–91630); St. John, O. (1580–1646); SSt. Leger, Sir Warham 1525?–1597); Salter, Th. (fl. 1580); Saltonstall, W. (fl. 1630–1640); Sandys, E. (1561–1629); Saville, J. (1545–1607); Saville, J. (1556–1630); Saville, Th. (1590?–1658); Scalter, E. (1623–1699?).

vol. 51: Scoloker, A. (fl. 1548); Searchfield, R. (1565?–1622); Selby, W.D. (1845–1889); Senhouse, W. (d. 1505); Seres, W. (d. 1579?); Sever, H. (d. 1471); Seymour, C. (1538?–1568); Seymour, E. (1506?–1552); Seymour, E. (1539?–1621); Seymour, Fr. (1590?–1664); Seymour, Th. (1508?–1549); Sharington, W. (1495?–1553); Sharp, G. (1735–1813).

vol. 52: Shelley, R. (1513?–1589?); Shelley, W. (1480?–1549); Shelton, R. (d. 1647); Sherborne, R. (1440?–1536); Shirley, J. (1366–1456); Shute, R. (d. 1590).

Review: *The Girlhood of Maria Josepha Holroyd (Lady Stanley of Alderley), recorded in Letters of a Hundred Years Ago: from 1776 to 1796*. Ed. J.H. Adeane. London, 1896. *E.H.R.* 12 (1897), pp. 376–377.

Review: G. Isambert, *La vie à Paris pendant une année de la Révolution (1791–1792)*. Paris, 1896. *E.H.R.* 12 (1897), pp. 591.

Review: J. Perrin, *Le Cardinal de Loménie de Brienne, archevêque de Sens; ses dernières années: épisodes de la Révolution*. Paris, 1896. *E.H.R.* 12 (1897), p. 805.

1898

'The Protector Somerset and Scotland' in *E.H.R.* 13 (1898), pp. 464–472.

D.N.B. vol. 53: Smith, R. (1752–1838); Smith, Th. (1513–1577); Smith, Th. (1556?–1609); Somerset, E. (1553–1628); Somerset, E. (1601–1667); Somerset, W. (1526–1589); Soulemont, Th. (d. 1541); Speed, J. 1552?–1629); Spencer, R. (d. 1627); Spottiswood, J. (1567–1645); Squire, E. (d. 1598); Stafford, E. (1478–1521); Stafford, E. (1552?–1605); Stafford, H. (1501–1563); Stafford, H. (1439–1469); Stafford, W. (1554–1612); Stanbury, J. (d. 1474); Stanford, W. (1509–1558).

vol. 54: Stanhope, J. (1545?–1621); Stanhope, Ph.H. (1805–1875); Stanley, Ch. (1599–1664); Stanley, E. (1460?–1523); Stanley, H. (1531–1593); Stanley, J. (1465?–1515); Stan-

ley, J. (1607–1651); Staples, E. (1490?–1560); Starkey, R.
(d. 1628); Stawell, J. (1599–1662); Stephens, J. (fl. 1615);
Sterne, R. (1596?–1683); Stewart, A. (1375?–1435);
Stewart, W. (1481?–1550?); Stokesley, J. (1475?–1539);
Stone, A. (1703–1773); Stone, G. (d. 1417); Story, J.
(1510?–1571).

vol. 55: Stretes, G. (fl. 1546–1556); Stubbs, Ph. (fl. 1581–1593);
Stucley, Th. (1525?–1578); Sweetman, M. (d. 1380);
Swift, R. (1534?–1599); Swinburne, H. (1560?–1623);
Swinnerton, Th. (d. 1554); Swynfen, J. (1612–1694);
Talbot, F. (1500–1560); Talbot, G. (1468–1538); Talbot,
R. (1302?–1356); Talbot, R. (d. 1449); Talbot, R. (1505?–
1558); Talbot, Th. (fl. 1580); Talbot, W. (d. 1633); Tate,
Fr. (1560–1616); Taverner, R. (1505?–1575); Taylor, J.
(d. 1534); Taylor, J. (1503?–1554); Taylor, J. (1600?–
1655); Taylor, R. (d. 1555).

vol. 56: Tenison, R. (1640?–1705); Ternan (d. 431?); Thomas
(fl. 1200); Thompson, J. (fl. 1382); Thorton, R. (fl. 1440);
Throckmorton, J. (d. 1445); Thweng, R. (1205?–1268);
Tidferth (d. 823?); Tindal, N. (1687–1774); Tiptoft, J.
(1375?–1443); Tobias (d. 726).

Review: A. Lang, *Pickle the Spy; or, the Incognito of Prince Charles*, London,
1897. *E.H.R.* 13 (1898), pp. 378–380.
Review: W. Cunningham, *Alien Immigrants to England*, London, 1897. *E.H.R.*
13 (1898), pp. 768–769.

1899

D.N.B. vol. 57: Tooke, W. (1744–1820); Tournay, S. (fl. 1184–1200);
Townshend, Ch. (1725–1767); Townshend, R. (d. 1493);
Townshend, Th. (1733–1800); Toy, H. (1540?–1577);
Tracy, R. (d. 1569); Traheron, B. (1510?–1558?); Tregury,
M. (d. 1471); Trengrouse, H. (1772–1854); Tresham, F.
(1567?–1605); Tresham, Th. (d. 1471); Tresham, Th. (d.
1559); Tresham, W. (d. 1450); Trumbull, W. (d. 1635);
Trussell, J. (fl. 1620–1642); Tuke, B. (d. 1545); Tunstall,
C. (1474–1559); Tunstall, Th. (d. 1616); Turner, J. (1615–
1686); Turswell, Th. (1548–1585); Twyford, N. (d. 1390);
Twyne, B. (1579?–1644); Twyne, J. (1501?–1581); Twyne,
L. (fl. 1576); Tymme, Th. (d. 1620); Tyrwhitt, R. (d.
1428).

vol. 58: Ughtred, Th. (1291?–1365); Uhtred (1315?–1396); Under-
hill, E. (fl. 1539–1561); Unwona (d. 800?); Upton, N.
(1400?–1457); Urswick, Ch. (1448–1522); Urswick, Th.
(d. 1479); Ussher, A. (1582?–1629); Valognes, Ph. (d.
1215); Vannes, P. (d. 1562); Vaughan, G. (d. 1447);

Vaughan, R. (1550?–1607); Vaughan, St. (d. 1549); Vermuyden, C. (1595?–1683?); Villiers, Ch. (1593?–1630); Villiers, E. (1585?–1626); Villiers, J. (1591?–1657); Villiers, Th. (1709–1786); Waad, A. (d. 1568); Waad, W. (1546–1623); Wadding, P. (1581?–1644); Wadham, N. (1532–1609).

vol. 59: Waller, R. (1395?–1462?); Walrond, H. (1600?–1670?); Walsh, W. (1512?–1577); Walsingham, E. (fl. 1643–1659); Walton, J. (fl. 1410); Walton, J. (d. 1490); Walton, Th. (1370?–1437?); Washbourn, J. (1760?–1829); Washbourne, Th. (1606–1687).

vol. 60: Watson, J. (1520–1584); Watson, Th. (1513–1584); Watson, W. (1559?–1603); Wendy, Th. (1500?–1560); Wentworth, Th. (1501–1551); Wentworth, Th. (1525–1584); West, Fr. (1586–1633); West, Th. (1577–1618); Weston, H. (1505?–1558); Weston); Weston, J. (1605–1663); Weston, R. (1577–1635); Weston, W. (1550?–1615); Wey, W. (1407?–1476); Whalley, R. (1499?–1583); Wharton, Th. (1495?–1568); Whelpdale, R. (d. 1423).

Review: M.A.S. Hume, *The Great Lord Burghley: a Study in Elizabethan Statecraft*, London, 1898. *E.H.R.* 14 (1899), pp. 162–164.

Review: *Calendar of Inquisitions Post Mortem and other analogous documents preserved in the Public Record Office. Henry VII.* vol. I., London, 1898. *E.H.R.* 14 (1899), pp. 558–559.

Review: *Lasciana, nebst den ältesten evangelischen Synodalprotokollen Polens, 1555–1561.* Hrsg. H. Dalton, Berlin, 1898. *E.H.R.* 14 (1898), p. 559.

Review: *Calendar of Letters, Despatches and State Papers relating to the Negotiations between England and Spain.* vol. VII. Ed. P. de Gayangos. Introd. M.A.S. Hume. London, 1899. *E.H.R.* 14 (1899), pp. 770–773.

Review: *The Archpriest Controversy: Documents relating to the Dissensions of the Roman Catholic Clergy, 1597–1602.* Ed. Th. G. Law, London, 1898, vol. II. *E.H.R.* 14 (1899), pp. 778–779.

1900

England under Protector Somerset. An Essay. London, 1900.

D.N.B. vol. 61: Whitehead, D. (1492?–1571); Whithorne, P. (fl. 1543–1563); Whittingham, W. (1524?–1579); Wilford, J. (1516?–1550); Wilkes, Th. (1548?–1598); William of Drogheda d. 1245); William of Durham (d. 1249); Williams, J. (1500?–1559); Williams, Th. (1513?–1566).

vol. 62: Wilmot, Ch. (1570?–1644?); Wilson, Th. (1525?–1581); Wilson, Th. (1560?–1629); Winchcombe (d. 1520); Windebank, Fr. (1582–1646); Windsor, Th. (1627?–1687); Wingfield, A. (1485?–1552); Wingfield, A. (1550?–1615); Win-

niffle, Th. (1576–1654); Winter, J. (1600–1673); Winter-
bourne, W. (1225?–1305); Wisdom, R. (d. 1568); Wode-
noth, A. (1590–1650?); Woodcock, M. (1603–1646); Wood-
ford, W. (fl. 1380–1411).

vol. 63: Worsley, W. (1435?–1499); Wotton, A. (1561?–1626);
Wotton, E. (1489–1551); Wotton, E. (1492–1555); Wotton,
E. (1548–1626); Wotton, N. (1497?–1567); Wriothesley,
Ch. (1508?–1562); Wriothesley, J. (d. 1504); Wriothesley,
Th. (d. 1534); Wriothesley, Th. (1505–1550); Wroth, Th.
(1516–1573); Wroth, Th. (1584–1672); Wrottesley, W.
(d. 1473); Wulford, R. (1479?–1499); Wulfric (d. 1010);
Wyndham, Th. (1510?–1553); Yates, J. (fl. 1582); Yaxley,
Fr. (d. 1565); Yeamans, R. (d. 1643); Yelverton, Ch.
(1535?–1612); Yelverton, W. (1400?–1472?); Yevele, H.
(d. 1400); Yonge, J. (fl. 1423); Yonge, Th. (1405?–1476);
Yonge, W. (1581?–1649); Young, J. (1514–1580); Young,
J. (1534?–1605); Zouche, E. la (1556?–1625).

Review: *Select Cases in the Court of Requests. A.D. 1497–1569.* Ed. I.S. Leadam,
London, 1898. *E.H.R.* 15 (1900), pp. 168–170.
Review: *Acts of the Privy Council.* New Series, vols. XIII–XIX, 1581–1590.
Ed. J.R. Dasent. London, 1896–1899. *E.H.R.* 15 (1900), pp. 581–585.

1901

D.N.B. Suppl. vol. 1: Acland, Th. D. (1809–1898); Albert, V.C.E. (1864–
1892); Allman, C.J. (1812–1896); Archdale, J. (fl.
1664–1707); Arnold, N. (1507?–1580); Bagnal, H.
(1556?–1598); Bagnal, N. (1510?–1590); Bardolf, Th.
(1368–1408); Barnato, B.I. (1852–1897); Beaufort,
E. (1438?–1471); Beaufort, H. (1436–1464); Beaufort, J. (1373?–1410); Blagdon, F.W. (1778–1819);
Blew, W.J. (1808–1894); Booth, W. (1390?–1464);
Brady, H. (d. 1584); Brand, H.B.W. (1814–1892);
Brantingham, Th. (d. 1394); Brereton, W. (d. 1541);
Bridgett, Th. E. (1829–1899); Burgon, J.W. (1813–
1888); Burke, J.B. (1814–1892); Busher, L. (fl. 1614);
Chaundler, Th. (1418?–1490); Cheyne, Th. (1485?–
1558).

Suppl. vol. 2: Clark, L. (1822–1898); Clement of Llanthony (d.
1190?); Colquhoun, Sir P. Macchombaich (1815–
1891); Crofts, W. (1611?–1677); Cromwell, R.
(1394?–1456); Danby, R. (d. 1471?); Dashwood, F.
(1708–1781); Dillon, L. (d. 1593); Dillon, R. (1500?–
1580); Dillon, R. (d. 1597); Dimock, J.F. (1810–
1876); Doudney, D.A. (1811–1894); Dowell, St.
(1833–1898); Dudley, H. (d. 1565); Erpingham,

Th. (1357–1428); Eveleigh, J. (1748–1814); Everdon, Silvester de (d. 1254); Fane, F.W.H. (1825–1891); Fenner, G. (d. 1600?); Fenner, Th. (d. 1590); Forster, J. (1520?–1602); Froude, J.A. (1818–1894); Gau, J. (1493?–1553?); Geddes, W.D. (1828–1900); Gentleman, T. (fl. 1614); Gibbon, Ch. (1843–1890); Goulburn, E.M. (1818–1897); Grosvenor, R. (1801–1893); Hamilton, R.C. Crookshank (1836–1895); Henry Maurice of Battenberg (1858–1896); Hexham, H. (1585?–1650?); Hitchcock, R. (fl. 1580–1591); Hoddesdon, Ch. (1534–1611).

Suppl. vol. 3: Keppel, W.C. (1832–1894); Kettlewell, S. (1822–1893); Keymer, J. (fl. 1610–1620); Lacy, E. (1370?–1455); Lindsay, C. (1819–1892); Macknight, Th. (1829–1899); Mitchell, A.F. (1822–1899); Mowbray, J.R. (1815–1899); O'Neill, B. MacPhelim (d. 1574); Ottley, F. (1601–1649); Parr, H. (1828–1900); Phillips, Molesworth (1755–1832); Pocock, N. (1814–1897); Pole, W. (1814–1900); Stansfield, J. (1820–1898); Stephens, Th. (1549?–1619); Torry, P. (1763–1852).

Review: M. MacColl, *The Reformation Settlement examined in the Light of History and Law*. London, 1901. *E.H.R.* 16 (1900), pp. 376–379.

Review: *Letters and Papers, Foreign and Domestic, of the Reign of Henry VIII*. Arranged and Catalogued by J. Gairdner and R.H. Brodie. Vol. XVII. London, 1900. *E.H.R.* 16 (1901), pp. 567–569.

Review: *Calendar of Letters and State Papers relating to English Affairs preserved in, or originally belonging to, the Archives of Simancas*. Vol. IV, Elizabeth, 1587–1603. Ed. M.A.S. Hume. London, 1899. *E.H.R.* 16 (1901), pp. 572–577.

Review: J.S. Corbett, *The Successors of Drake*, London, 1900. *E.H.R.* 16 (1901), pp. 577–578.

Review: G.C. Lee, *Leading Documents of English History, together with Illustrative Material from Contemporary Writers and a Bibliography of Sources*. London, 1900. *E.H.R.* 16 (1901), pp. 810–812.

1902

Henry VIII, London, 1902. (1905, 1951, 1966).

Review: R.W. Dixon, *History of the Church of England from the Abolition of the Roman Jurisdiction*. Vols. V–VI, 1558–1570, Oxford, 1902. *E.H.R.* 17 (1902), pp. 577–580.

Review: *Historical Essays by Members of the Owens College, Manchester*. Ed. T.F. Tout and J. Tait. London, 1902. *E.H.R.* 17 (1902), pp. 813–814.

1903

Tudor Tracts, ed. A.F. Pollard. London, 1903.

'National Opposition to Rome in Germany'; 'Social Revolution and Catholic Reaction in Germany'; 'The Conflict of Creeds and Parties in Germany'; 'Religious War in Germany'; 'The Reformation under Edward VI' in *The Cambridge Modern History*, ed. A.W. Ward, G.W. Prothero, S. Leathes, Cambridge, 1903, vol. II, pp. 142–274, 474–511.

Review: *Letters and Papers, Foreign and Domestic, of the Reign of Henry VIII preserved in the Public Record Office, the British Museum, and elsewhere in England.* Arranged and catalogued by J. Gairdner and R.H. Brodie. Vol. XVIII, 1,2. London, 1901–1902. *E.H.R.* 18 (1903), pp. 166–167.
Review: *Calendar of State Papers preserved in the Record Office, Foreign Series, 1577–1578.* Ed. A.J. Butler. London, 1901. *E.H.R.* 18 (1903), pp. 365–367.
Review: *Acts of the Privy Council of England.* New Series. Vols. XX–XXVII, 1590–1597. Ed. J.R. Dasent. London, 1900–1903. *E.H.R.* 18 (1903), pp. 567–569.

1904

Thomas Cranmer and the English Reformation, 1489–1556, London, 1904.

Review: *Calendar of State Papers, Foreign Series, of the Reign of Elizabeth, 1578–1579, preserved in the Public Record Office.* Ed. A.J. Butler, London, 1903. *E.H.R.* 19 (1904), pp. 782–783.

1906

Review: W.W. Rockwell, *Die Doppelehe des Landgrafen Philipp von Hessen*, Marburg, 1904. *E.H.R.* 21 (1906), pp. 157–158.
Review: K. Haebler, *Die überseeischen Unternehmungen der Welser und ihrer Gesellschafter*, Leipzig, 1903. *E.H.R.* 21 (1906), pp. 158–159.
Review: A. Lang, *John Knox and the Reformation*, London, 1905. *E.H.R.* 21 (1906), pp. 163–164.
Review: H. Barge, *Andreas Bodenstein von Karlstadt*, Leipzig, 1905. *E.H.R.* 21 (1906), pp. 374–375.
Review: *Calendar of Letters, Despatches, and State Papers relating to the Negotiations between England and Spain, preserved in the Archives at Simancas, Vienna, Brussels and elsewhere.* Vol. VIII, 1545–1546. Ed. M.A.S. Hume, London, 1904. *E.H.R.* 21 (1906), pp. 800–803.

1907

Factors in Modern History, London, 1907 (1926, 1932, 1948).

'The Germanic Federation' in *The Cambridge Modern History*, ed. A.W. Ward, G.W. Prothero, S. Leathes, Cambridge, 1907, vol. X, pp. 340–382.

Review: *Calendar of State Papers, Foreign Series, of the Reign of Elizabeth, 1574–1580, preserved in the Public Record Office.* Ed. A.J. Butler, London, 1904. *E.H.R.* 22 (1907), pp. 169–170.

Review: J.N. Learned, *History for Ready Reference: from the best Historians, Biographers and Specialists.* 6 vols. London, 1906. *E.H.R.* 22 (1907), pp. 392–393.

Review: *Letters and Papers, Foreign and Domestic, of the Reign of Henry VIII, preserved in the Public Record Office, the British Museum and elsewhere in England.* Arranged and catalogued by J. Gairdner and R.H. Brodie. Vol. XIX, parts I and II. London, 1903–1905. *E.H.R.* 22 (1907), pp. 795–797.

1908

Review: *Calendar of State Papers, Foreign Series, of the Reign of Elizabeth, 1581–1582, preserved in the Public Record Office.* Ed. A.J. Butler, London, 1907, *E.H.R.* 23 (1908), pp. 151–153.

Review: *Letters and Papers, Foreign and Domestic, of the Reign of Henry VIII, preserved in the Public Record Office, the British Museum and elsewhere in England.* Arranged and catalogued by J. Gairdner and R.H. Brodie. Vol. XX, parts I and II. London, 1905–1907. *E.H.R.* 23 (1908), pp. 358–361.

Review: Von Charlotte, Lady Blennerhassett, *Maria Stuart, Königin von Schottland.* Kempten, 1908. *E.H.R.* 23 (1908), pp. 786–787.

Review: Sir Thomas Smith, *De Republica Anglorum*, ed. L. Alston. With a Preface by F.W. Maitland, Cambridge, 1906. *E.H.R.* 23 (1908), pp. 788–789.

1909

The British Empire, ed. A.F. Pollard, London, 1909.

Review: W.M. Kennedy, *Archbishop Parker*, London, 1908. *E.H.R.* 24 (1909), pp. 795–797.

1910

From the Accession of Edward VI to the Death of Elizabeth, 1547–1603. Vol. VI of
The Political History of England in Twelve Volumes, ed. W. Hunt and R.L.
Poole, London, 1910.

'The Coronation of Queen Elizabeth' in *E.H.R.* 25 (1910), pp. 125–126.

E.B. (11th): vol. 1: Aconcio, G. (1492–1566); vol. 2: Askew, A. (1521?–
1546); vol. 3: Balnaves, H. (1512?–1579); Barnes, R. (1495–1540);
Bilney, Th. (d. 1531); vol. 4: Bonner, E. (1500?–1569); Burghley,
W.C. (1521–1598); vol. 7: Coverdale, M. (1488–1569); Cox, R. (1500?–
(1581); Craig, J. (1512?–1600); Cranmer, Th. (1489–1556); Cromwell,
Th. (1485?–1540); Crowley, R. (1518?–1588); vol. 8: Edward VI
(1537–1553); vol. 9: Elizabeth (1533–1603); Emser, J. (1477–1527);
Englefield, Fr. (1520–1596); English History, VII: The Reformation
and The Age of Elizabeth (1528–1603); XIII: Sources and Writers of
English History.
vol. 10: Ferrar, R. (d. 1555); Fox, E. (1496–1538); Fox, R. (1448–
1528); vol. 12: Grindal, E. (1519–1583); vol. 13: Heath, N. (1501–
1578); Henry VIII (1491–1547); Hooper, J. (d. 1555); Humphrey, L.
(1527?–1590).

1911

On The Educational Value of the Study of History, London, 1911. (Historical
Association).

'The Letters and Papers of Henry VIII' in *E.H.R.* 26 (1911), pp. 257–266.

E.B. (11th): vol. 15: Jewel, J. (1522–1571); vol. 16: Lambert, F. (c. 1486–
1530); Lambert, alias Nicholson, J. (d. 1538); vol. 17: Macalpine, J.
(d. 1557); vol. 18: Morton, J. (1420–1500); vol. 19: Nicholas, H.
(c. 1501–1580); Northumberland, John Dudley (1502–1553); vol. 20:
Parker, M. (1504–1575); vol. 21: Perne, A. (1519–1589); vol. 24:
Sanders, N. (1530–1581); vol. 25: Somerset, E. Seymour (1506–1552);
vol. 26: Taylor, R. (d. 1555); Tetzel, J. (1460–1519); vol. 27: Vermigli,
Pietro Martire (1500–1562).

Review: K. Stählin, *Sir Francis Walsingham und seine Zeit,* Heidelberg, 1908.
    E.H.R. 26 (1911), pp. 176–177.
Review: *Calendar of State Papers, Foreign Series, of the Reign of Elizabeth.* Vol.
    XVI, May-December 1582. Ed. A.J. Butler, London, 1909. *E.H.R.* 26
    (1911), pp. 177–179.
Review: *Geschichte des fränkischen Kreises; Darstellung und Akten.* Erster Band:
    Die Geschichte des fränkischen Kreises. von 1521–1559. Bearbeitet von
    F. Hartung, Leipzig, 1910; A. Neukirch, *Der niedersächsische Kreis und*

die Kreisverfassung bis 1542, Leipzig, 1909. *E.H.R.* 26 (1911), pp. 780–781.
Review: J.W. Thompson, *The Wars of Religion in France, 1559–1576*, Chicago, 1909. *E.H.R.* 26 (1911), pp. 783–785.
Review: *The Collected Papers of F.W. Maitland*, ed. H.A.L. Fisher. 3 vols. Cambridge, 1911. *The Morning Post*, 20-7-1911.

1912

The History of England. A Study in Political Evolution, London, 1912.

'Ireland as a Dependency' in *The New Irish Constitution*, ed. J.H. Morgan, London 1912, pp. 251–267.

Review: *Chroniken der Stadt Bamberg. II: Chroniken zur Geschichte des Bauern-krieges und der Markgrafenfehde in Bamberg*, ed. A. Chroust. Leipzig, 1910. *E.H.R.* 27 (1912), pp. 153–154.
Review: M.G. Constant, *Rapport sur une mission scientifique aux Archives d'Autriche et d'Espagne*, Paris, 1910. *E.H.R.* 27 (1912), pp. 157–159.
Review: A.O. Meyer, *England und die Katholische Kirche unter Elisabeth und den Stuarts*, Rome, 1911. *E.H.R.* 27 (1912), pp. 159–161.
Review: H. Pirenne, *Histoire de Belgique*, t. IV, Bruxelles, 1911. *E.H.R.* 27 (1912), pp. 362–364.
Review: *Archives du Musée Teyler*. Série II, vol. XII. Deuxième Partie: *Correspondance inédite de Robert Dudley, Comte de Leycester, et de François et Jean Hotman*. Publiée par P.J. Blok. Haarlem, 1911. *E.H.R.* 27 (1912) pp. 364–365.
Review: A. Cauchie, L. van der Essen, *Inventaire des Archives Farnésiennes de Naples au point de vue de l'histoire des Pays-Bas catholiques*, Bruxelles, 1911. *E.H.R.* 27 (1912), pp. 572–573.
Review: T.E. May, *The Constitutional History of England since the Accession of George III.* Ed. and continued to 1911 by F. Holland. 3 vols. London, 1912. *E.H.R.* 27 (1912), pp. 576–578.
Review: J. Vota, *Der Untergang des Ordensstaates Preussen und die Entstehung der preussischen Königswürde*, Mainz, 1911. *E.H.R.* 27 (1912), pp. 779–780.

1913

The Reign of Henry VII from Contemporary Sources, ed. A.F. Pollard. 3 vols., London 1913–1914. (1968).

'Contenementum in Magna Carta' in *E.H.R.* 28 (1913), pp. 117–118.

Review: G.P. Gooch, *History and Historians in the Nineteenth Century*, London, 1913. *E.H.R.* 28 (1913), pp. 753–755.
Review: F. López de Gómara, *Annals of the Emperor Charles V*. Translated by R.B. Merriman, Oxford, 1912. *E.H.R.* 28 (1913), pp. 778–779.

Review: 'The Evolution of Joint Stock Enterprise'; W.R. Scott, *The Constitution and Finance of English, Scottish, and Irish Joint Stock Companies to 1720*, Cambridge, 1913, 3 vols., *T.L.S.*, 18-9-1913, p. 384.

1914

'The Authenticity of the Lords' Journals in the Sixteenth Century' in *T.R.H.S.* 3rd. ser. 8 (1914), pp. 17–40.

Review: E. Barker, *The Dominican Order and Convocation. A Study of the Growth of Representation in the Church during the Thirteenth Century*, Oxford, 1913. *E.H.R.* 29 (1914), pp. 146–148.

Review: *Calendar of the Letters, Despatches and State Papers relating to the Negotiations between England and Spain, preserved in the Archives at Vienna, Simancas and elsewhere*. Vol. IX, Edward VI, 1547–1549. Ed. M.A.S. Hume and R. Tyler, London, 1912. *E.H.R.* 29 (1914), pp. 572–574.

Review: R. Lechat, S.J., *Les réfugiés anglais dans les Pays-Bas espagnols durant le règne d'Elisabeth*, Louvain, 1914. *E.H.R.* 29 (1914), pp. 761–762.

Review: *Calendar of the State Papers, Foreign Series, of the Reign of Elizabeth, January–June 1583, and Addenda, preserved in the Public Record Office*. Ed. A.J. Butler and S.C. Lomas. London, 1913. *E.H.R.* 29 (1914), pp. 764–766.

Review: 'England under Edward VI': *Calendar of Letters, Despatches, and State Papers, relating to the Negotiations between England and Spain, preserved in the Archives at Vienna, Brussels, Simancas and elsewhere*. Vol. X. Edward VI. 1550–1552. Ed. R. Tyler. London, 1914. *T.L.S.*, 17-12-1914, p. 572.

1915

'The Lords' Journals and the Privy Council Register' in *E.H.R.* 30 (1915), p. 304.

'Plenum Parliamentum' in *E.H.R.* 30 (1915), pp. 660–662.

Review: *Calendar of Letters, Despatches and State Papers relating to the Negotiations between England and Spain, preserved in the Archives at Vienna, Brussels, Simancas and elsewhere*. Vol. X, Edward VI, 1550–1552. Ed. R. Tyler. London, 1914. *E.H.R.* 30 (1915), pp. 142–144.

Review: *Calendar of Inquisitions post Mortem*, Henry VII, vol. II. London, 1915; *Calendar of Patent Rolls*, Henry VII, vol. I, 1485–1494. London 1914. *E.H.R.* 30 (1915), pp. 719–720.

Review: P. Guilday, *The English Catholic Refugees on the Continent, 1558–1795*. Vol. I: 'The English Colleges and Convents in the Catholic Low Countries. London, 1914. *E.H.R.* 30 (1915), pp. 724–725.

1916

'History and Science: A Rejoinder' in *History* 1 (1916–1917), pp. 25–39.

'The Growth of an Imperial Parliament' in *History* 1 (1916–1917), pp. 129–146.

Review: *Calendar of State Papers, Foreign Series, of the Reign of Elizabeth, July 1583–July 1584, preserved in the Public Record Office,* ed. S.C. Lomas. London, 1914. *E.H.R.* 31 (1916), pp. 163–164.

Review: *Calendar of Letters, Despatches and State Papers relating to the Negotiations between England and Spain, preserved in the Archives at Vienna, Simancas, Besançon and Brussels.* Vol. XI, Edward VI and Mary, 1553. Ed. R. Tyler. *E.H.R.* 31 (1916), pp. 493–494.

Review: C.S. Terry, *A Short History of Europe from the Dissolution of the Holy Roman Empire to the Outbreak of the German War, 1806–1914,* London, 1915. *History* 1 (1916–1917), pp. 55–56.

Review: L. van der Essen, *A Short History of Belgium,* Chicago, 1916. *History* 1 (1916–1917), pp. 116–117.

Review: N. Forbes, A·J. Toynbee, D. Mitrany, D.G. Hogarth, *The Balkans: A History of Bulgaria, Serbia, Greece, Rumania, Turkey,* Oxford, 1915. *History* 1 (1916–1917), pp. 118–119.

Review: O. Browning, *A History of the Modern World, 1815–1910,* London, 1916. *History* 1 (1916–1917), pp. 185–186.

Review: *The False Dimitri, a Russian Romance and Tragedy. Described by British Eye-wittnesses, 1604–1612.* Ed. with a Preface by S.E. Howe, London, 1916. *History* 1 (1916–1917), pp. 243–244.

Review: A·J. Grant, A Greenwood, J.D.I. Hughes, P.H. Kerr and F.F. Urquhart, *An Introduction to the Study of International Relations,* London, 1916. *History* 1 (1916–1917), pp. 250–251.

1917

The Commonwealth at War, London, 1917.

'The Growth of an Imperial Parliament: A Rejoinder' in *History* 2 (1917–1918), pp. 1–11.

'Magna Carta' in *History* 2 (1917–1918), pp. 170–173.

Review: E. Law, *England's First Great War Minister,* London, 1916. *E.H.R.* 32 (1917), pp. 295–296.

Review: *Calendar of State Papers, Foreign Series, of the Reign of Elizabeth, preserved in the Public Record Office.* Vol. XIX, August 1584–August 1585. Ed. S.C. Lomas, London, 1916. *E.H.R.* 32 (1917), pp. 440–441.

Review: *Calendar of State Papers relating to English Affairs, preserved principally at Rome in the Vatican Archives and Library.* Vol. I, Elizabeth 1558–1571, ed. J.M. Rigg. London, 1916. *E.H.R.* 32 (1917), pp. 608–611.

Review: J.W. Jeudwine, *The Manufacture of Historical Material: An Elementary Study in the Sources of Story,* London, 1916. *History* 2 (1917–1918), pp. 56–57.

Review: E. Lipson, *Europe in the Nineteenth Century. An Outline History,* London, 1916. *History* 2 (1917–1918), pp. 121–122.

Review: P. Milyoukov, P. Struve, A. Lappo-Danilevsky, R. Dmowski and H. Williams, *Russian Realities and Problems,* ed. J.D. Duff, Cambridge, 1917. *History* 2 (1917–1918), p. 185.

Review: 'Mr. Chesterton's Latter-day Pamphlet': G.K. Chesterton, *A Short History of England,* London 1917. *T.L.S.,* 22-11-1917, p. 564. (Cf. *T.L.S.,* 23-11-1967).

1918

The League of Nations: An Historical Argument, Oxford, 1918.

The League of Nations in History, Oxford, 1918.

'The two Houses of Parliament and their Separation' in *History* 3 (1918–1919), pp. 33–35.

'No Taxation without Representation' in *History* 3 (1918–1919), pp. 162–164.

'Lord Morley on History' in *History* 3 (1918–1919), pp. 210–221.

Review: Ch. L. Powell, *English Domestic Relations, 1487–1653. A Study of Matrimony and Family Life in Theory and Practice, as revealed by the Literature, Law and History of the Period,* New York, 1917. *E.H.R.* 33 (1918), pp. 109–111.

Review: H.E. Egerton, *British Foreign Policy in Europe to the End of the Nineteenth Century. A Rough Outline,* London, 1917; A. Oakes and R.B. Mowat, *The Great European Treaties of the Nineteenth Century,* Oxford, 1918; A. Ponsonby, *Wars and Treaties, 1815 to 1914,* London, 1918; *The Secret Agreements* (National Labour Press), Preface C.R. Buxton, London, 1918. *History* 3 (1918–1919), pp. 180–182.

Review: W.H. Dawson, *Problems of the Peace,* London, 1917; H.L. Hart, *The Bulwarks of Peace,* London, 1918; E. Bevan, *The Pan-German Programme,* London, 1918; Viscount Grey of Fallodon, *The League of Nations,* Oxford, 1918. *History* 3 (1918–1919), pp. 182–184.

Review: G.B. Adams, *Outline Sketch of English Constitutional History,* New Haven, 1918. *History* 3 (1918–1919), pp. 187–188.

Review: W.E. Weyl, *American World Policies,* New York, 1917; J.L. Beer, *The English Speaking People,* New York, 1917. *History* 3 (1918–1919), pp. 242–243.

1919

'The Nature of History' in *T.L.S.*, 25-9-1919, pp. 505–506.

'The Chair of American History. Studies for Home Understanding' in *The Times*, 6-12-1919.

'The Universities. A Plea for a National Policy' in *The Times*, 17-12-1919.

Review: B. Gourko, *Memories and Impressions of War and Revolution in Russia, 1914–1917*, London, 1918; R. Butler, *The New Eastern Europe*, London, 1919. *History* 4 (1919–1920), pp. 230–233.
Review: *The Work of The Hague*. Vol. I. W. Schücking, *The International Union of The Hague Conferences*. Vol. II. H. Wehberg, *The Problem of an International Court of Justice*, Oxford, 1919. Translated by C.G. Fenwick. *History* 4 (1919–1920), pp. 236–238.

1920

A Short History of the Great War, London, 1920.

The Evolution of Parliament, London, 1920 (1926, 1968).

'Local History' in *T.L.S.*, 11-3-1920, pp. 161–162.

'Historical Criticism' in *History* 5 (1920–1921), pp. 21–29.

'The Balance of Power' in *History* 5 (1920–1921), pp. 103–104.

Review: *Select Cases before the King's Council, 1243–1482*. Ed. I.S. Leadam and J.F. Baldwin, Cambridge Mass., 1918 .*E.H.R.* 35 (1920), pp. 591–593.

1921

'The Elizabethans and the Empire' in *Proceedings of the British Academy* 10 (1921–1923), pp. 139–156.

'An Essay in Historical Method: the Barbellion Diaries' in *History* 6 (1921–1922), pp. 23–31.

'The Dominions and Foreign Affairs' in *History* 6 (1921–1922), pp. 84–98.

Review: F.J.C. Hearnshaw (ed.), *Mediaeval Contributions to Modern Civilisation*, London, 1920. *History* 6 (1921–1922), pp. 203–204.
Review: H. Newbolt, *A Naval History of the War, 1914–1918*, London, 1920. *History* 6 (1921–1922), pp. 213–215.
Review: H.A.L. Fisher, *Studies in History and Politics*, Oxford, 1920; H.A.L.

Fisher, *Political Prophecies*, Oxford, 1919; H.A.L. Fisher, *An International Experiment*, Oxford, 1921. *History* 6 (1921–1922), pp. 285–286.

Review: C.H. Firth, *Modern History in Oxford, 1841–1918*, Oxford, 1920. *History* 6 (1921–1922), pp. 286–287.

1922

'Council, Star Chamber and Privy Council under the Tudors. I. The Council' in *E.H.R.* 37 (1922), pp. 337–360. II. 'The Star Chamber' in *E.H.R.* 37 (1922), pp. 516–539.

'An Apology for Historical Research' in *History* 7 (1922–1923), pp. 161–177.

'Lord Bryce and Modern Democracies' in *History* 7 (1922–1923), pp. 256–265.

1923

'Council, Star Chamber and Privy Council under the Tudors. III. The Privy Council' in *E.H.R.* 38 (1923), pp. 42–60.

'History and Progress' in *History* 8 (1923–1924), pp. 81–97.

'Balance of Power' in *Journal of the British* (later *Royal*) *Institute of International Affairs* 2 (1923), pp. 51–64.

Review: *Calendar of State Papers, Foreign Series, of the Reign of Elizabeth, preserved in the Public Record Office*. Vol. XX, September 1585–May1586. Ed. S.C. Lomas, London, 1921. *E.H.R.* 38 (1923), pp. 441–443.

Review: C.K. Webster, *British Diplomacy, 1813–1815*, London, 1921. *History* 8 (1923–1924), pp. 70–71.

Review: *Oxford Studies in Social and Legal History*, ed. P. Vinogradoff. Vol. VI, no. 11: H. Cam, *Studies in the Hundred Rolls: Some Aspects of Thirteenth Century Administration*, Oxford, 1921; no. 12: L. Ehrlich, *Proceedings against the Crown (1216–1377)*, Oxford, 1921; T.F.T. Plucknett, *Statutes and their Interpretation in the First Half of the Fourteenth Century*, Cambridge, 1922. *History* 8 (1923–1924), pp. 135–138.

Review: R. Muir, *A Short History of the British Commonwealth*, London, 1920–1922. 2 vols. *History* 8 (1923–1924), pp. 226–227.

Review: M. Epstein (ed.), *The Annual Register*. New Series, vols. 163, 164 (1921–1922 and 1922–1923), London, 1924. *History* 8 (1923–1924), pp. 227–229.

Review: J. Buchan, *A History of the Great War*, London, 4 vols. *History* 8 (1923–1924), pp. 301–303.

1924

Review: Baron G. von Romberg, *The Falsifications of the Russian Orange Book*, London, 1923. *History* 9 (1924–1925), pp. 71–73.

Review: *Sources and Documents, illustrating the American Revolution, 1764–1788, and the Formation of the Federal Constitution*, ed. S.E. Morison, London, 1923; C.H. McIlwain, *The American Revolution: a Constitutional Interpretation*, New York, 1923; H.E. Egerton, *The Causes and Character of the American Revolution*, Oxford, 1923. *History* 9 (1924–1925), pp. 249–251.

1925

Factors in American History, Cambridge, 1925.

'History and the Law' in *History* 10 (1925–1926), pp. 203–211.

1926

'Sir Sidney Lee and the Dictionary of National Biography' in *B.I.H.R.* 4 (1926–1927), pp. 1–13.

'History, English and Statistics' in *History* 11 (1926–1927), pp. 15–24.

'Some Causes of the Reformation' in *The Churchman* 40 (1926), pp. 8–18.

'Henry VIII' in *The Churchman* 40 (1926), pp. 89–100.

'Bacon as a Historian' in *T.L.S.*, 8-4-1926, pp. 253–254.

'What is History?' in *T.L.S.*, 16-12-1926, pp. 921–922.

E.B., Suppl. Vol. (1926): English History, 1911–1926.

Review: F.J.C. Hearnshaw (ed.), *Social and Political Ideas of Some Great Thinkers of the Renaissance and the Reformation*, London, 1925. *History* 11 (1926–1927), pp. 66–68.

Review: W.S. Holdsworth, *A History of English Law*, London, 1924, vols. IV and V. *History* 11 (1926–1927), pp. 251–254.

Review: 'Cranmer and Gardiner': C.H. Smyth, *Cranmer and the Reformation under Edward VI*, Cambridge, 1926; J.A. Muller, *Stephen Gardiner and the Tudor Reaction*, New York, 1926. *T.L.S.*, 29-7-1926, p. 504.

1927

'Political Philosophy from Hobbes to Mazzini' in *History* 12 (1927–1928), pp. 13–22.

'The Use and Abuse of Capital Letters' in *B.I.H.R.* 5 (1927–1928), pp. 1–12.

'Council Memoranda in 1528' (In co-operation with C.H. Williams) in *B.I.H.R.* 5 (1927–1928), pp. 23–27.

'Bias in History' in *T.L.S.*, 28-4-1927, pp. 285–286.

Review: *The Anonimalle Chronicle, 1333 to 1381*, ed. V.H. Galbraith, Manchester, 1927. *History* 12 (1927–1928), pp. 255–257.
Review: 'Rome and Queen Elizabeth': *Calendar of State Papers relating to English Affairs preserved principally at Rome in the Vatican Archives and Library.* Vol. II, Elizabeth 1572–1578, London, 1927. *T.L.S.*, 17-3-1927, p. 175.
Review: 'Morocco and the Elizabethans': *Les Sources inédites de l'histoire du Maroc.* Par le Comte Henry de Castries, 2 vols., Paris, 1918–1925. *T.L.S.*, 2-6-1927, p. 386.

1928

'Biographers and Historians' in *History* 13 (1928–1929), pp. 315–324.

'The Oslo Congress' in *B.I.H.R.* 6 (1928–1929), pp. 65–70.

1929

Wolsey, London, 1929 (1952, 1965).

'Tudor Gleanings. I. The De Facto Act of Henry VII' in *B.I.H.R.* 7 (1929–1930), pp. 1–12.

'Tudor Gleanings. II. Wolsey and the Great Seal' in *B.I.H.R.* 7 (1929–1930), pp. 85–97.

Review: H.A.L. Fisher, *The Whig Historians*, London, 1928. *E.H.R.* 44 (1929), pp. 689–690.
Review: *A Dialogue concerning Heresies and Matters of Religion made in 1528 by Sir Thomas More*, ed. W.E. Campbell and A.W. Reed, London, 1927. *History* 14 (1929–1930), pp. 72–75.
Review: W. Albery, *A Parliamentary History of Horsham*, 1295–1885, London, 1927. *History* 14 (1929–1930), pp. 267–268.

1930

'An Early Parliamentary Election Petition' in *B.I.H.R.* 8 (1930–1931), pp. 156–166.

'History à la Mode' in *Proceedings of the Royal Institution of Great Britain* 26 (1929–1931), pp. 197–198.

Review: Ifan ab Owen Edwards, *A Catalogue of Star Chamber Proceedings relating to Wales*, Cardiff, 1929. *History* 15 (1930–1931), pp. 153–154.

1931

'Thomas Cromwell's Parliamentary Lists' in *B.I.H.R.* 9 (1931–1932), pp. 31–43.

'Edward Hall's Will and Chronicle' in *B.I.H.R.* 9 (1931–1932), pp. 171–177.

Review: J.H. Round, *Family Origins and Other Studies*, London, 1930. *History* 16 (1931–1932), pp. 279–280.
Review: *Letters and Papers, Foreign and Domestic, of the Reign of Henry VIII, preserved in the Public Record Office*. Addenda, Vol. I, part 1, London, 1929. *E.H.R.* 46 (1931), pp. 127–128.

1932

'A Changeling Member of Parliament' in *B.I.H.R.* 10 (1932–1933), pp. 20–27.

'Sir Thomas More's Richard III' in *History* 17 (1932–1933), pp. 317–323.

'Clio's Recessional' in *T.L.S.*, 3-3-1932, pp. 141–142.

'The First M.P. Journalist. A Reporter of Things Seen. Edward Hall' in *The Times*, 1-10-1932.

'Parliamentary History' in *T.L.S.*, 13-10-1932, pp. 717–718.

Review: M. McKisack, *The Parliamentary Representation of the English Boroughs during the Middle Ages*, Oxford, 1932. *History* 17 (1932–1933), pp. 257–259.

1933

'The Making of Sir Thomas More's Richard III' in *Historical Essays in honour of James Tait,* ed. J.G. Edwards, V.H. Galbraith, E.F. Jacob, Manchester, 1933, pp. 223–238.

'The Great Queen of England' in *The Observer,* 3-9-1933.

'A Missing Link in History. The Great Chronicle of London' in *The Times,* 4-12-1933.

Review: *International Bibliography of Historical Sciences,* ed. by the International Committee. London, 1932. *History* 18 (1933–1934), pp. 248–249.
Review: H.L. Gray, *The Influence of the Commons on Early Legislation: a Study of the Fourteenth and Fifteenth Centuries,* Cambridge Mass., 1932. *History* 18 (1933–1934), pp. 262–263.
Review: 'A Diplomatist Dean': J. Wegg, *Richard Pace. A Tudor Diplomatist,* London, 1932. *T.L.S.,* 5-1-1933, p. 4.

1934

'The Great Chronicle of London' in *Essays of the Year, 1933–1934,* London, 1934.

'Hayward Townshend's Journals. I. The Parliaments of 1597–1598' (In co-operation with M. Blatcher) in *B.I.H.R.* 12 (1934–1935), pp. 1–31.

'Documents Astray. The Problem of Ownership' in *The Times,* 1-9-1934.

'The Royal Supremacy' in *The Listener* (17-10-1934), pp. 643–645.

'Fusion of Church and State' in *The Listener* (7-11-1934), pp. 778–780.

'Religious Liberty' in *The Listener* (21-11-1934), pp. 867–869.

Review: *International Bibliography of Historical Sciences,* London, 1933. *History* 19 (1934–1935), pp. 81–83.

1935

'Henry VIII' in *The Great Tudors,* ed. K. Garvin, New York, pp. 23–33.

'Hayward Townshend's Journals. II. The 'Historical Collections' and D'Ewes Journals' in *B.I.H.R.* 13 (1935–1936), pp. 9–34.

'A First Silver Jubilee. No Precedent for To-day' in *The Times,* 6-5-1935.

Review: *International Bibliography of Historical Ssciences,* London, 1934. *History* 20 (1935–1936), pp. 185–186.
Review: H. Hornyold-Strickland, *Biographical Sketches of the Members of Parliament of Lancashire, 1290–1550,* Manchester, 1935. *History* 20 (1935–1936), pp. 270–271.

Review: 'The Earliest Parliamentary Journal': *The Fane Fragment of the 1461 Lords' Journal*, ed. W.H. Dunham, London, 1935. *T.L.S.*, 5-9-1935, p. 545.

1936

Parliament in the Wars of the Roses, Glasgow, 1936.

'The Reformation Parliament as a Matrimonial Agency and its National Effects' in *History* 21 (1936–1937), pp. 219–229.

'Hayward Townshend's Journals. III. The Journal for 1601' in *B.I.H.R.* 14 (1936–1937), pp. 149–165.

Review: J.B. Code, *Queen Elizabeth and the English Catholic Historians*, Louvain, 1935. *History* 21 (1936–1937), pp. 162–163.
Review: *European Civilization: its Origin and Development*, ed. E. Eyre. Vol. IV: The Reformation, London, 1936. *History* 21 (1936–1937), pp. 266–267.
Review: J.B. Black, *The Reign of Elizabeth 1558*–1603, Oxford, 1936. *History* 21 (1936–1937), pp. 368–370.

1937

'Hayward Townshend's Journals. IV. Elizabeth's Last Parliament' in *B.I.H.R.* 15 (1937–1938), pp. 1–18.

'Fifteenth Century Clerks of Parliament' in *B.I.H.R.* 15 (1937–1938), pp. 137–161.

'Marriage and Divorce' in *The Times*, 5-8-1937.

Review: *The Usurpation of Richard the Third. Dominicus Mancinus ad Angelum Catonem de occupatione regni Anglie per Riccardum tercium libellus*, ed. C.A.J. Armstrong, London, 1936. *E.H.R.* 52 (1937), pp. 325–326.
Review: S.B. Chrimes, *English Constitutional Ideas in the Fifteenth Century*, Cambridge, 1936. *History* 22 (1937–1938), pp. 162–165.
Review: F.W. Maitland, *Selected Essays*, ed. H.D. Hazeltine, G. Lapsley, P.H. Winfield, Cambridge, 1936. *History* 22 (1937–1938), pp. 179–180.

1938

'The Authorship and Value of the 'Anonimalle' Chronicle' in *E.H.R.* 53 (1938), pp. 577–605.

'Two Notes on Parliamentary History' in *B.I.H.R.* 16 (1938–1939), pp. 19–23.

'Bibliographical Note' in *B.I.H.R.* 16 (1938–1939), p. 47.

'The Mediaeval Under-Clerks of Parliament' in *B.I.H.R.* 16 (1938–1939), pp. 65–87.

'The Under-Clerks and the Commons' Journals' in *B.I.H.R.* 16 (1938–1939), pp. 144–167.

Review: *Irish Historical Studies: the Joint Journal of the Irish Historical Society and the Ulster Society for Irish Historical Studies*. Editors: R. Dudley Edwards and T.W. Moody. Dublin, vol. I, no. 1 (1938). *B.I.H.R.* 16 (1938–1939), p. 31.

'The History of Parliament. An Editor for Each Period' in *The Times*, 7-11-1938.

1939

'Queen Elizabeth's Under-Clerks and their Commons' Journals' in *B.I.H.R.* 17 (1939–1940), pp. 1–12.

'Fighting An Ideology. I. The Natural History of War' in *T.L.S.*, 18-11-1939, p. 668.

'Fighting An Ideology. II. The Science of War and Peace' in *T.L.S.*, 25-11-1939, p. 684.

1940

'Chronology, Synchronology and History' in *History* 25 (1940–1941), pp. 193–207.

'New Year's Day and Leap Year in English History' in *E.H.R.* 55 (1940), pp. 177–193.

'A Protean Clerk of the Commons' in *B.I.H.R.* 18 (1940–1941), pp. 49–51.

Review: W. Nelson, *John Skelton, Laureate*, New York, 1939. *E.H.R.* 55 (1940), pp. 124–128.

1941

'The Growth of the Court of Requests' in *E.H.R.* 56 (1941), pp. 300–303.

Review: F. Le Van Baumer, *The Early Tudor Theory of Kingship*, New Haven, 1940. *E.H.R.* 56 (1941), pp. 310–313.
Review: *The Annual Register. A Review of Public Events at Home and Abroad for 1940*, London, 1941. History 26 (1941–1942), pp. 303–305.

1942

'The Clerical Organization of Parliament' in *E.H.R.* 57 (1942),pp. 31–58.

'Receivers of Petitions and Clerks of Parliament' in *E.H.R.* 57 (1942), pp. 202–226.

'The Clerk of the Crown' in *E.H.R.* 57 (1942), pp. 312–333.

Review: Sir John Fortescue, *De Laudibus Legum Anglie*, ed. S.B. Chrimes, Cambridge, 1942. *History* 27 (1942), pp. 155–156.
Review: *The Annual Register. A Review of Public Events at Home and Abroad for 1941*, London, 1942. *History* 27 (1942), pp. 156–158.

1944

Why We Study History, London, 1944 (Historical Association Pamphlet no. 131) pp. 13–15.

Review: *The Annual Register, 1942*, ed. M. Epstein, New Series, 184th issue. London, 1943. *History* 29 (1944), pp. 211–212.

SOURCES AND LITERATURE

A. SOURCES

Cambridge

Cambridge University Library
Lord Acton, Letters (35) to R.L. Poole. Add. MS. 7472.

A.F. Pollard, Letters (2) to F.W. Maitland. Add. MS. 7007 (219, 221).
W. Stubbs, Letters (3) to F.W. Maitland. Add. MS. 7006 (11, 29, 37).
T.F. Tout, Letters (2) to F.W. Maitland. Add. MS. 7008 (336, 352).
J. Gairdner, Letters (5) to Lord Acton. Add. MS. 6443 (154–158).

S.R. Gardiner, Letters (3) to Lord Acton. Add. MS. 6443 (159–161).
R.L. Poole, Letters (7) to Lord Acton. Add. MS. 6443 (219–225).
J.H. Round, Letters (3) to Lord Acton. Add. MS. 6443 (246–248).
W. Stubbs, Letters (2) to Lord Acton. Add. MS. 6443 (256–257).

London

University of London Library

Institute of Historical Research Manuscripts (I.H.R. MS.) Letters to J.H. Round:
no. 613, Letters (7) from G.B. Adams.
no. 629, Letters (3) from W.J. Courthope.
no. 633, Letters (3) from C.H. Firth.
no. 638, Letters (9) from S.R. Gardiner.
no. 646, Letters (32) from H. Hall.
no. 647, Letters (2) from C. Haskins.
no. 648, Letters (2) from W. Hunt.
no. 656, Letters (3) from W.S. McKechnie.
no. 658, Letters (3) from H. Maxwell Lyte.
no. 664, Letters (72) from R.L. Poole.
no. 680, Letters (2) from J. Tait.
no. 683, Letters (3) from T.F. Tout.

also:

no. 743, Cromwell and the Electorate.

no. 744, An Address on Oliver Cromwell delivered by J.H. Round at Colchester.

no. 745, Fairfaix and his 'Short Memorials.'

no. 770, The 'Garrison theory' of the borough. A paper read by J.H. Round at the International Congress of Historical Studies (1913).

no. 797, (a/b), Criticism of Vinogradoff's English Society in the Eleventh Century.

Public Record Office

P.R.O. 1/124, Correspondence of B. Thorpe and J. Stevenson relating to the materials for English History (1842–1865).

P.R.O. 1/128, Papers of Sir T.D. Hardy: personal (1859).

P.R.O. 1/148, J.R. Dasent. Acts of the Privy Council (1887/1894).

P.R.O. 1/150, J. Gairdner. State Papers, Foreign and Domestic, Henry VIII.

P.R.O. 1/155, M.A.S. Hume. State Papers in Spain.

P.R.O. 1/158, J.H. Round. Documents preserved in France and various other matters (1886–1924).

P.R.O. 1/168, Literary enquiries etc. addressed to Sir Henry Maxwell Lyte (1886–1906).

P.R.O. 1/169, Correspondence of Sir Henry Maxwell Lyte with the Treasury (1887–1905).

P.R.O. 8/6, Press cuttings of reviews of publications, articles etc. (1846–1864).

P.R.O. 8/14, Press cuttings of reviews of publications, articles etc. (1865–1876).

P.R.O. 8/20, Press cuttings of reviews of publications, articles etc. (1876–1886).

P.R.O. 36/19, An Account on the Parliamentary Petitions lately discovered in the Tower (1805, 24 June).

P.R.O. 36/46, Report of C.W. Williams Wynn, John Allen, Sir James Mackintosh, Henry Hallam and Sir Robert Inglis, a Committee appointed by the Board on the the work to be carried on by Sir Francis Palgrave (1831, May).

P.R.O. 36/49, Sir Francis Palgrave. Reports on work done at the Chapter House (1837–1840).

P.R.O. 37/1, Correspondence. Chronicles and Memorials (1859–1879).

P.R.O. 37/34, J.R. Green. Memorials of St. Dunstan (1866–1869).

P.R.O. 37/35, H. Hall. Red Book of the Exchequer (1890–1896).

P.R.O. 37/47, I.S. Leadam. Ranulf de Glanvill (1891–1901).

P.R.O. 37/52, F.W. Maitland. Memoranda de Parliamento (1889–1897).

P.R.O. 37/54, L.O. Pike. Year Books, Edward III (1886, 1904–1911).

P.R.O. 37/61, W. Stubbs. Chronicles and Memorials, Richard I (1862–1870).

University College

College Collection, DP 77 Pollard, A.F.: A Collection of press-cutting mainly of the 1930's in pamphlet box, together with articles in The Listener 1934.

College Collection, DP 77.9, Pollard, A.F.: To the electors of the University of London. Parliamentary election for the University of London (1923).

A.F. Pollard, Notebooks (2) for lectures taken down at Oxford University (1887–1888). Notebooks (3) for seminar lectures given at U.C. London (1909–1911). MS. Add. 80.

Notes taken by Miss E.J. Davis on various matters, including some of A.F. Pollard's lectures. MS. Add. 119.

Historical Letters and Personal Papers of Sir Francis Palgrave, 12 vols. (G. Palgrave Barker, London).

Oxford

Bodleian Library

H.A.L. Fisher, Papers (Box 1, 2, 12, 27).
A.F. Pollard, Letters to Sir Sidney Lee. MS. Eng. Misc. d. 179.
A.F. Pollard, Notes on J.F. Bright's Lectures. MS. top. oxon. d. 442.
A.F. Pollard, Notes on University Lectures by A.L. Smith and R. Lodge, 1889. MS. Eng. hist. d. 224.
R.L. Poole, Letters of 1896. MS. Eng. Misc. d. 125.
G.W. Prothero, Letters to Sir Sidney Lee. MS. Eng. Misc. d. 179.
W. Stubbs, Letters (144) to E.A. Freeman. MS. Eng. Misc. e 148.
Letters and Notes relative to Haddan and Stubbs's Councils. MS. Eng. hist. c. 204.
T.F. Tout, Letters to Sir Sidney Lee. MS. Eng. Misc. d. 181.

B. LITERATURE

The date of publication usually refers to the year in which the copy consulted by us was printed, which is not necessarily the year of the first edition. The date of the first edition was added between brackets, however, whenever relevant for the knowledge of the development of historiography.

ABBOTT, W.C., 'The Long Parliament of Charles II' in *E.H.R.* 21 (1906), pp. 21–56, 254–285.

—, 'The Fame of Cromwell' in *Yale Review* 2 (1913), pp. 315–349.

—, 'Macaulay and The New History' in *Yale Review* 18 (1929), pp. 539–557.

ABRAMS, PH., 'The Failure of Social Reform' in *Past and Present* no. 24 (1963), pp. 43–64.

ACTON, LORD, *Selections from the Correspondence of the First Lord Acton*, ed. J.N. Figgis and R.V. Laurence, London, 1917, vol. I.

—, *Essays on Freedom and Power*, sel. by G. Himmelfarb, New York, 1955.

'Acton and the Cambridge Modern History' in *T.L.S.*, 29-2-1971, pp. 195–198.

ADDISON, W.G., *J.R. Green*, London, 1946.

ALLAN, M., *Palgrave of Arabia. The Life of William Gifford Palgrave*, 1826–1888, London, 1972.

ALLEN, J., 'Cortes of Spain' in *E.R.* 23 (1814), pp. 347–384.

—, 'Constitution of Parliament' in *E.R.* 26 (1816), pp. 338–383.

—, 'Annual Parliaments and Universal Suffrage' in *E.R.* 28 (1817), pp. 126–150.

—, 'Hallam's Middle Ages' in *E.R.* 30 (1818), pp. 140–172.

—, 'History of the English Legislature' in *E.R.* 35 (1821), pp. 1–43.

—, 'Palgrave's Rolls of Parliament' in *E.R.* 46 (1827), pp. 471–489.

—, *A Short History of the House of Commons with reference to Reform*, London, 1831.

—, *Inquiry into the Rise and Growth of the Royal Prerogative in England*, London, 1849.

ALLEN, V.L., 'Valuations and Historical Interpretation: A Case Study' in *British Journal of Sociology* 14 (1963), pp. 48–58.

ANDERSON, O., *A Liberal State at War*, London, 1967.

—, 'The Political Use of History in Mid-Nineteenth Century England' in *Past and Present* no. 36 (1967), pp. 87–105.

—, 'The Growth of Christian Militarism in Mid-Victorian Britain' in *E.H.R.* 86 (1971), pp. 46–72.

ANDREWS, C.M., *The Old English Manor. A Study in English Economic History*, Baltimore, 1892.

ANNAN, N.G., *Leslie Stephen*, London, 1951.

—, *The Curious Strength of Positivism in English Political Thought*, Oxford, 1959.

ANON., 'The Future of Liberalism' in *Fortnightly Review* 63 (1898), pp. 1–21.

ANSON, W.R., 'The Cabinet in the Seventeenth and Eighteenth Centuries' in *E.H.R.* 29 (1914), pp. 56–78.

ASHLEY, M., 'Sir Charles Firth: a Tribute and a Reassessment' in *History Today* 7 (1957), pp. 251–256.

ASHLEY, W.J., *Surveys. Historic and Economic*, London, 1900.

ASHTON, T.S., 'R.H. Tawney' in *Proceedings of the British Academy* 48 (1962), pp. 461–480.

ASPINALL, A., 'English Party Organization in the Early Nineteenth Century' in *E.H.R.* 41 (1926), pp. 389–411.

ATHERLY-JONES, L.A., 'The New Liberalism' in *Nineteenth Century* 26 (1889), pp. 186–193.

AUSTIN, J., 'Centralization' in *E.R.* 85 (1847), pp. 221–258.

BAGEHOT, W., *The English Constitution*, intr. R.H.S. Crossman, New York, 1966.

BANASCHEWSKI, P., *Macaulay und Acton*, München, 1960.

BARKER, E., *The Dominican Order and Convocation*, Oxford, 1913.

—, 'The Origin and Future of Parliament' in *E.R.* 234 (1921), pp. 58–73.

—, 'History and Philosophy' in *History* 7 (1922–1923), pp. 81–91.

—, *Change and Continuity*, London, 1949.

—, *Age and Youth*, Oxford, 1953.

BARRACLOUGH, G., *History in a Changing World*, Oxford, 1957.

BAYLEY, C.J., 'The Early Administrations of George III' in *E.R.* 126 (1867), pp. 1–43.

BAYNES, N.H., *A Bibliography of the Works of J.B. Bury*, Cambridge, 1929.

BEARD, C.A., *An Economic Interpretation of the Constitution of the United States*, New York, 1913.

—, 'The Teutonic Origins of Representative Government' in *American Political Science Review* 26 (1932), pp. 28–44.

BECKER, C.L., 'Horace Walpole's Memoirs of the Reign of George the Third' in *A.H.R.* 16 (1910–1911), pp. 255–272, 496–507.

BEER, E.S. DE, 'Sir Charles Firth, 1857–1936' in *History* 21 (1936–1937), pp. 1–13.

BEER, S.H., *Modern British Politics*, London, 1969.

BELL, A., 'Lord Acton gets his Chair' in *T.L.S.*, 8-2-1974, p. 137.

BELL, H.E., *Maitland. A Critical Examination and Assessment*, London, 1965.

BEN-ISRAEL, HEDVA, *English Historians on the French Revolution*, Cambridge, 1968.

BETTI, E., *Allgemeine Auslegungslehre als Methodik der Geisteswissenschaften*, Tübingen, 1967.

BIRCH, A.H., *Representative and Responsible Government*, London, 1964.

BLACK, E.C., *The Association*, Cambridge Mass., 1963.

BLAKE, R., *Disraeli*, London, 1969.

BOCK, K.E., 'History and a Science of Man; an appreciation of George Cornewall Lewis' in *Journal of the History of Ideas* 12 (1951), pp. 599–608.

BÖCKENFÖRDE, E.W., *Die deutsche verfassungsgeschichtliche Forschung im 19. Jahrhundert*, Berlin, 1961.

—, 'Die historische Rechtsschule und das Problem der Geschichtlichkeit des Rechts' in *Collegium Philosophicum. Studien Joachim Ritter zum 60. Geburtstag*, Basel, 1965, pp. 9–36.

BOOGMAN, J.C., *Vaderlandse Geschiedenis in Hedendaags Perspectief*, Groningen, 1959.

BRANDS, M.C., *Historisme als Ideologie*, Assen, 1965.

BRATCHEL, M.E., *E.A. Freeman and the Victorian Interpretation of the Norman Conquest*, Ilfracombe, 1969.

BRENTANO, R., 'The Sound of Stubbs' in *Journal of British Studies* 6 (May 1967), pp. 1–14.

BREWER, J.S., 'New Sources of English History' in *Q.R.* 130 (1871), pp. 373–407.

—, 'Green's History of the English People' in *Q.R.* 141 (1876), pp. 285–323.

BRIGGS, A., *Victorian People*, Harmondsworth, 1965.

BRIGHTFIELD, M.F., *John Wilson Croker*, London, 1940.

BRINK, H. v.d., 'Typen van rechtshistorie' in *Lof der historie*, Rotterdam, 1973, pp. 33–46.

—, *The Charm of Legal History*, Amsterdam, 1974.

BRODRICK, G.C., *Political Studies*, London, 1879.

—, 'A Nation of Amateurs' in *Nineteenth Century*, 48 (1900), pp. 521–535.

BROOKE, J., 'Namier and Namierism' in *Studies in the Philosophy of History* ed. G.H. Nadel, New York, 1965, pp. 97–113.

—, 'Horace Walpole and the Politics of the Early Years of the Reign of George III' in *Horace Walpole: Writer, Politician and Connoisseur*, ed. W.H. Smith, New Haven, 1967, pp. 3–23.

BROUGHAM, H., 'Allen's Inquiry into the Rise and Growth of the Royal Prerogative in England' in *E.R.* 52 (1830), pp. 139–157.

—, 'Defects of the Reform Bill-Parliamentary Business' in *E.R.* 66 (1837), pp. 208–219.

—, *The British Constitution*, London, 1861.

BROWNING, A., 'Lord Macaulay, 1800–1859' in *The Historical Journal* 2 (1959), pp. 149–160.

BROWNING, O., *Memories of Sixty Years*, London, 1910.

BRUNNER, O., a.o., 'Der Historiker und die Geschichte von Verfassung und Recht' in *Historische Zeitschrift* 209 (1969), pp. 1–36.

BURN, W.L., 'The Historian and the Lawyer' in *History* 28 (1943), pp. 17–36.

—, *The Age of Equipoise*, London, 1968.

BURROW, J.W., *Evolution and Society*, Cambridge, 1970.

BURY, J.B., *The Ancient Greek Historians*, London, 1909.

—, *The Imperial Administrative System in the Ninth Century*, London, 1911.

—, *The Idea of Progress*, introd. by C.A. Beard, New York, 1955, (1920).

—, *Selected Essays of J.B. Bury*, ed. H.W.V. Temperley, Cambridge, 1930.

BUTTERFIELD, H., *The Whig Interpretation of History*, London, 1931.

—, *The Englishman and his History*, London, 1944.

—, *George III and the Historians*, London, 1957.

—, 'Some Reflections on the Early Years of George III's Reign' in *Journal of British Studies* 4 (May 1965), pp. 78–101.

—, 'Delays and Paradoxes in the Development of Historiography' in *Studies in International History*, ed. K. Bourne and D.C. Watt, London, 1967, pp. 1–15.

—, *Magna Carta in the Historiography of the Sixteenth and Seventeenth Centuries*, Reading, 1969.

—, 'Some Trends in Scholarship, 1868–1968, in the field of modern history' in *T.R.H.S.* 5th ser. 19 (1969), pp. 159–184.

'CALCHAS'(J.L. GARVIN), 'The Test of Efficiency' in *Fortnightly Review* 72 (1902), pp. 405–418.

CAM, H., 'Stubbs Seventy Years After' in *The Cambridge Historical Journal* 9 (1948), pp. 129–147.

—, 'The Theory and Practice of Representation in Medieval England' in *History* 38 (1953), pp. 11–26.

CAMERON, J.R., *F.W. Maitland and the History of English Law*, Norman, 1961.

CANTOR, N.F., 'Medieval Historiography as Modern Political and Social Thought' in *Journal of Contemporary History* 3 (1968), pp. 55–73.

CARLYLE, TH., *Heroes, Hero-worship and the Heroic in History*, London, 1841.

—, *Oliver Cromwell's Letters and Speeches*, introd. W.A. Shaw, 3 vols. London, 1908 (Everyman's Library).

CARR, E.H., *What is History?*, Harmondsworth, 1964.

CECIL, A., 'Sir George Prothero' in *Q.R.* 238 (1922), pp. 213–218.

CECIL, R., 'Lord Stanhope's Life of Pitt' in *Q.R.* 109 (1861), pp. 531–565.

—, 'Stanhope's Life of Pitt' in *Q.R.* 111 (1862), pp. 516–561.

—, 'Political Lessons of the War' in *Q.R.* 130 (1871), pp. 256–286.

CHADWICK, E., 'The New Poor Law' in *E.R.* 63 (1836), pp. 487–537.

CHAMBERLAIN, J., 'Shall We Americanise our Institutions?' in *Nineteenth Century* 28 (1890), pp. 861–875.

CHAMBERS, J.D., 'The Tawney Tradition' in *The Economic History Review* 24 (1971), pp. 355–369.

CHANDLER, A., *A Dream of Order. The Medieval Ideal in Nineteenth-Century English Literature*, Lincoln, U.S.A., 1970.

CHAPMAN-HUSTON, D., *The Lost Historian. A Memoir of Sir Sidney Low*, London, 1936.

CHRIMES, S.B., *English Constitutional Ideas in the Fifteenth Century*, Cambridge, 1936.

—, *Lancastrians, Yorkists and Henry VII*, London, 1964.

CLAPHAM, J.H., *The Study of Economic History*, Cambridge, 1929.

CLARK, G.K., 'Statesmen in Disguise: Reflexions on the History of the Neutrality of the Civil Service' in *The Historical Journal* 2 (1959), pp. 19–39.

—, *The Making of Victorian England*, London, 1966.

CLARK, G.N., 'The Study of Economic History' in *History* 17 (1932–1933), pp. 97–110.

—, 'R.L. Poole' in *E.H.R.* 55 (1940), pp. 1–7.

—, *Historical Scholarship and Historical Thought*, Cambridge, 1944.

—, 'The Origin of the Cambridge Modern History' in *The Cambridge Historical Journal* 8 (1945), pp. 57–64.

—, 'General Introduction: History and the Modern Historians' in *The New Cambridge Modern History*, ed. G.R. Potter, vol. I, Cambridge, 1957, pp. XVII–XXXVI.

CLARK, P., 'Henry Hallam Reconsidered' in *Q.R.* 305 (1967), pp. 410–419.

CLARKE, M.V., *Medieval Representation and Consent*, London, 1936.

CLARKE, P.F., *Lancashire and The New Liberalism*, Cambridge, 1971.

CLIVE, J., *Scotch Reviewers. The Edinburgh Review, 1802–1815*, London, 1957.

—, 'Macaulay, History and the Historians' in *History Today* 9 (1959), pp. 830–836.

—, *Thomas Babington Macaulay*, London, 1973.

COHN, G., *Gneist und Stuart Mill*, Berlin, 1869.

COLLINGWOOD, R.G., *The Idea of History*, Oxford, 1946.

CONWAY, M., 'Is Parliament a mere Crowd?' in *Nineteenth Century* 57 (1905), pp. 898–911.

COULTON, D.T., 'The First Decade of George III' in *Q.R.* 90 (1852), pp. 503–543.

COULTON, G.G., 'An Episode in Canon Law' in *History* 6 (1921–1922), pp. 67–76.

—, 'Two Ways of History' in *History* 9 (1924–1925), pp. 1–13.

—, 'Monastic History' in *The Scottish Historical Review* 25 (1927–1928), pp. 318–326.

—, *Fourscore Years*, Cambridge, 1944.

COURT, W.H.B., *Scarcity and Choice in History*, London, 1970.

COURTHOPE, W.J., 'The Crown and the Constitution' in *Q.R.* 145 (1878), pp. 277–328.

—, 'Party Government' in *Q.R.* 146 (1879), pp. 264–292.

—, 'The English Monarchy' in *Q.R.* 148 (1879), pp. 1–32.

COWPER, LORD, 'Desultory Reflections of a Whig' in *Nineteenth Century* 13 (1883), pp. 729–739.

—, 'The Whigs. A Rejoinder' in *Nineteenth Century* 14 (1883), pp. 23–30.

CRAWLEY, C.W., 'Sir George Prothero and His Circle' in *T.R.H.S.* 5th ser. 20 (1970), pp. 101–127.

CREASY, E., *The Rise and Progress of the English Constitution*, London, 1886 (1853).

CREIGHTON, M., *Life and Letters of Mandell Creighton by his wife*, 2 vols., London, 1904.

CRICK, B., *The American Science of Politics*, London, 1959.

CROKER, J.W., 'Walpole Memoirs' in *Q.R.* 27 (1822), pp. 178–215.

—, 'Municipal Reform' in *Q.R.* 54 (1835), pp. 231–294.

—, 'Horace Walpole' in *Q.R.* 74 (1844), pp. 395–416.

—, 'Memoirs of the Reign of King George III' in *Q.R.* 77 (1845), pp. 253–298.

—, 'Horace Walpole's Letters to the Countess of Ossory' in *Q.R.* 83 (1848), pp. 110–127.

—, 'Correspondence of Walpole and Masson' in *Q.R.* 89 (1851), pp. 135–169.

—, 'The Garland. By the Hon. Horace Walpole' in *Q.R.* 90 (1852), pp. 311–313.

CROMWELL, V., 'The Losing of the Initiative by the House of Commons' in *T.R.H.S.* 5th ser. 18 (1968), pp. 1–23.

CRONNE, H.A., 'E.A. Freeman' in *History* 28 (1943), pp. 78–92.

CROOK, D.P., *American Democracy in English Politics, 1815–1850*, Oxford, 1965.

CROSBY, G.R., 'George III: Historians and a Royal Reputation' in *Essays in Modern English History in honour of W.C. Abbott*, Cambridge Mass., 1941, pp. 295–313.

CUNNINGHAM, A., *William Cunningham*, London, 1950.

CUNNINGHAM, W., 'A Plea for Pure Theory' in *The Economic Review* 2 (1892), pp. 25–41.

—, 'The Relativity of Economic Doctrine' in *The Economic Journal* 2 (1892), pp. 1–16.

—, 'The Perversion of Economic History' in *The Economic Journal* 2 (1892), pp. 491–506.

DANCE, E.H., *The Victorian Illusion*, London, 1928.

DARLINGTON, R.R., *Anglo-Norman Historians*, London, 1947.

—, *The Norman Conquest*, London, 1963.

DAVIES, C.J., *The Baronial Opposition to Edward II. Its Character and Policy, A Study in Administrative History*, Cambridge, 1918.

DAVIES, G., 'The Treatment of Constitutional History in Macaulay's *History of England*' in *The Huntington Library Quarterly* 2 (1938–1939), pp. 179–204.

DAVIS, H.W.C., *The Study of History*, Oxford, 1925.

DELABORDE, F., 'Notice sur la vie et les travaux de M. Paul Viollet' in *Bibliothèque de L'Ecole des Chartes* 79 (1918), pp. 147–175.

DIBDIN, T., 'Wolsey' in *History* 15 (1930–1931), pp. 18–26.

DICEY, A.V., *The Privy Council*, London, 1887.

—, *The Law of the Constitution*, London, 1902.

DICKENS, A.G., 'Introduction' in A.F. Pollard, *Henry VIII* ,New York 1966 (Harper Torchbook), pp. IX–XXIII.

DICKINS, B., 'John Mitchell Kemble and Old English Scholarship' in *Proceedings of the British Academy* 25 (1939), pp. 51–84.

'The Dictionary of National Biography. A Statistical Account' in *D.N.B.* vol. 63 (1900), pp. V–XIX.

DINWIDDY, J.R., 'Charles James Fox as Historian' in *The Historical Journal* 12 (1969), pp. 23–34.

DOBSON, J.G., 'Position and Prospects of Parties' in *E.R.* 125 (1867), pp. 269–301.

DONNE, W.B., 'The Saxons in England' in *E.R.* 89 (1849), pp. 151–184.

—, 'The Marquis of Rockingham and His Contemporaries' in *E.R.* 96 (1852), pp. 110–142.

—, 'The Youth of Milton' in *E.R.* 111 (1860), pp. 312–347.

DONNE, W.B. (ed.) *George III 's Letters to Lord North from 1768 to 1783*, 2 vols., London, 1867.

DOUGLAS, D., *English Scholars*, London, 1943.

—, *The Norman Conquest and British Historians*, Glasgow, 1971 (1946).

DRION, J., *Stare Decisis. Het Gezag van Precedenten*, The Hague, 1950.

DUNBABIN, J.P.D., 'The Politics of the Establishment of County Councils' in *The Historical Journal* 6 (1963), pp. 226–252.

—, 'Expectations of the New County Councils and their Realization' in *The Historical Journal* 8 (1965), pp. 353–379.

DUNN, W.H., *J.A. Froude. A Biography*, 2 vols., Oxford, 1961–1963.

EDWARDS, E., *Libraries and Founders of Libraries*, London, 1865.

EDWARDS, J.G., 'The Personnel of the Commons in Parliament under Edward I and Edward II' in *Essays in Medieval History presented to T.F. Tout*, ed. A.G. Little and F.M. Powicke, Manchester, 1925, pp. 197–214.

—, 'Re-election and the Medieval Parliament' in *History* 11 (1926–1927), pp. 204–210.

—, 'Sir John Cecil Power' in *B.I.H.R.* 23 (1950), pp. 139–146.

—, *William Stubbs*, London, 1952, (Historical Association).

—, 'Justice in Early Parliaments' in *B.I.H.R.* 27 (1954), pp. 35–53.

—, *The Commons in Medieval English Parliament*, London, 1958.

—, *Historians and the Medieval English Parliament*, Glasgow, 1970 (1960).

EISENSTEIN, E.L., 'Clio and Chronos' in *History and the Concept of Time*, Beiheft 6 of *History and Theory*, 1967, pp. 36–63.

ELIAS, N., *Über den Prozess der Zivilisation*, 2 Bde., Bern, 1969 (1939).

—, 'Problems of Involvement and Detachment' in *British Journal of Sociology* 7 (1956), pp. 226–252.

—, *Die höfische Gesellschaft*, Neuwied, 1969.

ELLIS, T.F., 'Sir F. Palgrave's Merchant and Friar' in *E.R.* 66 (1838), pp. 465–476.

ELTON, G.R., 'Fifty Years of Tudor Studies at London University' in *T.L.S.*, 6-1-1956, p. VIII.

—, *Henry VIII*, London, 1967 (1960). (Historical Association).

Elton, G.R. (ed.), *The Tudor Constitution. Documents and Commentary*, Cambridge, 1960.

—, 'Introduction' in A.F. Pollard, *Wolsey*, London, 1965 (Fontana Library), pp. XI-XXXVII.

—, 'The Problems and Significance of Administrative History in the Tudor Period' in *Journal of British Studies* 4 (May 1965), pp. 18–28.

—, *The Practice of History*, London, 1967.

—, *The Future of the Past*, Cambridge, 1968.

—, *The Body of the Whole Realm. Parliament and Representation in Medieval and Tudor England*, Charlottesville, 1969.

ELTON, O., *F.Y. Powell*, 2 vols., Oxford, 1906.

ELWIN, W., 'Causes of the Civil War – Mr. Guizot' in *Q.R.* 99 (1856), pp. 105–159.

ENSOR, R.C.K., *England, 1870–1914*, Oxford, 1936.

Essays on the Teaching of History, ed. W.A.J. Archbold, Cambridge, 1901.

EVANS, E., 'Of the Antiquity of Parliaments in England: Some Elizabethan and Early Stuart Opinions' in *History* 23 (1938–1939), pp. 206–221.

EVERETT, E.M., *The Party of Humanity. The Fortnightly Review and its Contributors, 1865–1874*, Chapel Hill, N-C, 1939.

Fabian Essays in Socialism, London, 1920 (1889).

FAHEY, D.M., 'Henry Hallam – a Conservative as Whig Historian' in *The Historian* 28 (1966), pp. 625–647.

—, 'Gardiner and Usher in Perspective' in *Journal of Historical Studies* 1 (1968), pp. 137–150.

FIFOOT, C.H.S., *Pollock and Maitland*, Glasgow, 1971.

—, *F.W. Maitland. A Life*, Cambridge Mass., 1971.

FIGGIS, J.N., *The Divine Rights of Kings*, introd. by G.R. Elton, New York, 1965 (1896).

FINLAYSON, G.B.A.M., 'The Municipal Corporation Commission and Report, 1833–1835' in *B.I.H.R.* 36 (1963), pp. 36–52.

FIRTH, C.H., 'Cromwell and the Insurrection of 1655' in *E.H.R.* 3 (1888), pp. 323–350 and *E.H.R.* 4 (1889), pp. 313–338; 525–535.

—, *Oliver Cromwell and the Rule of the Puritans*, introd. by G.M. Young, Oxford, 1968 (1900).

—, *Cromwell's Army*, introd. by P.H. Hardacre, London, 1962 (1902).

—, *A Plea for the Historical Teaching of History*, Oxford, 1904.

—, 'Modern History in Oxford, 1724–1841' in *E.H.R.* 32 (1917), pp. 1–21.

—, 'S.R. Gardiner's Historical Method' in *T.L.S.*, 6–11, 27–11–1919, pp. 630, 695.

—, *Modern History in Oxford, 1841–1918*, Oxford, 1920.

—, *A Commentary on Macaulay's History of England*, London, 1938.

FISHER, H.A.L., *F.W. Maitland*, Cambridge, 1910.

—, *P. Vinogradoff*, Oxford, 1927.

—, 'The Whig Historians' in *Proceedings of the British Academy* 14 (1928), pp. 297–339.

—, *An Unfinished Autobiography*, London, 1941.

FLEISHMANN, A., *The English Historical Novel*, Baltimore, 1971.

FORBES, D., *The Liberal Anglican Idea of History*, Cambridge, 1952.

—, 'Scientific Whiggism: Adam Smith and John Millar' in *The Cambridge Journal* 7 (1954), pp. 643–670.

—, 'Introduction' in A. Ferguson, *An Essay on the History of Civil Society*, 1767, Edinburgh, 1966, pp. XIII–XLI.

—, 'Introduction' in D. Hume, *The History of Great Britain*, Harmondsworth, 1970, pp. 7–54.

FORSTER, J., 'The Civil Wars and Cromwell' in *E.R.* 103 (1856), pp. 1–54.

FOURNIER, P., 'Paul Viollet' in *Nouvelle Revue Historique de droit français et étranger* 38 (1914–1915), pp. 816–827.

FRASER, P., 'The Growth of Ministerial Control in the Nineteenth-Century House of Commons' in *E.H.R.* 75 (1960), pp. 444–463.

—, 'Public Petitioning and Parliament Before 1832' in *History* 46 (1961), pp. 195–211.

FREEMAN, E.A., 'Sir F. Palgrave's Normandy and England' in *E.R.* 109 (1859), pp. 486–513.

—, 'Sir F. Palgrave's History of England and Normandy' in *E.R.* 121 (1865), pp. 1–41.

—, *The Growth of the English Constitution*, London, 1872.

—, *The History of the Norman Conquest of England*, 5 vols., Oxford, 1870–1876.

—, *The Methods of Historical Study*, London, 1886.

—, *Historical Essays*, Fourth Series, London, 1892.

—, *The Life and Letters of E.A. Freeman*, ed. W.R.W. Stephens, 2 vols., London, 1895.

FREIDEL, F., *Francis Lieber. Nineteenth-Century Liberal*, Baton Rouge, 1947.

FUETER, E., *Geschichte der neueren Historiographie*, München, 1911.

FULLER, L.L., 'What motives give rise to the historical legal fiction'? in *Recueil d'études sur les sources du droit en l'honneur de François Gény*, Paris, 1935, vol. 2, pp. 157–176.

GADAMER, H.G., *Wahrheit und Methode*, Tübingen, 1960.

—, *Kleine Schriften*, 2 Bde, Tübingen, 1967.

GAIRDNER, J., 'The House of Lords. Its Functions' in *The Antiquary* 9 (1884), pp. 149–156, 255–259.

GALBRAITH, V.H., 'Historical Research and the Preservation of the Past' in *History* 22 (1937–1938), pp. 303–314.

—, *Roger Wendower and Matthew Paris*, Glasgow, 1970 (1944).

—, 'James Tait' in *E.H.R.* 60 (1945), pp. 129–135.

—, *Studies in the Public Records*, London, 1948.

—, *Historical Study and the State*, Oxford, 1948.

—, 'A.F. Pollard' in *Proceedings of the British Academy* 35 (1949), pp. 257–274.

—, *An Introduction to the Study of History*, London, 1964.

—, 'Sir Frank Stenton,' 1880–1967' in *A.H.R.* 76 (1971), pp. 1116–1123.

GARDINER, S.R., *Cromwell's Place in History*, London, 1897.

—, *Oliver Cromwell*, London, 1901.

GASH, N., *Politics in the Age of Peel*, London, 1953.

—, *Reaction and Reconstruction in English Politics, 1832–1852*, Oxford, 1965.

GASKELL, C.M., 'The position of the Whigs' in *Nineteenth Century* 10 (1881), pp. 901–912.

GERARD, J., 'An Apologist for Henry VIII' in *The Month, a Catholic Magazine* 106 (1905), pp. 474–487.

GERSCHENKRON, A., *Continuity in History and Other Essays*, Cambridge Mass., 1968.

Geschichte, Fischer Lexikon, Hrsg. W. Besson, Frankfurt a. Main, 1961.

GLADSTONE, W.E., 'The Declining Efficiency of Parliament' in *Q.R.* 99 (1856), pp. 521–570.

—, 'Lord Macaulay' in *Q.R.* 142 (1876), pp. 1–50.

—, 'Liberty in the East and West' in *Nineteenth Century* 3 (1878), pp. 1154–1174.

—, *Gleanings of Past Years*, 7 vols., London, 1879.

GNEIST, R. VON, *Self-government*, Berlin, 1871.

—, *Englische Verfassungsgeschichte*, Berlin, 1882.

—, *Das englische Parlament in tausendjährigen Wandelungen*, Berlin, 1886.

GOMME, G.L., 'Systems of English Local Government' in *The Local Government Review* 2 (1910), pp. 14–17, 119–121.

GOOCH, G.P., *History and Historians in the Nineteenth Century*, London, 1920.

—, *Under Six Reigns*, London, 1958.

GOODHART, A.L., *Essays in Jurisprudence and the Common Law*, Cambridge, 1931.

GOODNOW, F.G., *Politics and Administration*, New York, 1900.

GRAS, N.S.B., 'The Rise and Development of Economic History' in *The Economic History Review* 1 (1927–1928), pp. 12–34.

GRAY, H.L., *The Influence of the Commons on Early Legislation*: *A Study of the Fourteenth and Fifteenth Centuries*, Cambridge Mass., 1932.

GREEN, J.R., *A Short History of the English People*, London, 1916 (1874).

—, *Letters of John Richard Green*, ed. L. Stephen, London, 1902.

—, *Historical Studies*, London, 1903.

GREG, W.R., 'The Newspaper Press' in *E.R.* 102 (1855), pp. 470–498.

—, 'French Judgments of England: Montalembert and Rémusat' in *E.R.* 103 (1856), pp. 558–590.

—, 'Representative Reform' in *E.R.* 106 (1857), pp. 254–286.

GREY, EARL, 'The House of Commons' in *Nineteenth Century* 15 (1884), pp. 507–536.

—, 'In Peril from Parliament' in *Nineteenth Century* 28 (1890), pp. 694–698, 1012–1030.

GRUYS, C., *De Strijd over de Historische Interpretatie*, Utrecht, 1933.

GUIZOT, F., *Histoire des origines du gouvernement représentatif en Europe*, 2 vols., Paris, 1851.

—, *Life of Oliver Cromwell*, London, 1899 (1854).

GUTCHEN, R.M., 'Local Improvements and Centralisation in Nineteenth-Century England' in *The Historical Journal* 4 (1961), pp. 85–96.

GUTTSMAN, W.L. (ed.), *The English Ruling Class*, London, 1969.

GWYN, W.B., *The Meaning of the Separation of Powers*, New Orleans, 1965.

HABER, S., *Efficiency and Uplift. Scientific Management in the Progressive Era, 1890–1920*, Chicago, 1964.

HABERMAS, J., *Zur Logik der Sozialwissenschaften*, Tübingen, 1967.

HADSEL, F.L., 'G.P. Gooch' in *Some 20th Century Historians*, ed. S.W. Halperin, Chicago, 1961, pp. 255–276.

HALBWACHS, M., *La mémoire collective*, Paris, 1950.

'Haldane Centenary Essays' in *Public Administration* 35 (1957), pp. 217–265.

HALEVY, E., *A History of the English People in the Nineteenth Century*, 6 vols., London, 1949.

HALL, H., 'New Methods of Historical Enquiry' in *Q.R.* 184 (1896), pp. 122–138.

HALLAM, H., *View of the State of Europe during the Middle Ages*, 3 vols., London, 1855 (1817).

—, *The Constitutional History of England*, 3 vols., London, 1863 (1827).

—, 'Palgrave's Rise and Progress of the English Commonwealth' in *E.R.* 55 (1832), pp. 305–337.

HAMER, D.A., *John Morley*, Oxford, 1968.

HAMER, W.S., *The British Army. Civil-Military Relations, 1885–1905*, Oxford, 1970.

HANHAM, H.J., *The Reformed Electoral System in Great Britain, 1832–1914*, London, 1968 (Historical Association).

Hansard's Parliamentary Debates. Third Series, vols. 2–9 (1831).

HARDCASTLE, J.A., 'Principles and Prospects of the Liberal Party' in *E.R.* 147 (1878), pp. 274–300.

HARDING, A., *A Social History of English Law*, Harmondsworth, 1966.

HARRISON, F., 'The Deadlock in the House of Commons' in *Nineteenth Century* 10 (1881), pp. 317–340.

—, *Oliver Cromwell*, London, 1912 (1888).

—, 'The Historical Method of Professor Freeman' in *Nineteenth Century* 44 (1898), pp. 791–806.

—, *Autobiographic Memoirs*, 2 vols., London, 1911.

HART, J., 'Nineteenth-Century Social Reform: a Tory Interpretation of History' in *Past and Present* no. 31 (1965), pp. 39–61.

HASKINS, G.L., *The Statute of York and the Interest of the Commons*, Cambridge Mass., 1935.

—, *The Growth of English Representative Government*, Oxford, 1948.

HAYWARD, A., 'Macaulay and His School' in *Q.R.* 124 (1868), pp. 287–333.

—, *A Selection from the Correspondence of Abraham Hayward. From 1834 to 1884*, ed. H.E. Carlisle, 2 vols., London, 1886.

HAZLEHURST, C., 'Asquith as Prime Minister, 1908–1916' in *E.H.R.* 85 (1970), pp. 502–531.

HERRICK, F.H., 'The Second Reform Movement in Britain, 1850–1865' in *Journal of the History of Ideas* 9 (1948), pp. 174–192.

HEXTER, J.H., *Reappraisals in History*, London, 1961.

HIGHAM, J., KRIEGER, L., GILBERT, F., *History*, Englewood Cliffs, 1965.

HILL, B.W., 'Executive Monarchy and the Challenge of Parties, 1689–1832: Two Concepts of Government and Two Historiographical Interpretations' in *The Historical Journal* 13 (1970), pp. 379–401.

HILL, C., 'The Norman Yoke' in *Puritanism and Revolution*, London, 1958, pp. 50–122.

HIMMELFARB, G., *Victorian Minds*, New York, 1968.

—, 'The Intellectual in Politics: The Case of the Webbs' in *Journal of Contemporary History* 6 (1971), pp. 3–11.

HINTON, R.W.K., 'History Yesterday: Five Points about Whig History' in *History Today* 9 (1959), pp. 720–728.

HIRSCH, E.D., *Validity in Interpretation*, New Haven, 1967.

The Historical Association, 1906–1956, London, 1957.

Historical Studies of the English Parliament, ed. E.B. Fryde and E. Miller, 2 vols., Cambridge, 1970.

Historical Study in the West, introd. by B.C. Shafer, New York, 1968.

HOBHOUSE, H., 'Local Government and State Bureaucracy in Great Britain' in *The Local Government Review* 2 (1910), pp. 229–231.

HOBHOUSE, L.T., 'The New Spirit in America' in *Contemporary Review* 100 (1911), pp. 1–10.

—, *Liberalism*, introd. by A.P. Grimes, Oxford, 1964 (1911).

HOBSON, J.A., *Traffic in Treason*, London, 1914.

HOETINK, H.R., *Historische Rechtsbeschouwing*, Haarlem, 1949.

—, 'Uber anachronistische Begriffsbildung in der Rechtsgeschichte' in *Zeitschrift der Savigny-Stiftung für Rechtsgeschichte*, Romanistische Abteilung 72 (1955), pp. 39–53.

—, 'Les notions anachroniques dans l'historiographie du droit' in *Tijdschrift voor Rechtsgeschiedenis* 23 (1955), pp. 1–20.

HOLDSWORTH, W.S., *The Historians of Anglo-American Law*, Hamden, 1966.

—, *Essays in Law and History*, Oxford, 1946.

HOLLENBERG, G., *Englisches Interesse am Kaiserreich*, Wiesbaden, 1974.

HOLLISTER, C.W., 'King John and the Historians' in *Journal of British Studies* 1 (May 1961), pp. 1–19.

HOLT, J.C., *Magna Carta*, Cambridge, 1969.

HORTON, R.F., *Oliver Cromwell. A Study in Personal Religion*, London, 1897.

HOUGHTON, W.E., *The Victorian Frame of Mind*, New Haven, 1967.

HUGENHOLTZ, F.W.N., 'Adriaan Kluit en het onderwijs in de mediaevistiek' in *Forum der Letteren* 6 (1965), pp. 142–160.

HUGHES, E., 'Sir Erskine May's Views on Parliamentary Procedure in 1882' in *Public Administration* 34 (1956), pp. 419–424.

—, 'The Changes in Parliamentary Procedure, 1880–1882' in *Essays presented to Sir Lewis Namier*, ed. R. Pares and A.J.P. Taylor, London, 1956, pp. 289–319.

HUIZINGA, J., *The Waning of the Middle Ages*, Harmondsworth, 1955.

HUME, D., *The History of England*, London, 1825.

HUMPHREYS, R.A., *The Royal Historical Society, 1868–1968*, London, 1969.

HUNT, E.M., 'S.R. Gardiner' in *Some Modern Historians of Britain*, ed. H. Ausubel, a.o. New York, 1951, pp. 99–110.

HUTTON, W.H., 'The Collected Papers of A.W. Ward' in *Q.R.* 238 (1922), pp. 314–326.

HUXLEY, T.H., 'Administrative Nihilism' in *Fortnightly Review* 10 (1871), pp. 525–543.

HYNES, S., *The Edwardian Turn of Mind*, Princeton, 1968.

IMBART DE LA TOUR, P., 'Achille Luchaire' in *Revue des Deux Mondes* 52 (1909, pp. 876–901.

Interim Report of the Committee on House of Commons Personnel and Politics, 1264–1832, London 1932.

JAMES, R.R., *Rosebery*, London, 1963.

JEFFREY, F., 'Cobbett's Political Register' in *E.R.* 10 (1807), pp. 386–421.

—, 'Brodie's Constitutional History and Corrections of Mr. Hume' in *E.R.* 40 (1824), pp. 92–146.

JENKINS, J.E., 'Bismarckism in England' in *Contemporary Review* 22 (1873), pp. 107–125.

JENKINS, R., *Mr. Balfour's Poodle*, London, 1968.

JENKINSON, C.H., 'The First Parliament of Edward I' in *E.H.R.* 25 (1910), pp. 231–242.

JENKS, E., *The Constitutional Experiments of the Commonwealth*, Cambridge, 1890.

—, 'Fustel de Coulanges as an Historian' in *E.H.R.* 12 (1897), pp. 209–224.

—, 'The Story of the Habeas Corpus' in *Law Quarterly Review* 18 (1902), pp. 64–77.

—, *Parliamentary England. The Evolution of the Cabinet System*, London, 1903.

—, 'The Myth of Magna Carta' in *The Independent Review* 4 (1904–1905), pp. 260–273.

—, 'Central and Local Government' in *The Local Government Review* 3 (1910–1911), pp. 8–11, 55–59, 103–107, 157–159.

JOHNSON, C.B., *William Bodham Donne and His Friends*, London, 1905.

JOHNSON, D., *Guizot. Aspects of French History, 1787–1874*, London, 1963.

JOHNSON, J.W., *The Formation of English Neo-Classical Thought*, Princeton, 1967.

JOHNSTON, W.M., *The Formative Years of R.G. Collingwood*, The Hague, 1967.

JONES, G.S., 'The Pathology of English History' in *New Left Review* no. 46 (1967), pp. 29–43.

JUDD IV, G.P., *Horace Walpole Memoirs*, New York, 1959.

KAMERBEEK, J., 'Huizinga en de Beweging van Tachtig' in *Tijdschrift voor Geschiedenis* 67 (1954), pp. 145–164.

KEITH-LUCAS, B., *The English Local Government Franchise*, Oxford, 1952.

KELLEY, D.R., *Foundations of Modern Historical Scholarship. Language, Law and History in the French Renaissance*, New York, 1970.

—, 'History, English Law and the Renaissance' in *Past and Present* no. 65 (1974), pp. 24–51.

KELLEY, R., 'Asquith at Paisley: the Content of British Liberalism at the End of its Era' in *Journal of British Studies* 3 (November 1964), pp. 133–159.

KNOWLES, D., *Great Historical Enterprises*, London, 1963.

—, 'Some Trends in Scholarship, 1868–1968, in the field of medieval history' in *T.R.H.S.* 5th ser. 19 (1969), pp. 139–157.

KOCKA, J., 'Otto Hintze' in *Deutsche Historiker*, Hrsg. H.U. Wehler, Göttingen, 1972, Band III, pp. 41–64.

KRAMNICK, J., 'Augustan Politics and English Historiography: The Debate on the English Past, 1730–1735' in *History and Theory* 6 (1967), pp. 33–56.

LACOMBE, P., *De l'histoire considérée comme science*, Paris, 1894.

LAING, R., 'The First Stewart in England' in *Q.R.* 139 (1875), pp. 1–40.

LAMBERT, R., 'Central and Local Relations in Mid-Victorian England: The Local Government Act Office, 1858–1871' in *Victorian Studies* 6 (1962), pp. 121–150.

LANGLOIS, C.V., *Le Règne de Philippe III Le Hardi*, Paris, 1887.

—, 'The Comparative History of England and France during the Middle Ages' in *E.H.R.* 5 (1890), pp. 259–263.

LANGLOIS, C.V. and SEIGNOBOS, C., *Introduction aux études historiques*, Paris, 1898.

LANGLOIS, C.V., *Questions d'histoire et d'enseignement*, Paris, 1902.

LAPRADE, W.T., 'The Present State of the History of England in the Eighteenth Century' in *Journal of Modern History* 4 (1932), pp. 581–603.

LAPSLEY, G., 'Some Recent Advance in English Constitutional History' in *The Cambridge Historical Journal* 5 (1936), pp. 119–161.

LASLETT, P., *The World We Have Lost*, London, 1968.

LEE, R.W., 'Edward Jenks, 1861–1939' in *Proceedings of the British Academy* 26 (1940), pp. 399–423.

LEFEBVRE, G., *La Naissance de l'historiographie moderne*, Paris, 1971.

LE GOFF, J., 'Is Politics Still the Backbone of History?' in *Deadalus* (Winter 1971), pp. 1–19.

'The Lessons of the War. A Proposed Association' in *Nineteenth Century* 48 (1900), pp. 1–3, 173–183, 859–880.

LETWIN, S.R., *The Pursuit of Certainty*, Cambridge, 1965.

LEWIS, G.C., *Remarks on the Use and Abuse of Some Political Terms*, London, 1832. New Edition with introd. essay by C.F. Mullett, Columbia, 1970.

—, 'Marshall on the Representation of Minorities' in *E.R.* 100 (1854), pp. 226–235.

—, 'Modern English History' in *E.R.* 103 (1856), pp. 305–357.

—, 'History and Prospects of Parliamentary Reform' in *E.R.* 109 (1859), pp. 264–292.

—, *Letters of Sir George Cornewall Lewis*, ed. G.F. Lewis, London, 1870.

LEWIS, W.S., *Horace Walpole*, London, 1961.

The Liberal Tradition. From Fox to Keynes, ed. A. Bullock and M. Shock, Oxford, 1967.

LIEBER, F., *Manual of Political Ethics*, London, 1839.

—, *On Civil Liberty and Self-Government*, London, 1859.

LIEBERMANN, F., 'New Light on Medieval England' in *Q.R.* 236 (1921), pp. 361–365.

LINK, A.S. (ed.), *The Papers of Woodrow Wilson*, vol. V, Princeton, 1968.

LIPPINCOTT, B.E., *Victorian Critics of Democracy*, Minneapolis, 1938.

LITTLE, A.G., 'Professor Tout' in *History* 14 (1929–1930), pp. 313–324.

LLOYD, D., *The Idea of Law*, Harmondsworth, 1964.

LOCHER, Th. J.G., 'Over Historisch Relativisme' in *Forum der Letteren* 5 (1964), pp. 147–163.

LODGE, M., *Sir Richard Lodge*, London, 1946.

LOW, S., 'If the House of Commons were abolished' in *Nineteenth Century* 36 (1894), pp. 846–863.

—, 'The Decline of the House of Commons' in *Nineteenth Century* 37 (1895), pp. 567–578.

—, *The Governance of England*, London, 1904.

LUBENOW, W.C., *The Politics of Government Growth. Early Victorian Attitudes Toward State Intervention, 1833–1848*, Newton Abbot, 1971.

LUCHAIRE, A., *Histoire des institutions monarchiques de la France sous les premiers Capétiens*, 2 vols., Paris, 1891.

—, *La Société française au temps de Philippe Auguste*, Paris, 1909.

MACAULAY, T.B., *The History of England*, 3 vols., London, 1906. (Everyman's Library).

—, *Critical and Historical Essays*, 2 vols., London, 1907. (Everyman's Library).

—, *Miscellaneous Essays*, London, 1910 (Everyman's Library).

MACKENZIE, K., *The English Parliament*, Harmondsworth, 1963.

MACKENZIE, W.J.M., *Theories of Local Government*, London, 1961.

MACKINTOSH, J., 'Parliamentary Reform' in *E.R.* 34 (1820), pp. 461–501.

—, 'Sismondi's History of France' in *E.R.* 35 (1821), pp. 488–509.

MAITLAND, F.W., *Justice and Police*, London, 1885.

MAITLAND, F.W. (ed.) *Records of the Parliament holden at Westminster on 28 February 1305. Memoranda de Parliamento*, London, 1893.

MAITLAND, F.W., *Domesday Book and Beyond*, London, 1960 (1897).

—, *Township and Borough*, Cambridge, 1898.

—, *The Constitutional History of England*, Cambridge, 1961 (1908).

—, *The Collected Papers of Frederic William Maitland*, 3 vols., Cambridge, 1911.

—, *Selected Historical Essays of F.W. Maitland*, introd. by H. Cam, Cambridge, 1957.

—, *The Letters of F.W. Maitland*, ed. C.H.S. Fifoot, Cambridge, 1965.

MANNING, W.W., 'Parliamentary Procedure' in *E.R.* 155 (1882), pp. 205–221.

MANSFIELD, H.C., 'Sir Lewis Namier Considered' in *Journal of British Studies* 2 (November 1962), pp. 28–55.

—, 'Sir Lewis Namier Again Considered' in *Journal of British Studies* 3 (May 1964), pp. 109–119.

MARRIOTT, J.A.R., 'Cabinet Government or Departmentalism?' in *Nineteenth Century* 48 (1900), pp. 685–694.

MARWICK, A., *The Nature of History*, London, 1970.

MASON, T.W., 'Nineteenth-century Cromwell' in *Past and Present* no. 40 (1968), pp. 187–191.

MASSEY, W.N., 'May's *Constitutional History of England*' in *E.R.* 115 (1862), pp. 211–242.

—, 'The Constitution and the Crown' in *E.R.* 148 (1878), pp. 262–294.

MASTERMAN, C.F.G. (ed.), *The Heart of the Empire*, London, 1901.

MATTHEW, H.C.G., *The Liberal Imperialists*, Oxford, 1973.

MAY, T.E., 'The Machinery of Parliamentary Legislation' in *E.R.* 99 (1854), pp. 243–282.

—, *The Constitutional History of England, 1760–1860*, 3 vols., London 1882, (1861).

McCLELLAND, C.E., *The German Historians and England*, Cambridge, 1971.

McDOWELL, R.B., *A. Stopford-Green*, Dublin, 1967.

McILWAIN, C.H., *The High Court of Parliament and its Supremacy*, New Haven, 1910.

—, *Constitutionalism. Ancient and Modern*, New York, 1966.

McKISACK, M., 'Borough Representation in Richard II's Reign' in *E.H.R.* 39 (1924), pp. 511–522.

—, *The Parliamentary Representation of the English Boroughs during the Middle Ages*, Oxford, 1932.

McLACHLAN, J.O., 'The Origin and Early Development of the Cambridge Historical Tripos' in *The Cambridge Historical Journal* 9 (1947), pp. 78–104.

MERIVALE, H., 'George III and Charles James Fox' in *Q.R.* 105 (1859), pp. 463–504.

—, 'Character of George III' in *Q.R.* 122 (1867), pp. 281–310.

MILL, J.S., 'Recent French Historians – Michelet's History of France' in *E.R.* 79 (1844), pp. 1–39.

—, 'Centralisation' in *E.R.* 115 (1862), pp. 323–358.

—, *Utilitarianism, Liberty and Representative Government*, ed. A.D. Lindsay, London, 1964.

MILLER, E., *The Origins of Parliament*, London, 1960. (Historical Association).

MILMAN, A., 'The House of Commons and the Obstructive Party' in *Q.R.* 145 (1878), pp. 231–257.

—, 'The Peril of Parliament' in *Q.R.* 178 (1894), pp. 263–288.

—, 'Parliamentary Procedure versus Obstruction' in *Q.R.* 178 (1894), pp. 486–503.

MILNE, A.T., 'The Historical Association and its Founders' in *History Today* 16 (1966), pp. 279–281.

—, *A Centenary Guide to the Publications of the Royal Historical Society, 1868–1968 and of the Former Camden Society, 1838–1897*, London, 1968.

MITTEIS, H., *Vom Lebenswert der Rechtsgeschichte*, Weimar, 1947.

MOIR, E., *The Justice of the Peace*, Harmondsworth, 1969.

MONCREIFF, J., 'Extension of the Franchise' in *E.R.* 123 (1866), pp. 263–296.

MOORE, D.C., 'The Other Face of Reform' in *Victorian Studies* 5 (1961), pp. 7–34.

—, 'Concession or Cure: The Sociological Premises of the First Reform Act' in *The Historical Journal* 9 (1966), pp. 39–59.

MORISON, J.C., *Macaulay*, London, 1882.

MORLEY, J., *Oliver Cromwell*, London, 1900.

MUIR, R., *How Britain is Governed*, London, 1933.

NAMIER, J., *Lewis Namier*, London, 1971.

NAMIER, L., *The Structure of Politics at the Accession of George III*, London, 1961 (1929).

—, *Avenues of History*, London, 1952.

—, *Personalities and Powers*, London, 1955.

—, *Crossroads of Power*, London, 1962.

NEALE, J.E., 'The Commons' Privilege of Free Speech in Parliament' in *Tudor Studies*, ed. R.W. Seton-Watson, London, 1924, pp. 257–286.

—, 'A.F. Pollard' in *E.H.R.* 64 (1949), pp. 198–205.

—, *The Elizabethan House of Commons*, Harmondsworth, 1963 (1949).

—, *Elizabeth I and Her Parliaments*, 2 vols., London, 1965 (1953–1957).

—, *Essays in Elizabethan History*, London, 1958.

NELSON, J.G., *The Sublime Puritan. Milton and the Victorians*, Madison, 1963.

NEWLAND, H.O., 'Local Government and Free Institutions' in *The Local Government Review* 1 (1909–1910), pp. 264–267.

NICHOLLS, D., 'Positive Liberty, 1880–1914' in *American Political Science Review* 56 (1962), pp. 114–128.

NOBLE, D.W., *The Paradox of Progressive Thought*, Minneapolis, 1958.

NOTESTEIN, W., *The Winning of the Initiative by the House of Commons*, London, 1924.

NUSCHELER, F., *Walter Bagehot und die englische Verfassungstheorie*, Meisenheim am Glan, 1969.

OAKESHOTT, M., *Experience and its Modes*, Cambridge, 1966 (1933).

OGG, D., *Herbert Fisher, 1865–1940*, London, 1947.

OMAN, C., *Inaugural Lecture on the Study of History*, Oxford, 1906.

—, *Memories of Victorian Oxford*, London, 1941.

OSBORNE, J.W., *John Cartwright*, Cambridge, 1972.

PALGRAVE, F., 'Poor Laws' in *Q.R.* 33 (1826), pp. 429–455.

—, 'Proposal for a Museum of National Antiquities' in *Q.R.* 37 (1828), pp. 485-489.

—, *On the Legal Right of Dormant Parliamentary Boroughs*, London, 1830.

—, *An Essay upon the Original Authority of the King's Council*, London, 1834.

—, 'Election Committees and Registration of Electors' in *Q.R.* 71 (1843), pp. 478–501.

—, 'Convocation' in *Q.R.* 75 (1845), pp. 464–484.

—, *The Collected Historical Works of Sir Francis Palgrave*, ed. Sir R.H. Inglis Palgrave, 10 vols., Cambridge, 1919–1921.

PALGRAVE, R., 'Pym and Shaftesbury: two Popish Plots' in *Q.R.* 147 (1879), pp. 402–430.

—, 'Fall of the Monarchy of Charles I' in *Q.R.* 154 (1882), pp. 1–32.

—, 'Oliver Cromwell: His Character Illustrated by Himself' in *Q.R.* 162 (1886), pp. 414–442.

—, 'Cromwell and the Insurrection of 1655. A Reply to Mr. Firth' in *E.H.R.* 3 (1888), pp. 521–539, 722–751 and in *E.H.R.* 4 (1889), pp. 110–131.

—, *Oliver Cromwell. The Protector*, London, 1890.

PALLISTER, A., *Magna Carta. The Heritage of Liberty*, Oxford, 1971.

PANTIN, W.A., 'F.M. Powicke' in *E.H.R.* 80 (1965), pp. 1–9.

PARKER, H.T., 'Herbert Butterfield' in *Some 20th Century Historians*, ed. S.W. Halperin, Chicago, 1961, pp. 75–101.

PARSLOE, G., 'Recollections of the Institute, 1922–1943' in *B.I.H.R.* 44 (1971), pp. 270–283.

PASQUET, D., *Essai sur les origines de la Chambre des Communes*, Paris, 1914.

PATERSON, A., *Oliver Cromwell. His Life and Character*, London, 1899.

PEARDON, Th. P., *The Transition in English Historical Writing, 1760–1830*, New York, 1933.

PENSON, L.M., 'Harold Temperley, 1879–1939' in *History* 24 (1939–1940), pp. 121–124.

PERRIN, C.E., *Un Historien français. Ferdinand Lot, 1866–1952*, Genève, 1968.

PICOT, G., *L'Histoire des États-Généraux*, 5 vols., Paris, 1888.

PICTON, J.A., *Oliver Cromwell. The Man and his Religion*, London, 1882.

PLAYNE, C.E., *The Pre-War Mind in Britain. An Historical Review*, London, 1928.

PLUCKNETT, T.F.T., 'The Place of the Council in the Fifteenth Century' in *T.R.H.S.* 4th ser. 1 (1918), pp. 157–189.

—, 'The Lancastrian Constitution' in *Tudor Studies*, ed. R.W. Seton-Watson, London 1924, pp. 161–181.

—, 'Maitland's View of Law and History' in *Law Quarterly Review* 67 (1951), pp. 179–194.

PLUMB, J.H., *The Growth of Political Stability in England, 1675–1725*, London, 1967.

—, *The Death of the Past*, London, 1969.

—, 'The Atomic Historian' in *New Statesman*, 1-8-1969, pp. 141–143.

—, 'The Function of History' in *Encounter* (June 1971), pp. 71–78.

POCOCK, J.G.A., *The Ancient Constitution and the Feudal Law*, Cambridge, 1957.

—, 'Burke and the Ancient Constitution: a Problem in the History of Ideas' in *The Historical Journal* 3 (1960), pp. 125–143.

—, 'The Origins of the Study of the Past: a Comparative Approach' in *Comparative Studies in Society and History* 4 (1961–1962), pp. 209–246.

—, 'Time, Institutions and Action: an essay on Traditions and their Understanding' in *Politics and Experience*, ed. P. King and B.C. Parekh, Cambridge, 1968, pp. 209–237.

POLLARD, A.F., See Bibliography of A.F. Pollard's Writings, pp. 374–397.

POLLOCK, F. and MAITLAND, F.W., *The History of English Law*, introd. by S.F.C. Milson, 2 vols., Cambridge, 1968 (1895).

POLLOCK, F., *History of the Science of Politics*, London, 1911.

POOLE, A.L., 'F.W. Maitland and R.L. Poole' in *The Cambridge Historical Journal* 10 (1952), pp. 318–351.

POSTAN, M.M., *The Historical Method in Social Science*, Cambridge, 1939.

POUND, R., *Interpretations of Legal History*, Cambridge, 1930.

POWELL, F.Y., 'The École des Chartes and English Records' in *T.R.H.S.* N.S. 11 (1897), pp. 31–40.

POWICKE, F.M., 'Sir Francis Palgrave' in *T.L.S.*, 22-5-1919, p. 272.

—, 'The Historical Method of Mr. Coulton' in *History* 8 (1923–1924), pp. 256–268.

—, *Medieval England, 1066–1485*, London, 1931.

—, *History, Freedom and Religion*, London, 1938.

—, *Three Lectures*, Oxford, 1947.

—, 'Administrative History' in *T.L.S.* 6-1-1956, pp. XXVI–XXVII.

—, *Modern Historians and the Study of History*, London, 1956.

PRESTWICH, J.O., 'Anglo-Norman Feudalism and the Problem of Continuity' in *Past and Present* no. 26 (1963), pp. 39–57.

PREYER, R., *Bentham, Coleridge and the Science of History*, Bochum Langendreer, 1958.

PRICE, J.M., 'Party, Purpose and Pattern: Sir Lewis Namier and His Critics' in *Journal of British Studies* 1 (November 1961), pp. 71–93.

PROTHERO, G.W., 'Gneist on the English Constitution' in *E.H.R.* 3 (1888), pp. 1–33.

—, *Why Should We Learn History?* Edinburgh, 1894.

—, 'Presidential Address' in *T.R.H.S.* N.S. 16 (1902), pp. VII–XXV; 18 (1904), pp. 1–31; 19 (1905), pp. 1–26.

RABB, Th.K., 'Parliament and Society in Early Stuart England: The Legacy of Wallace Notestein' in *A.H.R.* 77 (1972), pp. 705–714.

RADBRUCH, G., 'Arten der Interpretation' in *Recueil d'études sur les sources du droit en l'honneur de François Gény*, Paris, 1935, vol. 2, pp. 217–226.

—, *Der Geist des englischen Rechts*, Heidelberg, 1947.

—, *Einführung in die Rechtswissenschaft*, Stuttgart, 1952.

RAIT, R.S., 'Frederick York Powell' in *E.H.R.* 19 (1904), pp. 484–492.

RANDALL, H.J., *The Creative Centuries. A Study in Historical Development*, London, 1944.

REDLICH, J., *Englische Lokalverwaltung*. Leipzig, 1901.

REDLICH, J., and HIRST, F.W., *The History of Local Government in England*, ed. B. Keith-Lucas, London, 1970.

REEVE, H., 'Earl Grey on Parliamentary Government' in *E.R.* 108 (1858), pp. 271–297.

—, 'Todd on Parliamentary Government' in *E.R.* 125 (1867), pp. 578–596.

—, 'Plain Whig Principles' in *E.R.* 151 (1880), pp. 257–280.

—, 'A Whig Retort' in *E.R.* 155 (1882), pp. 279–290.

—, *Memoirs of the Life and Correspondence of Henry Reeve*, ed. J.K. Laughton, 2 vols., London, 1893.

Report from Select Committee on Public Petitions in *Parliamentary Papers*, vol. XII (1833).

Reports from the Lords Committees appointed to search the Journals of the House, Rolls of Parliament and other Records and Documents, for all matters touching the Dignity of a Peer of the Realm (1819–1822) London, 1826.

REX, M.B., 'C.H. Firth' in *Some Modern Historians of Britain*, ed. H. Ausubel, a.o. New York, 1951, p.p 192–214.

RICHARDSON, H.G., 'The Commons and Medieval Politics' in *T.R.H.S.* 4th ser. 28 (1946), pp. 21–45.

RICHARDSON, H.G. and SAYLES, G.O., *Parliaments and Great Councils in Medieval England*, London, 1961.

—, 'William Stubbs: The Man and The Historian' in *The Governance of Mediaeval England from the Conquest to Magna Carta*, Edinburgh, 1963, pp. 1–21.

RICHTER, M., *The Politics of Conscience*, London, 1964.

RIESS, L., *Geschichte des Wahlrechts zum englischen Parlament im Mittelalter*, Berlin, 1885.

ROACH, J., 'Liberalism and the Victorian Intelligentsia' in *The Cambridge Historical Journal* 13 (1957), pp. 58–81.

ROBBINS, C., *The Eighteenth-Century Commonwealthman*, New York, 1968.

ROBERTSON, J.M., *New Essays towards a Critical Method*, London, 1897.

—, 'Cromwell and The Historians' in *The Reformer* (June–July 1899), pp. 334–343, 391–400.

ROGERS, H., 'Revolution and Reform' in *E.R.* 88 (1848), pp. 360–403.

ROGERS, J.E.Th., *The Economic Interpretation of History*, London, 1929 (1888).

ROGERS, J.G., 'Chatter versus Work in Parliament' in *Nineteenth Century* 16 (1884), pp. 396–411.

ROGERS, J.G., a.o. 'The Liberal Collapse' in *Nineteenth Century* 45 (1899), pp. 1–38.

Rogers, J.G., 'Liberalism and its Cross-currents' in *Nineteenth Century* 46 (1899), pp. 527–540.

—, 'Wanted a Leader' in *Nineteenth Century* 48 (1900), pp. 149–158.

ROMEIN, J., *Het Onvoltooid Verleden*, Amsterdam 1937.

—, *Carillon der Tijden*, Amsterdam, 1953.

—, *Op Het Breukvlak van Twee Eeuwen*, 2 vols., Leyden-Amsterdam, 1967.

ROORDA, D.J., 'Sir Lewis Namier, een inspirerend en irriterend historicus' in *Tijdschrift voor Geschiedenis* 75 (1962), pp. 325–347.

—, *Een eigenaardige bureaucratie*, Leyden, 1973.

ROSKELL, J.S., 'Perspectives in English Parliamentary History' in *Bulletin of the John Rylands Library* 46 (1963–1964), pp. 448–475.

ROUND, J.H., *Feudal England*, London, 1909 (1895).

—, 'Village Communities in Spain' in *Q.R.* 182 (1895), pp. 483–507.

—, 'Historical Research' in *Nineteenth Century* 44 (1898), pp. 1004–1014.

—, 'As Established by Law' in *Contemporary Review* 75 (1899), pp. 814–822; 76 (1899), pp. 220–230.

—, 'Cromwell and the Electorate' in *Nineteenth Century* 46 (1899), pp. 947–956.

—, 'Colchester during the Commonwealth' in *E.H.R.* 15 (1900), pp. 641–664.

—, *Studies in Peerage and Family History*, London, 1901.

—, *Peerage and Pedigree*, 2 vols., London, 1910.

—, 'The House of Lords and the Model Parliament' in *E.H.R.* 30 (1915), pp. 385–397.

—, *Family Origins and Other Studies*, ed. W. Page, London, 1930.

ROWLAND, P., *The Last Liberal Governments. The Promised Land, 1905–1910*, London, 1968.

ROWLEY, J., 'Mr. Green's Short History of the English People; Is It Trustworthy?' in *Fraser's Magazine* 12 (1875), pp. 395–410, 710–724.

ROWSE, A.L., *The Use of History*, London, 1946.

RUSSELL, G.W.E., 'A Protest against Whiggery' in *Nineteenth Century* 13 (1883), pp. 920–927.

—, 'The New Liberalism: A Response' in *Nineteenth Century* 26 (1889), pp. 492–499.

RUSSELL, J., *An Essay on the History of the English Government and Constitution,* London, 1865 (1821).

—, *Selections from Speeches of Earl Russell (1817–to 1841) and from Despatches (1859 to 1865)*, 2 vols., London, 1870.

—, *The Early Correspondence of Lord John Russell, 1805–1840*, ed. R. Russell, 2 vols., London, 1913.

SALEILLES, R., 'École historique et droit naturel' in *Revue trimestrielle de droit civil* 1 (1902), pp. 80–112.

SAMUEL, H., *Memoirs*, London, 1945.

SANDERS, LLOYD, *The Holland House Circle*, London, 1908.

SAYLES, G.O., *The Medieval Foundations of England*, London, 1966 (1948).

—, 'The Changed Concept of History: Stubbs and Renan' in *Aberdeen University Review* 35 (1953–1954), pp. 235–247.

SCARISBRICK, J.J., *Henry VIII*, London, 1968.

SCHREUDER, D.M., 'Gladstone and Italian Unification, 1848–70: the Making of a Liberal?' in *E.H.R.* 85 (1970), pp. 475–501.

SCHUYLER, R.L., 'Some Historical Idols' in *Political Science Quarterly* 47 (1932), pp. 1–18.

—, 'The Usefulness of Useless History' in *Political Science Quarterly* 56 (1941), pp. 23–47.

—, 'John Richard Green and His Short History' in *Political Science Quarterly* 64 (1949), pp. 321–354.

—, *F.W. Maitland. Historian*, Berkeley, 1960.

—, 'History and Historical Criticism: Recent Work of Richardson and Sayles' in *Journal of British Studies* 3 (May 1964), pp. 1–23.

SEARLE, G.R., *The Quest for National Efficiency*, Oxford, 1971.

SEDGWICK, R., 'Horace Walpole' in *From Anne to Victoria*, ed. B. Dobrée, London, 1937, pp. 265–278.

SEDGWICK, R. (ed.), *Letters from George III to Lord Bute, 1756–1766*, London, 1939.

SEEBOHM, F., *The English Village Community*, London, 1884.

SEELEY, J.R., *The Expansion of England*, London, 1925 (1883).

—, *Lectures and Essays*, London, 1895.

—, *The Growth of British Policy. An Historical Essay*, 2 vols., Cambridge, 1895.

—, *Introduction to Political Science*, Cambridge, 1923. (1896).

SEELEY, L.B., *Horace Walpole and His World*, London, 1895.

SEELIGER, G., 'Juristische Konstruction und Geschichtsforschung' in *Historische Vierteljahrsschrift* 7 (1904), pp. 161–191.

SEIGNOBOS, C., *La Méthode historique appliquée aux sciences sociales*, Paris, 1909.

SEMMEL, B., *Imperialism and Social Reform*, London, 1960.

SHANNON, R.T., 'John Robert Seeley and the Idea of a National Church' in *Ideas and Institutions of Victorian Britain*, ed. R. Robson, London, 1967, pp. 236–267.

SHEA, D.F., *The English Ranke: John Lingard*, New York, 1969.

SIDGWICK, H., 'The Historical Method' in *Mind* 11 (1886), pp. 203–219.

SIMKHOVITCH, V.G., 'Approaches to History' in *Political Science Quarterly* 44 (1929), pp. 481–497; 45 (1930), pp. 481–526; 47 (1932), pp. 410–439; 48 (1933), pp. 23–61.

SMITH, A., 'Lieber's Political Ethics' in *E.R.* 73 (1841), pp. 55–76.

SMITH, A.L., *F.W. Maitland*, Oxford, 1908.

SMITH, GOLDWIN, *The United Kingdom. A Political History*, 2 vols., London, 1899.

—, 'The Failure of Party Government' in *Nineteenth Century* 45 (1899), pp. 729–732.

SMITH, L.P., *The English Language*, Oxford, 1952.

SMITH, P. (ed.), *Lord Salisbury on Politics: A Selection from his Articles in the Quarterly Review, 1860–1883*, Cambridge, 1972.

SOUTHERN, R.W., *The Shape and Substance of Academic History*, Oxford, 1961.

—, 'The Letters of Frederic William Maitland' in *History and Theory* 6 (1967), pp. 105–111.

SOUTHGATE, D., *The Passing of the Whigs, 1832–1886*, London, 1962.

SPENCER, H., *The Man Versus The State*, ed. D. Macrae, Harmondsworth, 1969.

STARZINGER, V.E., *Middlingness. Juste Milieu. Political Theory in France and England, 1815–48*, Charlottesville, 1965.

STENTON, F.M., 'J.H. Round' in *D.N.B.* (1922–1930), London, 1937, pp. 727–731.

—, 'The History of Parliament' in *T.L.S.*, 6-1-1956, p. XII.

—, 'Early English History, 1895–1920' in *Preparatory to Anglo-Saxon England. Being the Collected Papers of F.M. Stenton*, ed. D.M. Stenton, Oxford, 1970, pp. 346–356.

STEPHEN, J.F., 'Buckle's History of Civilization in England' in *E.R.* 107 (1858), pp. 465–512.

—, 'Parliamentary Government' in *Contemporary Review* 23 (1873–1874), pp. 1–19, 165–181.

STEPHEN, L., *Hobbes*, London, 1904.

—, *Hours in a Library*, 3 vols., London, 1907.

STOKES, E., *The English Utilitarians and India*, Oxford, 1959.

STONE, L., 'Prosopography' in *Daedalus* (Winter 1971), pp. 46–79.

STONE DE MONTPENSIER, R., 'Maitland and the Interpretation of History' in *American Journal of Legal History* 10 (1966), pp. 259–281.

STRACHEY, L., *Biographical Essays*, London, 1948.

STUART, C.H., 'The Prince Consort and Ministerial Politics, 1856–1859' in *Essays in British History. Presented to Sir Keith Feiling*, ed. H.R. Trevor-Roper, London, 1964, pp. 247–269.

STUBBS, W., *The Constitutional History of England*, 3 vols., Oxford, 1874–1878.

—, *The Early Plantagenets*, London, 1889 (1876).

—, *Seventeen Lectures on The Study of Medieval and Modern History*, New York, 1967 (1887).

—, *Letters of William Stubbs*, ed. W.H. Hutton, London, 1904.

Studies in History. British Academy Lectures, selected and introd. by L.S. Sutherland, London, 1966.

'The Study of History' in *T.L.S.*, 5-8-1955, pp. 437–438.

TAIT, J., 'J.H. Round' in *E.H.R.* 43 (1928), pp. 572–577.

—, 'T.F. Tout' in *E.H.R.* 45 (1930), pp. 78–85.

TANNER, J.R., 'J.R. Seeley' in *E.H.R.* 10 (1895), pp. 507–514.

—, *Tudor Constitutional Documents*, 1485–1603, Cambridge, 1930 (1922).

—, *English Constitutional Conflicts of the Seventeenth Century, 1603–1689*, Cambridge, 1966 (1928).

TEMPERLEY, H.W.V., 'Inner and Outer Cabinet and Privy Council, 1689–1783' in *E.H.R.* 27 (1912), pp. 682–699.

TEMPLEMAN, G., 'The History of Parliament to 1400 in the Light of Modern Research' in *University of Birmingham Historical Journal* 1 (1947–1948), pp. 202–231.

—, 'Edward I and The Historians' in *The Cambridge Historical Journal* 10 (1950), pp. 16–35.

THOMPSON, F.M.L., *English Landed Society in the Nineteenth Century*, London, 1971.

THOMPSON, P., *Socialist, Liberals and Labour. The Struggle for London, 1885–1914*, London, 1967.

THOMSON, D., *England in the Twentieth Century*, Harmondsworth, 1965.

TOUT, T.F., *Edward I*, London, 1893.

—, 'W. Stubbs' in *D.N.B.*, sec. suppl. vol. III, London, 1912, pp. 444–451.

—, *The Place of the Reign of Edward II in English History*, Manchester, 1914.

—, *Chapters in the Administrative History of Medieval England*, 6 vols., Manchester, 1920–1933.

—, 'The Place of the Middle Ages in the Teaching of History' in *History* 8 (1923–1924), pp. 1–18.

—, *Collected Papers*, 3 vols. Manchester, 1932–1934.

TREVELYAN, G.M., 'Carlyle as an Historian' in *Nineteenth Century* 46 (1899), pp. 493–503.

—, 'The Latest View of History' in *The Independent Review* 1 (1903–1904), pp. 395–414.

—, *England under The Stuarts*, Harmondsworth, 1960 (1904).

—, *The Two-Party System in English Political History*, Oxford, 1926.

—, *Sir George Otto Trevelyan. A Memoir*, London, 1932.

—, *The English Revolution*, London, 1938.

—, *An Autobiography and Other Essays*, London, 1949.

TREVELYAN, G.O., *The Life and Letters of Lord Macaulay*, London, 1959 (1876).

—, *The Early History of Charles James Fox*, London, 1928 (1880).

TREVOR-ROPER, H.R., *History: Professional and Lay*, Oxford, 1957.

—, *Historical Essays*, London, 1957.

—, *The Romantic Movement and The Study of History*, London, 1969.

TURBERVILLE, A.S., 'History Objective and Subjective' in *History* 17 (1932–1933), pp. 289–302.

UNWIN, G., *Studies in Economic History. The Collected Papers of George Unwin*, ed. R.H. Tawney, London, 1927.

USHER, R.G., *A Critical Study of the Historical Method of Samuel Rawson Gardiner*, St. Louis, 1915.

VENEMA, C.A. UNIKEN, *Van Common Law en Civil Law*, Zwolle, 1971.

VERAX (ps.), *The Crown and the Cabinet*, Manchester, 1878.

VERNON, V.F., 'Parliamentary Reapportionment Proposals in the Puritan Revolution' in *E.H.R.* 74 (1959), pp. 409–442.

VILE, M.J.C., *Constitutionalism and the Separation of Powers*, Oxford, 1967.

VINCENT, J., *The Formation of the Liberal Party*, London, 1966.

VINOGRADOFF, P., *Villainage in England*, Oxford, 1892.

—, 'F.W. Maitland' in *E.H.R.* 22 (1907), pp. 280–289.

—, *English Society in the Eleventh Century*, Oxford, 1908.

VIOLLET, P., *Histoire des institutions politiques et administratives de la France*, 3 vols., Paris, 1890–1903.

VOGT, J., 'Geschichte und Gegenwartsverständnis' in *Geschichte und Gegenwartsverständnis. Festschrift für Hans Rothfels*, Göttingen, 1963, pp. 49–65.

WALCOTT, R., '"Sir Lewis Namier Considered"' Considered' in *Journal of British Studies* 3 (May 1964), pp. 85–108.

WALLACE, E., *Goldwin Smith. Victorian Liberal*, Toronto, 1957.

WALLAS, G., *Human Nature in Politics*, London, 1914.

—, *Our Social Heritage*, New Haven, 1921.

WALPOLE, H., *Memoirs and Portraits*, ed. M. Hodgart, London, 1963.

WALPOLE, S., *The Life of Lord John Russell*, 2 vols., London, 1889.

WALSH, W.H., *An Introduction to Philosophy of History*, London, 1951.

WARD, A.W., 'Presidential Address' in *T.R.H.S.* N.S. 14 (1900), pp. 1–18.

—, *The Collected Papers of A.W. Ward*, 5 vols., Cambridge, 1921.

WEBB, B., *Our Partnership*, London, 1948.

WEBB, C.C.J., 'R.L. Poole' in *Proceedings of the British Academy* 25 (1939), pp. 311–320.

WEBB, S. and B., *Industrial Democracy*, 2 vols., London, 1897.

WEBB, S., *Twentieth Century Politics: A Policy of National Efficiency*, London, 1901.

WEDGWOOD, C.V., *The Last of the Radicals. Josiah Wedgwood, M.P.*, London, 1951.

Wellesley Index to Victorian Periodicals, 1824–1900, ed. W.E. Houghton, 2 vols., London, 1966–1972.

WERNHAM, R.B., 'The Public Record Office, 1838–1938' in *History* 23 (1938–1939), pp. 222–235.

WESTON, C.C., 'Henry Hallam' in *Some Modern Historians of Britain*, ed. H. Ausubel, a.o. New York, 1951, pp. 20–34.

—, 'The Theory of Mixed Monarchy under Charles I and After' in *E.H.R.* 75 (1960), pp. 426–443.

WHITE, A., *The English Democracy*, London, 1894.

—, *Efficiency and Empire*, London, 1901. (Ed. with an introduction and notes by G.R. Searle, The Harvester Press, Brighton, 1973).

WHITE, H.V., 'The Burden of History' in *History and Theory* 5 (1966), pp. 111–134.

WHITELOCK, D., 'F.M. Stenton' in *E.H.R.* 84 (1969), pp. 1–11.

Why We Study History, London, 1944 (Historical Association Pamphlet no. 131).

WIEACKER, F., *Wandlungen im Bilde der historischen Rechtsschule*, Karlsruhe, 1967.

Wiener, M.J., *Between Two Worlds, The Political Thought of Graham Wallas*, Oxford, 1971.

WILLEY, B., *More Nineteenth Century Studies*, London, 1956.

WILLIAMS, B., 'The Value of History' in *The Scottish Historical Review* 23 (1925–1926), pp. 128–140.

WILLIAMS, C.H., 'A.F. Pollard' in *B.I.H.R.* 22 (1949), pp. 1–10.

WILLIAMS, P., 'Dr. Elton's Interpretation of the Age' in *Past and Present* no. 25 (1963), pp. 3–8.

—, 'The Tudor State' in *Past and Present* no. 25 (1963), pp. 39–58.

WILLIAMS, R., *Culture and Society, 1780–1950*, Harmondsworth, 1963.

WILLIAMS, T., 'The Cabinet in the Eighteenth Century' in *History* 22 (1937–1938), pp. 240–252.

WILLIAMS, W.J., 'Stubbs's Appointment as Regius Professor, 1866' in *B.I.H.R.* 33 (1960), pp. 121–125.

WILSON, T., *The Downfall of the Liberal Party*, London, 1966.

WINGFIELD-STRATFORD, E., *Truth in Masquerade*, London, 1951.

WINKLER, H.R., *The League of Nations Movement in Great Britain*, Kingsport, 1952.

—, 'G. M. Trevelyan' in *Some 20th Century Historians*, ed. S.W. Halperin, Chicago, 1961, pp. 31–55.

WINSTANLEY, D.A., *Later Victorian Cambridge*, London, 1947.

WINTER, J.M., 'R.H. Tawney's Early Political Thought' in *Past and Present* no. 47 (1970), pp. 71–96.

WINTER, P.J. VAN, *Engeland en Cromwell*, Groningen, 1939.

WOODWARD, C. VANN, 'The Age of Reinterpretation' in *A.H.R.* 66 (1960). pp. 1–29.

—, 'The Future of the Past' in *A.H.R.* 75 (1970), pp. 711–726.

WOODWARD, L., 'The Rise of the Professional Historian in England' in *Studies in International History*, ed. K. Bourne and D.C. Watt, London, 1967, pp. 16–34.

WUNDT, W., *Ethik, eine Untersuchung der Thatsachen und Gesetze des sittlichen Lebens*, Stuttgart, 1892.

YOUNG, G.M., *Victorian England*, New York, 1954.

ZELDIN, T., 'English Ideals in French Politics during the Nineteenth Century' in *The Historical Journal* 2 (1959), pp. 40–58.

INDEX OF NAMES

INDEX OF SUBJECTS